FOUNDATIONS OF INVENTORY MANAGEMENT

THE IRWIN/MCGRAW-HILL SERIES

Operations and Decision Sciences

OPERATIONS MANAGEMENT

Bowersox and Closs
Logistical Management: ***The Integrated Supply Chain Process***
First Edition

Chase, Aquilano, and Jacobs
Production and Operations Management
Eighth Edition

Chu, Hottenstein, and Greenlaw
PROSIM for Windows
Third Edition

Cohen and Apte
Manufacturing Automation
First Edition

Davis, Aquilano, and Chase
Fundamentals of Operations Management
Third Edition

Dobler and Burt
Purchasing and Supply Management
Sixth Edition

Flaherty
Global Operations Management
First Edition

Fitzsimmons and Fitzsimmons
Service Management: ***Operations, Strategy, Information Technology***
Second Edition

Gray and Larson
Project Management: ***The Managerial Process***
First Edition

Hill
Manufacturing Strategy: ***Text & Cases***
Third Edition

Hopp and Spearman
Factory Physics
Second Edition

Lambert and Stock
Strategic Logistics Management
Third Edition

Leenders and Fearon
Purchasing and Supply Chain Management
Eleventh Edition

Melnyk and Denzler
Operations Management
First Edition

Moses, Seshadri, and Yakir
HOM Operations Management Software for Windows
First Edition

Nahmias
Production and Operations Analysis
Third Edition

Nicholas
Competitive Manufacturing Management
First Edition

Pinedo and Chao
Operations Scheduling
First Edition

Sanderson and Uzumeri
Managing Product Families
First Edition

Schroeder
Operations Management: ***Contemporary Concepts and Cases***
First Edition

Schonberger and Knod
Operations Management: ***Customer-Focused Principles***
Sixth Edition

Simchi-Levi, Kaminsky, and Simchi-Levi
Designing and Managing the Supply Chain: ***Concepts, Strategies, and Case Studies***
First Edition

Sterman
Business Dynamics: ***Systems Thinking and Modeling for a Complex World***
First Edition

Stevenson
Production/Operations Management
Sixth Edition

Vollmann, Berry, and Whybark
Manufacturing Planning & Control Systems
Fourth Edition

Zipkin
Foundations of Inventory Management,
First Edition

BUSINESS STATISTICS

Alwan
Statistical Process Analysis
First Edition

Aczel
Complete Business Statistics
Fourth Edition

Bowerman and O'Connell
Applied Statistics: ***Improving Business Processes***
First Edition

Bryant and Smith
Practical Data Analysis: ***Case Studies in Business Statistics, Volumes I and II***
Second Edition;
Volume III
First Edition

Butler
Business Research Sources
First Edition

Cooper and Schindler
Business Research Methods
Sixth Edition

Delurgio
Forecasting Principles and Applications
First Edition

Doane, Mathieson, and Tracy
Visual Statistics
First Edition

Gitlow, Oppenheim, and Oppenheim
Quality Management: ***Tools and Methods for Improvement***
Second Edition

Hall
Computerized Business Statistics
Fifth Edition

Lind, Mason, and Marchal
Basic Statistics for Business and Economics
Third Edition

Mason, Lind, and Marchal
Statistical Techniques in Business and Economics
Tenth Edition

Merchant, Goffinet, Koehler
Basic Statistics Using Excel
First Edition

Merchant, Goffinet, Koehler
Basic Statistics Using Excel for Office 97
First Edition

Neter, Kutner, Nachtsheim, and Wasserman
Applied Linear Statistical Models
Fourth Edition

Neter, Kutner, Nachtsheim, and Wasserman
Applied Linear Regression Models
Third Edition

Siegel
Practical Business Statistics
Fourth Edition

Webster
Applied Statistics for Business and Economics: *An Essentials Version*
Third Edition

Wilson and Keating
Business Forecasting
Third Edition

QUANTITATIVE METHODS AND MANAGEMENT SCIENCE

Bodily, Carraway, Frey, Pfeifer
Quantitative Business Analysis: *Casebook*
First Edition

Bodily, Carraway, Frey, Pfeifer
Quantitative Business Analysis: *Text and Cases*
First Edition

Bonini, Hausman, and Bierman
Quantitative Analysis for Business Decisions
Ninth Edition

Hesse
Managerial Spreadsheet Modeling and Analysis
First Edition

Hillier, Hillier, Lieberman
Introduction to Management Science: *A Modeling and Case Studies Approach with Spreadsheets*
First Edition

FOUNDATIONS OF INVENTORY MANAGEMENT

Paul H. Zipkin
Fuqua School of Business
Duke University

Boston Burr Ridge, IL Dubuque, IA Madison, WI New York San Francisco St. Louis
Bangkok Bogotá Caracas Lisbon London Madrid
Mexico City Milan New Delhi Seoul Singapore Sydney Taipei Toronto

McGraw-Hill Higher Education
*A Division of The **McGraw-Hill** Companies*

FOUNDATIONS OF INVENTORY MANAGEMENT

This book is printed on acid-free paper.

1 2 3 4 5 6 7 8 9 0 DOC/DOC 0 9 8 7 6 5 4 3 2 1 0

ISBN 0-256-11379-3

Publisher: *Jeffrey J. Shelstad*
Executive editor: *Richard T. Hercher, Jr.*
Marketing manager: *Zina Craft*
Project manager: *Jim Labeots*
Manager, new book production: *Melonie Salvati*
Freelance design coordinator: *Craig E. Jordan*
Cover design: *Maureen McCutcheon*
Senior supplement coordinator: *Becky Szura*
Compositor: *Carlisle Communications, Ltd.*
Typeface: *10/12 New Times Roman*
Printer: *R.R. Donnelley & Sons Company*

Library of Congress Cataloging-in-Publication Data

Zipkin, Paul Herbert.
Foundations of inventory management / Paul H. Zipkin.
p. cm.
Includes index.
ISBN 0-256-11379-3
1. Inventory control. I. Title.
HD40.Z56 2000
658.7'87--dc21 **99-40847**

http:\\www.mhhe.com

P R E F A C E

During the making of this book I have often reflected on my good fortune—so many fine people helped me, directly or indirectly. Here I can express only a small fraction of my gratitude to them.

My grandparents were four quite different people, but they shared certain qualities—all were extraordinarily generous and remained cheerful even in harsh circumstances. They were very proud of us, their children, and grandchildren, and they would have been proud to see this book (never mind whether it deserves such pride). My late mother was a source of strength, warmth, and humor to all around her.

My father has taught me many things, but two especially come to mind. He showed me the importance of carefully analyzing things, of looking below surface appearances. And, he demonstrated the importance of empathy and interest towards all people. I have not always been the most responsible or responsive son, in these respects among others, but give the man credit, he tried.

My wife Karen and my children Joe and Leah patiently and graciously endured countless hours when I occupied myself with the computer screen instead of them. For that, and for their constant love and support, I am deeply grateful.

How can I adequately thank the great teachers I have learned so much from? The faculty of the IEOR Department at the University of California, Berkeley, introduced me to the field of Operations Research. I wish to thank especially C. Roger Glassey, William Jewell, the late Ronald Shephard, Donald Topkis, and Ronald Wolff for encouraging my fledgling efforts and tolerating my many mishaps. Later, during my doctoral studies at Yale University, I was fortunate to receive the guidance and encouragement of Ron Dembo, Donald Brown, Eric Denardo, and Ward Whitt, among others. I owe special thanks to Harvey Wagner, whose wisdom played a great role in forming my understanding of the field. Finally, to my advisor and mentor, Matthew J. Sobel, who gave so much of his time and effort to my dissertation work and taught me so much about the tasks and meaning of scholarship, and who kindly put up with all the egregious nonsense I subjected him to, I offer my heartfelt thanks and appreciation.

I have had wonderful colleagues, first at Columbia University and later at Duke University. I owe a special debt of gratitude to my research collaborator and friend Awi Federgruen. Side by side we fought many battles, intellectual and otherwise, and from them I learned much about science and life.

This book grew out of lecture notes and assignments for courses I have given at Columbia and Duke over the last 18 years. It represents my view of the key concepts of inventory management—how they really work and why they really matter. Chapter 1 sets forth the goals of the book more fully.

To the students who suffered through those courses, I offer my apologies and thanks. Their questions and suggestions contributed greatly to my understanding of the subject and to the coherence of this book. And what superb students I have had! I cannot resist mentioning in particular Shoshana Anily, Mark Ferguson, Arie Harel, Oded Koenigsberg, Sang-Bum Lee, Yong-Joo Lee, Agnes Peña-Perez, Antony Svoronos, Michal Tsur, Weiming Zhang, Shaohui Zheng, and Yu-Sheng Zheng. The greatest joy of my professional life has been to watch you grow to surpass at least this one of your teachers. (My apologies also to future students, whose wrists and minds this book may strain.)

Very special thanks go to Jing-Sheng (Jeannette) Song, former student and now collaborator, friend, and true scholar. Over the years she read many drafts and offered countless suggestions for improvement, and the book is much better than it would have been without her efforts. Moreover, her continuing encouragement and (mostly) gentle prodding helped to counter my habitual sloth. Finally, after learning a few tricks from me, she has taught me much more, from the technical to the philosophical, by both precept and example.

Sincere thanks to the reviewers of the book, whose suggestions were so helpful: Harry Groenevelt, University of Rochester; Ananth V. Iyer, Purdue University; Hau L. Lee, Stanford University; Kamran Moinzadeh, University of Washington; Steven Nahmias, Santa Clara University; Leroy B. Schwarz, Purdue University; and Robert T. Sumichrast, Virginia Polytechnic Institute and State University.

Finally, thanks to all the talented, hard-working and patient people at Irwin/McGraw-Hill who contributed to the creation of the book. Especially hearty thanks to my editor, Richard Hercher, who kept kindly suggesting that I click the "print" button, but whose patience never faltered when I procrastinated.

Paul H. Zipkin
Durham
August, 1999

BRIEF CONTENTS

C O N T E N T S

C H A P T E R

1 General Introduction

Outline

1.1 Inventories Are Important—So Are Foundations

1.1.1 Inventories Everywhere

In the desk in my office, in the bottom right-hand drawer, I keep pads of lined paper. I use a lot of paper in my work. About once a month I go to the supply room to get more. These trips are mildly irritating. I would hate to have to go every time I need a sheet of paper, or even a single pad. On the other hand, I never take more than a few pads. Why? Well, my desk is full of other things, and my office expense budget is limited.

Change of scene: I'm driving through a steel plant on an island in Tokyo Bay. On my right is the company's inventory of coal. It's stored outside in piles, each about 4 m high. There are thousands of these piles, stretching as far as the eye can see. (Question: Why do they need so much coal? The answer will come later.)

That stack of paper is one familiar example of an *inventory.* Every one of us deals with dozens of inventories daily, usually without thinking too hard about them. Even at home we stock supplies of food, soap, and many other items, because they make life easier than it would be otherwise. We don't keep too much, however, because otherwise we would run out of room or money. Thus, we are all familiar at an intuitive level with the need to *manage* inventories.

Large enterprises too, like the Japanese steel company I visited, need to manage inventories. Often, doing that well spells the difference between corporate success and failure.

None of this is new. Inventory management is hardly a modern innovation. The earliest humans kept caches of food and stone tools. As for recorded history, well, the whole business started with inventory management—writing was invented, it seems, for that very purpose. Readers familiar with the Bible will recall that Joseph was, among other things, a remarkably proficient inventory manager. (True, he did enjoy some unusual advantages—intimate access to senior management, not to mention a superb forecasting system.)

Returning to here and now, the person who runs the supply room has a different viewpoint on inventories. This operation serves about 250 busy, demanding people, and provides several dozen types and sizes of paper, as well as hundreds of other kinds of office supplies, from paper clips and staples to computer diskettes. It takes a serious, conscious effort to monitor all these items, to estimate their usages, to order new supplies from our office-supplies wholesaler at the appropriate times, to decide when to discontinue rarely used items and when to add attractive new ones, and so forth. These are the typical concerns of inventory management at the retail level; the operators of most retail stores face basically the same set of problems.

Behind the supply room and the retail store lies the vast global network of industry, every part of which is permeated by inventories. Consider what has to happen before I obtain my small stack of paper: Wood-products companies maintain inventories of growing trees; paper companies keep logs waiting to be processed; the logs are transformed into wood pulp, which is made into paper at paper mills; finished paper is held in inventory at the mills themselves and then at one or more warehouses, until it reaches the wholesaler; from the wholesaler's stocks the paper is sent to our supply room, where I pick it up. (As for paper clips, some of that Japanese steel may end up in them.)

Even this picture is simplified: Between these steps there are inventories in transit, floating on rivers or carried in ships, trains, or trucks. In addition, wood is only one of the components of pulp and paper; a variety of other inputs (mainly chemicals) are also needed, all of which are stored as inventories before they are used. Finally, the complexities of scope are enormous. There are thousands of different types, grades, sizes, and colors of paper, for example.

The management of these manufacturing inventories involves many of the same issues as a retail operation, but with a different emphasis. One key difference is that producers have to *coordinate* inventory-producing and -consuming activities at several related processing stages and locations; logs, chemicals, pulp, and paper must be managed in concert for the overall system to work.

A similar story could be told about every single item we use at home or at work (including paper clips). We could not eat or drink or bathe or keep warm, were it not for a huge, intricate chain of production and distribution activities, all of them fed by diverse inventories of raw materials, components, spare parts, and finished goods.

Inventories are also critical in the service industries, a fact you may find surprising. After all, a service, according to one popular definition, is something you can't drop on your foot. Haircuts, brain surgery, auto insurance, college teaching—none of these can be kept in a warehouse until needed. Nevertheless, the provision of any service depends on a supply chain of supporting materials and equipment, just as much as a manufacturing process does. Fast food restaurants could not operate without inventories of food; the airlines would be grounded without their inventories of working aircraft engines and jet fuel.

The scale of all these inventory-related operations is simply immense: As of March 1999, businesses in the United States held about *$1.1 trillion* worth of inventories. This is about *1.35* times their total sales for the month. (This figure does *not* include all the stocks carried by governments and not-for-profit agencies.) Changes in inventories, by industry and in aggregate, are watched closely by economists and reported in newspapers, for these numbers are closely associated with the overall direction and health of the economy. Stocks of particularly critical items (such as crude oil) make front-page news.

At the individual company level, inventories are if anything even more important. Customers do not easily forgive shortages or delivery delays, and for good reason: From the customer's viewpoint a shortage may mean a minor annoyance (if the supply room doesn't have *my* favorite kind of paper), or a severe disruption (if the steel company runs out of coal), or even life and death (in the case of medicines). For some products in some situations occasional shortages can be tolerated, but generally too-frequent shortages can erode a company's reputation and market position. On the other hand, bloated stocks are a serious drain on a company's financial resources. Short-sighted attempts to correct these extremes, through frequent production changes or emergency orders, often just make matters worse. Either widespread shortages or slow-moving inventories (and often both) are clear signals of a company in trouble.

We have understood for some time, at least in principle, that sound, careful inventory management is critical to a firm's strategic viability. Recent events have sharpened our appreciation of this fact, however: One of the most significant developments in the world economy over the last two decades has been the extraordinary success of Japanese companies in Western markets for automobiles, machine tools, copiers, and numerous other products. Among the key factors underlying this phenomenon seems to be the ability of Japanese firms to operate with substantially lower inventories than their Western counterparts. Thus, inventory has become one of the dimensions upon which companies compete on a global scale. Many of the success stories of the last few decades in retailing (Wal-Mart), automobiles (Toyota), computers (Dell), and other industries are founded on operational capabilities that, among other things, keep inventories lean.

Question: Why are internet retailers like Amazon.com growing so rapidly? *Answer:* They can operate without the huge inventories that retail stores require. (Anyway, that's part of the answer.) This is one example of a broader phenomenon: Innovations in inventory management enabled by technology can lead to the restructuring of entire industries.

Commercial enterprises are by no means the only ones concerned with inventory management. The crucial functions of a hospital depend, among other things, on reliable supplies of medicines, surgical equipment, blood for transfusions, bedpans, and many other items. Armed forces must stock ammunition, spare parts of all sorts, food and clothing, etc. Napoleon's famous quip, "An army travels on its stomach," can be reasonably read as an assertion of the importance of inventory management in military operations.

Now, why does that Japanese steel company need so much coal? Because they ship it in from Australia. A steel company in Germany, situated near a coal mine, needs a far smaller inventory. Both are acting reasonably.

1.1.2 Principles and Practice

As its title suggests, this book focuses on the *foundations* of inventory management. Let us take a moment to think about what this means.

First of all, there is a remarkable claim inherent in the title. The book is not about inventories of paper, specifically, or about coal; nor is it about ball bearings, photo film, computer screens, automobile door handles or insurance forms. It is not about Western or Eastern inventories or inventories carried by large or small organizations, in the public or private sectors. Rather, it is about inventories of *all* of these items in *all* these places and more, inventories in general. That is, there are fundamental principles, general concepts, basic ideas, that underlie the management of inventories *per se,* transcending the apparent differences in the physical nature of the items involved and in organizational and geographical circumstances. Such differences do matter at some level, of course, and another reason for exploring foundations is to discern which are the essential differences and why.

Many of these ideas have implications beyond the realm of inventories as we usually think of them. For example, an order backlog is not exactly a physical stock, but as we shall see it can be usefully viewed in very similar terms. In fact, this connection is crucial in understanding how *both* inventories and backlogs function.

Ranging a bit further afield, we would not normally regard a pile of garbage or other undesirable waste as an inventory, but the principles developed here can be usefully applied to waste management nonetheless. Likewise, consider a portfolio of securities. This is somewhat like an inventory, insofar as both are stores of value that evolve over time. So, it should not surprise you to learn that, at the level of basic principles at least, inventory management and financial management are quite closely related. (Important and interesting as such connections are, however, we shall touch upon them only in passing. The main focus will remain inventories in the usual sense.)

More broadly, the subject of this book is the science of material processing systems, or supply chains—how to describe and classify them, how goods and information flow within them, how to manage them, and how to design and improve them. Inventories are important features of such systems, but not the only ones.

These principles, concepts, and ideas, furthermore, really are fundamental and basic; they are *important.* If you learn them well, you will come to understand the central issues of supply-chain and inventory management better than you did before, and this knowledge will serve you well as a manager, analyst, engineer, consultant, or researcher.

The development of these principles and ideas has been pursued vigorously for most of the twentieth century. They represent an extraordinary intellectual achievement, to which many people have contributed, people from all over the world, including academics, professional engineers, and managers. Also, while the field will doubtless grow and evolve in the future, it is likely that such developments will build on the foundation established so far. We can be reasonably confident that these basic ideas will have continuing validity and value for years to come.

We pay a price, however, to delve deeply into fundamental concepts, to achieve a broad scope of generality. These basic ideas are *abstract,* and an abstract language is required to express them clearly. Specifically, we shall employ the language of mathematics throughout the book, and you will need to be fairly conversant with it to follow much of what we have to say. Just how conversant you need to be will be explained a bit later. I have tried to keep the mathematical demands of the book to a minimum, but these minimal demands are still fairly hefty.

Also, the focus on foundations means there are many practical aspects of inventory management that lie outside our scope. Day-to-day inventory control involves a myriad of details that we cannot hope to cover. There are no pictures of billing invoices in the book. Our discussions of such matters as forecasting and database management are sketchy, and there are even some (like warehouse layout) that we do not touch at all. (Chapter 2 treats some of these topics briefly.) Thus, the book is not intended to be a complete guide to the *practice* of inventory management.

Do not read this as an apology. Billing invoices have become obsolete in many industries, replaced by electronic data interchange (EDI). To set up an inventory database, or *any* database for that matter, you must know something about its purposes, what functions it is expected to accomplish. The varied tasks of management make no sense without an intellectual framework, a foundation. Without a foundation, we are prisoners of habit or hyperbole, unable to see opportunities for fruitful change or limits to change. That foundation is what this book seeks to provide.

Another name for our subject is *inventory theory.* This label has the advantage of brevity, and I do use it here sometimes for that reason. But it is rather unfortunate, because it connotes something ethereal, quite removed from practical concerns, interesting perhaps, but irrelevant. As I shall try to convince you, that is not the case. I do believe in the saying, "Nothing is more practical than a good theory."

1.2 About the Book

1.2.1 What and Whom Is the Book for?

This book is intended, first and foremost, as a course textbook. It is designed to be used as the basic text for courses on the theory of inventories, offered by schools of management and engineering for graduate students and advanced undergraduates.

To explain further, the focus of the book is on the formulation, analysis, and use of *mathematical models* of inventory systems. The book thus presumes a fairly strong technical background, and while it aims to take students closer to applications than many theoretically oriented texts do, it is by no means a complete guide to the management of inventories, as indicated above. In particular, the book is probably not an appropriate text for a basic course on inventory management for undergraduate or professional masters-level business students, though it may serve as a useful background reference for such a course.

The intended audience comprises doctoral students in management, industrial engineering, and operations research, along with well-prepared professional students in those fields. Students in other areas (especially economics and some of the other engineering disciplines) where inventories are important may also find the book of value.

When during their programs should students take such a course? The nature of the field makes this question problematic: Inventory theory draws on virtually all of the basic methodologies of operations research, so ideally students should already be familiar with at least the rudiments of optimization theory, stochastic processes, and dynamic programming. On the other hand, the subject is much more than a collection of miscellaneous illustrations of those methodologies, as explained further below; indeed, it has its own intellectual core. Also, because its focus is close to applications and practical managerial concerns, it can serve as a powerful motivator for further learning in advanced methodological courses. Furthermore, the material covered in the course underlies a good deal of the research literature in operations management and industrial engineering broadly construed, not just in the inventory area.

As the theory itself tells us, when faced with contradictory criteria, the best solution is a compromise. (Well, sometimes.) In my experience the course works best for most students early in the second year of graduate study; the book is designed primarily for students with that level of preparation. There are exceptions, however: The course can also work well for first-year graduate students, and even undergraduates and MBA students, provided they have solid technical backgrounds and are able to learn some things on their own. And, of course, it is never too late.

Partly to accommodate students with diverse preparations, and also to provide instructors with a degree of flexibility in designing the course, I have included fairly extensive appendices to make the book self-contained, or nearly so.

For similar reasons I have adopted a somewhat mixed approach toward mathematical generality and rigor. There are some theorems and proofs in the book, included without apologies: One of its purposes, certainly, is to expose the basic techniques of research in the field. Also, the proofs often embody insights that cannot be conveyed fully otherwise. I have, nonetheless, tried to motivate these arguments as best I can, and very often I forego full generality in favor of simplicity. Also, I have tried to identify and encapsulate the more difficult and technical material, so that instructors can choose to work around some of it without losing continuity.

In addition to constructing a pedagogical device, I have also aimed to convey certain ideas to my academic and professional colleagues—and to students as future colleagues—which I hope they will find interesting, useful, or at least provocative. *This is a book with a message, indeed a mission.*

First, the book comprises what I view to be the fundamental concepts of inventory theory as it now stands, the core, the backbone. Besides its function as a textbook, it is designed to serve as a reference on the subject for practicing professionals and academic researchers. While some of these concepts have been around for decades, many are treated in nonstandard ways or revived here after long neglect, and others are products of quite recent research.

In forming this selection I have necessarily had to omit much of value and interest. I have tried to compensate somewhat for these omissions in the notes and the problems following the chapters. (Still, I remain painfully aware of how many beautiful and significant results I have been unable to include; I hope my colleagues will accept my profuse apologies on this score.)

Also, the book expresses, in some cases implicitly, certain judgments and convictions concerning the connections between these concepts, the relation of the field to other disciplines, and especially its role and value in the practice of inventory management. I explain these ideas, views, judgments, and convictions a bit more in § 1.2.3.

1.2.2 Structure and Contents

1.2.2.1 Elements of Inventory Systems

Inventory systems are extraordinarily diverse, and they differ along many dimensions. The overall structure of the book reflects, necessarily, a certain classification or taxonomy of these systems. Ours is by no means the only way to classify them, but it is true that the major divisions of the book correspond to fundamental differences among real systems. To understand what the various parts of the book are about, and the connections between them, therefore, we need to appreciate some of these basic distinctions.

Let us begin with a general, abstract way of looking at an inventory. We focus first on the inventory of one item only in a single location. Every inventory lies *between* two activities or processes, which we call the *supply process* and the *demand process.* As Figure 1.2.1 indicates, the supply process comprises the production, transportation, and/or other activities that *add* new stock to the inventory, while the demand process describes the various activities that use and thus *subtract* material from the inventory.

Like any abstraction, this picture omits a great deal. The arrows indicate directions of movement, but otherwise the figure lacks a temporal dimension; it represents structure, not activity. Also, there is nothing here to suggest information and control; we cannot see who or what directs the supply process to perform its tasks or what knowledge guides these decisions.

Furthermore, the figure gives no hint as to what lies inside the circles depicting the supply and demand processes. These processes might be quite simple or enormously complex systems themselves. Consider the inventory of one specific type of finished paper at a paper mill, for example. The supply process here is that extensive chain of processing and shipping activities that turns trees into paper, including many different inventories along the way. The demand process too is a complex web, stretching from the mill to all the final users of paper, and perhaps even further to include certain factors that influence those

FIGURE 1.2.1

Inventory—between supply and demand.

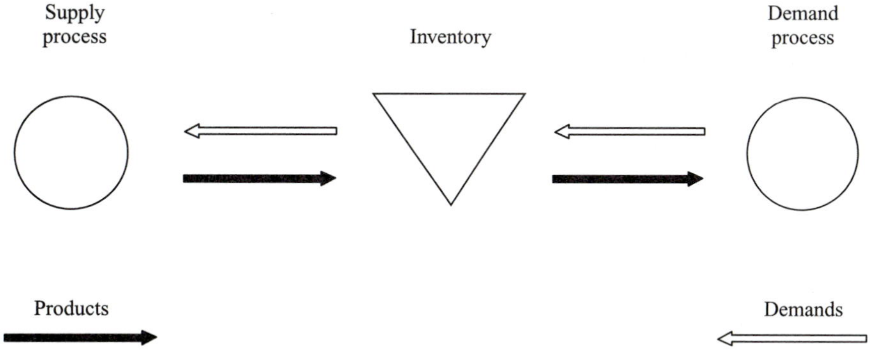

FIGURE 1.2.2

Procurement, production, and distribution.

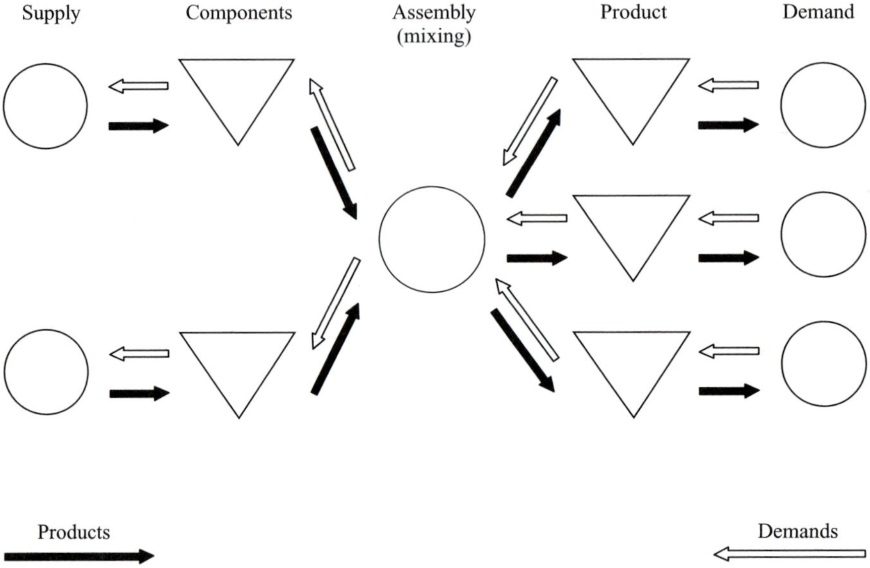

users (like the general level of the economy). The same supply and demand processes, moreover, typically affect many other kinds of paper and other goods as well.

Nevertheless, this is a *useful* abstraction, and we shall refer to it repeatedly throughout the book.

For one thing, this basic structure can be used as a building block to compose diagrams of much larger, more complex systems. Figure 1.2.2 suggests some of the possibilities. Here, two different components are procured and then assembled or mixed to form one final product, which is then shipped to three separate stocking locations.

Indeed, one critical distinction among inventory systems rests on their *degrees of structural complexity:* There are some inventories that can be reasonably, plausibly viewed in the simple terms of Figure 1.2.1 by itself, independently of other items in other places. There are other cases, however, where multiple items and/or locations are essential, where the distinct inventories in the system cannot sensibly be considered in isolation.

Even as it stands, Figure 1.2.1 expresses a fundamental point about inventories in general, their "between-ness": To understand what an inventory does, how it works, why it is held, the basic functions it performs, and to begin to think seriously about how to manage it effectively, we must first understand the basic characteristics of the supply and demand processes that drive it. Indeed, the real subject of this book is supply and demand and the transactions between them. Inventory is just one aspect of supply-demand interaction, albeit a crucial one.

To appreciate this point, it is helpful to imagine a situation where an inventory is *not* needed and would serve no useful purpose. For this to be so, we would have to find (or design or adapt) a supply process capable of providing instantly the exact amounts needed to fill the demands arising from the demand process. Furthermore, such a perfect supply process must be not just physically possible, but also reasonably inexpensive to build and operate.

The possibility and practicality of an ideal supply process, of course, depend in part on the nature of the demand process. For example, if we could be sure from the beginning that demands will occur at a regular rate, with only minor variations over time, then a supply process capable of providing goods at that same rate, and of responding immediately to variations within the expected range, would do the job.

No such perfect match exists in the real world, but there are situations that come close: Most of us do not keep an inventory of cold water in our residences. Our sinks and tubs are connected to a very effective supply process, the network of pipes, pumps, and reservoirs that make up the public water system, which normally meets virtually all of our domestic demands. These demands are *not* regular at all, but the supply process is easily controlled to respond to our demands, by opening and closing the valves we call taps. (Of course, it is only in the industrialized countries and only quite recently that such modern water systems have been created; elsewhere and in earlier times, people do and did keep inventories of water, to minimize trips to the well.)

This example of water serves as a nice paradigm for the notion of perfectly matched supply and demand processes. If we can envision an ideal supply process, we can further imagine attaching it directly to the demand process by means of pipes and valves. We would then have a system where the product *flows* directly from the supply system to meet the demands.

In most situations, unfortunately, supply and demand processes *cannot* be matched perfectly; most products do *not* flow smoothly in this way. Indeed, most of the important functions of inventories can be understood in terms of the various types of *mismatches* that arise between supply and demand processes. In other words, inventory serves as a *buffer* between supply and demand processes that do not fit neatly together, to mitigate the costly disruptions that would otherwise occur. The most obvious type of disruption is a *shortage,* a failure to meet demand as it occurs; inventories are often held, then, to prevent or reduce shortages. Most of the other significant potential disruptions are strains of various kinds on the supply process itself.

Here is a short (and by no means comprehensive) list of common and important characteristics of actual supply and demand processes which, alone or in combination, lead to such mismatches.

Demand processes:

- Smooth or lumpy demand
- Variations in demand over time
- Unpredictable demand variations

Supply processes:

- Economies of scale in supply
- Capacity limits
- Delays in response—leadtimes
- Imperfect quality

A good part of this book is devoted to understanding these factors and their interactions, but for now we explain each one briefly:

Smooth or lumpy demand: When demand can be envisioned as a continuous stream, drawing down inventory at some rate (constant or variable), then we say demand is *smooth.* Lumpy demand, in contrast, occurs in large, discrete chunks. (Of course, these two are extreme cases; real demands often have both smooth and lumpy components.) Even smooth demand can lead to a mismatch, depending on the nature of the supply process, as explained below. Normally, lumpy demand increases the difficulties further.

Variations in demand over time: Seasonal changes in demand, and other temporal variations, often lead to mismatches, especially when the capacity of the supply process is severely limited. Then, inventory must be built up during slack periods to have sufficient stock to meet later, heavier demands. Even with virtually unlimited capacity, however, the presence of other complicating factors (supply leadtimes and demand uncertainties, for example) means that temporal changes must be anticipated somehow.

Unpredictable demand variations: Random fluctuations in demand, in conjunction with supply leadtimes and capacity limits, are among the major reasons for maintaining inventories. In these cases, the supply process is unable to respond quickly to unanticipated demand surges and declines, so inventory is needed in order to fill demands in a timely manner.

Economies of scale in supply: In many situations the technology and economics of the supply process favor long production runs or large deliveries, relative to short-term demand. Examples include long production setup or changeover times and shipments over great distances. Also, if we purchase goods from an independent supplier, the supplier may simply charge less per unit for a large order. Thus, even if it is possible to supply small quantities, it may be expensive. This explains why even smooth demand can lead to a problematic mismatch. In such cases there will be sizable inventories for some time after a batch is produced or a shipment received.

Capacity limits: Every real supply process has limited capacity, and so has limited ability to respond to changes or lumps in demand, whether anticipated or not. Thus, inventories are required to compensate for this inflexibility. Capacity limits are more significant in some cases than others; often they can be safely ignored for practical purposes, but just as often they cannot.

Delays in response—leadtimes: As mentioned above, supply leadtimes and demand fluctuations together lead to shortages, unless inventories are held to prevent or at least mitigate them. When the leadtimes themselves are unpredictable, these difficulties become even more severe, for the same reasons.

Imperfect quality: Imperfect quality exacerbates many of the problems discussed so far. Defects waste precious capacity, and they add elements of uncertainty to the supply process, somewhat like random leadtimes.

There are other reasons to hold inventory besides these supply-demand mismatches. For example, gold and other precious metals are used as inputs to certain production processes, but some people own them for purely speculative reasons, hoping their prices will rise. In retail settings inventories often serve a marketing purpose; customers want to examine goods before buying. Most of our attention here, however, will be focused on mismatches such as those described above.

Once we understand the characteristics of supply and demand, we can design a good inventory strategy. But, the job of management does not stop there. We must then step back and envision the total system, including supply and demand as well as inventory. From that larger perspective we must ask, what can be done to *improve* the system?

1.2.2.2 Organization of the Book

These basic characteristics of supply and demand processes, along with differences in structural complexity, define the primary divisions between the several parts, chapters, and sections of the book.

The distinction between predictable (or deterministic) and unpredictable (or stochastic) processes is perhaps the single most significant dividing line between different systems. One of the crucial functions of inventory, to protect against unforeseen contingencies, simply does not arise when supplies and demands are (or can be usefully regarded as) predictable. Only in the stochastic case must we be concerned with all the issues surrounding information, what we know and when. For just these reasons, moreover, stochastic models involve different and rather more complex mathematics.

The book's major partition is defined by this distinction: After the two introductory chapters of Part I, Part II (Chapters 3 to 5) deals with predictable supply and demand, while Part III (Chapters 6 to 9) treats stochastic models.

Another key distinction rests on the difference between stationary processes and those that change over time. The need to anticipate temporal variations significantly complicates the problems of inventory management, as explained above. Models incorporating time-varying data, accordingly, require their own special techniques of analysis and solution. Within Part II, Chapter 3 focuses on stationary data. Models with temporal variation are introduced in Chapter 4. (Chapter 5 includes both cases.) Similarly, in Part III, Chapters 6 to 8 deal mainly with stationary, stochastic models, while the nonstationary case is taken up in Chapter 9.

It turns out to be convenient to introduce, along with nonstationarity, certain distinct approaches to model formulation and analysis. In particular, we model time as *discrete* in Chapters 4 and 9 (for reasons explained there), whereas time is *continuous* in most of the rest of the book. Another difference requires a bit more explanation: We often *assume* that a specific type or form of control policy will be used; then we try to evaluate different policies and to choose a good one, but always within this policy class. Sometimes, however, we ask, what form does a truly optimal control policy take among *all* possible policies? Both kinds of investigations are valuable, but for different reasons, and they involve quite different methods of analysis. Chapters 4 and 9 consider optimal control, whereas the other chapters mostly focus on particular policy forms.

Regarding structural complexity, Parts II and III both begin with one or two chapters on single-item, single-location models, followed by chapters on more complex networks. (Chapter 9 considers both simple and complex structures, but in different sections.)

Most of the other specific characteristics of supply and demand processes mentioned above are dealt with in different sections of the individual chapters. For example, in the context of the stationary, deterministic systems of Chapter 3, limited capacity is treated in Section 3.4.

1.2.3 Guiding Lights

Several principles have guided the writing of this book. These ideas have grown gradually out of the process of teaching this material over the years, from discussions with hundreds of practicing managers, and through shared reflections with colleagues and students. It is worth reviewing them briefly here, for otherwise some of the selections and treatments of topics may seem merely eccentric.

1.2.3.1 Inventory Theory Is a Coherent, Unified Body of Knowledge

This is partly an assertion and partly a goal or ideal. Inventory models (like inventories themselves) come in many different shapes, sizes, and flavors, and the techniques used to analyze them are equally diverse. At first glance the field appears to be a motley collection of unrelated topics, each a special case of some larger subject, such as dynamic programming or queuing theory.

Yet there *are* common ideas, concepts and methods that link the central model formulations. There *are* threads linking the most abstract theory with practical methods. For example, consider the simple but powerful idea of viewing backorders as the mirror image of physical stock. This notion underlies the analysis of supply leadtimes, through the construct of the inventory position (because the dynamics of the inventory position are linear in a key sense). This approach cuts across the distinctions between deterministic and stochastic demands and between continuous and discrete time. To make clear the generality of this idea, I have introduced it much earlier than usual, in the context of the economic-order-quantity (EOQ) model in Chapter 3. Later, in the context of stochastic demand, we are led naturally to a fundamental observation, that leadtimes and random demand fluctuations have their greatest impact *in combination.* (Also, the breakdown of this approach in the lost-sales and certain other models explains why they are so difficult.)

For similar reasons I have tried to point to several other subsequent developments during the treatments of the EOQ model and its cousins, which consequently are slightly more elaborate than usual. I regard this as a small price to pay for continuity. Likewise, I have emphasized the interplay between the classic equilibrium analyses and the equally classic dynamic-programming formulations of Part III, which are usually presented as entirely distinct approaches.

More generally, as will be evident from a perusal of the book's contents, I have sometimes grouped and sequenced familiar topics in somewhat unusual ways, to clarify what I feel are the key structural relationships between them. I hope that I have revealed structure, not imposed it.

Unity is a good thing, but it can be overdone. While stressing coherence, I have also tried to suggest the richness and variety of the field, especially through the problems. (I recommend that students read *all* the problems, not just those assigned as homework.)

1.2.3.2 Inventory Theory Is Strengthened through Its Connections to Other Disciplines

This principle might seem to contradict the previous one, but I do not think it does.

Within operations research, as mentioned above, inventory theory has long-standing ties to most of the other subdisciplines, ties that have enriched all of these subjects. In certain cases I have emphasized these connections somewhat more or differently than usual, however.

In particular, I have highlighted the connection between inventory theory and the theory of queues. In this respect the book revives a tradition established in the classic work of Morse [1958] (or rather continues the revival begun by Heyman and Sobel [1982] in a somewhat different manner). For queueing theory remains our richest source of models for what I call here supply processes. Recent developments in both fields (for instance, the flowering of queueing-network models, and the "discovery" of the effects of batching on congestion and leadtimes) further enhance this interaction. In addition, I find that several of the classic inventory models are most clearly expressed in the language of queues. The lost-sales model in Chapter 6 is one prominent example.

On the other hand, the central concerns of inventory theory are rather different from those of mainstream queueing theory; neither field subsumes the other. The challenge for me, then, has been to establish this link without turning the book into a text on queues or requiring students to have had a full course on the subject. (The approach here seems to work pretty well in my experience.)

There are also strong links with subjects outside operations research, or more precisely, outside typical operations-research curricula. The theory of dynamical systems and control, in particular, is prominently represented in the book. The systems approach, I believe, is a compelling metaphor for the functions of management.

Inventory systems *are* dynamical systems, as much as any real system is, and the unified picture of information, estimation and control provided by systems theory is a valuable one in the context of inventory management. This remains true, even when inventory theory cannot, so far at least, follow the entire program exemplified in the analysis of the simple linear-quadratic control model. Thus, I have included the production-smoothing model of Holt, Modigliani, Muth, and Simon [1960] (the celebrated HMMS model). I do think this model is worth learning, even though most of inventory theory and practice have followed other paths. There are *reasons* the HMMS assumptions are problematic, and these reasons are *interesting.*

Also, the systems-theoretic framework can be used to pose a rich class of demand-process models, which are consistent with standard modern forecasting methods. The book does not treat forecasting methods *per se,* beyond informal discussions; other books and other courses are the places to learn statistical forecasting properly. Still, I believe it is important to include demand models that *could* be specified using modern estimation methods. Then, I have indicated what we know about how to use the information provided by such models to control and to manage inventories. I have not hesitated to mention rules of thumb, though I have tried to be careful to identify them as such.

Furthermore, several recent lines of research in inventory theory have exploited the extraordinary flexibility of the linear-systems approach, its capacity to accommodate extensions and elaborations, such as multiple products and stages. In their details these models are quite different from the HMMS model, but they are similar in spirit. I expect this style of modeling to become more prominent in the future.

Finally, this framework has come to play a large role in other areas of management and engineering (finance and electrical engineering, to name just two). Indeed, the HMMS model itself has formed the basis of a good deal of the empirical work on the economics of inventories. When it is reasonably convenient and natural, it is a good thing to show students that what they are learning is part of a broader body of knowledge, not an isolated island of technique.

1.2.3.3 Advances in Technology Have Radically Changed What Is Practical

This should come as no surprise. We hear constantly that computers and communications technology have transformed our lives. Our thinking, however, often lags behind. In particular, many of the standard tools of inventory control were developed at a time when the only "practical" computational methods were those that could be carried out with a slide rule and statistical tables, with data that could be collected manually in a short time. This is no longer true, to put it mildly.

These changes have influenced the book in a variety of ways. Generally, I have tried to strike a balance between past and future, to say enough about standard, current practice (regardless of whether or not it is *good* practice) that students can understand it, even while indicating where I feel better methods or approaches are now available.

For example, I give far less weight to normal approximations than previous writers have done. I do include them, partly because they are indeed widely used, and partly because the properties of the normal distributions facilitate certain modes of analysis, but *not* because they are more widely available in tables than others. Anyone today can easily and cheaply buy and run programs to evaluate virtually any conceivable distribution.

For similar reasons I downplay manual solution methods, when standard, reliable codes are widely available. It may be that students will not understand these methods as deeply as those of us who have performed them on paper, but I believe their time is better spent on other things.

More fundamentally, I have not hesitated to suggest the implementation of fairly large, complex models and methods requiring extensive data and number crunching. The availability of these resources is rarely an issue today, as noted above. (There are other reasons, of course, to try to keep models simple.)

Obviously, no one will read the current state of technology and its implications precisely as I do. Also, the future will no doubt bring further changes, and what we do today will then likely seem old-fashioned. Well, that's progress. The best we can do is to try to adapt, keeping our sights as clear as we can.

1.2.3.4 Inventory Management Is More Than Inventory Control

The world has changed in other ways as well. Our view of the scope of inventory management, in particular, has broadened substantially. Thirty years ago, say, inventory control was seen as a fairly static, technical function. The technology embodied in the supply process was regarded as stable, demand was viewed as, if not quite predictable, then at least fairly regular in its fluctuations, and both were determined externally, by the environment or by managerial decisions at a much higher level. The job of inventory control was to understand these processes and to determine appropriate responses to them in the form of control policies. (This is an exaggerated picture, but still not an unfair one.) Most of the models and analyses of inventory theory up to that time were developed to support the inventory-control function as thus conceived.

Today, inventory management encompasses a far wider span of activities and issues. The most striking change has come in our picture of supply activities. We now understand much more clearly than before that production and distribution technologies can *improve,* and indeed with effort we can drive these improvements. Furthermore, the cumulative effects of seemingly mundane reductions in supply leadtimes, production setup times, quality defects, and so forth have a profound impact on the strategic health of the organization. This is the central message of the just-in-time (JIT) approach to operations, developed first by Japanese manufacturers, and widely recognized as a major factor in their competitive successes.

Recently, there has been an explosion of interest in supply-chain management. This means managing across entire supply networks, even when they cross organizational or geographical boundaries. This approach offers opportunities for substantial system improvements, but it also raises new challenges that the traditional inventory-control paradigm cannot address.

Does this mean that all of our inventory models are obsolete? No. But it does mean that we need to expand and enrich our models in certain directions, and also that we need to analyze, use, and teach even the older models somewhat differently.

First, the basic economic fundamentals embodied in these models have not changed. For example, it has been suggested, frequently and seriously, that the JIT approach teaches that every lot size should be one, and thus all the models that calculate lot sizes should be scrapped. This is utter nonsense. What is true is that, *if* we succeed in reducing setup costs and leadtimes to negligible values, relative to holding costs and other factors, *then* the lot size should be small, just as the models prescribe. Furthermore, we *should* strive to achieve such process improvements, for they lead to tangible overall benefits, as the models predict. There is no harm in calling attention to these facts with a rhetorical flourish, *provided* we remember to distinguish flourish from fact. "Inventory is evil," says another JIT slogan. I say, tell it to the squirrels.

Likewise, the *kanban* system is often promoted as a radically different and superior substitute for the control methods addressed by the models. This view rests on a misunderstanding of the *kanban* system, the earlier methods, or both. In fact, the *kanban* system is a variant of certain older methods, perhaps an improvement, but a variant nonetheless, and its use does not fundamentally change the issues of inventory management.

True, the *kanban* system can be *implemented* with less centralized short-term information and control than we are accustomed to, and this is important, for it has led us to rethink the whole issue of effective implementation in fresh terms. Nevertheless, the key managerial decisions (setting production rates and numbers of *kanbans,* for instance) involve the same logic, the same economic tradeoffs, as traditional systems of control. (To anyone who thinks these concerns don't matter in Japan, I strongly recommend reading Shingo [1985], a summary of JIT by one of its inventors. My own views on this and related issues are aired more fully in Zipkin [1991a].)

Second, prodded in part by the JIT phenomenon, researchers in academia and industry have been working furiously to extend our models to incorporate such elements as quality defects and *kanban*-style controls. While this work is by no means complete, substantial progress has been made; I have tried to include in the book some of the more significant and accessible of these recent achievements.

Third, in managing a supply chain, it is not enough to know that reducing leadtimes is a good thing. Even a network of modest size may include thousands of items over dozens of locations. In each case there may be many possible alternative improvements, some of them costly, some not. The key questions, then, are *where* should improvement efforts be focused, and *what* are the anticipated benefits? Similar questions arise concerning all sorts of other operational improvement projects. Managers, engineers, and analysts, whether or not their jobs are primarily concerned with inventories, are being called on to answer such questions with increasing frequency.

The models and methods of inventory theory, in my view, constitute the most accurate, tractable, thorough, and reliable set of tools now available to address questions of this nature. To use the tools for this purpose, however, requires a shift of focus. Most of the models, as noted above, are explicitly addressed to the problems of control, given all the environmental parameters. We need to ask further, what are the effects of *changes* in these parameters? This style of parametric analysis is certainly not new; it falls under the heading of *sensitivity analysis.* In the past, however, sensitivity analysis played a rather minor role in most expositions of the models. I have placed considerably greater emphasis on it.

1.2.3.5 Inventory Theory and Inventory Practice Are Closely Linked

This is another ideal. Yet, I believe there is far more actual truth to it than is commonly realized, partly because of the changes in technology and the roles of inventory managers discussed above. Although there are differences in style and vocabulary between the academic and the managerial cultures, they are less than they were a generation ago, and I do not regard them as fundamental. The ultimate concerns of theorists and practitioners are the same.

In any event I have tried to bridge some of those gaps here. Notwithstanding the warnings above concerning all the book does not purport to do, I remain mindful of the fact that, with very rare exceptions, today's students of inventory theory will someday have to talk to managers (or future managers). Thus, where possible, I have tried to explain how certain commonly used heuristic techniques appear when viewed from the perspective of the theory, and, conversely, how certain ideas derived from the theory can be and are used, sometimes in less-than-obvious ways.

A case in point is the discussion of material requirements planning (MRP) in Chapter 5. A glance at that section will immediately reveal that it stops far short of a full exposition of MRP on its own terms. Much of the MRP vocabulary and virtually all of its specific techniques are missing. The purpose here is rather to present the basic structure of the model underlying MRP and its overall approach to production control and to relate these to structures and approaches addressed in the theory. Viewed from this somewhat distant vantage point, the disjunction between MRP and other methods seems far less sharp than it may appear closer up. The goal, then, is to provide a framework within which this and other popular techniques can be comprehended; the details can be learned elsewhere.

1.2.3.6 Coping with Inventories Requires Both Management and Engineering

Do inventories fall under the purview of management or engineering? This sounds like a clear-cut question. The training and the daily activities of managers and engineers are typically quite different, after all. One might even say that management and engineering embody different views of the world, different philosophies. Which of these perspectives, then, is the most appropriate one from which to formulate the conceptual issues and to handle the practical problems raised by inventories?

In my view the subject of inventories is one place where the arts and sciences of management and engineering intersect. *Both* perspectives are necessary to obtain an adequate grasp of it, whether conceptual or practical. To deal intelligently with inventories as a professional, a consultant, or a researcher, a person trained in management must learn to think like an engineer, while an engineer must become something of a manager.

The managerial viewpoint is essential, simply because all the major functions of a business, from financial control to sales to production, strongly affect and are strongly affected by inventories. Effective inventory management entails *at least* satisfying customers, keeping capital requirements modest, and avoiding excessive operational costs. To balance all of these criteria, one must have some appreciation of where they come from and what they mean in a larger context.

The larger context, the broad view, the big picture, however, are not enough. The inventories maintained by the typical organization and the activities that feed and consume them compose an enormously complex system. Thousands of items, hundreds of locations, all interrelated, along with records, forecasts, orders and vast amounts of other information—this is the usual situation. To cope with such complexity involves a substantial task of systems engineering. There is simply no substitute here for the engineering approach to problem solving, the application of basic principles through a process of careful, systematic analysis and design. The big picture can be misleading if it oversimplifies the complex reality.

Thus, I really do mean the book to be addressed to students of *both* management and engineering. The interplay between the management and engineering points of view is, to my mind at least, one of the fascinations of the whole subject. There is a special challenge and reward in forging a conception, a picture, a *model* that is true to the essential details of a problem while encompassing the larger whole, particularly when the task involves something so critical to all of our economic lives as inventories. If I have conveyed some portion of this fascination here, the book will have accomplished one of its main purposes.

Notes

Here is a very brief overview of the development of the theory of inventories. Further discussions of specific topics will be found at the end of each chapter.

Modern inventory theory began with the derivation of the EOQ formula by Harris [1913], an engineer, inventor, and lawyer. Over the next few decades, numerous variations were elaborated, most printed in popular magazines, written by and for managers. Many of these results were collected in Raymond [1931], the first published book on inventory management. The fascinating details of this early history are explored in Erlenkotter [1989,1990]. Chapter 3 is based on this pioneering work.

These pioneers were certainly aware of the need to plan for uncertainties. However, the rigorous analysis of models with explicitly stochastic features really began in the 1950s, starting with the seminal papers of Arrow, Harris, and Marschak [1951] and Dvoretzky, Kiefer, and Wolfowitz [1952]. High points of this work are represented in the books by Whitin [1953], Arrow, Karlin, and Scarf [1958], Morse [1958], and Holt, Modigliani, Muth, and Simon [1960]. Most of the basic analytical methods of the field (dynamic programming and stationary analysis, for example) were established during this period, as were the research-oriented journals in which this work increasingly appeared.

The classic, monumental text of Hadley and Whitin [1963], a comprehensive summary of the field to that date, represents the culmination of this period, in a sense, and it has had a profound effect on all subsequent developments. Appearing shortly afterwards, the survey of Veinott [1966a] was also influential. Much of the work on single-item, single-location models since then can be seen as elaboration and extension of the ideas set forth in these works. This is not to say that nothing important has happened; the cumulative effect of these elaborations and extensions has been a substantial broadening and deepening of the field.

The study of complex systems with multiple items and stocking locations has progressed somewhat more slowly. Research along these lines began in the late 1950s and has continued actively ever since. See Scarf, Gilford, and Shelly [1963] for a collection of influential early papers. The achievements in this area up to about 1970 are summarized in Clark [1972], and those of the following decade in Schwarz [1981]. Many important results are quite recent and appear here for the first time in book form.

Good recent surveys of the research literature can be found in Porteus [1990] and the reviews collected in Graves et al. [1993] and Tayur et al. [1999]. Chikán [1990] has compiled an extensive bibliography.

C H A P T E R

2 Systems and Models

Outline

2.1 Introduction

This chapter provides a brief overview of the *context* of inventory management. It touches on some of the information technologies used in operations, who in the organization should be concerned with inventories and how they should interact with others, etc. It also presents some observations on models and their uses.

Inventory management employs a wide range of information technologies. These include databases, cost accounting, and statistical forecasting. It is important that you be conversant with these technologies, at least enough to be an intelligent consumer of them. This chapter provides a brief account of what they do, how they relate to inventory management, and where to get more information about them.

In this respect I am articulating an essentially conservative position. Many books and articles about inventory management say or imply that you should do your *own* accounting, forecasting, etc. Maybe so, 30 years ago. In those days many companies were unsophisticated in their uses of these technologies. Since then, however, the technologies and companies' uses of them have developed considerably. Today, in my view, it makes no sense to develop, say, your own personal cost accounting system. You are unlikely to do better than the experts, there are organizational and legal dangers in maintaining two sets of books, and you have other tasks to occupy your energies.

2.2 Contexts

2.2.1 Computer Systems

Look at some inventory-control software. Ask to see the systems used in your company or university. Go to a local retail store, and ask whether you can see the system used there. On the World Wide Web (WWW), go to one of the shareware sites, and download a couple of the inventory programs. Try them out. Do a search for inventory software; many commercial sites have demonstration packages.

Chances are that what you will find is, essentially, a database. It may be built on a general-purpose database program (e.g., Access, Paradox, Oracle) or on another type of application with database functions (e.g., Excel, 1-2-3). Even if it is a stand-alone program, however, it will look and act much like a database.

This is the beginning of wisdom about inventory control in practice. *An inventory system is, first and foremost, a database.* Such a system is structured as a database, and much of what it actually does is carried out through database functions.

The simplest and most common inventory systems are structured around a collection (or table) of *items*. These represent the goods available in a store, or the parts stored in a repair shop. The items are *independent* of each other. (Such systems are discussed in §§5.2 and 8.2. Later, we shall mention more complex databases, where the items are not independent.) There is a record for each item, containing basic descriptive information about it (name, code number, etc.). Typically, there are pointers to other structured information (e.g., a list of suppliers). In addition, there is a transaction history, including all orders, receipts, and withdrawals for each item; this is analogous to the ledger in a basic accounting system.

What does the system do? Well, people enter transactions. They add, delete, and change items. They compile summary reports for management. In sum, they do all the things that people do with other kinds of databases.

The quality and value of the system, moreover, depend to a large extent on how well it performs its database functions. Is it easy or hard to use, flexible or rigid, dependable or not? The answers depend entirely on the underlying database. People often complain about errors in inventory data, but that's true of all data. Good database programs include error control capabilities, and these are precisely the techniques available to control inventory errors, no more and no less.

Nevertheless, an inventory system is special in certain ways, namely, in the nature of the decisions and actions it supports. Specifically, *an inventory system triggers orders.* It may do so indirectly, by just signaling when an item's stock is low, leaving the action to a person. Or, it may place the order automatically. In either case, the system requires some logic to perform this task. (Other databases can support actions too; for example, a contact manager may indicate when it is time to phone a certain client.)

This is where models, the subject of this book, come in. An inventory model, among other things, provides the logic required by a computer-based inventory system to trigger orders. Although the model typically is a tiny fraction of the code of the system, it is a very important part. A bad model triggers bad decisions, and bad decisions lead to furious customers, irate suppliers, unhappy bankers, and stressed-out managers.

By the way, this answers a question that students of inventory theory often raise: How do you implement an inventory model? In most cases, the answer is simple: Code it up, and insert the code into an inventory system built on a database. The database program will take care of most of the technical difficulties that implementation entails (nice interface, pretty reports, etc.). (There are other issues in implementation, however, as discussed below.)

The answer today is of course very different from what it was 20 years ago. Then, before database programs were so widely available, it was often necessary to code the whole system from scratch, and so to worry about interfaces, reports, and all that. (And, since few modelers are good at all those things, the result was a lot of awful systems.) Today, on the other hand, one must know something about database technology to use it in an intelligent way.

Now, not every existing inventory system will allow you to insert code. Some have the decision logic "hard wired" (that is, buried in an inaccessible place in the program). In selecting such a system, therefore, look for one that is sufficiently modular to allow the decision logic to be revised and replaced. (Be warned, however: No such system is as flexible as you would like.)

Standard inventory systems, as mentioned above, treat the items as independent. In a production setting, however, the relevant items include materials, parts, components, subassemblies, and finished goods. These are *not* independent. They are related, in that the demand for one is generated by the needs for others. A different type of software is required for such situations. A *material requirements planning* (MRP) system is designed to capture and use such relationships. Such a system is still a database, but it is considerably more complex than an independent-item system. (See Chap. 5 for more information.) There are similar systems for other applications; for example, a distribution requirements planning (DRP) system applies the same structure to distribution. You can find a lot of MRP and DRP software via the WWW. Try some.

Even more ambitious are *enterprise resource planning* (ERP) systems. Such systems extend a common database technology to all the information needs of the enterprise. They differ from other databases mainly in scope and scale. Major providers of ERP software include SAP and Baan; many other companies provide related products. They are all on the Web too.

Finally, there are consulting and software companies that provide inventory applications tailored for particular industries.

Thus, there are a variety of off-the-shelf programs to support inventory management. None may fit a particular business perfectly, but they provide good starting points. There are cases, however, where no existing product adequately captures the real system. Thus, there is still a role for customized systems. Do remember that this is a costly and hazardous undertaking, and carefully consider the alternatives.

2.2.2 Monitoring

Inventory is driven by demand and supply. To control an inventory system, it is necessary to monitor and record demands and supplies as they occur. Does this sound obvious? Perhaps it is. Still, many companies neglect these basic chores.

Mind you, monitoring can be tricky. Nearly every company adequately records *sales,* but *demands* are something else. A demand is a potential sale. But, if the goods are unavailable, the customer may go elsewhere. Even if the customer is content to wait, and purchases the goods when they become available, it is important to record the time of the original demand as well as that of the later sale. Otherwise, we will have a distorted record of the time-pattern of demand.

In some situations it is easy to monitor demands. The customers of a catalogue retailer, for example, communicate with the company only by mail or phone or email, so it is easy to record each such contact, whether or not it leads to a sale. Likewise, in most industrial markets, demands arrive in the form of orders.

In other situations, however, monitoring demands is hard or impossible. Consider a grocery store. If a customer enters seeking almond-flavored herbal tea, but the store has none, the customer will leave empty-handed, or perhaps buy another flavor. There is no way to discern the customer's actual demand. There are special statistical methods to *estimate* demands from sales data (e.g., Nahmias [1994]), but these are difficult.

There are still other situations where demands can be recorded, but only with some effort. In a high-end clothing store, for instance, the sales staff try to talk to every customer who walks in the door. If a customer wants something that isn't there, it is likely that a salesperson knows about it. The trick, then, is to train the sales staff to record such events. Information technologies (e.g., with point-and-click item selection) can make this process easier.

On the supply side, similarly, it is important to record when each replenishment order is placed and when it is actually received. (The difference is precisely what we call the leadtime. As you will find throughout the book, this is a very important driver of performance.) Obvious? Yes. Does everybody do it faithfully? No. Be sure that your organization does.

Again, modern information technologies make this task much easier and more reliable than it once was. For example, bar-code scanners have vastly simplified the recording of deliveries.

2.2.3 Organizational Issues

Suppose a company has two main divisions, production and marketing. Production makes the products, and marketing distributes and sells them. Who should manage the inventories of finished goods?

One possible answer is production. They are the ones who actually make the goods, so it is natural that they control the end products. But wait: Those inventories are there to meet the needs of marketing, who use them to serve the ultimate customers. So, marketing should control the inventories. Here's yet another answer: Marketing people always demand more of everything, and production people always make excuses for not doing what they promised. Who looks out for the firm as a whole and its owners? Finance people, that's who. Let them manage the inventories.

Or, since these existing groups can't seem to agree, why not set up a separate department to manage the inventories? There's just one problem: Where should this department be located, to whom should it report? Oh dear, it looks like we're back where we were before.

This sort of dilemma confronts most organizations. Indeed, it is inherent in the very nature of inventory. Recall, inventories arise at the boundaries between firms, divisions, or plants, in order to facilitate supply-demand transactions. We should not be surprised that all sides want to control them for their own respective purposes. Such contention is natural and inevitable. (As one professional acquaintance put it, inventory management is part science and part blood sport.)

In truth, there is no universal answer to the question of who should manage inventory. Any of the answers above can work. The key point is, no matter who manages it, there must be mechanisms in place to ensure that all parties' desires and constraints are properly acknowledged and balanced.

Many firms recently have created *teams* to run supply chains, including managing inventories, comprising people from all the interested groups. Such teams sometimes even span company boundaries. This can be an effective approach. It is important to recognize, however, that a team simply localizes the natural contention between groups. The team must still work out methods to resolve conflicting goals.

A model typically aims to represent the concerns of different parties in its parameters. The production division's concerns, for example, might be captured through the cost of setups, while marketing's are represented by a stockout penalty. The model's solution, then, aims to serve the overall organization's goals by balancing those of the divisions.

This is good, but remember, compromise is a difficult art. A compromise, even for the common good, rarely silences all complaints. A model cannot eliminate contention. On the other hand, it can serve as a point of common reference, through which conflicts can be worked out.

2.3 Models

2.3.1 Overview

Modeling is a wonderful and mysterious art. It underlies much of science and engineering and hence is a basic element of modern life. It is a mode of thinking about and understanding the world and a mode of problem solving. A good model can be beautiful as well as useful.

Still, nobody really understands what a model is. Many have tried to define the term, none satisfactorily to my mind. Part of the problem is that different fields use models in different ways. Some of the models of physics (e.g., general relativity, quantum electrodynamics) are incredibly accurate depictions of the segments of reality they address. Those models essentially capture all our knowledge of their domains. The models of the social sciences, in contrast, are far less precise. They aim to capture some important broad features of their domains, while suppressing other less important details. In that setting, the construction of a model requires design decisions—what to include and what to leave out. Furthermore, engineers and scientists use models for quite different purposes. A scientist, whether physical or social, is trying to understand something; an engineer is trying to build something that works.

Operations research (OR), which includes the subject of this book, is more like engineering than science, and closer to the social realm than the physical. OR models always leave out more than they include, and their ultimate goal is practical utility, not pure knowledge. (This point, by the way, explains much of the unfortunate and sometimes amusing misunderstanding between operations researchers and economists. The models they use are quite similar, but their purposes are altogether different.)

Even among operations researchers there is quite a range of styles in making those design decisions. Some prefer to include as much relevant detail as possible, while others aim for simplicity above all. Inventory theory tends toward the latter style. Many of its basic models are radically simple. This approach, then, includes only the most important features of the problem, suppressing everything else. It takes some getting used to, but it's effective. (I happen to think that these models are beautiful too, but you can decide for yourself.)

There is another difficulty with the word *model.* People use it to describe both a piece of mathematics and a piece of computer software. These are different things. They may be related, that is, a computer model may implement a mathematical one. But, there are many ways to implement a given mathematical model, and the software always includes more than the mathematics. What you will find here in this book are mainly models of the mathematical kind, though many of them have indeed been implemented in software.

What else does the software implementing a model include? A model is a powerful but crude device. Because it omits much, some deviations between model and reality are inevitable, and a raw, naked model on its own may behave foolishly. To prevent this, it is often essential to surround the model with buffers, i.e., various functions to preprocess the data, postprocess the solution, and so forth. Most successful computer models are amply buffered in this manner.

Finally, a word about applications. Many have observed that applying a model is fraught with difficulties. The main reason, I believe, is that a computer model is a piece of technology. Just like a new type of machine, a computer model requires people to learn different skills and to work with others in different patterns. Such adjustments are difficult, costly and time-consuming. It is no wonder that people are conservative in adopting a new computer model. The model may seem perfectly natural to its creator, but to the people who have to use it, it's a strange and threatening device. Furthermore, again like a new machine, a model has political implications; it will increase some people's power and reduce others'. This is certainly true in the inventory arena, which is inherently political, as explained above.

Indeed, a vast majority of successful applications have one thing in common: They have been used elsewhere first. Nobody wants to be the first to try a brand new technology. Truly innovative models are rare.

If you understand these points and undertake applications keeping them in mind, your chances of success will improve considerably. I'm not saying never innovate. Just remember that every innovative feature of your model will require more effort in the application phase. And try to anticipate the technical and political difficulties your users will face in employing the model.

2.3.2 Cost Estimation

Many of the models in this book require cost factors—purchase costs, production setup costs, inventory holding costs, etc. Where do these come from? The short answer is, they come from cost (or managerial) accounting. That discipline is largely concerned with estimating costs of various kinds, including those used in inventory models. (See, e.g., Zimmerman [1997].) This answer, of course, begs the question: What do cost accountants do?

Well, much of what they do is addition. An item's purchase cost, for example, typically consists of several components. There is the actual price charged by the provider, taxes, transportation cost, physical handling cost, etc. The accountant's job is to find all these sources of cost and add them up. (The total acquisition cost is sometimes called the "all-in cost," to emphasize that it includes everything, not just the list price.) The same goes for the setup cost, holding cost, and so forth.

In a system with only one item, this job is straightforward. It becomes harder, however, when there are hundreds of thousands of items (not an unusual situation). It is impossible to do a separate study to determine the cost factors for each item. Moreover, often many of the cost components are not item-specific, but rather come from shared resources. The truck used for transportation, for example, may carry many items, not just one. Cost accountants have to know division too.

For a large, complex system, a cost accountant will try to identify the key *drivers* of cost, and then to use these to estimate the individual items' costs. Volume (in the geometric sense), for example, may serve as the driver of transportation cost. That is, determine the volume of each item, and divide the total transportation cost among the items by volume. If the results are not precise enough, add another driver, e.g., weight. This approach is sometimes called *activity-based costing* (ABC). It is entirely analogous to regression analysis, in that a few variables (the drivers) are used to estimate many other quantities (the items' costs).

There remains a thorny problem. Our models are supposed to represent the effects of alternative actions on the financial condition of the enterprise. In a model where the order quantity is a variable, for example, the objective function includes the holding cost, which is supposed to be correct for any possible order quantity. Consequently, the holding-cost factor, which multiplies the order quantity, should be a *prospective, marginal* value; it should measure the per-unit holding cost in the future. The trouble is that cost-estimation methods typically provide the *historical, average* value. They look backward instead of forward in time. They are based on actual past holding costs, the result of actual past order quantities. The result, as a predictor of future costs, is a pure extrapolation. Furthermore, such methods *allocate* the historical costs of shared resources across items. Even when that allocation is done cleverly, using well-chosen drivers, it mixes variable and fixed costs together. (Accountants are aware of this problem, and have tried to devise means to ameliorate it, with modest success.)

It may be some consolation that we are not the only ones with this problem. Nearly every sort of analysis tries to say something useful about the future based on past data. And so, it is customary for analysts to complain about accounting numbers (and to hate accountants). But could we do better? It's hard to see how. The key point is to recognize that cost estimates, even the most careful ones, are imperfect, and to use them with appropriate caution.

Stockout-penalty costs present a special problem. Whereas inventory holding costs, say, are internal to the firm, a stockout mainly affects somebody else. One can measure a holding cost (subject to the caveats above), but it is harder to imagine measuring the cost of a stockout to a customer. In any case, accounting systems typically do not touch such costs.

Faced with this difficulty, many people simply give up. As we shall see, it is possible to formulate an inventory model without stockout-cost parameters, using constraints instead, and those people find this approach more comfortable. If you are one of those people, rest assured, the book includes such formulations. My own view, however, is that this just translates the problem to different terms. The basic problem remains to understand what stockouts mean to customers.

This is essentially a problem of market research. Fortunately, marketers have come to recognize the importance of customer response time and have devised methods to assess its importance to customers. (The methods are basically the same as those used to measure other dimensions of product quality.) We are rapidly passing beyond the point where the inventory analyst had to pick a number out of the air, whether a penalty cost or a constraint.

Incidentally, the difficulties of cost estimation have influenced the structure of the book. There is an emphasis throughout on policy evaluation in physical terms, which doesn't require cost estimates, before policy optimization, which does. Policy evaluation is always useful, but especially when reliable cost numbers are hard to get.

2.3.3 Demand Forecasting

Inventories, among other things, are largely driven by forecasts, especially of demand. To manage inventories effectively, therefore, one must know something about demand forecasting.

Here is my view on the matter: A forecast is one kind of statistical estimate. Forecasting methods *are* statistical methods. To learn forecasting, therefore, study statistics.

Of course, there is more to statistics than forecasting. Much of statistics concerns static or cross-sectional data, e.g., the fraction of people over 6 feet tall at one particular time. Many basic statistics books and courses focus on cross-sectional problems and say little about forecasting. Forecasting is about dynamic or longitudinal or time-series data. A forecast is a statement about the future, which no one has observed yet. Even so, the basic approach of forecasting is precisely that of statistical estimation in general: Take some information you know and use it to estimate something you don't know. That unknown something can be a parameter of a static population or a demand value in the future.

For instance, you probably know that a point estimate is one particular number, the best (most likely or average or some such) guess for an unknown quantity. You probably know too that, while a point estimate is better than nothing, it is incomplete. It is wise to supplement a point estimate with some measure of its accuracy or precision, such as the sample variance or range. This is the rationale for interval estimates, like confidence intervals.

Now, forecasts are often presented in the form of point estimates. "We expect demand next month to be 3508 cases." This is what people expect a forecast to look like. Even forecasters who know statistics consider their jobs to be the creation of such statements. But forecasts have different degrees of precision, just like other estimates, and the usefulness of any forecast is a direct function of its precision. This is true in general, and it is certainly true in inventory management. As emphasized throughout the book, one of the key drivers of inventory policies and performance is demand uncertainty, that is, forecast error. Without some measure of forecast accuracy, it is impossible to manage inventory intelligently.

This raises another point about monitoring. To assess forecast accuracy, it is essential to monitor actual demands, as discussed above. But it is equally essential to keep records of past forecasts. You would be amazed how many companies simply discard old forecasts. It is necessary to set up a database to store those old forecasts, but it is well worth the effort.

Many discussions of forecasting concentrate on methods, techniques, algorithms. "Here are the directions for the exponential-smoothing method. . . ." This emphasis is misplaced, in my view. It is exactly analogous to learning the technique of regression analysis without understanding the basic concept.

The whole purpose of the forecasting activity is to construct a concept, or story, or picture, of the world out there, the system that drives demand. The numbers are important, to be sure, but they make little sense without this broader context. Every forecast is based on a *model* of demand. That model may be implicit in some cases, but it is there all the same. (It is analogous to the linear model which underlies regression analysis.) Every forecasting method, moreover, can be interpreted as fitting the parameters of such a model. It is important to understand the underlying models, because they are quite different. (§C.6.4 in Appendix C discusses the model underlying one popular forecasting method.)

A word about software: If you are actually doing forecasting, you should get one of the available packages. This is cheaper and more reliable than writing your own code. The manuals and help screens of these packages are, in some cases, good introductions to the whole subject of forecasting.

Notes

The World Wide Web is an excellent source of information about many of the topics of this chapter. To find out more about databases, for example, use any of the popular search engines with the keyword *database.*

Here are a few web sites that you may find of interest:

http://www.mhhe.com/business/opsci/pom/ This is the Operations Management Center, hosted by our publisher. It has lots of information about operations in general.

http://www.apics.org/ APICS is the American Production and Inventory Control Society. It is a good source for many topics, especially MRP and ERP.

http://www.clm1.org/ The Council of Logistics Management, another professional society.

http://www.informs.org/ The Institute for Operations Research and the Management Sciences, a professional and academic organization.

http://www.lmi.org/ The Logistics Management Institute, a nonprofit corporation that advises government agencies on logistics issues.

For an overview of cost accounting, see Zimmerman [1997].

The notes to Appendix C cite some books on forecasting. Also, the magazine *OR/MS Today* conducts and reports a yearly survey of forecasting software.

C H A P T E R

3 One Item with a Constant Demand Rate

Outline

3.1 Introduction

This chapter undertakes a detailed exploration of the meaning and impact of *economies of scale* in supply. Except for this characteristic, the supply and demand processes are as simple as they could be. The systems here are structurally simple too, involving a single product at a single location.

Time and the product itself are both continuous, or in other words, *infinitely divisible.* This is a modeling choice. In reality, products like orange juice, petroleum, wood pulp and bauxite *are* infinitely divisible, while airplanes, computers and steel mills are not. (3.62 gallons of orange juice has a specific value, but a fraction of an airplane is worthless.) Things like screws, finished paper, and medicine bottles are intermediate cases; such items may be thought of as infinitely divisible for some purposes, even though they are not really so.

Demand for the item occurs at a known, constant rate, continuously over time; the demand over 1.672 years is precisely 1.672 times the annual demand rate. The complicating features of other demand processes are abstracted away: Demand is smooth, not lumpy; there are no variations over time, neither predictable nor unpredictable ones; et cetera.

The supply process is also simple. However, it *cannot* supply the item at the precise, constant rate of the demand process. Supply and demand are not perfectly matched, and they cannot be linked in an ideal flow system. Supply occurs in discrete *batches* or *lots,* because of its underlying technology and economics. Each batch, no matter how small, incurs a *fixed cost.* This is the simplest form of economy of scale. (Much of the chapter is concerned with how large these lots should be; the topic is sometimes called *lot sizing.*) Also, the supply process responds to replenishment orders only after a fixed *leadtime.* As we shall see, this feature is not very significant here.

We start with a very basic model in Section 3.2, the economic-order-quantity (EOQ) model. The key assumption is that demand must be filled immediately; stockouts are forbidden. The subsequent sections treat important variations of this model.

Section 3.3 relaxes the no-stockout assumption to allow planned backorders.

The next three sections explore variants of the supply system. Section 3.4 focuses on a production process which produces the item at a constant, finite rate. This model incorporates a simple capacity limit. Section 3.5 treats more complex economies of scale arising from quantity discounts. Section 3.6 examines the effects of imperfect quality.

Section 3.7 reformulates the EOQ model using a different cost objective. The EOQ model aims to minimize the long-run *average* cost over time. This new model is based instead on the *present value* of future costs. We then reinterpret the original EOQ model as an approximation to the new one.

Many other variants of the EOQ model have been developed in response to diverse practical needs. Some are explored in the problems at the end of the chapter.

The models of this chapter are highly stylized, with all their simplifying assumptions, but they are nonetheless widely used in practice. Also, the methodology and the intuition we build up here will provide a solid basis for understanding the more elaborate and realistic models presented later.

This chapter requires little mathematics beyond basic calculus.

Before getting started, let us set forth some basic vocabulary: We need two units of measurement, a unit of *time* (days, months, years, etc.) and a unit of physical *quantity* (tons, bushels, gallons, etc.). For now we use the abstract terms "time-units" and "quantity-units." In a real application, of course, we would choose specific units of measurement instead.

3.2 The Economic-Order-Quantity Model

3.2.1 Setting the Scene

Our task is to manage a single product at a single location over time. Demand occurs continuously at a constant rate:

$$\lambda = \text{demand rate (quantity-units/time-units)}$$

Imagine that we start with some inventory. The inventory decreases at rate λ as stock is depleted to fill the demand. At some point, we must replenish the stock. To accomplish this, we send an order to the supply system. An order is a request for a specific amount of product. The supply process delivers that quantity after a constant leadtime, denoted

$$L = \text{leadtime (time-units)}$$

FIGURE 3.2.1

Inventory over time.

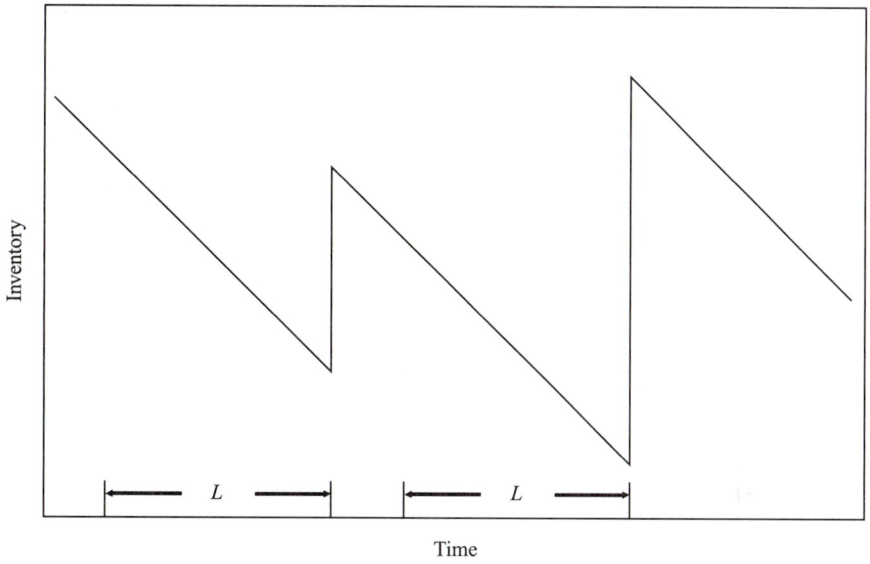

(*L* does not depend in any way on the time or size of the order. We are assuming, in effect, that the supplier has unlimited quantities available.) Subsequently, demands further deplete the inventory, and we continue to place and receive orders for supplies.

This scenario roughly describes the situation at a retail outlet, which receives finished goods from a supplier and sells them to customers; the leadtime represents order-processing and transportation time. With minor changes in wording, however, the same model depicts a simple production process. An "order" becomes a signal to produce a certain amount. The entire batch is completed after *L* time units and then becomes available to meet demand. For example, *L* might represent the time required to procure raw materials and set up a machine, actual production being virtually instantaneous. (This story presumes no capacity limit. Section 3.4 treats a limited-capacity production process.)

Figure 3.2.1 describes the net effects of supply and demand on inventory. Most of the time, inventory decreases linearly with slope $-\lambda$. When we place an order, nothing happens until *L* time units later, when the corresponding batch arrives. At that point, the inventory jumps up by the amount received.

What would happen if we neglected to order, and inventory dropped to zero? After that, for a while at least, we would be unable to meet demand. Such stockouts are forbidden: We always order far enough in advance that *stock is available to meet all demand.* (Section 3.3 drops this restriction.)

To control an inventory under this scenario means to answer two questions: *When should an order be placed, and how much should be ordered?* (These basic questions capture the essence of inventory control under a variety of circumstances.)

To focus the search for answers, we make two further assumptions. First, subject to the requirement that all demand be filled immediately, we never order earlier than necessary. In other words, each order arrives precisely at a moment when we would otherwise run out of stock. (This is sometimes called the *zero-inventory property.*) Second, each order is of the same size. (These rules should seem reasonable. Problems 3.1 and 3.2 provide rigorous support for them.)

Define the following functions (measured in quantity-units) of time t (measured in time-units) for $t \geq 0$:

$I(t)$ = *inventory* at time t

$IO(t)$ = *inventory on order,* the total stock ordered before t but not yet received by t

$IP(t)$ = *inventory position* at time $t = I(t) + IO(t)$

This double-letter notation (IO and IP) allows us to distinguish different quantities, all related to inventories. By convention all these functions are right-continuous. For example, if an order arrives at time t, $I(t)$ is the inventory *after* the arrival, not before. To indicate the inventory just *before* the arrival, write $I(t^{-})$. Figure 3.2.2 depicts these functions.

Also, let

$$D = \lambda L = \text{demand during a leadtime}$$

Think of time t as now, so the current inventory is $I(t)$. How does it change from t to $t + L$? The new supplies arriving in that interval total exactly $IO(t)$, and the demand is $\lambda L = D$. Consequently,

FIGURE 3.2.2

Inventory and inventory position.

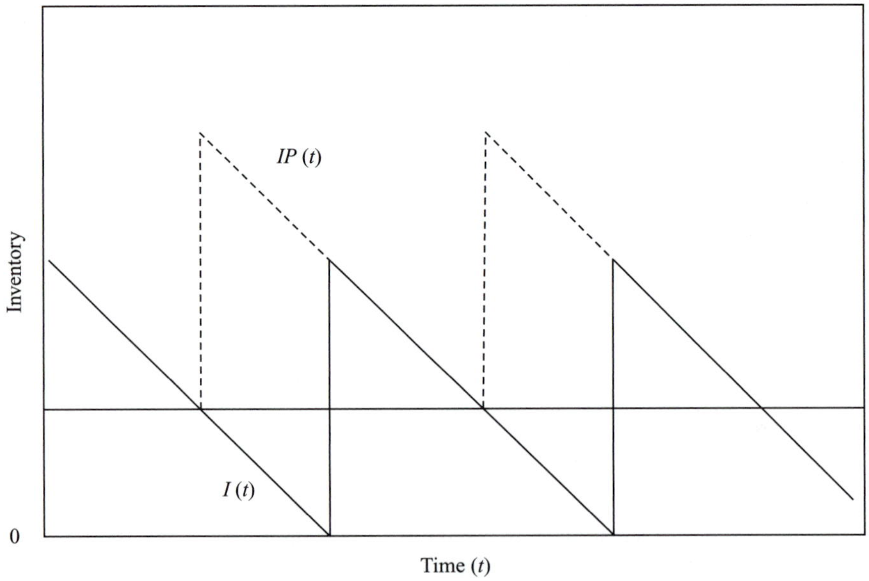

$$I(t + L) = I(t) + IO(t) - D \tag{3.2.1}$$
$$= IP(t) - D$$

(This relation between $I(t)$ and $I(t + L)$ is a *conservation-of-flow* law. Such laws are important characteristics of many inventory systems.) Thus, the inventory position $IP(t)$ neatly summarizes information about the present, namely $I(t)$ and $IO(t)$, to help predict future inventory. In particular, the zero-inventory rule can be expressed as follows:

> Monitor the inventory position $IP(t)$ constantly. When $IP(t^-) = D$, place a new order at time t.

Having settled the issue of when to order, we must still specify the amount. (Remember, all orders are of the same size.) For now, we give it a name:

$$q = \text{order or batch size (quantity-units)}$$

This is a policy variable. We now develop a model and analyze it, in order to determine the best value of q.

3.2.2 *Performance Criteria*

There are two relevant criteria for the performance of the system: We do not want to order too frequently, because of scale economies, nor do we want to carry too much inventory. These guidelines are too broad to guide action; we need to translate them into more precise criteria. The approach here focuses on *long-run averages* over time. (This formulation should seem natural, but Section 3.7 describes a different one.) The system operates forever, over the time interval $[0,\infty)$, and we measure performance by the following quantities:

$$\overline{I} = \text{average inventory}$$
$$= \lim_{T\to\infty}\{(1/T)\textstyle\int_0^T I(t)\,dt\}$$
$$\overline{OF} = \text{order frequency}$$
$$= \lim_{T\to\infty}\{(1/T)(\text{number of orders in } [0, T])\}$$

Notice that in Figure 3.2.2 $IP(t)$ and $I(t)$ are periodic. We can thus determine the long-run averages $\overline{I}$ and $\overline{OF}$ by examining what happens during one *cycle,* the time interval between the receipts of two successive orders. The length of each cycle is q/λ, and there is one order per cycle. Therefore,

$$\overline{OF} = \frac{1}{q/\lambda} = \frac{\lambda}{q}$$

Also, during a cycle, $I(t)$ decreases linearly from q to 0, so the average inventory during the cycle is $\tfrac{1}{2}q$. Thus,

$$\overline{I} = \tfrac{1}{2}q$$

We now have a simple formula for each performance measure.

Incidentally, we have implicitly assumed that inventory on order is of no concern. In effect, we take ownership of goods only when we actually receive them. (Otherwise, if we pay on ordering, an additional term is needed in the total average inventory. This extra term happens to be D, a constant, independent of q.)

Notice that $\overline{I}$ is increasing in q, while $\overline{OF}$ is decreasing. *These two criteria are in direct conflict:* We can exploit economies of scale in the supply process by choosing a large q, but this leads to large average inventory; we can economize on inventory, but only at the expense of a high order frequency.

So, how should we select q? There are two basic approaches. Sometimes the world outside the model imposes a *constraint* on $\overline{I}$ or $\overline{OF}$. Either the inventory or the order frequency cannot exceed a prescribed upper limit. In either case it is clear what to do: An upper bound on $\overline{I}$ implies an upper bound on q. So, to minimize $\overline{OF}$, set q as large as possible, precisely at its upper bound. Likewise, given a limit on $\overline{OF}$, set q so as to hit the limit precisely.

Without such constraints, the conflict remains. To resolve it, suppose we can translate the two criteria to a common scale, monetary cost. That is, we compute the costs entailed by orders and inventory, and combine them into an overall cost measure.

To do this, we estimate *cost factors* for procurement and inventory holding. These cost factors remain constant over time. We measure all costs in some standard monetary unit; here, we use the abstract term "moneys." Specifically,

k = fixed cost to place an order (moneys)

c = variable cost to place an order (moneys/quantity-unit)

h = cost to hold one unit in inventory for one unit of time (moneys/[quantity-unit · time-unit])

The definition of h means, in effect, that at time t an inventory of $I(t)$ causes cost to accumulate at the rate of $hI(t)$.

The estimation of these cost factors is discussed in Chapter 2 and elsewhere in the book. For now we mention a few basic facts: The fixed cost k represents all order costs that are independent of the order size. It typically includes administrative order-processing costs as well as transportation and receiving costs. In a production setting k may include a setup cost. Thus, k reflects *economies of scale* in the supply process. The variable cost c comprises the unit purchase cost as well as any other costs that do depend on the order size. The total cost per order is thus $k + cq$.

The holding cost h typically includes two major components. The first comprises all direct costs associated with inventory itself, including costs for physical handling, insurance, refrigeration, and warehouse rental. Denote all these direct costs by $\underline{h}$. The second component is a financing cost αc, where α is an interest rate, reflecting the fact that holding inventory ties up capital. (Section 3.7 discusses this point further.) Thus, $h = \underline{h} + \alpha c$.

These cost factors, along with the physical performance measures $\overline{OF}$ and I, determine the average costs per unit time: The long-run average order cost is $(k + cq)\overline{OF}$, and the average inventory-holding cost is $h\overline{I}$. The overall performance criterion is the sum of these two quantities:

FIGURE 3.2.3

Total average cost.

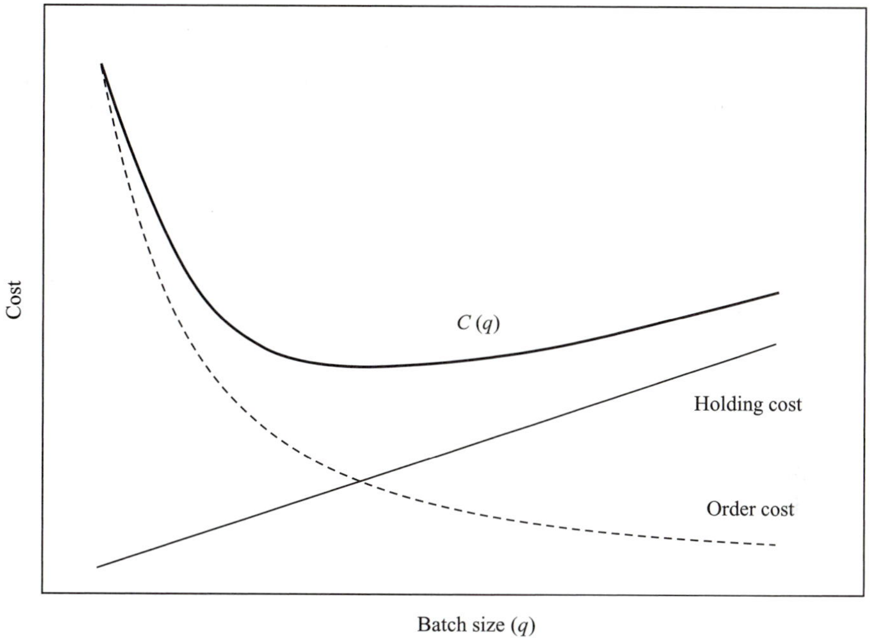

$$\begin{aligned} C(q) &= \text{total average cost (moneys/time-unit)} \\ &= (k + cq)\overline{OF} + h\overline{I} \\ &= c\lambda + k\lambda/q + \tfrac{1}{2}hq \qquad q > 0 \end{aligned}$$

Figure 3.2.3 graphs this function.

We have now completed the formulation of the basic model of this section, the classic *economic-order-quantity* (EOQ) model.

This is as good a time as any to issue a friendly *WARNING:* Before using $C(q)$, or any of the other results in this section, chapter, and book, it is essential to *convert all parameters to the same units.* For example, λ might be expressed originally in metric tons per month, and h in dollars per carton per year. One or both must be adjusted, so that both use the same quantity-unit and time-unit. Otherwise, $C(q)$ is meaningless. (Problem 3.4 requires such a conversion.)

Of course, careful attention to units is necessary in any calculation. You know that; you probably learned it in high school, if not before. The world of inventory management, however, is pitted with traps for the unwary. This may be because the data are drawn from numerous sources, each with its own unit conventions. Whatever the cause, mistakes are common. To avoid them, experienced people routinely take extra precautions. You would be wise to do the same.

EXAMPLE 3.2.A, PART 1

You are responsible for paper supplies in the copying room in a medium-sized office. Paper usage averages 8 boxes per week. Each box costs $25. The shipping cost per order, regardless of size, is $50, and receiving an order takes about an hour of your time, which costs the company $80. Each order takes a week to arrive. The company figures financing costs at 15% per year. Keeping the boxes organized costs about $1.10/week per box. Currently, you order 2 weeks' worth of supplies with each order. What is the average cost of this policy? Use boxes, weeks, and $ as the units. In the notation above,

$$\lambda = 8 \qquad c = 25 \qquad k = 50 + 80 = 130$$

$$\alpha = \frac{0.15}{52} = 0.0029$$

$$h = 1.10 + (0.0029)(25) = 1.173 \qquad q = (2)(8) = 16$$

$$C(q) = (25)(8) + \frac{(130)(8)}{16} + \frac{1}{2}(1.173)(16)$$

$$\approx 200 + 65 + 9 = 274$$

3.2.3 The Optimal Policy

The function $C(q)$ measures the total cost for any possible order size, q. Our goal now is to find the *optimal* value of q, denoted q^*, the one that minimizes this function. The plan is to apply a classic technique of calculus: Compute the derivative $C'(q)$ and equate it to zero.

(This technique works only under certain conditions. Here, fortunately, those conditions are met. The domain of C is the open interval $(0, \infty)$, and on that domain C is continuously differentiable and strictly convex. These properties imply that $C'(q) = 0$ is necessary and sufficient for optimality, and the optimal solution is unique. See Appendix A if any of these notions is unfamiliar.)

Here goes:

$$C'(q) = -\frac{k\lambda}{q^2} + \frac{1}{2}h = 0$$

This equation has the unique positive solution

$$q^* = \sqrt{2k\lambda/h} \tag{3.2.2}$$

This formula is called the *economic order quantity* (EOQ). It is a truly fundamental result: It is widely applied in practice. And, as we consider more complex settings later on, we shall encounter it and variations of it again and again.

It is sometimes convenient to work with the alternative variable

$$u = \text{time between orders, or order interval} = q/\lambda$$

The entire analysis above can be conducted in terms of u instead of q. In particular, $\overline{OF} = 1/u$ and $\overline{I} = ½\lambda u$. The average cost can then be expressed as a function of u. (A graph of this function looks just like Figure 3.2.3; since u is a linear transformation of q, we are just rescaling the horizontal axis.) Some of the models of Chapter 5 follow this approach. Meanwhile, the optimal order interval here can be obtained immediately from (3.2.2):

$$u^* = \sqrt{2k/\lambda h}. \tag{3.2.3}$$

We can implement the optimal policy using u^* instead of q^*: Place the first order L time units before we would otherwise run out of stock. From then on place a new order each u^* time units. Under this rule, clearly, the functions $IP(t)$ and $I(t)$ have precisely the same values as before. Since the demand rate is constant, we can equivalently monitor the inventory position or time. (This notion can be expressed in a pleasant little rhyme: Watch the stock or watch the clock.) In the context of stochastically varying demands, however, time-based and quantity-based controls are quite different, as we shall see later.

Substituting (3.2.2) back into $\overline{I}$ and $\overline{OF}$ yields

$$\overline{I} = \sqrt{\frac{k\lambda}{2h}} \qquad \overline{OF} = \sqrt{\frac{\lambda h}{2k}}$$

and so

$$h\overline{I} = k\overline{OF} = \sqrt{\frac{k\lambda h}{2}}$$

Thus, the average holding cost and the average (fixed) order cost are equal at the optimal $q = q^*$. By itself this identity is just an odd coincidence, but it leads to a formula for the optimal cost:

$$C^* = C(q^*) = c\lambda + \sqrt{2k\lambda h} \tag{3.2.4}$$

EXAMPLE 3.2.A, PART 2

For the paper supply problem above,

$$q^* = \left[\frac{2(130)(8)}{1.173}\right]^{1/2} \approx 42$$

$$u^* = \left[\frac{2(130)}{(8)(1.173)}\right]^{1/2} \approx 5.25$$

$$C^* = 200 + [2(130)(8)(1.173)]^{1/2} \approx 249$$

The optimal policy orders more boxes (25 instead of 16) less frequently (every 5.25 weeks instead of 2) than the current policy. The optimal total cost is less (249 instead of 274).

3.2.4 Sensitivity Analysis

The simple form of the EOQ formula (3.2.2) allows us to address directly "what-if" questions. Here is an important example: What is the effect on q^* of a change in the demand rate, say from λ to λ'? Denote the new value of q^* by $q^{*\prime}$. Then,

$$q^{*\prime}/q^* = \sqrt{\lambda'/\lambda}$$

The formula says that

1. The optimal order size changes in the *same direction* as the demand rate, *but*
2. The *relative* change in the optimal order size is *smaller* than that of the demand rate (i.e., $q^{*\prime}/q^*$ is closer to 1 than λ'/λ).

Thus, if demand doubles ($\lambda'/\lambda = 2$), $q^{*\prime}/q^*$ is only $\sqrt{2} \approx 1.414$. In order to lower q^* by half ($q^{*\prime}/q^* = ½$), λ must decrease by 75% ($\lambda'/\lambda = ¼$).

In other words, q^* is *robust* with respect to changes in λ. This is a crucial property in practice. In the real world, none of our assumptions will be fulfilled strictly. We must estimate λ, and the estimate is virtually sure to contain some error. Nevertheless, provided the relative error is not too large, the q^* computed with the estimated λ is close to the true value. Moreover, λ is likely to change over time. Still, as long as the relative change is small, the q^* given by (3.2.2) remains useful. (Chapter 4 discusses this point in greater detail.) This robustness is one reason the EOQ formula is used so widely, in spite of the rather heroic assumptions on which it is based.

These observations follow from the fact that q^* varies as the square root of λ. Evidently, q^* depends on the cost factors k and h in the same manner. Thus, q^* is robust with respect to changes in k and h as well.

EXAMPLE 3.2.A, PART 3

For the paper supply problem above, if λ increases from 8 to 12, then q^* increases by the factor $\sqrt{1\frac{1}{2}} \approx 1.22$, from 42 to about 51. Returning to $\lambda = 8$, if we can reduce k from130 to 100 (by lowering the shipping cost, not your salary!), then q^* becomes $(1/\sqrt{1.3})\,(42) \approx 37$.

There is another sense in which the EOQ model is robust: Omit the variable purchase cost $c\lambda$ from $C(q)$ and C^* for the moment. Define the function

$$\epsilon(x) = \frac{1}{2}\left(x + \frac{1}{x}\right) \qquad x > 0$$

With a bit of algebra you can show (see Prob. 3.6) that

$$\frac{C(q)}{C^*} = \epsilon\left(\frac{q}{q^*}\right) \tag{3.2.5}$$

Suppose we use the "wrong" value q instead of q^*, because of errors in parameter estimates, or additional constraints not included in the model, or any other reason. Then, the relative cost of this suboptimal policy, compared to the true optimal cost, depends only on the relative error in q itself, as indicated by (3.2.5). The formula is entirely independent of the cost and demand parameters. (ϵ is sometimes called the *EOQ error function.*)

Formula (3.2.5) always produces values greater than 1 (unless of course $q = q^*$). However, $\epsilon(x)$ grows slowly as x departs from 1, so the relative cost penalty is *small,* provided q is reasonably close to q^*. For example, suppose we overestimate q^* by one-third, so $q/q^* = 4/3$. Then, $C(q)/C^* = 25/24$, a cost penalty of only 1/24 or just over 4%. The cost penalty is the same if q underestimates q^* by 25%, so $q/q^* = 3/4$.

This finding has another practical implication: It has been suggested that there are advantages to setting lot sizes systematically lower than the EOQ model prescribes. Lower lot sizes and inventories, the reasoning goes, encourage managers and workers to seek opportunities to improve the system. This is one element of the just-in-time (JIT) approach to operations. Now, there is some dispute as to whether this is really an effective way to motivate people. (I'm skeptical; see Zipkin [1991a].) Even so, the cost penalty for *trying* this approach is modest, provided we don't overdo it. For instance, if we purposely set q to 90% of q^*, the cost will increase only slightly. On the other hand, if we set q to 5% of q^*, the cost penalty will be substantial indeed.

The simple cost formula (3.2.4) also makes it easy to estimate the benefits of operational improvements in the system. For example, suppose the supply process models a production activity, and k represents a setup cost. We may be able to *reduce* k through engineering changes or training programs. (There is now a fairly well developed technology for reducing setups. This is another element of the JIT approach; see Shingo [1985], for example.) This will permit us to lower q and hence save on inventory holding costs. Assuming we use the appropriate q^* both before and after the improvement, we can use (3.2.4) to estimate the overall cost reduction. This approach is discussed further in § 3.7 and Problems 3.7 and 3.27.

It is worth remarking that some parameters have no effects. First, q^* does not depend at all on the variable-cost parameter c. The intuitive reason is that the long-run average supply rate must equal the demand rate λ, so the average variable order cost must be $c\lambda$, a constant independent of q. (However, as mentioned above, h usually depends partly on c, so changing c does change q^* indirectly.) Also, neither q^* nor C^* depends on the leadtime L. The leadtime merely introduces a delay between actions (orders) and their effects. If the leadtime were to increase, we would need to order earlier, but this would happen automatically via the trigger quantity $D = \lambda L$ in the order rule. All this reflects the fact that, given the current inventory position, we know *exactly* when we will run out of stock. Thus, according to this model, there is no advantage to reducing the leadtime. (Of course, such perfect foresight rests on the assumption of perfectly known leadtimes and demands. As we shall see later, in a stochastic system the leadtime *does* have an impact, and leadtime reduction is valuable indeed.)

3.3 Planned Backorders

3.3.1 The Setting

Consider the same EOQ system, but relax the requirement that all demand be met from stock on hand. All demands are ultimately filled, though perhaps after a delay. That is, demands not filled immediately are *backordered.* Customers are willing to wait, and we are committed to meet their demands. (An alternative scenario is *lost sales,* where demands not filled immediately are never filled. We discuss this case below in Section 3.3.7.) We always use any inventory on hand to fill demands; backorders accumulate only when we run out of stock entirely.

Of course, we could choose to operate the system without backorders by following the policy described for the EOQ model. Permitting backorders enlarges the set of feasible operating policies.

Many businesses do operate with substantial backlogs. This is certainly true of capital-goods firms and the service industries. There, the products are expensive (or, in the case of services, impossible) to store. These are extreme cases, but even in other markets (industrial materials, for example) occasional backorders are pervasive.

3.3.2 Reorder-Point/Order-Quantity Policies

Let us define some new functions and redefine some of those used in Section 3.2:

$$I(t) = \text{inventory at time } t$$

$$B(t) = \text{backorders at time } t$$

$$IN(t) = \text{net inventory at time } t = I(t) - B(t)$$

$$IO(t) = \text{stock on order at time } t$$

$$IP(t) = \text{inventory position at time } t = IN(t) + IO(t)$$

The new functions are $B(t)$ and $IN(t)$, and $IP(t)$ has a new meaning.

The net inventory $IN(t)$ captures the information in both $I(t)$ and $B(t)$: At any given time, at least one of those two functions is zero, since we use any available stock to fill demand. Therefore,

$$IN(t) = \begin{cases} I(t) & \text{when } IN(t) \geq 0 \\ -B(t) & \text{when } IN(t) \leq 0 \end{cases}$$

or

$$I(t) = [IN(t)]^+ \qquad B(t) = [IN(t)]^-$$

The definition of $IN(t)$ treats backorders as negative inventories, and indeed they function in this way: Between receipts of orders, $IN(t)$ decreases at the constant rate λ, regardless of whether $IN(t)$ is positive or negative. When an order arrives, $IN(t)$ jumps up by precisely q in all cases; some of the batch may be used to fill backorders, and the rest is added to inventory. Thus, $IN(t)$ behaves much like $I(t)$ did before, when backorders were forbidden, while now $I(t)$ itself is more complex. See Figure 3.3.1. ($IN(t)$ is sometimes called the inventory level.)

Also,

$$\begin{aligned} IN(t+L) &= IN(t) + IO(t) - D \\ &= IP(t) - D \end{aligned} \tag{3.3.1}$$

This relation is the direct analogue of (3.2.1), with $IN(\cdot)$ replacing $I(\cdot)$. It is the conservation-of-flow law for this system: Between t and $t + L$, $IO(t)$ gets added to the net inventory, and D gets subtracted. Thus, $IP(t)$ summarizes all the information needed to predict the net inventory a leadtime into the future.

FIGURE 3.3.1

Net inventory.

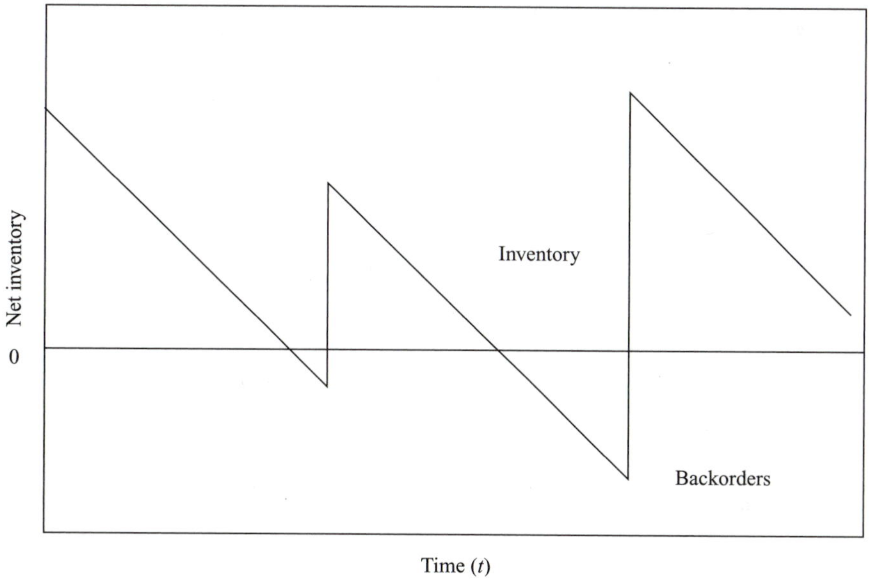

As in the EOQ model, assume that all orders are of the same size $q > 0$. The issue of *when* to order is now more complex. We need a second policy variable in addition to q:

$$r = \text{reorder point (quantity-units)}$$

This variable can take on any real value, positive or negative. Consider the following policy:

> Monitor the inventory position $IP(t)$ constantly. When $IP(t^-) = r$, place a new order of size q at time t.

(The EOQ model's policies are special cases with $r = D$.) In honor of the two variables, a policy of this kind is called a *reorder-point/order-quantity* or (r, q) policy. Figure 3.3.2 illustrates the behavior of $IN(t)$ and $IP(t)$ under such a policy. Note the similarity of Figures 3.3.2 and 3.2.2. The graph retains the same sawtooth pattern, but now the pattern can shift vertically, depending on the choice of r.

3.3.3 Performance Criteria

The relevant criteria still include $\overline{I}$ and $\overline{OF}$, but we need more. While the model allows backorders, that does not mean they are welcome. Customers do not like to wait, and if we hope to please them, we had better not make them wait too often or too long. Moreover, just as we do not have to pay for orders prior to delivery, so customers typically delay payments until their demands are filled. Sometimes there is even a direct monetary

FIGURE 3.3.2

IP(t) and IN(t) under an (r, q) policy.

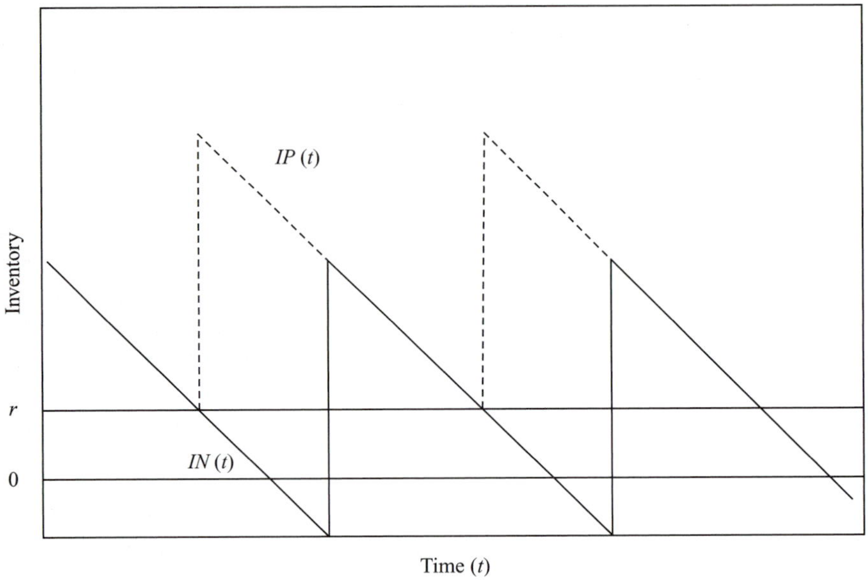

cost for backorders, as in a contractual penalty for late delivery. For a variety of reasons, then, we need to measure and control backorders.

The primary backorder-related performance measure is the following:

$$\begin{aligned}\overline{B} &= \text{long-term average outstanding backorders}\\ &= \lim_{T\to\infty}\{(1/T)\textstyle\int_0^T B(t)\,dt\}\end{aligned}$$

(The limit here is analogous to the one defining $\overline{I}$.) There is another criterion which plays a secondary but still important role:

$$\begin{aligned}A(t) &= \mathbf{1}\{IN(t) \le 0\}\\ \overline{A} &= \text{long-run fraction of time out of stock, or stockout frequency}\\ &= \lim_{T\to\infty}\{(1/T)\textstyle\int_0^T A(t)\,dt\}\end{aligned}$$

(Here, $\mathbf{1}\{\cdot\}$ is the indicator function and $A(t)$ is an indicator variable, taking the value 1 when $IN(t) \le 0$ and 0 otherwise.) Clearly, $\overline{A}$ also measures the fraction of demands backordered. Thus, the average *number* of demands backordered per unit time is $\lambda\overline{A}$, and the *fill rate,* the fraction of demands met from stock, is $1 - \overline{A}$. (Terminology alert: We often call $\overline{B}$ the backorders for short. Because $\overline{A}$ measures the backorder frequency, however, some writers call *it* the backorders, referring to $\overline{B}$ as the *time-weighted* backorders.)

Let us now compute the criteria as functions of the policy variables q and r. It is convenient to replace r by the equivalent variable

$$v = \text{safety stock} = r - \mathrm{D}$$

(The phrase *safety stock* suggests a positive quantity, but v can be negative! Still, this definition is consistent with standard usage in stochastic-demand models. There, the safety stock is usually positive.) Again, call a cycle the time between the receipts of successive orders, and u the cycle time. Also, define a time-equivalent to v,

$$y = \text{safety time} = \frac{v}{\lambda}$$

Like v, y can be negative.

For any given q, only certain values of v make sense: Equation (3.3.1) implies that the net inventory $IN(t^-)$ just at the end of a cycle is precisely v, so $IN(t) = v + q$ at the beginning of a cycle. Therefore,

1. If $v > 0$, then for all t

$$I(t) > v > 0 \qquad \text{and} \qquad B(t) = 0$$

2. If $v < -q$, then for all t

$$I(t) = 0 \qquad \text{and} \qquad B(t) > -(v + q) > 0$$

Neither conclusion is appealing: In case 1, we have more inventory than we actually need, and in case 2 we never fill all backorders. So, we can and do restrict attention to the range $-q \leq v \leq 0$. So, v *is* negative (more precisely, nonpositive), as is y, and each arriving order fills all current backorders.

Thus, a cycle consists of two parts, one of length $u + y = (q + v)/\lambda$, during which inventory is held, and a second part of length $-y = -v/\lambda$, when backorders accumulate. (See Figure 3.3.3.) These intervals correspond to the fractions $(q + v)/q$ and $-v/q$, respectively, of the full cycle. In particular,

$$\overline{A} = -\frac{v}{q}$$

The average inventory is simply ½$(q + v)$ during the first part and zero during the second. The average over a full cycle is a weighted average of these quantities:

$$\overline{I} = \left(\frac{q+v}{q}\right)\left[\frac{1}{2}(q+v)\right] + \left(\frac{-v}{q}\right)(0) = \frac{1}{2}\frac{(q+v)^2}{q}$$

Likewise, the average backorders in the first part of the cycle is zero, and ½$(-v)$ in the second, so

$$\overline{B} = \left(\frac{q+v}{q}\right)(0) + (-v/q)\left[\frac{1}{2}(-v)\right] = \frac{1}{2}\frac{v^2}{q}$$

Finally, the cycle length is $u = q/\lambda$, so

$$\overline{OF} = \frac{\lambda}{q}$$

Clearly, these criteria are in direct conflict. Let us translate them into monetary terms. (Section 3.3.5 discusses constraints on the criteria.) We continue to use the cost

FIGURE 3.3.3

The two parts of a cycle.

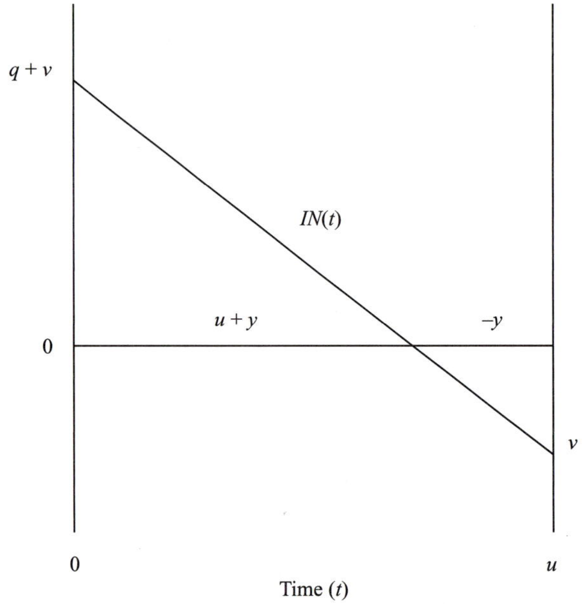

factors k, c, and h defined earlier. Suppose we can also estimate a factor for backorders, analogous to h:

b = penalty cost for one unit backordered during one time-unit (moneys/[quantity-unit · time-unit])

This parameter summarizes all the drawbacks of backorders mentioned above. The total average cost then becomes

$$C(v, q) = (k + cq)\overline{OF} + h\overline{I} + b\overline{B}$$
$$= c\lambda + \frac{k\lambda}{q} + \frac{1}{2}\frac{h(q+v)^2}{q} + \frac{1}{2}\frac{bv^2}{q}$$

(This formulation does not explicitly include $\overline{A}$. The backorder cost results, not from the *occurrence* of a backorder, but rather from its *continuation* in time. The reason for this focus will become clear later.)

3.3.4 The Optimal Policy and Sensitivity Analysis

The cost $C(v, q)$ is now a function of two variables. To minimize it, we equate its partial derivatives to zero. (C is continuously differentiable and strictly convex on its domain, so this approach works.) That is,

$$\frac{\partial C}{\partial v} = \frac{h(q+v)}{q} + \frac{bv}{q} = 0$$

$$\frac{\partial C}{\partial q} = -k\lambda/q^2 + \frac{1}{2}\frac{h(q^2 - v^2)}{q^2} - \frac{1}{2}\frac{bv^2}{q^2} = 0$$

Defining the cost ratio

$$\omega = \frac{b}{b+h}$$

gives the unique solution to these equations as

$$q^* = \sqrt{\frac{2k\lambda}{h}}\sqrt{\frac{1}{\omega}} \tag{3.3.2}$$

$$v^* = -(1-\omega)q^*$$

The optimal reorder point is $r^* = D + v^*$. The optimal cycle time and safety time are given by

$$u^* = \sqrt{\frac{2k}{\lambda h}}\sqrt{\frac{1}{\omega}}$$

$$y^* = -(1-\omega)u^*$$

Direct substitution of (3.3.2) into $C(v, q)$ yields

$$C^* = C(v^*, q^*) = c\lambda + \sqrt{2k\lambda h\omega} \tag{3.3.3}$$

These results are strikingly similar to those for the original EOQ model: The expression for C^* includes the average variable cost $c\lambda$, of course, plus the same square-root term as the EOQ model, but multiplied by the factor $\sqrt{\omega}$. Since ω lies between 0 and 1, so does this factor. Thus, the optimal total cost is *less* than in the EOQ model. This should come as no surprise: The solution to the EOQ model (with $v = 0$) is *one* feasible solution to the model here. A wider range of solutions can only improve the total cost.

Also, q^* is similar to the EOQ formula. The square-root term in (3.2.2) is divided by $\sqrt{\omega}$ here, so the optimal order size is *larger* than in the EOQ model. The reason is a bit subtle: For any given q, the order cost is fixed, but the variable v provides a degree of freedom to adjust the mix of holding and penalty costs to achieve the best combination. With this flexibility we can afford to take on more of these latter costs, by increasing q, to save on order costs.

It may be surprising that v^* is always negative; every system should operate with some backorders. But, imagine starting with $v = 0$. A tiny reduction in v causes a tiny amount of backorders, and only for a short period at the end of a cycle. This change reduces inventory, also by a tiny amount, but over nearly the whole cycle. Thus, even for a large penalty cost b, the total cost will decline.

On the other hand, as $b \to \infty$ with h held fixed, $\omega \to 1$. Thus, $v^* \to 0$, and q^* and C^* approach the corresponding values in the EOQ model. We can think of the EOQ model as a limiting case with $b = \infty$.

Interestingly, $\overline{A}$ takes on a remarkably simple form in the optimal solution:

$$\overline{A} = \frac{-v^*}{q^*} = 1 - \omega \tag{3.3.4}$$

Although the model does not restrict or penalize $\overline{A}$, the optimal policy controls it anyway, as a by-product, so to speak.

EXAMPLE 3.3.A, PART 1

Reconsider the paper supply problem above, assuming that backorders are allowed. This can mean that copying work waits when paper runs out, or you borrow paper from a neighboring copying room. In any case, you figure the backorder cost to be $b = \$15$ per box-week. The other data are the same as before. Then, $\omega = 15/(15 + 1.173) \approx 0.927$, and $\sqrt{\omega} \approx 0.963$. So, q^* increases to 42/0.963 or about 44, and $v^* = -(0.073)(44) \approx -3$. The optimal cost declines from 249 to $C^* = 200 + (0.963)(49) \approx 247$.

The sensitivity analysis of this model is similar to that of the EOQ model. Again, q^* and C^* are robust with respect to changes in λ and k, because of the square-root operations. Also, think of ω as a relative-cost index, independent of h itself. With the parameters viewed in this way, the optimal solution is robust with respect to ω and h.

Also, fix q to any value, and suppose we set the safety stock optimally, to $v = -(1 - \omega)q$. Let $C(q)$ denote the cost of this solution, excluding the term $c\lambda$. One can show that

$$C(q) = \frac{k\lambda}{q} + \frac{1}{2}h\omega q \tag{3.3.5}$$

This is precisely $C(q)$ in the EOQ model, except for the adjusted inventory cost. The ratio $C(q)/C^*$ thus reduces to $\epsilon(q/q^*)$, as in (3.2.5). Consequently, there is little cost penalty for a modest deviation of q from q^*. Now, suppose $q = q^*$, but we choose $v \neq v^*$. The cost $C(v, q^*)$ is a quadratic function of v. Thus, a small deviation of v from v^* does not increase the cost much, but a large one does.

3.3.5 Constrained Stockouts

Backorders cause a variety of unpleasant effects, as mentioned above. The penalty cost b is supposed to represent all those negative impacts in economic terms. It is not easy, however, to measure the economic value of keeping customers happy; b typically includes intangible factors. Actually, estimating k and h is also difficult in practice, but b is no doubt the most problematic of the three cost factors. We discuss these measurement issues in Chap. 2.

These difficulties lead us to consider alternative approaches to the control of backorders. The most common is to impose a constraint on one of the service measures, usually the stockout frequency $\overline{A}$ or the fill rate $1 - \overline{A}$, foregoing explicit calculation of a backorder cost.

So, suppose there is an upper limit $1 - \omega_{-}$ on $\overline{A}$, where $0 < \omega_{-} < 1$. The fraction ω_{-} need not have any relation to a cost ratio like ω; it is an exogenously determined service requirement. (Problem 3.12 asks you to explore a constraint on a different service measure.) The remaining total cost is $c\lambda + k\overline{OF} + h\overline{I}$.

To see the impact of this constraint, fix q for now, leaving v variable. The order frequency $\overline{OF}$ is independent of v, so apart from $\overline{A}$ itself, the only relevant criterion is $\overline{I}$. Now, $\overline{I}$ is increasing in v, while $\overline{A}$ is decreasing. So, starting from $v = 0$, we want to reduce v (thus lowering $\overline{I}$ and raising $\overline{A}$) as far as the constraint permits. That is, set $v = -(1 - \omega_-)q$, so that $\overline{A} = 1 - \omega_-$. Thus, the inequality we began with should be satisfied as an equality. At this value of v, $\overline{I} = \frac{1}{2}\omega_-^2 q$.

Recall, the solution to the cost-optimization model above yields the similar identity (3.3.4), $\overline{A} = 1 - \omega$. The cost ratio ω plays the same role there as the fill-rate limit ω_-. Assuming we set v as above, the total cost becomes (3.3.5), with ω_-^2 replacing ω. With the same replacement, formula (3.3.2) gives the optimal q.

To conclude, there is no fundamental difference between the cost-minimization and service-constraint approaches. The fraction ω_- enforces essentially the same effect as a backorder cost. (Technically, the constrained model is equivalent to a cost-optimization model with the same h, an inflated fixed cost k/ω_-, and b chosen so that $\omega = b/(b + h) = \omega_-$.) It may be more *convenient* sometimes to specify ω_- than b, but each one implies a value for the other. The basic managerial issue of balancing competing objectives remains the same, regardless of which approach is used.

3.3.6 *Space and Time*

The quantities $\overline{A}$ and $\overline{B}$ are related to the service experienced by customers, but it is instructive to consider a more direct measure:

$$\overline{BW} = \text{average customer backorder waiting time.}$$

Again, assume $-q \le v \le 0$. A glance at Figure 3.3.3 should convince you that there is no waiting in the first part of a cycle, while in the second part, after stock runs out, the average wait is $\frac{1}{2}(-y) = \frac{1}{2}(-v/\lambda)$. Thus, the overall average is

$$\begin{aligned}\overline{BW} &= \left(\frac{q+v}{q}\right)(0) + \left(\frac{-v}{q}\right)\left[\frac{1}{2}\left(\frac{-v}{\lambda}\right)\right] \\ &= \left(\frac{1}{\lambda}\right)\left(\frac{1}{2}\frac{v^2}{q}\right) \\ &= \left(\frac{1}{\lambda}\right)\overline{B}\end{aligned}$$

This is an important conclusion: *The average waiting time of a customer demand is proportional to the average outstanding backorders,* with constant of proportionality $1/\lambda$, the reciprocal of the demand rate. This is one reason why the measure $\overline{B}$ is so important. (We shall see later that this same relation holds for a wide variety of models.)

EXAMPLE 3.3.A, PART 2

For the paper supply problem above, under the optimal policy, $\overline{B} \approx \frac{1}{2}(-3)^2/44 \approx 0.10$ boxes, so $\overline{BW} \approx 0.10/8 \approx 0.013$ weeks.

The average inventory $\overline{I}$ is related similarly to what we call the average *stocking time,* denoted $\overline{IW}$, the time a unit of physical goods remains in inventory, from the moment its order is received to the instant it is used to fill demand. That is, $\overline{I}/\lambda = \overline{IW}$. (The reciprocal of the stocking time $1/\overline{IW} = \lambda/\overline{I}$ is called the *inventory turnover,* or *turnover* for short. This measure is widely used in practice.)

These connections suggest an alternative way to think about the tradeoff between performance criteria: Instead of the physical quantities measured by $\overline{I}$ and $\overline{B}$, we can focus on the equivalent time measures $\overline{IW}$ and $\overline{BW}$. In these terms, we can choose to reduce customer waiting by keeping stock on hand longer. The order frequency $\overline{OF}$ is just the reciprocal of the cycle time u, which is already a time-oriented measure.

These are more than mathematical tricks: An inventory or a backlog *is* the net result of the interactions between the times of various events. For example, $I(t)$ is the number of physical units whose arrivals (due to order receipts) precede t, but whose departures (due to demands) occur after t. In a very real sense, *all of inventory management concerns the management of time.* (The time dimension is crucial in other managerial arenas as well; see Stalk and Hout [1990].) This perspective underlies the specification of inventory-related cost factors such as h, as discussed in Section 3.7.

3.3.7 Costs for Backorder Occurrences

We now explore a variant of the model, using the stockout frequency $\overline{A}$ as the customer-service criterion instead of $\overline{B}$. That is, replace $b\overline{B}$ by $b\overline{A}$ in the definition of C. [Of course, b has an entirely new meaning here. For instance, suppose we incur a cost b' each time a demand is backordered. Set $b = \lambda b'$. The average stockout cost is then $b'(\lambda\overline{A}) = b\overline{A}$.]

The optimal policy is peculiar: Either never allow backorders ($v^* = 0$), or never order at all and let all demands be backordered forever; provide perfect customer service, or get out of the business altogether. Furthermore, a small change in the model's parameters can flip the solution from one case to the other.

To see this, first note that v should lie between $-q$ and 0, for the reasons cited above. Assume for now that $v^* < 0$. Solving $\partial C/\partial v = 0$ leads to $v = b/h - q$. Substituting this into $C(v, q)$ yields the cost function

$$C(q) = (c\lambda + b) + \frac{2k\lambda h - b^2}{2hq}$$

There are two cases to consider, depending on the sign of the numerator of the last term:

1. $b^2 > 2k\lambda h$: The numerator is negative, so to minimize $C(q)$ we want q as small as possible. But we must stop at $q = b/h$ with $v = 0$. Thus, $v^* = 0$, and so q^* is just the EOQ formula. [More precisely, one can show that any solution (v, q) with $v < 0$ has cost at least $C(q) > C(b/h) > c\lambda + (2k\lambda h)^{1/2}$.]
2. $b^2 \leq 2k\lambda h$: Here, we want q to be large. But there is no upper limit, so the model seems to prescribe $q^* = \infty$, which is meaningless. What is going on? In this case, $b < C(q)$ for any q. The average cost of never ordering (b) is less than the cost of any other policy, so it is optimal never to order.

Perhaps there are situations where this odd conclusion makes sense. In my opinion, however, the result is an artifact of an odd model: The model's cost is linear in $\overline{A}$, even for $\overline{A}$ near 0 and 1. This is not credible; in real systems, a small stockout frequency is usually tolerable, whereas a large one means disaster. The optimization exploits this linearity all it can, resulting in the extreme solution above. (In technical terms, $\overline{A}$ is not a convex function of v and q, hence neither is C. Strange things can happen when we minimize a nonconvex function.) In contrast, the model of Section 3.3.5, which constrains $\overline{A}$, yields a perfectly reasonable answer. By restricting $\overline{A}$ to a narrow range, it avoids the problems above. That model is equivalent to a cost-minimization model, but one based on $\overline{B}$, not $\overline{A}$.

Moreover, although $\overline{A}$ is a useful and widely used customer-service measure, it conveys only limited information. Do customers really care only *whether* they have to wait, not *how long?* Rarely. Thus, $\overline{B}$ captures more of customers' actual experience than $\overline{A}$. For all these reasons, we focus more on $\overline{B}$.

3.3.8 Lost Sales

The planned-backorders models above assume that customers are willing to wait for their demands to be filled. Now assume the opposite: Demands that occur when no inventory is available are lost.

Equivalently, there is a special, emergency supply channel which we draw on when inventory is exhausted. The "lost" sales are not really lost. Rather, they are filled directly by this special source. The source has zero fixed cost, so it can fill demands continuously as they occur, but a high variable cost, so we use it only in stockout emergencies.

Consider the analogue of the (r, q) policy above: Order arrivals are separated by the cycle time u, and every order is of size q. It is no longer necessarily true that $q = \lambda u$, only that $q \leq \lambda u$. After an order arrives, inventory declines until it reaches zero. Then, there is a period of no stock during which sales are lost, until the next order arrives. Define

$$q' = \text{demand during a cycle} = \lambda u$$

$$v' = \text{minus the lost sales in each cycle}$$

Then, $q = q' + v' \leq q'$,

$$\overline{OF} = \frac{\lambda}{q'} \qquad \overline{I}\frac{1}{2}\frac{(q' + v')}{q'} \qquad \overline{A} = -\frac{v'}{q'}$$

and the average lost sales per unit time is $\lambda\overline{A}$. These criteria have the same form as in the original backorders model, with v' and q' replacing v and q.

[Incidentally, to implement the policy, we can no longer rely on the simple rule above based on the inventory position, for (3.3.1) no longer holds. Under lost sales, there is no simple relation between $IP(t)$ and $IN(t + L)$. This is not a major problem; there are other ways to implement the policy. In a stochastic-demand setting, however, this fact makes the lost-sales case much more difficult.]

The order cost is now $k + c(q) = k + c(q' + v')$. Suppose we incur the penalty b for each lost sale. (Equivalently, b is the unit cost for the emergency supply source.) Then, the total average cost is

$$C(v', q') = [k + c(q' + v')]\overline{OF} + h\overline{I} + b\lambda\overline{A}$$
$$= (k + cq')\overline{OF} + h\overline{I} + (b - c)\lambda\overline{A}$$

This has exactly the same form as the model in the prior subsection, assuming backorders but using $\overline{A}$ to measure service. Consequently, the solution is also the same: Either never lose sales, or abandon the business. (Problem 3.13 asks you to work out the details.)

3.4 A Finite Production Rate

3.4.1 The Setting

Return to the stipulation that all demand be filled immediately from stock.

Recall, the supply process in the EOQ model can model a production process. The leadtime L is required to get the process going, but after that, production of a batch is instantaneous. Now, suppose instead that the process produces a *continuous stream* of output at a finite rate until the batch is complete. The process then shuts down until the next batch begins. Assume for now that, once production begins, the output becomes available immediately to satisfy demand. (Section 3.4.5 below discusses the opposite case, where none of the output can be used until the entire batch is complete.)

Define

$$\mu = \text{production rate (quantity-units/time-units)}$$

When the processor is on, it *must* produce at rate μ, no less; the output rate is inflexible. Assume that $\mu > \lambda$. Otherwise, if $\lambda > \mu$, we can never hope to catch up with demand, even by producing continuously. We even disallow $\lambda = \mu$. (In that case, once production starts, we can meet all demand by producing continuously; supply and demand are perfectly matched! Alas, for some reason, this is impossible.) The *utilization* of the process is $\rho = \lambda/\mu < 1$, the fraction of time it spends actually producing.

3.4.2 Performance Criteria

Assume a constant batch size, q. Production begins precisely when the inventory hits zero. The inventory position can be used to implement this policy, as in the EOQ model: When $IP(t^-) = r = D$, issue a production order for the amount q.

Figure 3.4.1 illustrates the dynamics of the system. A cycle now means the time between successive production starts. Each cycle consists of an *active period* when production occurs and an *idle period* following production. The full cycle time is again $u = q/\lambda$, so $\overline{OF} = \lambda/q$. The active period yields total output q at rate μ, so its length is $q/\mu = \rho u$. The idle period is the remainder $(1 - \rho)u$ of the cycle.

At the end of the active period, the output inventory reaches its maximum value of

$$q - (\text{demand during the active period}) = q - \lambda\left(\frac{q}{\mu}\right) = (1 - \rho)q$$

FIGURE 3.4.1

A finite processing rate.

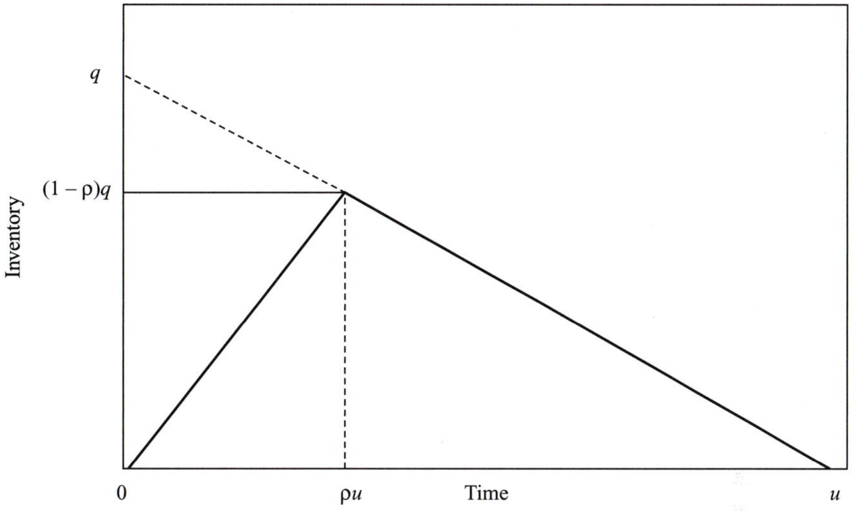

The average inventory during the active period is half this value, and so is the average inventory during the idle period. Thus, the overall average is

$$\bar{I} = \frac{1}{2}(1 - \rho)q$$

Now, assume that each production start incurs the fixed cost k, the variable production cost is c, and h measures the output-inventory-holding cost, as in the EOQ model. (There is no holding cost for inputs.) The total average cost is then

$$C(q) = c\lambda + \frac{k\lambda}{q} + \frac{1}{2}h(1 - \rho)q \tag{3.4.1}$$

3.4.3 The Optimal Policy and Sensitivity Analysis

The function $C(q)$ here has precisely the same form as in the EOQ model: The constant h there becomes $h(1 - \rho)$. Therefore,

$$q^* = \sqrt{\frac{2k\lambda}{h(1 - \rho)}} \tag{3.4.2}$$

$$C^* = C(q^*) = c\lambda + \sqrt{2k\lambda h(1 - \rho)} \tag{3.4.3}$$

Observe that q^* is *larger* than in the EOQ model: For any q, the average inventory is lower here, because stock accumulates gradually. The solution exploits this effect to reduce the order cost. The EOQ model is a limiting case of this one with $\mu = \infty$.

EXAMPLE 3.4.A, PART 1

Consider an English soft-drink bottler. It measures physical quantities in thousands of cases, time in days, and money in £. By an amazing coincidence, the data in these units are exactly the same as in the paper supply problem above, i.e., $\lambda = 8$, $k = 130$, and $h = 1.173$. The bottler's processing rate is $\mu = 10$, so $\rho = 0.8$. So,

$$q^* = \left[\frac{2(130)(8)}{(1.173)(0.2)}\right]^{1/2} \approx 94$$

$$u^* = \frac{q^*}{\lambda} \approx 12$$

$$C^* = 200 + [2(130)(8)(1.173)(0.2)]^{1/2} \approx 222$$

The effects of changes in k and h on q^* and C^* are similar to those in the EOQ model. The optimal batch size and cost are robust with respect to such changes. The magnitudes of these effects, of course, are influenced by the factor $(1 - \rho)$. Furthermore, formula (3.2.5) still applies; the cost is insensitive to suboptimal choices of q.

Because of the limit imposed by μ, however, the demand rate λ has very different effects. In the notation of Section 3.2.4,

$$\frac{q^{*\prime}}{q^*} = \sqrt{\frac{\lambda'}{\lambda}}\sqrt{\frac{1-\rho}{1-\rho'}}$$

When $\lambda' > \lambda$, both factors on the right are greater than 1. The first is the same as in the EOQ model; it reflects the relative change in demand. The second, however, depends on how close λ and especially λ' are to the limit μ. If λ' is close to μ, this factor can be quite large. Thus, when the system nears full utilization (i.e., when ρ is near 1), the optimal order size is very sensitive to demand changes. Conversely, to take the optimistic view, under the same conditions a slight increase in the production rate μ can substantially reduce q^*.

3.4.4 Setup Time

Next, we introduce an additional element into the model: Prior to starting each production run, a positive setup time is required, during which no output is produced. Denote

$$\tau = \text{setup time (time-units)}$$

You may have been thinking of the leadtime L as a setup time, but there is a crucial difference: When the batch size q is small, there may be several orders outstanding at any given moment; that is, several leadtimes may overlap. Furthermore, a production run can begin during the leadtime of a later batch. In short, the leadtime L does not tie up the production facility. During a setup, in contrast, there can be no output, and certainly setups cannot overlap.

This distinction is sometimes expressed as the difference between *internal* and *external* setups. An internal setup is one that ties up the production facility; this is what we call a "setup." An external setup can take place while the facility is doing other work; in our terms an external setup is part of the leadtime. Sometimes it is possible in practice to modify the production technology, so as to convert all or part of an internal setup to an external setup. This is yet another technique of the just-in-time approach to production; see Shingo [1985].

For example, body parts for automobiles are made from sheet metal by a stamping machine. To make one particular part, say a right fender, one must install a mold or *die* for that part on the stamping machine. This die must be hot to work properly. Traditionally, dies were heated after being installed. This was an internal setup. Toyota invented a method of heating dies before installation, thus converting this step to an external setup.

Intuitively, we expect a larger setup time to result in larger batches, for if we try to make many small ones, the production facility will be constantly tied up performing setups, leaving insufficient time for actual production. Indeed, the setup time imposes a *constraint* on the batch size: The fraction of time spent in actual production is $\rho = \lambda/\mu$, which we previously called the *utilization*. This is independent of q. The fraction of time spent in setups is $\tau/u = \tau\lambda/q$, which does depend on q. The overall utilization, then, is $\tau\lambda/q + \rho$, and this quantity cannot exceed 1. That is, q must satisfy

$$q \geq \frac{\tau\lambda}{1 - \rho} \tag{3.4.4}$$

As long as this constraint is met, the setup time does not affect the inventory cost. In effect, part of the idle time of each cycle is shifted to become the setup time in the next cycle, so the graph of inventory over time is shifted to the right by τ. Such a shift does not change the average inventory. The setup time may affect the setup cost k, but whatever value k has, the average setup cost is still $k\lambda/q$. [The setup also requires a slight adjustment in policy implementation. To avoid running out of stock, initiate a production order when $IP(t^-) = r = \lambda(L + \tau)$.]

In sum, the problem now is to minimize the same cost function $C(q)$ defined in (3.4.1), subject to the constraint (3.4.4). This problem can be solved easily:

1. Compute q^* as in formula (3.4.2), ignoring the constraint.
2. Check whether q^* satisfies (3.4.4).
   a. If so, then q^* is optimal.
   b. If not, reset q^* to $\tau\lambda/(1 - \rho)$.

(This does work: In case *a* the minimum-cost q^* is feasible, so it is optimal. In case *b*, since $C(q)$ is strictly convex, it is increasing for $q > q^*$, so the smallest feasible q is optimal.)

EXAMPLE 3.4.A, PART 2

Suppose the bottling process requires setup time $\tau = 3$ days. The lower bound on q is (3)(8)/(0.2) = 120. The original $q^* = 94$ does *not* satisfy (3.4.4), so step 2 passes to case *b*, and $q^* = 120$. The cost of this solution is $C^* = 200 + (130)(8)/120 + \frac{1}{2}(1.173)(0.2)(120) \approx 223$. This is more than the original C^* of 222, though not much.

Clearly, the setup time can increase the overall cost. In case *b* we are forced to use a larger q than would otherwise be optimal. This is one real benefit of reducing the setup time and converting an internal to an external setup. Also, a reduction in τ often entails a simultaneous reduction in k. As we shall see later, these effects become even stronger when demand and supply are influenced by random factors.

3.4.5 Demand-Ready Output in Whole Batches

We have assumed until now that output immediately becomes available to meet demand. Therefore, we could wait until inventory dropped to zero before beginning production. In many cases, however, the finished product cannot be used until an entire batch is complete, perhaps because the batch must be moved to a warehouse, or because some finishing operation or cooling is required.

Here, we must start production when inventory is just sufficient to meet the demand during the production run itself. The length of a run is again q/μ, so demand in this period is $\lambda(q/\mu) = \rho q$. This is now the minimum inventory over a cycle. The maximum occurs when a batch is completed. At this point inventory must be sufficient to cover demand until the next batch is completed, that is, over an entire cycle. So, the maximum inventory is just q.

Problem 3.14 asks you to show that the average inventory is simply the average of these maximum and minimum values, that is,

$$\bar{I} = \frac{1}{2}(1 + \rho)q$$

Reasoning as above leads to

$$q^* = \max\left\{\frac{\tau\lambda}{(1 - \rho)}, \sqrt{\frac{2k\lambda}{h(1 + \rho)}}\right\}$$

Assuming the setup-time constraint is not binding,

$$C^* = C(q^*) = c\lambda + \sqrt{2k\lambda h(1 + \rho)}$$

Compare this formula with the optimal cost in the earlier case (3.4.2). You may have found it odd that previously the optimal cost was *increasing* in the production rate; according to that model, faster production costs more! There, a slower production rate tends to smooth the inventory, while imposing no delays whatsoever in our capacity to meet demand. Such delays do occur in the current model, and additional stock is required to cover them. As a result, the total cost is now *decreasing* in the production rate.

This difference is no minor technical point. The basic production economics are totally different in the two cases. It is important to know whether an "improvement," like an increase in the production rate, will help or hurt cost performance!

EXAMPLE 3.4.A, PART 3

In this case, assuming a negligible setup time τ, the bottler's optimal solution is

$$q^* = \left[\frac{2(130)(8)}{(1.173)(1.8)}\right]^{1/2} \approx 31$$

$$u^* = \frac{q^*}{\lambda} \approx 4$$

$$C^* = 200 + [2(130)(8)(1.173)(1.8)]^{1/2} \approx 266$$

If $\tau = 3$, as above, the lower bound on q is 120, so $q^* = 120$. The cost of this solution is $C^* \approx 335$, a substantial increase over 266.

Improvements in the details of materials handling can have major benefits. If we can change the system so that output is available immediately, we switch from the current model to the earlier one with correspondingly reduced costs. (This is true even though the switch increases the optimal batch size, contrary to what you might suppose.)

3.5 Quantity Discounts

3.5.1 *Alternative Specifications of Purchase Costs*

In the basic EOQ model of Section 3.2, the variable cost c is constant for orders of all sizes. However, it is common for suppliers to offer price breaks for large orders. This section shows how to extend the EOQ model to incorporate such quantity discounts. Actually, there are two kinds of discounts, *incremental* and *all-units*.

Consider the *incremental* case first: Suppose the purchase price changes at the breakpoint χ. The variable cost is c_0 for any amount up to χ. For an order larger than χ, the *additional* amount over χ incurs the rate c_1, where $c_1 < c_0$. Thus, the total order cost is $k + c(q)$, where

$$c(q) = \begin{cases} c_0 q & 0 < q \leq \chi \\ c_0\chi + c_1(q - \chi) & q > \chi \end{cases}$$

Alternatively, define $k_0 = k$ and $k_1 = k + (c_0 - c_1)\chi$. Then, the order cost is

$$k + c(q) = \begin{cases} k_0 + c_0 q & 0 < q \leq \chi \\ k_1 + c_1 q & q > \chi \end{cases}$$

This function describes more elaborate economies of scale than the original fixed-plus-linear form. In a production setting, it represents costs that depend on the production quantity in a complex, nonlinear way.

With an *all-units* discount, if $q > \chi$, the entire order is priced at the lower rate c_1, so

$$c(q) = \begin{cases} c_0 q & 0 < q < \chi \\ c_1 q & q \geq \chi \end{cases}$$

Figure 3.5.1 illustrates $c(q)$ for both cases.

3.5.2 *Incremental Discounts*

Given the revised order cost for the incremental case, the formulation proceeds as in the EOQ model. The holding cost is a bit tricky, however. In addition to direct handling costs, which occur at rate $\underline{h}$, there is also a financing cost, which occurs at rate $\alpha[c(q)/q]$. Here, α is the interest rate, and $c(q)/q$ is the *average* variable purchase cost. (Financing costs are discussed at greater length below in Section 3.7.) Thus, the total average cost is

$$C(q) = [k + c(q)]\frac{\lambda}{q} + \frac{1}{2}\left[\underline{h} + \frac{\alpha c(q)}{q}\right]q$$

FIGURE 3.5.1

Order cost with a quantity discount.

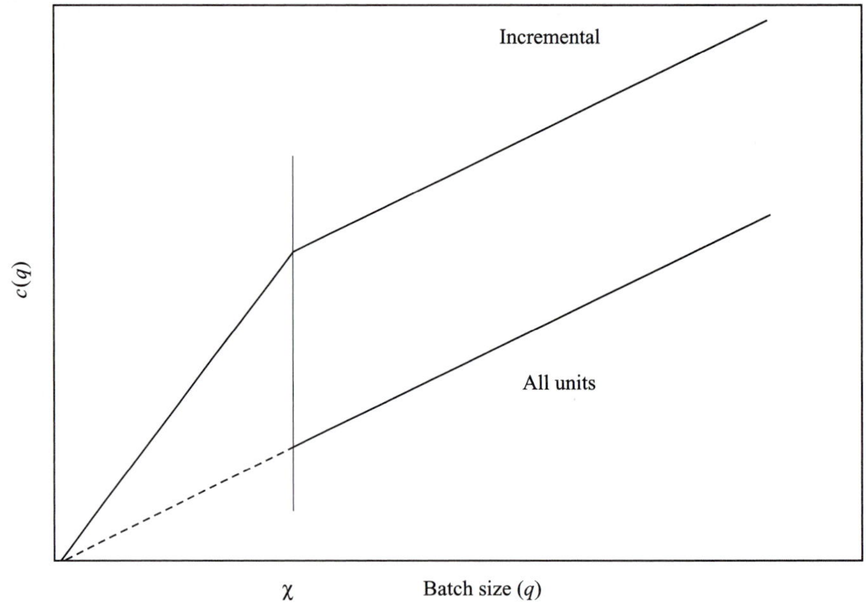

(C is not differentiable at $q = \chi$, so we cannot hope simply to differentiate to obtain the optimal solution. Also, C is not convex.)

Observe that

$$c(q) = \min\{k_0 + c_0 q,\ k_1 + c_1 q\} - k \qquad q > 0$$

That is, $c(q)$ is the smaller of two positive, linear functions that cross at χ. Therefore,

$$C(q) = \min\{C_0(q), C_1(q)\}$$

where $$C_0(q) = c_0\lambda + \frac{k_0\lambda}{q} + \frac{1}{2}(\underline{h} + \alpha c_0)q$$

$$C_1(q) = c_1\lambda + k_1\lambda/q + \frac{1}{2}(\underline{h} + \alpha c_1)q + \frac{1}{2}\alpha(c_0 - c_1)\chi$$

Both C_0 and C_1 have the form of the EOQ model's cost function. Both are strictly convex and differentiable, and their graphs cross at χ. Let q_0^* and q_1^* be the respective minimizing values of q.

Also,

$$C_0'(q) = \frac{-k_0\lambda}{q^2} + \frac{1}{2}(\underline{h} + \alpha c_0)$$

$$C_1'(q) = \frac{-k_1\lambda}{q^2} + \frac{1}{2}(\underline{h} + \alpha c_1)$$

Evidently, $C_0'(q) > C_1'(q)$, so $q_0^* < q_1^*$. There remain three possible cases:

1. $q_0^* < q_1^* \leq \chi$
2. $q_0^* < \chi < q_1^*$
3. $\chi \leq q_0^* < q_1^*$

In case 1, for $q \geq \chi$,

$$C(q) = C_1(q) \geq C_1(\chi) = C_0(\chi) > C_0(q_0^*)$$

so q_0^* is optimal. In case 3, by a parallel argument, q_1^* is optimal. Only in case 2 is there any doubt. In that case, calculate both $C_0(q_0^*)$ and $C_1(q_1^*)$ to determine which one is smaller. [Apply formula (3.2.4) to compute these costs.]

In sum, it is easy to determine an optimal policy: Compute both q_0^* and q_1^* using EOQ-like formulas, compare them with χ to determine which case applies, and if necessary (in case 2) compare their costs.

Problem 3.16 asks you to extend the analysis to several breakpoints and cost rates.

3.5.3 All-Units Discounts

In the all-units case the average cost becomes

$$C(q) = \begin{cases} C_0(q) & 0 < q < \chi \\ C_1(q) & q \geq \chi \end{cases}$$

where

$$C_i(q) = c_i\lambda + \frac{k\lambda}{q} + \frac{1}{2}(\underline{h} + \alpha c_i)q$$

This C_0 is the same as the one above, but C_1 is different. Since $c_0 > c_1$, $C_0(q) > C_1(q)$ for all q. Also, $C_0'(q) > C_1'(q)$, so $q_0^* < q_1^*$. This leaves the same three cases above.

In cases 2 and 3, since $q_1^* \geq \chi$, the cost $C_1(q_1^*)$ is attainable. This is the smallest possible cost, so q_1^* is optimal. In case 1, for any $q \geq \chi$, $C_1(q) \geq C_1(\chi)$, so the only possible solutions are χ itself and q_0^*. In that case, compare $C_1(\chi)$ and $C_0(q_0^*)$ and pick the smallest. Again, a couple of EOQ-like calculations suffice to find the optimal policy.

3.5.4 Discussion

The overall effect of a quantity discount, compared to the case where the variable cost $c = c_0$ is constant, can only be to increase order sizes. Depending on the other parameters, either there is no effect ($q^* = q_0^*$), or the optimal order size is larger than it would have been otherwise.

Why then do suppliers offer quantity discounts in practice? The supplier may achieve economies of scale from large orders. Or, the supplier may hope to attract new customers with the lower price and/or to induce existing customers to buy more. Researchers have investigated these and other mechanisms to explain price breaks, but there is no clear consensus so far on which are the primary reasons. In fact, it is not easy to construct a plausible scenario where a quantity discount makes sense.

My own experience suggests that, often, suppliers offer discounts more out of habit than reasoned analysis. ("It's stupid, but our customers are used to it," one told me.) It may be possible and mutually beneficial to negotiate a revised cost schedule without quantity discounts. The supplier and the customer might agree to a constant cost rate c, say some average of c_0 and c_1, leaving both parties better off. The model above can help guide such discussions. (See Problem 3.17 for an illustration.)

3.6 Imperfect Quality

3.6.1 Where Do Defects Occur and When Are They Found?

Up to this point, we have assumed that the goods received from the supply system are free from defects, and the product remains in perfect condition through final delivery to the customer. This section relaxes these assumptions, but only a bit: Now, defects do occur. However, there are only two quality levels; a unit is either perfect or useless. Also, *all defects are entirely predictable.*

As we shall see, such defects do not complicate the analysis much. In most cases we can account for them by adjusting the model parameters, and the solution remains the same or changes only slightly. (In reality, of course, poor quality does complicate life, for both analysts and managers. The worst effects, however, arise because of unpredictable defects, or because the system includes other stochastic features, such as leadtimes or demands, which defects exacerbate. Chapter 7 illustrates this point.)

The first questions to ask about quality are, where do defects occur and when are they found? Even in a structurally simple system, defects can arise in several places. The supply process itself may generate them. Or, they may appear in the inventory itself, as in a product prone to spoilage. Also, regardless of where the defects *occur*, in some situations they are *discovered* immediately, while in others they are detected only at some later stage. Even under the simple assumptions above, these distinctions do matter. It is a general maxim of quality control that immediate inspection is always better; see Juran [1988], for instance. Still, it is useful to consider other possibilities, in part just to evaluate the benefits of earlier inspection. Also, in some cases immediate inspection is physically impossible or very costly.

There are additional important questions: Do we pay for defective units? If we are reimbursed by the supplier, when do those payments occur?

The next two subsections consider defects in the supply process and nowhere else. Section 3.6.2 explores the basic EOQ model, while Section 3.6.3 extends the finite-production-rate model. Then, Section 3.6.4 examines a perishable product, which tends to spoil in inventory.

3.6.2 The EOQ Setting

Begin with the basic EOQ model of Section 3.2. Suppose now that each batch the supply system sends contains a fixed fraction of defective product, independent of the batch size. (Problem 3.18 considers an alternative scenario.) Denote

$$\delta = \text{defect rate}$$

$$\xi = \text{yield rate} = 1 - \delta$$

There are four cases, depending on when the defects are detected (immediately or later) and whether or not we must pay for them.

- *Case 1 (immediate detection, reimbursement).* First, suppose that we discover the defective units immediately on receipt; at that moment we discard them or return them to the supplier. Also, we do not have to pay for them; we are reimbursed immediately. This system operates just as if the order size were ξq. Therefore, it is easy to account for defects: Analyze the EOQ model, assuming no defects, interpreting q as the nondefective yield of each batch. When it comes time to implement the policy, order q^*/ξ instead of q^*. The overall cost C^* is independent of δ.
- *Case 2 (immediate detection, no reimbursement).* Sometimes, alas, we pay for all units ordered, defective or not. To yield q, we must again order q/ξ, so the order cost becomes $k + (c/\xi)q$. In effect, the cost rate c is inflated by the factor $1/\xi$. Recall, changing c does not directly affect the optimal policy, but it does so indirectly through h. The latter includes a direct cost $\underline{h}$ and a financing cost αc, so h now becomes

$$h = \underline{h} + \frac{\alpha c}{\xi}$$

  Thus, q^* is smaller than it would be with $\delta = 0$, because h is larger. (Again, we must inflate q^* as above to determine the actual order size. The net effect, clearly, is an increase in the order size.) Also, the square-root term in C^* is larger than before, and of course the term $c\lambda$ also increases to $(c/\xi)\lambda$. Not surprisingly, when we pay for defects, they do increase the overall cost.
- *Case 3 (delayed detection, no reimbursement).* Now, suppose we do not discover defects on receipt of a batch. Instead, the defective units are placed in inventory along with the good ones. The defects are found at the moment of demand. (Imagine, for example, that demands originate from a subsequent processing stage, which is able to detect and reject defective units before using them.) Then, we discard or return the defective units, as before, without reimbursement. Assume the defects are evenly spread through the inventory, so at each time t it includes exactly $\delta I(t)$ of defective product. Thus, inventory is depleted by demand at rate λ/ξ instead of λ.

  This model too reduces to the EOQ model with revised parameters: Again, q indicates the yield of each batch. Also, reinterpret $I(t)$ as the nondefective stock only. This good inventory is depleted by demand at rate λ. So, $I(t)$ behaves just as in the EOQ model with no defects. Accordingly, replace $\underline{h}$ by $\underline{h}/\xi$, since the whole inventory incurs direct handling costs. Also, divide c and αc by ξ, as in case 2. Thus, the entire holding cost h is inflated by the factor $1/\xi$, i.e.,

$$h = \frac{\underline{h} + \alpha c}{\xi}$$

Consequently, q^* is even smaller, and C^* larger, than in case 2. Compared to their values in the EOQ model, the actual order size and the square-root term in C^* are larger by $1/\sqrt{\xi}$. Delayed detection does cost money, due to the increase in $\underline{h}$.

- *Case 4 (delayed detection, reimbursement).* Finally, consider the same scenario as case 3, but assume that we are reimbursed for defects. Specifically, we pay for the full batch on receipt, including defects. Later, we are reimbursed for each defective unit as it is found. It turns out that the effects on h are precisely the same as in case 3, as if we had to pay for defects! (To show this requires the methods of Section 3.7 below; see Problem 3.29.) Consequently, q^* and the square-root term of C^* are also the same as in case 3. Reimbursement does help, of course, because the $c\lambda$ term remains uninflated.

To summarize, all four cases reduce to the EOQ model with appropriately adjusted parameters. Those adjustments and their effects depend on the details of inspection and cost reimbursement. Except in case 1, defects increase the overall cost, though not by much. So, improving quality brings real, albeit modest, economic benefits. (It is worth reemphasizing that the impacts of bad quality are much worse in a stochastic system. The benefits of quality improvement are, accordingly, much greater.)

3.6.3 Limited Capacity

Next, consider the system of Section 3.4 with a finite production rate μ. For the moment assume there is no setup time ($\tau = 0$). While we are actually producing, defective goods emerge from the production process at rate $\delta\mu$, while nondefective goods are produced at the rate $\xi\mu$.

Assume the case 1 scenario; we detect defects immediately and do not have to pay for them. (Problem 3.30 explores another case.) So, the production process belongs to another organization from which we purchase goods. This system works precisely like one with no defects but a reduced μ, namely $\xi\mu$. Thus, the ratio ρ now becomes ρ/ξ. The model can thus be analyzed as if there were no defects, but these parameter shifts do change the optimal policy: If output becomes available to meet demand immediately, then q^* increases, according to (3.4.2):

$$q^* = \sqrt{\frac{2k\lambda}{h(1 - \rho/\xi)}}$$

Otherwise (as in Section 3.4.5), q^* decreases:

$$q^* = \sqrt{\frac{2k\lambda}{h(1 + \rho / \xi)}}$$

(Again, q^* indicates the yield of a production run, so the total run size is q^*/ξ.)

All this assumes that the effective production rate $\xi\mu$ remains larger than the demand rate λ. If not, the problem becomes entirely infeasible. Thus, defects can have the drastic effect of transforming an adequate production process into one that is unable to meet demand.

Now, suppose there is a positive setup time, τ. Even if $\lambda < \xi\mu$, so the problem is still feasible, the optimal policy can change radically. The setup time imposes a lower limit on q, now $\tau\lambda/(1 - \rho/\xi)$. This bound increases in δ, and if the original ρ is near 1, it increases sharply. In that case q^* and C^* increase sharply too.

We are thus led to an observation, which in retrospect is obvious, but worth emphasizing nonetheless: *Defects waste production capacity.* No such effect was apparent in the context of the EOQ model, for its supply process has unlimited capacity. The consequences of such waste depend on the details of the problem, but in general they are unwelcome indeed.

3.6.4 Perishable Products

Now, suppose that the supply system operates perfectly, but defects arise while the product is held in inventory. Actually, this is true of virtually all items to some extent. Boxes are dropped or mislabeled; containers and roofs leak. The focus here, however, is on *perishable products,* such as food, medicines, certain chemicals, and blood in blood banks. Such products, because of their physical nature, systematically deteriorate over time.

The actual pattern of deterioration over time can be quite complex and largely unpredictable; also, it may be difficult to determine whether a particular unit is spoiled or not. Partly for these reasons, and also because the consequences of using spoiled goods can be catastrophic (think of food poisoning), it is quite common to find a *limit* on the time a unit can remain in storage. Here, for practical purposes, all the inventory becomes defective when this time limit is reached.

It is simple to incorporate such a time limit in the EOQ model. The limit becomes an upper bound u^+ on the cycle time u. Equivalently, constrain $q \leq \lambda u^+$. To solve this model, follow a procedure like that of Section 3.4.4: Compute q^* with the EOQ formula (3.2.2), ignoring the constraint. Check whether q^* satisfies the constraint. If not, reset $q^* = \lambda u^+$.

When there is no time limit, we need a *model* to describe spoilage. Here is the simplest model: Inventory decays at a constant rate over time, independent of its age or past experience. That is, redefining δ to be the *decay rate*, inventory deteriorates at rate $\delta I(t)$ for all t. For reasons explained shortly, this is sometimes called the *exponential decay model.* Assume the defective product is detected immediately and discarded, and we pay for all goods without reimbursement, as in case 2 above.

Even for this simple case, the analysis and the results are fairly complex. As in the EOQ model, suppose every order is of size q, placed so as to arrive just when stock would otherwise run out. So, $I(t)$ is periodic. Assuming time 0 is the beginning of a cycle, $I(0) = q$. Within the cycle, taking both spoilage and demand into account, we have

$$I'(t) = -\delta I(t) - \lambda \tag{3.6.1}$$

(The prime indicates a derivative.) This is a first-order linear differential equation with exogenous input and initial condition $I(0) = q$. Its solution, as you can check directly, is

$$I(t) = qe^{-\delta t} - (\lambda/\delta)(1 - e^{-\delta t})$$

(The phrase *exponential decay* refers to the $e^{-\delta t}$ terms.)

Now, the cycle time u is just that value of t with $I(t) = 0$. It is convenient to use u as the decision variable. Given u, $q = (\lambda/\delta)(e^{\delta u} - 1)$. It is not hard to show (Problem 3.19) that

$$\bar{I} = \frac{(\lambda/\delta)(e^{\delta u} - \delta u - 1)}{\delta u} \tag{3.6.2}$$

Also, $\overline{OF} = 1/u$. The average cost is

$$C(u) = (k + cq)\overline{OF} + \underline{h}\bar{I} + ½\alpha cq \tag{3.6.3}$$

$$= \frac{k + c(\lambda/\delta)(e^{\delta u} - 1)}{u} + \frac{\underline{h}(\lambda/\delta)(e^{\delta u} - \delta u - 1)}{\delta u} + \frac{1}{2}\alpha c(\lambda/\delta)(e^{\delta u} - 1)$$

(Only the direct handling cost $\underline{h}$ multiplies $\bar{I}$ here. The financing-cost term $½\alpha cq$ has the same form as in the EOQ model, because we pay for the entire batch. This reasoning may seem mysterious now, but the concept will become clear in the next section.) To minimize this function, solve $C'(u) = 0$. (C is smooth and convex, so this approach works.) This equation is too complex to yield a formula for u^*. It must be solved numerically with a computer.

We can get a rough notion of the effects of spoilage by an approximation: For small δ, $q^* \approx [2k\lambda/(\underline{h} + \alpha c + \delta c)]^{1/2}$. (The technique underlying this result is explained in Section 3.7.3.) So, spoilage effectively adds an additional component to the holding cost, forcing q^* to be smaller. Intuitively, we want to keep the inventory low to avoid substantial losses.

3.7 The Present-Value Criterion

3.7.1 Objectives and Holding Costs

The objective of each model above is the total average cost per unit time. This seems plausible. But, does it truly reflect the economic impacts of alternative policies? A policy affects the whole pattern of costs over time. Does the average cost really capture the significant differences in these cost patterns?

This section attacks the issue of comparing cost patterns from a different perspective. We define a new objective, called the *present value* or *discounted cost,* and use it to reformulate the EOQ model of Section 3.2. The average-cost EOQ model can be understood as an approximation to this new one.

The present-value objective has several advantages. It represents the financing component of the holding cost in real, tangible terms. Financing charges arise from the time gaps between purchasing expenditures and sales revenues. To bridge such gaps, firms must borrow money and pay interest. A unit in inventory has been purchased but not sold, so we can think of it as "generating" interest costs at rate αc. This story underlies the average-cost formulation, but it is only a rough heuristic. A box sitting in a warehouse does not really generate interest costs. The new approach includes financing costs as they actually occur.

This approach is especially helpful, indeed essential, in analyzing complex models with intricate costs and revenues. See Problems 3.27 and 3.29, for example.

3.7.2 Definition of Present Value

To set the stage, let us sketch a bit of financial theory: Suppose we can invest money at a constant, continuously compounding interest rate α. An investment of 1 now (time 0) will be worth $e^{\alpha t}$ at time t. For the investment to be worth 1 at time t, the initial investment must be $e^{-\alpha t}$. In general, a cash flow f at time t can be exchanged for a cash flow $e^{-\alpha t}f$ now. This latter quantity is the *present value* of the original cash flow. The operation of multiplying f by the fraction $e^{-\alpha t}$ is called *discounting;* another name for the present value is the *discounted value.*

Suppose that we can also borrow money at rate α. If we must pay a cost of 1 now, we can borrow the money, wait until time t, and then pay the larger amount $e^{\alpha t}$. Similarly, an obligation to pay f at time t is equivalent to a cost of $e^{-\alpha t}f$ today. This quantity is called the *discounted cost.* Thus, a cost works just like a negative cash flow.

Now, suppose we face a *sequence* of cash flows $\{f_j\}$ at times $\{t_j\}$. Some of these f_j may be positive and some negative, representing costs. As above, we can replace each cash flow by its present value. The sum of these present values $\Sigma_j \exp(-\alpha t_j) f_j$ is the *net present value* of the entire sequence. Given the assumptions above, this provides an unambiguous means of ordering and choosing among alternative sequences.

This idea extends directly to a continuous cash-flow stream. Let $f(t)$ be the rate at which cash flow accumulates at time t, positive or negative. The net present value of this stream is $\int_0^\infty e^{-\alpha t} f(t)\,dt$.

These assumptions are rather special. In reality, for example, one cannot borrow and invest at the same interest rate; the borrowing rate is higher. Still, the present-value criterion does reflect the fact that a cost today is more burdensome than a cost tomorrow. This is, I believe, a real advantage over the average-cost measure.

Not everyone agrees. The present-value logic puts little weight on events far into the future. Critics charge that this leads people and companies to make shortsighted decisions. Defenders counter that the real problem lies elsewhere. Enough already; you get the idea. For a vivid debate on this issue, see Hayes and Garvin [1982] and Kaplan [1986].

3.7.3 Formulation and Analysis

Let us reformulate the EOQ model using this new objective. Assume for simplicity that there is no direct handling cost and no leadtime, i.e., $\underline{h} = L = 0$. (Problem 3.25 shows how to incorporate a positive $\underline{h}$.) Also, as before, the order size is the constant q, and the cycle time is the constant u.

We incur the cost $k + cq = k + c\lambda u$ when we receive each order. We sell goods in response to demand at price p, so we receive a stream of revenue at the constant rate $p\lambda$. Suppose $I(0^-) = 0$, so we order at time 0. Thus, we order at times $t = 0, u, 2u, \ldots$, incurring cost $k + c\lambda u$ every time. The present value of all these costs, or the total discounted cost, is thus

$$C(u) = \Sigma_{n=0}^{\infty} e^{-\alpha n u}(k + c\lambda u) = \frac{(k + c\lambda u)}{(1 - e^{-\alpha u})}$$

Also, the present value of the revenue stream is $\int_0^\infty e^{-\alpha t}(p\lambda)\,dt = p\lambda/\alpha$. The net present value of all the cash flows is thus $p\lambda/\alpha - C(u)$. The revenue term is a constant, so to maximize the net present value, we can equivalently minimize the discounted cost.

To optimize $C(u)$, we solve $C'(u) = 0$. (This works; the function C has the right properties. See Problem 3.22.) A bit of algebra reduces this equation to

$$\frac{f(\alpha u)}{\alpha} = \frac{k}{c\lambda} \tag{3.7.1}$$

where

$$f(x) = e^x - x - 1$$

Unfortunately, there is no formula for the solution of equation (3.7.1). Fortunately, it is easy to solve numerically with a computer. It is interesting that the parameters k, c, and λ appear only in the ratio $k/c\lambda$.

3.7.4 Comparison of Average-Cost and Present-Value Models

At first glance (3.7.1) appears totally unrelated to the original EOQ model. However, there is a close connection: Recalling the power series for e^x, $e^x = \Sigma_{n=0}^{\infty} x^n/n!$, $f(x)$ just omits the first two terms:

$$f(x) = \Sigma_{n=2}^{\infty} \frac{x^n}{n!}$$

Now, suppose α and $k/c\lambda$ are both small, so the relevant values of $x = \alpha u$ in (3.7.1) are also small. In that range we can approximate f by the first term in the series, $f(\alpha u) \approx \frac{1}{2}(\alpha u)^2$. Solving (3.7.1) with this approximation yields

$$u^* \approx \sqrt{\frac{2k}{\alpha c \lambda}}$$

or

$$q^* \approx \sqrt{\frac{2k\lambda}{\alpha c}}$$

Identifying h with αc, this is precisely the EOQ formula!

Plugging this u into (3.7.1) makes the left-hand side *more* than the right-hand side (since this solution neglects positive terms in f). Also, the left-hand side is increasing in u. To solve the equation exactly, therefore, means reducing u. Thus, the *true* u^* is always *less* than the EOQ model's. Likewise, the true q^* is less than the EOQ formula.

The average-cost EOQ model is far more widely applied than the model above. This is partly because the EOQ model was developed earlier, and an explicit formula is easier to understand than an equation. Also, the average-cost objective is built on concrete, physical measures like the average inventory. The economic justification for the present-value model is stronger, however.

How closely does the EOQ formula approximate the discounted-cost solution? We know it is close when α and $k/c\lambda$ are small, but what if they are not? Look at Figure 3.7.1. It shows u^* for the discounted-cost and average-cost models, graphed against the ratio $k/c\lambda$. The time-unit is years. Two different interest rates are used, 12½% and 25% (α = 0.125 and 0.25); values in this range are common in practice. As expected, the differences between the two models are negligible when $k/c\lambda$ is small, becoming larger when $k/c\lambda$ is large. Also, the relative differences are greater for larger α.

The differences are significant, however, only when $k/c\lambda$ is so large that the optimal cycle times are huge. Even for $\alpha = 0.25$, the u^* curves diverge noticeably only when u^*

FIGURE 3.7.1

Discounted versus average cost.

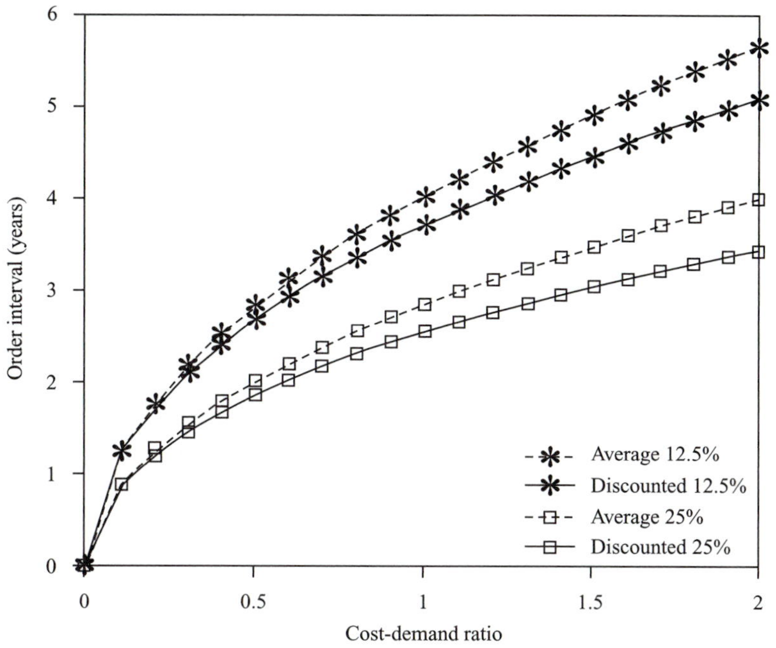

is nearly 2 years. Thus, for items ordered several times per year (i.e., most cases of practical interest), the EOQ approximation is reasonably accurate. Only for an extremely low-cost, low-usage item (with small $c\lambda$) is this not so.

Also, remember that the cost penalty for choosing a suboptimal q in the average-cost model is small. The same is true, it turns out, in the present-value model. So, if we calculate u and q using the "wrong" objective, the resulting cost penalty is usually small.

The EOQ model can be somewhat misleading, however, as the basis for economic analysis. For example, suppose we can purchase some technology (e.g., production machinery or communications equipment) to reduce the fixed cost k. This new technology requires a one-time expenditure but no ongoing costs. Is the reduction in k worth the cost?

To address this question with the EOQ model, one must convert the average cost (3.2.4) into an equivalent discounted cost. Imagine, as an approximation, a constant cash-flow stream with this value. The present value of this stream is

$$C^0(k) = \int_0^\infty e^{-\alpha t}(c\lambda + \sqrt{2k\lambda h})\,dt = \frac{c\lambda}{\alpha} + \sqrt{\frac{2k\lambda c}{\alpha}}$$

where $h = \alpha c$. This function estimates the operating cost over time for any fixed k. To evaluate the technology, compare its cost to the change in $C^0(k)$. With the present-value criterion, we don't need to imagine or approximate. For each k, compute the optimal u^*,

FIGURE 3.7.2

Discounted versus average cost.

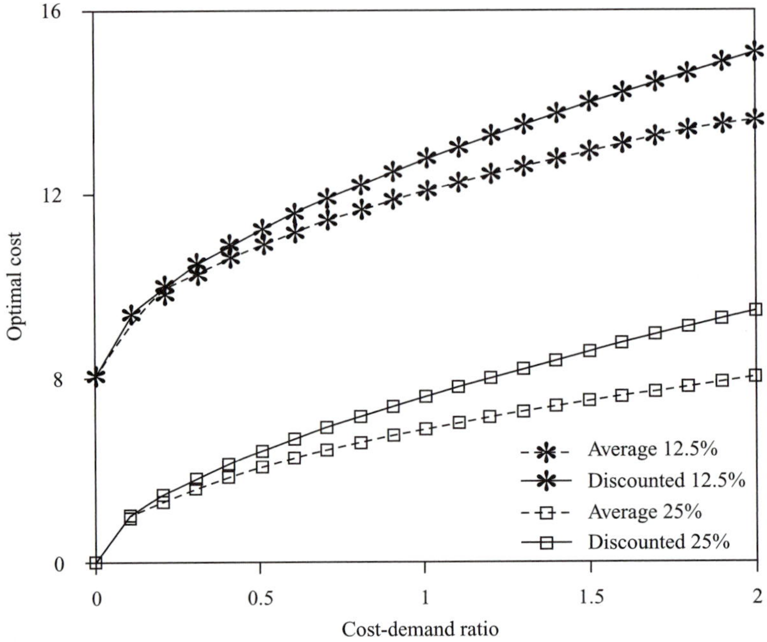

plug it into $C(u)$, and call the result $C^*(k)$. Use this function instead of $C^0(k)$. (There is no simple formula for it.)

Figure 3.7.2 compares the functions $C^0(k)$ and $C^*(k)$ for the same two values of α. Here, $c = \lambda = 1$, so the ratio $k/c\lambda$ is now just k. The differences become significant earlier, for smaller values of k, than in the previous figure. (This is not surprising, because $C^*(k) > k$, while $C^0(k)$ grows only as the square root of k.) In fact (see Problem 3.26), for any $k_1 < k_2$,

$$C^*(k_2) - C^*(k_1) > C^0(k_2) - C^0(k_1)$$

That is, assuming C^* measures the true operating cost, C^0 always *underestimates* the benefits of the technology. An analysis based on C^0 might reject the investment, even though it is really worthwhile according to C^*.

The rest of this book includes various models based on one or the other objective. In some places (e.g., Chapter 9), results for both criteria are presented. Others focus on just one, but mainly for the sake of brevity. In most cases it is possible to construct and analyze a model based on either criterion. And the two models usually yield similar results for a small interest rate. In practice, the choice of objective is a matter of modeling art. These criteria each have their own advantages, as discussed above. The choice is yours.

Notes

Much of the material in this chapter was developed in the early twentieth century, as outlined in the Notes to Chapter 1. Since then, the literature has continued to accumulate. It is now vast and still growing. I know of no single source that surveys it all. Useful points of entry include Aggarwal [1974] and Lee and Nahmias [1993].

Recent investigations of quantity discounts include Monahan [1984] and Weng [1995]. The material on imperfect quality in Section 3.6, straightforward as it is, is mostly original here. Alternative scenarios are explored by Porteus [1986b] and Lee and Rosenblatt [1987]. Nahmias [1982] reviews the literature on perishable products.

The discussions of process improvement (e.g., setup reduction, quality improvement) are inspired, in spirit if not in detail, by Porteus [1985, 1986a, 1986b].

Problems

3.1 In Section 3.2.1 we assume that an order is placed at time t only if $I(t^-) = 0$ (the zero-inventory property). This problem suggests why. For simplicity assume that $L = 0$ and $I(0^-) = IO(0^-) = 0$, so we must order at time 0. Any policy can be described through an increasing sequence of order times $\{t_i : i \geq 1\}$ and a corresponding sequence $\{q_i : i \geq 1\}$ of positive order sizes. Consider only feasible policies, with $I(t) \geq 0$, and those with finitely many order times t_i in every finite interval.

Consider a policy that violates the zero-inventory assumption. Choose j to be the smallest i for which $I(t_i^-) > 0$. Construct a new policy by delaying the order at time t_j until $t_j^* = \min\{t_j + I(t_j^-)/\lambda, t_{j+1}\}$. Show how to adjust some of the q_i if necessary, so that $I(t)$ remains the same as before for $t \geq t_j^*$. Argue that the new policy is feasible and dominates the old one, i.e., its cost over every finite time interval is lower.

3.2 This problem justifies another assumption of Section 3.2.1, that all orders are of the same size. Consider a policy with the zero-inventory property. Let $OF(t)$ be the number of orders and $C(t)$ the total cost in the time interval $[0, t)$. (In the notation of the previous problem, $OF(t) = \max\{i : t_i < t\}$.) Fix t and $OF(t)$. Prove that, among all feasible policies with this $OF(t)$, the one that orders equal amounts $q = \lambda t/OF(t)$ at equal intervals $u = t/OF(t)$ minimizes $C(t)$. (Set up and solve an optimization problem with variables q_i, $1 \leq i \leq OF(t)$.) Also, show that the minimal value of $C(t)$ is $[k/u + \tfrac{1}{2}h\lambda u]t$. Explain that, for every feasible policy and all t, $C(t) \geq (2k\lambda h)^{1/2}t$.

3.3 Consider the function $C(q)$ in Section 3.2.2, the average total cost in the EOQ model. Show that this function is strictly convex in q.

3.4 In the EOQ model of Section 3.2, suppose the fixed cost to place an order is \$100, demand is 50 tons/year, and the holding cost is \$0.015385/pound-week. (There are 2000 pounds/ton and 52 weeks/year.) Calculate the optimal order size and the optimal average cost.

3.5 Consider the following variation on the EOQ model: We own storage space for only I_+ quantity-units. Whenever the inventory exceeds I_+, we have to rent additional space to store the excess. The cost rate for this rented space is $h_+ > h$. Show that the total average cost now becomes

$$C(q) = c\lambda + \frac{k\lambda}{q} + \frac{1}{2}hq + \{\frac{1}{2}\frac{h_+(q^2 - I_+^2)}{q} - \frac{1}{2}\frac{h(q - I_+)^2}{q} \quad \text{if } q > I_+\}$$

Show that this function is continuously differentiable and convex. (Be careful: C is *not* twice continuously differentiable at $q = I_+$.)

Argue that q^* can be computed as follows: First, compute q^* as in the EOQ formula. If $q^* \leq I_+$, stop. Otherwise, reset

$$q^* = I_+ + \sqrt{\frac{2k\lambda - hI_+^2}{h_+}}$$

3.6 Verify equation (3.2.5) describing the relative cost of a suboptimal q in the EOQ model. Evaluate this quantity for $q/q^* = 2$ and $1/\sqrt{2}$. (Notice, these values are small.)

3.7 Define the function $F(x)$ over $x > 0$ by

$$F(x) = ax^{-\alpha} + bx^{\beta}$$

where a, α, b, and β are positive constants. Consider the problem of minimizing F over x. Show that the unique optimal solution is $x^* = (\alpha a/\beta b)^{1/(\alpha+\beta)}$. (We have not assumed $\beta \geq 1$, so F is *not* necessarily convex!) Show also that $F(x^*) = (\alpha + \beta)[(a/\beta)^{\beta}(b/\alpha)^{\alpha}]^{1/(\alpha+\beta)}$.

(This problem generalizes the EOQ model and several others in the text; in these cases $x = q$, and $\alpha = \beta = 1$. Here is another application: The optimal average cost C^* in the EOQ model is a simple function of the fixed cost k; setting $x = k$ gives $C^* = bx^{\beta}$, where $b = (2\lambda h)^{1/2}$ and $\beta = ½$. Now, suppose the current fixed cost is x_0, and there is a range of investments we can make to reduce it. The investment required to achieve any value of $x < x_0$ is $ax^{-\alpha} - ax_0^{-\alpha}$. Thus, the problem of selecting the amount to invest reduces to the problem above.)

3.8 Throughout this chapter we have assumed that the product is infinitely divisible and demand occurs continuously. This problem demonstrates that the EOQ model, with a slight modification, also describes a discrete scenario.

Suppose that demands occur at discrete points in time, spaced $1/\lambda$ apart, in units of size 1. We order batches of size q, a positive integer, so that each batch arrives at the latest feasible moment. Show that $\overline{OF} = \lambda/q$, $\bar{I} = ½(q - 1)$, and

$$C(q) = c\lambda + \frac{k\lambda}{q} + \frac{1}{2}h(q - 1)$$

Denote the first difference operator $\Delta C(q) = C(q + 1) - C(q)$. The optimal $q = q^*$ satisfies $\Delta C(q - 1) < 0 \leq \Delta C(q)$. (This is the analogue of $C'(q) = 0$ in the continuous setting.) Show that this condition is equivalent to

$$q(q - 1) < \frac{2k\lambda}{h} \leq q(q + 1)$$

Let q_c^* indicate the EOQ formula, the optimal q for continuous demand. Argue that, if q_c^* happens to be an integer, then $q^* = q_c^*$, and otherwise q^* is obtained by rounding q_c^* to an integer, either up or down.

The same idea works, clearly, when the demand size is some number Y other than 1. (Just redefine the quantity unit to recover unit demands.) Now, return to the continuous scenario, but suppose that the order interval u is constrained to be integral. Show how to compute u^*, adapting the methods above. Finally, explain what to do when u must be an integer multiple of some arbitrary base period, $\underline{u}$.

3.9 In the model with planned backorders of Section 3.3, suppose the parameters are

$$\lambda = 1000 \qquad k = 60 \qquad h = 0.75 \qquad \omega = 0.81$$

Compute the optimal policy and the optimal average cost (excluding $c\lambda$). Now, suppose we install a computer system to process orders, reducing k from 60 to 33.75. What are the effects on the optimal policy and the optimal cost?

3.10 Define the functions $\hat{C}(x) = h[x]^+ + b[x]^-$ and $C_-(y) = \hat{C}(y - D)$. Show that the cost function for the EOQ model with backorders can be expressed as

$$C(r, q) = c\lambda + \frac{k\lambda + \int_r^{r+q} C_-(y)\,dy}{q}$$

3.11 Here is another approach to backorders: Instead of imposing a cost penalty or a constraint, we explicitly model the effects of waiting time $\overline{BW}$ on the market for the product. $\overline{BW}$ affects the price p that customers are willing to pay, or the amount they are willing to purchase, as expressed in the demand rate λ, or both. Specifically, p, λ, and $\overline{BW}$ are related by the equation

$$\lambda = \alpha[pf(\overline{BW})]^{-\beta}$$

where α and β are positive constants with $\beta > 1$, and f is an increasing function with $f(0) = 1$. So, as $\overline{BW}$ gets larger, λ declines or p declines or both. (Think of $pf(\overline{BW})$ as the total per-unit cost to customers.) The per-unit purchase cost c remains fixed.

Use the time variables u and y to describe an inventory policy. Recall, $\overline{BW} = \tfrac{1}{2}y^2/u$. First, consider u, y, and hence $\overline{BW}$ fixed. So, it remains only to choose p, or equivalently λ. Calculate the value of λ that maximizes the total average profit $P(\lambda)$, that is, the average revenue $p\lambda$ minus all relevant costs.

Now, treat u and y as well as λ as variables. *Formulate* a function $P(u, y, \lambda)$ = total average profit per unit time. Write the first-order necessary conditions for an overall optimal policy. (Do not attempt to solve them.)

3.12 In the planned-backorders model, suppose there is no penalty cost b, but rather an upper limit on $\overline{BW}$, say BW_+. The problem then becomes

$$\begin{aligned} \text{Minimize} \quad & c\lambda + \frac{k\lambda}{q} + \frac{1}{2}\frac{h(q+v)^2}{q} \\ \text{subject to} \quad & \overline{BW} \le BW_+ \\ & -q \le v \le 0 \end{aligned}$$

Argue that the last pair of inequalities can be eliminated, and the remaining constraint reduces to $\tfrac{1}{2}v^2/q = \lambda BW_+$. Introduce a Lagrange multiplier (dual variable) π for this equation, define an appropriate Lagrangian function, and derive the first-order necessary conditions for an optimum. Use these to obtain formulas for v^* and q^* in terms of π^*, and a simple polynomial equation for π itself. Argue that π plays essentially the same role here as b does in a pure cost-optimization model.

3.13 The optimal policy for the lost-sales model of Section 3.3.8 is one of two extremes: Either never lose sales or never order. When precisely does each case apply?

3.14 Consider the model of Section 3.4.5 with a finite production rate μ, where product becomes available to meet demand only after a whole batch is complete. Show that, to avoid running out of stock, we must begin production when $I(t) = \rho q$. Also, show that, when a batch is completed, $I(t) = q$. Draw a graph of $I(t)$ versus t. Show that $\overline{I} = ½(1 + \rho)q$.

3.15 In the model of Section 3.4 suppose the parameters are

$$\lambda = 90 \qquad \mu = 150 \qquad k = 500 \qquad h = 8$$

First, assume each unit produced can be used to meet demand immediately. Compute the optimal policy and the optimal cost. Second, repeat the analysis, assuming that only whole batches can be used to meet demand. Finally, for both cases, determine the effect of increasing the demand rate λ from 90 to 120.

3.16 Consider the incremental quantity-discount model of Section 3.5.2. Instead of only one breakpoint, suppose now there are n breakpoints $\chi_0 < \chi_1 < \cdots < \chi_{n-1}$ and $n + 1$ cost rates $c_0 > c_1 > \cdots > c_n$. For $0 < i < n$, the cost rate c_i applies to those units between χ_{i-1} and χ_i in an order; the highest cost rate c_0 applies to amounts from 0 up to χ_0, and the lowest rate c_n to amounts above χ_{n-1}. Write down an expression for the average cost $C(q)$, and describe how to compute the optimal policy.

3.17 In the incremental quantity-discount model of Section 3.5.2 (with one breakpoint) compute the optimal policy and cost for the following data:

$$\lambda = 10{,}000 \qquad k = 200 \qquad \alpha = 0.10 \qquad \underline{h} = 8$$

$$c_0 = 80 \qquad c_1 = 60 \qquad \chi_0 = 314$$

Now, suppose the supplier approaches us with a proposal to set the variable cost c to 62, regardless of the order size. Determine whether this new arrangement is beneficial for us. Why might the supplier prefer it? (*Hint:* Compare the new optimal policy to the earlier one.)

3.18 The EOQ model with imperfect quality of Section 3.6.2 presumes a fixed defect rate. Suppose now that the defect-generation process depends on the order size. Each increment has its own defect rate $\delta(x)$, and the total defect quantity in an order of size q is $\Delta(q) = \int_0^q \delta(x)\,dx$. Assume that $\delta(x)$ is increasing in x. (Think of the supply system as a production process. As it works on an order, the system deteriorates, and its defect rate grows.) On the other hand, a defective unit is not entirely worthless; instead of scrapping it, we can and do fix it at cost c_f, where $0 < c_f < c$. In effect, we receive the full amount q in each order, but we pay the extra cost $c_f\Delta(q)$.

Write down $C(q)$, the total average cost, and compute its derivative $C'(q)$. Argue that the equation $C'(q) = 0$ has a unique positive solution, q^*. (Do not try to show that C is convex; it need not be. Instead, reduce the equation to an equivalent one with q^2 on the left-hand side and another function of q on the right-hand side. Assume that $\delta(x)$ is differentiable, and show that the right-hand side is decreasing in q.) Show that q^* is *less* than the value given by the EOQ formula.

3.19 Verify the expression (3.6.2) for $\overline{I}$ in the perishable-product model. *Hint:* Integrate both sides of (3.6.1), and use the fact that $\overline{I} = (1/u)\int_0^u I(t)\,dt$.

3.20 For the perishable-product model of Section 3.6.4 show that the average cost $C(u)$ in (3.6.3) is increasing as a function of δ for each fixed value of u. Then, argue that the optimal cost C^* is increasing in δ.

3.21 This problem generalizes the exponential-decay model of Section 3.6.4. Presuming a cycle begins at time 0, inventory deteriorates during the cycle at the rate $\delta(t)I(t)$, where the decay rate $\delta(t)$ is some specified function of time, no longer a constant. Set up a differential equation to describe the evolution of $I(t)$, analogous to (3.6.1). Define $\Delta(t) = \int_0^t \delta(s)\, ds$. Verify that the following function solves the differential equation:

$$I(t) = e^{-\Delta(t)}[q - \lambda \int_0^t e^{\Delta(s)}\, ds]$$

Use this to express q and $\overline{I}$ in terms of u. Specialize these results to a linear decay rate, that is, $\delta(t) = \delta t$ for some constant δ. (Leave $\overline{I}$ as an integral; don't try to express it in closed form.)

3.22 Consider the function $C(u) = (k + c\lambda u)/(1 - e^{-\alpha u})$, the objective function of the present-value model of Section 3.7. Show that $C(u)$ is strictly convex. *Hint:* Show that the function $g(x) = x(1 + e^{-x}) - 2(1 - e^{-x})$ is positive for $x > 0$. *Further hint:* Clearly, $g(0) = 0$; show that $g'(x) \geq 0$.

3.23 Again, consider the function $C(u)$ of Section 3.7. This problem explores its behavior as a function of α, treating u as fixed. First, argue that $\lim_{\alpha \to 0} C(u) = \infty$ for any $u > 0$. Next, compute $\lim_{\alpha \to 0} \alpha C(u)$. (Use l'Hôpital's rule from calculus.) Compare the result with the EOQ model.

3.24 In Section 3.7 we assume that $I(0^-) = 0$. Now assume we begin with inventory $I(0^-) = I_0 > 0$. Argue that the total discounted cost now becomes $\exp[-\alpha I_0/\lambda]\, C(u)$, where $C(u)$ is defined as before, assuming $I_0 = 0$. Conclude that the policy chosen to minimize $C(u)$ is optimal here as well.

3.25 In the discounted-cost model of Section 3.7, suppose that, in addition to the order costs, there is a direct inventory-handling cost rate $\underline{h}$, so cost is incurred continuously at rate $\underline{h}I(t)$. Show that the total-cost function $C(u)$ now has the additional term

$$\underline{h}(\lambda/\alpha^2)[(\alpha u - 1) + \frac{\alpha u e^{-\alpha u}}{(1 - e^{-\alpha u})}]$$

Differentiate $C(u)$ to show that the optimal u satisfies the equation

$$\frac{f(\alpha u)}{\alpha} = \frac{\alpha k}{\lambda(\alpha c + \underline{h})}$$

where $f(x) = e^x - x - 1$. [This reduces to equation (3.7.1) when $\underline{h} = 0$.] Now, approximate f as in the text to obtain an approximate value for u^*. Compare this with the EOQ formula.

3.26 This problem explores further the relation between the present-value optimal cost function $C^*(k)$ and the average-cost function $C^0(k)$ in Section 3.7. Let $u^*(k)$ be the optimal u for given k in the present-value model. Show that

$$\frac{dC^*(k)}{dk} = \frac{1}{1 - e^{-\alpha u^*(k)}}$$

Use this expression, and the fact that $e^{-\alpha u} > 1 - \alpha u$, $u > 0$, to show that

$$\frac{dC^*(k)}{dk} > \frac{dC^0(k)}{dk} \qquad k > 0$$

Explain that this implies

$$C^*(k_2) - C^*(k_1) > C^0(k_2) - C^0(k_1)$$

for $k_1 < k_2$, as asserted in the text. Also, show that $u^*(k) \to \infty$ as $k \to \infty$, so

$$\lim_{k \to \infty} \frac{dC^*(k)}{dk} = 1 \qquad \lim_{k \to \infty} \frac{dC^0(k)}{dk} = 0$$

(So, in the limit, $C^*(k)$ grows linearly at rate 1, while $C^0(k)$ becomes essentially flat. Thus, the two functions behave quite differently for large k.)

3.27 The present-value model of Section 3.7 forbids backorders, and revenue accrues at the constant rate $p\lambda$. Now, relax this restriction. Suppose we follow an order-quantity/reorder-point policy, as in Section 3.3, with $-q < v < 0$. We receive revenue only when a demand increment is actually met. There is no direct backorder-penalty cost.

Derive an expression for the total present value of profit, as a function of u and y, where $y = v/\lambda$ is the safety time. Differentiate this function to obtain two equations describing u^* and y^*. What can you say about these values, compared to the optimal policy in the average-cost case?

(Section 3.7 observes that the usual inventory-holding cost consists of two parts, a physical handling cost and a financing cost. The present-value model represents the financing cost directly, through the discounting of order costs. We see here that there is a financing component in the backorder-penalty cost too, to account for delayed receipt of revenues.)

3.28 Suppose there is a finite production rate μ, as in Section 3.4, and the variable production cost is incurred continuously at rate $c\mu$ while production actually occurs. Analyze this system using the present-value criterion. (Assume there is no direct holding cost, and each unit produced is immediately available to meet demand.) Show that the total discounted cost is

$$C(u) = \frac{k + (c\lambda/\alpha\rho)(1 - e^{-\alpha\rho u})}{1 - e^{-\alpha u}}$$

Differentiate this function to show that u^* solves the equation

$$\frac{\rho f[(1 - \rho)\alpha u] + (1 - \rho)f[-\rho\alpha u]}{\rho\alpha} = \frac{k}{c\lambda}$$

where $f(x) = e^x - x - 1$, as before. Use the approximation $f(x) \approx \frac{1}{2}x^2$ to obtain an approximate formula for u^*. Compare this with the optimal policy of the average-cost model.

How do the model and its solution change when the variable cost for a batch cq is paid in a lump sum at the moment the lot begins production? (This is so, for instance, when cq represents the cost of materials, all of which must be on hand when production begins.)

3.29 Consider case 4 of Section 3.6.2: The supply system generates defects which are discovered only at the moment of demand. We pay for the entire batch on receipt, but we are reimbursed for defective units as they are found. Formulate this model using the present-value criterion. Argue that it reduces to a model with no defects, variable cost c/ξ, and revenue rate $p + c\delta$. Conclude that, in the average-cost approximation of this model, the appropriate holding cost is $h = \alpha c/\xi$, as if there were no reimbursement.

3.30 Consider the model of Section 3.6.3: There is a finite production rate μ, and a fraction δ of the output is defective. We discover and discard the defective goods immediately as they are produced. Suppose, however, that we pay the variable production cost c for every unit produced, defective or not, as in case 2. (This is so, for instance, when a defective unit must be scrapped entirely.)

Formulate the model using the present-value criterion. (*Hint:* Use the result of Problem 3.28 as a starting point.) Then, approximate the model to derive the appropriate parameters for the average-cost model.

C H A P T E R

4 TIME-VARYING DEMANDS

Outline

4.1 Introduction

This chapter considers situations where demand changes over time. It also allows for time-varying purchase costs. Real demand rates and purchase costs do change, of course, because of seasonal factors, or growing or shrinking markets, or other shifts in the economic landscape. The central managerial dilemma, as in Chapter 3, is to find the right balance between the cost of holding inventory and the cost of ordering, including scale economies. This issue is complicated here by temporal variations.

In practice, our current picture of future demand is a forecast. It is important to mention that the models of this chapter treat such forecasts as perfect. Demands change, but the changes are entirely predictable.

Section 4.2 explores some simple cases. A crude, heuristic analysis reveals the broad effects of time-varying demands. The rest of the chapter is quite different in style. It aims for exact answers to the general problem. This program is more challenging here than in Chapter 3. Partly for this reason, starting in Section 4.3, we model time as discrete instead of continuous, with a finite time horizon. We derive *algorithms* to compute solutions, but we shall see few simple, appealing formulas. This emphasis on computation continues throughout Section 4.3 and Section 4.4. Numerical examples relate the results back to the intuitive findings of Section 4.2.

Section 4.5 introduces a *smoothing model.* This model represents *diseconomies of scale,* the opposite of economies of scale, where large orders incur substantial cost penalties. The major virtues of the model—and its primary faults—are certain fundamental *symmetries* in its formulation. These symmetries are not very realistic, but they lead to wonderfully simple, interesting results.

4.2 Extreme Cases

Consider a scenario like that of the EOQ model in all respects but one: The demand rate is now a function of time, say $\lambda(t)$. The cost factors remain constant. The general case of this model is quite difficult. There are a few special cases, however, whose solutions can be described in simple terms, at least approximately. Understanding these special cases will help build our intuition about the overall effects of time-varying demands.

4.2.1 Small Changes

First, suppose the demand rate $\lambda(t)$ changes over time, but only a little; there is some overall average demand rate λ, and $\lambda(t)$ deviates from λ by only a few percent. (This condition is vague, of course, and we shall leave it so; we could specify a precise range for $\lambda(t)$, but we won't. We are not aiming for precise conclusions here.)

Since $\lambda(t)$ is *almost* constant, the EOQ model with constant demand rate λ is *almost* correct. If we use a constant order quantity q, the EOQ's cost function $C(q)$ measures the actual cost quite accurately. Alternatively, if we use a constant cycle time u, $C(u)$ is a good approximation. There is no compelling reason to consider radically different policies. In sum, EOQ model's optimal policy (q^* or u^*) should work well, and its optimal cost C^* should accurately approximate the true optimal cost.

In Section 3.2 we found that the EOQ model is robust with respect to demand-rate changes. That analysis concerned *persistent* changes, changes over all time. Here, the deviations are *transient.* If anything, we should expect the EOQ model to be *more* robust in this setting.

4.2.2 Fast Changes

The scenario above limits the demand fluctuations' *amplitude.* The next two cases restrict their *frequency.*

First, suppose $\lambda(t)$ fluctuates quickly around an overall average λ. Again, we define this condition loosely: For each t, let $\underline{\lambda}(t)$ denote the average of $\lambda(\cdot)$ over a small interval near t. Call $\lambda(t)$ a fast-changing demand rate, if $\underline{\lambda}(t)$ is nearly constant and equal to λ. (For example, compute $u^* = [2k/\lambda h]^{1/2}$, as in (3.2.3), and take $\underline{\lambda}(t)$ to be the average over $[t, t + \frac{1}{4}u^*]$.) The fluctuations may be large, but they are so rapid, the averaging process damps them out.

Figure 4.2.1 shows what happens. The demand-rate fluctuations cause only tiny ripples in $D(t)$, and hence in $I(t)$. Clearly, the EOQ model accurately measures the costs of alternative policies. Again, we can ignore the fluctuations and apply the EOQ model as is.

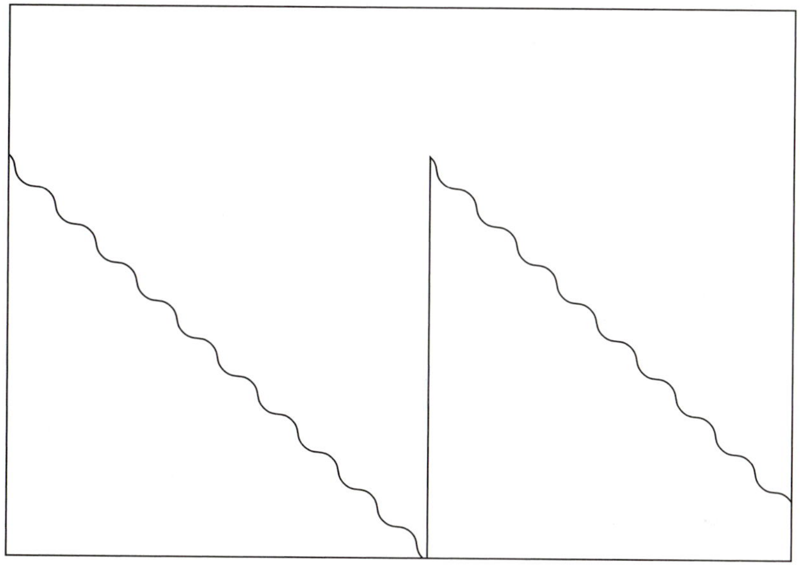

4.2.5 A Finite Production Rate

Now, suppose there is a finite production rate μ, as in Section 3.4. Small or rapid changes in $\lambda(t)$ can again be ignored, following the arguments above. Consider a slow-changing demand rate. For simplicity, assume $\lambda(t)$ is continuous.

The simplest case is where $\lambda(t) < \mu$ for all t. The heuristic approach above can be adapted directly: Define $\rho(t) = \lambda(t)/\mu$, and redefine

$$q(t) = \sqrt{\frac{2k\lambda(t)}{h[1 - \rho(t)]}} \tag{4.2.3}$$

combining (4.2.1) with (3.4.2). Arguing as in Section 4.2.3, the policy using the $q(t)$ as batch sizes will likely perform reasonably well. (This formula presumes that stock produced can be used immediately to meet demand. Otherwise, revise it, replacing $1 - \rho(t)$ by $1 + \rho(t)$ as in Section 3.4.5.)

This approach will *not* work, obviously, when $\lambda(t) > \mu$ for some t. In that case, demand exceeds capacity, at least in the short run, and we must somehow anticipate such heavy-load periods. Figure 4.2.2 illustrates the situation. The horizontal line represents the capacity μ, and the curve is $\lambda(t)$. (The notation will be explained in a moment.)

Let $D(t) = \int_0^t \lambda(s)\,ds$ denote the cumulative demand. Feasibility requires $D(t) \leq \mu t$ for all t. Suppose there is a finite time t_+, such that $\lambda(t) \leq \mu$ for $t \geq t_+$. There are no capacity shortages after t_+, and we can apply (4.2.3) as above; the difficulties come before t_+. Choose t_+ as small as possible. By continuity, $\lambda(t_+) = \mu$, and for t below but near t_+, $\lambda(t) > \mu$ and

$$D(t_+) - D(t) > \mu(t_+ - t)$$

Reducing t further, this inequality certainly holds as long as $\lambda(t) > \mu$, and it continues to hold for a while even when $\lambda(t)$ falls below μ. At some point, however, cumulative supply catches up with cumulative demand, and

$$D(t_+) - D(t) = \mu(t_+ - t)$$

Set t_- to be the *largest* $t < t_+$ satisfying this equation. Thus, if we should arrive at time t_- with no inventory, we *must* produce continuously at least until t_+. The lightly shaded area in Figure 4.2.2 is the total excess demand before t_+, which must be anticipated by earlier production, and t_- is the point where the darker area equals the light one.

Clearly, $\lambda(t_-) < \mu$. For the moment, suppose $\lambda(t) \leq \mu$ for all $t \leq t_-$, as in Figure 4.2.2. In this case the original heuristic fails only during the interval $[t_-, t_+]$. This suggests the following modified heuristic: Apply (4.2.3) until t_-, then produce continuously until t_+, and from then on return to (4.2.3). (Minor adjustments may be needed to hook up the long production run in $[t_-, t_+]$ with the short ones before and after.)

Conversely, suppose that some $t < t_-$ has $\lambda(t) > \mu$. Thus, at some time *before* t_-, the situation looks just like Figure 4.2.2. So, repeat the same approach: Identify a new interval like $[t_-, t_+]$, and schedule production around it in the same way. Continue in this manner to identify such intervals, each requiring a relatively long production cycle to compensate for its short-term capacity shortage. Outside these intervals, apply (4.2.3) as above. (This procedure, like everything else in this section, is a heuristic.)

FIGURE 4.2.2
Excess demand and capacity.

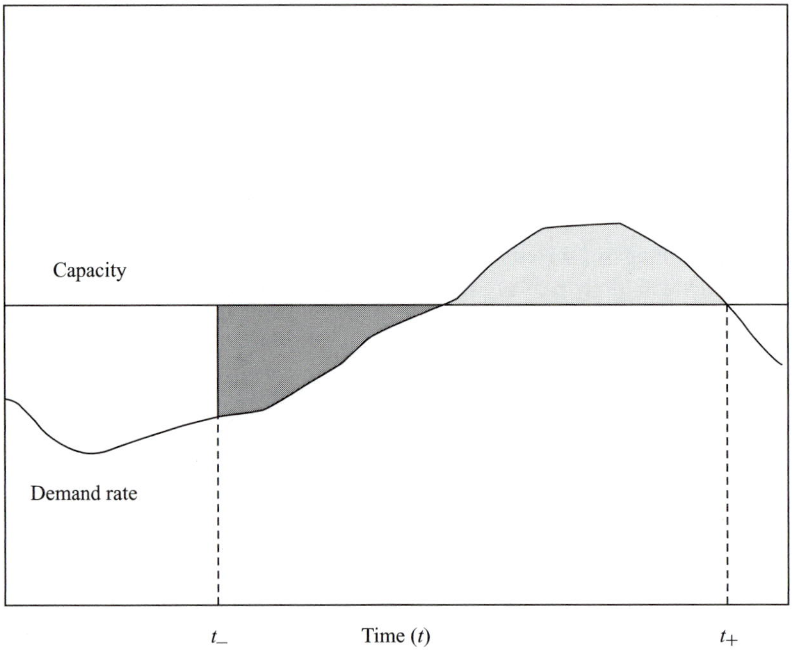

The broad effect of these extended production cycles on performance is clear: The early part of each cycle builds up inventory in order to meet demand in the later part when demand is heaviest. Thus, we end up holding larger inventories than we would otherwise. (This effect can be quantified; see Problem 4.2.)

The same ideas cover situations where the production rate also changes over time, i.e., $\mu = \mu(t)$. One special case deserves mention, where $\mu(t)$ is proportional to $\lambda(t)$, so $\rho(t) = \lambda(t)/\mu(t)$ is the constant $\rho < 1$. Here, capacity expands and contracts in direct response to demand variations. Equation (4.2.3) reduces to

$$q(t) = \sqrt{\frac{2k\lambda(t)}{h(1 - \rho)}}$$

As in the uncapacitated model, $q(t)$ varies as the square root of $\lambda(t)$.

This discussion covers extreme cases only. The general case requires intricate computational methods; see Section 4.4.5.

4.3 The Dynamic Economic Lotsize Model

4.3.1 Discrete-Time Formulation

This section formulates and analyzes an analogue of the EOQ model, where the demand and the purchase cost can vary over time in any manner. To attain this level of general-

FIGURE 4.2.1

Inventory with fast-changing demand.

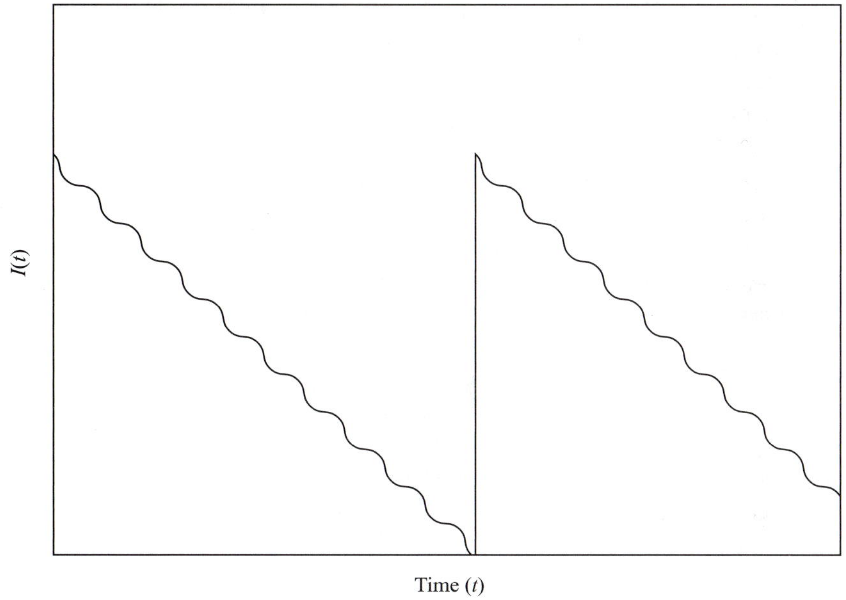

4.2.3 Slow Changes

Next, consider the opposite case: Suppose $\lambda(t)$ changes slowly. The idea, roughly, is that $\lambda(t)$ remain nearly constant over every plausible order interval. For instance, define

$$u(t) = \sqrt{\frac{2k}{\lambda(t)h}}$$

This is just the optimal order interval, computed for each t as if the demand rate were constant at the current value $\lambda(t)$. One way to define a slow-changing demand rate is to stipulate that $\lambda(\cdot)$ change only a little over the interval $[t, t + u(t)]$, for all t. (Evidently, this condition depends on the cost ratio k/h.)

Here is a plausible policy: Order only when stock would run out otherwise, and if t is such a moment, order the quantity

$$q(t) = \sqrt{\frac{2k\lambda(t)}{h}} \tag{4.2.1}$$

That is, use the EOQ formula, treating the demand rate as constant at its current value. Alternatively, order just enough to meet demand until $t + u(t)$.

Why should this heuristic work? Here is an intuitive argument: Consider a time period of intermediate length, covering several order cycles but no large shifts in $\lambda(t)$ and $q(t)$. If $\lambda(t)$ really were constant, the EOQ model's optimal q^* would nearly minimize the average cost over this period. Actually, $\lambda(t)$ does change, but only slightly, and each $q(t)$ is near q^*. So, the heuristic policy nearly minimizes the average cost over the period.

But, this is true for all such periods. Thus, the policy nearly minimizes the overall average cost.

Of course, this is not a rigorous proof, and a good deal of work would be required to make it so. Nevertheless, the basic idea is clear: The demand rate will change significantly only in the distant future, and we can ignore such changes in the current order cycle. (This is a *myopic* heuristic, one that focuses on the near future only. Such methods are effective in a variety of situations. We shall encounter them again later.)

The same reasoning suggests an approximation C^* of the optimal average cost: Following (3.2.4), define

$$C^*(t) = c\lambda(t) + \sqrt{2k\lambda(t)h} \tag{4.2.2}$$

$$C^* \quad = \lim_{T\to\infty}\left(\frac{1}{T}\right)\int_0^T C^*(t)\,dt$$

(Think of $C^*(t)$ as the approximate instantaneous cost rate. The integral can be evaluated exactly, of course, only for certain special forms of $\lambda(t)$.)

This model inherits the robustness properties of the EOQ model. For instance, $q(t)$ and C^* change only slightly in response to a modest change in k, and if the entire function $\lambda(t)$ doubles, each $q(t)$ increases only by $\sqrt{2}$, as does C^*. Moreover, $q(t)$ is *dynamically robust* as well. That is, consider one fixed function $\lambda(t)$. If $\lambda(t)$ changes modestly over some interval of time, then $q(t)$ changes even less over that interval.

For this reason, an even cruder heuristic works fairly well: Keep the order size (or the cycle time) constant most of the time. Change it only when $q(t)$ (or $u(t)$), as computed above, departs too far from the current policy. It is often easier to administer a policy whose variables change infrequently.

4.2.4 Discussion

To summarize: If the changes in $\lambda(t)$ are small and/or rapid, focus on the long-run average λ, ignoring the current demand rate. If $\lambda(t)$ evolves slowly, focus on the current $\lambda(t)$, and ignore longer-run changes. The numerical examples of Section 4.3.5 support these suggestions.

We can even combine these three cases: Suppose $\lambda(t)$ is the sum of three functions, a small-, a fast-, and a slow-changing one. That is, suppose the local average $\underline{\lambda}(t)$ does change over time, but only slowly. Following the arguments above, a reasonable heuristic policy is to set $q(t)$ according to (4.2.1), using $\underline{\lambda}(t)$ instead of $\lambda(t)$.

This is still a rather extreme case. What about more typical cases, where $\lambda(t)$ includes changes of substantial size that are neither slow nor fast, but somewhere in between? The following crude guideline appears to work well: Suppose $\lambda(t)$ varies within a certain range. Compute the corresponding range of values for the EOQ formula, and set each order quantity within this range.

Of course, when the range of $\lambda(t)$ is wide, this guideline leaves a great deal of leeway. As discussed below, there seem to be no more precise, simple, reliable guidelines for finding a truly optimal or even close-to-optimal policy. Algorithmic methods, exact or approximate, appear to be essential.

ity, we introduce a very different conception of time. We model time as a finite sequence of discrete *time points.* We casually refer to *time periods,* the intervals between the time points, but in this view of the world all the significant events occur precisely *at* the time points themselves.

There are situations where discrete time describes reality better than continuous time. For instance, it may well be that, by prior arrangement, we can order only at certain times, say once per week on Mondays at 9:00 A.M. Alternatively, a discrete-time model can be employed to approximate a continuous-time system. (As in any such discretization, of course, the approximation is more accurate when the time points are close together.) We may think of the time periods as being of equal length, though this is not necessary. In fact, it is sometimes better to use short periods near the beginning and longer ones toward the horizon.

The world of discrete time takes some getting used to; the terminology, notation, and overall style are rather different from anything we have seen before. Indeed, the connection to continuous-time models may not be immediately apparent. Rest assured, the connection exists, as explained later.

The problem, in words, is the following: Demand for a product occurs at each of several time points. We must meet all demand as it occurs; no backorders or lost sales are permitted. We can order or produce supplies at each point, and we can carry inventory from one point to the next. Replenishment decisions take effect immediately; there is no order leadtime. Each order incurs a fixed cost regardless of the size of the order, and also a variable cost proportional to the order quantity. There is a cost to hold inventory between any two successive points. These costs as well as the demands may change over time. The goal is to determine a feasible ordering plan which minimizes the total cost over all time points.

To formulate this problem, denote

T = time horizon
t = index for time points, $t = 0, \ldots, T$

The horizon T is finite. Time period t is the time from point t until just before $t + 1$. The data of the problem include

$$d(t) = \text{demand at time } t$$

These are arbitrary nonnegative constants. The decision variables are

$$x(t) = \text{inventory at time } t$$

$$z(t) = \text{order size at time } t$$

The starting inventory at time $t = 0$ is the known constant x_0.

We use the notation $d(t)$ instead of $\lambda(t)$ to emphasize that demand occurs in discrete chunks, not continuously. Also, we use $z(t)$ for the order size, not $q(t)$. We reserve $q(t)$ to describe a *policy,* indicating the amount to order *if* certain conditions are met, whereas $z(t)$ specifies precisely what to order with no conditions attached. This is the most common usage in the literature on discrete-time models, perhaps because $z(t)$ *looks* more like a decision variable than $q(t)$. For similar reasons we denote inventory by $x(t)$ instead of $I(t)$. (In Section 4.4, $x(t)$ will have the more general meaning of net inventory or inventory position.)

The precise sequence of events at each time point $t < T$ is as follows:

1. We observe the inventory $x(t)$.
2. We decide the order size $z(t)$.

Then, sometime during period t, the order $z(t)$ arrives and the demand $d(t)$ occurs. We don't care precisely when these events happen, provided they are complete by the end of the period, in time to determine $x(t + 1)$ at point $t + 1$. The story concludes at step 1 of the last time point T; the terminal inventory $x(T)$ is important, but there is no order or demand at the horizon.

The cost parameters are the following:

$k(t)$ = fixed order cost at time t
$c(t)$ = variable order cost at time t
$h(t)$ = inventory holding cost at time t.

These are all nonnegative. Let $\delta(\cdot)$ denote the *Heaviside function,* that is, $\delta(z) = 1$ for $z > 0$, and $\delta(z) = 0$ for $z \leq 0$. The total order cost at time t is thus $k(t)\delta(z(t)) + c(t)z(t)$. The holding cost at t is $h(t)x(t)$. We ignore the constant cost $h(0)x(0) = h(0)x_0$, but we do include the terminal holding cost $h(T)x(T)$.

We are now prepared to formulate the model:

Initial conditions:

$$x(0) = x_0 \tag{4.3.1}$$

Dynamics:

$$x(t + 1) = x(t) + z(t) - d(t) \qquad t = 0, \ldots, T - 1 \tag{4.3.2}$$

Constraints:

$$x(t) \geq 0 \qquad t = 1, \ldots, T \tag{4.3.3}$$

$$z(t) \geq 0 \qquad t = 0, \ldots, T - 1$$

Objective:

$$\text{Minimize} \quad \Sigma_{t=0}^{T-1} [k(t)\delta(z(t)) + c(t)z(t)] + \Sigma_{t=1}^{T} h(t)x(t) \tag{4.3.4}$$

This optimization problem is called the *dynamic economic lotsize* (DEL) model. It is also called the *Wagner-Whitin problem* after its inventors, Wagner and Whitin [1958]. (It is a special instance of a general modeling framework for discrete-time *dynamical systems* and *optimal control.* In those terms, $x(t)$ describes the *state* of the system, $z(t)$ is the *control* variable, and $d(t)$ is the exogenous *input.* See Appendix B. The dynamics (4.3.2) express a conservation-of-flow law for this system.)

There are alternative scenarios, where time is less strictly discrete, which lead to the same mathematical model. For instance, as explained in Section 4.4.3, holding costs can accrue continuously throughout the period. The crucial assumption is the restriction of order decisions to the discrete time points.

Here is some additional notation, used below:

$D(t)$ = cumulative demand through time $t = \Sigma_{s=0}^{t} d(s)$
$D[t, u)$ = demand from time t through $u - 1 = D(u-1) - D(t-1), t \le u$
$\tilde{c}[t, u)$ = variable cost to order a unit at t and hold it until $u = c(t) + \Sigma_{s=t+1}^{u} h(s)$, $t \le u$

(For $u = t$, $\tilde{c}[t, u) = c(t)$.)

The DEL model can be reformulated to eliminate the nonlinear function δ from the objective by introducing additional binary indicator variables $v(t)$. Here, $v(t)$ is 1 if we order at time t, and 0 if not. (If you are familiar with integer programming, you will recognize this as a standard trick.) The model requires some new constraints in addition to (4.3.3),

$$v(t) \in \{0,1\} \tag{4.3.5}$$

$$z(t) \le D[t, T)v(t) \qquad t = 1, \ldots, T-1$$

and the objective (4.3.4) now becomes linear:

$$\text{Minimize} \qquad \Sigma_{t=0}^{T-1}[k(t)v(t) + c(t)z(t)] + \Sigma_{t=1}^{T} h(t)x(t) \tag{4.3.4$'$}$$

Thus, the DEL model can be expressed as a linear mixed-integer program. (This reformulation is interesting; the same trick can be applied to more complex systems, as in Chapter 5. But it is not immediately practical, for integer programs are hard to solve.)

4.3.2 The Linear-Cost Case

The linear-cost case, where all the $k(t) = 0$, is easy to solve, and the solution is interesting.

First, suppose that all the $c(t)$ equal some constant $c \ge 0$. The solution is obvious: Assuming $x_0 = 0$, set each $z(t) = d(t)$ and $x(t) = 0$. Likewise, if $x_0 > 0$, order nothing until the initial stock runs out, and from then on order the minimal amount required to keep $x(t) \ge 0$. In general, order as little and as late as possible, while still meeting demand as it occurs. This is the discrete-time version of a perfect flow system—it meets all demands while holding no inventory (except any remaining from the initial stock).

Now, suppose the variable costs $c(t)$ do depend on t. The basic economic issue here is the balance of purchase and holding costs: We can avoid projected cost increases by ordering earlier than necessary, but then we incur holding costs.

Assume $x_0 = 0$ for now. Consider any time t and any single unit of demand within $d(t)$. To fill that demand unit, we can order a unit at any time $s \le t$. If we choose time s, the total cost is just $\tilde{c}[s, t)$. This includes both the purchase cost $c(s)$ and the holding costs between s and t. To minimize this cost, compute

$$\tilde{c}[*, t) = \min_s\{\tilde{c}[s, t) : 0 \le s \le \text{t}\} \tag{4.3.6}$$

Let $\tilde{s}(t)$ denote the largest s achieving this minimum.

This calculation applies to *all* the demand units in $d(t)$. Thus, to solve the overall problem, we need only determine the best order time $\tilde{s}(t)$ to meet time t's demand, separately for each t. These optimal order times are *independent* of the demand quantities $d(t)$; they depend solely on the cost factors.

The following recursive scheme streamlines the calculation:

$$\tilde{c}[*, 0) = c(0) \tag{4.3.7}$$
$$\tilde{c}[*, t+1) = \min\{\tilde{c}[*, t) + h(t+1), c(t+1)\}$$

That is, there are only two possible values for $\tilde{s}(t+1)$: If the first quantity in brackets is smaller, then $\tilde{s}(t+1) = \tilde{s}(t)$, while if the second is smaller, then $\tilde{s}(t+1) = t+1$. (Problem 4.3 asks you to validate this approach.) For each $t > 0$, (4.3.7) requires the smaller of *two* numbers instead of the $t+1$ in (4.3.6). Also, in (4.3.7) there is no need to compute the $\tilde{c}[s, t)$ in advance. If we do order at some time *s*, we order enough to meet demand at several *consecutive* time points (those $t \geq s$ for which $\tilde{s}(t) = s$). (This latter property holds for positive $k(t)$ too, as we shall see shortly.)

When $x_0 > 0$, calculate the $\tilde{s}(t)$ as above. Not all of these times represent actual orders, however. Use the initial inventory to meet demands until it runs out, thus replacing some of the earliest orders.

Incidentally, when $\tilde{s}(t) < t$, we say there is a *speculative motive* for holding inventory, for this means we anticipate an increase in the purchase cost from period $\tilde{s}(t)$ to *t*, large enough to offset the intervening holding costs. If on the other hand $\tilde{s}(t) = t$ for all *t*, as in the case of constant $c(t)$, we say the problem offers *no speculation opportunities.* This latter case is important, even when there are additional complexities like fixed costs.

4.3.3 The Zero-Inventory Property

The general DEL model with positive $k(t)$, as formulated above, is a hard-to-solve nonlinear program or an equally hard linear mixed-integer program. The model possesses a remarkable property, however, which we shall exploit later to devise a simple solution procedure.

Given a feasible solution, call *t* an *order time* if $z(t) > 0$. The central result describes the optimal schedule in terms of the optimal order times, and is called *the zero-inventory property.* It is simplest to state assuming $x_0 = 0$: Orders should be planned so as to run out of stock just as each order is received. This rule works in the general case $x_0 \geq 0$ too, with a slight qualification: The first order may arrive when there is positive inventory, but only the first. Here is a formal statement:

THEOREM 4.3.1. There exists an optimal solution $x^*(t)$, $z^*(t)$ to equations (4.3.1) to (4.3.4) such that $z^*(t) > 0$ only when $x^*(t) = 0$, for every *t* except possibly the earliest order time.

Recall, we assumed essentially the same property for the EOQ model in Section 3.2 (and verified it in Problem 3.1). The theorem asserts that this property continues to hold even with nonstationary data.

The zero-inventory property implies that, at each order time, we order precisely the amount needed to cover demand until the next order time. In particular, the order times completely determine the order quantities. This point is crucial for the reformulation of the next subsection. (Also, assuming $x_0 = 0$, when the $d(t)$ are all integers, so are the

$z^*(t)$. This fact is useful: Sometimes it is important that the $z(t)$ be integral, though the DEL model itself contains no such restrictions. It doesn't need them; they hold automatically. This is even true, it turns out, when x_0 is positive but integral.)

PROOF OF THEOREM 4.3.1. For simplicity suppose $x_0 = 0$, all $d(t) > 0$, and all $k(t) > 0$. For this case, we prove that every optimal solution has the zero-inventory property. (Problem 4.4 asks you to prove the result in the general case.) Call an order time t *bad* if it violates the assertion, that is, if $x(t) > 0$. Consider a feasible solution with a bad order time. Let u be the smallest one and t the order time just prior to u. (This t exists, because 0 is a non-bad order time.)

We now construct a new feasible solution, in which u is no longer a bad order time, and whose cost is less than the original's, by shifting some of $z(u)$ to $z(t)$ or vice versa. Define

$$\bar{c}[t, u) = \tilde{c}[t, u) - c(u)$$

This is the change in the overall cost to increment $z(t)$ by 1, reduce $z(u)$ by 1, and adjust the inventories between t and u accordingly [as determined by the dynamics (4.3.2)]. Consider two cases, depending on the sign of this quantity: If $\bar{c}[t, u) \leq 0$, modifying the solution in this way improves the cost (or at worst leaves it unchanged), and further such changes are equally beneficial. So, make the largest possible such change; that is, replace $z(t)$ by $z(t)+z(u)$ and reduce $z(u)$ to 0, so that u is no longer an order time. The total cost change is $\bar{c}[t, u)z(u) \leq 0$, and we also save the fixed cost $k(u)$. On the other hand, if $\bar{c}[t, u) > 0$, make the maximal change in the opposite direction. That is, increase $z(u)$ by $x(u)$, reduce $z(t)$ by the same amount, and again adjust the inventories between t and u; this change drives $x(u)$ itself to 0, so u is no longer bad. This reduces the cost by $\bar{c}[t, u)x(u) > 0$ (or even more if $z(t)$ too is driven to 0).

In constructing this new solution we have created no new bad order times. Indeed, any remaining ones must all be greater than u. We can thus repeat this procedure until all the bad order times are eliminated, reducing the total cost at each step. Certainly, an *optimal* solution can have no bad order times. ■

Incidentally, there is another way to demonstrate the zero-inventory property: The objective is a *concave* function of the variables over the *convex* set defined by the constraints and the dynamics. Its minimum can be found, therefore, at an extreme point of the feasible region. (See Section A.3.) It is possible to show that every extreme point has the zero-inventory property, so the optimal solution does too. We shall not pursue this approach here, but it is worth being aware of it. Several extensions of the DEL model can be analyzed in this way.

4.3.4 Network Representation and Solution

To solve the DEL model, then, the primary problem is to select the order times. Focus on the case $x_0 = 0$. This selection problem can be expressed in terms of a network: The nodes correspond to the time points $t = 0, \ldots, T$. There is a directed arc from t to u for every node pair (t, u) with $t < u$. Any specific choice of order times corresponds to a *path* in this network from node 0 to node T, and vice versa. The nodes encountered

FIGURE 4.3.1

Network for DEL model.

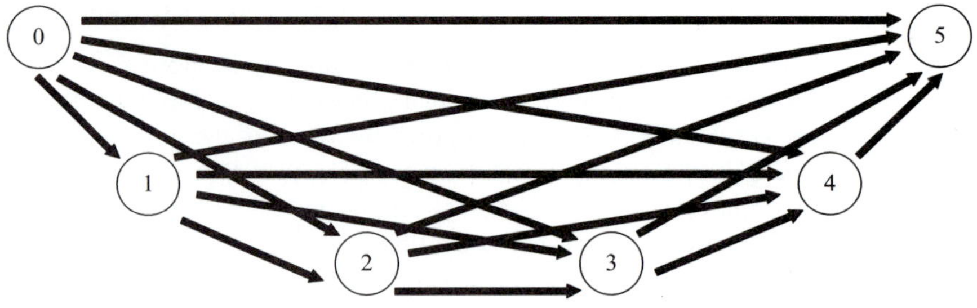

FIGURE 4.3.2

One possible path.

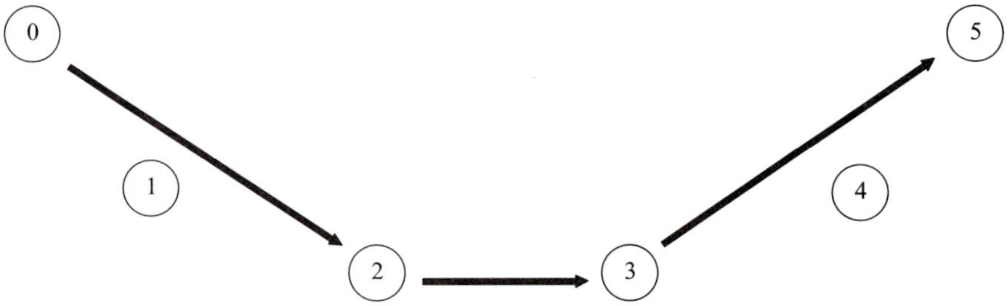

along the path (excluding T itself) identify the order times. Figure 4.3.1 illustrates this network for a problem with $T = 5$. Figure 4.3.2 shows one possible path; the order times are 0, 2, and 3.

Now, consider any one path and a particular arc (t, u) along the path. Choosing this arc means that t is an order time, and we order just enough at t to meet the demands at points t through $u - 1$. Let $k[t, u)$ denote the total cost incurred by this decision. The dynamics imply that $z(t) = D[t, u)$, $x(t + 1) = z(t) - d(t) = D[t + 1, u)$, and $x(s + 1) = x(s) - d(s) = D[s + 1, u)$ for $t < s < u$. Thus,

$$\begin{aligned} k[t, u) &= k(t) + c(t)z(t) + \Sigma_{s=t+1}^{u} h(s)x(s) \\ &= k(t) + c(t)D[t, u) + \Sigma_{s=t+1}^{u} h(s)D[s, u) \\ &= k(t) + \Sigma_{s=t}^{u-1} \tilde{c}[t, s)d(s) \end{aligned} \tag{4.3.8}$$

Now, add the $k[t,u)$ over all arcs encountered on the path. This sum accounts for the all costs in all periods—it *is* the cost of choosing the order times along the path.

EXAMPLE 4.3.A, PART 1

Here is an example with $T = 5$:

t	$d(t)$	$k(t)$	$c(t)$	$h(t)$
0	10	40	2	—
1	2	40	2	1
2	12	40	2	1
3	4	40	2	1
4	14	40	2	1
5	—	—	—	1

The arc costs $k[t, u)$ are:

	u				
t	1	2	3	4	5
0	60	66	114	134	218
1		44	80	96	166
2			64	76	132
3				48	90
4					68

So, compute $k[t, u)$ for every arc (t, u) in the network, and think of $k[t, u)$ as the travel cost along arc (t, u). To determine an optimal sequence of order times, *find a path of minimum total cost.* In sum, the DEL model reduces to a shortest-path calculation. There are very efficient solution procedures for such problems. (See Gallo and Pallottino [1986], for example.) This network is acyclic (there is no path from a node to itself), and the nodes are naturally ordered by t, which makes the calculation even easier.

Let us look at one method in detail. It is called *forward recursion.* The idea is to compute the minimum-cost path from node 0 to *every* node t, starting with $t = 1$, then $t = 2$, and continuing until $t = T$. This method solves the DEL model with horizon t for each t. Let $V^*(t)$ denote the optimal cost of the t-horizon problem, so $V^*(T)$ is the optimal cost of the original DEL model.

Step t aims to determine the *last* order time in the t-horizon problem, denoted $s^*(t)$. But, *assuming* $s^*(t) = s$ for some fixed $s < t$, we should set all earlier order times according to the optimal solution of the s-horizon problem, so the total cost is $V^*(s) + k[s, t) \equiv V^*(s, t)$. To find the best such s, the actual $s^*(t)$, compute the smallest of the $V^*(s, t)$. The following algorithm embodies this idea:

Algorithm Forward_DEL:

Set $V^*(0) = 0$

For $t = 1, \dots, T$:

$V^*(s, t) = V^*(s) + k[s, t) \qquad 0 \le s < t$

$V^*(t) = \min_s \{V^*(s, t) : 0 \le s < t\}$

$s^*(t) =$ largest s achieving this minimum

Once this calculation is done, recover the optimal order times by tracing the $s^*(t)$ back from T. That is, $s^*(T)$ is the last order time, $s^*(s^*(T))$ is the next to last, and so on.

EXAMPLE 4.3.A, PART 2

For the example above, the solution is

t	$V^*(t)$	$s^*(t)$	$x^*(t)$	$z^*(t)$
0	0		0	12
1	60	0	2	0
2	66	0	0	30
3	114	0	18	0
4	134	0	14	0
5	198	2	0	

The solution tells us to plan two orders: Order 12 units at the beginning to cover the demands at points 0 and 1, and then order 30 at point 2 to cover the remaining demands. The total optimal cost is $V^*(5) = 198$.

Incidentally, there is another approach to the problem called *backward recursion:* Take Figure 4.3.1, turn it upside down, reverse all the arrows, and apply Algorithm Forward_DEL to this network. In terms of the original problem, this method works in the opposite direction, finding the optimal path *from* each t to T. The cost of that path, say $V^*(t)$, measures the optimal cost over times t through T, starting with $x(t) = 0$. The optimal cost of the full DEL model is $V^*(0) = V^*(t)$.

This method is essentially equivalent to Algorithm Forward_DEL, but it is worth knowing about anyway: People do use it. It recovers not just a solution but a full optimal *policy.* Letting $q(t)$ be the first order in the t-to-T subproblem, $q(t)$ prescribes the amount to order at time t, *if* $x(t) = 0$, as in § 4.2.3. Finally, this approach is similar conceptually to that of Chapter 9 for stochastic models; both are sometimes called *dynamic programming* approaches.

How much effort does Algorithm Forward_DEL require? There are T iterations, and the tth entails t similar calculations. The total number of calculations is thus proportional to $\Sigma_t t = \frac{1}{2}T(T + 1)$. The quadratic term is the dominant one for large T. So, we say the algorithm requires $O(T^2)$ time. (This notation has a precise meaning, but this informal definition will do here. Setting up the $k[s, t)$ also requires $O(T^2)$ time.) This summarizes the capability of the algorithm to handle large problems: As T increases, the time required grows roughly as T^2.

Quadratic growth is not bad as these things go; other algorithms for other problems are far more sensitive to their primary size parameters. (See Section 4.4.5, for instance.) Even so, researchers have recently developed refined procedures requiring only $O[(T) \log (T)]$ time in general, and only $O(T)$ for problems with no speculation opportunities. These methods are thus faster than Algorithm Forward_DEL for large T. (Federgruen and Tzur [1991] report that theirs runs about 3 times faster for $T = 500$ and 70 times faster for $T = 5000$. Such huge T's can arise, for instance, in a discretization of an originally continuous model.) They require some additional computational overhead, however, and for small T they are a bit slower.

The basic idea is simple: To determine $s^*(t)$, Algorithm Forward_DEL searches over *all* $s < t$. Even for large t, it continues to consider even the smallest s's. The new algorithms extract information from prior iterations to help guide the search, specifically, to eliminate some of the s's. [The same idea underlies the streamlined recursion (4.3.7) for the linear-cost case. See also Problem 4.5*a*.]

The asymptotic growth rates expressed in the $O(\cdot)$ notation do not tell the whole story. If an algorithm took 3 years to solve a problem with $T = 1$, it would be little comfort to know that a problem with $T = 100$ requires "only" $3(100^2)$ or even 3(100) years!

The DEL model, fortunately, has no such problem. The individual calculations in Algorithm Forward_DEL are *very* simple. The newer methods are nearly as simple. Provided some care is given to efficient programming, most practical-sized problems can be solved quickly. For example, with $T = 26$ (half a year of weekly time periods), the entire calculation requires a fraction of a second on any decent personal computer.

One additional fact deserves mention: In some instances of the DEL model, it is possible to identify (see Problem 4.5*b*) a *planning horizon*. This is a time point, say t_H, which essentially separates earlier times from later ones. Specifically, for $s < t_H - 1$, the $z^*(s)$ in the t_H-horizon problem remain optimal in the t-horizon problem for all $t > t_H$. (*Terminology alert:* Sometimes people refer to T as *the* planning horizon. Usually, it is clear in the context what "planning horizon" means.)

A planning horizon is very convenient: Often in practice, we actually use the solution values only for early time points. In that case, we can terminate the algorithm at step t_H. Also, the $z^*(s)$ are entirely independent of the data after t_H, so we need not worry about estimating those data. Thus, a planning horizon justifies a myopic approach. Unfortunately, it is hard to predict if and when a planning horizon will occur.

4.3.5 Examples–Opacity

Let us solve a few examples with many periods. Think of these as discretized versions of originally continuous-time models. They all have $T = 200$, but we display the solution only up to $t = 150$. All have constant cost factors, indicated in the figures below.

First, consider a model with slowly varying demand, shown in Figure 4.3.3. The demand $d(t)$ is the heavy curve near the bottom, which undulates gently between 2 and 6. The lighter curve above shows $q(t)$, the solution to an EOQ model for each t assuming

FIGURE 4.3.3

Optimal order sizes (k = 50, c = 2, h = 1).

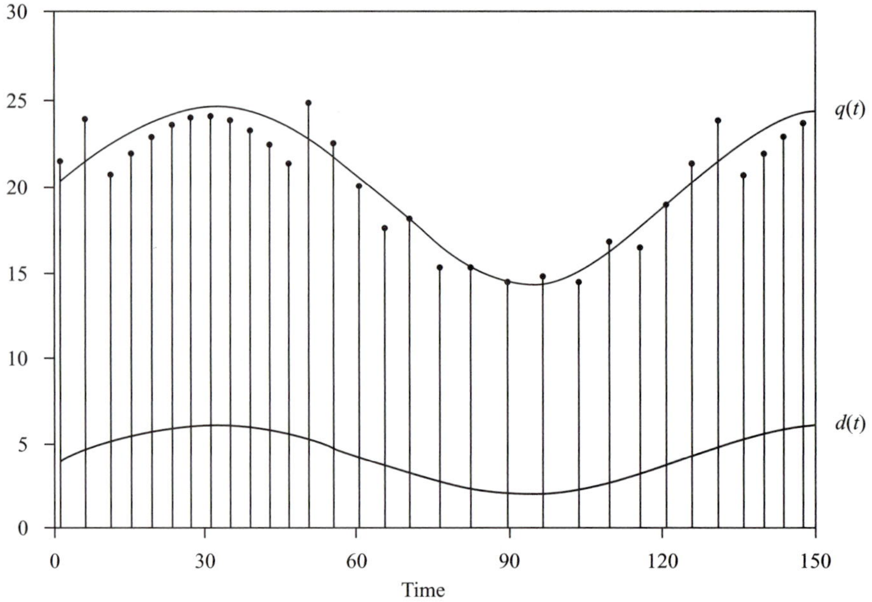

the demand rate remains constant at the current value $d(t)$. Finally, the vertical lines indicate the optimal orders in the DEL model.

It is striking how closely the positive $z^*(t)$ track the $q(t)$. The spacing of the lines, moreover, indicates that orders are more frequent as well as larger when demand is large. (The EOQ model exhibits similar behavior.) The correspondence is not perfect, mainly because of the DEL model's discrete time. This example illustrates one of the special cases of Section 4.2: When demand changes slowly, the EOQ model using the current demand rate works well.

Next, Figure 4.3.4 presents a model with fast-changing $d(t)$. The positive $z^*(t)$ are all equal to 32. (The exact equality here is somewhat coincidental. For other values of k, for example, the $z^*(t)$ do change, though not much.) This common value is near the EOQ model's q^* of 28.3, based on the average demand rate of 4. This example illustrates another extreme case of Section 4.2: Rapid fluctuations can essentially be ignored.

Figure 4.3.5 shows a model with a highly irregular demand pattern. In this case the *ranges* of the orders generated by the DEL and EOQ models are about the same. It is hard to discern any precise correspondence between them, however. The fine structure of the optimal solution exploits the demand fluctuations in subtle ways.

Most instances of the DEL model have similarly subtle solutions. In this sense, compared to the EOQ model with its simple formulas, the DEL model is opaque. Except in the extreme cases of Section 4.2, it is hard to see why the algorithm makes the precise choices it does. In fact, a tiny change in the model parameters can cause the solution to shift markedly. We *need* a clever algorithm to find the optimal solution; no simple formula will

FIGURE 4.3.4

Optimal order sizes (k = 100, c = 2, h = 1).

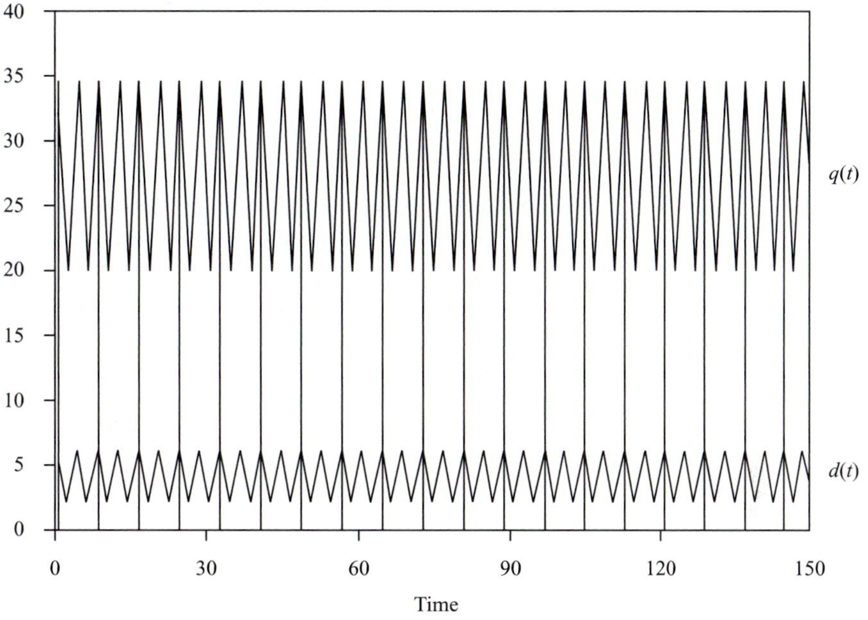

FIGURE 4.3.5

Optimal order sizes–k = 50, c = 2, h = 1.

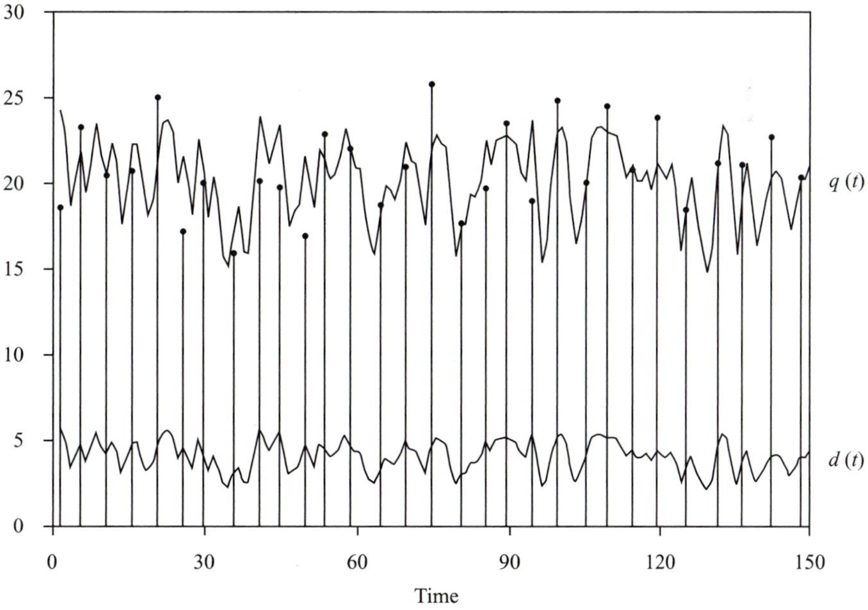

do. On the other hand, the range of order sizes is usually within the range of values indicated by the myopic use of the EOQ model, as suggested in Section 4.2.4.

This opacity rules out sensitivity analysis, or at least simple, transparent results like those in Chapter 3. There do exist some limited sensitivity results; see Problems 4.6 and 4.7 and Zangwill [1987], for instance.

4.3.6 Heuristics

Even though it is not hard to solve the DEL model exactly, several heuristic methods have been developed, for reasons explained below. We describe one popular approach, the Silver-Meal heuristic (Silver and Meal [1973]). Most of the others are similar in spirit. The idea is to look ahead only a few periods, not all the way to the horizon, to set each order quantity. (This is a common analytical tactic, sometimes called the *greedy* or *myopic* approach; we saw the idea in Section 4.2.) The heuristic itself determines how far ahead to look as it works.

Assume $x_0 = 0$. Focus on the first order, restricting attention to values consistent with the zero-inventory property. So, $z(0)$ may cover just the initial demand $d(0)$, or $D[0, 2) = d(0) + d(1)$, or $D[0, 3) = d(0) + d(1) + d(2)$, et cetera. If it covers $D[0, u)$, then the total cost over this interval is $k[0, u)$, so the average cost is $k[0, u)/u$. The heuristic aims to make this average cost small: Starting with $u = 1$, it increments u by 1 *as long as the average cost decreases;* once it finds that a further increment would increase the average cost, it stops. This rule determines $z(0)$.

If the heuristic stops at u, setting $z(0) = D[0, u)$, then $x(u) = 0$. It then restarts, treating u as the initial period, and computes $z(u)$ as above. It continues in this manner until it reaches the horizon.

EXAMPLE 4.3.A, PART 3

Reconsider the small example of § 4.3.4. To select $z(0)$, the heuristic computes

$$\frac{k[0, 1)}{1} = \frac{60}{1} = 60$$

$$\frac{k[0, 2)}{2} = \frac{66}{2} = 33 < 60$$

$$\frac{k[0, 3)}{3} = \frac{114}{3} = 38 > 33$$

So, the heuristic sets $z(0) = D[0, 2) = 12$. Next,

$$\frac{k[2, 3)}{1} = \frac{64}{1} = 64$$

$$\frac{k[2, 4)}{2} = \frac{76}{2} = 38 < 64$$

$$\frac{k[2, 5)}{3} = \frac{132}{3} = 44 > 38$$

So, $z(2) = D[2, 4) = 16$. Next,

$$\frac{k[4,5)}{1} = \frac{68}{1} = 68$$

We have hit the horizon $T = 5$, so $z(4) = D[4, 5) = 14$.

The cost of this solution is 210, about 5% above optimal. (The optimal solution does not order at time 4.)

In the larger examples of Section 4.3.5, the heuristic's solutions are similar, though not identical, to the optimal ones, and their costs are quite close to optimal.

How good is the heuristic in cost terms? First, it is designed mainly for stationary cost factors. (It performs poorly with rapid cost changes.) In that case it usually performs well, but not always: If the demands are stationary also and T is infinite, the heuristic recovers the optimal solution. (In that case the DEL model is a discrete-time version of the EOQ model.) With slowly changing $d(t)$, it performs quite well. It sets the $z(t)$ near the corresponding EOQ values, consistent with the guideline suggested in Section 4.2.3. Even with changes of moderate speed, the heuristic is fairly effective.

Sharply varying demands, however, can defeat it. It terminates when it finds a *locally* minimal average cost, and fast demand shifts can lead to poor local optima. For example, in the model of Figure 4.3.4 above with $k = 90$ instead of 100, the true optimal solution remains the same, i.e., $z^*(t) = 0$ or 32, but the heuristic sets the positive $z(t)$ to 16, covering only one demand cycle instead of two. The optimal average cost is 32.25, while the heuristic's is 35.5, about 10% more. Indeed, Axsäter [1982] demonstrates that the heuristic can perform awfully; its cost can be arbitrarily large relative to the optimal cost. (Bitran et al. [1984] show that another heuristic is better in this sense.)

This negative result is based on a worst-case analysis, which, by design, focuses on extreme cases. What about more "typical" cases? A good deal of research has been devoted to empirical performance testing, including Wemmerlov [1982], Blackburn and Millen [1985], and Baker [1990, 1993]. They find that the Silver-Meal heuristic and related methods perform reasonably well over a wide range of problems, on average.

Why bother with a heuristic when the exact algorithms are so fast? Well, the heuristic is even faster. It requires $O(T)$ time, which certainly beats Algorithm Forward_DEL for large T. The newer algorithms also require $O(T)$ time (for stationary costs). But, simple as those algorithms are, the heuristic's internal mechanics are even simpler, so it is still faster.

This speed advantage was more important in 1973 when the heuristic was introduced than it is now, for computers then were far slower and far less accessible, and the newer algorithms were unknown. Today, in my view, the exact procedures are fast enough for most practical purposes.

Apart from the speed issue, there are other reasons that follow to consider the heuristic.

4.3.7 Modeling and Implementation Issues

The DEL model is widely used. (Often, it is part of a larger model with many products or locations, as discussed in Sections 5.7 and 5.8 of Chapter 5.) In virtually every application, the real situation differs considerably from the world envisioned by the model: The demands are more-or-less imperfect forecasts, and the costs are rough estimates. Typically, the model is solved repeatedly over time with frequently updated data. (That is, the horizon length T is fixed, but the time interval $[0, T]$ shifts ahead as time passes, so that "now" always means time point 0.) This is called a *rolling-horizon scenario.*

Such discrepancies between a model and reality are hardly unique here. *Every* applied model functions within a far more complex world. This fact is cause for neither despair nor complacency. A good model is valuable partly *because* it focuses on simple essentials, ignoring real-world complexities. On the other hand, a good modeler has to know both the world and the model, and to navigate the gaps between them.

In the context of the DEL model, these general concerns include a variety of specific modeling and implementation issues. Let us briefly discuss a couple of them:

One issue is the choice of solution method. As mentioned above, the optimal solution is usually a few percent better than the Silver-Meal heuristic's, and occasionally much better. The question is, how meaningful is the difference in the real world? The heuristic is myopic, ignoring the distant future where the parameter forecasts are least certain. Does it therefore extract most of the useful information in the data? The optimal solution cleverly exploits every opportunity embodied in the model parameters to minimize cost. But, when the parameters are only estimates, are these opportunities real or just fleeting mirages?

It would be nice to have a clear-cut answer, but unfortunately there is none, not yet at least. This issue is a contentious one, and there is evidence to support both sides. Some of the empirical studies cited above simulate rolling-horizon scenarios, and in some of those the heuristics seem to work as well as optimization, or even better. On the other hand, it is easy to construct a plausible scenario where optimization clearly wins.

The "right" answer, of course, depends a great deal on just *how* precise the parameter estimates are. People disagree about this too. In my experience, real-world settings differ widely in this respect; in some cases the estimates are sharp, while in others they are crude. So, I sit squarely on the fence; I believe that optimization and heuristics both have their places.

If the estimates are *too* noisy, the DEL model itself ceases to be useful, and no computational technique can save it. The primary issue becomes modeling, not method. One option is to expand the model to include imperfect forecasts explicitly. Such stochastic models are discussed in Chapter 9. Some are much more complex than the DEL model, but others are only little more. The philosophy there is to seek a *robust* policy, one that works well for a range of possible future outcomes, instead of the best schedule for one particular forecast.

Another option is to adjust the DEL model by adding *safety stock* (sometimes called *buffer stock*). This means changing the lower bound on $x(t)$ in the constraints from 0 to some positive value, say $x_{-}(t)$, for some or all t. This variant of the DEL model, it turns out, is no harder to solve than the original. (In fact, the new model is equivalent to an instance of the DEL model itself, as Problem 4.8 asks you to show.) It is no easy matter, however, to determine "good" values for the $x_{-}(t)$. Most practical methods borrow guidelines from the analysis of stochastic models, like those of Chapter 9. Thus, the safety-stock approach tries to mimic a stochastic analysis within a deterministic model.

Another, related issue is *nervousness.* This refers to the fact, mentioned above, that the optimal solution of the DEL model can shift abruptly in response to small parameter changes. In a rolling-horizon scenario, one solution can schedule a large order at some future time, and then a subsequent solution, based on updated parameters, can move that entire order to a different time, or combine it with another, or split it into two.

Well, so what? If the data change, the schedule *should* change, shouldn't it? The difficulty lies in how the model is used: The DEL model is often used to guide not just the orders inside the model, but also other decisions outside it, such as workforce levels and maintenance schedules. All these decisions, the orders themselves (as discussed in Section 4.4.1) but especially the others, often require substantial leadtimes. In this context, nervousness can be highly disruptive.

This is another contentious issue. There is no consensus on how to think about nervousness, let alone what to do about it. Some people favor relieving its symptoms with *ad hoc* tactics, while others insist on the radical cure of expanding the model.

One *ad hoc* approach focuses on solution technique: The Silver-Meal heuristic tends to be less nervous than the exact algorithms, simply because of the way it processes the data. The danger, as above, is that the heuristic may miss *real* cost-saving opportunities. An occasional disruption may be tolerable if the savings are sufficient.

Another approach directly suppresses nervousness by partially *freezing* the solution. That is, it selects a *scheduling horizon,* some fairly small $T_{-} < T$. Whenever an instance of the model is solved, the orders $z^*(t)$ for $t < T_{-}$ become final; these $z^*(t)$ become fixed constants in subsequent runs. (Alternatively, fix the order times for $t < T_{-}$, but allow the quantities to shift with revisions in demand forecasts.) This approach too has dangers: If T_{-} is too large, the solution ceases to be responsive to important changes in the environment, and it is hard to know in advance what is too large in a particular instance.

Yet another tactic adds terms to the objective to penalize deviations from a previous solution. If this is done in a certain way, the resulting model reduces to an instance of the DEL model (Problem 4.18). It is not easy, however, to select appropriate penalties. If they are too low, the effect is negligible, but if they are too high, they dominate the rest of the objective and enforce the previous solution. (By the way, adding safety stocks does nothing to reduce nervousness.)

Nervousness can be anticipated and reduced somewhat by using planning-horizon techniques (mentioned in Section 4.3.4). See Federgruen and Tzur [1994], for example.

These tactics all build on the established technology of the DEL model. They are therefore relatively easy to implement; they use the same data structures and computational methods. Those who favor the radical cure argue that nervousness itself is a symptom of a model under stress. The real ailment is parameter uncertainty; to treat it directly, expand the model. Don't try to trick the DEL model into doing something it doesn't want to do.

One final note: Nervousness tends to be most severe when the fixed costs $k(t)$ are large. (It is much more benign in the linear-cost case.) So, reducing the $k(t)$ relieves nervousness, in addition to its direct cost-saving benefits.

4.4 Extensions

Many extensions of the basic DEL model have been developed. Some are straightforward, while others require extensive analysis. We cover only a few of them here and those only briefly. We discuss them separately, but it should be clear that they can be combined. Extensions to multiple products and locations are considered in Chapter 5.

4.4.1 Leadtimes

The DEL model has no explicit order leadtime, but it is easy to include one. Let L denote the leadtime, a fixed, positive integer. An order placed at time t arrives at the end of period $t + L - 1$, in time to be counted in the inventory at time $t + L$. (By this convention, the original DEL model has leadtime 1, not 0.)

Just change the meanings of the variables and cost factors: Now, $z(t)$ means the quantity ordered at time $t - L + 1$, and $k(t)$ and $c(t)$ describe the costs incurred by this order. This $z(t)$ still arrives just before time $t + 1$, so the dynamics (4.3.2) are still valid. The initial conditions require a slight adjustment. The $z(t)$ for $t < L - 1$ and the $x(t)$ for $t < L$ have been determined already before time $t = 0$; they become fixed constants. Thus, as in the EOQ model, we can account for the leadtime by keeping careful track of the calendar.

There is another, equivalent way to revise the formulation, focusing on physical stock instead of time: Return $z(t)$ to its original meaning, the order placed at time t, but redefine $x(t)$ as the *inventory position* at step (1) of time t, and x_0 as the initial inventory position. Also, use the symbol $\hat{x}(t)$ for the actual inventory at time t. Clearly, these variables are related by the identity

$$\hat{x}(t + L) = x(t) - D[t, t + L).$$

This is the discrete-time analogue of (3.2.1). With these definitions the initial conditions (4.3.1) and the dynamics (4.3.2) remain valid as stated, but $\hat{x}(t)$ replaces $x(t)$ in the constraints (4.3.3) and the objective (4.3.4).

Now, use the equations above to eliminate the $\hat{x}(t)$. The end result is another instance of the DEL model. [The lower bound on $x(t)$ in (4.3.3) is now $D[t, t + L) > 0$ instead of zero, but that difference is inessential, as Problem 4.8 demonstrates. This lower bound serves as a reorder point. Also, the objective has an additional constant term.]

The time-based approach above is simpler, but this stock-based approach is worth knowing too. We shall use similar transformations in the stochastic-demand models of Chapter 9.

4.4.2 Discounted Costs

The objective of the DEL model is the *total* cost from now until the horizon. This is equivalent, of course, to the *average* cost over that time. It is easy to adjust the DEL model to represent the discrete-time analogue of the discounted-cost criterion of Section 3.7.

How do the present-value calculations work in a discrete-time context? For the moment, suppose that time is really continuous, and the length of each of our periods is exactly 1, so the time index t correctly measures time on the continuous scale. Letting α denote the interest rate, the present value of a unit cash flow at time t is $e^{-\alpha t}$, as before. Equivalently, defining $\gamma = e^{-\alpha}$, the present value is γ^t. If the period length is different from 1, say w, redefine $\gamma = e^{-\alpha w}$, so that the present value of a unit cash flow at *time point* t is again γ^t. The fraction γ is called the *discount factor*.

Now, suppose that time is really discrete. The story in Section 3.7 can be retold entirely in discrete-time terms. Here, α is the one-period interest rate (regardless of the period length), and $\gamma = 1/(1 + \alpha)$. The conclusion is the same: The present value of a unit cash flow at time point t is γ^t.

Turning to the DEL model, suppose $c(t)$, $k(t)$, and $h(t)$ are the actual cost factors. To reformulate the objective (4.3.4), just perform the replacements $c(t) \leftarrow \gamma^t c(t)$, $k(t) \leftarrow \gamma^t k(t)$, and $h(t) \leftarrow \gamma^t h(t)$. Then, (4.3.4) measures the total discounted cost, as desired. In sum, the discounted-cost DEL model reduces to an instance of the original DEL model with altered cost factors.

As in Chapter 3, the $h(t)$ here should include only physical handling costs, not financing charges. Indeed, the discounted-cost model is conceptually simpler when the (original, undiscounted) $c(t)$ change over time: In this case it is not at all clear how to specify an appropriate financing cost in the total- or average-cost model; we *choose* the order costs, hence the financing charges, through our decisions. There are ways to resolve this dilemma, but they rely on intricate assumptions and arguments. The discounted-cost objective bypasses the difficulty altogether.

4.4.3 Continuously Accumulating Costs

Returning to the total-cost criterion, suppose we use the DEL model to approximate a continuous-time problem. In the real problem, demand occurs and holding costs accumulate continuously over time. For simplicity, scale time so that the time periods are each of length 1.

Given the data of the DEL model, we typically do not know the actual demand and holding-cost rates at each instant, nor the precise moment an order is received. Provided the time periods are short, it is reasonable to assume that these rates are the constants $d(t)$ and $h(t+1)$ over the entire period from t to $t+1$, and the order $z(t)$ is received at the beginning of the period. Then, for s between t and $t+1$,

$$x(s) = x(t) + z(t) - (s-t)d(t),$$

and the total holding cost over the period is

$$\begin{aligned} h(t+1)\textstyle\int_t^{t+1} x(s)\,ds &= h(t+1)[x(t) + z(t) - \textstyle\int_t^{t+1}(s-t)d(t)\,ds] \\ &= h(t+1)[x(t) + z(t) - \tfrac{1}{2}d(t)] \\ &= h(t+1)[x(t+1) + \tfrac{1}{2}d(t)] \end{aligned}$$

Thus, the objective function (4.3.4) correctly accounts for the controllable holding costs in all periods. The actual total cost includes the additional constant $\tfrac{1}{2}\Sigma_t\, h(t+1)\, d(t)$.

If we do know the true demand rate $\lambda(t)$ and retain the other assumptions above, the end result is the same; only the constant term changes. Alternative assumptions lead to similar results. In sum, the DEL model requires only slight adjustments to account for continuously accumulating costs.

4.4.4 Backorders

Now, suppose that backorders are allowed, as in Section 3.3 of Chapter 3. Redefine the state variable $x(t)$ to mean the *net inventory* (inventory minus backorders). The initial conditions (4.3.1) and the dynamics (4.3.2) remain valid as stated. Omit the constraints $x(t) \geq 0$ in (4.3.3), but retain $z(t) \geq 0$. In the objective (4.3.4), replace the term $h(t)x(t)$ by $\hat{C}(t, x(t))$, where $\hat{C}(t, x) = h(t)[x]^+ + b(t)[x]^-$ and $b(t)$ is the backorder-cost rate.

Incidentally, a standard formulation trick recovers a linear objective (apart from the $\delta(z)$ terms): Define two new variables for each t, the inventory $x^+(t)$ and the backorders $x^-(t)$. Replace $x(t)$ in the dynamics by the difference $x^+(t) - x^-(t)$ and $\hat{C}(t, x(t))$ in the objective by $h(t)x^+(t) + b(t)x^-(t)$, and add the constraints $x^+(t) \geq 0$ and $x^-(t) \geq 0$. (For this to work $x^+(t)$ and $x^-(t)$ cannot both be positive. The constraints do not enforce this condition, but the objective ensures that it holds anyway.)

In the original DEL model, the zero-inventory property implies that each order covers the entire demand over several consecutive time points. It turns out (see Problem 4.10) that this is true also in the model with backorders. In the original model, however, the interval covered by an order always begins with the order time itself, whereas here it may begin earlier. That is, each order (except perhaps the first) covers the demand at its own time, plus some earlier and later times.

Thus, the overall behavior of the net inventory is much the same as in the continuous-time, constant-demand model of Section 3.3. It decreases at most times, increasing only at order times. Typically, an order raises $x(t)$ from a negative to a positive value. So, a solution divides time into cycles, each consisting of a part with inventory followed by a part with backorders. (Because time is discrete, however, the inventory or backorder part can disappear.)

Using this property, one can construct a network whose paths correspond to potential solutions of the problem, as in Section 4.3.4. There is one node for $t = T$, labeled $T-$, but *two* nodes for each $t < T$, indicated by $t-$ and $t+$. The arcs connect pluses to minuses and minuses to pluses. Specifically, there is an arc $(t-, u+)$ for all $t \leq u$ and an arc $(t+, u-)$ for all $t < u$. See Fig. 4.4.1. A path from $0-$ to $T-$ corresponds to a solution as follows: The nodes $t+$ encountered along the path describe the order times, while the nodes $t-$ specify the amounts ordered: If the path contains the arcs $(s-, t+)$ and $(t+, u-)$ for $s \leq t < u$, the order at time t covers the demands at time points s through $u - 1$.

It is possible to assign a cost to each arc, as in (4.3.8), so that the total cost of a solution equals the sum of the arc costs on the corresponding path. (Problem 4.11 asks you to supply the details.) Thus, as in the DEL model, to compute the optimal solution, just determine the minimum-cost path in the network.

FIGURE 4.4.1

Network for DEL model with backorders.

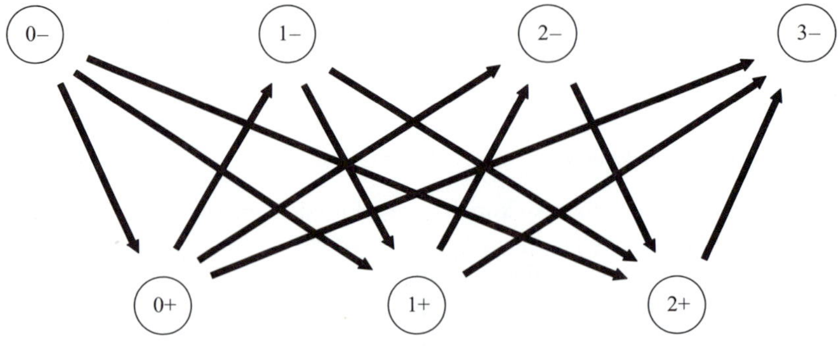

Many other extensions of the DEL model can be analyzed by the same logic: First, derive some qualitative characteristic of an optimal solution, analogous to the zero-inventory property. Second, use this property to construct a network whose paths correspond to possible solutions. Third and finally, calculate the minimum-cost path in the network.

4.4.5 Limited Capacity

Return to the DEL model, but suppose there is an upper limit $z_+(t)$ on the order quantity at time point t. Thus, the $z(t)$ must respect the upper bounds

$$z(t) \leq z_+(t) \qquad t = 0, \ldots, T-1 \tag{4.4.1}$$

in addition to the original constraints (4.3.3). When the $z(t)$ represent production quantities, we can interpret the $z_+(t)$ as production capacities. (This interpretation is somewhat problematic, however, as explained below.) For simplicity, assume that $x_0 = 0$, and to ensure feasibility, assume that $\Sigma_{s=0}^{t} z_+(s) \geq \Sigma_{s=0}^{t} d(s)$ for all t.

Incidentally, we can reformulate the model as a mixed-integer program using the binary variables $v(t)$, replacing the inequalities in (4.3.5) and (4.4.1) by the single constraint

$$z(t) \leq \min \{D[t, T), z_+(t)\} v(t) \qquad t = 0, \ldots, T-1$$

The qualitative effect of limited capacities is the same as in the continuous-time model of Section 4.2.5: The capacity constraints (4.4.1) force us to anticipate large demands, i.e., to order (or produce) earlier than we might otherwise. So, capacity constraints lead to larger inventories. Part of this effect can be quantified as follows: Recursively define

$$\begin{aligned} x_>(T) &= 0 \\ x_>(t) &= [d(t) - z_+(t) + x_>(t+1)]^+ \qquad 0 \leq t < T \end{aligned} \tag{4.4.2}$$

This quantity is the excess demand from time t onward. It is not hard to show that *every* feasible solution must have $x(t) \geq x_>(t)$. A group of successive periods with positive $x_>(t)$ is the discrete-time analogue of an interval $[t_-, t_+]$, in the notation of Section 4.2.5.

Interestingly, it is possible to use these quantities to derive an equivalent model in which demand never exceeds capacity. The demands in this new model are $d(t) = d(t) + x_>(t+1) - x_>(t)$, and the initial inventory is $x_0 = x_0 - x_>(0)$; the cost factors are just the original ones. (See Problem 4.13.) Even in this revised formulation, however, we *cannot* ignore the capacity constraints.

The analogue of the zero-inventory property here is fairly subtle: Every feasible solution divides the periods into what we call *inventory cycles.* An inventory cycle consists of successive periods s, with $t \leq s < u$ say, starting with $x(t) = 0$ but with positive inventory at all other times s. (Since u begins the next cycle, we also have $x(u) = 0$.) There is some optimal solution whose inventory cycles each have the following property: *For every time* s *except at most one,* we produce nothing or at full capacity, i.e., $z(s)$ equals 0 or $z_+(s)$.

Unfortunately, this property, while interesting, does not always lead to a tractable algorithm. The general version of the problem is *very* hard. (In technical terms it is NP-hard; the time required by every known algorithm grows exponentially in the problem size.)

In certain special but important cases, however, it is possible to solve the problem with relative ease. In the linear-cost case, the problem is a linear program. (This linear program has a useful special structure—it can be recast as a minimum-cost network-flow problem, and this in turn can be expressed as a transportation problem. See Problem 4.14. There are very fast specialized algorithms to solve such problems; see Chvátal [1983], for example.)

Also, consider the case with positive fixed costs but equal capacities $z_+(t) = z_+$. Here, the inventory-cycle property can be exploited to devise a reasonably tractable algorithm. Here is the basic idea: Focus on any potential inventory cycle, specified by the pair (t, u). The inventory-cycle property implies that the cumulative production at each time s can take on only a small number of values. Using this fact, one can compute the optimal solution *within* the cycle, *assuming* $x(t) = x(u) = 0$. (See Problem 4.15.) Call the cost of this solution $k[t, u)$. Now, use these costs within Algorithm Forward_DEL. This procedure determines the optimal set of inventory cycles, hence the optimal overall solution. The calculation of the $k[t, u)$ is more involved than in the DEL model, and the overall algorithm runs in $O(T^4)$ time.

The capacitated DEL model is an important one, but it is not a perfect model of a production process: If there are orders in several consecutive periods, every one incurs a fixed cost. A typical production system, however, incurs a setup cost only at the beginning of a production run. If the time periods are short, and we expect a production run to cover many of them, then the capacitated DEL model presents a distorted picture of production-setup costs.

Here is an alternative formulation: Say that t begins a *production run* if $z(t) > 0$ *and* either $t = 0$ or $z(t-1) < z_+(t-1)$. The setup cost $k(t)$ is incurred at such time points and only those. If $z(t) > 0$ but $z(t-1) = z_+(t-1)$, an earlier production run continues through t, so $z(t)$ incurs no setup cost.

In certain cases, this model is easier to solve than the capacitated DEL model. Suppose there are no speculation opportunities ($\tilde{s}(t) = t$), and $d(t) \leq z_+(t)$ (following the transformation above, if necessary). One can show that every production run begins with zero inventory, except perhaps the first. Let $k[t, u)$ be the cost of beginning a production run at t and producing a total of $D[t, u)$ to meet demand through time $u - 1$. (This is easy to compute.) Using these costs within Algorithm Forward_DEL solves the problem.

An even simpler model is the *all-or-nothing* formulation: Each $z(t)$ can take only two possible values, 0 or $z_+(t)$. (Thus, $z(t) = z_+(t)v(t)$, so the variables $z(t)$ can be eliminated.) This is the discrete-time analogue of the finite-capacity EOQ model of Section 3.4 and Section 4.2.5. Here, every solution corresponds to a path in a network similar to Figure 4.4.1. (Node $t+$ indicates a possible beginning of a production run, and node $t-$ an end.) Thus, a shortest-path calculation determines the optimal solution.

4.4.6 Quantity Discounts

Now, suppose the supplier offers an incremental quantity discount, as in Section 3.5.2 of Chapter 3. Let $c(t, z)$ denote the variable cost of placing an order for z units at time t. In the original DEL model $c(t, z)$ is linear in z for each t, but now it is piecewise linear. (It has the same form as the function $c(q)$ in Section 3.5.) So, replace each term $c(t)z(t)$ in the objective (4.3.4) by $c(t, z(t))$.

Each $c(t, z)$ is a concave function of z, because the purchase price is smaller for larger orders. The objective function (4.3.4) thus remains concave. As noted after the proof of Theorem 4.3.1, therefore, the zero-inventory property remains valid.

Consequently, Algorithm Forward_DEL again solves the model. The $k[t, u)$ are calculated differently, to account properly for the order-cost discounts, but that is the only modification required. (Under an all-units discount, however, $c(t, z)$ is not concave, nor even continuous, so this approach does not work.)

4.5 Smoothing Models

4.5.1 Formulation and Discussion

The next model is similar in some ways to the DEL model with backorders, but in others it is radically different. The demands $d(t)$ have the same meaning as before, as do the variables $z(t)$ and $x(t)$. ($x(t)$ denotes net inventory, not just inventory.) Again, these are related by the initial condition

$$x(0) = x_0 \qquad (4.5.1)$$

and the dynamics

$$x(t + 1) = x(t) + z(t) - d(t) \qquad t = 0, \ldots, T - 1. \qquad (4.5.2)$$

However, there are *no* other constraints on the variables; $z(t)$ as well as $x(t)$ can be negative. The objective function is quite different:

$$\text{Minimize} \quad \tfrac{1}{2}\textstyle\sum_{t=0}^{T-1} c(t)z^2(t) + \tfrac{1}{2}\sum_{t=1}^{T} h(t)x^2(t) \qquad (4.5.3)$$

Here, the $c(t)$ and $h(t)$ are all positive. Call this the *basic smoothing model.*

What an odd model! Let us try to understand the story it represents: First, a negative "order" $z(t)$ represents disposal of excess stock. For both actual positive orders and disposal, there are *diseconomies* of scale, expressed by the quadratic term $c(t)z^2(t)$. That is, the unit ordering cost increases in the amount ordered (and similarly for the disposal cost). Moreover, these costs are *symmetric;* the cost of $-z(t)$ is the same as $z(t)$. Likewise, there are diseconomies of scale for inventory and backorders, and these costs too are symmetric; the coefficient $h(t)$ measures backorder costs as well as holding costs.

Frankly, this model is not very realistic. It is indeed possible to dispose of stock in some situations, and diseconomies of scale do arise in practice. The problem lies in the symmetry assumptions: It is just not credible that the disposal cost precisely equal the purchase cost, nor that backorders and inventory have identical cost effects.

Why should we study an unrealistic model? The answer, in a word, is simplicity: The solution is easy to compute, and it has an appealingly simple form. The model can be extended in many directions while retaining comparable simplicity. Also, although the model is unrealistic, the solution accounts for demand variations in a plausible way. The details reflect this particular formulation, but the general idea suggests practically useful heuristics. Finally, this model helps us to understand others. More realistic models are *asymmetric* in crucial places; those asymmetries help to explain precisely how and why such models are more complex.

4.5.2 Solution: The Linear Decision Rule

Consider the form of the basic smoothing model: The objective function is quadratic, and the constraints are all linear equations. The first-order optimality conditions thus comprise a system of linear equations. This system, moreover, is highly structured, and its solution can be expressed in a concise recursive form:

THEOREM 4.5.1. For each $t = 0, \ldots, T - 1$, suppose we are given $x(t)$. Then, the optimal order policy is given by

$$q(t) = \Sigma_{u=t}^{T-1} \beta(t, u)\, d(u) - \beta(t, t)x(t). \tag{4.5.4}$$

The coefficients $\beta(t, u)$ can be computed recursively: Treating $c(T) = \beta(T, T) = 0$, set

$$\Delta(t) = c(t) + h(t+1) + c(t+1)\beta(t+1, t+1)$$

$$\beta(t, t) = 1 - \frac{c(t)}{\Delta(t)}$$

$$\beta(t, u) = \left[\frac{c(t+1)}{\Delta(t)}\right]\beta(t+1, u) \qquad t < u < T$$

Moreover, $0 < \beta(t, u) < 1$, and $\beta(t, u)$ is decreasing in u for each t. ■

The actual optimal solution can be recovered recursively from (4.5.4): First, substitute x_0 for $x(0)$, and set $z^*(0) = q(0)$. This determines $x^*(1)$ through (4.5.2). Next, using $x(1) = x^*(1)$ in (4.5.4), set $z^*(1) = q(1)$. Continue in this manner.

The coefficients $\beta(t, u)$ depend on the cost factors, but *not* on the demands. Thus, $q(t)$ is a linear function of $x(t)$ and the $d(u)$, $u \geq t$. In this sense the policy prescribes a *linear decision rule.*

The form of this linear function, moreover, is intuitively appealing: Given the current net inventory $x(t)$, $q(t)$ depends only on future demands, not past ones. This relationship is positive; an increase in any of the $d(u)$ can only increase $q(t)$. On the other hand, the relationship is stable; an increase in $d(u)$ causes a *smaller* increase in $q(t)$. Also, $q(t)$ depends most strongly on the imminent demand $d(t)$; subsequent demands $d(u)$ are decreasingly important. (This result is broadly consistent with the myopic approach above.)

Thus, we can view each $z^*(t)$ as a smoothed version of the forecasted demands $d(u)$, $u \geq t$. One unusually large demand increases *all* the prior orders, not just one or a few nearby ones. Thus, there is typically less variation in the $z^*(t)$ than in the $d(t)$ themselves. (This observation inspires the name *smoothing model.* Clearly, the DEL model is qualitatively different in this respect. There, economies of scale induce sharply unequal orders, since $z^*(t) = 0$ except at order times.)

The infinite-horizon version of this model leads to similar results (provided certain technical conditions are met), and for some special cases the solution is even simpler: Suppose $c(t) = \gamma^t c$ and $h(t) = \gamma^t h$, where c and h are positive constants and $0 < \gamma < 1$. Let β denote the (unique) root in the interval (0, 1) of the quadratic equation

$$\gamma x^2 + [1 - \gamma + \gamma\left(\frac{h}{c}\right)]x - \gamma\left(\frac{h}{c}\right) = 0$$

Then, each $\beta(t, u) = \beta[\gamma(1 - \beta)]^{u-t}$, and

$$q(t) = \beta\Sigma_{n=0}^{\infty} [\gamma(1 - \beta)]^n d(t + n) - \beta x(t)$$

Again, $q(t)$ is a weighted sum of future demands and $x(t)$. But here the weights are constant over t, and they decay geometrically in $n = u - t$. This result holds approximately when T is finite but large, and the costs are nearly discounted-stationary.

PROOF OF THEOREM 4.5.1. Let $\zeta(t)$ denote the dual variable for the tth equation of (4.5.2). The first-order optimality conditions are

$$c(t)z(t) = \zeta(t) \tag{4.5.5}$$

$$h(t + 1)x(t + 1) = \zeta(t + 1) - \zeta(t) \qquad 0 \leq t < T \tag{4.5.6}$$

where $\zeta(T) = 0$.

The proof is by induction: The result is easy to check for $t = T - 1$, so suppose it holds for some $t + 1$, where $t < T - 1$. Substitute (4.5.5) and (4.5.4) into (4.5.6), setting $z(t) = q(t)$, to obtain

$$\begin{aligned} h(t + 1)x(t + 1) &= c(t + 1)z(t + 1) - c(t)z(t) \\ &= c(t + 1)\{\Sigma_{u=t+1}^{T-1} \beta(t + 1, u)\, d(u) - \beta(t + 1, t + 1)x(t + 1)\} - c(t)z(t) \end{aligned}$$

or

$$[\Delta(t) - c(t)]x(t + 1) + c(t)z(t) = c(t + 1)\Sigma_{u=t+1}^{T-1} \beta(t + 1, u)\, d(u)$$

This and (4.5.2) comprise a pair of simultaneous equations in the unknowns $x(t + 1)$ and $z(t)$, regarding everything else as fixed. Eliminate $x(t + 1)$ to obtain

$$\Delta(t)z(t) = c(t + 1)\Sigma_{u=t+1}^{T-1} \beta(t + 1, u)\, d(u) + [\Delta(t) - c(t)][d(t) - x(t)]$$

Solving this for $z(t)$ and resetting $q(t) = z(t)$ yields (4.5.4); the $\beta(t, u)$ are computed as in the assertion.

Since $c(t) < \Delta(t)$, it is clear that $0 < \beta(t, t) < 1$. Moreover,

$$\beta(t, t) > \frac{c(t + 1)\beta(t + 1, t + 1)}{\Delta(t)} = \beta(t, t + 1)$$

Finally, since $\beta(t + 1, u)$ is decreasing in u for $u \geq t + 1$, by assumption, so is $\beta(t, u)$. ■

4.5.3 Extensions

Suppose at each time t there is some ideal order quantity $z_*(t)$, and we incur a cost for deviating from it. That is, the term $c(t)z^2(t)$ in (4.5.2) becomes $c(t)[z(t) - z_*(t)]^2$. This model is equivalent to an instance of the original one. Just redefine $z(t) \leftarrow z(t) - z_*(t)$ and $d(t) \leftarrow d(t) - z^*(t)$. Similarly, the model can incorporate a nonzero ideal net inventory $x_*(t)$.

Also, we can add linear terms to the objective function. The results are nearly as simple as before. [Formula (4.5.4) now includes an additional constant term.]

These extensions allow us to employ the model as an approximation of a more realistic one: Suppose the "real" model is just like the basic smoothing model, but with a more complex objective function of the form

$$\text{Minimize} \qquad \Sigma_{t=0}^{T-1} c(t, z(t)) + \Sigma_{t=1}^{T} h(t, x(t))$$

Each of the component functions $c(t, \cdot)$ and $h(t, \cdot)$ is convex (reflecting diseconomies of scale) and smooth, but not necessarily symmetric. Suppose we solve this model; let $z_*(t)$, $x_*(t)$ denote the optimal solution.

Now, suppose we wish to investigate how the model responds to demand changes. Construct a second-order approximation, that is, replace each $c(t, \cdot)$ and $h(t, \cdot)$ by a quadratic function centered at the original optimal solution. This approximation is precisely an instance of the smoothing model (with the extensions above). Its solution accurately predicts the effects of small deviations from the original demands. (This is a classic approach to parametric analysis. What is special here is the structure of the linearized optimality conditions.)

Here is another interesting extension: Suppose that, in addition to the original costs, there is also a cost to *change* the order quantity from one time to the next. Assume that these costs too are quadratic; add the term $e(t)[z(t-1) - z(t)]^2$ to the objective function, where $e(t)$ is a positive constant, for $0 < t < T - 1$. Some production activities (especially high-volume continuous processes) entail costs of this sort. This is called the *production smoothing model,* because the objective itself favors even production levels.

In control-systems terms there are now two state variables, $z(t-1)$ as well as $x(t)$. To avoid confusing states and controls, define a new state variable $x_=(t)$ to represent the previous order, and include the equation $x_=(t+1) = z(t)$ in the dynamics. The smoothing-cost term becomes $e(t)[x_=(t) - z(t)]^2$.

The objective of this production-smoothing model is quadratic, so the optimality conditions form a system of linear equations. The optimal policy is similar to the basic smoothing model's, as described in Theorem 4.5.1: Given $x(t)$ and $x_=(t)$, $q(t)$ is a linear function of these state variables and the demands $d(u)$ for $u \geq t$. (The β coefficients are different from those above, of course. Problem 4.17 asks you to work out the details.)

The basic smoothing model and the production smoothing model are instances of an important family of discrete-time control models, called *linear-quadratic control* (LQC) models: The state of the system, the control, and the input are each described by a vector. The dynamics comprise linear equations, and there are no additional constraints. Finally, the objective is a quadratic function of the state and control variables. See Appendix B.

Provided certain technical conditions are met, the solution of such a model can be characterized in terms fully analogous to Theorem 4.5.1. That is, given the current state, the current action is a linear function of the state and of current and future inputs. The coefficients of this linear function can again be computed recursively.

Smoothing models have the remarkable virtue that certain types of stochastic demands can be incorporated readily. Indeed, sometimes the solution is identical to that of the original deterministic model! This insensitivity property is less wonderful than it may seem, however; it is essentially an artifact of the symmetry assumptions. The solutions of more realistic models *do* depend on demand uncertainties, and for good reasons, as shown in Chapter 9. Even so, stochastic models of this general style, albeit with different details, are often used to gain insight into complex systems. (Section 9.4.8.3, for example, employs what is essentially a symmetry approximation.)

Finally, multiproduct smoothing models can be formulated and analyzed in the same spirit. The state and the control become fairly large vectors. But while the scale of the model grows, its complexity does not; essentially the same methods can be used to solve it. In fact, in some cases, one can aggregate the products in a simple way, thus collapsing the large model to the single-product model above. As we shall see later, more realistic models *cannot* be reduced so easily. In some cases, however, a partial, approximate reduction can be achieved; see Section 8.6, for instance.

Notes

Section 4.2: The essential idea here is presented in Daganzo [1991]. A few very special cases can be solved exactly; see Resh et al. [1976] and Barbosa and Friedman [1978]. § 4.2.5 on the finite-production-rate model borrows ideas from Shulman and Smith [1992].

Section 4.3: The DEL model was introduced by Wagner and Whitin [1958]; they also developed the original shortest-path algorithm. Since then a huge literature has accumulated. Recent overviews are provided by Salomon [1990] and Baker [1992]. Evans [1985] discusses the details of implementation. Denardo [1982] provides a broad exposition of the dynamic-programming approach to modeling and computation. Three groups of researchers, namely Aggarwal and Park [1993], Federgruen and Tzur [1991], and Wagelmans et al. [1992], independently and around the same time, developed asymptotically faster algorithms. Additional results on planning horizons can be found in Eppen et al. [1969] and Lundin and Morton [1975]. For more on nervousness and its prevention, see Kropp and Carlson [1984] and Federgruen and Tzur [1994].

Section 4.4: Zangwill [1966,1968,1969] extended the DEL model to permit backorders. Federgruen and Tzur [1993] provide a refined algorithm for this model also.

The DEL model with capacity constraints was posed by Florian and Klein [1971]. Florian et al. [1980] and Bitran and Yanasse [1982] demonstrate that the general, unequal-capacity problem is NP-hard (indeed several special subclasses are themselves NP-hard). Solution procedures can be found in Baker et al. [1978]. Alternative formulations are discussed by Karmarkar et al. [1987] and Fleischmann [1990].

Other extensions not covered here include Sogomonian and Tang [1993], who consider a system where demands are not exogenous, but rather are influenced by promotions.

Section 4.5: Smoothing models were introduced by Holt et al. [1960]. These were among the earliest discrete-time control models, and they inspired much subsequent work in diverse fields. They have deeply affected our views of the role of inventory at the macroeconomic level; see Blinder and Maccini's [1991] review article and the historical studies of Blanchard [1983] and Kashyap and Wilcox [1993].

Schneeweiss [1974] discusses the use of such models as approximations when the true costs are not quadratic. Stochastic models with something of the overall spirit of smoothing models are analyzed by Akella et al. [1992], Denardo and Tang [1992], and Graves [1999], for example. For multiproduct smoothing models see Gaalman [1978] and Zipkin [1982].

Problems

4.1 Suppose the finite production rate μ in Section 4.2.5 is itself a function of time, say $\mu(t)$. Both $\lambda(t)$ and $\mu(t)$ change slowly. (For instance, we may be able to adjust production capacity to anticipate the known changes in $\lambda(t)$. For now, consider $\mu(t)$ as a given, positive, continuous function.) Describe a reasonable policy, and explain why you expect it to work well.

4.2 Consider the finite-production-rate model of Section 4.2.5 (with constant rate μ). First, assume $\lambda(t) \leq \mu$ for all t. Modify the definitions of $C^*(t)$ and C^* in (4.2.2) appropriately to approximate the optimal average cost. Next, assume $\lambda(t) > \mu$ for some t, but there is only one interval $[t_-,t_+]$ requiring an extended production cycle. Estimate the average cost over a *finite* interval $[0, T]$, where $T > t_+$. Write a simple formula for the inventory $x(t)$, $t_- \leq t \leq t_+$, assuming $x(t_-) = x(t_+) = 0$, and use it to approximate the average cost.

4.3 Consider the linear-cost case of the DEL model in Section 4.3.2. Argue that the recursion (4.3.7) correctly computes the minimal costs $\tilde{c}[*, t)$ and the order times $\tilde{s}(t)$.

4.4 The proof of Theorem 4.3.1 in the text begins with the simplifying assumptions that $x_0 = 0$, all $d(t) > 0$, and all $k(t) > 0$. Prove the result in the general case, i.e., assuming only that these quantities are nonnegative.

4.5 In the DEL model suppose there are no speculation opportunities, so for every fixed t, the quantities $\tilde{c}[s, t)$ are nonincreasing in s. Let $s^{\star}(t)$ denote the last order time in the t-horizon problem, as in Algorithm Forward_DEL.

(*a*) Using the definition of $k[s, t)$ in (4.3.8), show that $s^{\star}(t)$ is nondecreasing in t. (Thus, to determine $s^{\star}(t)$ in iteration t, we need only search over $s \geq s^{\star}(t-1)$.)

(*b*) Suppose that, for some t_H, $s^{\star}(t_H) = t_H - 1$. Using part (*a*), prove (by induction) that $t_H - 1$ is an order time in the t-horizon problem for all $t \geq t_H$. Then, explain that this implies that t_H is a planning horizon.

4.6 This problem conducts a partial sensitivity analysis of the DEL model: Let d denote the entire sequence of demands $\{d(t), 0 \leq t < T\}$, regarded as a nonnegative T-vector, and $C^*(d)$ the optimal cost of the DEL model with demand sequence d, assuming the cost parameters are fixed. Argue that $C^*(d)$ is a continuous, nondecreasing, concave function of d. (*Hint:* Let π denote any fixed sequence of order times, and $C(d|\pi)$ the cost of using the order times π to meet the demand sequence d. Express $C^*(d)$ in terms of the $C(d|\pi)$. Now, derive certain relevant properties of the $C(d|\pi)$, and use these to arrive at the desired conclusion.)

What does this tell us about $C^*(2d)$, assuming we know $C^*(d)$? Compare this finding to the effect of doubling λ in the EOQ model.

4.7 As in the previous problem, let k and c denote T-vectors describing the order-cost parameters, and $C^*(k, c)$ the optimal cost, assuming all other parameters are held fixed. Prove that $C^*(k, c)$ is continuous, nondecreasing, and concave. Can we draw a similar conclusion about $C^*(k, c, d)$ or at least $C^*(k, d)$? Why?

4.8 The DEL model includes constraints $x(t) \geq 0$ prohibiting negative inventories. Suppose instead that there are lower bounds $x(t) \geq x_-(t)$, where the $x_-(t)$ are any nonnegative constants. Transform the parameters and the variables of the problem to obtain an instance of the original DEL model which is equivalent to this new one. Restate the zero-inventory property in terms of the new model.

4.9 The DEL model envisions a world in which time stops at $t = T$. This is a fiction, of course. The optimal solution can depend strongly on the choice of T, a phenomenon called the *horizon effect,* and there are several ways to reduce it. One is simply to choose a large T whenever possible. This is certainly wise, but it is generally hard to know when T is large enough. This problem explores another approach.

Suppose the objective (4.3.4) includes an additional term of the form $V(T, x(T))$. Here, V is a *function* of $x(T)$, representing the costs of alternative terminal inventory levels. Think of V as measuring future costs after T. Suppose there is a specified, finite set of possible values of $x(T)$. Show how to solve this problem by determining the shortest path in a certain network. (*Hint:* If $x(T)$ is fixed to one particular value, the result is an instance of the DEL model, as in the previous problem.)

4.10 Consider the DEL model with backorders, as in Section 4.4.4. Prove that each order covers the entire demand for an interval of consecutive periods. (*Hint:* Follow the proof of Theorem 4.3.1. Or, reformulate the model using the variables $x^+(t)$ and $x^-(t)$, so that the objective function is concave, and then show that every extreme point of the feasible set shares the property above.)

4.11 Consider the network describing the DEL model with backorders, as illustrated in Figure 4.4.1. Show how to assign a cost to each arc, so that the cost of a solution equals the sum of the arc costs on the corresponding path.

4.12 In the limited-capacity DEL model, verify that every feasible solution must satisfy $x(t) \geq x_>(t)$, where the anticipated excess demand $x_>(t)$ is defined in (4.4.2).

4.13 Consider the model with revised demands $\underline{d}(t)$, as defined in Section 4.4.5. For any feasible solution to the original capacitated DEL model, construct a solution to this new model, setting $\underline{z}(t) = z(t)$ and $\underline{x}(t) = x(t) - x_>(t)$. Argue that this solution is feasible in the revised model. Also, show that the cost of the revised solution differs from that of the original by a constant. Thus, the revised model is equivalent to the original. Finally, show that $d(t) \leq z_+(t)$.

4.14 Consider the linear-cost case (all $k(t) = 0$) of the capacitated DEL model of Section 4.4.5. Explain that the model is a minimum-cost network-flow problem. [The dynamics (4.3.2) provide the flow-conservation constraints.] Now, revise the model to obtain an equivalent transportation problem. (*Hint:* The cost coefficients become $\tilde{c}[s, t]$.)

4.15 Consider the limited-capacity DEL model with equal capacities $z_+(t) = z_+$. Given a potential inventory cycle specified by the pair of times (t, u), we want to determine the optimal solution within the cycle. The total demand over the cycle can be written in the form $mz_+ + r$, where m is a nonnegative integer and r is the remainder, $0 \leq r < z_+$; the total production during the cycle must equal this quantity.

Argue that, for each time s in the cycle, the cumulative production from the beginning of the cycle until just before s (excluding $z(s)$ itself) must be of the form nz_+ or $nz_+ + r$, where n is an integer between 0 and min $\{m, (s - t + 1)\}$. Now, define a network: Each node indicates a time s and a possible value of cumulative production up to s. (There is only one value at t, namely 0.

Include a node for time u with production $mz_+ + r$.) Explain exactly which nodes are included and which arcs connect them. Also, show how to calculate an appropriate cost for each arc. Now, argue that the shortest path in this network determines the optimal production schedule within the cycle.

4.16 Consider the alternative formulation of the capacitated DEL model, in which a setup cost is paid only at the beginning of a production run. Assuming $\tilde{s}(t) = t$ and $d(t) \leq z_+(t)$ for all t, show that this model enjoys the zero-inventory property. That is, each production run begins with zero inventory. (Follow the proof of Theorem 4.3.1.)

4.17 Consider the production-smoothing model of Section 4.5.3. Following the proof of Theorem 4.5.1, verify that the optimal order-policy variable $q(t)$ is a linear function of the state variables $x(t)$ and $x_=(t)$ and the demands $d(u)$, $u \geq t$.

4.18 Let $z_*(t)$ denote a previous solution to the DEL model. Suppose we modify the DEL model to penalize deviations from this solution, adding the following term to the objective for each t:

$$e^+(t)\delta[\delta(z(t)) - \delta(z_*(t))] + e^-(t)\delta[\delta(z_*(t)) - \delta(z(t))]$$

Thus, if t is an order time in the new solution but not in the old one, we incur the fixed cost $e^+(t)$, and in the opposite case we incur $e^-(t)$. Assume that $e^+(t)$ and $e^-(t)$ are both positive, and $e^-(t) < k(t)$. Derive an instance of the DEL model that is equivalent to this one, and explain why it is equivalent. (*Hint:* Modify the $k(t)$.)

C H A P T E R

5 Several Products and Locations

Outline

5.1 Introduction

This chapter explores systems with several products, or several locations, or both. The goal is to understand, both in detail and in broad terms, what is needed to coordinate diverse and dispersed activities, so that the overall system functions effectively. This theme continues in Chapter 8 in the context of stochastic demands. These two chapters, then, constitute the core of the theory of supply chains.

This chapter mostly follows the scenario of Chapter 3 (continuous time, constant demand rates). Only at the end does it treat time-varying demands.

5.1.1 Items: Product-Location Pairs

We begin with an important observation: Multiproduct systems and multilocation systems are fundamentally identical. The same models and analytical techniques can be applied just as well to one as the other. Indeed, a system with multiple products *and* locations can be approached in the same way. The differences, such as they are, are mainly differences in wording.

This parallel should not be too surprising. Demand for one product cannot be met by supply of another, just as demand in one place cannot be met by supply elsewhere. To meet the demand, it is necessary to *transform* the available goods, either by moving them or by processing them into something else. Production and transportation are both physical transformations; both require time and money. There are differences in detail, certainly, but for our purposes such differences are superficial. So are distinctions among modes of transportation and types of production processes.

So universal is this likeness that we build on it from the beginning. Instead of products or locations, we work with generic entities called *items.* Items can indicate locations, or products, or product-location pairs. A multi-item model can represent either geographically separated points, or physically distinct products, or both.

There are a few apparent exceptions, models designed originally to capture specific production- or transportation-oriented features. Even then, the specificity is more a matter of interpretation than intrinsic structure. Virtually every production-specific feature has some analogue in the context of transportation, and vice versa.

This is a powerful abstraction. Many innovations in distribution management have been adapted from the production sphere, and the other way around. The item approach allows us to conceptualize, model, and manage production *and* transportation activities in a unified manner. It may take a while to get accustomed to this idea, but it is worth the effort.

5.1.2 Structural Complexity: Networks of Items

There are important and interesting things to learn about multiple items, even when each item is entirely independent of the others. Section 5.2 examines such systems.

The rest of the chapter is concerned with items that are intrinsically linked, either through supply-demand relationships or through a shared supply process. Consider supply-demand relationships first. For example, a large retailer may purchase goods centrally, stock them in a central warehouse, and supply its several stores from the warehouse. Or a manufacturer may acquire raw materials, fabricate them into various components, and assemble the components into finished products.

In such situations the items and the relationships between them form a *network,* specifically a directed graph. The nodes represent the items, and the arcs depict the supply-demand relationships. It is important to distinguish several broad network structures:

The simplest structure is a *series system* (Figure 5.1.1). Here, the items represent the outputs of successive production stages or stocking points along a supply chain. Each product is used as input to make the next one; or each location supplies the next one. Only the first item receives supplies from outside the system, and only the last one meets exogenous customer demands. (The figure omits the exogenous supply and demand processes as well as all internal processing steps. Only the items' inventories and their links are shown.) Section 5.3 shows how to construct a good policy for such a system and to compute a simple, accurate estimate of its overall cost.

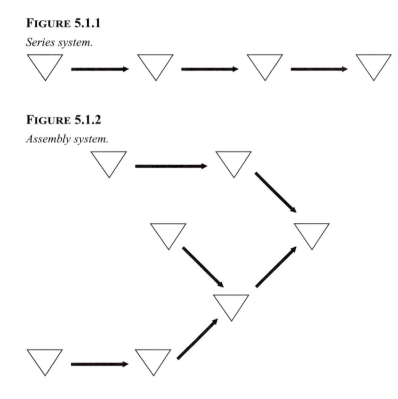

FIGURE 5.1.1

Series system.

FIGURE 5.1.2

Assembly system.

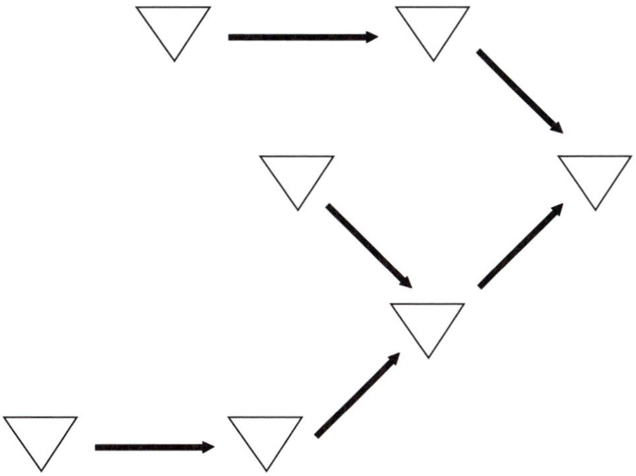

The next simplest structure is an *assembly system* (Figure 5.1.2). This usually represents production activities. As in a series system, there is only one finished product. There may be several raw materials, however, all supplied exogenously. These are processed and/or combined ("assembled") into components, which in turn are assembled further, ultimately forming the final product. Some arcs in the network may represent transportation, moving materials, components, or the final product from one location to another.

A *distribution system* looks like a backwards assembly system (Figure 5.1.3). In production terms, there is one raw material and several final products. The raw material is successively specialized or refined as it moves through the production stages. In transportation terms, the first node represents a central warehouse, and the ending nodes are retail outlets; the nodes in the middle are intermediate stocking points, such as regional warehouses. Of course, a series system is a special case of both an assembly and a distribution system.

A *tree system* (Figure 5.1.4) combines the features of an assembly system and a distribution system, roughly in that order.

A fully *general system* (Figure 5.1.5) represents still more intricate relationships. Compare Figures 5.1.4 and 5.1.5: The general system includes distributionlike activities whose outputs are later combined in assembly operations, while the tree system does not. This distinction is important. As we shall see, general systems are fundamentally more

FIGURE 5.1.3

Distribution system.

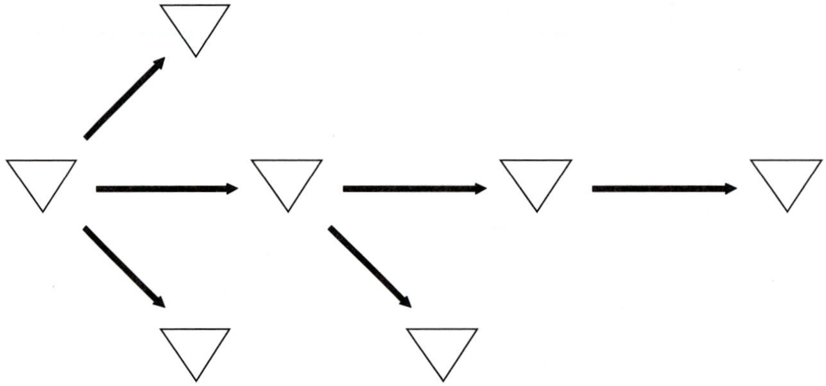

FIGURE 5.1.4

Tree system.

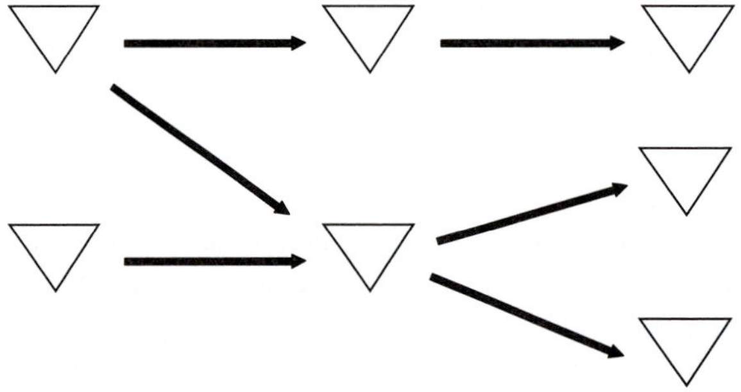

FIGURE 5.1.5

General system.

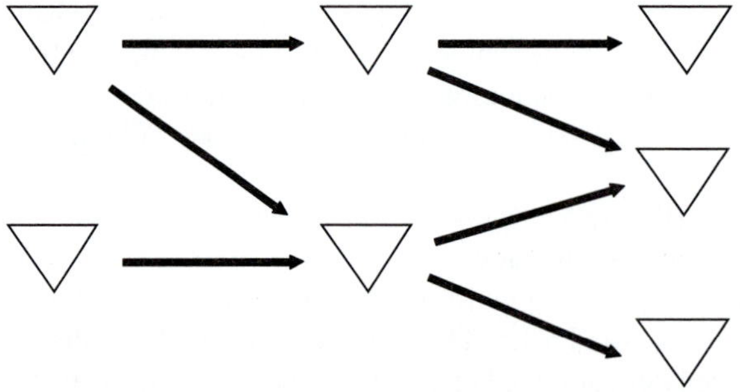

complex than tree systems. All these more complex networks, from assembly to general systems, are discussed in Section 5.4. Again, the main objective is to construct a good policy and an accurate cost estimate.

We can even think of purely independent items as forming a network, though a trivial one with no arcs. In light of the classification above we might call this a *parallel system.* This notion is useful conceptually: For instance, a distribution system combines the features of the series and parallel structures.

5.1.3 Shared Supply Processes

Items can be linked in other ways besides supply-demand relations. Their demand processes may be driven by some common underlying factors. For example, each arriving customer may demand several items, not just one; or all items' demands may be influenced by general economic conditions. But most of the chapter assumes known, constant demand rates for all items, and it really doesn't matter how these rates are determined. Such demand links play no direct role in the model formulations. (Common demand drivers are relevant for sensitivity analysis, when we step back from a model and view it in a larger context, and also in certain of the variable-demand models of Section 5.7.)

Likewise, the supply processes may be linked. At the extreme, the items may share a common supply process. There are several types of supply links. We explore two of them.

First, Section 5.5 discusses the *joint-replenishment problem.* This model portrays a situation where there is an economic advantage to ordering several items at the same time, that is, *economies of scope.* Economies of scope arise, for example, when all the items come from a single supplier, so we can save shipment charges by synchronizing their orders. Section 5.5 shows how to exploit these economies of scope effectively. The key idea is to reduce the problem to an equivalent distribution system and then apply the methods of Section 5.4.

Section 5.6 explores a different type of supply link, where several items share a supply process of limited capacity. One example is a flexible production facility: The items are products, and the supply process consists of a single machine, capable of producing only one product at a time. This model is called the *economic lot scheduling problem.* We develop effective heuristic methods for this problem.

5.1.4 Time-Varying Demands

The chapter concludes with two sections on time-varying demands. Section 5.7 approaches the issue much in the same spirit as Chapter 4, using discrete-time formulations. Following a brief discussion of simple cases, it explores discrete-time versions of supply-demand networks and limited-capacity systems.

Then, we abruptly change pace in Section 5.8 to consider a broad, widely applied approach to managing operations known as *material requirements planning* (or *MRP*). This is a large topic; our treatment of it is selective, not exhaustive. The aim is to provide a brief overview and assessment, focusing on MRP's basic logic and its relation to the models discussed earlier. Also, we describe several other popular approaches in passing.

5.2 Independent Items

5.2.1 Aggregate Performance Measures

Consider a system with many items, each satisfying the assumptions of the EOQ model. The items are independent; there are no supply-demand links between them, and their supply and demand processes are distinct. This scenario describes a retail store or a parts warehouse fairly well. Because the items do not interact in any way, we can control each one separately from the others. That is, for each individual item, we can estimate the parameters, solve the EOQ model, and implement the results.

This is essentially what most commercial inventory control programs do. Such a program, typically, is structured as a database with one record for each item. The order-triggering function and the supporting calculations are performed on an item-by-item basis. (These calculations are sometimes more sophisticated than the EOQ model's, sometimes less, but that is beside the point here.)

This parallel approach to a multi-item inventory is not the only possible one, however, or necessarily the best one. Imagine a system with thousands of distinct items. It would be tedious to estimate each item's cost factors separately; maintaining consistency, let alone accuracy, would be brutally difficult. In the end, moreover, we would have no coherent picture of the overall operation.

This section describes a different perspective: Most inventory-related costs arise when, to order or stock an item, we draw on a few key firmwide *resources,* such as working capital and stockroom labor. (Such resources are referred to, appropriately, as *cost drivers* in accounting parlance.) The central managerial concerns are the total usages of these resources over all items, expressed as *aggregate performance measures.* The most important measures are the total inventory investment and the aggregate order-handling workload. In this view the individual items still matter, but mainly insofar as they contribute to these aggregates.

Senior managers and even investors pay close attention to aggregate performance measures. In situations involving thousands of items, no individual can possibly grasp the details of each one. Aggregate-level information enables managers to monitor the effectiveness of the inventory-control function and the overall health of the enterprise, and to set broad, consistent operating policies.

Even so, ultimately we (or someone) must take action. To strike an appropriate balance between aggregate inventory and workload, as we shall see, entails measuring or specifying their relative costs, implicitly or explicitly. The aggregate approach, however, does this once, at the aggregate level, not for each item separately.

Nevertheless, this approach is entirely consistent with the individual-item EOQ model; it arrives at the same result by a different path. Given each item's resource usage and each resource's cost, as required by the aggregate approach, we can use these data to compute the individual-item costs. What we have, then, is a plausible, relatively tractable cost-estimation procedure for the EOQ model. Both perspectives are useful in practice.

Denote

$$J = \text{number of items}$$

$$j = \text{item index}, j = 1, \ldots, J$$

We need three basic pieces of information about each item:

$$\lambda_j = \text{demand rate for item } j$$

$$c_j = \text{unit purchase cost for item } j$$

$$w_j = \text{workload imposed by one order of item } j$$

Assume that c_j captures the aggregate resource usage in stocking item j. Holding inventory ties up working capital, and c_j measures how much, but it also consumes other valuable resources, such as warehouse space, labor, and energy. We assume, in effect, that the consumption of such resources is proportional to c_j. Likewise, *assume* that the single coefficient w_j captures the critical resources consumed in all the activities (setting up a machine, filling out a form, etc.) required to place and receive an order of item j.

Define three aggregate-level statistics describing the system itself. The first is a measure of overall demand activity:

$$\begin{aligned} c\lambda &= \text{aggregate purchase-cost rate} \\ &= \Sigma_j c_j \lambda_j \end{aligned}$$

(Think of $c\lambda$ as a single symbol. Each term in the sum, and $c\lambda$ itself, are measured in moneys per time-unit. Alternatively, think of $c\lambda$ as the product of two quantities, c and λ, where $\lambda = \Sigma_j \lambda_j$ is the total demand rate, and $c = \Sigma_j (\lambda_j/\lambda) c_j$ is the demand-weighted average of the c_j. This second interpretation makes sense when all the items have the same quantity units, but not otherwise.) Second, let

$$w = \text{weighted-average order-workload} = \Sigma_j \left(\frac{c_j\lambda_j}{c\lambda}\right) w_j$$

The product of w and $c\lambda$ is just the sum $wc\lambda = \Sigma_j w_j c_j \lambda_j$. Finally, define

$$J_* = \text{variety index} = \frac{(\Sigma_j \sqrt{w_j c_j \lambda_j})^2}{wc\lambda}$$

There are good reasons for this name: It is not hard to show (Problem 5.1) that

$$1 \le J_* \le J \tag{5.2.1}$$

Within this range, J_* measures the dispersion among the quantities $w_j c_j \lambda_j$ over j. If they are very different, then J_* is small, while if they are similar, J_* is large. As we shall see, J_* captures the impact of the number of items on performance; in this sense it measures the *effective* variety among them. (This usage may seem backwards; different $w_j c_j \lambda_j$ mean less variety. A high-variety system here means a system with many items, even if their parameters are identical, or one that performs similarly.)

Now we define the performance measures themselves. Even in aggregate, performance depends on the choice of the policy variables

$$q_j = \text{batch size for item } j$$

The individual-item performance measures are

$$\bar{I}_j = \text{average inventory of item } j = \tfrac{1}{2}q_j$$

$$\overline{OF}_j = \text{order frequency of item } j = \lambda_j/q_j$$

The aggregate performance measures are

$$cI = \text{average total investment in inventory} = \Sigma_j c_j \bar{I}_j$$

$$wO = \text{aggregate average workload} = \Sigma_j w_j \overline{OF}_j$$

(Again, it is simplest to think of cI as a single symbol, and likewise wO.) Given the assumptions above about c_j and w_j, these two measures capture all the relevant information about aggregate resource usage.

On the other hand, like all time-averages, these measures suppress the actual patterns of resource usage over time. Local peaks and valleys can be important for capacity-constrained resources, especially those measured by wO. For now, simply ignore this issue; Section 5.6 revisits it.

5.2.2 The Inventory-Workload Tradeoff Curve

The aggregate measures cI and wO are related through the q_j, of course. This relationship can be expressed in a clear and simple way:

Suppose for now that there is a fixed target level for the total inventory investment, and use cI to indicate that target. The remaining problem is to allocate this total investment among the items, so as to minimize the aggregate workload wO. This problem can be expressed as a mathematical optimization problem over the positive variables q_j:

$$\begin{aligned} &\text{Minimize} && \Sigma_j w_j\left(\frac{\lambda_j}{q_j}\right) \\ &\text{subject to} && \Sigma_j c_j(\tfrac{1}{2}q_j) = cI \end{aligned} \tag{5.2.2}$$

Use wO to indicate the optimal objective value.

This is a pure classical optimization problem, which can be solved directly: Let ζ denote the dual variable (or Lagrange multiplier) for the equation. The first-order optimality conditions are

$$\frac{w_j\lambda_j}{q_j^2} = \frac{1}{2}\zeta c_j$$

or

$$q_j = \sqrt{\frac{2w_j\lambda_j}{\zeta c_j}} \qquad j = 1, \ldots, J \tag{5.2.3}$$

(Notice the similarity to the EOQ formula!) Now, substitute these expressions into the equation and solve for ζ; use this ζ in (5.2.3) to compute the optimal q_j^*; and substitute the q_j^* back into the objective function. The end result is the strikingly simple formula

FIGURE 5.2.1

Inventory-workload tradeoff curve.

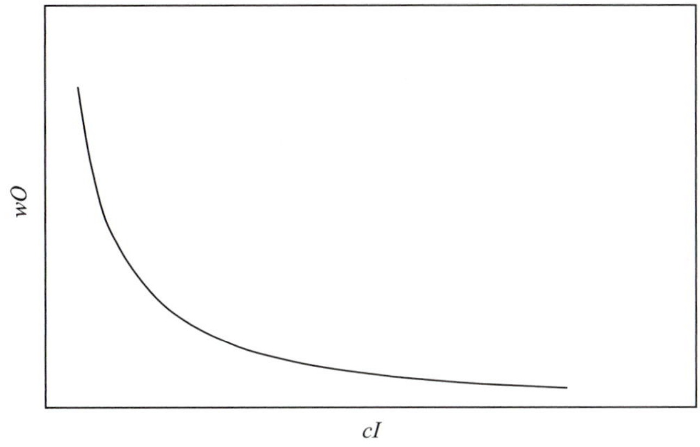

$$wO = \frac{1}{2}\frac{(wc\lambda)J_*}{cI} \tag{5.2.4}$$

(Problem 5.2 asks you to work out the details.)

Equation (5.2.4) holds for every value of cI. It describes a functional relationship between the aggregate inventory cI and the aggregate workload wO. The graph of this equation is called the *inventory-workload tradeoff curve.* Figure 5.2.1 illustrates one such curve.

It is important to understand what the tradeoff curve does and does not do: In the language of economics, a curve of this kind is an *efficient set.* For any given cI, the curve tells us the best (i.e., smallest) achievable wO. The relationship works in the opposite direction too; given wO, the curve indicates the best possible cI. The curve does *not* prescribe a particular optimal solution, however. That means selecting a single point on the curve, and to make such a choice requires knowing or deciding the relative importance of inventory and workload. Equivalently (as explained below), we need more specific cost information.

Still, the tradeoff curve can be immensely useful. First, it can be used in a diagnostic mode. Only certain combinations of the q_j correspond to efficient points. Any other is *inefficient;* the corresponding point (cI, wO) lies above (or to the right of) the curve. Thus, we can compare current operations with the curve to assess their efficiency.

Also, the curve can serve to sharpen discussion among managers, for it summarizes what is and is not possible. For example, financial and competitive pressures often suggest reducing inventory investment. Presuming current operations are efficient, the curve indicates precisely the corresponding increase in workload. Thus informed, we can then seriously discuss whether such an increase is tolerable or not. In sum, the curve enables managers to explore broad policy directions, even without detailed cost information.

Finally, the curve depends on the underlying system parameters in a remarkably simple way, through the quantity $(wc\lambda)J_* = [\Sigma_j(w_jc_j\lambda_j)^{1/2}]^2$. Keeping everything else fixed, the aggregate workload wO required for a given investment cI is proportional to this quantity. This fact is useful in sensitivity analysis, as indicated below in Section 5.2.4.

5.2.3 Cost Estimation and Optimization

Now, suppose we can estimate a positive constant κ, summarizing the unit cost of the aggregate resources measured in wO. Likewise, suppose the constant η measures the cost of aggregate inventory, cI. (Recall, α denotes the interest rate, and interest is certainly one of the costs of cI. Here, η includes α, plus any other relevant costs proportional to cI.) The problem of choosing a particular point on the tradeoff curve can then be expressed as the following two-variable classical optimization problem:

$$\begin{aligned} &\text{Minimize} \quad && \kappa(wO) + \eta(cI) \\ &\text{subject to} \quad && (5.2.4) \end{aligned} \qquad (5.2.5)$$

This problem is easy to solve: Just find the point on the tradeoff curve with slope $-\eta/\kappa$.

Here is an equivalent approach: Given the parameters κ and η, directly estimate the cost factors required for the EOQ model, item by item:

$$k_j = \kappa w_j \qquad h_j = \eta c_j \qquad j = 1, \ldots, J$$

Thus, we determine the k_j and h_j in two steps, first measuring the "physical" quantities w_j and c_j, and then using the factors κ and η to convert them into cost rates.

Next, use these cost factors in a separate EOQ model for each item. The EOQ formula now takes the form

$$q_j^* = \sqrt{\frac{2(\kappa w_j)\lambda_j}{\eta c_j}} \qquad j = 1, \ldots, J$$

Comparing this with (5.2.3) above, the ratio η/κ corresponds precisely to the dual variable ζ. Substituting these q_j^* into the sums defining wO and cI yields

$$wO = \sqrt{(\tfrac{1}{2}wc\lambda J_*)(\tfrac{\eta}{\kappa})} \qquad cI = \sqrt{(\tfrac{1}{2}wc\lambda J_*)(\tfrac{\kappa}{\eta})} \qquad (5.2.6)$$

Multiplying these two equations eliminates η and κ entirely, and the end result is (5.2.4). Thus, this point (cI, wO) lies on the tradeoff curve. Moreover, it is easy to check that the slope of the curve at this point is indeed $-\eta/\kappa$.

In fact, the individual-item approach can recover the entire tradeoff curve: Just let the ratio η/κ range over all positive values. Using (5.2.6), each value generates a point (wO, cI) lying on the curve, and the locus of these points is the curve itself. Thus, these two approaches are truly equivalent.

Given η and κ, the optimal total average cost is simply

$$\begin{aligned} C^* &= c\lambda + \kappa(wO) + \eta(cI) \\ &= c\lambda + \sqrt{2(\kappa w)(\eta c\lambda)J_*} \\ &= c\lambda + \sqrt{2(\kappa\eta)(wc\lambda)J_*} \end{aligned} \qquad (5.2.7)$$

Thus, fixing the other parameters (and neglecting the constant term $c\lambda$), C^* is proportional to the square root of J_*. For systems with identical items, C^* is proportional to the square root of the number of items.

Clearly, the two-step approach to cost estimation depends on the assumptions above about c_j and w_j. Those assumptions rarely hold exactly in practice, but they often hold approximately. Otherwise, if the assumptions are seriously violated, aggregate resource usage *cannot* be captured in a single measure cI with a uniform cost rate η, and likewise for wO and κ. In such cases it is necessary to work with additional aggregate measures and cost rates. For instance, it may be possible to identify *two* key stocking-cost drivers. The procedure then becomes the following: Estimate two coefficients for each item, say c_{j1} and c_{j2}, and two corresponding cost rates η_1 and η_2, and then compute $h_j = \eta_1 c_{j1} + \eta_2 c_{j2}$.

Similar cost-estimation approaches are frequently used to cope with large numbers of items. The better inventory-control programs include cost-estimation modules of this kind.

5.2.4 *Aggregate Sensitivity Analysis*

The formulas above embody a clear message: Consider two systems, identical in every way, except that the items of one exhibit greater effective variety, as measured by J_*. (Remember, high variety does not mean different parameters across items; on the contrary, given J, such differences reduce variety.) The low-variety system performs better, along every dimension, than the high-variety system: The low-variety tradeoff curve dominates (lies entirely below) the high-variety curve. And, in the cost-optimization model, C^* is smaller for the low-variety system.

In other words, it is less costly to have a few items, each with large demand, than many items with small demands. There are tangible benefits to *consolidating* a product line into relatively few items, and conversely tangible costs to allowing the line to proliferate.

These costs and benefits reflect the *operational* criteria of workload and inventory. In most businesses *marketing* considerations push in the opposite direction. To enhance total sales, or just to protect them against competitors—these are strong arguments for a highly *differentiated* product line, with each item aimed at a small segment of the overall market. To make intelligent product-line decisions, executives must carefully address both operations and marketing issues; neither consolidation nor differentiation is a universally workable strategy.

It is important to remember these points in addressing sensitivity-analysis issues at the aggregate level. In practice, one frequently confronts questions like the following: If total demand doubles, how should the total inventory change? In the notation above, how does the aggregate inventory investment cI respond to changes in some measure of aggregate demand, say the purchase-cost rate $c\lambda$?

In some special cases such questions can be answered easily, using the results for the EOQ model: Suppose all J items are identical, and each of the λ_j doubles, all else remaining the same. Then, each q_j^* is raised by the factor $\sqrt{2}$, so each $\bar{I}_j$ and cI are also. On the other hand, suppose each individual item remains the same, but the number of items J doubles. Each $\bar{I}_j$ is unchanged, but there are now twice as many of them, so cI itself doubles. This is a much larger increase than in the first case.

As these simple examples illustrate, it is not enough to know the change in $c\lambda$ itself. We need to know something about *how the change is distributed* among the items. Recalling the formulas above, two additional pieces of information are relevant, namely, the changes in the average workload w and the variety index J_*. Now, it often happens that the w_j are nearly constant, so w changes little in response to demand shifts. This leaves J_* as the remaining determinant of performance. In the first example above J_* does not change at all, but in the second J_* doubles along with $c\lambda$; this accounts for the difference in performance in the two cases.

The variety index J_* requires a great deal of information about the individual items. Sometimes it is possible to specify a particular distributional form for the item-specific data, and thus to compute J_* in terms of a few parameters. See Problem 5.3.

Aggregate-level sensitivity issues are often expressed in terms of *turnover.* Recall, in the single-item context, the turnover is just the ratio $\lambda/\bar{I}$. The aggregate turnover is the corresponding ratio $c\lambda/cI$. Thus, if $c\lambda$ increases, we expect turnover to increase, *provided* J_* does not increase too much. In general, we need to know how J_* changes, as well as $c\lambda$, to predict the effects on turnover.

The name "turnover" is sometimes attached to alternative measures. One is $p\lambda/cI$, where

$$\begin{aligned} p\lambda &= \text{total revenue rate} \\ &= \Sigma_j p_j \lambda_j \end{aligned}$$

In this usage, turnover means the ratio of sales to inventory investment. This is a complex measure, and it is hard to interpret sensibly. It is helpful to express it as the product of two more basic ratios:

$$\frac{p\lambda}{cI} = \left(\frac{p\lambda}{c\lambda}\right)\left(\frac{c\lambda}{cI}\right)$$

The second term is the original turnover discussed above. The first ratio $p\lambda/c\lambda$ is the *aggregate markup.* This too can be affected in subtle ways by demand changes. For instance, a shift in demand towards high-margin items increases it, and this can occur even while $c\lambda$ and cI remain constant.

Generally, in working with aggregate performance measures, it is wise to learn precisely how the calculations are performed, and to reckon carefully the various factors that influence them. This may sound obvious, but it is easy to forget.

5.2.5 Aggregate Sensitivity Analysis in Action

One particular experience taught me the importance of care in these matters: Some years ago I was asked to advise the executives of a large conglomerate. Every month they reviewed the financial performance of their subsidiaries. There were several hundred of these, and many were themselves quite large, complex businesses. So, the reviews tended to focus on a few aggregate performance measures. Total sales ($p\lambda$) and turnover ($p\lambda/cI$) received close attention.

Some of the European subsidiaries had enjoyed rapidly increasing sales in recent months. The executives were concerned, however, that turnover had actually declined somewhat. What was wrong? Had the European managers lost control of their inventories?

First, we looked at the aggregate markup ($p\lambda/c\lambda$). These figures had fluctuated over that same period, but in no clear, systematic direction. A more detailed examination revealed that there had in fact been a shift toward higher-margin products, but their prices had been reduced also, and these two effects more or less cancelled each other.

Then, we estimated the variety index (J_*). This was not easy: We had no item-specific workloads (w_j), and the expenditure data ($c_j\lambda_j$) were incomplete. So, we assumed all $w_j = w$ for each subsidiary. Then, with the limited expenditure data and additional assumptions (along the lines of Problem 5.3), we patched together an estimate of J_*. (We were a bit uncomfortable with this crude approach, but the practical need for a quick answer overrode our reservations.)

The results were clearcut: Most of the subsidiaries' J_*'s had increased substantially. Further investigation provided the explanation: The sales expansion had come mainly through opening new markets in widespread geographic regions. The effective number of items had grown even faster than revenues, so the inventory needed to support them had increased sharply. (This also explained the price reductions; managers were cutting prices aggressively to attract new customers.) In such circumstances, declining turnover was perfectly natural. Far from losing control, the European managers were apparently doing their jobs well.

5.2.6 ABC Analysis

ABC analysis is another tactic for coping with a large number of items. Essentially, it means dividing the items into a few groups. Commonly, three groups are used, labeled A, B, and C on the basis of sales volume. The A items have the largest values of $p_j\lambda_j$, the B items medium values, and the C items the smallest. Normally, the A group includes only a few items (say, 10%), the B group is larger (30%), and the C group is the largest (60%). Even so, the A items typically account for the bulk of total sales (often as much as 80%), while the C items cover only a small fraction, with the B items somewhere in between.

Thus, ABC analysis identifies the most important items, the A group, and the least important ones, the C group, putting the rest in the B group. This is a preliminary step to other modes of analysis, such as parameter estimation and modeling. The idea is to focus effort where it counts the most. Thus, the A items deserve the most intensive data-collection and model-formulation efforts, while relatively crude methods can be used for the B items, and even cruder ones for the C items.

Some writers offer much more specific advice, recommending particular models for particular groups (e.g., the EOQ model for B items). This is, in my view, too specific. The "right" model depends, as usual, on many other factors. The B items in one system may be far more important and complex than the B items in another system, and thus require entirely different models and methods.

The basic notion of dividing items into groups can be usefully applied to any large data set. It is not just a technique of inventory analysis, but rather much more general.

5.3 Series Systems

5.3.1 The Setting

This section analyzes a series system. There are J items numbered $j = 1, \ldots, J$ from first to last. The items represent the outputs of successive production stages, or stocking points along a supply chain. Demand occurs, at rate λ, only for item J, and an external source supplies item 1. All other supply links are internal; item 1 supplies item 2, item 2 feeds item 3, and so on. See Figure 5.3.1. Another word for "item" in this context is *stage.* A series system is sometimes called a multistage system.

Stock moves in discrete batches, as in the EOQ model. An *order* is a decision to move a batch *to* any stage, whether the batch comes from the supplier or a prior stage. The stages do not make their own order decisions, however; information and control are fully centralized. The order decisions must be *coordinated;* it makes no sense to order a batch to be sent to one stage, when the prior stage has insufficient inventory. (Nevertheless, we shall see later that the system can be operated effectively in a decentralized manner.) The external supplier always has ample stock available.

All demand must be met as it occurs; stockouts are forbidden. There are economies of scale in the form of fixed costs for all orders. (If not, the entire system could operate as a perfect flow system.) So, the basic issue here, as in the EOQ model, is to find a good balance between these fixed costs and inventory holding costs. Denote

$$k_j = \text{fixed cost for orders of item } j$$

$$h'_j = \text{inventory holding-cost rate for item } j$$

$$I'_j(t) = \text{inventory of item } j \text{ at time } t$$

(The reason for the primes will become apparent shortly.)

Each stage requires precisely one unit from its predecessor to produce a unit of its own item. This is no real restriction: If a stage requires more or less than one unit, just redefine the quantity units of items $j < J$ to reflect their usages in the end product. For example, consider a two-stage system, where both items are originally measured in tons, and it requires *two* tons of item 1 to make one ton of item 2. Measure item 1 in two-tons instead; just one of these new units is needed to produce a unit of item 2. Accordingly, revise h'_j to be twice its original value.

There is a constant leadtime L'_j for stage-j orders. (So, implicitly, there are no capacity limits.) Shipments in transit between stages comprise *pipeline inventories.* These

FIGURE 5.3.1

Series system.

are distinct from the $I'_j(t)$, which measure inventories *at* the stages. Still, a shipment from j to $j + 1$ essentially consists of stock of item j, so it incurs holding cost at rate h'_j, just like $I'_j(t)$. (Shipments from the source to stage 1 incur no such costs.) But, under any plausible policy, on average, there must be exactly $\lambda L'_{j+1}$ units in transit from j to $j + 1$, so the total average pipeline-holding cost is $\lambda\Sigma_{j<J}h'_jL'_{j+1}$. This is a constant. Consequently, we ignore these costs from now on. Likewise, we ignore variable purchase and shipment costs, since these are constant over all sensible policies.

Also, as in the EOQ model, we can anticipate leadtimes just by shifting the orders in time appropriately, as explained below. For simplicity, then, assume each $L'_j = 0$. So, it is possible to order stock from the supplier and pass it through the successive stages, even all the way to stage J, instantaneously. Assume the system starts empty, i.e., $I'_j(0^-) = 0$ for all j.

All the proofs in this section are collected at the end, in Section 5.3.8.

5.3.2 Echelons and Echelon Inventories

Here is a fundamental concept in multiitem systems: The *echelon* of stage j (or echelon j for short) comprises stage j itself and all downstream stages, i.e., all stages $i \geq j$. The echelons of a four-stage system are indicated by rectangles in Figure 5.3.2. This notion captures the supply-demand relationships in a useful manner: First, stage J is its own echelon. The external supplier and all the prior stages can be viewed as stage J's supply process. Likewise, consider echelon $J - 1$, i.e., the last two stages. This is another subsystem, whose supply process includes the earlier stages $i < J - 1$. Continuing in this manner, the entire system can be viewed as a hierarchy of nested subsystems, the echelons, each with a clearly defined supply process.

(In military usage the word *echelon* is a generic term for a group of troops. Thus, an echelon may refer to a division, or a battalion, or a company. A division includes several smaller groups, which include still smaller groups, and so on.)

Imagine a multistage production process. Item 1 is a raw material. At each stage the material is transformed somehow, or various enhancements are added, until the final product emerges as item J. So, in a sense, a unit of item $i > j$ includes one of item j. The total system inventory of item j thus comprises, not just $I'_j(t)$, but also the inventories downstream. To express this idea, define

FIGURE 5.3.2

Echelons.

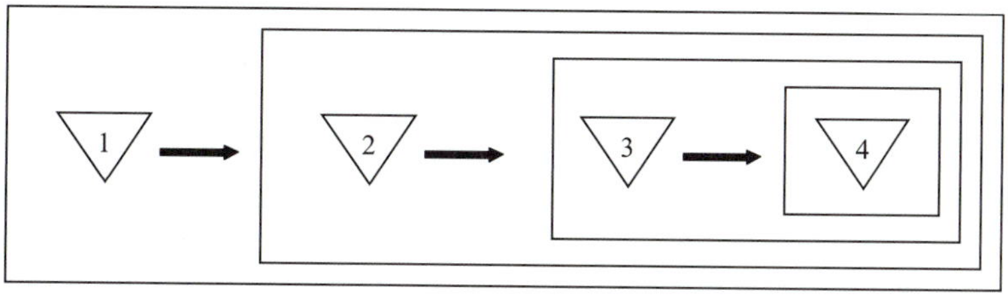

$$I_j(t) = \text{echelon inventory of item } j \text{ at time } t$$
$$= \Sigma_{i \geq j} I'_j(t)$$

The original $I'_j(t)$ is sometimes called the *local* or *installation* inventory of item j. The prime indicates that it is a local quantity.

Also, let

$$h_j = \text{echelon-inventory holding-cost rate for item } j$$
$$= h'_j - h'_{j-1}$$

where $h_0 = 0$. Assume that each $h_j > 0$. (This is usually the case: Suppose c_j is the variable order-cost rate for item j, and h'_j includes financing costs only. To create a unit of item j incurs *all* the costs c_i, $i < j$, so $h'_j = \alpha\Sigma_{i \leq j} c_i$, where α is the interest rate. Thus, the echelon holding cost is just $h_j = \alpha c_j$, that is, h_j reflects the *value added* at stage j. And $c_j > 0$ immediately implies $h_j > 0$. If h'_j also includes a physical handling cost $\underline{h}'_j$, the $\underline{h}'_j$ must also increase, or at least not decrease too fast. This is usually true also; physical handling tends to be more expensive downstream.)

With these definitions the systemwide inventory cost rate becomes

$$\Sigma_j h'_j I'_j(t) = \Sigma_j h_j I_j(t) \qquad \text{for all } t$$

Thus, the echelon inventories track stocks and their costs throughout the system just as well as the local inventories.

Echelon inventories offer distinct advantages: Consider a two-stage system. Figure 5.3.3 graphs the local inventories of the two items. Item 2's inventory $I'_2(t)$ behaves like that of a single-item system: It decreases at the constant rate λ, except at order epochs, when it jumps up by the order amount. However, $I'_1(t)$ describes a fairly complex step function.

Figure 5.3.4 shows the corresponding echelon inventories. Of course, $I_2(t) = I'_2(t)$, but $I_1(t) = I'_1(t) + I'_2(t)$ too looks like the inventory of a single-item system. (The dashed lines show $I'_1(t)$.) The jumps occur at stage 1 orders only; when stage 2 orders but stage 1 does not, $I_1(t)$ does not change.

Clearly, this idea extends to general J: For every j, $I_j(t)$ decreases at rate λ, except at stage-j order epochs, when it jumps by the amount ordered. Thus, echelon inventories simplify the task of inventory-cost accounting.

Reconsider the positive-leadtime case for a moment. Let

$$\underline{L}_j^- = \text{forward echelon leadtime for item } j$$
$$= \Sigma_{i>j} L'_i$$

This is the minimal time required to move a unit of item j through the subsequent stages to the customer; note, $\underline{L}_J^- = 0$. Given a feasible policy for the zero-leadtime system, one can construct a corresponding feasible policy for the "real" positive-leadtime system: Just shift each order arrival of item j back in time by $\underline{L}_j^-$. Equivalently, shift the start of each shipment to j back by $\underline{L}_j = L'_j + \underline{L}_j^-$. (Thus, the initial order arrivals for $j < J$ occur at negative times. This is necessary for feasibility, assuming the system starts empty and demand begins at time $t = 0$.) It is easy to see that, except for a similar time shift, the

FIGURE 5.3.3

Local inventories over time.

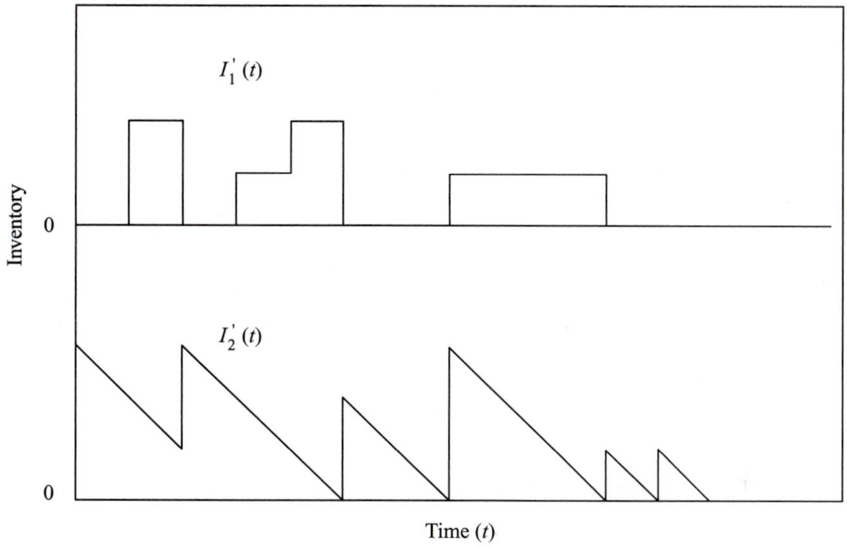

FIGURE 5.3.4

Echelon inventories over time.

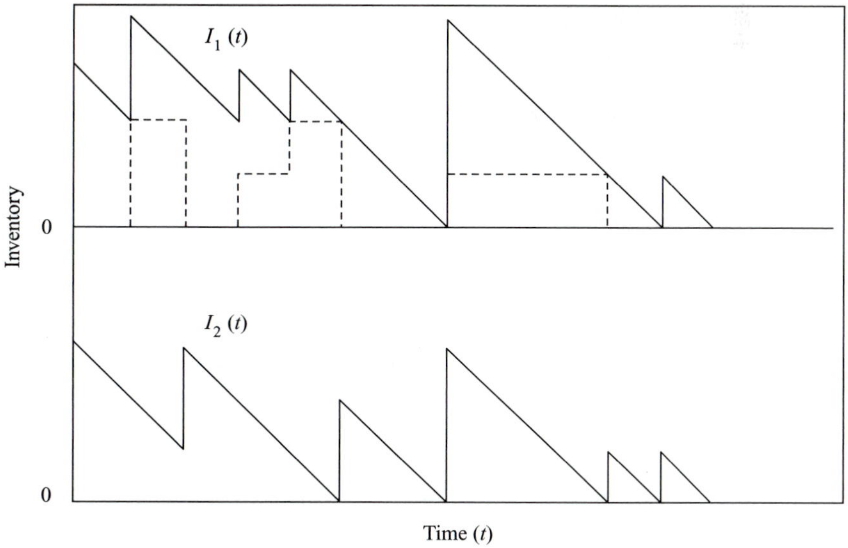

$I_j(t)$ are identical in the two systems. Conversely, given a feasible policy for the real system, we can construct a policy for the zero-leadtime system by the reverse transformation. So, we can and do focus on zero-leadtime systems.

5.3.3 Policy Characteristics

For practical purposes, and analytical purposes too, we would like to focus on relatively simple policies. Fortunately, good policies share certain simplifying qualitative characteristics.

A policy is *nested* if, for all j, whenever stage j orders, so does stage $j+1$. Here, an order at one stage triggers orders at all downstream stages; in other words, all stages in an echelon order together. Consequently, stage J orders most frequently among all the stages, and stage 1 least. It turns out that nested policies are the only ones we need consider:

THEOREM 5.3.1. Every non-nested policy is dominated by a nested policy. (The nested policy has lower inventories and no more orders.)

(Remember, the proofs of this and subsequent results are postponed until Section 5.3.8.)

Another important policy characteristic is the zero-inventory property, encountered in Chapter 3. Under a *zero-inventory policy,* each item orders only when its inventory $I'_j(t^-)$ is zero. (Recall, $I'_j(0^-) = 0$, so the first order certainly satisfies this condition.)

THEOREM 5.3.2. Every non-zero-inventory policy is dominated by a zero-inventory policy.

Thus, we can restrict attention to policies with both these characteristics. Note, under a nested, zero-inventory policy, item j orders only when its echelon inventory $I_j(t)$ is zero.

A *stationary-interval* policy means just that: For each item the time intervals between orders are equal. Such policies are generally easier to implement than others, and they are certainly easier to analyze. (Stationary intervals imply equal order quantities, of course. For the complex networks of the next section, however, it is more natural to work with order intervals, so we do the same here to maintain consistency. One can show that stationary-interval policies do dominate all others. We do not actually use this fact, however.)

Consider a policy with all three properties, i.e., a nested, zero-inventory, stationary-interval policy. Let

u_j = order interval for item j
$\mathbf{u}$ = the vector $(u_j)_j$
$g_j = h_j\lambda$
$C(\mathbf{u})$ = average cost of the policy specified by $\mathbf{u}$

Each $I_j(t)$ describes the periodic pattern familiar from the EOQ model. Therefore, applying the EOQ model's calculations to each item,

$$C(\mathbf{u}) = \Sigma_j[k_j/u_j + \tfrac{1}{2}g_j u_j] \tag{5.3.1}$$

Each u_j is a positive-integer multiple of u_{j+1}. The problem of selecting the best such policy can be stated as follows:

$$
\begin{aligned}
&\text{Minimize} \quad C(\mathbf{u}) \\
&\text{subject to} \quad u_j = \xi_j u_{j+1} \\
&\qquad\qquad \xi_j = \text{a positive integer}, j < J
\end{aligned}
\tag{5.3.2}
$$

Problem (5.3.2) is a nonlinear mixed-integer program and far too difficult to work with directly. (A technical point: There is no guarantee even that a truly optimal solution exists. That is, in principle, it may be possible to find a sequence of better and better solutions, without ever reaching a best one.) Here is the plan: First, we solve a simpler problem called the *relaxed problem.* Its optimal cost is a *lower bound* on the actual minimal cost. Next, by carefully rounding off the relaxed problem's solution, we construct a feasible solution. Also, we compute a simple upper bound on this feasible solution's cost; this provides an *upper bound* on the minimal cost. These two bounds are close together; they differ by only a few percent. Consequently, the feasible solution is a good one, and the lower bound is an accurate estimate of the optimal cost.

5.3.4 The Relaxed Problem

Clearly, any feasible vector **u** in problem (5.3.2) satisfies $u_j \geq u_{j+1}$. Define another optimization problem based on this property:

$$
\begin{aligned}
C^{-} = &\text{ minimize} \quad C(\mathbf{u}) \\
&\text{subject to} \quad u_j \geq u_{j+1} \qquad j < \mathrm{J}
\end{aligned}
\tag{5.3.3}
$$

This is called the *relaxed problem,* because its constraints relax those of problem (5.3.2). Thus, its optimal cost C^{-} is a lower bound on the minimal cost of problem (5.3.2), but that's not all:

THEOREM 5.3.3. The optimal cost C^{-} of the relaxed problem is a lower bound on the average cost of any feasible policy.

The relaxed problem (5.3.3) is obviously simpler than the original (5.3.2). All the variables are continuous, and the constraints are linear inequalities. Moreover, the objective function is strictly convex, so (see Proposition A.3.6 of Appendix A) the optimal solution is *unique.* Call it **u***.

Thus, (5.3.3) is a standard nonlinear program; one way to solve it is to use a standard nonlinear-programming algorithm. But there is a better way. Problem (5.3.3) has a great deal of special structure. We shall apply an algorithmic strategy (a variant of the active-set strategy; see, e.g., Luenberger [1984], pp. 326–330) that exploits this special structure to develop a simple, fast method to solve (5.3.3).

The key idea is to distinguish which constraints in (5.3.3) are binding at the optimal solution. Let $N = \{1, \ldots, J\}$ denote the set of items, and let $A = \{1, \ldots, J-1\}$ index the constraints. For any subset $A_{=} \subseteq \mathrm{A}$, construct a modified version of the relaxed problem: Tighten the constraints for $j \in A_{=}$ to equations, and omit the others:

$$
\begin{aligned}
&\text{Minimize} \quad C(\mathbf{u}) \\
&\text{subject to} \quad u_j = u_{j+1} \qquad j \in A_{=}
\end{aligned}
\tag{5.3.3[$A_{=}$]}
$$

FIGURE 5.3.5

Clusters.

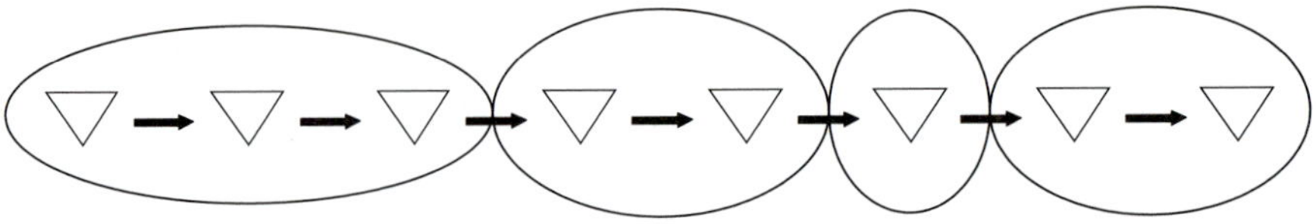

It is easy to solve this problem for any $A_=$, as shown below, and it turns out that, for the right subset $A_=$, say $A^*_=$, the solution to (5.3.3[$A^*_=$]) also solves (5.3.3) itself. (Given **u***, set $A^*_= = \{j \in A : u^*_j = u^*_{j+1}\}$. As Problem 5.7 asks you to prove, **u*** is the unique solution to (5.3.3[$A^*_=$]).) So, the problem becomes, find an optimal subset $A^*_=$.

First, let us solve (5.3.3[$A_=$]) for any given subset $A_=$. Any $A_=$ divides the items N into groups or *clusters,* where the items within each cluster are forced to have equal u_j. Let N_m denote an individual cluster, setting the index m to the largest item-number j in the cluster. The collection of clusters is the *partition* $\mathbf{N} = \{N_m, m \in N \backslash A_=\}$. ($\mathbf{N}$ is a special partition. The items in each cluster are consecutive, and the clusters are ordered by their indices m. To emphasize this fact, $\mathbf{N}$ is sometimes called a *directed partition.*) Figure 5.3.5 shows one possible partition. The ovals designate the clusters. The set $A_=$ corresponds to arcs inside ovals, i.e., those that do not cross cluster boundaries. Also, let

$$\text{prev}(m) = \text{cluster index just before } m$$

$$\text{next}(m) = \text{cluster index just after } m \qquad m \in N\backslash A_=$$

where $\text{next}(J) = 0$, and $\text{prev}(m) = 0$ for the lowest index m. So, for all m, $N_m = \{\text{prev}(m) + 1, \ldots, m\}$.

Now, (5.3.3[$A_=$]) separates into $|\mathbf{N}|$ independent subproblems, one for each cluster. The subproblem for cluster N_m is

$$\text{Minimize} \quad \Sigma_{j \in N_m} \left[\frac{k_j}{u_j} + \frac{1}{2} g_j u_j\right]$$

$$\text{subject to} \quad u_j = u_{j+1} \qquad j \in N_m, j < m$$

or equivalently, using one additional variable u,

$$\text{Minimize} \quad \Sigma_{j \in N_m} \left[\frac{k_j}{u} + \frac{1}{2} g_j u\right]$$

$$\text{subject to} \quad u_j = u \qquad j \in N_m$$

For any subset $M \subseteq N$ denote

$$k(M) = \Sigma_{j \in M} k_j$$

$$g(M) = \Sigma_{j \in M} g_j$$

$$\pi(M) = k(M)/g(M)$$

The objective function above can be written compactly as

$$C_m(u) = \frac{k(N_m)}{u} + \frac{1}{2}g(N_m)u$$

But this is the cost function of an EOQ model. Its minimum occurs at $u = u(m) = [2k(N_m)/g(N_m)]^{1/2} = [2\pi(N_m)]^{1/2}$. Thus, the solution to (5.3.3[$A_=$]) is

$$u(m) = [2\pi(N_m)]^{1/2} \qquad m \in N \backslash A_=$$

$$u_j \quad = u(m) \qquad\qquad j \in N_m \tag{5.3.4}$$

This solution need not be feasible for (5.3.3) itself. It *is* feasible, if (but only if) the ratios $\pi(N_m)$ are ordered in the right way:

$$\pi(N_m) \geq \pi(N_{\text{next}(m)}) \qquad m < J \tag{5.3.5}$$

Even then, the solution need not be optimal. For that, it turns out, one additional condition is required: No finer partition satisfies (5.3.5), at least not strictly. In other words, choose any $j \in A_=$, and identify the cluster N_m to which j belongs (so that prev(m) $< j < m$). Now, drop j from $A_=$, or equivalently *cut* N_m into a pair of clusters (N_m^-, N_m^+), where $N_m^- = \{\text{prev}(m) + 1, \ldots, j)$ and $N_m^+ = \{j + 1, \ldots, m\}$. Optimality requires that, for every choice of j (i.e., for any such cut),

$$\pi(N_m^-) \leq \pi(N_m^+) \tag{5.3.6}$$

THEOREM 5.3.4. Conditions (5.3.5) and (5.3.6) on a partition **N** are necessary and sufficient for the solution u given by (5.3.4) to be optimal in the relaxed problem (5.3.3).

While the optimal solution **u*** is unique, the optimal partition need not be. For instance, suppose **N** satisfies (5.3.5) and (5.3.6), and one of the inequalities in (5.3.5) holds with equality, say $\pi(N_m) = \pi(N_{\text{next}(m)})$. Form a new partition by merging the clusters N_m and $N_{\text{next}(m)}$. This new partition also satisfies (5.3.5) and (5.3.6); indeed, it generates the same solution **u***. Continuing in this manner, one can construct an optimal partition with strict inequalities in (5.3.5). Conversely, suppose some cut satisfies (5.3.6) with equality, say $\pi(N_n^-) = \pi(N_n^+)$. Form a new partition, splitting N_n into separate clusters N_n^- and N_n^+. This partition too satisfies (5.3.5) and (5.3.6) and generates the same solution **u***.

Here is a graphical interpretation of the optimality conditions: Define the subsets $N^j = \{1, \ldots, j\}, j = 1, \ldots, J$. Plot the points $[k(N^j), g(N^j)]$ and also (0, 0), and connect them by line segments, as in Figure 5.3.6. The resulting curve is a function of g, for g in the interval $[0, g(N^J)]$; this function is piecewise-linear and increasing. It shows how the cumulative fixed cost $k(N^j)$ varies with the cumulative holding cost $g(N^j)$. Now, *concavify* this function. That is, construct the smallest concave function lying above or on the original function. This new function, indicated by the solid line in Figure 5.3.7, is also piecewise-linear and increasing; it connects some but not all of the original points. Use the concave function to specify a partition **N:** The points on the new curve, excluding (0, 0), correspond to indices m of clusters N_m. (Include only extreme points, i.e., those at "kinks" of the curve.) Equivalently, $A_=$ consists of points below the curve (including those between kinks).

FIGURE 5.3.6

Cumulative costs.

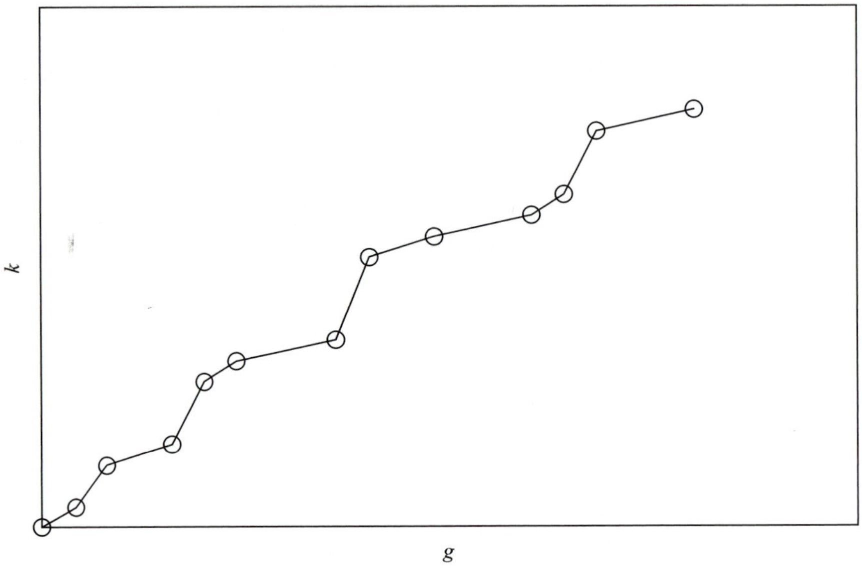

FIGURE 5.3.7

Concavified cumulative costs.

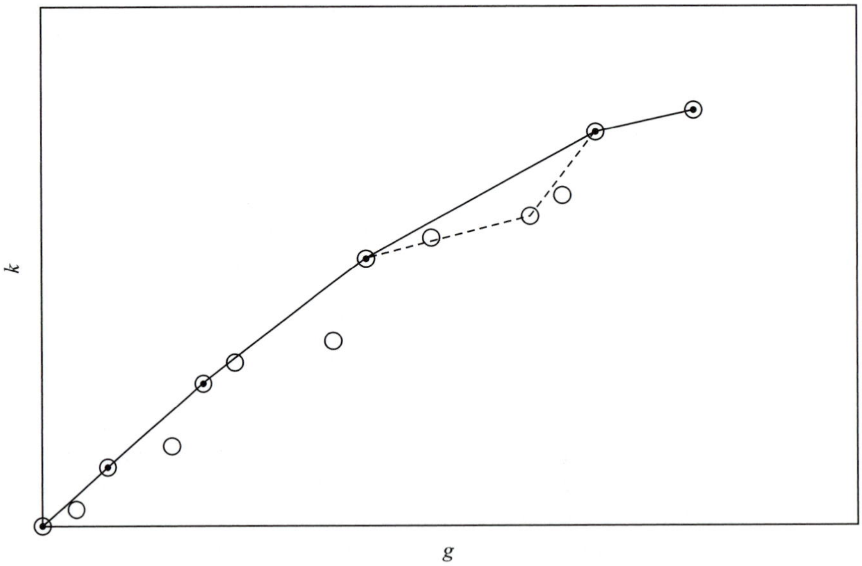

This partition satisfies the optimality conditions: The slopes of the new function's line segments are precisely the $\pi(N_m)$. These are nonincreasing, by concavity, so (5.3.5) holds. Also, to cut any N_m means to add a point $j \in A_= \cap N_m$ to the curve, replacing N_m's line segment by two segments, like the dashed lines in Figure 5.3.7, one each for N_m^- and N_m^+. That new point lies below (or on) N_m's segment, so the new segments have nondecreasing slopes, i.e., $\pi(N_m^-) \le \pi(N_m^+)$. Thus, the cut satisfies (5.3.6).

Thus, to determine an optimal partition **N** and thereby solve the relaxed problem, we need only concavify a piecewise-linear function. There are several ways to do this. The following algorithm, in essence, concavifies the curve through (0, 0) and the next j points, first for $j = 1$, and then for each successive j up to J:

Algorithm Series_Relaxed:

Set $N_j = \{j\}, j = 1, \ldots, J$

For $j = 1, \ldots, J$:

While $\text{prev}(j) \ne 0$ and $\pi(N_{\text{prev}(j)}) \le \pi(N_j)$:

Reset $N_j = N_{\text{prev}(j)} \cup N_j$

At the beginning, each $\text{prev}(j) = j - 1$ and $\pi(N_j) = k_j/g_j$. The reset operation recomputes $k(N_j) = k(N_{\text{prev}(j)}) + k(N_j)$, $g(N_j) = g(N_{\text{prev}(j)}) + g(N_j)$, $\pi(N_j) = k(N_j)/g(N_j)$, and $\text{prev}(j) = \text{prev}(\text{prev}(j))$.

THEOREM 5.3.5. Algorithm Series_Relaxed determines an optimal partition, and so the corresponding solution (5.3.4) solves the relaxed problem.

This algorithm is easy to implement, and its calculations are simple. (One can show that it requires $O(J)$ time.) Let **N*** denote an optimal partition, and $u^*(m)$ the optimal $u(m)$ in (5.3.4).

EXAMPLE 5.3.A, PART 1

Consider a system with $J = 4$ and $\lambda = 1$. All $h_j = 1$, so all $g_j = 1$. The k_j are

$$k_1 = 4 \qquad k_2 = 8 \qquad k_3 = 2 \qquad k_4 = 2$$

Apply Algorithm Series_Relaxed:

<u>Initialize</u>:

$$N_1 = \{1\} \qquad N_2 = \{2\} \qquad N_3 = \{3\} \qquad N_4 = \{4\}$$

$$\pi(N_1) = 4 \qquad \pi(N_2) = 8 \qquad \pi(N_3) = 8 \qquad \pi(N_4) = 2$$

<u>$j = 1$</u>:

prev(1) = 0, so no change

$\underline{j=2}$:

$$\pi(N_1) = 4 < 8 = \pi(N_2), \text{ so reset } N_2 = \{1,2\}$$

$$k(N_2) = 12, g(N_2) = 2, \pi(N_2) = 6, \text{prev}(2) = 0$$

$$\text{prev}(2) = 0, \text{ so no change}$$

$\underline{j=3}$:

$$\pi(N_2) = 6 > 2 = \pi(N_3), \text{ so no change}$$

$\underline{j=4}$:

$$\pi(N_3) = 2 = \pi(N_4), \text{ so reset } N_4 = \{3, 4\}$$

$$k(N_4) = 4, g(N_4) = 2, \pi(N_4) = 2, \text{prev}(4) = 2$$

$$\pi(N_2) = 6 > 2 = \pi(N_4), \text{ so no change.}$$

The optimal partition is $\mathbf{N}^* = \{N_2, N_4\}$, where $N_2 = \{1, 2\}$, $N_4 = \{3, 4]$. The optimal solution to the relaxed problem is

$$u_1^* = u_2^* = u^*(2) = \left(\frac{2 \cdot 12}{2}\right)^{1/2} \approx 3.464$$

$$u_3^* = u_4^* = u^*(4) = \left(\frac{2 \cdot 4}{2}\right)^{1/2} = 2$$

and its cost is $C^- \approx 10.928$.

Incidentally, there is an intriguing and useful interpretation of the solution, based on the duality theory for nonlinear programming. Let ζ_j be the dual variable for the constraint $u_j \geq u_{j+1}$, and ζ_j^* its optimal value, $j < J$, and let $\theta_j^* = 2(\zeta_j^* - \zeta_{j-1}^*)$ with $\zeta_0^* = \zeta_J^* = 0$. The optimality conditions for (5.3.3) imply that $u_j^{*2} = 2k_j/(g_j + \theta_j^*) = 2\pi(N_m), j \in N_m$. Thus, given the $\pi(N_m)$ for an optimal partition, we can directly recover the θ_j^*. Also, $\Sigma_j\, \theta_j^* = 2\Sigma_j\, (\zeta_j^* - \zeta_{j-1}^*) = 0$. So, the θ_j^* essentially *reallocate* the holding costs, or more precisely the g_j, among the items, to recover the optimal solution. There is an entirely analogous construction which reallocates the fixed costs k_j instead. (Just restate the constraints as $1/u_j \leq 1/u_{j+1}$, and proceed as above.) These are just interesting facts for now, but we shall use them later in Section 5.7.

5.3.5 Constructing a Feasible Policy Using a Base Period

Next, we use the solution of the relaxed problem to construct a low-cost, feasible solution to (5.3.2).

Fix some *base period* $\underline{u}$. This can be any convenient time interval, such as a day or a week (not necessarily the same as the original time-unit used to measure t). We shall construct a solution where each u_j is an integer-power-of-two multiple of $\underline{u}$. (That is, u_j is $\underline{u}$, or $2\underline{u}$, or $4\underline{u}$, et cetera, or $\frac{1}{2}\underline{u}$, or $\frac{1}{4}\underline{u}$, et cetera) There are often practical reasons to impose a base period; it is simpler to speak about days, or even half-days, than some bizarre interval like 0.962 days. In any case, the base period will help us construct a feasible policy; any $\underline{u}$ will do. (Section 5.3.6 drops this base-period restriction.)

Given $\underline{u}$, here is a rule to construct a feasible policy, denoted $\mathbf{u}^+$:

$$
\begin{aligned}
n(m) &= \text{closest integer to } \log_2\left(\frac{u^*(m)}{\underline{u}}\right) \\
u^+(m) &= 2^{n(m)}\underline{u} \qquad m \in N\backslash A_= \\
u_j^+ &= u^+(m) \qquad j \in N_m \\
\mathbf{u}^+ &= (u_j^+)_j
\end{aligned}
$$

(If $\log_2(u^*(m)/\underline{u}) = 3\frac{1}{2}$ say, which is squarely between 3 and 4, set $n(m) = 3$. In general, resolve ties by rounding down.) This policy *is* feasible: Since the $u^*(m)$ are nonincreasing in m, so are the $n(m)$ and the $u^+(m)$, hence the u_j^+ are nonincreasing in j. Moreover, each u_j^+ is an integer multiple of u_{j+1}^+. (Specifically, u_j^+ is a nonnegative-integer-power-of-two multiple of $u_{j+1}^+, j < J$. A policy with this property is called a *power-of-two* policy.)

How good is this policy? Let $C^+ = C(\mathbf{u}^+)$. Recall the EOQ error function $\epsilon(x) = \frac{1}{2}(x + 1/x)$ for $x > 0$, defined in (3.2.5).

THEOREM 5.3.6. $C^+ \leq \epsilon(\sqrt{2})C^-$.

A direct calculation reveals that $\epsilon(\sqrt{2}) \approx 1.06$. So, *the cost of the policy is, at worst, 6% more than that of any other policy.* This is quite good performance. The result holds for *any* choice of base period $\underline{u}$.

EXAMPLE 5.3.A, PART 2

In the example above, let us use $\underline{u} = 1$. $\log_2(u^*(2)/\underline{u}) \approx 1.79$, so $n(2) = 2$, and $\log_2(u^*(4)/\underline{u}) = 1 = n(4)$. So, $u^+(2) = 2^2 = 4$, $u^+(4) = 2^1 = 2$, and

$$C^+ = \left[\frac{12}{4} + \frac{1}{2}(2)(4)\right] + \left[\frac{4}{2} + \frac{1}{2}(2)(2)\right] = 11$$

Thus, $C^+/C^- \approx 11/10.928 \approx 1.007$; that is, the solution is at most 0.7% above optimal. This is much better than the theorem's guarantee of 6%.

5.3.6 Constructing a Feasible Policy with No Base Period

Now drop the base-period restriction. The method above seems attractive nevertheless, so continue to use it. Let $C^+(\underline{u})$ be the cost C^+ above, now regarded as a function of $\underline{u}$. Choose $\underline{u}$ to minimize this function.

This, it turns out, is not terribly difficult. First, observe that $\underline{u}$ can be restricted to the fairly small interval $[1, 2)$: Starting with any $\underline{u}$ and then doubling it, each $n(m)$ drops by 1, so $u^+(m)$ remains unchanged. Likewise, halving $\underline{u}$ increases each $n(m)$ by 1, so again $u^+(m)$ is unchanged.

Second, consider what happens to any one $u^+(m)$ as $\underline{u}$ increases from 1 to 2. For a while, $n(m)$ stays constant, so $u^+(m)$ is linear in $\underline{u}$. At some point, $n(m)$ drops by 1 and $u^+(m)$ jumps to a new value. After that point, $u^+(m)$ again changes linearly. There is precisely one such *breakpoint* within $(1, 2)$. Thus, each $u^+(m)$ is a piecewise-linear function with two linear pieces. (The exact expression for $u^+(m)$ is given in the proof of Theorem 5.3.7 in Section 5.3.8.)

Now, there is typically a different breakpoint for each m. Still, the entire vector $\mathbf{u}^+$ is a piecewise-linear function of $\underline{u}$ with at most $|\boldsymbol{N}| + 1$ pieces. Within each piece $C^+(\underline{u})$ is an EOQ-like cost function, so it is easy to optimize. Select the best of these solutions. (Problem 5.8 asks you to work out the technical details.)

Let C^{+*} denote its cost. Of course, this is one possible value of C^+, so Theorem 5.3.6 bounds it above. Here is a stronger result:

THEOREM 5.3.7.

$$C^{+*} \leq \left[\frac{1}{\ln(2)\sqrt{2}}\right] C^-$$

The peculiar constant here is about 1.02. *The cost of this policy is no more than 2% above that of any other policy.* This is truly outstanding performance.

EXAMPLE 5.3.A, PART 3

Let $\chi(m)$ denote the breakpoint for $u^+(m)$. By calculations explained in Section 5.3.8,

$$\chi(2) \approx 1.225 \qquad \chi(4) = \sqrt{2} \approx 1.414$$

$$u^+(2) = \begin{cases} 4\underline{u} & 1 \leq \underline{u} < \chi(2) \\ 2\underline{u} & \chi(2) \leq \underline{u} < 2 \end{cases}$$

$$u^+(4) = \begin{cases} 2\underline{u} & 1 \leq \underline{u} < \chi(4) \\ \underline{u} & \chi(4) \leq \underline{u} < 2 \end{cases}$$

We must evaluate $C^+(\underline{u})$ over three intervals, $[1, \chi(2))$, $[\chi(2), \chi(4))$, and $[\chi(4), 2)$. Over the third one,

$$C^+(\underline{u}) = \left[\frac{12}{2\underline{u}} + \frac{1}{2}2(2\underline{u})\right] + \left[\frac{4}{\underline{u}} + \frac{1}{2}2\underline{u}\right]$$

$$= \frac{10}{\underline{u}} + \frac{1}{2}6\underline{u}$$

By the EOQ formula, the best value of $\underline{u}$ is $\underline{u}^* = (2\cdot 10/6)^{1/2} \approx 1.826$, and the cost of this solution is $C^+(u^*) \approx 10.954$. The calculations for the other intervals are similar. The third one turns out to be best.

The solution is thus $u^+(2) = 2\underline{u}^* \approx 3.651$, $u^+(4) = \underline{u}^* \approx 1.826$, and its cost is $C^{+*} \approx 10.954$. So, $C^{+*}/C^- \approx 10.954/10.928 \approx 1.002$. This solution is at most 0.2% above optimal, much better than the guaranteed 2%.

5.3.7 Discussion: Coordination and Sensitivity

To summarize, determine a policy in two steps. Solve the relaxed problem, and then round off its solution in a careful way, depending on whether or not a base period is specified. If so, the policy's cost is no worse than 6% above optimal; if not, the error bound reduces to 2%. These worst-case bounds are conservative; often, the cost of the heuristic policy is even better (closer to the lower bound) than the bound indicates.

We spoke at the outset of the need to coordinate the items. How exactly does the policy do this? The key idea is to coordinate the *timing* of events throughout the system. The stages are partitioned into clusters. Within each cluster, the policy tells us to synchronize the stages; order for all of them at the same times. Between clusters, the power-of-two policy enforces a partial synchronization. Each cluster's orders coincide with some, but not necessarily all, of those of the next downstream cluster, specifically, either with every downstream order, or every other order, or every 4, etc. Finally, cluster N_J's orders, and therefore every cluster's orders, occur regularly, at equal time intervals.

Among conceivable coordination mechanisms, this is a very simple one. It is remarkable that it performs so well.

Still, this is a centralized control scheme. It is possible, however, to implement the same policy with a minimal degree of central direction: Because the stages within each cluster all use the same order interval (and order quantity), only the last one actually holds inventory. Whenever any earlier stage receives a batch, it processes the batch immediately and passes it through to the next stage. With this rule in place, we need only manage the flow of goods between clusters. Imagine that each cluster operates an EOQ-like policy, based on its own local inventory. The last cluster N_J orders $q^+(J) = \lambda u^+(J)$ quantity-units every $u^+(J)$ time-units, and transmits these orders upstream to cluster $N_{\text{prev}(J)}$. Cluster $N_{\text{prev}(J)}$ views these orders as discrete demands; it fills them as they occur, as if they were exogenous, by transferring batches downstream to cluster N_J. Cluster $N_{\text{prev}(J)}$ in turn places orders with *its* predecessor, cluster $N_{\text{prev}(\text{prev}(J))}$. In actual physical units, each of $N_{\text{prev}(J)}$'s orders is for the quantity $q^+(\text{prev}(J)) = \lambda u^+(\text{prev}(J))$; in terms of the implicit demands $N\text{prev}_{(J)}$ sees, each order is the integer $q^+(\text{prev}(J))/q^+(J) = u^+(\text{prev}(J))/u^+(J)$. So, cluster $N_{\text{prev}(J)}$ operates just like the single-item, discrete-demand EOQ model of Problem 3.7. Likewise, every other cluster receives orders from its successor, treats these orders as its own demands, and places orders with its predecessor.

Clearly, this approach correctly implements the policy. It is necessary, of course, to specify the clusters in advance and tell each one its order interval (or order size). In real time, however, there is no need for centralized information and control. Each cluster monitors only its own local inventory. The orders passed between them provide sufficient information to coordinate the system as a whole.

This equivalence between local and centralized control is a powerful idea in practice, for a local-control scheme is often much easier to manage. This issue is revisited in Section 5.8 and Chapter 8. Also, whether local or centralized, the policy's orders can be driven by time or stock quantities, as in the EOQ model; in certain situations, one may be more convenient than the other.

Let us now consider the overall performance of the system. The relaxed problem's cost C^- accurately estimates the total optimal cost and the cost of the heuristic policy. Given an optimal partition $\mathbf{N}^*$, this quantity is

$$C^- = \Sigma_m \sqrt{2k(N_m)g(N_m)} \tag{5.3.7}$$

We can use this formula to address sensitivity issues:

Suppose λ changes. Examining (5.3.5) and (5.3.6), we see that the optimal partition $\mathbf{N}^*$ remains the same. Each term of C^- in (5.3.7) is proportional to $\sqrt{\lambda}$, so C^- itself is too. Thus, the effect of λ on the overall cost (as approximated by C^-) is the same as in the EOQ model.

Also, each $u^*(m)$ changes as $1/\sqrt{\lambda}$, so the (relaxed) relative order frequency $u^*(m)/u^*(\text{next}(m))$ is insensitive to λ. Consequently, $u^+(m)$ is approximately proportional to $1/\sqrt{\lambda}$, though not exactly. And while the true relative frequency $u^+(m)/u^+(\text{next}(m))$ may change with λ, the change is limited. (In fact, this ratio may go up or down by a factor of 2, but no more, and of course it always remains at least 1. See Problem 5.10.)

Similarly, cost-factor changes affect C^- as in the EOQ model, *provided* the k_j all change by a common multiple, and likewise the h_j. For instance, if $k_j = \kappa w_j$ and $h_j = \eta c_j$ as in Section 5.2, and κ and η change but not the w_j and c_j, then C^- is proportional to $\sqrt{\kappa\eta}$.

In this special case, moreover, one can easily construct an aggregate inventory-workload tradeoff curve, estimating wO and cI by their values in the relaxed problem. The optimal partition **N*** must be determined only once, since it is independent of κ and η. The tradeoff curve is precisely (5.2.4), the same form as in an independent-item model, with the aggregate system parameters redefined as follows: For any subset $M \subseteq N$ let

$$w(M) = \Sigma_{j \in M}\, w_j$$

$$c(M) = \Sigma_{j \in M}\, c_j$$

Then redefine

$$c\lambda = \Sigma_m\, c(N_m)\lambda = (\Sigma_j\, c_j)\lambda$$

$$w = \Sigma_m \left[\frac{c(N_m)\lambda}{c\lambda}\right] w(N_m)$$

$$J_* = \frac{(\Sigma_m \sqrt{w(N_m)c(N_m)\lambda})^2}{wc\lambda}$$

Problem 5.11 asks you to verify these formulas. Also, the optimal cost C^- can be written in terms of these parameters, as in (5.2.6). (The index J_* here characterizes effective variety among the *clusters* of the optimal partition. This is related to dispersion among the original items, but indirectly.)

Also, let C^{--} denote the optimal cost, omitting the constraints of the relaxed problem and optimizing each item separately. Obviously, $C^- \geq C^{--}$. They are equal when the ratios $\pi(\{j\}) = k_j/g_j$ are nonincreasing. Thus, C^- is forced above C^{--} only when a downstream stage has a larger ratio than an upstream stage.

This observation suggests a crude but useful guideline for fixed-cost (or order-workload or setup-time) reduction efforts: Focus attention on downstream stages. While reductions anywhere are welcome, downstream fixed costs have the greatest system-wide performance effects.

EXAMPLE 5.3.A, PART 4

Recall that all $g_j = 1$, so $\pi(\{j\}) = k_j$. In this case,

$$C^{--} = (2\cdot4\cdot1)^{1/2} + (2\cdot8\cdot1)^{1/2} + (2\cdot2\cdot1)^{1/2} + (2\cdot2\cdot1)^{1/2} \approx 10.828$$

$C^- \approx 10.928$ is larger, because $k_2 = 8$ is more than $k_1 = 4$. (The k_j further downstream are both 2, i.e., less.) So, focusing on the first two stages, k_2 is more critical than k_1.

Performance evaluation is important also in the context of *system design.* In logistics, typically, we have some choice over the number and placement of stocking points. In a production setting there may be several alternative processes, and numerous alternative ways to combine basic operations into stages. To compare alternative designs, of course, we should estimate their initial costs of construction, equipment, and the like. We should also estimate their ongoing operating costs, and for this purpose we can calculate C^- for each alternative.

5.3.8 Proofs

THEOREM 5.3.1. Every non-nested policy is dominated by a nested policy. (The nested policy has lower inventories and no more orders.)

PROOF. We prove the result for a two-stage system. (Problem 5.5 asks you to extend it to general J.) Consider a feasible, non-nested policy. Suppose in particular that, at time t, stage 1 orders but stage 2 does not. Let u be the earliest time after t when stage 2 does order. Thus, all stock arriving at stage 1 at time t must remain there at least until u. Now, consider an alternative policy, where the stage-1 order at t is postponed until u; otherwise (before t and after u), the new policy is identical to the old one. Clearly, $I_2'(s)$ is the same in both policies, but $I_1'(s)$ is lower in the new one, $t \leq s < u$, and the total numbers of orders at both stages remain the same. Thus, the new policy dominates the old one. Clearly, this construction can be repeated to eliminate all non-nested order times t.

THEOREM 5.3.2. Every non-zero-inventory policy is dominated by a zero-inventory policy.

PROOF. The basic idea here is the same as in Problem 3.1 and Theorem 4.3.1, but with an extra twist. Again, focus on the case $J = 2$; see Problem 5.6 for the general case.

Consider a non-zero-inventory policy. Let u be the earliest bad order time, i.e., a time when some item orders, yet has positive inventory. Choose j to be the *largest-numbered* such item. Let t be the previous time j orders. Construct a better policy: Postpone all or part of j's order at t until u. Specifically, reduce the order at t by as much as possible, i.e., the smaller of $I_j'(u^-)$ and the original order quantity at t, while increasing the order at u by the same amount. This new policy is clearly feasible. The number of orders for item j is no more than before, and the other item's orders are unaffected. Also, $I_i(s)$ is the same as before for $i \neq j$, but $I_j(s)$ is less, $t \leq s < u$. Outside this time interval nothing changes. So, the new policy dominates the original one. If $I_j'(u^-)$ remains positive, repeat this procedure until it is driven to zero.

Now, if $j = 1$, this process creates no new bad order times. If $j = 2$, however, it increases $I_1'(s)$ over certain intervals before u, and so may create some bad order times involving item 1. In this case, apply the same method to eliminate them.

At this point, the earliest bad order time, if any, comes after u. We can repeat this procedure as long as there are any bad order times, pushing the earliest one later and later, while improving the policy at each step.

THEOREM 5.3.3. The optimal cost C^- of the relaxed problem is a lower bound on the average cost of any feasible policy.

(We remarked in Section 5.3.3 that stationary-interval policies dominate all others. In view of the previous two theorems, then, we already know that this assertion is true. The following argument, however, uses only the nestedness and zero-inventory properties.)

PROOF. Consider any feasible, zero-inventory policy. Let $OF_j(t)$ denote the total number of orders for item j during the time interval $(0, t)$, and $C(t)$ the total cost. Thus,

$$C(t) = \Sigma_j\,[k_j OF_j(t) + h_j \textstyle\int_0^t I_j(s)\,ds]$$

Now, for each j, consider the integral here as a mathematical quantity, ignoring all the other items, constrained only by $I_j(s) \geq 0$ and the demand rate λ. *Given* $OF_j(t)$, this quantity is minimized by spacing the orders out equally over $(0, t)$ (as in Problem 3.2), in which case $\int_0^t I_j(s)\,ds = ½\lambda[t/OF_j(t)]t$. Thus,

$$C(t) \geq \Sigma_j\,[k_j OF_j(t) + \frac{1}{2}g_j\left[\frac{t}{OF_j(t)}\right]t]$$

Equivalently, *defining* $u_j = t/OF_j(t)$,

$$C(t) \geq t\cdot\Sigma_j\left[\frac{k_j}{u_j} + \frac{1}{2}g_j u_j\right] = tC(\mathbf{u})$$

By Theorem 5.3.1 we can assume the policy is nested, so $OF_j(t) \leq OF_{j+1}(t)$ or $u_j \geq u_{j+1}$. That is, $\mathbf{u}$ is feasible in the relaxed problem, so $C(u) \geq C^-$. Consequently, $C(t)/t \geq C^-$: The average cost *over any finite time t* is bounded below by C^-. Surely, this inequality holds too when $t \to \infty$.

THEOREM 5.3.4. Conditions (5.3.5) and (5.3.6) on a partition $\mathbf{N}$ are necessary and sufficient for the solution $\mathbf{u}$ given by (5.3.4) to be optimal in the relaxed problem (5.3.3).

PROOF.

Necessity. Fix $A_=$ and $\mathbf{N}$, and let $\mathbf{u}^-$ be the solution to (5.3.3[$A_=$]), as given by (5.3.4). Equation (5.3.5) is necessary for feasibility. Assume it holds. Indeed, assume the inequalities (5.3.5) are all strict. (If not, one can construct an equivalent partition with strict inequalities, as remarked in Section 5.3.4 after Theorem 5.3.4.) Now, suppose some cut (N_m^-, N_m^+) violates (5.3.6). Construct a new partition $\mathbf{N}'$ by splitting N_m into the two clusters N_m^- and N_m^+, let $\mathbf{u}'$ be the corresponding solution (5.3.4), and set $\mathbf{u}^\gamma = \gamma\mathbf{u}' + (1-\gamma)\mathbf{u}^-$, $0 < \gamma < 1$. For sufficiently small γ, $\mathbf{u}^\gamma$ is feasible for the relaxed problem. (The u_j^γ are equal within each cluster of $\mathbf{N}'$, (5.3.5) holds strictly for $\mathbf{N}$, and $\pi(N_m^-) > \pi(N_m^+)$.) Also, $C(\mathbf{u}') < C(\mathbf{u}^-)$, so $C(\mathbf{u}^\gamma) < C(\mathbf{u}^-)$, $0 < \gamma < 1$. (This follows from the strict convexity of C.) That is, $\mathbf{u}^-$ cannot be optimal for the relaxed problem.

Sufficiency. Suppose $A_=$ and **N** satisfy (5.3.5) and (5.3.6). Consider the special case $A_= = A$, so there is only one cluster, N itself. Here, (5.3.5) is vacuous, and (5.3.6) says that, for every cut (N^-, N^+) of N, $\pi(N^-) \le \pi(N^+)$. Assume to the contrary that $\mathbf{u}^* \ne \mathbf{u}^-$ solves the relaxed problem. Defining $A_=^* = \{j \in A : u_j^* = u_{j+1}^*\}$, as above, $\mathbf{u}^*$ also solves (5.3.3[$A_=^*$]). The corresponding partition $\mathbf{N}^* = \{N_m^*\}$ satisfies (5.3.5) (since $\mathbf{u}^*$ is feasible for the relaxed problem), and at least one of those inequalities is strict (otherwise $\mathbf{u}^* = \mathbf{u}^-$), say $\pi(N_n^*) > \pi(N_{\text{next}(n)}^*)$. Set $N^- = \{j : j \le n\}$ and $N^+ = \{j : j > n\}$. Now, $\pi(N^-)$ is a weighted average of the $\pi(N_m^*)$, $m \le n$, using weights $g(N_m^*)/g(N^-)$, and similarly $\pi(N^+)$ is a weighted average of the $\pi(N_m^*)$, $m > n$. Moreover, all the $\pi(N_m^*)$ in $\pi(N^-)$ are strictly greater than those in $\pi(N^+)$, and so $\pi(N^-) > \pi(N^+)$. This contradicts (5.3.6), so $\mathbf{u}^* = \mathbf{u}^-$.

Turn to the general case $A_= \subseteq A$. By (5.3.5), $\mathbf{u}^-$ is feasible for the relaxed problem, so $C(\mathbf{u}^-) \ge C^-$. Consider the problem

$$\begin{aligned} &\text{Minimize} \quad C(\mathbf{u}) \\ &\text{subject to} \quad u_j \ge u_{j+1} \qquad j \in A_= \end{aligned} \tag{5.3.8}$$

This problem relaxes the constraints of both (5.3.3) and (5.3.3[$A_=$]). It suffices to show that $\mathbf{u}^-$ solves (5.3.8), for then $C(\mathbf{u}^-) \le C^-$, so $C(\mathbf{u}^-) = C^-$. But (5.3.8), like (5.3.3[$A_=$]), separates into several independent subproblems, one for each cluster N_m. Each subproblem, moreover, is a smaller version of the relaxed problem (5.3.3). Applying the argument above (for the special case $A_= = A$), we see that the optimal partition for N_m's subproblem has a single subcluster, N_m itself, and the optimal solution is the subvector $(u_j^-)_{j \in Nm}$. Thus, $\mathbf{u}^-$ solves (5.3.8).

THEOREM 5.3.5. Algorithm Series_Relaxed determines an optimal partition, and so the corresponding solution (5.3.4) solves the relaxed problem.

PROOF. It suffices to show that the algorithm concavifies the function illustrated in Figure 5.3.6. We argue, by induction on j, that step j concavifies the first j points. The result is true for $j = 1$. (Since prev(1) = 0, step 1 leaves $N_1 = \{1\}$.) Suppose it is true for $j - 1$. During step j, N_j is reset until either prev(j) = 0 or $\pi(N_{\text{prev}(j)}) > \pi(N_j)$. At that moment, the slopes $\pi(N_m)$ for $m \le j$ are decreasing, so the function is concave up to point j. Also, each time N_j is reset, two line segments are replaced by a single segment lying on or above both of them. So, all points remain on or below the curve.

THEOREM 5.3.6. $C^+ \le \epsilon(\sqrt{2})C^-$.

PROOF. Given an optimal partition $\mathbf{N}^*$, $C_m[u^*(m)] = [2k(N_m)g(N_m)]^{1/2}$. By equation (3.2.5) in Chapter 3,

$$C_m[u^+(m)] = \epsilon\left[\frac{u^+(m)}{u^*(m)}\right] \cdot [2k(N_m)g(N_m)]^{1/2}$$

Now, the definition of $n(m)$ implies

$$-\tfrac{1}{2} \le n(m) + \log_2(\underline{u}) - \log_2(u^*(m)) < +\tfrac{1}{2}$$

or

$$2^{-1/2} \leq \frac{u^+(m)}{u^*(m)} < 2^{+1/2}$$

For x within this interval, the largest value of $\epsilon(x)$ occurs at $x = 2^{+1/2} = \sqrt{2}$. Consequently,

$$C_m[u^+(m)] \leq \epsilon(\sqrt{2}) \cdot [2k(N_m)g(N_m)]^{1/2}$$

Summing these inequalities over m yields the result.

THEOREM 5.3.7.

$$C^{+*} \leq \left[\frac{1}{\ln(2)\sqrt{2}}\right] C^-$$

PROOF. The quantity C^{+*} is the minimal value of $C^+(\underline{u})$ over the interval [1, 2). Certainly, any weighted average of $C^+(\underline{u})$ over this interval is an upper bound on C^{+*}. Define the function

$$f(\underline{u}) = \frac{1}{\ln(2) \cdot \underline{u}}$$

It is not hard to check that this is a probability density function over [1, 2). So,

$$C^{+*} \leq \textstyle\int_1^2 f(\underline{u}) C^+(\underline{u})\, d\underline{u}.$$

Write $C^+(\underline{u}) = \Sigma_m C_m^+(\underline{u})$, where $C_m^+(\underline{u})$ is the quantity $C_m[u^+(m)]$, now expressed as a function of $\underline{u}$. Thus,

$$C^{+*} \leq \Sigma_m \textstyle\int_1^2 f(\underline{u}) C_m^+(\underline{u}) d\underline{u}$$

$$= \Sigma_m [2k(N_m)g(N_m)]^{1/2} \textstyle\int_1^2 f(\underline{u}) \epsilon\left[\frac{u^+(m)}{u^*(m)}\right] d\underline{u}$$

We now evaluate this integral for each m. (We skip some details; Problem 5.9 asks you to supply them.) Let

$$\nu(m) = \text{fractional part of } [\log_2 (u^*(m)) - \tfrac{1}{2}]$$

$$\chi(m) = 2^{\nu(m)}$$

Then, $\chi(m)$ is the breakpoint in [1, 2) of $u^+(m)$. Indeed,

$$u^+(m) = \begin{cases} u^*(m)\left[\frac{2^{+1/2}}{\chi(m)}\right]\underline{u} & 1 \leq \underline{u} < \chi(m) \\ u^*(m)\left[\frac{2^{-1/2}}{\chi(m)}\right]\underline{u} & \chi(m) \leq \underline{u} < 2 \end{cases}$$

Thus,

$$\textstyle\int_1^2 f(\underline{u})\, \epsilon\left[\frac{u^+(m)}{u^*(m)}\right] d\underline{u} =$$

$$\left[\frac{1}{\ln(2)}\right] \cdot \left\{\int_1^{\chi(m)} \epsilon\left(\left[\frac{2^{+1/2}}{\chi(m)}\right]\underline{u}\right)\left(\frac{d\underline{u}}{\underline{u}}\right) + \int_{\chi(m)}^{2} \epsilon\left(\left[\frac{2^{-1/2}}{\chi(m)}\right]\underline{u}\right)\left(\frac{d\underline{u}}{\underline{u}}\right)\right\}$$

Change variables in the two integrals; use $x = [2^{+1/2}/\chi(m)]\underline{u}$ in the first, and $x = [2^{-1/2}/\chi(m)]\underline{u}$ in the second. The sum of the two (the expression in braces) then reduces to

$$\int_{2^{-1/2}}^{2^{+1/2}} \left[\frac{\epsilon(x)}{x}\right] dx = \frac{1}{\sqrt{2}}$$

The overall integral thus equals $1/[\ln(2)\sqrt{2}]$.

Substituting this value above yields

$$C^{+*} \le \Sigma_m [2k(N_m)g(N_m)]^{1/2}\left[\frac{1}{\ln(2)\sqrt{2}}\right]$$

$$= \left[\frac{1}{\ln(2)\sqrt{2}}\right] C^{-}$$

5.4 Tree Systems

5.4.1 Network Structure

Next, consider a tree system. Wonderfully, the overall approach of the last section for series systems works here too. Some adjustments are needed, mainly in setting up and solving the relaxed problem, but the central ideas remain valid.

Actually, the approach works even for fully general systems, but only under a severe restriction involving leadtimes, as explained below. Also, the notation and analysis become more complex in the general case. For these reasons we focus on tree systems.

Let us formalize the network expressing the system's structure: It is a directed graph, specified by the pair of sets (N, A). The *nodes* N represent the items; $J = |N|$ is the number of items. The *arcs* A describe the supply-demand or input-output relations. An arc from i to j, denoted $(i, j) \in A$, means that some of item i is used to produce or supply item j. (If there are several i with $(i, j) \in A$, then *all* the inputs i are required for item j.)

This graph is connected but acyclic; no group of items is independent of the others, and no item is used, directly or indirectly, to produce itself. We can (and do) number the items so that $i < j$ whenever $(i, j) \in A$. If $(i, j) \in A$, we say i is an (immediate) *predecessor* of j, and j is a *successor* of i. Define

$Pre(j)$ = set of predecessors of j
$Suc(i)$ = set of successors of i

These sets list each item's immediate inputs and outputs. A *start item* is one with no predecessor, and an *end item* is one with no successor. Only start items receive supplies from outside the system; in a production setting they represent the raw materials. Only end items have exogenous demands.

In these terms an *assembly system* has one end item J, and each $i < J$ has only one successor. An item may have several predecessors, however (unlike a series system). A *distribution system,* conversely, has one start item 1, and each $j > 1$ has only one predecessor. An item may have several successors. The official definition of a *tree system* is a bit more intricate: Ignoring the directions of the arcs for the moment, the undirected network has no circuits; in other words, there is a unique (undirected) path connecting any two nodes. Provided this condition holds, an item may have several predecessors and successors. In all these cases the number of arcs is precisely $|A| = |N| - 1 = J - 1$.

The cost factors k_j and h'_j have the same meaning as in a series system, as do the local inventories $I'_j(t)$. Also, let

$$\lambda'_j = \text{demand rate for item } j$$

Only an end item may have $\lambda'_j > 0$. (This is no real restriction. If some non-end item does have $\lambda'_j > 0$, add a new item j'' to the network with $(j, j'') \in A$, $k_{j''} = 0$, $h'_{j''} = h'_j$, and $\lambda'_{j''} = \lambda'_j$, and reset $\lambda'_j = 0$. Usually, every end item has $\lambda'_j > 0$, but this is not strictly necessary; see Section 5.4.7.)

5.4.2 Leadtimes and Quantity Units

Each arc (i, j) has an associated leadtime L'_{ij}. Also, each start item j has order leadtime L'_j. These are non-negative constants. The corresponding *zero-leadtime system* has the same data, except all L'_{ij} and L'_j are 0.

Consider some item j with several predecessors. The L'_{ij} may include item-specific transportation times as well as assembly time, so in general the L'_{ij} need not be equal over i. Now, for a batch of j to be finished and available at time t, a corresponding batch of item i must be released at time $t - L'_{ij}$ from every $i \in Pre(j)$. It makes no sense to speak of *placing* an order for item j at a certain time if these L'_{ij} are different. Rather, the key events are now the departure and arrival times of batches on specific arcs. The inventory $I'_j(t)$ depends on all arrivals to and departures from j.

Later, we shall assume the L'_{ij} and L'_j are zero. But, suppose some are really positive. Is this system equivalent to the corresponding zero-leadtime one? The answer, fortunately, is yes for tree systems, but not otherwise.

For an *assembly system*, the transformation is essentially the same as for a series system: Let $\underline{L}_i^-$ be the sum of the arc leadtimes along the path from i to J. (In a series system this is the forward echelon leadtime. Note, $\underline{L}_J^- = 0$.) Starting with a policy for the zero-leadtime system, shift each order event (arrival or departure) at i back in time by $\underline{L}_i^-$, to obtain an equivalent policy for the real system. For example, suppose that $\underline{L}_3^- = 15$, and in the zero-leadtime system an order of item 3 arrives at time $t = 122$. In the real system, that order arrives at time $122 - 15 = 107$.

To visualize this transformation, draw the network as in Figure 5.4.1. Here, each arc (i, j) is drawn horizontally with length proportional to L'_{ij}, so $\underline{L}_i^-$ is just the horizontal distance from i to J. Suppose some event affects the zero-leadtime system at time t. To determine the appropriate shift, imagine placing a copy of the network on the time axis so that item J lines up with t. Then, if the event affects item i, find the location of i on the graph, and schedule the event at that time, namely at $t - \underline{L}_i^-$. In the example above, putting node 5 at $t = 122$, node 3 appears at time 107.

Incidentally, this sort of drawing is used in project scheduling, and it is interesting to interpret the network in that context. Forget about demands and inventories for the mo-

FIGURE 5.4.1

Assembly system with leadtimes.

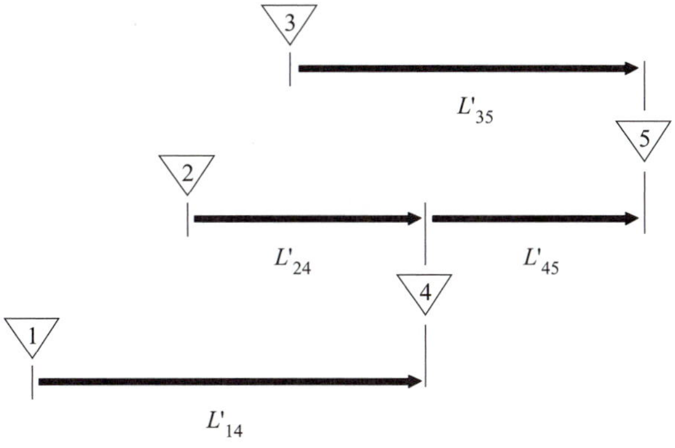

ment. The "project" is the creation of one isolated unit of the end product, item $J = 5$. The arcs represent activities that must be performed to complete this project, and the L'_{ij} are their durations. Of course, there are additional activities corresponding to the L'_j, but ignore them for now. Some activities can be performed simultaneously, but certain activities require others to be completed first; the structure of the network captures such precedence relations. Evidently, Figure 5.4.1 depicts a feasible schedule for the entire project.

We can draw a *distribution system* in the same way. See Figure 5.4.2. Let L_j^- be the sum of the arc leadtimes along the path from 1 to j. Renumber the items, if necessary, so that item J has the longest such L_j^-, and set $\underline{L}_j = L_J^- - L_j^-$. (In the figure, $J = 6$.) Thus, $\underline{L}_j$ is the horizontal distance from node j to J in Figure 5.4.2. Again, shift the events affecting item j back in time by $\underline{L}_j$.

The same idea applies to a *tree system,* as illustrated in Figure 5.4.3. The procedure for drawing the diagram and calculating the time shifts is a bit more intricate in this case, but the concept is clear from the figure.

This approach does not work for a *general system.* Figure 5.4.4 illustrates what goes wrong. There are two paths from 1 to 5, and their total leadtimes are different; the dashed line indicates the discrepancy. (This discrepancy is analogous to slack time in project scheduling.) We can construct a feasible policy by using the longest path leadtime, ignoring arc (1, 3). But then each batch intended for node 3 must sit at node 1, accumulating cost, for the discrepancy interval. The real holding cost is thus more than the zero-leadtime system's. Moreover, it is not clear how to transform a feasible policy for the real system into one for the zero-leadtime system.

Only under a very special condition, called *leadtime balance,* do we avoid such dilemmas. In the example of Figure 5.4.4 this means $L'_{13} + L'_{35} = L'_{14} + L'_{45}$. Larger networks typically require many more such identities. This condition rarely holds in practice.

In truth, we do not yet clearly understand how to coordinate the operations of non-tree systems. Tree systems are fundamentally simpler in this respect.

Next, consider the issue of quantity units. The set *Pre* (j) identifies *which* items are used to make a unit of j, but not *how much.* It is possible to transform any tree system,

FIGURE 5.4.2

Distribution system with leadtimes.

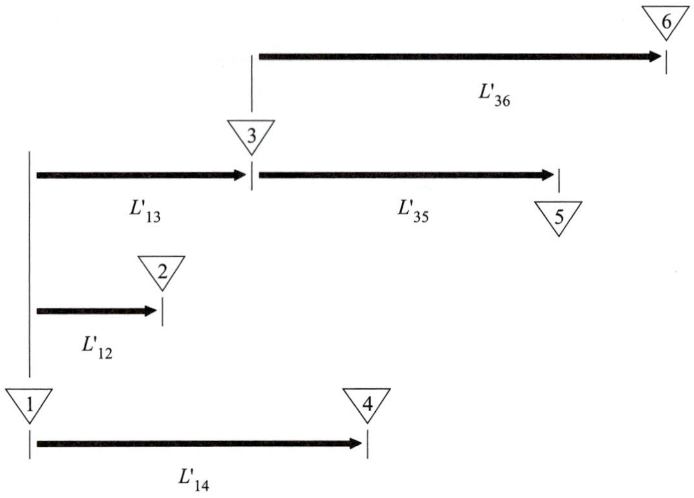

FIGURE 5.4.3

Tree system with leadtimes.

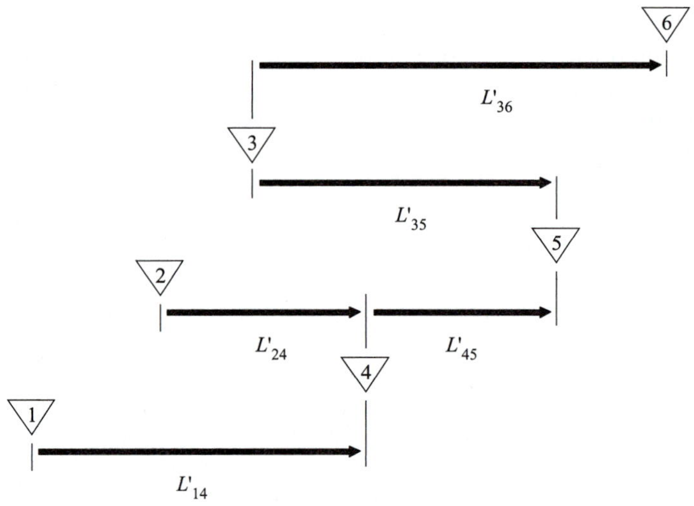

so that every j requires precisely one unit of each $i \in Pre(j)$, as in a series system. The basic idea is similar to the leadtime transformation above: Choose item J as a reference point or anchor. Then, follow each (undirected) path leading from J, successively revising the quantity units of the items encountered along the way, until they are all consistent with one-for-one usage. Of course, the h'_j and λ'_j must be revised accordingly. In

FIGURE 5.4.4

General system with leadtimes.

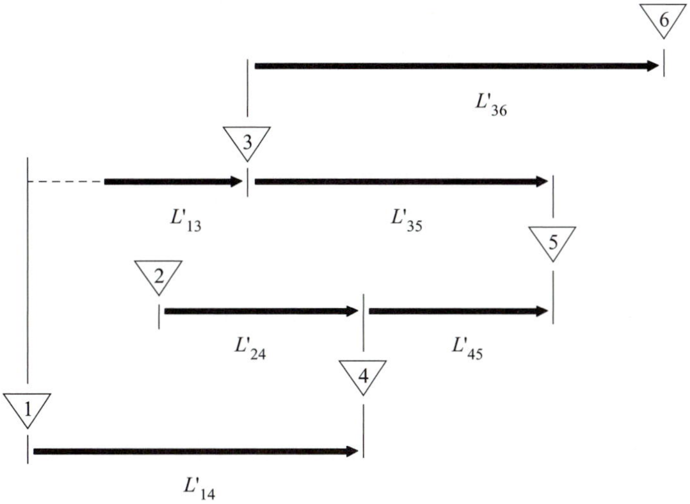

an assembly system, this means that all items are measured in terms of their usage in the end product. (A *general system* cannot be simplified in this manner, again because of multiple paths between items. The model must include input usages explicitly. Apart from the extra notation required, however, this is not a serious difficulty like the leadtime-balance issue.)

From now on assume all L'_{ij} and L'_j are zero, and every input requirement is one.

5.4.3 Echelons and Echelon Inventories

Echelon *i* comprises item *i* itself, its successors, *their* successors, and so on. That is, echelon *i* includes *i* and all subsequent items which use *i* as input, directly or indirectly.

The echelon inventory of item *i* is all the inventory in echelon *i,* and its echelon demand rate is the total demand over items in echelon *i.* These quantities can be computed recursively, starting with the end items:

$$I_i(t) = I'_i(t) + \Sigma_{j \in Suc(i)} I_j(t)$$

$$\lambda_i = \lambda'_i + \Sigma_{j \in Suc(i)} \lambda_j$$

The echelon holding cost is

$$h_j = h'_j - \Sigma_{i \in Pre(j)} h'_i$$

In an assembly system, for example, echelon *i* comprises the items along the path from *i* to *J,* each λ_i is just $\lambda_J = \lambda$, and, if *j* is the (unique) element of *Suc*(*i*),

$$I_i(\mathrm{t}) = I'_i(\mathrm{t}) + I_j(t)$$

As in Section 5.3, these echelon-level quantities are simpler than local ones. Again, $I_j(t)$ declines at a constant rate, now λ_j, except at order epochs, when it jumps up by the order quantity. Also, the total holding-cost rate at time t is again $\Sigma_j h'_j I'_j(t) = \Sigma_j h_j I_j(t)$.

5.4.4 Policy Characteristics

Zero-inventory policies continue to dominate others. (The proof of Theorem 5.3.2 continues to hold nearly as is; only modest technical formalities must be added.) On the other hand, *stationary-interval policies* are not necessarily dominant. Still, they are convenient, and, as shown below, they do perform well.

A *nested policy* is one where an order for item i triggers an order for each of its successors, and hence throughout echelon i. In an assembly system, nested policies dominate others, as in a series system. (The proof of Theorem 5.3.1, with minor adaptations, still applies.) Otherwise, nested policies need not be dominant. For example, consider the simple distribution system shown in Figure 5.4.5, where a warehouse (item 1) supplies two retailers (items 2 and 3). Suppose $\lambda_2 = \lambda_3$, all the h_j are equal, $k_1 = k_2$, but k_3 is much larger than k_1 and k_2. It makes sense to order items 1 and 2 relatively often, but item 3 less frequently. (Since item 1 sometimes orders when 3 does not, such a policy is not nested.) Under a nested policy the system either incurs the cost k_3 too often or carries too much inventory (at 1 or 2) to supply stage 2.

Nevertheless, some situations require a nested policy, not because it is less costly as measured by the model, but rather because it is easier to implement. If so, we say the *system* is nested. This distinction is unnecessary, of course, for an assembly system. For now, we focus on *nested tree systems* only. (Section 5.4.7 describes the adjustments required to deal with non-nested systems.)

Consider a policy with all three properties. Redefine

$$g_j = h_j \lambda_j$$

Then, the average cost of policy $\mathbf{u}$ is precisely (5.3.1); that is,

$$C(\mathbf{u}) = \Sigma_j \left[\frac{k_j}{u_j} + \frac{1}{2} g_j u_j \right]$$

FIGURE 5.4.5

Simple distribution system.

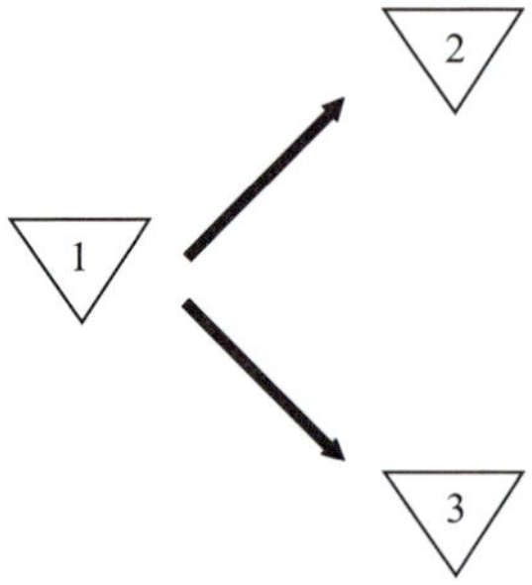

The problem of choosing the best such policy, analogous to (5.3.2), becomes

$$\begin{aligned} &\text{Minimize} && C(\mathbf{u}) \\ &\text{subject to} && u_i = \xi_{ij} u_j \\ & && \xi_{ij} = \text{a positive integer} \qquad (i, j) \in A \end{aligned}$$

5.4.5 The Relaxed Problem

The *relaxed problem,* analogous to (5.3.3), is the following:

$$\begin{aligned} C^- = \text{minimize} \quad & C(\mathbf{u}) \\ \text{subject to} \quad & u_i \geq u_j \qquad (i, j) \in A \end{aligned} \tag{5.4.1}$$

As in Theorem 5.3.3, C^- is a lower bound on the cost of any (nested) policy. Let $A_=$ be any subset of $A,$ and define the problem

$$\begin{aligned} \text{Minimize} \quad & C(\mathbf{u}) \\ \text{subject to} \quad & u_i = u_j \qquad (i, j) \in A_= \end{aligned} \tag{5.4.1[$A_=$]}$$

As in Section 5.3.4, the principal idea is to identify the "right" subset, $A_=^*$; the solution to (5.4.1[$A_=^*$]) also solves (5.4.1) itself.

Again, any subset $A_=$ determines a partition **N** of N: Remove all the arcs in the network *except* those in $A_=$. The result is a collection of connected subnetworks. The nodes in each subnetwork form a cluster N_m. (As for a series system, we can set the index m to the largest item-number in the cluster, but this is not essential.) Let A_m denote the arcs connecting them. Figure 5.4.6 illustrates this idea. Notice that each subnetwork (N_m, A_m) is itself a tree system. (If the original network is an assembly system, then so is each subnetwork, and likewise for distribution systems.) Also, the clusters form a *cluster network:* The nodes $\underline{N}$ are the cluster indices $m,$ and the arcs $\underline{A}$ are pairs (m, n) such that $(i, j) \in A$ for *some* $i \in N_m$ and $j \in N_n$. (These (i, j) are precisely $A \backslash A_=$. For each cluster-arc $(m, n) \in \underline{A}$, there is a unique original arc (i, j) connecting N_m and N_n.) The cluster network too is a tree system.

The solution to (5.4.1[$A_=$]) is precisely (5.3.4), i.e.,

$$\begin{aligned} u(m) &= [2\pi(N_m)]^{1/2} \qquad && m \in \underline{N} \\ u_j &= u(m) && j \in N_m \end{aligned}$$

The feasibility condition, the analogue of (5.3.5), is

$$\pi(N_m) \geq \pi(N_n) \qquad (m, n) \in \underline{A} \tag{5.4.2}$$

To cut a cluster, just remove some arc in the corresponding subnetwork; equivalently, remove an arc (i, j) from $A_=$. This breaks the cluster N_m containing i and j into the pair (N_m^-, N_m^+), where (i, j) points from N_m^- to N_m^+. The optimality condition requires that (5.3.6) hold for all such cuts, i.e.,

$$\pi(N_m^-) \leq \pi(N_m^+) \tag{5.4.3}$$

FIGURE 5.4.6

Clusters.

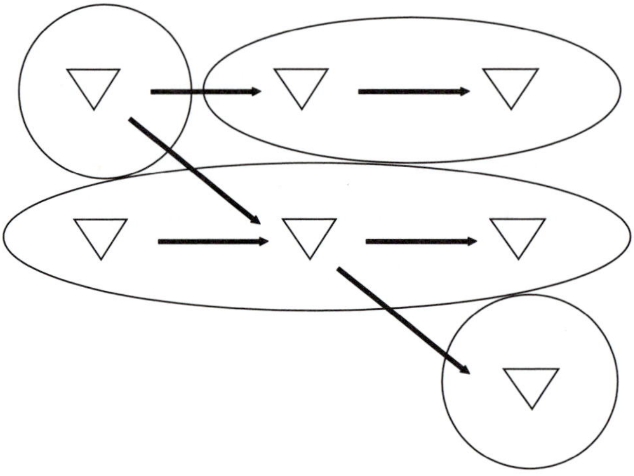

As in Theorem 5.3.4, these two conditions are necessary and sufficient for the corresponding solution to be optimal for (5.4.1).

Here is a useful way to express the optimality condition: Define

$$\gamma(N_m^-, N_m^+) = \frac{k(N_m^+)}{\pi(N_m)} - g(N_m^+)$$

$\gamma(N_m^-, N_m^+)$ is called the *net capacity* of the cut (N_m^-, N_m^+). A bit of algebra shows that (5.4.3) is equivalent to $\gamma(N_m^-, N_m^+) \geq 0$.

There are several ways to determine an optimal partition. Here is one: It starts with all items grouped into a single cluster, i.e., $\mathbf{N} = \{N\}$, and successively cuts it into smaller ones, using cuts that violate (5.4.3). Let M denote any possible cluster and B the arcs connecting its items, so (M, B) is a subtree of (N, A). The method uses a recursive procedure that takes any (M, B) as input.

Procedure Tree_Relaxed(*M, B*)

If $|M| = 1$ (i.e., $B = \emptyset$),

Set $\gamma^* = 0$ and STOP.

Else,

For each arc in B, compute $\gamma(M^-, M^+)$ for the corresponding cut (M^-, M^+).

Set $\gamma^* = \gamma(M_*^-, M_*^+) = \min\{\gamma(M^-, M^+)\}$.

If $\gamma^* < 0$,

Call **Procedure Tree_Relaxed**(M_*^-, B_*^-)

(where B_*^- is the subset of arcs connecting M_*^-).

Call **Procedure Tree_Relaxed**(M_*^+, B_*^+)

(where B_*^+ is the subset of arcs connecting M_*^+).

The overall algorithm just invokes this procedure once with $(M, B) = (N, A)$. The final partition **N*** consists of clusters M with $\gamma^* \geq 0$, and so it does satisfy the optimality condition (5.4.3). The procedure uses the minimal-capacity cut (M_*^-, M_*^+) in order to maintain the feasibility condition (5.4.2). (This works, by an argument like the proof of Theorem 5.3.4.)

This algorithm is not quite as simple as Algorithm Series_Relaxed. There are simpler specialized methods for assembly and distribution systems. (Actually, there is a faster one for tree systems too, but it is harder to explain.)

5.4.6 Constructing a Feasible Policy

With the solution to the relaxed problem in hand, apply precisely the same round-off procedures as in Section 5.3 to construct a feasible policy. The error bounds of Theorems 5.3.6 and 5.3.7 remain valid.

We now have all the pieces of a complete approach to analyze nested systems. Because an assembly system is naturally nested, this approach is entirely sufficient for that case.

5.4.7 Non-Nested Systems

For a distribution system or more generally a tree system, however, unless there is some special reason to exclude non-nested policies, something more is needed. We illustrate the idea with the three-item distribution system of Figure 5.4.5.

Consider a zero-inventory, stationary-interval, but not necessarily nested policy. In the average-cost function $C(\mathbf{u})$ above, the order-cost terms are correct, as are the echelon holding costs for items 2 and 3, but the holding cost for item 1 is not. To calculate its holding cost correctly, we need to think carefully about the function of item-1 inventory:

Every unit of item 1 will be sent ultimately to either node 2 or node 3. Indeed, we can decide which units go where in advance, at the instant they arrive, and keep the inventory of item 1 in two separate stores, one destined for node 2 and the other for node 3. To keep track of these inventories, imagine that we split node 1 into two artificial nodes, labeled 12 and 13, as in Figure 5.4.7. All item-1 stock destined for node j is held at node $1j$, $j = 1, 2$. Call this the *expanded network.* (Node 1 is still there, but it has an entirely new role, explained below. Notice, the expanded network is a tree system.)

Even the shipments from the source to node 1 can be divided in this way. So now, conceptually, the source sends separate shipments to nodes 12 and 13. Since the rest of the policy uses stationary intervals, it makes sense that these shipments too occur at regular intervals, say u_{1j}.

It turns out that, in these terms, the policy should be nested. That is, a shipment to node $1j$ (i.e., a shipment of item 1 that includes units destined for node j) should trigger a shipment from $1j$ to j itself. (The argument is essentially the same as in Theorem 5.3.1.) So, u_{1j} is an integer multiple of u_j. Consequently, by the standard calculation for a nested system, the average echelon inventory of item $1j$ is $\bar{I}_{1j} = \frac{1}{2}\lambda_{1j}u_{1j} = \frac{1}{2}\lambda_j u_{1j}$. The original

FIGURE 5.4.7

Expanded network.

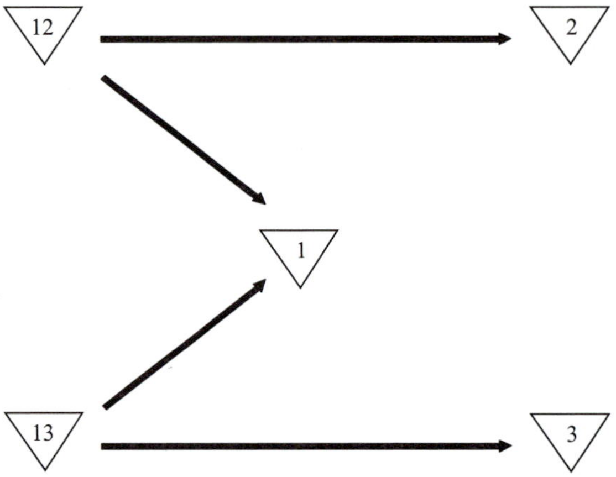

item 1's echelon inventory is the sum of these quantities, i.e., $\bar{I}_1 = \bar{I}_{12} + \bar{I}_{13} = ½(\lambda_2 u_{12} + \lambda_3 u_{13})$. (Problem 5.18 asks you to work out the details.) Thus, we can write the holding cost for item 1 as $½(g_{12}u_{12} + g_{13}u_{13})$, where

$$g_{1j} = h_{1j}\lambda_{1j} \qquad \lambda_{1j} = \lambda_j \qquad h_{1j} = h_1$$

This has the same form as the other holding-cost terms in $C(\mathbf{u})$.

As for the fixed cost, we incur k_1 when a shipment arrives at node 12 or node 13 or both. So, we cannot just set k_{1j} to k_1, for that would double-count the fixed cost when both nodes receive shipments. Instead, set $k_{1j} = 0$, but reintroduce node 1, as in Figure 5.4.7, with its original fixed cost k_1. Interpret the expanded network as a nested system. So, an order for 12 or 13 or both triggers an order for 1, and thus incurs the cost k_1, as required. Thus, the average fixed cost remains k_1/u_1. Also, set $\lambda_1 = 0$. (The λ_j and λ_{1j} above already account for the physical flows and holding costs.) Thus, the shipments to node 1 are only logical shipments of quantity zero.

In sum, the (nested) expanded network is entirely equivalent to the original system. Its costs correctly measure the true costs, even for a non-nested policy.

We are virtually done: Just apply the nested-system methods above, first to solve the relaxed problem, and then to round its solution. (What about the peculiar data? Do they create problems? Fortunately, the answer is no. For instance, if item 1 were isolated in its own cluster, since $g(\{1\}) = 0$, the ratio $\pi(\{1\})$ would be ill defined. It turns out that the algorithm never isolates item 1, so this problem never arises.) The result is a policy for the expanded system, which determines a policy for the original system. The error-bound theorems remain valid. So, once again, the policy performs well, and C^- accurately estimates the optimal cost.

This approach extends to any tree system. The key step is the construction of an expanded network, with new items corresponding to certain (directed) paths in the original network, so that a policy in the original system corresponds to a nested policy in the expanded network. Then, apply the nested-system methodology to this expanded network. (Unfortunately, the expanded network is not always a tree system; if not, its relaxed problem requires a somewhat more complex algorithm than Procedure Tree_Relaxed.)

The end result is a stationary-interval policy for the original system. If the policy happens to be non-nested, however, the order *quantities* need not be stationary. In the example above, suppose $u_2^+ = u_1^+$ and $u_3^+ = 2u_1^+$. Then, item 1's batch sizes alternate between $\lambda_2 u^+$ and $\lambda_2 u_2^+ + \lambda_3 u_3^+$. In general, the order quantities are periodic, though the pattern may be more intricate than simple alternation.

5.4.8 Coordination and Sensitivity Revisited

The basic principles of coordination here are thus the same as in a series system, described in Section 5.3.7: Synchronize the items within each cluster, partially synchronize across clusters, and use stationary intervals for all clusters.

Recall that, for a series system, a decentralized control mechanism coordinates the stages properly. The same idea, with minor variations, works here too. The simplest case is an assembly system. Each cluster itself looks like a small-scale assembly system with a single end item. Only this last item holds inventory. To communicate between clusters, we need only direct each cluster to order when necessary from all its predecessor clusters, and to send each outgoing order to the appropriate item in its successor cluster. Otherwise, each cluster operates its own EOQ-like policy.

A tree system is more complex, especially in the non-nested case, where the order quantities need not be stationary. Even so, it is possible to construct a fairly simple, locally controlled order rule that correctly implements the policy. (We omit the details.)

Let us turn to sensitivity analysis. Many of the results for series systems remain valid here. Assuming the cost factors are given by $k_j = \kappa w_j$ and $h_j = \eta c_j$, the optimal partition $\mathbf{N}^*$ is independent of κ and η. In this case we can construct an aggregate tradeoff curve, as in Section 5.3.7, and C^- is given by formula (5.3.7).

For an assembly system, $\mathbf{N}^*$ is also independent of the demand rate $\lambda_J = \lambda$, so C^- is again proportional to $\sqrt{\lambda}$. Otherwise, demand-rate changes have more intricate effects. If there are several positive λ'_j, and they change arbitrarily, $\mathbf{N}^*$ can indeed change; one must recompute C^- from scratch.

Suppose, however, that the λ'_j all change in the same proportions. That is, for some common factor λ and fixed base demand rates λ'_j, the λ'_j are determined through $\lambda_j^{0\prime} = \lambda\lambda_j^{0\prime}$. (For example, λ might be an index of general economic conditions.) Then, the echelon demand rates λ_j and the g_j are also proportional to λ, and therefore $\mathbf{N}^*$ is independent of λ, and C^- is proportional to $\sqrt{\lambda}$.

5.5 Coordinated Supply: Economies of Scope

5.5.1 The Joint-Replenishment Problem

Now consider systems whose items are linked through their supply processes. This section focuses on one type of supply link; the next section treats another type.

Imagine for now that the items represent several locations but only one product. This product is supplied by a sole source, from which all the locations must order. The locations could order separately, but it may be advantageous to pool their orders. This way, especially if the source is far away, we can consolidate the shipments over part of the distance and thus trim transportation costs. Likewise, we can centralize and simplify the administrative tasks of order processing. (And, if the supplier offers quantity discounts, joint purchasing exploits them better. This sort of scale economy is not the focus here, however.)

In multiproduct systems, joint replenishment offers similar advantages. When the products are all supplied by the same source, we can save transportation charges, as above. In any case it may be simpler to process occasional orders, each including many products, than frequent single-product orders. In addition, when ordering means production, we can sometimes pool setup operations.

In such situations the supply process offers *economies of scope.* Whereas scale economies enable us to order large *quantities* cheaply, economies of scope refer to a large *number* of diverse activities, in this case the orders for many items.

Here is a model that captures this notion in a simple way: The fixed order cost now consists of two components. There is an item-specific cost k_j, incurred by each order of item *j*, as before. In addition, there a cost k_0, incurred on ordering *any* item or combination of items. For instance, if we order item 1 alone, the total fixed cost is k_0+k_1. If we order items 1 and 2 together, the total is $k_0 + k_1 + k_2$ (not $2k_0 + k_1 + k_2$). In a production setting, k_0 is called a *major* setup cost, and the other k_j *minor* setup costs. (This wording suggests that k_0 is larger than the other k_j, but no such assumption is required.) This model is called *the joint-replenishment problem.* For the moment assume all leadtimes are zero. (We discuss positive leadtimes later on.)

To exploit the economies of scope to the fullest extent, we can choose to order all the items together. In this case every item uses the same order interval, say *u*. Define

$$k = k_0 + \Sigma_{j=1}^{J} k_j$$

$$g_j = h_j\lambda_j$$

$$g = \Sigma_{j=1}^{J} g_j$$

Given *u*, the overall average cost is $C(u) = k/u + \frac{1}{2}gu$. This is just the cost function of a single-item EOQ model! Thus, the best order interval u^* can be computed in the usual way.

This need not be the best approach, however. There are disadvantages to joint replenishment. By forcing all items to conform to a common order interval, we give up the flexibility to optimize each one individually. (If k_0 is tiny compared to the other k_j, clearly, joint ordering makes little sense.) A less rigid approach would be better, one which recognizes both the advantages and the disadvantages of synchronization.

One reasonable approach is to partition the items into groups. Each group contains similar items, as measured by the ratios k_j/g_j. Then, order each group's items together, as above, but manage each group independently of the others. This approach retains flexibility between groups, while exploiting economies of scope within groups. (It is not that hard to determine the best partition. Interestingly, the calculation is much like the algorithm for solving the DEL model of Chapter 4.)

This approach can miss clear cost-saving opportunities, however. For example, suppose that it constructs two groups, and the second group's order interval is precisely 2.01

times the first's. Hardly ever do the groups' orders coincide. But, consider the following revised policy: Adjust the order intervals so that the ratio becomes 2, and then alternate between ordering all items together and just those of the second group. This policy avoids paying k_0 to order the first group alone, while only slightly increasing other costs.

It would be nice to extend the approach to identify and evaluate such opportunities. As of now, however, it is unclear how to do this systematically.

Let us explore a different approach, closer in spirit to those of the last two sections. This method too partitions the items into groups, each with a common order interval, but it also synchronizes the groups in a controlled manner.

The key idea is to construct a distribution system that is equivalent to the joint-replenishment system. Then, we apply the techniques developed earlier to this distribution system. The resulting policy is thus guaranteed to perform well.

5.5.2 An Equivalent Distribution System

Reconsider for a moment the multilocation system above. The formulation of the fixed costs suggests a specific two-step transportation scenario: First, consolidated orders are shipped from the source to some central point at cost k_0. From there, each order is shipped separately to its designated location. The location-specific costs k_j are incurred during this second step.

Call this central point location 0. The overall system is essentially the two-level distribution system shown in Figure 5.5.1. Location 0 is special, however, in that it never holds inventory. (In practice, such a location is sometimes called a *break-bulk point* or a *trans-shipment center.*) This requirement forces the distribution system to follow an *antinested policy,* where location 0 orders precisely when one or more original locations order. Clearly, a multiproduct or a general multi-item system can be interpreted similarly as a special distribution system of this kind. The original data (λ_j, h_j, and k_j) continue to describe item $j > 0$. The new item 0 has demand rate $\lambda'_0 = 0$ and fixed cost k_0; since it never holds inventory, set $h_0 = h'_0 = 0$.

This antinested system can be analyzed in the same way as a nested system: Consider the mirror image of Figure 5.5.1 with all arcs reversed but the same h_j and λ_j. This is an assembly system, and it is equivalent to the original one. The original antinestedness condition translates into the usual nestedness property for the assembly system. So, just analyze this assembly system as above. This approach determines a policy whose cost is no more than 2% above optimal. If there are positive leadtimes in the original system, simply adjust the zero-leadtime solution for the distribution system in the usual way.

The optimal partition $\mathbf{N}^*$ happens to be especially simple in this case. Number the original items so that the ratios $\pi(\{j\}) = k_j/g_j$ are increasing in j. Then, for some index j^*, items $j \le j^*$ are clustered with item 0, and each item $j > j^*$ forms its own cluster. Knowing this, the algorithm for the relaxed problem can be streamlined: Let N_0 denote the large cluster including item 0. Starting with all items in one cluster ($N_0 = N$), first cut off item J, then $J - 1$, and so forth. Keep cutting as long as $\pi(N_0 \backslash \{j\}) < \pi(\{j\})$. Stop with $j^* = j$ the first time this condition fails. (Incidentally, this same procedure can be used to solve the relaxed problem for any two-stage assembly system.)

FIGURE 5.5.1

Equivalent distribution system.

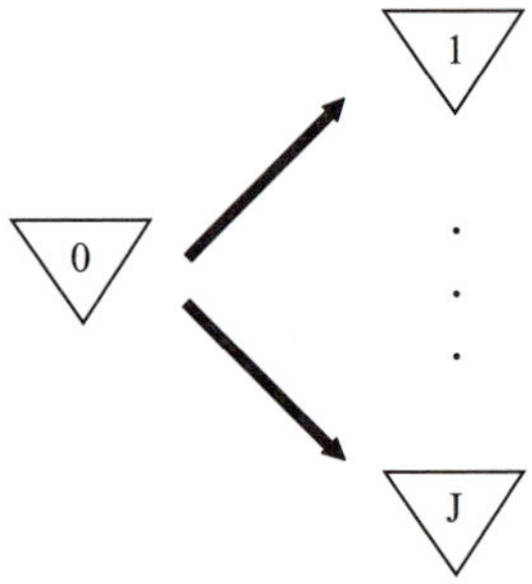

Following the round-off procedure, the final policy has a simple form: Items $j \le j^*$ order together, with order interval $u^+(0)$. The other items order less often, but always with the larger group, since their intervals are positive-integer multiples of $u^+(0)$.

5.5.3 Complex Economies of Scope

The joint-replenishment problem embodies the simplest form of economy of scope. Far more intricate forms are encountered in practice. For example, suppose the items represent products. There are several suppliers, each the sole source for a family of products. There are transportation economies of scope within each supplier's family, but not across suppliers. Also, the products have different physical characteristics; some are fragile, some refrigerated, some are both, and some neither. On receipt of an order, each type requires special handling, perhaps with special equipment; there are common setup activities for fragile items and other activities for refrigerated ones. Consequently, there are economies of scope over items of the same type. Each supplier's family may include fragile and nonfragile items, refrigerated and nonrefrigerated.

In such situations the fixed cost of an order has many components. For each supplier, there is a cost when any item or combination of items in its family is ordered; there is a cost to order one or more fragile items and a different cost for refrigerated items; there are item-specific costs as well. In general, the total fixed cost depends in a complex way on the *subset* of items included. That is, the fixed cost is some function $k(M)$, where M is any subset of items.

The approach above for the basic joint-replenishment problem can be extended to accommodate virtually any plausible fixed-cost function! That is, the problem can be solved by the methods developed earlier for supply-demand networks. (Which functions are plausible? The condition is a technical one: $k(M)$ must be increasing and submodular. If you don't know what that means, never mind; the example above does satisfy the condition. To deal with such $k(M)$, the techniques of Sections 5.3 and 5.4 must be revised somewhat, but the essential ideas remain the same, and the key results remain valid.)

Moreover, consider a system with supply-demand relationships *and* economies of scope. Examples include an assembly system whose raw materials (items with no predecessors) all come from a single source, and a tree system with certain products sharing setup operations. The same general approach applies even here! (Alas, we haven't room to cover the details.)

5.5.4 The Inventory-Routing Problem

Again consider a multilocation system: A single source supplies one product to several locations. The joint-replenishment problem corresponds to a two-step transportation scenario. Here is an alternative scenario:

There is a single vehicle, say a truck. When the locations place orders, the truck picks them up at the source and delivers them to their designated locations. The truck need not return to a central point between visits to successive locations. Rather, the truck follows some *route* among them. (Since the truck must return to the source for later orders, it may as well park at the source between deliveries. So, the route starts and ends at the source. For simplicity, imagine that the entire delivery process takes negligible time; that is, treat all leadtimes as zero. Also, ignore any limits on the truck's capacity.)

Suppose all locations use the same order interval u, and all order together. Thus, the route passes through all locations, including the source. To model the corresponding costs, define

$$k_{ij} = \text{travel cost from location } i \text{ to location } j$$

(The index 0 represents the source, so k_{0j} is the cost to travel from the source to location j, and k_{j0} is the travel cost in the opposite direction.) The total travel cost is the sum of the k_{ij} along the route.

There are many possible routes, and we want to design one of minimal total travel cost. This is a version of the *traveling salesman problem* (TSP), a celebrated problem in combinatorial optimization. It is difficult to find the true optimal solution, but there are effective heuristic methods. (See Lawler et al. [1985] for an overview.) Suppose we use some method, exact or approximate, to determine a solution, and let k denote its total cost.

Each order incurs the fixed cost k. Given the order interval u, therefore, the average total cost is precisely $C(u) = k/u + \frac{1}{2}gu$. The EOQ model yet again! To summarize, solve the TSP to determine a good route, use its cost k to formulate an EOQ model, and then solve the EOQ model to compute the best order interval u^*. *Assuming* all locations order together, this approach completely solves the problem.

However, as in the simple joint-replenishment problem, there may be good reasons not to force all locations to order at the same frequency. Here, though, it is more difficult to balance the pluses and minuses of synchronization.

The best approach to date is essentially the first one in Section 5.5.1 above: Partition the locations into groups, and operate each group independently of the others, using a common order interval for all locations in each group. Given a partition, determine each group's route and order interval as above. (Form the groups mainly by geography, grouping locations that are close together and so have small k_{ij}.)

Again, this approach can miss cost-saving opportunities, but these are less likely here. For suppose there are two groups with relative order frequency 2.01. It may be advantageous to synchronize them, as above, but only if they are geographically adjacent.

This approach has no simple performance guarantees like the theorems of Section 5.3. On the other hand, it performs well when the number of locations is large. (Technically speaking, it is "asymptotically optimal" as J grows.) Also, it has been extensively tested, and it seems to work well.

The same model describes a multiproduct system, where the setup costs depend on the production sequence. We explore a similar model in the next section.

5.6 Shared Production Capacity: Economic Lot Scheduling

5.6.1 *Average Resource Usage*

Now, suppose the items share a common production resource of limited capacity. Actually, there are several different ways to model shared production capacity. We begin with a simple one.

Reconsider the independent-item system of Section 5.2, where the EOQ model describes each item. Suppose the quantity wO now measures the aggregate average usage of a limited production resource. Further, suppose we can express the capacity limit as a bound on *average* usage. That is, we let wO denote the capacity itself:

$$\Sigma_j \, w_j\left(\frac{\lambda_j}{q_j}\right) \leq wO \tag{5.6.1}$$

The remaining problem is to minimize the aggregate inventory investment, cI. Clearly, the constraint (5.6.1) is always binding, so we can replace it by the equation

$$\Sigma_j \, w_j\left(\frac{\lambda_j}{q_j}\right) = wO$$

This problem is the reverse of problem (5.2.2), which minimizes wO subject to a constraint on cI. As discussed in that context, these two problems are essentially equivalent—they generate the same tradeoff curve. Moreover, this new problem, like (5.2.2), can be solved by selecting appropriate aggregate costs κ and η, using them to compute item costs k_j and h_j, and then solving a separate EOQ model for each item.

The same idea can be applied to supply/demand networks. Consider a series system. Orders for all stages draw on a common resource, constrained by (5.6.1) as above. Here is the approach in rough outline: Choose κ and η, form the k_j and h_j accordingly, and then solve the uncapacitated series system as in Section 5.3. Adjust κ and η, repeating this process until the constraint (5.6.1) is just barely satisfied.

5.6.2 *The Economic Lot Scheduling Problem (ELSP)*

For some purposes in some situations, it suffices to limit the average resource usage as above, ignoring the time pattern of usage. This is so, for instance, in preliminary system-design studies. Real capacities, however, impose more stringent constraints. The actual usage must respect capacity limits at every point in time.

Suppose the items are products, each described by the EOQ model with a finite production rate, as in Section 3.4. The production resource consists of a single machine,

FIGURE 5.6.1

Inventories in the ELSP.

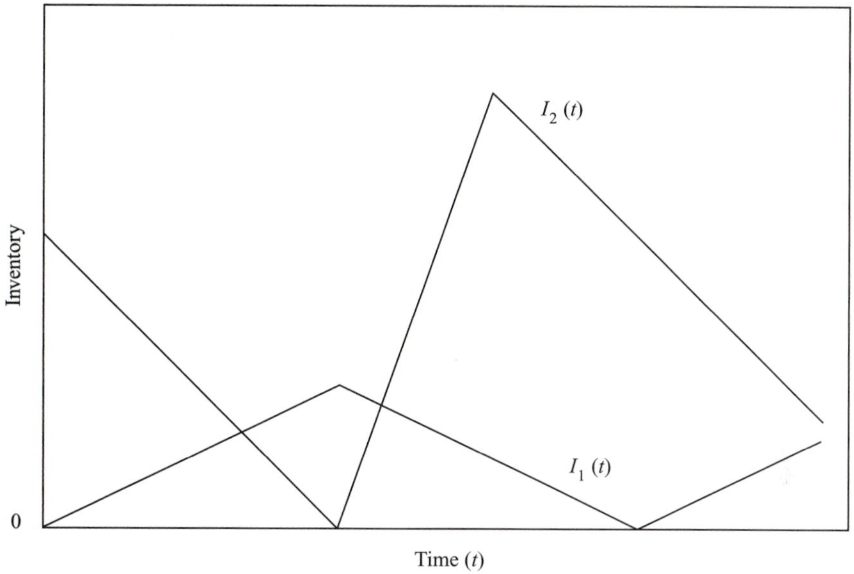

which can produce only *one product at a time.* Figure 5.6.1 describes one possible policy for a two-product system. The key point is that the production runs of the products (the intervals where their inventory curves increase) cannot overlap. (Assume that output can meet demand immediately as it emerges from the machine. The other case, where only full batches can be used, is no more difficult; see Problem 5.19.)

Let μ_j denote product j's production rate, and $\rho_j = \lambda_j/\mu_j$. Let $\rho = \Sigma_j \rho_j$, and assume $\rho < 1$. The fixed cost k_j represents the setup cost to begin a production run of product j. For now, assume that this cost depends only on j itself, not on which product was produced previously. There is no setup time. This model (and several of its variants) is called the *economic lot scheduling problem* (ELSP).

As in the joint-replenishment problem, we must coordinate the items, but for a different reason and in the opposite way: There, economies of scope favor ordering items at the same time. Here, the limited-capacity machine forces us to produce items at different times. In effect, there are extreme *diseconomies of scope.*

The simplest approach is a *cyclic schedule:* Produce the products in some fixed sequence, and repeat that same sequence over and over. Among cyclic schedules, the simplest type is a *rotation schedule,* where each product appears only once in the sequence. (For a two-product system, this means alternating production between the products.) Renumber the products so that they are sequenced in numerical order; i.e., the sequence is $\{1, \ldots, J\}$.

Under a rotation schedule, a *production cycle* is the time between successive starts of product 1's production runs. It is reasonable that all production cycles be equal, say to u. Thus, every product shares the common interval u between production starts. During each cycle, for each item j, as in Section 3.4, the machine must produce exactly $\lambda_j u$, so the run length is precisely $\rho_j u$, and the average inventory is $\bar{I}_j = \frac{1}{2}(1 - \rho_j)\lambda_j u$. The total production time over all products is ρu, and the machine is idle for time $(1 - \rho)u$. (This idle time can be inserted anywhere during the cycle.)

Define

$$k = \Sigma_{j=1}^{J} k_j$$

$$g_j = h_j(1 - \rho_j)\lambda_j$$

$$g = \Sigma_{j=1}^{J} g_j$$

The overall average cost is $C(u) = k/u + \frac{1}{2}gu$. Again, compute the optimal cycle time $u^* = (2k/g)^{1/2}$ as in the EOQ model! The end result is markedly similar to the simple common-cycle approach to the joint-replenishment problem, notwithstanding the radically different characters of the two problems.

The rotation-schedule approach certainly is simple, but as in the joint-replenishment problem, there are disadvantages to imposing a common cycle time on all products. Let $u_j^* = (2k_j/g_j)^{1/2}$ be the optimal cycle time for product j alone, ignoring the others. When the u_j^* are very different, the products' individual economics favor producing some more frequently than others.

EXAMPLE 5.6.A, PART 1

Consider a 3-product system:

j	k_j	λ_j	μ_j	h_j	ρ_j	g_j	u_j^*
1	9.61	1.0	5.0	2.500	0.2	2.0	3.1
2	69.62	1.5	5.0	3.810	0.3	4.0	5.9
3	19.84	0.4	2.0	3.125	0.2	1.0	6.3
	99.07				0.7	7.0	

Here, $u^* = (2 \cdot 99.07/7.0)^{1/2} \approx 5.32$. The cost of this solution is $C(u^*) \approx 37.24$.

Notice that u_2^* and u_3^* are nearly the same, but u_1^* is about half of those values. These data suggest producing product 1 twice as often as the others.

Unlike the joint-replenishment problem, the ELSP does *not* reduce to a simple network-type model. It appears to be fundamentally more difficult. There is a fairly simple heuristic. Here is the basic idea:

1. Compute the u_j^*.
2. Use the u_j^* within a rounding procedure like that of Section 5.3 to determine the products' *relative* production frequencies. That is, treat each product as its own cluster, compute the $u^+(j)$, set $u^{++} = \max_j \{u^+(j)\}$, and $\text{ROF}_j = u^{++}/u^+(j)$. Then, ROF_j is the relative frequency of product j.
3. Treat ROF_j as the number of times product j is produced within each cycle. Compute $k = \Sigma_j \text{ROF}_j k_j$ and $g = \Sigma_j g_j/\text{ROF}_j$, and solve the EOQ model above to yield u^*.

4. Construct a "good" sequence based on the relative frequencies.
5. Combine u^* with the sequence to yield a feasible cyclic schedule.

(The last two steps are quite intricate, in general, and we omit the details.) This heuristic seems to perform well. There is no performance guarantee, however.

EXAMPLE 5.6.A, PART 2

Applied to the example above, the heuristic works as follows:

1. The u_j^* are given in the table above.
2. Choose the base-period $\underline{u} = 3$. The rounding procedure yields $u^+(1) = 3$, $u^+(2) = u^+(3) = 6$. So, $u^{++} = 6$, $\text{ROF}_1 = 2$, $\text{ROF}_2 = \text{ROF}_3 = 1$.
3. $k = 108.68$, $g = 6$, $u^* \approx 6.02$.
4. Within each cycle, produce the products in the sequence (1, 2, 1, 3).
5. Here is a feasible schedule based on these results:

Activity	*Time*
Product 1	0.60
Product 2	1.81
Idle	0.60
Product 1	0.60
Product 3	1.20
Idle	1.21
Total	6.02

The cost of this solution is about 36.11, a bit less than that of the rotation schedule above.

5.6.3 *Extensions*

The setup costs in the basic ELSP are independent of the production sequence. Suppose instead that there is a *changeover cost* k_{ij} to switch from product i to product j. Also, there is a cost k_{0j} to start producing j when the machine is idle, and a cost k_{j0} to turn the machine off after producing j. Restrict attention to rotation schedules. The following is a reasonable heuristic; it is similar to the heuristic for the inventory-routing problem of Section 5.5.4: Solve a TSP to find a good product sequence. Calling its cost k, determine the optimal cycle time u^* through the EOQ model above.

Now, consider another system, which combines the features of the ELSP and a series system: There are several products *and* several production stages. The stages are arranged in a fixed sequence, and every product requires processing at each of the stages in that order. At each stage there is one machine, capable of processing only one product at a time.

In essence, this system is a sequence of ELSPs in series, where the outputs of one stage become inputs to the next. Put another way, there is an item corresponding to each product-stage pair. Leaving aside the machine capacities for the moment, the supply-demand relationships among these items form several separate series systems, one for each product. The shared machines link these series systems together.

Thus, this model adds realistic capacity constraints to the series systems of Section 5.3. Research on this type of model has only just begun. Preliminary results suggest that a simple heuristic, related to the one above for the ELSP, works quite well.

5.7 Time-Varying Demand

Every model in this chapter is driven by one or more demand rates. In many practical instances, those demand rates change over time, for the same reasons and in the same ways as in Chapter 4. This section explores a few of the possibilities.

First, we explore some simple cases, in the spirit of Section 4.2. Then we turn to discrete-time formulations, analogous to the DEL model of Section 4.3. Keep your expectations modest: These formulations are important to know but hard to solve. Researchers have devised heuristic approaches for some of these models; refer to the Notes.

5.7.1 Supply-Demand Networks: Extreme Cases

In certain extreme cases, like those of Section 4.2, it is possible to sketch what a good policy looks like and how the system works. Again, the reasoning is entirely heuristic.

Consider the series system of Section 5.3, but suppose its demand rate is $\lambda(t)$, a function of time. Recall, in the constant-demand case, the optimal partition $\mathbf{N}^*$ is insensitive to the demand rate. It is reasonable, therefore, to use the same partition for the variable-demand system. That is, all the items in each cluster N_m always order together.

First, suppose the changes in $\lambda(t)$ are small and/or fast. Then, as in Section 4.2, it makes sense to ignore the demand fluctuations. That is, use constant order intervals $u^+(m)$, or alternatively constant order quantities $\lambda u^+(m)$, based on the average demand rate λ.

Next, suppose that $\lambda(t)$ changes slowly. Then, a policy should focus on the current rate $\lambda(t)$, ignoring long-run changes. There are several plausible ways to implement this idea. Here is one: Use a nested, zero-inventory policy. Recompute all the order intervals $u^+(m)$ each time cluster N_1 must order, applying the methods of Section 5.3, treating the current demand rate $\lambda(t)$ as constant. Use these $u^+(m)$ until the next time cluster N_1 orders. Within each such cycle, adjust the order quantities to retain feasibility, given the actual changes in $\lambda(t)$. (Alternatively, use the stationary quantities $\lambda(t)u^+(m)$ until cluster N_1 must order again.)

These ideas extend directly to a tree system whose demand rates $\lambda'_j(t)$ change with time. If the changes are small and/or fast, again ignore them. Slow-changing demands require a bit more care: Suppose some common factor drives all the rates; that is, for some function $\lambda(t)$ and constant base rates $\lambda_j^{0\prime}$, $\lambda'_j(t) = \lambda(t)\lambda_j^{0\prime}$. When $\lambda(t) = \lambda$, remember, the optimal partition $\mathbf{N}^*$ is insensitive to λ. So, again it is reasonable to fix $\mathbf{N}^*$. Then, apply the approach above for series systems.

5.7.2 Supply-Demand Networks: Discrete-Time Formulation

5.7.2.1 Formulation

Consider a supply-demand network like that of Section 5.4, where time is now discrete, as in Section 4.3. We shall formulate a multi-item analogue of the DEL model.

For now, consider a *general system*. Assume that, for every item, one output unit requires precisely one input unit from each of its predecessors. (This is not a severe restriction; see Problem 5.22.) Also, for the moment suppose there are no leadtimes.

The notation closely follows that of Section 4.3, but subscripts i and j distinguish the items. The model data are the following:

T = time horizon
t = index for time points, $t = 0, \ldots, T$
$d_i'(t)$ = local demand for item i at time t
$k_i(t)$ = fixed order cost for item i at time t
$c_i(t)$ = variable order cost for item i at time t
$h_i'(t)$ = local inventory holding cost for item i at time t
x_{i0}' = initial local inventory of item i

The decision variables are:

$x_i'(t)$ = local inventory of item i at time t
$z_i(t)$ = order size for item i at time t

Again, δ denotes the Heaviside function.

Here is the model:

Initial conditions:

$$x_i'(0) = x_{i0}' \qquad i = 1, \ldots, J \tag{5.7.1}$$

Dynamics:

$$x_i'(t+1) = x_i'(t) + z_i(t) - d_i'(t) - \Sigma_{j \in Suc(i)} z_j(t),\ t = 0, \ldots, T-1,\ i = 1, \ldots, J \tag{5.7.2}$$

Constraints:

$$x_i'(t) \geq 0 \qquad t = 1, \ldots, T,\ i = 1, \ldots, J \tag{5.7.3}$$
$$z_i(t) \geq 0 \qquad t = 0, \ldots, T-1,\ i = 1, \ldots, J$$

Objective:

$$\text{Minimize} \qquad \Sigma_i \Sigma_{t=0}^{T-1} [k_i(t)\delta(z_i(t)) + c_i(t)z_i(t)] + \Sigma_i \Sigma_{t=1}^{T} h_i'(t)x_i'(t) \tag{5.7.4}$$

Apart from the summation in (5.7.2), this model's structure is identical to the DEL model's. This summation links the items together: An order for item $j \in Suc\ (i)$ draws down the inventory of item i. (It is possible to reformulate the model in terms of echelon quantities. See Problem 5.23.)

The nonlinearities in the objective can be eliminated by introducing binary indicator variables, as in Section 4.3: Let

$$v_i(t) = 1 \text{ if } z_i(t) > 0, \text{ and } 0 \text{ otherwise}$$

Also, let $D_i[t, T)$ denote the cumulative demand from t onward *and* over all items in echelon i. Add the constraints

$$v_i(t) \in \{0,1\}$$
$$z_i(t) \leq D_i[t, T)v_i(t) \qquad t = 0, \ldots, T-1,\ i = 1, \ldots, J \tag{5.7.5}$$

and replace the objective (5.7.4) with the linear function

$$\text{Minimize} \quad \Sigma_i \Sigma_{t=0}^{T-1} [k_i(t)v_i(t) + c_i(t)z_i(t)] + \Sigma_i \Sigma_{t=1}^{T} h_i'(t)x_i'(t) \qquad (5.7.4')$$

This model is a linear mixed-integer program.

It turns out that the optimal solution enjoys the zero-inventory property. Can one use this fact to construct a simple method to solve the problem? In general, alas, the answer is no.

To obtain a fully or nearly optimal solution requires the methodology of mixed-integer programming. Among the tools of that trade are techniques to exploit special structure, and the model has a great deal of that. Such techniques do help. Still, the current state of the art allows us to solve only fairly small problems.

Several heuristic methods are available. Section 5.8 discusses an important one, the MRP heuristic, and the Notes mention others. Roundy's [1993] approach is especially interesting, for it builds on methods for the stationary models of Sections 5.3 and 5.4. Assume stationary costs. The heuristic constructs the optimal partition $\mathbf{N}^*$ for the stationary-demand case, and in the nonstationary-demand problem, it forces the items within each cluster to order together, as in Section 5.7.1 above. This step reduces the scale of model (5.7.1) to (5.7.4); essentially, it now represents clusters instead of items. Then, the heuristic constructs a related system where the clusters are arranged in series. Finally, it applies the algorithm below in Section 5.7.2.2 to solve this series system. Roundy proves that the cost of the solution is at most 44% above optimal; his numerical examples suggest that its performance is often much better than that.

There are other ways to use information from stationary models. We mentioned near the end of Section 5.3.4 that the solution of the relaxed problem can be interpreted as a cost-reallocation scheme, using the parameters θ_j^*. That discussion focused on series systems, but the same idea applies to general systems. These θ_j^* capture the interactions between items in a stationary system. The idea is to use these θ_j^* to revise the cost coefficients of the nonstationary problem, and then to ignore the item interactions expressed in the dynamics (5.7.2) (or to apply the MRP heuristic, which ignores some of those interactions). See Blackburn and Millen [1982] and Rosling [1993] for elaborations of this notion.

5.7.2.2 Series Systems

There *is* a streamlined algorithm for series systems. The procedure requires $O(JT^4)$ time. There is an even simpler method, requiring only $O(JT^3)$ time, for *nested* series systems, which we present here. (The system is indeed nested, provided the cost factors satisfy certain plausible conditions. See Problem 5.24.)

Here is the basic idea: For each j, compute arc costs $k_j[t, u)$ just as in formula (4.3.8) in Chapter 4, using the echelon holding costs $h_i(t) = h_i'(t) - h_{i-1}'(t)$ and echelon cumulative demands $D_i[t, u) = D_J[t, u)$. Define

$V_j(s, t)$ = optimal cost of the system comprising stages j through J, starting at time s and ending with horizon t, $0 \leq s < t \leq T$

These quantities can be computed recursively, starting with $j = J$ and working backward: Set $V_{J+1}(s, t) = 0$. Given $V_{j+1}(s, t)$, define the augmented arc costs

$$k_j^+[t, u) = k_j[t, u) + V_{j+1}(t, u)$$

Construct the network of Figure 4.3.1 using these arc costs. Then, for every pair of nodes (s, t) with $s < t$, determine the minimum-cost path from s to t; the cost of this path is precisely $V_j(s, t)$. (One way to do this is to apply Algorithm Forward_DEL for each starting time s separately. Actually, there are quicker ways.)

For $j = 1$ we need only compute $V_1(0, T)$, the optimal total cost. The nodes on the optimal path are the optimal stage-1 order times. Now, take each pair (s, t) of successive order times, and recover the minimum-cost path for $V_2(s, t)$. Those nodes are the optimal stage-2 order times. Continue working forward in this way to reconstruct the full optimal solution.

The key to this approach is the echelon-cost-accounting scheme: At stage j, choosing arc (t, u) means ordering at time t to cover demand in periods t through $u - 1$. The original arc cost $k_j[t, u)$ includes the corresponding order and echelon-j holding costs; these costs are incurred regardless of what happens at stage $j + 1$ and beyond. Now, $V_{j+1}(t, u)$ represents the best way to manage those downstream stages during the same time interval, using a nested policy. The augmented arc cost $k_j^+[t, u)$ thus correctly measures the total cost of choosing arc (t, u).

5.7.2.3 Leadtimes

Returning to a general system, suppose there is a leadtime L'_{ij} to transfer item i to $j \in Suc(i)$. Each L'_{ij} is a positive integer. To create item j at time t requires pulling item-i stock at time $t - L'_{ij}$, for all $i \in Pre(j)$. Also, there is an order leadtime L'_j for each start item j. The original formulation above has $L'_{ij} = 1$ and $L'_j = 1$.

There are several equivalent ways to adapt the model to incorporate leadtimes, along the lines of Section 4.4.1. Here is one: Interpret $z_i(t)$ as the amount of item i *arriving* (or the production quantity *completed*) just before time $t + 1$. With this understanding, replace the dynamics (5.7.2) by

$$x'_i(t + 1) = x'_i(t) + z_i(t) - d'_i(t) - \Sigma_{j \in Suc(i)} z_j(t + L'_{ij} - 1)$$

$$t = 0, \ldots, T - 1, i = 1, \ldots, J \qquad (5.7.2')$$

Also, add appropriate initial conditions to (5.7.1). For example, consider a two-stage series system with $L'_1 = 3$ and $L'_{12} = 2$. The $z_1(t)$ for $t < L'_1 - 1 = 2$ and the $z_2(t)$ for $t < L'_{12} - 1 = 1$ are determined before time $t = 0$, so they become constants, specified by initial conditions of the form

$$z_1(0) = z_{1,0} \qquad z_2(0) = z_{2,0} \qquad z_1(1) = z_{1,1}$$

Moreover, the summation in (5.7.2′) for $i = 1$ and $t = T - 1$ is $z_2(T)$, a variable that exists nowhere else in the model. So, either omit that variable or fix it to zero with a terminal condition $z_2(T) = 0$. Alternatively, extend the horizon to $T + 1$ for stage 2 only.

One more adjustment is needed, to account for holding costs on stock in transit between items. Assume that the inventory of item i on its way to becoming another item j incurs the cost $h'_i(t)$. Add the terms $h'_i(t)z_j(u), j \in Suc(i), t \le u < t + L'_{ij} - 1$, to the objective (5.7.4) or (5.7.4′). That is, augment each $c_j(t)$ by $\Sigma_{i \in Pre(j)} \Sigma_{s=t-L'_{ij}+2}^{t} h'_i(s)$. (Actually, this adjustment is needed only when the $h'_i(t)$ change over t. Otherwise, if $h'_i(t) = h'_i$ for some constant h'_i, then the extra term in $c_j(t)$ becomes the constant $\Sigma_{i \in Pre(j)} (L'_{ij} - 1)h'_i$. This constant multiplies $z_j(t)$ for *every* t in the objective, but the total item-j orders $\Sigma_t z_j(t)$ is the minimal feasible quantity, and so itself is a constant. Thus, the extra term in $c_j(t)$ does not affect the solution, and hence can be omitted.)

There is another, simpler approach for tree systems: Just shift the time axis for each item, as in Section 5.4. In the two-stage series system above, for instance, interpret $x_2'(t)$ and $z_2(t)$ as before, but reinterpret $x_1'(t)$ as inventory at time $t - L_{12}' + 1$ and $z_1(t)$ as production of item 1 completed just before time $t - L_{12}' + 2$. Under this relabeling scheme, the original dynamics (5.7.2) remains valid. [As in Section 5.4, this idea does *not* work for a general system, unless the leadtimes happen to be balanced; the general case requires (5.7.2′) in place of (5.7.2), as above.]

5.7.3 Limited Capacity

Consider a multiproduct system, whose products share a production facility of limited capacity. Otherwise, the items are independent. Thus, the system is essentially that of Section 5.6, recast in a discrete-time framework.

Define

$$z_+(t) = \text{capacity available at time } t$$

$$a_i = \text{capacity usage per unit of item } i$$

Otherwise, borrow the notation of model (5.7.1) to (5.7.4) above. (Omit the primes; e.g., write $x_i(t)$ for $x_i'(t)$. Also, $D_i[t, T)$ means the cumulative demand from t onward of item i only.) Here is the linear mixed-integer programming formulation:

Initial conditions:

$$x_i(0) = x_{i0} \qquad i = 1, \ldots, J \tag{5.7.6}$$

Dynamics:

$$x_i(t+1) = x_i(t) + z_i(t) - d_i(t) \qquad t = 0, \ldots, T-1, i = 1, \ldots, J \tag{5.7.7}$$

Constraints:

$$x_i(t) \geq 0$$

$$z_i(t) \geq 0$$

$$v_i(t) \in \{0, 1\}$$

$$z_i(t) \leq D_i[t, T)v_i(t) \qquad t = 0, \ldots, T-1, i = 1, \ldots, J \tag{5.7.8}$$

$$\Sigma_i a_i z_i(t) \leq z_+(t) \qquad t = 0, \ldots, T-1 \tag{5.7.9}$$

Objective:

$$\text{Minimize} \qquad \Sigma_i \Sigma_{t=0}^{T-1} [k_i(t)v_i(t) + c_i(t)z_i(t)] + \Sigma_i \Sigma_{t=1}^{T} h_i(t)x_i(t) \tag{5.7.10}$$

This is a multi-item version of the limited-capacity DEL model of Section 4.4.5. (One could rescale the variables and the data so that all $a_i = 1$, but there is no real advantage to doing so.) It is also a discrete-time analogue of the ELSP. (However, the setup costs do not reflect continuing production runs, as discussed in Section 4.4.5. It is possible to revise the formulation along the lines suggested there.)

To solve this model too requires integer-programming techniques. The successful approaches to date all exploit the model's special structure: It *almost* consists of a separate DEL model for each item. Only the capacity constraints (5.7.9) link them together. Nevertheless, it remains quite difficult to compute the true optimal solution.

It is straightforward to extend the model to incorporate several limited resources (equipment and labor, for instance): Let $r = 1, \ldots, R$ index the resources. There are now resource-capacity and resource-usage parameters $z_{+r}(t)$ and a_{ir} for each resource. The constraints (5.7.9) now expand to become

$$\Sigma_i\, a_{ir} z_i(t) \leq z_{+r}(t) \qquad t = 0, \ldots, T-1, r = 1, \ldots, R \qquad (5.7.11)$$

One could add capacity limits like (5.7.9) or even (5.7.11) to the network model, (5.7.1) to (5.7.4). The resulting model combines the features of both earlier models. The multiple-resource model has an interesting interpretation: Suppose r indexes distinct machines. Each item utilizes only one machine, but several items may share a machine. So, for each i, there is only one positive a_{ir}; all the others are zero. Now, were it not for the supply-demand relationships embodied in the dynamics (5.7.2), the model would separate into R independent problems, one for each machine. These relationships now link the machines as well as the items.

This combined model is still more difficult to solve than the earlier ones. Nevertheless, it is worth seeing that even such intricate systems can be represented in the language of mixed-integer linear programming. We learn something about how things work in the act of formulation itself. When J, R, and T are small, one can indeed obtain the solution—with a powerful computer and some patience. Otherwise, one must use a heuristic method.

One heuristic approach for this model (and other intricate, large-scale problems) is called *hierarchical planning,* which determines a solution in two steps. First, it solves a relatively simple approximate model, called the aggregate model. This model suppresses the fixed costs $k_i(t)$ and aggregates the items into groups. The second step, called disaggregation, translates the aggregate model's solution into a solution of the original model. It solves a separate model for each group, which divides the group's production quantities among its original items.

It is worth mentioning that all the difficulties here are caused by the fixed-cost terms. If the $k_i(t) = 0$, the model becomes a linear program (LP); it is a large and intricate LP, but even those are easy to solve. (Hierarchical planning exploits this fact in its aggregate model.) Such models are used widely to plan production and distribution. If the $k_i(t)$ are positive but small, moreover, the model is easier to work with than it would be otherwise; exact methods work faster, and heuristics perform better. So, reducing the fixed costs simplifies analysis, in addition to its direct benefits.

5.8 Material Requirements Planning (MRP)

5.8.1 Overview

The phrase *material requirements planning* (MRP) describes a broad approach for managing operations, a type of computer program designed to support that approach, and a specific set of procedures underlying it. MRP is the *de facto* standard approach to production planning and control in the United States, and it is widely used elsewhere too; the number of companies using it runs easily into the hundreds of thousands.

Our aim in this section is not to give a comprehensive account of MRP. That would be impossible. MRP is virtually a managerial subculture with its own extensive vocabulary. A small but thriving industry provides MRP software and consulting services; a recent directory (APICS [1994]) lists 107 vendors. Rather, we offer a brief overview and assessment of MRP, focusing on its basic logic and its relation to other approaches.

5.8.2 The Core Model and the Heuristic

MRP is not usually presented as a model-based approach. But there *is* a model at the core of MRP. To understand MRP, it is crucial to understand the model and what MRP does with it. That model is precisely (5.7.1) to (5.7.4) above, with (5.7.2′) replacing (5.7.2). In words, the world as viewed by MRP consists of a set of items *N*, linked by a network (*N*, *A*) to form a general system with leadtimes, operating in discrete time.

Let us repeat the core model for easy reference:

Initial conditions:

$$x'_i(0) = x'_{i0} \qquad i = 1, \ldots, J \tag{5.7.1}$$

Dynamics:

$$x'_i(t+1) = x'_i(t) + z_i(t) - d'_i(t) - \Sigma_{j \in Suc(i)} z_j\,(t + L'_{ij} - 1)$$
$$t = 0, \ldots, T-1,\ i = 1, \ldots, J \tag{5.7.2′}$$

Constraints:

$$x'_i(t) \geq 0 \qquad t = 1, \ldots, T,\ i = 1, \ldots, J \tag{5.7.3}$$
$$z_i(t) \geq 0 \qquad t = 0, \ldots, T-1,\ i = 1, \ldots, J$$

Objective:

$$\text{Minimize} \qquad \Sigma_i \Sigma_{t=0}^{T-1} [k_i(t)\delta(z_i(t)) + c_i(t)z_i(t)] + \Sigma_i \Sigma_{t=1}^{T} h'_i(t)x'_i(t) \tag{5.7.4}$$

(There are additional initial conditions, fixing previously determined $z_i(t)$ to constants, as discussed in Section 5.7.2.3. Other variations are discussed below.)

MRP's scheduling procedures essentially constitute a heuristic solution method for this model. In broad terms this is a decomposition technique. It constructs a solution for one item at a time, beginning with downstream items and gradually working upstream.

To describe the method in detail, recall we number the items so that $i < j$ whenever $(i, j) \in A$. With this understanding, MRP treats the items in reverse numerical order.

Thus, MRP starts with item *J*. Now, item *J* has no successors; the summation in the dynamics (5.7.2′) for $j = J$ disappears. Item *J* does interact with other items, but only through their dynamics. MRP ignores these interactions. What remains, then, is a single-item DEL model, which MRP solves to determine a solution for item *J*. (To solve this DEL model, some versions of MRP use an exact method, such as Algorithm

Forward_DEL, but others use a heuristic, such as the Silver-Meal heuristic.) Let $z_J^0(t)$ denote the resulting order quantities.

Next, MRP focuses on item $J - 1$. Now, item $J - 1$ too may have no successors; in this case MRP treats it just like item J. Otherwise, its only successor is J. Thus, with the $z_J(t)$ fixed at $z_J^0(t)$, its dynamics become

$$x'_{J-1}(t + 1) = x'_{J-1}(t) + z_{J-1}(t) - d^0_{J-1}(t) \qquad t = 0, \ldots, T - 1$$

where

$$d^0_{J-1}(t) = d'_{J-1}(t) + z^0_J(t + L'_{J-1,J} - 1)$$

Again ignoring interactions with upstream items, MRP solves the DEL model for item $J - 1$ alone with demands $d^0_{J-1}(t)$. Call the result $z^0_{J-1}(t)$.

MRP continues in this manner as it works upstream. When it reaches item i, $z_j^0(t)$ has been determined already for all $j \in Suc(i)$, since $j > i$. Set

$$d_i^0(t) = d'_i(t) + \Sigma_{j \in Suc(i)} z_j^0(t + L'_{ij} - 1)$$

The dynamics (5.7.2′) then become

$$x'_i(t + 1) = x'_i(t) + z_i(t) - d_i^0(t) \qquad t = 0, \ldots, T - 1$$

Again, MRP uses these dynamics within a DEL model to determine $z_i^0(t)$. Thus, at each step, the order quantities for downstream items become additional demands.

Clearly, the overall procedure takes little time, and the end result is a feasible solution of the core model. That is no small accomplishment, in view of the complexity of the model.

It is interesting to compare this heuristic with the exact algorithm for series systems outlined in Section 5.7.2. That method too starts downstream and works upstream. But, it works harder at each stage to compute the function $V_j(s, t)$ for all pairs (s, t). Clearly, MRP loses information as it progresses from stage to stage.

The MRP heuristic is a plausible one, but there is little evidence concerning its performance in solving the core model. (Several alternatives have been proposed, as mentioned in Section 5.7.2.1 above and the Notes below, but to our knowledge none has been implemented in a commercial MRP system.)

5.8.3 The Larger Context

MRP is a great deal more than its core model and the heuristic. It has to be; the environment it operates in is much more complex than the core model. The issues discussed in Section 4.3.7 are all relevant here: Typically, MRP is used in a rolling-horizon scenario; the data of the core model are rough estimates which change often; nervousness is problematic.

Like most model-based approaches, MRP includes outer layers as well. Viewed from inside, from the model's viewpoint, these outer layers collect and process the data it requires, and send the solution where it needs to go. From an external managerial viewpoint, however, the outer layers are integral parts of the overall approach.

For example, consider the $d'_i(t)$, called *demands* above. In MRP these are not raw demand forecasts. Rather, there are one or more layers of analysis between forecasting and the model. The resulting $d_i'(t)$ are output targets, collectively called the *master production schedule* (MPS). There seems to be no uniform methodology for master production scheduling; this activity employs a variety of techniques, some formal, others informal. Still, the MPS embodies several important functions. Notably, it must plan for capacity limits, which do not appear in the core model (a point revisited below).

Another crucial layer is *buffering*. The core model includes no uncertainties in demand and supply, but such uncertainties do exist. Buffering refers to adjustments of the core model's data to account for uncertainties. There are two main buffering techniques, safety stock and safety time: Safety stock in this context means revising the lower bounds on the $x_i'(t)$ in (5.7.3) from 0 to positive values $x_{i-}(t)$, as discussed in Section 4.3.7. As mentioned there, it is hard to choose appropriate safety stocks even for the DEL model, and it is still harder here. Safety time means revising the L_i' and L_{ij}' upward. This too is hard, as explained below.

Still further out from the core, many MRP systems provide support for other activities besides production scheduling. Indeed, it is common to find all the firm's control and data-processing functions, including procurement, accounts payable and payroll, built around MRP.

Partly for this reason, some MRP systems, especially older ones, are slow and clumsy to work with. Other newer systems dispense with these extras, concentrating instead on efficient implementation of the core-model heuristic above. This approach is called *rapid MRP,* and indeed it is much faster than the traditional, full-featured MRP systems.

Enterprise resource planning (ERP) extends MRP's logic to the entire firm, encompassing multiple production and distribution facilities. Some versions are even capable of linking the activities of several firms, using modern communications technologies.

5.8.4 Evaluation: MRP versus OPT and JIT

People have strong feelings about MRP. Some view it as a blessing, others a curse. (In its early days, MRP's proponents shamelessly oversold it; the harsher negative views heard today, no doubt, reflect reactions to that earlier hyperbole.) Let us briefly review some of its key strengths and weaknesses from a broad managerial point of view:

MRP's primary strength is so obvious that it is easily missed. As explained in Section 5.1, complex production and distribution systems can be represented as networks. This idea is quite natural, once you see it. However, MRP was the first approach to embody this idea within practical, widely accessible software. Thus, MRP provided the first systematic procedures to coordinate large numbers of items with complex supply/demand relationships. This simple fact explains much of MRP's popularity.

One major weakness of MRP is the lack of capacity limits in its core model. Of course, real resource capacities *are* limited, so the heuristic solution may well be infeasible. To compensate, something must be done outside the core model. Several alternatives are employed in practice:

Some users add safety times; that is, they inflate the leadtimes L_i' and L_{ij}' to include anticipated delays due to congested resources. This cure, unfortunately, is often worse than the disease. Capacity limits hardly ever induce constant delays of this sort. The result, typically, is that many orders arrive well before they are expected, thus generating excessive inventories. Even so, occasionally there is more congestion than the L'_i and L'_{ij} account for, so the approach fails to meet the output targets of the MPS. (It is possible to augment the leadtimes intelligently, recognizing the potential costs involved. The trouble is that few users have the time and expertise required to exercise such care.)

Many MRP programs include a module called *capacity requirements planning* (CRP). CRP is a reporting function. After the MRP's heuristic is run, CRP computes and reports the solution's usage of key resources, highlighting those whose capacities are violated. At that point, some manual intervention is necessary, e.g., fix parts of the solution $z_i^o(t)$ to force feasibility, or adjust the MPS (the $d'_i(t)$). Then, rerun the heuristic. Of course, there is no guarantee that the revised solution is feasible; several iterations may be necessary.

Newer MRP programs provide support for this iterative CRP process, along with other enhancements. So different are these programs from the earliest MRP software that a new name has been coined to describe them, *MRP II.* The abbreviation MRP here now stands for *manufacturing resource planning.*

Thus, MRP II helps managers work around this limitation of the core model, but does not directly fix it. A totally different approach has gained favor recently. Called *finite-capacity scheduling,* it focuses on the resources and their capacities themselves, viewing the demands as jobs to be scheduled on those resources. Most such methods, however, suppress or ignore some of the detail of MRP's core model, specifically some of the supply-demand relations and/or later time periods. (Still better, of course, would be an integrated approach, based on a core model with explicit capacity limits *and* the full network structure. As indicated in Section 5.7.3, however, while we know how to formulate such models, we are just beginning to learn how to extract useful results from them.)

One finite scheduling technique is called *optimized production technology* (OPT). OPT's heuristic identifies one or a few *bottlenecks,* resources whose capacity limits are most severely strained. Then, to construct a solution, it aims to utilize the bottleneck resources efficiently. Unfortunately, the actual workings of this method remain shrouded in mystery; they are proprietary secrets. (Hyperbole is not the exclusive property of MRP; plenty of it surrounds OPT as well.) No one has seriously tested it, to our knowledge, so at this point we must regard OPT as an intriguing but unproved concept.

MRP's approach to uncertainties, as explained above, is a core model that ignores them, supplemented by a buffering layer to set safety stocks and times. It is not clear how well this approach works. (Chapters 8 and 9 examine networks with explicitly uncertain demands and supplies. The approaches that work effectively in that context seem radically different from MRP's. This fact does not settle the issue, however. Those models are special in several ways; for instance, most focus on series systems or other special structures with no fixed costs.)

Another weakness stems from the basic philosophy of central control underlying MRP. Under MRP, like any fully centralized approach (including OPT), all relevant data flow into one single point, where all key decisions are made; these control directives then flow out to be implemented at various points in the network. *In principle,* this is an ideal situation, *provided* everything works as planned.

In practice, of course, things do not always work as planned: Errors creep into the files containing current inventory data; machine breakdowns are not reported promptly; people misunderstand scheduling decisions; production lots turn out defective; et cetera, et cetera. MRP is a demanding and fairly rigid planning discipline, and it does not easily forgive such errors.

Also, as a managerial approach, centralized control is awkward: Generally, it entails substantial overhead costs (in the form of a substantial bureaucracy). People on the shop floor and in the warehouse often experience MRP as a distant, arbitrary master. They find little opportunity or motivation to take initiative, either to facilitate MRP itself (e.g., by reporting problematic conditions), or to improve the actual physical processes.

From this perspective it is easy to appreciate the appeal of a quite different philosophy, the *just-in-time* (JIT) approach. One central tenet of JIT is to decentralize control as much as possible. Here, demand *pulls* stock from downstream stages, which in turn pull stock from upstream stages, with minimal central direction; in contrast, MRP *pushes* stock through the system via the MPS and the core-model heuristic. Partly in this way, but also in others, JIT encourages process improvement, through small-scale initiatives as well as large-scale projects. (The JIT approach is discussed further in Section 8.8. *Caveat:* JIT's hyperbole exceeds even MRP's and OPT's.)

Different as their underlying philosophies are, it is nonetheless possible to integrate MRP and JIT, or at least parts of them. Certainly, there is nothing to stop a company from encouraging process improvements while adhering to MRP. Even at the level of control, MRP can be used to set longer-term output targets, leaving day-to-day or hour-to-hour control to JIT. Alternatively, one can relax central control within certain groups of related stages, but centrally control the flow of goods between groups. These by no means exhaust the possibilities; there are many others.

This brings us to a final and perhaps decisive issue—adaptability. On this score, MRP has a mixed record. The MRP industry has been less than eager to listen to ideas from elsewhere in the operations-management community. This was especially true in earlier years, but it remains so to some extent. One well-informed observer (Wagner [1993]) writes, "MRP has become a stern gatekeeper that guards the plant floor from incursions by operations research." In my view, this insularity has cost the MRP community dearly. Had it been more open to alternative formulations, solution techniques, and control mechanisms, MRP would surely be a more capable discipline today, and fewer people would regard it as a rigid monolith.

On the other hand, MRP has shown considerable adaptability in certain key directions. In extending the approach to MRP II and ERP, and incorporating elements of JIT, the industry has responded creatively to real needs of its customers. Based on that experience, some of its practitioners envision MRP becoming a flexible approach, capable of digesting a variety of new methods and ideas. That would be a welcome development indeed.

Notes

Section 5.2: The importance of the inventory-workload tradeoff curve was first recognized by Starr and Miller [1962]. See also Gardner and Dannenbring [1979]. De Groote [1994b] provides a detailed exploration and interpretation of the variety index.

Sections 5.3–5.5: The overall approach here is attributable to Maxwell and Muckstadt [1985] and Roundy [1985,1986]. (Parts of it were anticipated by Schwarz [1973], Schwarz and Schrage [1975], and Jackson et al. [1985].) Extensions and refinements can be found in Mitchell [1987], Federgruen and Zheng [1992a,1995], Federgruen, Queyranne, and Zheng [1992], and Atkins and Sun [1995]. Atkins [1990] and Muckstadt and Roundy [1993] review this literature.

Anily and Federgruen [1990] analyze the inventory-routing problem rigorously and provide extensive numerical results. For recent results and a guide to the literature, see Bramel and Simchi-Levi [1995] and Herer and Roundy [1997]. See also Burns et al. [1985] for a more intuitive, heuristic discussion.

Section 5.6: The primary early work on the ELSP was done by Hanssmann [1962] and Maxwell [1964]. Elmaghraby [1978] reviews the research on the problem through the late 1970s. Significant recent developments include Dobson [1987,1992], Jones and Inman [1989], Roundy [1989], Gallego [1990], and Zipkin [1991b]. The ELSP can be extended to incorporate planned backorders; see Gallego and Roundy [1992]. See Dobson and Yano [1990], El-Najdawi [1992], and El-Najdawi and Kleindorfer [1993] for extensions to series systems.

Section 5.7: Veinott [1969] demonstrates the zero-inventory property for model (5.7.1) to (5.7.4). Integer-programming methods are adapted to this model by Crowston and Wagner [1973], Afentakis et al. [1984] and Rosling [1986]. Efficient algorithms for series systems are developed by Zangwill [1966] and Love [1972]; see Erickson et al. [1987] for extensions. One heuristic for this model is MRP's. Alternative heuristics have been developed by Graves [1981], Blackburn and Millen [1982], Heinrich and Schneeweiss [1986], and Roundy [1993], among others.

The limited-capacity model (5.7.6) to (5.7.10) is discussed by Lasdon and Terjung [1971], Eppen and Martin [1987], and Diaby et al. [1992], among others. See Maes and Van Wassenhove [1988] for a review of heuristic methods and Salomon [1990] for an overall survey.

Billington et al. [1986] discuss a heuristic method (based on optimization principles) for the model combining supply/demand relationships and capacity limits. Hax and Candea [1984] provide an overview of the hierarchical-planning approach.

Section 5.8: Many books discuss MRP at length. An early introduction is Orlicky [1975]. The text by Chase and Aquilano [1992] includes an up-to-date overview, while that of Vollman et al. [1992] provides a more extensive exposition and bibliography. The issue of safety time is discussed at length by Karmarkar [1993]. For an interesting perspective on the sociology of MRP see Kling and Iacono [1984,1989].

Finite-capacity scheduling methods are discussed by Morton et al. [1988], Dobson et al. [1992], and Faaland and Schmitt [1993]. For introductions to OPT see Jacobs [1983], Aggarwal [1985], and the two texts mentioned above. The same two texts include summaries of JIT. One of the original sources on JIT is Shingo [1989]. See Zipkin [1991a] for a critical review of the popular literature and Groenevelt [1993] for a survey of the research literature. Karmarkar [1989] and Rao [1989] discuss alternative means of combining MRP with JIT. Krajewski et al. [1987] compare MRP and JIT by computer simulation.

Problems

5.1 Verify that the variety index J_* satisfies (5.2.1); i.e., $1 \leq J_* \leq J$. (*Hint:* Define $x_j = w_j c_j \lambda_j$. Think of the x_j as variables in an appropriate optimization problem.)

5.2 Carry out the steps outlined in the text to solve the optimization problem (5.2.2). Use the solution to verify equation (5.2.4), describing the inventory-workload tradeoff curve.

5.3 Consider an independent-item system with a very large number J of items. It may be difficult to obtain all the individual-item data. This problem suggests a statistical approach to estimating J_*.

First, it is often true that the w_j are similar across j. For simplicity, assume that they are equal (to w). Second, a useful empirical relationship has been observed in many multi-item inventories: The frequency distribution of the expenditure rates $c_j\lambda_j$ over the items is approximately lognormal. (If Y is a random variable having the normal distribution with mean μ and variance σ^2, then $X = e^Y$ has a lognormal distribution with these same two parameters.) Assume that J is so large, the items effectively form a continuum, and the fraction of items whose expenditure rates lie in the small interval $(x, x + dx)$ is $f(x)\,dx$, where $f(x)$ is the lognormal probability density function (*pdf*) with parameters μ and σ^2. Also, assume we have estimates of μ and σ^2.

For any positive number ϵ, $E[X^\epsilon] = \exp(\epsilon\mu + \frac{1}{2}\epsilon^2\sigma^2)$. For instance, in the notation of Section 5.2, $c\lambda/J = E[X] = \exp(\mu + \frac{1}{2}\sigma^2)$. Show that, under these assumptions, $J_* = J \cdot \exp(-\frac{1}{4}\sigma^2)$. Explain why it makes sense intuitively that J_* decreases in σ^2.

5.4 Consider the multi-item inventory of Section 5.2, but now suppose that planned backorders are allowed. Define a third aggregate performance measure,

$$cB = \text{aggregate cost-value of backorders}$$

$$= \Sigma_j c_j \overline{B}_j$$

where $\overline{B}_j$ is the average backorders for item j. (Actually, a more relevant measure is pB, defined by using the sales price p_j instead of c_j to weight $\overline{B}_j$. This case is more complex. Assume for now that the markup ratio p_j/c_j is the same for all items, so cB expresses the same information as pB.)

Show that the three measures are connected by the following functional relationship:

$$wO = \frac{\frac{1}{2}(wc\lambda)J_*}{(\sqrt{cI} + \sqrt{cB})^2}$$

This equation describes a two-dimensional surface in the three-space with coordinates (cI, cB, wO), analogous to the tradeoff curve of Section 5.2. It is sometimes called the *aggregate tradeoff surface.*

Now, drop the assumption above, that the markup ratio p_j/c_j is constant, and use pB instead of cB. There is no simple formula for the tradeoff surface in this case, but one can still generate the surface numerically: Let β denote the cost factor for aggregate backorders, analogous to κ and η, and $\omega = \beta/(\beta + \eta)$. Derive formulas for cI, cB, and wO in terms of the cost ratios η/κ and ω. Describe how to use these formulas to calculate points on the tradeoff surface.

5.5 For a series system with any number of stages J, show that a nested policy dominates a non-nested one, as in Theorem 5.3.1.

5.6 For a series system with any number of stages J, show that a zero-inventory policy dominates any other, as in Theorem 5.3.2.

5.7 Given the solution $\mathbf{u}^*$ to problem (5.3.3), define the subset $A^*_= = \{j \in A : u^*_j = u^*_{j+1}\}$. Prove that $\mathbf{u}^*$ is the unique solution to problem (5.3.3[$A^*_=$]). (Use a direct argument by contradiction. Assuming the contrary, construct a feasible solution to (5.3.3) having lower cost than $\mathbf{u}^*$.)

5.8 To construct a policy according to Section 5.3.6 entails minimizing the function $C^+(\underline{u})$ over the interval $[1, 2)$. The text outlines the approach in general terms. This problem fills in the details.

The proof of Theorem 5.3.7 (Section 5.3.8) shows how to compute the breakpoints, denoted $\chi(m)$, and provides a formula for $u^+(m)$ as a function of $\underline{u}$. Using this information, and notation of your invention, write an explicit expression for $C^+(\underline{u})$. The expression should clearly look like the cost function of an EOQ model over each of several subintervals. (For simplicity, assume the $\chi(m)$ are all distinct and strictly larger than 1.) Explain how to optimize $C^+(\underline{u})$ over each subinterval.

5.9 Fill in some of the details of the proof of Theorem 5.3.7: Show that $\chi(m)$ is indeed the breakpoint of $u^+(m)$, and verify the formula for $u^+(m)$ as a function of $\underline{u}$. Show that the sum of the two integrals in braces is $1/\sqrt{2}$, as asserted.

5.10 In the proof of Theorem 5.3.6 it is shown that

$$2^{-1/2} \leq \frac{u^+(m)}{u^*(m)} < 2^{+1/2}$$

This is true, evidently, for all m and any value of λ. Using this fact, argue that, if λ should change from one value to another, the relative order frequency $u^+(m)/u^+(\text{next }(m))$ changes by at most a factor of 2.

5.11 Consider a series system whose cost factors are specified by $k_j = \kappa w_j$, $h_j = \eta c_j$. The optimal partition $\mathbf{N}^*$ for the relaxed problem is then independent of κ and η. Suppose we use the relaxed problem and $\mathbf{N}^*$ to estimate wO and cI. Argue that the inventory-workload tradeoff curve is precisely (5.2.4), the same form as in an independent-item model, with aggregate system parameters redefined as in Section 5.3.7.

5.12 Consider a series system like that of Section 5.3, except that a fixed fraction δ_j of item j is defective. All defects are discovered immediately and must be scrapped. There is no reimbursement for defective items. (δ_1 is the defect fraction for supplies arriving from the outside source. For $j > 1$, stage j converts one unit of item $j - 1$ into $(1 - \delta_j)$ units of usable item j and δ_j units of scrap.) Construct an equivalent model with no defects.

5.13 Consider a series system where each stage has a finite production rate μ_j, as in Section 3.4. Stage 1 produces item 1 gradually, and stage $j + 1$ gradually converts item j to item $j + 1$. Assume that each increment of item J becomes available to meet demand the instant it is produced. Likewise, item-j production can be used instantaneously in stage $j + 1$. There are no leadtimes or setup times. So, in principle, a unit can pass through all stages instantaneously.

Assume $\mu_1 \geq \mu_2 \geq \cdots \geq \mu_J > \lambda$, and define $\rho_j = \lambda/\mu_j$. Consider a nested, zero-inventory, stationary-interval policy. Argue that any such policy is feasible. Explain that the echelon inventory $I_j(t)$ follows the same periodic pattern as in a single-item model for each j. Then, show that the average echelon inventory is $\bar{I}_j = \tfrac{1}{2}(1 - \rho_j)u_j\lambda$. Finally, explain how to redefine g_j so that the function $C(\mathbf{u})$ correctly measures the average cost. (So, from this point on, we can apply the approach of Section 5.3 as is to find a good policy of this type.)

5.14 As in the previous problem, consider a series system with finite production rates μ_j. Now, however, finished goods become available to meet demand only in whole batches, as in Section 3.4.5.

Likewise, stock produced during a production run at stage $j < J$ can be used at stage $j + 1$ only when the whole run is complete. After that, the production process at $j + 1$ gradually reduces $I'_j(t)$ as it increases $I'_{j+1}(t)$. Again set $\rho_j = \lambda/\mu_j$, and assume $0 < \rho_j < 1$ for all j. (The μ_j need not be monotonic, however.)

In this context, a policy is nested if stage $j + 1$ begins a production run each time stage j completes one. A zero-inventory policy is one where every production run at every stage begins at the last possible moment consistent with feasibility. The stationary-interval property has the same meaning as before. Consider only nested, zero-inventory, stationary-interval policies.

(*a*) Consider a concrete example with $J = 2$, $\lambda = 1$, $\mu_1 = \mu_2 = 4$, $u_1 = 8$, and $u_2 = 4$. Graph the $I'_j(t)$ for $0 \leq t \leq 16$, assuming a production run of item 1 starts at time 0, and setting $I'_1(0) = 0$ and $I_2(0) = 3$. Then, graph the echelon inventories $I_j(t)$ over the same interval.

(*b*) Now, consider the general case: For item J, as in a single-stage model, within each cycle (of length u_J) the production run lasts for time $\rho_J u_J$. Consequently, the production period must start with enough inventory to meet demand during this interval, namely $\rho_J u_{J;}\lambda$. Argue that, for similar reasons, in general, a production run for item j must start with echelon inventory $I_j(t) = (\Sigma_{i \geq j}\, \rho_i u_i)\lambda$. This is the smallest echelon inventory within each cycle. Then, argue that the largest is this quantity, plus $u_j\lambda$. Finally, show that the average echelon inventory is $\overline{I}_j = \frac{1}{2}(1 + \rho_j)u_j\lambda + (\Sigma_{i>j}\, \rho_i u_i)\lambda$.

(*c*) Set $h_j^+ = (1 + \rho_j)h_j + 2\rho_j \Sigma_{i<j} h_i$ and redefine $g_j = h_j^+\lambda$. Argue that $C(\mathbf{u})$ now correctly measures the average cost of a policy. (So, we can apply the approach of Section 5.3 to find a good policy.)

5.15 Consider a series system with the following data: $J = 4$, $\lambda = 10$, all $k_j = 80$, and

$$h_1 = 0.5 \qquad h_2 = 4.5 \qquad h_3 = 9.0 \qquad h_4 = 4.0$$

Solve the relaxed problem. Then, calculate a feasible solution using a base period of $\underline{u} = 2$. What is the ratio C^+/C^-?

5.16 Consider the tree system of Figure 5.4.3 with the following arc leadtimes:

$$L'_{14} = 6 \qquad L'_{24} = 3$$
$$L'_{35} = 5 \qquad L'_{45} = 3$$
$$L'_{36} = 6$$

Given a policy for the zero-leadtime system, explain precisely how to construct an equivalent policy for the real system.

5.17 Consider the distribution system of Figure 5.4.2. Suppose it describes a production process. Originally, all items are measured in kilograms (kg). To make 1 kg of end item 6 requires 4 kg of item 3. Item 5 requires 1 kg of item 3; 1 kg of item 3, in turn, requires 2 kg of item 1. Item 4 uses 2 kg of item 1, and item 2 uses 0.25 kg of item 1. Revise the items' quantity units, so that each item uses precisely one unit of its (single) predecessor. (Continue to measure item 1, the raw material, in kg.) If the original demand rates are

$$\lambda'_2 = 200 \qquad \lambda'_4 = 200 \qquad \lambda'_5 = 800 \qquad \lambda'_6 = 1600,$$

what are the revised rates?

5.18 Consider the three-item non-nested distribution system discussed in Section 5.4.7. Provide a detailed argument to verify the formulas given there for the average echelon inventories of the artificial items $1j$ and of item 1 itself.

5.19 The basic version of the ELSP in Section 5.6 assumes that stock becomes available to meet demand the instant it is produced. Show how to revise the formulation in the opposite case, where only full, completed batches can be used to meet demand. (Assume a rotation schedule.)

5.20 In the ELSP (assuming output is instantaneously available to meet demand), suppose each product requires a setup time τ_j in addition to the setup cost k_j. Assume a rotation schedule. Define the total setup time during a cycle $\tau = \Sigma_j \tau_j$. Using this quantity, show how to adapt the methods of Section 3.4 to determine the optimal cycle length u^*.

5.21 Consider a series system with a slow-changing demand rate $\lambda(t)$, as in Section 5.7.1. Suggest an approximation of the total average cost, analogous to (4.2.2). (*Hint:* Compute something like C^- for each point in time.) Provide the best argument you can to support this approximation.

5.22 Consider the optimization model (5.7.1) to (5.7.4) representing a general system in discrete time. That model presumes one-for-one input/output usage. Suppose instead that an output unit of item j requires precisely a_{ij} units of item i, for all $i \in Pre\,(j)$. Show how to modify the formulation. (*Hint:* Only one change is necessary.)

5.23 Consider problem (5.7.1) to (5.7.4). Let $d_i(t)$, $x_i(t)$, and $h_i(t)$ denote the echelon-i demand, inventory, and holding cost, respectively, at time t. Give expressions for these quantities in terms of local data and variables. Write down an equivalent formulation using these echelon-level quantities. [Notice, the dynamics become simpler than (5.7.2), but the constraints become more complex than (5.7.3).]

5.24 Consider problem (5.7.1) to (5.7.4) for the special case of a series system. Assume that $h'_j(t)$ is nondecreasing in j for each t, and $k_j(t)$ and $c_j(t)$ are nonincreasing in t for each j. Argue (by contradiction, as in the proof of Theorem 5.3.1) that the optimal solution is nested.

Actually, your argument should require only the following weaker condition: For all $t < u$ and all j, define

$$\bar{c}_j[t, u) = c_j(t) + \Sigma_{s=t+1}^{u} h_j(s) - c_j(u)$$

where $h_j(s) = h'_j(s) - h'_{j-1}(s)$. (This is analogous to the quantity $\bar{c}[t, u)$ in the proof of Theorem 4.3.1.) The condition is that $k_j(t)$ is nonincreasing in t and all $\bar{c}_j[t, u) \geq 0$.

5.25 Consider a three-item assembly system, where items 1 and 2 feed the final product, item 3. Suppose there are positive transfer leadtimes L_{13} and L_{23}. Show precisely how to augment the initial conditions (5.7.1) and add certain terminal conditions to reflect these leadtimes.

C H A P T E R

6 Stochastic Demand: One Item with Constant Leadtimes

Outline

6.1 Introduction

6.1.1 Major Themes

This chapter addresses some of the truly basic issues of operations management: How should we control a system whose demand is uncertain? What are the effects of such uncertainties on system performance?

Here, we explore these issues for an otherwise simple system; there is only one item, the supply process generates constant leadtimes and perfect quality, and demand is stationary. Subsequent chapters study more complex systems with stochastic leadtimes and imperfect quality (Chapter 7), multiple items (Chapter 8), and time-varying demand (Chapter 9). Also, this chapter assumes that stockouts are backlogged; Chapter 7 treats the lost-sales case.

Stochastic demand, in combination with an order leadtime, raises altogether new difficulties: As a result of the leadtime, there is a delay between the actions we take and their actual effects. Such lags raise no problems if demand is certain, as we have seen, for then we know what will happen during the leadtime, and we can adjust our current actions to compensate. Likewise, in the extreme (and rare) case of zero leadtime, even with random demands, we retain full control of the system. Here, this is no longer true; we must act in the dark, unable to foresee the ultimate effects of our actions. In particular, no matter what we do, an unexpected surge in demand can exhaust our stock, leaving us unable to meet subsequent demands; some degree of stockout risk is inevitable.

Generally, longer leadtimes and greater demand uncertainty both degrade the precision with which we can control the system. And the less precise the control is, the more inventory we need to serve customers adequately. The primary goal of this chapter is to probe and elaborate this intuitive insight, to understand precisely how these combined effects work.

One major conclusion is that the primary impact of these factors can be captured by a single summary measure, denoted σ, the *standard deviation of leadtime demand.* We shall explain what this means in due course. For now, think of σ as an index of imprecision, a measure of the noise or variation that impedes our efforts to control the system. (The next chapter shows that σ also captures the effect of leadtime uncertainty.) Along with other parameters examined earlier, such as the demand rate and the fixed order cost, σ is a major determinant of performance. Anything we can do to reduce it—and there are typically several ways—will improve the system.

On the other hand, reducing variation takes patient effort, and it is virtually never possible to eliminate it entirely. These simple facts are widely unappreciated: Too many firms proudly promulgate policies mandating perfect customer service *and* zero inventories, while neglecting to mobilize the resources needed to confront variation in a serious way. These are pieties, not policies. Our aim must be to *manage* stockout risk, and to do this intelligently we must understand its underlying sources.

6.1.2 Summary

Here is a brief overview of what lies ahead: Throughout the chapter we model time as continuous, but demand, inventory, and other quantities as discrete (integer-valued). We pose several models of demand and supply. In each case we specify a plausible type of control policy.

The initial goal is performance evaluation, to calculate the key measures of performance for any policy in the specified class. Sometimes we obtain exact formulas, but we also develop useful approximations. We explore some of the properties of these formulas, to learn how performance responds to alternative controls and to changes in the model parameters. This mode of analysis takes up Sections 6.2 to 6.4 and much of Sections 6.6 and 6.7.

Later (in Section 6.5 and parts of Sections 6.6 and 6.7), we introduce cost factors, define an overall cost function, and show how to determine the *best* policy (within a given class). Because the models here are so complex, we cannot always express the optimal solution in closed form. We do obtain such formulas for certain special cases and approximations. Otherwise, we show how to compute the optimal policy by fairly simple numerical methods. Even without closed-form formulas, moreover, we learn a good deal about the qualitative behavior of the optimal policy and its performance. It is here that we see most clearly the impact of the variation index σ.

6.1.3 Demand Models

The basic demand model is the *Poisson process,* the simplest model of random events over time: Demands occur one unit at a time. In every small time interval, a demand may or may not occur. Each such interval has the same potential to contain a demand, no matter what happens during other intervals. This potential is measured by a positive number λ, the average demand rate. Section 6.2 focuses on this type of demand process.

Section 6.3 introduces a more general model. Again, demands occur one at a time, and there is no predictable variation over time. So, there is again a constant demand rate λ. However, there is some exogenous system (conditions in the economy, for example) whose behavior partly determines the demands. The state of this system provides information about future demands. We call this system the *world,* and demand a *world-driven demand process.* Because of their dependence on the underlying world system, demands during different time intervals are correlated. (Chapter 9 treats a time-varying world system, as well as time-varying demand.)

We study one particular case in detail, where the world is represented by a continuous-time Markov chain. Here, the demand process is called a *Markov-chain-driven counting process,* or *MCDC process.* Such a process can be either more or less variable (and thus lead to a higher or lower σ) than a Poisson process, depending on its details.

Section 6.6 considers a model of lumpy demands, a *compound-Poisson process.* Customers arrive according to a Poisson process, but the *amount* each customer demands is random. Such a process generally leads to a larger σ than a Poisson process, because the demand sizes add another source of uncertainty, in addition to the timing of demands.

For all the differences in these models, the end results of their analysis—the performance formulas—nearly all share a common form. Consequently, many important qualitative properties of the performance measures hold universally. Moreover, the optimization methods of Section 6.5 apply to a wide variety of systems.

6.1.4 Policies

What is a reasonable control policy in a stochastic environment? Intuitively, we would like to respond sensibly to demand fluctuations, maintaining sufficient discipline to avoid overreaction. Also, any rule we adopt should be simple, i.e., easy to understand and to implement. The policies we explore here meet these requirements, and they are widely used in practice. (Chapter 9 proves that such a policy is optimal among all policies under certain reasonable assumptions. For now, however, we take these policy forms as given.)

The policies of Chapter 3, assuming deterministic demand at a constant rate, have two pleasing properties: The orders are all of the *same size,* and they are placed at *equal intervals* of time; in both quantity and timing orders are regular and predictable. With random demands, at least one of these regularities must be foregone. We can still place orders at regular intervals, but then the order quantities will vary. Or we can order equal amounts, so that the timing of orders becomes unpredictable. Each of these alternatives makes planning more difficult.

Here, we focus mainly on the second approach, that is, we base orders on observing the inventory position, not the clock or the calendar. In practice, this means we need an information system capable of tracking the inventory position, which requires recording demands as they occur. These are sometimes called *transaction reporting systems.* (Such systems are fairly common now, because of the advent of electronic point-of-sale terminals and related communication technologies.) Section 6.7.3 briefly discusses a periodic-review policy, where orders are placed at regular intervals. Chapter 9 treats discrete-time models, in which a regular grid of possible order times is imposed on the problem from the beginning.

Most of the chapter, assuming demands occur one unit at a time, focuses on the *order-quantity/reorder-point policy,* or (r, q) policy, introduced in Section 3.3. An important special case is the *base-stock policy,* where $q = 1$.

For the lumpy-demand case (Section 6.6), we consider *two* plausible extensions of the (r, q) policies. The first, also called an (r, q) policy, orders integer multiples of q. The second, called an (r, s) policy, orders enough to raise the inventory position to a fixed target level s. Also, Section 6.7.2 explores a more elaborate policy for world-driven demand, which bases order decisions on information about the world.

6.2 Policy Evaluation: Poisson Demand

6.2.1 Preliminaries

This section shows how to compute performance measures for a given policy. Throughout, demand is a Poisson process. This subsection sets forth some basic notation and technical preliminaries. The next two subsections present the main results; Section 6.2.2 focuses on the special case of a base-stock policy, while Section 6.2.3 treats the general (r, q) policy. Section 6.2.4 discusses customer waiting times. All proofs are collected in Section 6.2.5.

Denote

$$\lambda = \text{demand rate}$$

$$\mathrm{L} = \text{leadtime}$$

$$q = \text{batch size}$$

$$r = \text{reorder point}$$

$$E[\cdot] = \text{expectation}$$

$$V[\cdot] = \text{variance}$$

$$t = \text{continuous time variable, } t \geq 0$$

For each $t \geq 0$, let

$$D(t) = \text{cumulative demand through time } t\text{, i.e., demand in the interval } (0, t]$$

$$D(t, u] = \text{demand in the interval } (t, u]$$

$$= D(u) - D(t)\,,\ u \geq t$$

These are random variables. The *demand process* is a stochastic process, the collection of random variables $\mathbf{D} = \{D(t) : t \geq 0\}$.

FIGURE 6.2.1

Demands, orders, and receipts.

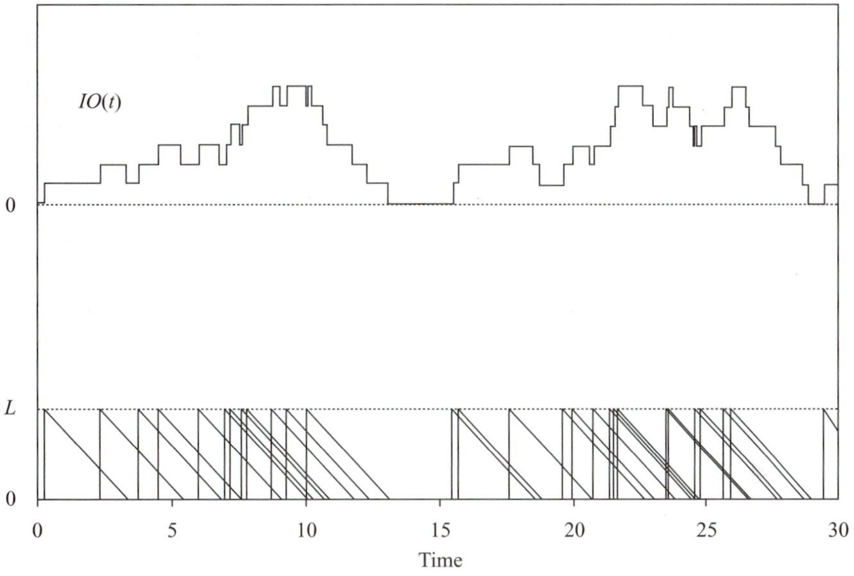

Here, **D** is a Poisson process with rate λ. That is, the probability of a demand occurring in a short time interval of length Δt is roughly $\lambda(\Delta t)$, independent of what happens in other intervals. Moreover, the chance that the interval contains more than one demand is negligible. (Technically, the probability of one demand is $\lambda(\Delta t) + o(\Delta t)$, and that of more than one is $o(\Delta t)$.)

This implies that $D(t)$ has the Poisson distribution with mean λt, that is,

$$Pr\,\{D(t) = d\} = \frac{(\lambda t)^d e^{-\lambda t}}{d!} \qquad d \geq 0$$

Also, $D(t, u]$ has the Poisson distribution with mean $\lambda(u - t)$, which depends on the interval $(t, u]$ only through its length, not its location. Finally, $D(t)$ and $D(t, u]$ are independent. (In technical terms, **D** has stationary, independent increments. See Section C.2.3.4 and Section C.5.6 in Appendix C for more about Poisson distributions and processes.)

Figure 6.2.1 illustrates (among other things) some demands generated by a Poisson process. The demands are quite irregular; in several places, they seem to occur in bunches, and there are long gaps with no demands at all. This behavior is typical.

A Poisson process is widely used to model demand for several reasons: It is easy to specify; the rate λ is its only parameter. In many practical situations, moreover, the model is fairly accurate; demand really does behave like a Poisson process. (One reason is that demand often comes from many small, nearly independent sources, e.g., customers spread over a large region, and a Poisson process approximates such an aggregate process reasonably well.) Finally, the mathematical simplicity of this model smooths the tasks of analysis and calculation.

Given a fixed policy, several state variables describe the evolution of the system over time. For each time $t \geq 0$,

$$I(t) = \text{inventory on hand}$$

$$B(t) = \text{backorders outstanding}$$

$$IN(t) = \text{net inventory} = I(t) - B(t)$$

$$A(t) = \text{stockout indicator} = \mathbf{1}\{IN(t) \leq 0\}$$

$$IO(t) = \text{inventory on order}$$

$$IP(t) = \text{inventory position} = IN(t) + IO(t)$$

Each of these quantities is a random variable. To indicate a quantity over *all t* we use bold letters, like **D** above, for example, $\mathbf{I} = \{I(t) : t \geq 0\}$. This is a stochastic process, as are **B, IN,** etc. The net inventory $IN(t)$ determines the stockout indicator $A(t)$, as above, and also both the inventory and backorders by

$$I(t) = [IN(t)]^+ \qquad B(t) = [IN(t)]^-$$

The performance measures of primary interest are the same as in Section 3.3:

$$\overline{A} = \text{average stockout frequency}$$

$$\overline{B} = \text{average backorders}$$

$$\overline{I} = \text{average inventory}$$

$$\overline{OF} = \text{average order frequency.}$$

These are long-run averages, e.g.,

$$\overline{I} = \lim_{T \to \infty} \{\left(\frac{1}{T}\right)\int_0^T I(t)\, dt\}$$

But it is not obvious that this limit exists or how to compute it. Fortunately, under the assumptions above, it turns out that **I** is well-behaved in two important senses: First, **I** is *ergodic.* The precise technical meaning of this property is not important here, but it implies that the limit above does exist (with probability 1). Indeed, it implies that **I** has a long-run frequency distribution; i.e., for every integer *i,* the following limit exists (with probability 1):

$$g_{\underline{I}}(i) = \lim_{T \to \infty} [\left(\frac{1}{T}\right)\int_0^T \mathbf{1}\{I(t) = i\}\, dt]$$

$\underline{I}$ denotes a random variable with this distribution; then, $\overline{I} = E[\underline{I}]$. Second, **I** has a *limiting distribution.* This means that the probability distributions of the random variables $I(t)$ converge to a limit as $t \to \infty$, and this limit does not depend on initial conditions. Let

I = equilibrium inventory, a random variable having the limiting distribution of $\boldsymbol{I}$

It is relatively easy to determine this distribution. The ergodic property further implies that the limiting distribution is precisely $g_{\underline{I}}$ above; that is, I has the same distribution as $\underline{I}$. So, $\overline{I} = E[I]$.

The other stochastic processes above are well-behaved in the same senses. In particular, **IN** is. So, we shall take the following general approach: Determine the distribution of

$$IN = \text{equilibrium net inventory}$$

Use this to determine the distributions of I and

$$A = \text{equilibrium stockout indicator}$$

$$B = \text{equilibrium backorders}$$

Then, compute $\bar{I} = E[I]$, $\bar{A} = E[A]$, and $\bar{B} = E[B]$.

To describe IN, it turns out, we need the distributions of two other random variables. The first is

$$IP = \text{equilibrium inventory position}$$

Its distribution is relatively simple. The second random variable is called the *leadtime demand,* denoted D. The variation index σ is precisely the standard deviation of D. It is mainly through D, and especially σ, that the demand and supply processes affect the system's performance.

6.2.2 Base-Stock Policies—A Unit Batch Size

6.2.2.1 Discussion

Suppose we follow an (r, q) policy with batch size $q = 1$, called a *base-stock policy.* Such a policy makes sense when economies of scale in the supply system are negligible relative to other factors. For example, when each individual unit is very valuable, holding and backorder costs clearly dominate any fixed order costs. Likewise, for a slow-moving product (one with a low demand rate), the economics of the situation clearly rule out large batch sizes. Also, sometimes there is a natural quantity unit for *both* demand and supply (e.g., a truckload), and in terms of that unit it makes sense to set $q = 1$.

Since q is fixed to 1, there is only one remaining policy variable, r. It is convenient to use the equivalent variable

$$s = \text{base-stock level} = r + 1$$

The policy aims to keep the inventory position at the constant value s: If the system starts with $IP(0^-) \leq s$, we immediately order the difference, so that $IP(0) = s$. If $IP(0^-) > s$, we order nothing until demand reduces $IP(t)$ to s. Once $IP(t)$ hits s, it remains there from then on. (This explains the names *base-stock level* and *base-stock policy.*) The policy is sometimes called a *one-for-one replenishment policy,* because from the moment $IP(t)$ first reaches s, each demand causes an order to be placed immediately. (The capital letter S is sometimes used instead of s; yet another name for a base-stock policy is an $(S - 1, S)$ policy.)

6.2.2.2 Analysis

Suppose for now that $s \geq 0$, and $IN(0) = I(0) = IP(0^-) = s$. Thus, orders coincide with demands. Also, each order remains outstanding for time L. So, $IO(t)$ (outstanding orders) does not depend on the choice of s.

Figure 6.2.1 helps to visualize how demands and orders interact. In the lower part of the figure, each demand is indicated by a vertical line of height L. There is a diagonal line attached to each one with slope -1. So, if there is a demand at t, the diagonal line meets the time axis at $t + L$, precisely the moment the corresponding order arrives. Now, pick an arbitrary time t, not necessarily a demand point, and count the number of diagonal lines above the time axis at t. The result is just $IO(t)$. The upper part of the figure graphs $IO(t)$. (This system has $\lambda = 1$ and $L = 3$.)

Choose any $t > L$. Any order placed *before* $t - L$ must have arrived before t, and so cannot be included in $IO(t)$; and of course, $IO(t)$ does not include any orders placed *after* t. The orders included in $IO(t)$ are precisely those placed in the interval $(t - L, t]$. But each such order corresponds to a demand, so $IO(t)$ is simply the demand during $(t - L, t]$, or

$$IO(t) = D(t - L, t]$$

Consequently, $IO(t)$ has the Poisson distribution with mean λL.

The definition of $IP(t)$ is

$$IP(t) = IN(t) + IO(t)$$

but $IP(t)$ is just the constant s. So,

$$IN(t) = s - IO(t) \tag{6.2.1}$$

The net inventory $IN(t)$ is just a translation of $IO(t) = D(t - L, t]$. Also, although we assumed $IP(0^-) = s$, (6.2.1) clearly holds regardless of starting conditions for sufficiently large t (i.e., such that $IP(t - L) = s$).

Since $IO(t)$ has the same distribution for all large t, certainly **IO** has a limiting distribution, and therefore so does **IN.** The limiting random variable IO has the Poisson distribution with mean λL, and

$$IN = s - IO \tag{6.2.2}$$

This is the main result. It is convenient to express it in slightly different terms: Call $D(t, t + L]$ the leadtime demand beginning at t, and let

$D =$ leadtime demand, a generic random variable with the Poisson distribution with mean λL

i.e., the same distribution as IO and $D(t, t + L]$. (The symbol D stood for the demand during a leadtime in Chapter 3 also, but there it was the constant λL.) Then,

$$IN(t + L) = s - D(t, t + L]$$

$$IN = s - D \tag{6.2.3}$$

As shown later (Theorem 6.2.3), this identity also describes the long-run frequency distribution of **IN.**

We can now compute the key system performance measures: Let g denote the probability mass function (pmf) of D, G^0 its complementary cumulative distribution (ccdf), and G^1 its loss function. (The latter is $G^1(d) = E[[D - d]^+]$, as in Section C.2.2.) From (6.2.3),

$$\overline{A} = Pr\,\{IN \leq 0\} = Pr\,\{D \geq s\} = G^0(s-1) \tag{6.2.4}$$

$$\overline{B} = E[[IN]^-] = E[[D-s]^+] = G^1(s) \tag{6.2.5}$$

$$\overline{I} = E[[IN]^+] = E[IN + [IN]^-] = s - \lambda L + \overline{B} \tag{6.2.6}$$

And, of course, $\overline{OF} = \lambda$.

There are no closed-form formulas for G^0 and G^1, so we must compute them directly; i.e., $\overline{A} = G^0(s-1) = 1 - \Sigma_{j<s}\, g(j)$ and $\overline{B} = G^1(s) = \lambda L - \Sigma_{0 \leq j < s}\, G^0(j)$. [Special care is needed to get good accuracy for very large s; see Section C.2.3.4. An alternative expression for G^1 is given below in (6.2.18).]

Formulas (6.2.4) to (6.2.6) are correct even for $s < 0$, with $G^0(s) = 1$ and $G^1(s) = -(s - \lambda L)$, $s < 0$. We would *never* choose a negative s in practice, however: For $s = 0$, $\overline{I} = 0$; inventory can be reduced no further. Making s negative leaves $\overline{I} = 0$, but increases $\overline{B}$.

Incidentally, for any model with Poisson demand, including this one, $\overline{A}$ is also the long-run fraction of demands backordered, so $1 - \overline{A}$ is the fill rate, the fraction of demands filled immediately. This fact reflects a fundamental property of Poisson processes, known by the acronym PASTA, which stands for "Poisson arrivals see time averages." The time average in question here is $\overline{A}$, and PASTA asserts that a typical arriving customer finds no inventory, and so is backordered, with frequency $\overline{A}$. We use the PASTA property again later on.

6.2.2.3 Behavior of Performance Measures

The performance measures above depend on the system parameters λ and L *only through their product* λL, the mean leadtime demand. You might guess that a system with a high demand rate and a short leadtime would behave quite differently from one with a low demand rate and a long leadtime. No: As long as λL is the same for the two systems, their performance characteristics are identical.

The formulas reveal the qualitative effects on performance of changes in s: First, $\overline{B}$ is *decreasing and convex* as a function of s; as the base-stock level increases, backorders decline, but at an ever slower rate. Similarly, $\overline{I}$ *is increasing and convex* in s. As for $\overline{A}$, it is *decreasing* in s; increasing the base-stock level reduces the stockout probability. (However, $\overline{A}$ is not generally convex in s. It happens to be convex when $\lambda L \leq 1$, but not otherwise.)

Figure 6.2.2 graphs $\overline{B}$ and $\overline{I}$ as functions of s for four different values of L with $\lambda = 10$. (Because $\overline{B}$ and $\overline{I}$ depend on λ and L only through λL, we would obtain the same family of curves were we to fix L at 1 but increase λ to 20, 30, and 40.) The decreasing curves describe $\overline{B}$, and the increasing curves $\overline{I}$. Clearly, all these functions are convex. (Also, for each L, the $\overline{B}$ and $\overline{I}$ curves cross near $s = \lambda L$, and they seem almost mirror images of one another; that is, if we reflect $\overline{B}$ around the vertical line at $s = \lambda L$, we obtain something close to $\overline{I}$.)

Next, compare the performance curves for different values of L. As L increases, the most visible effect is the *shift* of both curves to the right. So, as L grows, we must shift s accordingly to maintain performance at roughly the same levels. To see the effect of L on the shapes of the curves, consider Figure 6.2.3. Here, we translate all the curves to a common center, by changing the horizontal axis to $s - \lambda L$. Viewed in this way, *both* $\overline{B}$ and $\overline{I}$ grow larger as L increases. This effect is strongest near $s = \lambda L$.

FIGURE 6.2.2

Performance of base-stock policies.

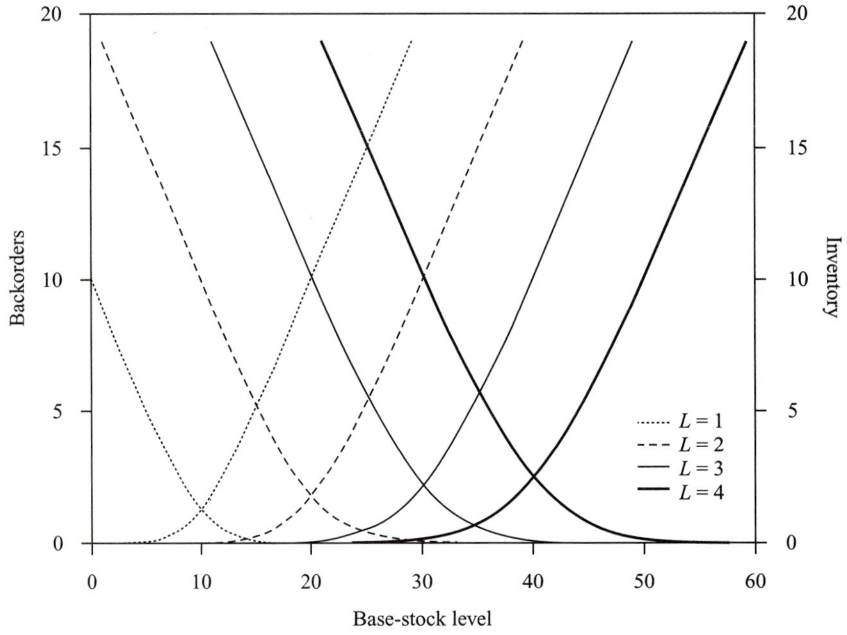

FIGURE 6.2.3

Performance of base-stock policies (centered).

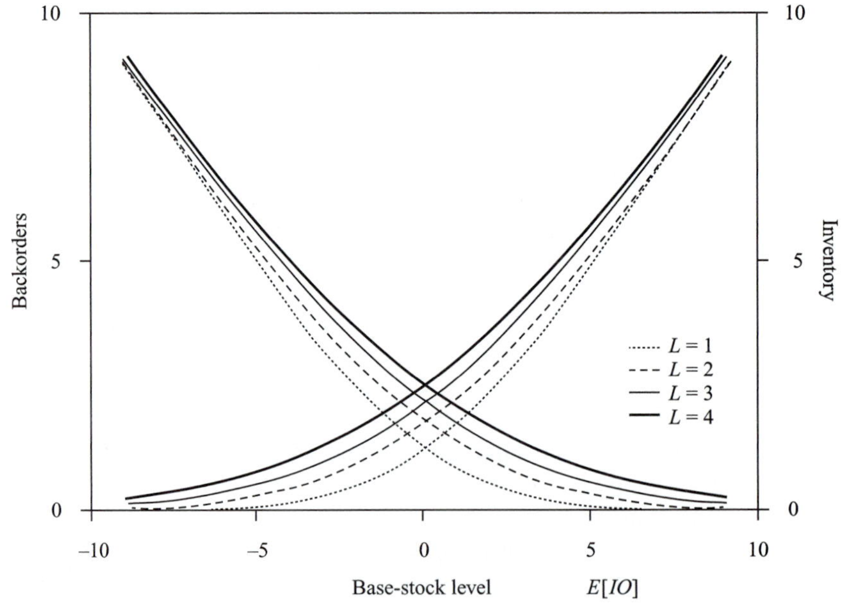

FIGURE 6.2.4

Stock-service tradeoff.

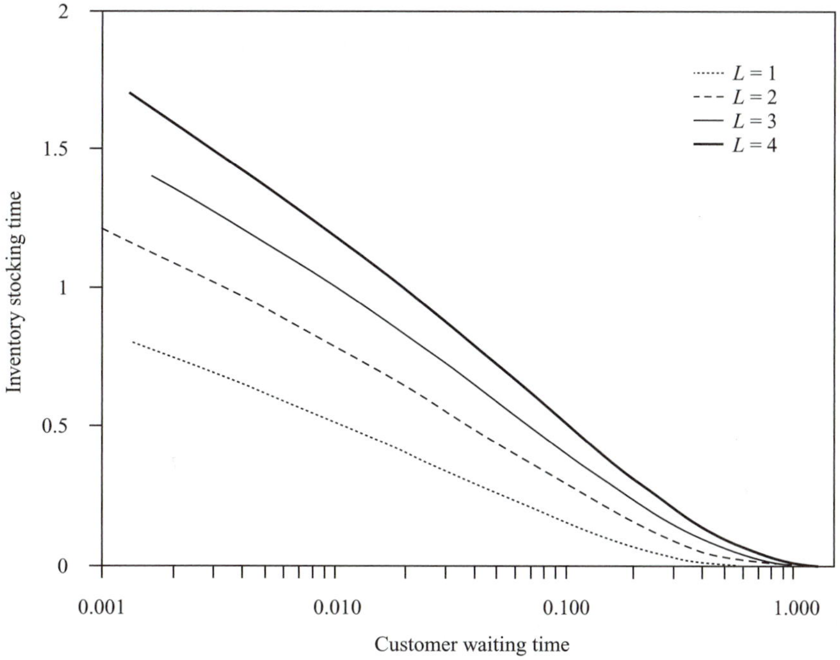

To judge the effect of L on overall performance, it is useful to graph the same data in a different form, as in Figure 6.2.4. Here, we use the rescaled performance measures

$$\overline{BW} = \text{average customer backorder waiting time}$$

$$\overline{IW} = \text{average stocking time, the time a unit spends in inventory}$$

instead of $\overline{B}$ and $\overline{I}$. Section 6.2.4 shows that $\overline{BW} = \overline{B}/\lambda$ and $\overline{IW} = \overline{I}/\lambda$. For each s the figure plots the corresponding values of $\overline{BW}$ and $\overline{IW}$. (The actual values of s are suppressed.) The resulting curves show how much stocking time is necessary to achieve a specified waiting time. (The logarithmic scale for waiting time reveals the relationships better.)

It is clear from the figure that performance deteriorates as the leadtime grows. To achieve a given desired waiting time, as L increases, we must increase the stocking time (by increasing s), or, to maintain a given stocking time, we must accept a longer waiting time. There is a clear, tangible benefit to reducing the leadtime.

6.2.2.4 Selecting a Policy to Meet a Service Constraint

Evidently, there is a conflict between the customer-service measures $\overline{A}$, $\overline{B}$, and inventory $\overline{I}$. Given a service-level target, e.g., an upper limit $1 - \omega_{-}$ on $\overline{A}$, we want to set s large enough to meet this constraint, but otherwise as small as possible. Conversely, given an upper limit on $\overline{I}$, set s as large as possible to minimize $\overline{A}$ and $\overline{B}$, while maintaining feasibility.

EXAMPLE 6.2.A, PART 1

The manager of a large urban classical record store is trying to determine a sensible stocking policy for a CD of Beethoven's Seventh Symphony (played by Bernstein and the New York Philharmonic). Demand for this particular item is a Poisson process of rate 3.6 per month, and the leadtime is 2 weeks. The manager aims to fill about 80% of demands directly from stock.

Express the leadtime as 0.5 months. So, the average leadtime demand is $\lambda L = (3.6)(0.5) = 1.8$. Direct calculation yields the performance of alternative base-stock policies:

s	$\overline{A}$	$\overline{I}$	$\overline{B}$
0	1.00	0.00	1.80
1	0.83	0.17	0.97
2	0.54	0.63	0.43
3	0.27	1.36	0.16
4	0.11	2.25	0.05
5	0.04	3.21	0.01
6	0.01	4.20	0.00

The performance target is $\overline{A} \leq 1 - \omega_2 = 0.2$, so the manager should set s $= 4$. With this policy, the average inventory will be 2.25.

You might wonder about the various assumptions here. Classical CDs do have roughly Poisson demands. Many customers, though not all, insist on a particular recording (they will not take, say, Karajan and the Berlin Philharmonic as a substitute), and are willing to wait a while if the item is not in stock. Popular CDs, in contrast, sometimes have more volatile demands (as discussed in Section 6.3 below), and stockouts are more likely to result in lost sales (see Section 7.2).

Another way to resolve the conflict is by cost optimization. We postpone that discussion until Section 6.5.

6.2.3 *General Batch Sizes*

Next, we evaluate a general (r, q) policy, where q is any positive integer. Figure 6.2.5 illustrates the behavior of **IP** and **IN.** The heavy curve is IN(t), and the lighter one is $IP(t)$. In this example $r = 4$ and $q = 3$. The demands are the same as in Figure 6.2.1; they occur at the times where $IN(t)$ jumps down. $IP(t)$ jumps up (from $r + 1$ to $r + q$) when an order is placed, while $IN(t)$ jumps up (by $q = 3$) when an order is received. Notice that there are a few intervals where $IN(t) = IP(t)$, so there are no outstanding orders. The rest of the time, $IN(t) < IP(t)$, which means there are some outstanding orders.

6.2.3.1 Analysis

Policy evaluation now requires a rather different approach, and more effort, than before. The analysis proceeds in four steps:

FIGURE 6.2.5

Inventory position and net inventory.

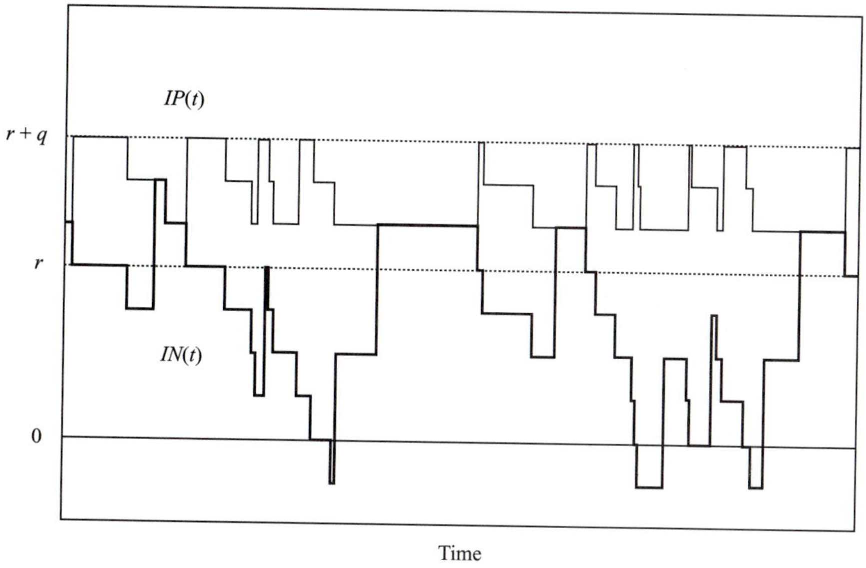

1. Determine the limiting distribution of **IP**, that is, the distribution of *IP.*
2. Describe the relation between **IP** and **D.**
3. Determine the limiting distribution of **IN,** that is, the distribution of *IN.*
4. Derive formulas for performance measures.

The end results are equations (6.2.8) to (6.2.13) below. (The proofs of all the results in this section are collected at the end in Section 6.2.5.)

Step 1 uses the following lemma:

LEMMA 6.2.1. The stationary, the limiting, and the long-run frequency distributions of **IP** are uniform on the integers in the interval $[r + 1, r + q]$. That is,

$$Pr\,\{IP = i\} = \frac{1}{q} \qquad i = r + 1, \ldots, r + q$$

Step 2: For fixed *t,* the random variables $IP(t)$ and $D(t, t + L]$ are *independent.* This follows directly from the fact that $IP(t)$ depends on the demand process up to time *t,* while $D(t, t + L]$ does not.

Step 3 begins with a lemma, the stochastic analogue of equation (3.3.1) in Chapter 3.

LEMMA 6.2.2. For all $t \geq 0$,

$$IN(t + L) = IP(t) - D(t, t + L] \tag{6.2.7}$$

The next result generalizes equation (6.2.3) to any $q > 0$:

THEOREM 6.2.3. The limiting distribution of the net inventory is described by the equation

$$IN = IP - D$$

where IP is uniformly distributed on the integers in the interval $[r + 1, r + q]$, D has the Poisson distribution with mean λL, and the two variables IP and D are independent. This also describes the stationary and long-run frequency distributions of **IN.**

Step 4: First, $\overline{B}$ is precisely the mean of the long-run frequency distribution of **B,** which is in turn a function of **IN.** It follows that $\overline{B} = E[B]$; similarly, $\overline{I} = E[I]$.

Theorem 6.2.3 tells us that IN is the difference of two independent random variables, IP and D. Condition on IP, say $IP = s$. The distribution of $[IN|IP = s]$ is given by (6.2.3). The (unconditional) distribution of IN is a simple average of these conditional distributions over $s = r + 1, \ldots, r + q$. This fact allows us to construct formulas for $\overline{A}$, $\overline{B}$, and $\overline{I}$ using their counterparts (6.2.4) to (6.2.6) for base-stock policies as building blocks. Let $\overline{A}(s)$, $\overline{B}(s)$, and $\overline{I}(s)$ denote the performance measures for a base-stock policy, now written as explicit functions of s. Likewise, let $\overline{A}(r; q)$, $\overline{B}(r; q)$, and $\overline{I}(r; q)$ denote the performance measures for an (r, q) policy. Then,

$$\begin{aligned}\overline{A}(r; q) &= Pr\{IN \le 0\} \\ &= \Sigma_{s=r+1}^{r+q}\left(\frac{1}{q}\right) Pr\{IN \le 0 \mid IP = s\} \\ &= \left(\frac{1}{q}\right)\Sigma_{s=r+1}^{r+q}\overline{A}(s) \qquad (6.2.8)\end{aligned}$$

Similarly,

$$\overline{B}(r; q) = \left(\frac{1}{q}\right)\Sigma_{s=r+1}^{r+q}\overline{B}(s) \qquad (6.2.9)$$

$$\overline{I}(r; q) = \left(\frac{1}{q}\right)\Sigma_{s=r+1}^{r+q}\overline{I}(s) \qquad (6.2.10)$$

Thus, system performance using a policy with $q > 1$ can be represented as a simple average of the performance of several base-stock policies.

We can write these quantities explicitly in terms of the first- and second-order loss functions of D, G^1, and G^2. The latter is $G^2(d) = \Sigma_{j>d}^{\infty} G^1(j) = ½(\lambda L)^2 - \Sigma_{0<j\le d} G^1(j)$. From (6.2.8) to (6.2.10) it immediately follows that

$$\overline{A} = \left(\frac{1}{q}\right)[G^1(r) - G^1(r + q)] \qquad (6.2.11)$$

$$\overline{B} = \left(\frac{1}{q}\right)[G^2(r) - G^2(r + q)] \qquad (6.2.12)$$

$$\overline{I} = ½(q + 1) + r - \lambda L + \overline{B} \qquad (6.2.13)$$

(Notice the close connection between $\overline{I}$ and $\overline{B}$. We observed a similar relation in the case of deterministic demand in Chapter 3. The only difference is that here we have a term

$\frac{1}{2}(q + 1)$ instead of $\frac{1}{2}q$. This difference is entirely a result of the demand quantities being discrete, as indicated in Problem 3.8.)

Finally, consider the order frequency $\overline{OF}$. Demands occur at rate λ, and an order is placed every q demands, so

$$\overline{OF} = \frac{\lambda}{q}$$

as in Chapter 3. We now have expressions for all the performance criteria.

These formulas are correct for all integer values of r, even negative ones. We would *never* wish to use a policy with $r < -q$, however, just as we would avoid a base-stock policy with $s < 0$: At $r = -q$, $\overline{I} = 0$. Reducing r below this value leaves $\overline{I} = 0$ but increases backorders. Thus, we can restrict $r \geq -q$.

Incidentally, the functions G^1 and G^2 can be written in terms of G^0 and g:

$$G^1(d) = -(d - \lambda L)G^0(d) + \lambda L g(d) \tag{6.2.14}$$

$$G^2(d) = \tfrac{1}{2}\{[(d - \lambda L)^2 + d]G^0(d) - \lambda L(d - \lambda L)g(d)\} \tag{6.2.15}$$

(See Problem 6.6. These expressions exploit the specific form of the Poisson distribution. They are not much easier to compute than the general loss-function definitions above. However, they give better numerical accuracy for large d, given accurate calculations of $G^0(d)$ and $g(d)$.)

6.2.3.2 Behavior of Performance Measures

Formulas (6.2.8) to (6.2.10) imply that $\overline{A}(r, q)$, $\overline{B}(r, q)$, and $\overline{I}(r, q)$, viewed as functions of r, inherit the qualitative properties of $\overline{A}(s)$, $\overline{B}(s)$, and $\overline{I}(s)$: For fixed q, $\overline{B}$ is decreasing and convex in r, while $\overline{I}$ is increasing and convex. (For $r \geq -q$, both functions are strictly convex.) $\overline{A}$ is decreasing in r, but not necessarily convex.

The effects of q are more subtle. Of course, $\overline{OF}$ is decreasing and convex in q. Also, we see immediately from (6.2.8) to (6.2.10) that $\overline{A}$ and $\overline{B}$ are decreasing in q for *fixed r*, and $\overline{I}$ is increasing. This fact by itself is not really germane, however. What matters is the effect of q on the available *ranges* of the performance measures as r *varies*.

We can see this effect by changing variables, as in Figure 6.2.6. For fixed $\lambda L = 20$ and several *odd* values of q, the figure graphs $\overline{B}$ and $\overline{I}$ against $s' = r + \frac{1}{2}(q + 1)$, not r itself. This s' is the center point of the integers $s = r + 1, \ldots, r + q$ over which the averages are computed. As q changes, we adjust r to compare $\overline{B}$ and $\overline{I}$ at the same center point s'. Viewed in this way, *both* $\overline{B}$ and $\overline{I}$ increase as q grows. (This property follows directly from the convexity of $\overline{B}(s)$ and $\overline{I}(s)$. See Problem 6.2.) The tradeoff between $\overline{B}$ and $\overline{I}$ becomes worse for larger q. This is the price we pay to reduce $\overline{OF}$.

For fixed q, by (6.2.8) to (6.2.10), performance deteriorates as L increases, as in the case $q = 1$. Though it is hard to see at this point, the same effect is felt overall, letting *both* r and q vary. (Section 6.5 verifies this statement.)

6.2.3.3 Selecting a Policy to Meet a Service Constraint

Again, there are conflicts between the performance measures. Suppose that q is fixed. Given the constraint $\overline{A} \leq 1 - \omega_-$, it is clear what to do: Set r large enough to meet the service requirement, but otherwise as small as possible.

FIGURE 6.2.6

Performance of (r, q) policies.

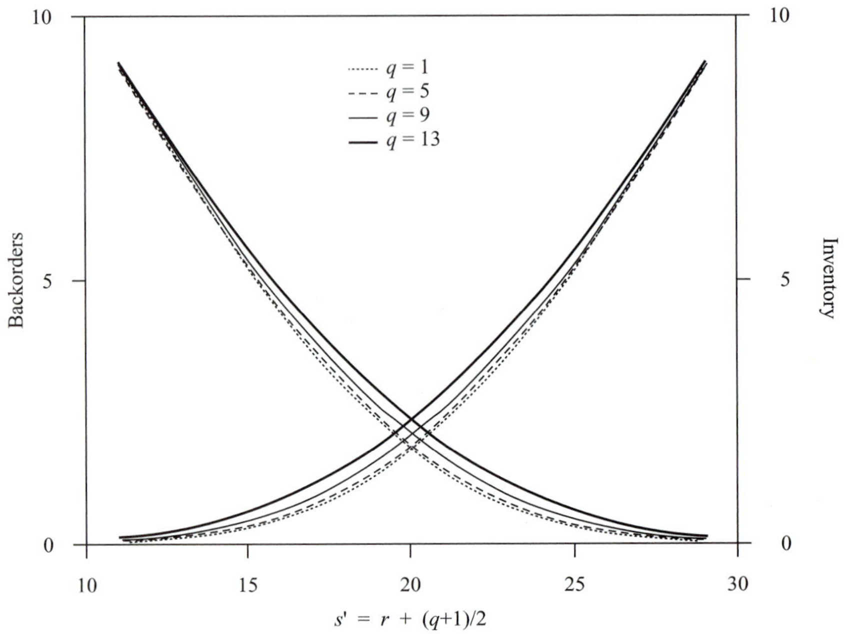

EXAMPLE 6.2.A, PART 2

The record store above must order CDs in batches of size $q = 2$, for some reason. The data remain $\lambda = 3.6$ and $L = 0.5$, and the service requirement remains $\overline{A} \leq 1 - \omega_{-} = 0.2$. The performance of certain (r, q) policies is as follows:

r	$\overline{A}$	$\overline{I}$
−1	0.92	0.09
0	0.69	0.40
1	0.41	1.00
2	0.19	1.81
3	0.08	2.73
4	0.03	3.71

So, the manager should set $r = 2$. This policy has $\overline{I} = 1.81$. (It is odd that this $\overline{I}$ is less than the base-stock policy's in Part 1 above. This is due entirely to the fact that integer policy variables cannot always hit a performance target exactly. Recall that the earlier policy with $s = 4$ has $\overline{A} = 0.11$, much lower than the required 0.2, while the (r, q) policy here just meets the requirement.)

FIGURE 6.2.7

Customer waiting times.

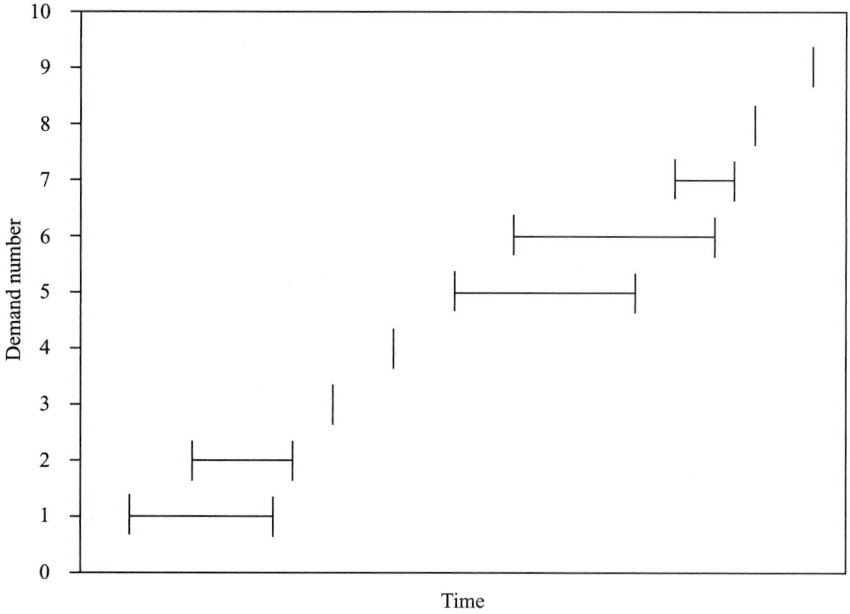

If q is not fixed, we still face a tradeoff between $\overline{OF}$ and $\overline{I}$. The cost-optimization framework of Section 6.5 addresses this issue.

6.2.4 Backorders and Waiting Time

Recall from Section 3.3.6 of Chapter 3 that, in that context, there is a close relation between the average backorders and the average customer waiting time, namely, $\overline{B} = \lambda\overline{BW}$. We now argue (somewhat heuristically) that the same relation applies here. Then, we prove (rigorously) an even stronger result.

Figure 6.2.7 depicts the waiting times experienced by a few customers. Each customer is represented by a horizontal bar, beginning when the demand occurs and ending when the demand is filled. Customers who do not wait (numbers 3, 4, 8, and 9 here) are indicated by short vertical lines—bars of zero length. Observe, $B(t)$ can be read by counting the bars above point t on the horizontal axis.

Now, let $\underline{BW}_n$ indicate the *cumulative total* waiting time experienced by the first n demands. Pick a value of t with $B(t) = 0$. Then, $\underline{BW}_{D(t)}$ is just the sum of the lengths of the bars ending before t. But, this quantity also equals the integral $\int_0^t B(u)\,du$.

For t with $B(t) \neq 0$ this is not quite true, since $\underline{BW}_{D(t)}$ includes parts of bars after t. Let $R(t)$ denote the difference, the sum of the bar lengths "hanging over" t. It seems intuitively clear that $R(t)$ should not grow systematically as t increases, specifically, that $\lim_{t\to\infty} R(t)/t = 0$. Therefore,

$$\begin{aligned}
\overline{B} &= \lim_{t\to\infty}\left(\frac{1}{t}\right)\int_0^t B(u)\,du \\
&= \lim_{t\to\infty}\left(\frac{1}{t}\right)(\underline{\mathrm{BW}}_{D(t)} - R(t)) \\
&= \lim_{t\to\infty}\left(\left\{\frac{D(t)}{t}\right\}\cdot\left\{\frac{\underline{\mathrm{BW}}_{D(t)}}{D(t)}\right\} - \left\{\frac{R(t)}{t}\right\}\right) \\
&= \lim_{t\to\infty}\left\{\frac{D(t)}{t}\right\}\cdot\lim_{t\to\infty}\left\{\frac{\underline{\mathrm{BW}}_{D(t)}}{D(t)}\right\} \\
&= \lambda\overline{BW}
\end{aligned}$$

(This result is analogous to Little's [1961] formula in the context of queues.) A similar argument shows that the average stocking time is related to the average inventory by $\overline{I} = \lambda\overline{IW}$.

By the way, this argument is valid for *any* processes where the averages $\overline{B}$, λ, and $\overline{IW}$ exist. It does not use the assumptions of Poisson demand and constant leadtimes. The result holds for quite general demand and supply processes, including those of Section 6.3 and Chapter 7.

Now, $\overline{BW}$ directly measures service to customers. The fact that it is proportional to $\overline{B}$ is the primary reason that $\overline{B}$ is important. Also, $\overline{BW}$ inherits the qualitative properties of $\overline{B}$ discussed above; for example, increasing s (or r) reduces the average customer waiting time.

EXAMPLE 6.2.A, PART 3

Reconsider the record store above (with $\lambda = 3.6$). Under the base-stock policy with $s = 4$, $\overline{B} = 0.05$, so $\overline{BW} = 0.05/3.6 = 0.014$ months, or about 0.4 days. Under the (r, q) policy with $q = r = 2$, $\overline{B} = 0.11$, so $\overline{BW} = 0.11/3.6 = 0.029$ months, or 0.9 days.

The following theorem is a sharper result. (It *does* assume Poisson demand and constant leadtimes. Actually, the result holds also for some of the more complex supply systems of Chapter 7, but not all; see Section 7.3.8.) Let BW denote the random variable describing the limiting distribution of waiting times, so $\overline{BW} = E[BW]$. Also, let $D(BW)$ indicate demand during the random time BW, where BW is independent of $\mathbf{D}$.

THEOREM 6.2.4. Assuming $r \geq -1$, $B = D(BW)$.

Thus, not only are the means of B and BW tightly linked, their distributions too are functionally dependent. Specifically, the theorem implies the following identity, relating the z-transform of B and the Laplace transform of BW:

COROLLARY 6.2.5.

$$\tilde{g}_B(z) = \tilde{f}_{BW}[\lambda(1 - z)] \tag{6.2.16}$$

In particular, (6.2.16) implies

$$E[B] = \lambda E[BW]$$
$$V[B] = \lambda E[BW] + \lambda^2 V[BW] \tag{6.2.17}$$

The first identity is simply $\overline{B} = \lambda\overline{BW}$, as above. The second enables us to compute the variance of BW from that of B.

So, what is $V[B]$? Consider the quantity $\tfrac{1}{2}E[B(B-1)]$. This is called the *second binomial moment* of B. For a base-stock policy, following the derivation of (6.2.5), one can show that

$$\tfrac{1}{2}E[B(B-1)] = G^2(s) \tag{6.2.18}$$

(See Problem 6.14. The function G^2 thus has several quite different uses!) For a general (r, q) policy, analogous to (6.2.9),

$$\frac{1}{2}\mathrm{E}[B(B-1)] = \left(\frac{1}{q}\right)\Sigma_{s=r+1}^{r+q} G^2(s)$$

Given this quantity, it easy to compute $V[B]$ and then $V[BW]$.

While $\overline{BW}$ is certainly the most important waiting-time measure, $V[BW]$ is also important. Together, they provide a more sensitive and thorough account of system performance from the customer's perspective than $\overline{BW}$ alone.

6.2.5 Proofs

PROOF OF LEMMA 6.2.1. It is convenient to work with a simple transformation of **IP:** Define $IP_c(t) = (r + q) - IP(t)$, $t \geq 0$, and $\mathbf{IP}_c = \{IP_c(t): t \geq 0\}$. Thus, $IP_c(t)$ measures the distance between $IP(t)$ and its maximum value $(r + q)$. For now, assume $IP(0) \leq r + q$, so $IP_c(t) \geq 0$.

The process $\mathbf{IP}_c$ is a continuous-time Markov chain. Think of its state space as the integers mod (q). A transition occurs at each demand epoch. At each such epoch t, provided $IP_c(t^-) < q - 1$, $IP_c(t)$ jumps up by 1. If $IP_c(t^-) = q - 1$, however, the jump is to 0 instead of q, reflecting the mod (q) operation. (These are precisely the demands that trigger orders according to the policy.) Thus, the process $\mathbf{IP}_c$ is remarkably simple; it just cycles through its q states, in the same order, forever. (The subscript c is meant to suggest the word *cyclic.*) Also, all the transition rates equal λ. Thus, the generator of $\mathbf{IP}_c$ is the matrix $\lambda(-I + I_+)$, where I is an identity matrix of order q and I_+ is the shift mod (q) matrix

$$\begin{pmatrix} 0 & 1 & & & & & \\ & 0 & 1 & & & & \\ & & 0 & 1 & & & \\ & & & \cdot & \cdot & & \\ & & & & \cdot & \cdot & \\ & & & & & \cdot & 1 \\ 1 & & & & & & 0 \end{pmatrix}$$

FIGURE 6.2.8

State-transition diagram for $\mathbf{IP}_c$.

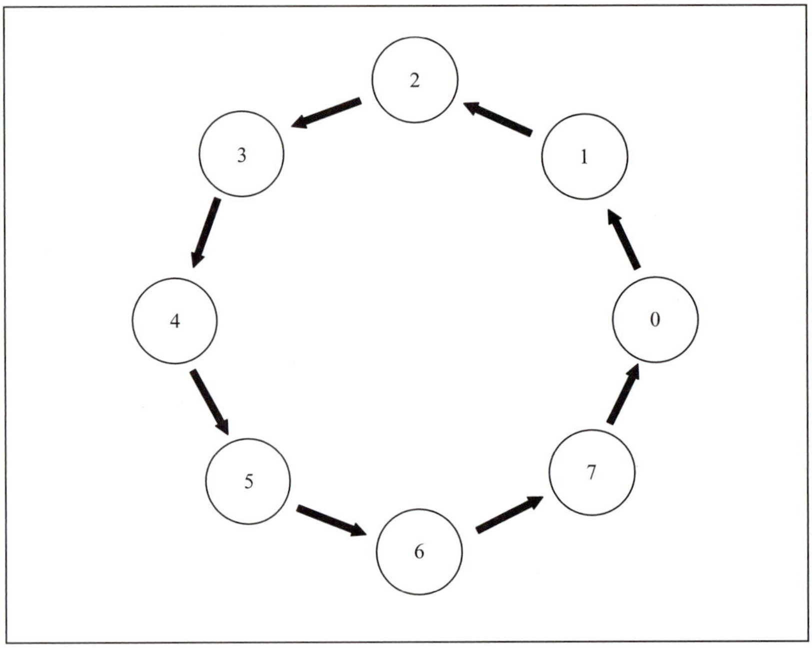

Figure 6.2.8 shows the state-transition diagram for the case $q = 8$.

Notice, this diagram is entirely symmetric over the states; rotating the figure changes nothing except the labels of the states. You might suspect, then, that *if* $\mathbf{IP}_c$ has a limiting distribution, it is *uniform* on the integers mod (q). This is true: The embedded discrete-time chain is irreducible, so Markov-chain theory (see Appendix C) tells us that $\mathbf{IP}_c$ has a unique stationary distribution, which is also its limiting distribution and its long-run frequency distribution. Moreover, letting **e** denote a column vector of ones, it is clear that $(1/q)\mathbf{e}'[\lambda(-I + I_+)] = \mathbf{0}$, so the uniform distribution is indeed stationary.

Actually, the full state space of $\mathbf{IP}_c$ also includes the negative integers, to account for the case $IP(0) > r + q$, or $IP_c(0) < 0$. But those states are transient. Thus, the result above is correct. Finally, $IP = (r + q) - IP_c$, so this has the uniform distribution on the integers from $r + 1$ to $r + q$, as asserted.

PROOF OF LEMMA 6.2.2. The quantity $IO(t)$ specifies the total amount of supplies arriving during the interval $(t, t + L]$, since orders placed *before* t must arrive before $t + L$, while those placed *after* t arrive after $t + L$. And, by definition, $D(t, t + L]$ is the demand during this same interval. Therefore,

$$IN(t + L) = IN(t) + IO(t) - D(t, t + L]$$
$$= IP(t) - D(t, t + L]$$

PROOF OF THEOREM 6.2.3. Define the *leadtime-demand process,* $\mathbf{DL} = \{D(t, t + L]: t \geq 0\}$, and consider the joint process (**IP, DL**). We have seen that **IP** has a limiting distribution, and of course **DL** has one also, since each $D(t, t + L]$ is distributed identically to D. Furthermore, $IP(t)$ and $D(t, t + L]$ are independent for all t. Therefore, the joint process has a limiting distribution: Denote the limiting random variable by $[IP, D]$, where IP is uniformly distributed, D has the Poisson distribution with mean λL, and the two variables are independent.

By equation (6.2.7), $IN(t + L)$ is just a function of this joint process. Since the joint process has a limiting distribution, so does this function of it, hence so does **IN.** Let IN denote the limiting random variable. Then, an equation like (6.2.7) must describe IN. This is precisely the assertion of the theorem.

Finally, this limiting distribution of **IN** also describes its stationary and long-run frequency distributions: Lemma 6.2.1 shows that this is true of **IP.** Since **DL** is also ergodic, and for each t $IP(t)$ and $D(t, t + L]$ are independent, the joint process (**IP, DL**) itself is ergodic, hence so is **IN.** Thus, IN fully characterizes the long-run behavior of **IN,** as asserted.

PROOF OF THEOREM 6.2.4. Suppose the system starts at time $t = 0$ with inventory $r + q$, no backorders, and no outstanding orders. Define

$$B_n^{\text{arr}} = \text{backorders observed by the } n\text{th arriving customer}$$

$$B_n^{\text{dep}} = \text{backorders remaining after the } n\text{th customer's demand is filled}$$

$$BW_n = \text{waiting time of customer } n$$

(Customer n is never included in B_n^{arr}; also, if the demands of customers n and $n + 1$ are filled simultaneously, we count customer $n + 1$ among B_n^{dep}.) The corresponding limiting random variables (as $n \to \infty$) are denoted B^{arr}, B^{dep}, and BW.

First, because demands are filled in order and the leadtimes are constant, B_n^{dep} is precisely the number of demands during the time BW_n following customer n's demand. Also, BW_n depends on **D** up to the moment n's demand occurs, but not afterwards. (This is because, for $n \geq r + q$, the order for the unit used to fill n's demand is triggered by the demand of some customer $m \leq n$. Here, we have used the assumption $r \geq -1$.) Consequently, B_n^{dep} has the same distribution as $D(BW_n)$, where we treat BW_n and **D** as independent. Thus, $B^{\text{dep}} = D(BW)$.

Second, apply what is called a level-crossing argument: Fix some positive integer i, and follow the function $B(t)$, focusing attention on when $B(t)$ changes between i and $i + 1$. A jump from i up to $i + 1$ must reflect the demand of some customer; that customer observes i backorders, so it is counted among those having $B_n^{\text{arr}} = i$. On the other hand, a change from $i + 1$ down to i means that some customer's demand is finally filled, and that customer is counted among those with $B_n^{\text{dep}} = i$. (Remember, if several demands are filled at once, so $B(t)$ jumps down by more than 1, we count this as several simultaneous unit jumps.) But each jump from i to $i + 1$ must be followed by a jump from $i + 1$ to i before the next such upward jump can occur. So, in the long run, the proportions of customers in these two groups must be equal. Since this is true for every i, $B^{\text{arr}} = B^{\text{dep}}$.

Third, because of the PASTA property of Poisson processes, $B^{\text{arr}} = B$. Combining all three of these identities, we have $B = B^{\text{arr}} = B^{\text{dep}} = D(BW)$.

PROOF OF COROLLARY 6.2.5. Let $\tilde{g}(z|t)$ denote the z-transform of $D(t)$, that is,

$$\tilde{g}(z|t) = e^{-(1-z)\lambda t} \qquad |z| \leq 1, t \geq 0$$

By Theorem 6.2.4,

$$\begin{aligned}\tilde{g}_B(z) &= E[\tilde{g}(z|BW)] = E[\exp(-(1-z)\lambda BW)] \\ &= \tilde{f}_{BW}[\lambda(1-z)]\end{aligned}$$

6.3 World-Driven Demand

6.3.1 Discussion

A Poisson process often closely approximates real demands. The approximation is rarely perfect, however, and some demand processes behave in a decidedly non-Poisson manner. This section explores a more general and complex demand model.

Suppose that demands still occur one at a time, but as time passes, events occur that affect future demands. (This is not true of a Poisson process.) Think of these events as changes in some system, which we call the *world.* We model the world by a stochastic process $\mathbf{W} = \{W(t) : t \geq 0\}$. This system is exogenous; nothing we do affects the evolution of **W.** The behavior of **W,** however, affects the demand process **D.** The overall model of demand is the joint process (**W, D**). Here are some examples:

Weather. The demand for many products depends on current weather conditions. Think of umbrellas, sun-tan lotion, and heating oil. Here, **W** includes the relevant variables, such as temperature and rainfall.

Economy. Alternatively, **W** might represent the general economic conditions in a country, region, or industry. Demands for such products as automobiles and office supplies tend to ary with the level of economic activity.

Competition. Suppose **W** represents the state of competition in the market for a product. It may include the current level of technology, the strengths of competing products, consumers' tastes, and so forth. Such factors do change over time, and our beliefs about subsequent demands change with them. A company introducing a new product, for example, faces just such uncertainties. Likewise, think of a mature product industry with a high rate of innovation, like computers and pharmaceuticals, or clothing, perfume, and other fashion goods; there, every product is in danger of partial or total obsolescence.

Customer status. Suppose demands represent orders from a few large customers. In this case **W** models the relevant conditions at each customer's site, including perhaps their own inventories.

Forecasting. Many demand-forecasting techniques are based, explicitly or implicitly, on a model of some world system. The forecasting methodology involves tracking certain variables, corresponding to **W,** which in turn are the main inputs to a forecast of future demand. In some cases the variables in **W** have real physical meaning (the weather, the economy, etc.), but in others they are just statistical constructs. (Section 9.7.1 discusses specific examples.)

At this point you may be worried: Yes, all sorts of factors may affect demand, but how can we model them all? Do we really need a full-scale model of the weather and/or the economy? (You may be aware that meteorologists and economists build huge, complex models, and even those don't always work very well.) It would take a marketing genius to measure competitive conditions, let alone to understand their dynamics!

Relax. Our purpose here is to understand what happens *given* a world-demand model (**W**, **D**). As we shall see, the central results of Section 6.2, even the performance formulas, continue to hold. The only difference is in the leadtime-demand random variable D. We do have to compute or estimate its distribution, but no more than that. Moreover, as shown in Section 6.4, for many practical purposes, it is sufficient to estimate just two parameters, the average demand rate λ and another one that measures demand variation.

So, to use the results entails *some* extra work, but we control how much. For a very important product, it may be worthwhile to construct a detailed, explicit model of (**W**, **D**), but in other cases we can get by with much less, a simpler, approximate model of (**W**, **D**) or just a couple of statistical estimates. Indeed, one can view the model as a technically convenient metaphor for complex demand in general. That is, think of $W(t)$ as comprising any and all relevant information we have concerning future demand.

We need some rather technical, not overly restrictive, assumptions: **W** is a *Markov process.* Essentially, this just means that **W** is complete, or self-contained. The variables in $W(t)$ constitute the *state* of the world system; they include all relevant information about the future evolution of **W** beyond time t. (Section C.3.2 provides a precise definition, but that is not critical here.) Also, **W** is well behaved, like the processes discussed in Section 6.2.1 above; it is ergodic and has a limiting distribution. So, it is meaningful to talk about equilibrium conditions. (So, if **W** includes a weather model, it is valid only for short time intervals, except perhaps in the tropics. Time-varying world models are discussed in Section 9.7.) Finally, **W** captures all events that affect **D.** That is, the joint process (**W**, **D**) is itself a Markov process; this process too is well behaved.

The results allow **W** to start in any initial state at time 0. An important special case arises when **W** begins in equilibrium, for then **W** is stationary and **D** has stationary increments (the distribution of $D(t, u]$ depends only on $u - t$). Define

D = leadtime demand, the random variable $D(L)$, assuming **W** starts in equilibrium

λ = demand rate

= $E[D(1)]$, assuming **W** starts in equilibrium.

Thus, D represents a (probabilistic) forecast of demand over a leadtime under typical or average conditions. Then, $E[D(t)] = \lambda t$ (so indeed λ is the average demand rate), and in particular $E[D] = \lambda L$.

Also, define

$$\psi^2 = \text{long-run variance-to-mean ratio}$$

$$= \lim_{t\to\infty} \{V[D(t)]/\lambda t\}$$

(This limit exists for virtually any process obeying the assumptions above.) For a Poisson process, since $V[D(t)] = \lambda t$, $\psi^2 = 1$. A world-driven demand process can have a larger or smaller ratio. This is the new demand parameter; it is a fundamental characteristic of the process. So, for large L, $V[D] \approx \psi^2 \lambda L$.

By the way, you might expect that the information embodied in the state $W(t)$ can be profitably used to help make ordering decisions. Indeed it can. Here, however, we evaluate an (r, q) policy with fixed r and q, which by definition does not adapt orders to $W(t)$. (r, q) policies are widely used in practice, because they are so simple to implement. It is often difficult or impossible to observe $W(t)$ in real time; even when $W(t)$ is observable, it is often hard to process and employ the information. Thus, it is worthwhile to see what happens under an (r, q) policy, even in settings like this one, where in principle some more complex policy works better. In the process, we shall see just how robust the techniques above are to the Poisson-demand assumption. (Section 6.7.2 and Section 9.7 consider more refined policies which do use the information in $W(t)$.)

6.3.2 The MCDC Process

Let us explore one particular class of world-driven demand processes. These are built from continuous-time Markov chains. (Section C.5 reviews this concept. If you are comfortable with it, the discussion here will help make the notion of world-driven demand more concrete. If not, you may prefer to skim this subsection.) While they are special in some ways, they still offer a great range of modeling flexibility, and they can be used to approximate still more general processes.

Assume that $\mathbf{W}$ is a finite-state, irreducible, continuous-time Markov chain. Let Q denote the generator of $\mathbf{W}$ and $\boldsymbol{\xi}$ its stationary probability vector. Also, conditional on $W(t)$, demand in the near future acts like a Poisson process. Specifically, decompose Q as follows:

$$Q = Q^0 - \Lambda^D + \Lambda$$

where Q^0 itself has the form of a generator (its off-diagonal elements are nonnegative and $Q^0\mathbf{e} = \mathbf{0}$, where $\mathbf{e}$ is a column-vector of ones); $\Lambda = (\lambda_{ww'})$ is nonnegative; and $\Lambda^D = \text{diag}(\Lambda\mathbf{e})$, a nonnegative diagonal matrix. These matrices represent different kinds of events: When a transition represented in Q^0 occurs, $\mathbf{W}$ changes state, but there is no demand. The matrix Λ, on the other hand, gives the rates of events that do generate demands; $\mathbf{W}$ may also change. Specifically, if $\mathbf{W}$ is now in state w, a demand occurs *and* $\mathbf{W}$ jumps from w to w' at rate $\lambda_{ww'}$. The diagonal entries in Λ describe demands that leave $\mathbf{W}$ unchanged. Finally, Λ^D simply summarizes the overall state-specific demand rates in Λ.

Thus, to specify the model fully, we need only specify the two matrices Q^0 and Λ, or equivalently Q and Λ. The joint process $(\mathbf{W}, \mathbf{D})$ is itself a continuous-time Markov chain. We call $\mathbf{D}$ a *Markov-chain-driven counting process,* or *MCDC process.*

Such models, like Markov chains generally, can differ greatly in complexity, depending on the number of states $\mathbf{W}$ has, which determines the sizes of the matrices. There is no limit to the complexity, in principle, but of course the modeling and computational difficulties increase as the number of states grows.

A couple of special cases are worth mentioning: $\mathbf{D}$ is a *Markov-modulated Poisson process,* or *MMP process,* when $\Lambda = \Lambda^D$, so the off-diagonal elements of Λ are all zero and $Q = Q^0$. In this case, transitions of $\mathbf{W}$ and demands are distinct events. During any interval between changes in $\mathbf{W}$, $\mathbf{D}$ behaves like a Poisson process, but the demand rate

(λ_{ww}) depends on the current state of **W**. Most of the examples above (the weather, economic conditions, etc.) correspond to demand processes of this form.

Alternatively, suppose demand is a *renewal process*. That is, the times between demands are i.i.d. random variables; see Section C.5.6. (By the way, any renewal process can be represented in the form (**W**, **D**), where **W** is the time since the last demand, and the results below are valid under mild conditions. Here, we consider a special case, using a different **W**.) Each interdemand time has a CPH distribution (Section C.5.5) with parameters ($\boldsymbol{\kappa}$, K), where $\boldsymbol{\kappa}\mathbf{e} = 1$. To recover the form above, set $Q = -K(I - \mathbf{e}\boldsymbol{\kappa})$ and $\Lambda = K\mathbf{e}\boldsymbol{\kappa}$. (Since $\mathbf{e}$ is a column vector and $\boldsymbol{\kappa}$ a row vector, $\mathbf{e}\boldsymbol{\kappa}$ is a matrix.) For instance, if our demands are orders from a single customer, whose own demand process is Poisson and who follows a (r, q) policy with $q > 1$, then our demand process has this form. The interdemand times have an Erlang-q distribution, and the world **W** is just the customer's **IP.**

Here are two examples. In both cases **W** has two states, and

$$Q = \begin{pmatrix} -20 & 20 \\ 20 & -20 \end{pmatrix}$$

Thus, $\boldsymbol{\xi} = (\frac{1}{2}, \frac{1}{2})$. The first example has

$$\Lambda = \begin{pmatrix} 0.5 & 0 \\ 0 & 19.5 \end{pmatrix}$$

This describes an MMP process, as defined above. Here, **W** switches back and forth between a low-demand state and a high-demand state. The second example has

$$\Lambda = \begin{pmatrix} 0 & 0 \\ 20 & 0 \end{pmatrix}$$

Again, **W** switches back and forth between its two states, and a demand occurs when switching from the second to the first. Here, **D** is a renewal process with Erlang-2 interdemand times.

In general, $\lambda = \boldsymbol{\xi}\Lambda\mathbf{e}.$ (Both examples above have $\lambda = 10$.) Also, letting β be a large positive number, one can show (Neuts [1981]) that

$$V[D] = [\lambda + 2\boldsymbol{\xi}(\Lambda - \lambda I)(\beta\mathbf{e}\boldsymbol{\xi} - Q)^{-1}\Lambda\mathbf{e}]L - 2\boldsymbol{\xi}\Lambda(I - e^{QL})(\beta\mathbf{e}\boldsymbol{\xi} - Q)^{-2}\Lambda\mathbf{e}$$

(Odd as it may seem, the result of this calculation does not depend on β, provided β is sufficiently large.) This may look ugly, but actually it is quite simple. The second term is a constant, plus some exponential terms which decay to zero as $L \to \infty$. The first term is linear in L. Thus,

$$\psi^2 = \frac{\lambda + 2\boldsymbol{\xi}(\Lambda - \lambda I)(\beta\mathbf{e}\boldsymbol{\xi} - Q)^{-1}\Lambda\mathbf{e}}{\lambda}$$

and for large L, we can ignore the second term above, using the first (i.e., $\psi^2\lambda L$) to approximate $V[D]$.

For the MMP process above, $\psi^2 = 1.45$, and for the renewal process, $\psi^2 = 0.5$. Figure 6.3.1 graphs $V[D]$ for different values of L. The dashed lines show the limiting linear functions. For reference, the straight line shows $V[D]$ for a Poisson process with the

FIGURE 6.3.1

World-driven demand: variance.

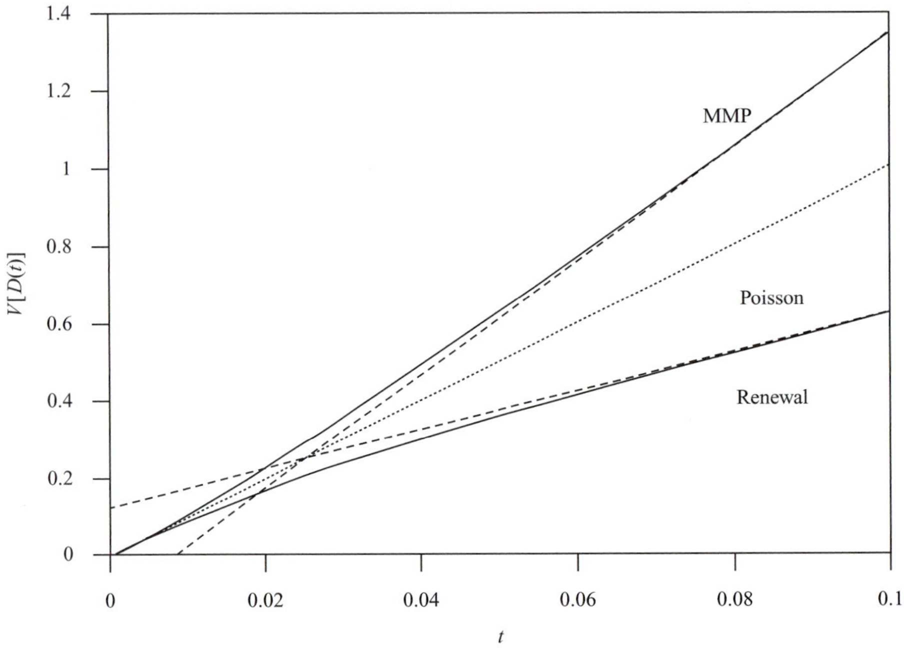

same rate, $\lambda = 10$. Observe, the MMP process is uniformly *more* variable than the Poisson process, while the renewal process is *less* variable.

It is not easy to compute the exact distribution of D. This requires solving the differential equations for the transient probabilities of the Markov chain (**W, D**). Specifically, let

$$g_w(d|t) = Pr\,\{D(t) = d,\, W(t) = w\} \qquad t \geq 0,\, d \geq 0$$

starting with $D(0) = 0$ and $W(0)$ distributed as $\boldsymbol{\xi}$, and let $\mathbf{g}(d|t)$ be the row-vector $[g_w(d|t)]_w$. To compute the $\mathbf{g}(d|t)$, solve the linear differential equations

$$\mathbf{g}'(0|t) = \mathbf{g}(0|t)(Q - \Lambda)$$

$$\mathbf{g}'(d|t) = \mathbf{g}(d|t)(Q - \Lambda) + \mathbf{g}(d-1|t)\Lambda \qquad d > 0$$

(the prime means derivative with respect to t) with initial conditions

$$\mathbf{g}(0|0) = \boldsymbol{\xi}$$

$$\mathbf{g}(\mathrm{d}|0) = \mathbf{0} \qquad d > 0$$

This is a conceptually straightforward, but practically tedious, numerical task. Then, $g(d) = Pr\,\{D = d\} = \mathbf{g}(d|L)\mathbf{e}$.

Figure 6.3.2 shows $g(d)$ for the examples above with $L = 0.2$, so $E[D] = \lambda L = 2$, as well as the Poisson pmf with the same mean. It is clear that the MMP process gener-

FIGURE 6.3.2

Probability mass functions (world-driven demand).

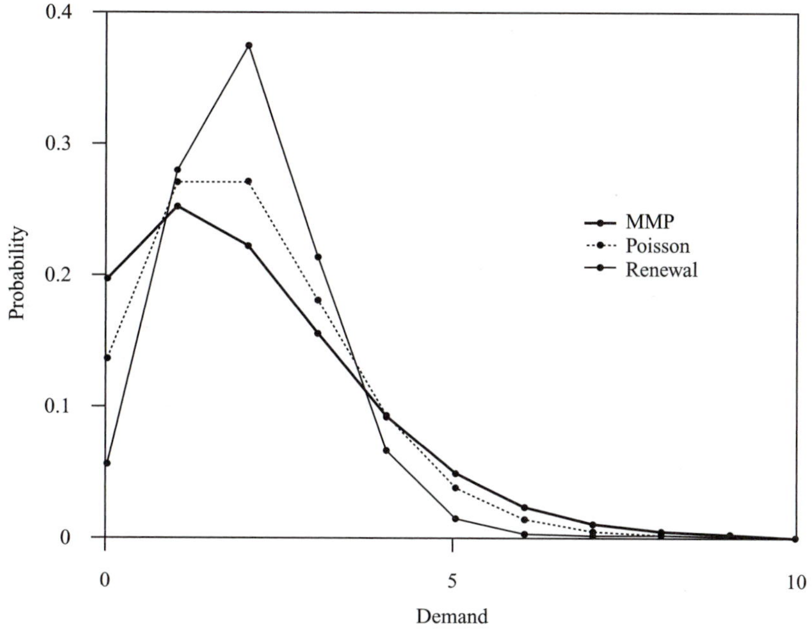

ates the most variable pmf of the three, and the renewal process the least variable, with the Poisson process in between.

6.3.3 Analysis

For simplicity, we state and prove the results assuming that demand is an MCDC process. They are valid more generally, however. We need a mild technical assumption:

ASSUMPTION. The joint process (**IP, W**) is irreducible.

This assumption holds for most reasonable models. For example, it is true when **D** is an MMP or a renewal process. (See Problem 6.4. Section 6.3.5 discusses the assumption further.)

LEMMA 6.3.1. Under the assumption above, the joint process (**IP, W**) has a limiting distribution, *IP* is uniformly distributed on the integers in the interval $[r + 1, r + q]$, and *IP* and *W* are independent.

In particular, the limiting behavior of the joint process is *insensitive* to the specification of **W** and **D,** except of course for the marginal distribution of *W* itself. Envision the result this way: As time passes, *IP*(t) cycles around its q possible values, and the *movement* of **IP** is determined in part by **W.** Nevertheless, after a sufficiently long time, the *position* of *IP*(t) contains negligible information about *W*(t).

The next result is analogous to Theorem 6.2.3:

THEOREM 6.3.2. Under the assumption above, the limiting distribution of the net inventory is described by the equation

$$IN = IP - D$$

where IP is uniformly distributed on the integers in the interval $[r + 1, r + q]$, D is the leadtime demand starting in equilibrium, and the two variables IP and D are independent. This also describes the long-run frequency distribution of **IN.**

We are thus led to a remarkable conclusion: Formulas (6.2.11) to (6.2.13) can *still* be used to calculate $\overline{A}$, $\overline{B}$, and $\overline{I}$. We need only redefine G^0, G^1, and G^2 to describe the new D. The performance measures depend *only* on this single distribution, not on finer details of the demand process. Also, $\overline{OF} = \lambda/q$, as before. In the special case $q = 1$, the simpler formulas (6.2.4) to (6.2.6) apply. Equations (6.2.8) to (6.2.10) continue to relate the results for general q to their counterparts for $q = 1$.

As for customer waiting, recall that the relation $\overline{B} = \lambda \overline{BW}$ continues to hold here. The sharper results of Section 6.2.4 (Theorem 6.2.4 and Corollary 6.2.5), however, do not. Still, analogous results can be used as approximations. For example, an approximate relation between $V[B]$ and $V[BW]$, analogous to (6.2.17), is given by

$$V[B] = \psi^2 \lambda E[BW] + \lambda^2 V[BW] \tag{6.3.1}$$

Regarding computation, G^0 can be computed directly from g, and recursions (6.2.16) and (6.2.17) can be used to compute G^1 and G^2 from G^0. As discussed above, however, it is rather difficult to calculate g. Thus, evaluating $\overline{A}$, $\overline{B}$, and $\overline{I}$ is no simple matter. [Formulas (6.2.14) and (6.2.15) depend on the specific form of the Poisson distribution; they do not apply here.] Section 6.4 develops a workable approximation. Also, oddly enough, exact performance evaluation becomes easier in certain stochastic-leadtime models; see Section 7.5.2.

One qualification is necessary: The quantity $\overline{A}$ is still the probability of being out of stock, but not the fraction of demands backordered. (The PASTA property does not hold for non-Poisson demand.) That fraction can be computed in another way, but we shall not do so.

6.3.4 Behavior of Performance Measures

Because the performance formulas retain the same form as in the Poisson-demand case, their qualitative properties remain the same: For base-stock policies, $\overline{B}$ is decreasing and convex in s, while $\overline{I}$ is increasing and convex (strictly, for $s \geq 0$). $\overline{A}$ is decreasing, but not convex. For general q, $\overline{B}$ is decreasing and convex in r, while $\overline{I}$ is increasing and convex (strictly, for $r \geq -q$). Also, $\overline{B}(s')$ and $\overline{I}(s')$ are increasing in q, in the manner of Figure 6.2.6.

It is interesting to explore how performance depends on the demand model itself. We focus here on base-stock policies. Figure 6.3.3 graphs $\overline{I}$ and $\overline{B}$ for the two examples above, as well as a Poisson process with the same demand rate, $\lambda = 10$, all with $L = 2$. Recall, the MMP process has the largest $V[D]$ among the three, and the renewal process the smallest. We see here that $\overline{I}$ and $\overline{B}$ seem to increase along with $V[D]$. That is, *the larger the demand variation, the worse the system performs.*

FIGURE 6.3.3

Performance of base-stock policies (world-driven demand).

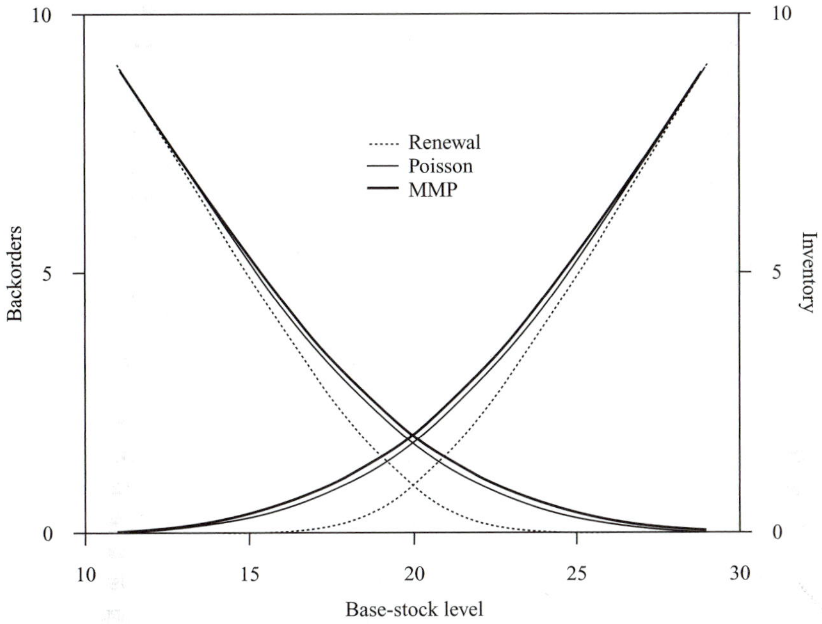

Figure 6.3.4 explores the MMP process further. It plots the tradeoff between waiting time and stocking time for different values of L, in the same format as Figure 6.2.4 above. Notice, the overall form of each curve, and the way performance degrades as L increases, are reminiscent of the Poisson-demand case. Comparing these two figures, we see that performance is worse for the more variable MMP process, as expected.

6.3.5 Technical Issues and Proofs

Before proving the results, let us explore the assumption of Section 6.3.3 at greater length: As noted above, most reasonable demand models satisfy it. However, here is a case where it does *not* hold: Suppose $\mathbf{W}$ has two states, 0 and 1, and it alternates between them as time passes. A demand occurs whenever $\mathbf{W}$ changes state, but never between transitions. (So, $Q^0 = 0$, and the diagonal elements of Λ are all 0. This $\mathbf{D}$ is an instance of what is called an alternating renewal process.) Now, suppose $q = 2$, so $\mathbf{IP}_c$ (defined in the proof of Lemma 6.2.1) also alternates between the values 0 and 1. Starting with $\mathrm{IP}_c(0) = W(0)$, $IP_c(t) = W(t)$ for all $t \geq 0$; more generally, the distance between $IP_c(0)$ and $W(0)$ will be preserved forever. Thus, the joint process cannot be irreducible.

It is fair to call this case pathological; it is hard to imagine a real demand process with this sort of periodic behavior. There are certain plausible demand models, however, which also violate the assumption: Suppose the current demand rate depends on the cumulative demand to date; in our terms $W(t)$ is just $D(t)$ itself. Such a model might describe the demand for a new product. The idea here is to model the possible saturation

FIGURE 6.3.4

Stock-service tradeoff (MMP demand).

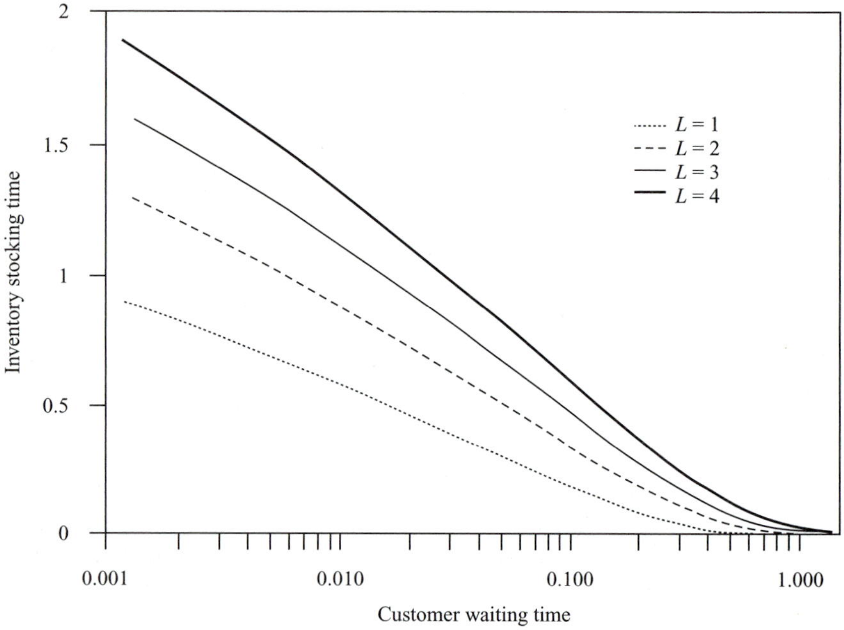

of the market, with the demand rate decreasing in $D(t)$. (See Mahajan and Wind [1986] for examples.) Clearly, the joint process is reducible.

On the other hand, suppose $W(t)$ increases whenever a demand occurs, but $W(t)$ can also decrease between demands. Such a construct could model a market with limited capacity to absorb *short-term* demand surges, provided the market adjusts so that recent demands are "forgotten" in the long run. It is not hard to check that, indeed, the assumption is now satisfied.

PROOF OF LEMMA 6.3.1. Because the joint process $(\mathbf{IP}, \mathbf{W})$ has a finite number of states, and in view of the assumption, we need only show that the distribution described in the lemma is stationary. We shall give two separate arguments, each instructive in its own way.

First, here is a direct algebraic argument. The generator of the joint process $(\mathbf{IP}_c, \mathbf{W})$ can be written

$$I \otimes Q^0 - I \otimes \Lambda^D + I_+ \otimes \Lambda$$

(I_+ is the shift mod (q) matrix in the proof of Lemma 6.2.1 above; Section C.5.3 in Appendix C explains the Kronecker product notation $\otimes$.) The first term corresponds to transitions of $\mathbf{W}$ without demands, while the second and third together describe demand events, hence changes in $\mathbf{IP}_c$, whether or not $\mathbf{W}$ changes at the same time. We wish to show that the probability row-vector $(1/q)(\mathbf{e}' \otimes \boldsymbol{\xi})$ is stationary for $(\mathbf{IP}_c, \mathbf{W})$; that is, when we multiply this vector by the matrix above, the result is zero. But, since $\mathbf{e}'I = \mathbf{e}'I_+ = \mathbf{e}'$ and $\boldsymbol{\xi}Q = \mathbf{0}$, we have

$$(\mathbf{e}' \otimes \boldsymbol{\xi})(I \otimes Q^0 - I \otimes \Lambda^D + I_+ \otimes \Lambda) = \mathbf{e}' \otimes [\boldsymbol{\xi}(Q^0 - \Lambda^D + \Lambda)] = \mathbf{e}' \otimes (\boldsymbol{\xi}Q) = \mathbf{0} \otimes \mathbf{0}$$

FIGURE 6.4.1

Performance of base-stock policies (normal versus Poisson).

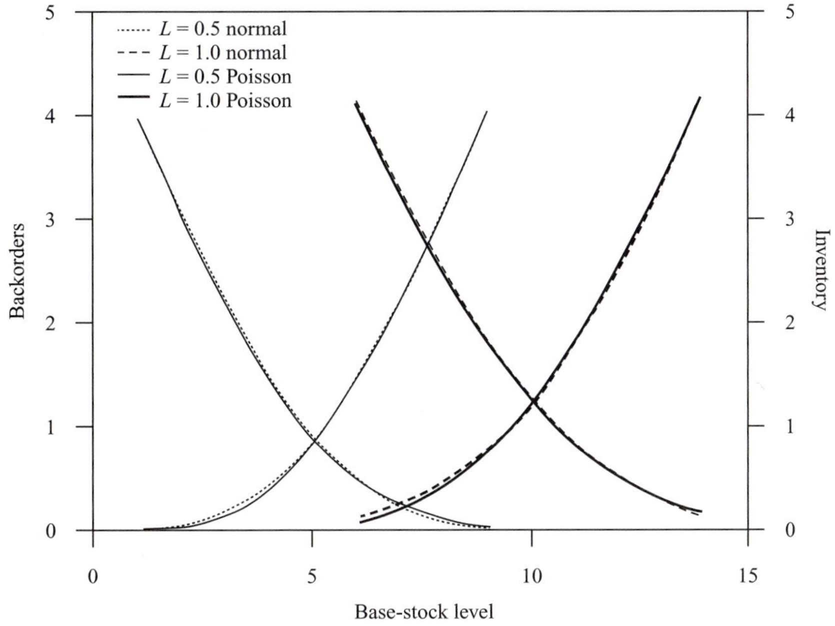

it is fairly good. (Part of the discrepancy, of course, is caused by the approximate value of σ^2.) Again, for larger *L,* the approximation becomes still more accurate.

The normal approximation makes some people uncomfortable, because it allows *D* to assume negative values. (This is not a weakness at all, of course, when customers can return items. For instance, retailers can usually return unsold CDs to manufacturers. While such situations are not uncommon, they are not the general rule.) Remember, we use the approximation, not to describe the dynamics of the system in detail, but rather to predict performance, and it does that very well in many cases. Still, the approximation tends to work best when it predicts a small $Pr\{D < 0\} = \Phi^0[-\nu/\sigma]$, namely, when the coefficient of variation σ/ν is small. For Poisson demand, $\sigma/\nu = 1/\sqrt{\lambda L}$, and this is one reason the approximation works poorly for small λL.

One note of caution: The normal approximation does capture the broad features of performance, but it is not precise when pushed to extremes. Suppose we have a stringent performance requirement, specifying a tiny value of $\overline{A}$, say 0.001. We know that s must be large, but how large? The normal approximation does not always give the right answer. In technical terms, it does not provide an asymptotically precise estimate of the tail probabilities; the ratio $\Phi^0(z)/G^0(s)$ does not go to 1 as $s \to \infty$. (This assumes, of course, that the model and the data are exactly correct. Errors from those sources usually dominate those of the approximation.)

In general, the appropriateness of the normal approximation depends partly on *L* being sufficiently large, but also on the context and purpose of the analysis: If we are analyzing one particularly important item, and we are unsure whether *L* is truly large

FIGURE 6.4.2

Performance of base-stock policies (normal versus MMP).

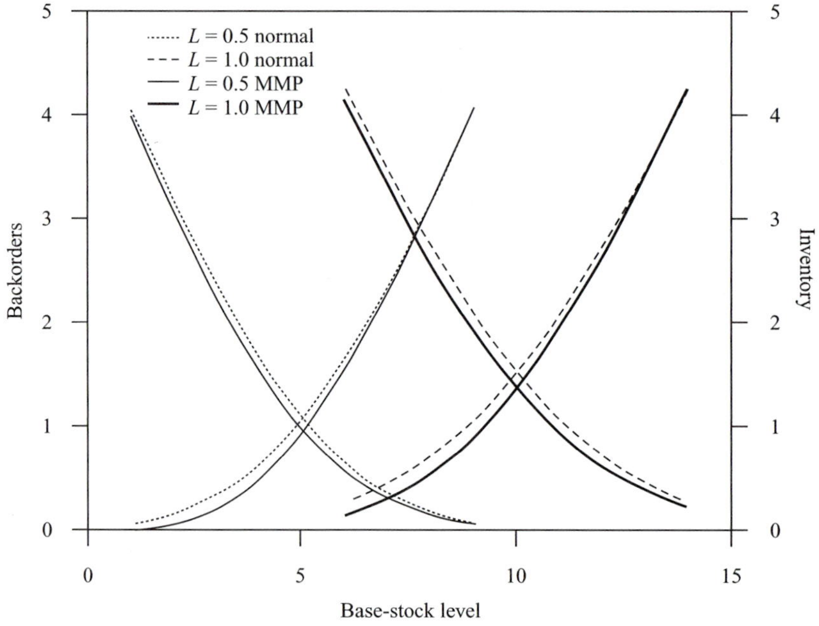

enough, then prudence dictates using the exact formulas. On the other hand, if we are conducting a large-scale analysis to support systems design, the approximation is usually quite adequate for any L. In that case, therefore, there is no need to model the world-demand system ($\mathbf{W}$, $\mathbf{D}$) explicitly, nor even to estimate the full distribution of D. It is enough to estimate λ and ψ^2 directly.

Suppose that we are comfortable with the approximation. Formulas (6.4.4) to (6.4.6) are quite easy to use. For instance, to meet a service-level requirement $\bar{A} = 1 - \omega_-$, find the value of z such that $\Phi^0(z) = 1 - \omega_-$ from a table of the standard normal distribution (or a computerized equivalent), and set $s = \nu + z\sigma$. (As mentioned in Section C.2.5.4, $\ln [\Phi^0(z)] \approx -\frac{1}{2}z^2$ for large z. So, for $1 - \omega_-$ near 0, $z \approx [-2 \ln (1 - \omega_-)]^{1/2}$ and $s \approx \nu + [-2 \ln (1 - \omega_-)]^{1/2}\sigma$. This is a rough, qualitative indication of how s grows as the service requirement becomes more stringent. However, as discussed above, the normal approximation loses accuracy in this range, so this estimate should be used with care.)

This z is sometimes called the *safety factor.* It depends only on ω_-. It is positive precisely when $\omega_- > \frac{1}{2}$, as is usually the case. If ν changes but σ doesn't, just shift s by the same amount to maintain z. If σ changes, the safety factor indicates the direction and magnitude of the appropriate change in s. Following these rules, the average inventory is then proportional to σ. Thus, the key parameter affecting performance is σ, the *standard deviation* of leadtime demand. (The cost-optimization approach of Section 6.5 leads to similar conclusions.)

By the way, some common practices deviate sharply from this approach. Certain firms follow guidelines of the form, "keep 2 weeks of inventory" or "keep 2 weeks of

This completes the first argument. For the second, suppose the system begins at time 0 with $[IP_c(0), W(0)]$ having the distribution described in the assertion. Now, for any $t \geq 0$,

$$[IP_c(t)|W(t)] = \{IP_c(0) + [D(t)|W(t)]\} \bmod (q)$$

The expression on the right-hand side consists of a random variable $IP_c(0)$ distributed uniformly on the integers mod (q), plus another random variable $[D(t)|W(t)]$ independent of $IP_c(0)$, all mod (q). Any such combination, it turns out, is also uniformly distributed. (This can be checked directly, as Problem 6.5 asks you to do; or see Feller [1971], page 64.) Thus, $[IP_c(t)|W(t)]$ has the uniform distribution on the integers mod (q); in particular, $\mathrm{IP}_c(t)$ and $W(t)$ are independent. Finally, $W(t)$ itself has the same distribution as $W(0)$, namely, the stationary distribution of **W**.

The assumption truly is necessary for the result. Consider the example above, where **W** has only two states and $q = 2$. It is still true that $(1/q)(\mathbf{e}' \otimes \boldsymbol{\xi})$ is *a* stationary vector for the joint process, but there are others as well; the stationary vector is not unique. Also, if the transition rates between the two states of **W** are different, then the limiting distribution of $\mathbf{IP}_c$ depends on the initial state, and typically this distribution is not uniform.

PROOF OF THEOREM 6.3.2. Consider the joint process (**IP, DL**), as in the proof of Theorem 6.2.3 above, but expand it to (**IP**, **W**, **DL**). By assumption, $D(t, t + L]$ depends on the past (through time t) of **IP**, **W**, and **D** only through $W(t)$. On the other hand, (**IP**, **W**) has a limiting distribution, in which IP and W are independent. Thus, the entire process (**IP**, **W**, **DL**) has a limiting distribution, and IP is independent of $[W, D]$. Furthermore, $IN(t + L)$ continues to be described by equation (6.2.7); in particular, **IN** is a function of (**IP**, **W**, **DL**). Taking the limit as $t \to \infty$, the result follows immediately.

6.4 Approximations

Thus far, we have derived *exact* performance measures for several different systems. We now turn to *approximations.* Approximations are important for two reasons: The first and most obvious is convenience. These approximations require less data than the exact formulas, and they are easier to calculate. Second, a simple approximation sometimes reveals important relationships better than an exact expression. We shall see, for instance, approximations that indicate which are the most significant characteristics of demand and supply and how they affect performance.

The most important approximation uses the normal distribution. The normal approximation works well in many situations, though not universally. (Its validity depends strongly on the assumption of constant leadtimes. As shown in Chapter 7, it also works well for *some* kinds of stochastic leadtimes, but not others.)

6.4.1 Base-Stock Policies—Normal Approximation

We first focus on base-stock policies. Consider the Poisson-demand model, where D has a Poisson distribution with mean and variance λL. As you may know, a Poisson distribution with a large mean can be approximated closely by a normal distribution. The idea, then, is to replace the actual leadtime demand D by a normally distributed random variable with the same mean and variance:

$$\nu = E[D] = \lambda L \qquad \sigma^2 = V[D] = \lambda L$$

For most plausible world-driven demand processes too, D is approximately normal for large L. (This is true of every MCDC process.) Again, $\nu = E[D] = \lambda L$. It is possible to compute the exact variance $V[D]$, but in the interest of simplicity, let us use the linear approximation $V[D] \approx \psi^2 \lambda L$, where ψ^2 is the asymptotic variance-to-mean ratio. That is, set

$$\nu = \lambda L \qquad \sigma^2 = \psi^2 \lambda L$$

We need some basic facts about normal distributions (see Section C.2.5.4): ϕ denotes the standard normal probability density function (pdf), and Φ^0 the standard normal ccdf. The function

$$\Phi^1(z) = \int_z^\infty (x - z)\phi(x)\, dx \tag{6.4.1}$$

is the *standard normal loss function;* it is the standard-normal analogue of G^1. The following identities are useful:

$$\Phi^1(z) \quad = \int_z^\infty \Phi^0(x)\, dx = -z\Phi^0(z) + \phi(z) \tag{6.4.2}$$

$$\Phi^1(-z) = z + \Phi^1(z) \tag{6.4.3}$$

Now, following the analysis of Section 6.2.2, using the normal approximation to D in (6.2.3), we obtain

$$\bar{A} = \int_s^\infty \left(\frac{1}{\sigma}\right)\phi\left(\frac{x-\nu}{\sigma}\right) dx = \Phi^0\left(\frac{s-\nu}{\sigma}\right)$$

$$\bar{B} = \int_s^\infty (x - s)\left(\frac{1}{\sigma}\right)\phi\left(\frac{x-\nu}{\sigma}\right) dx = \Phi^1\left[\frac{s-\nu}{\sigma}\right]\sigma$$

$$\bar{I} = s - \nu + \bar{B} = \left[\frac{s-\nu}{\sigma} + \Phi^1\left(\frac{s-\nu}{\sigma}\right)\right]\sigma = \Phi^1\left(\frac{-s+\nu}{\sigma}\right)\sigma$$

Use z to denote the standardized value of s; that is,

$$z = \frac{s-\nu}{\sigma}$$

The formulas above can then be written even more simply:

$$\bar{A} = \Phi^0(z) \tag{6.4.4}$$

$$\bar{B} = \Phi^1(z)\sigma \tag{6.4.5}$$

$$\bar{I} = \Phi^1(-z)\sigma \tag{6.4.6}$$

How accurate is this approximation? First, consider the Poisson-demand case. Figure 6.4.1 graphs exact and approximate performance measures for $\lambda = 10$ and two values of L, 0.5 and 1. In these cases, evidently, the approximation is extremely accurate. For larger λL, the approximation is even closer. Only for very small λL does the approximation give poor results.

The corresponding results for the MMP process of Section 6.3.2 (with $\psi^2 = 1.45$) are shown in Figure 6.4.2. The approximation is not quite as precise as before, but still safety stock." In practical terms this means setting either $s = 2\lambda$ or $s = \nu + 2\lambda$ (presuming time is measured in weeks). So, σ plays no role at all. There is *no* justification for rules of this kind. They are recipes for trouble.

Now, σ itself is proportional to the *square root* of λL. So, a shorter leadtime improves performance; we observed the same phenomenon in Figures 6.2.4 and 6.3.4. Likewise, as the demand rate grows (with ψ^2 fixed), so do $\bar{I}$ and $\bar{B}$. However, σ grows more slowly than λL itself; that is, the performance measures display a sort of *statistical economy of scale.* If λ doubles, for example, and we adjust s to maintain the same value of z, then $\bar{I}$ and $\bar{B}$ both increase by only $\sqrt{2}$, not 2.

This pattern of sensitivity is similar to the EOQ model's, though the reason here is entirely different. When we double λ, the new D is the sum of two *independent* copies of the original. The standard deviation only increases by $\sqrt{2}$, essentially because a small value in one copy may cancel a large value in the other. (This is the familiar principle underlying statistical estimation; an estimate becomes more precise as the sample size grows.) The same thing happens if we double L, because $\mathbf{D}$ has independent increments—exactly in the case of Poisson demand, approximately for MCDC demand—so $V[D]$ is linear (exactly or approximately) in L.

Also, σ is proportional to ψ, the square root of the variance-to-mean ratio ψ^2. Thus, reducing demand variation improves performance. (Problem 6.1 explores another way to obtain better demand information.)

The approximation also helps to explain more subtle performance phenomena: Notice that $\bar{I}$ here is *precisely* $\bar{B}$ reflected about the value $z = 0$; the exact measures exhibit nearly the same symmetry, as shown in Figures 6.2.3 and 6.3.3. Also, it is not hard to show that

$$\frac{\partial \bar{B}}{\partial \sigma} = \frac{\partial \bar{I}}{\partial \sigma} = \phi(z) \tag{6.4.7}$$

Thus, both $\bar{B}$ and $\bar{I}$ are increasing in σ, and their sensitivity to σ is greatest for $z = 0$, that is, for $s = \nu$. The figures above show that the exact $\bar{B}$ and $\bar{I}$ behave similarly.

6.4.2 Base-Stock Policies—Other Continuous Approximations

The normal approximation is one particular *continuous approximation.* In general, replacing G^0 by a continuous ccdf F^0 leads to the following formulas:

$$\bar{A} = F^0(s) \qquad \bar{B} = F^1(s)$$

$$\bar{I} = s - \nu + \bar{B}$$

where $F^1(s) = \int_s^\infty F^0(x)\,dx$ is the continuous loss function. [Clearly, (6.4.4) to (6.4.6) specialize these results to the normal case.] These approximate formulas have the same qualitative properties as the exact ones: For instance, $\bar{B}$ is decreasing and convex as a function of s, while $\bar{I}$ is increasing and convex.

For example, consider an exponential distribution with mean $\nu = E[D]$, so $F^0(x) = e^{-x/\nu}$. Then, $F^1(x) = \nu e^{-x/\nu}$. (This approximation works well for certain stochastic-leadtime systems, as explained in Section 7.3.11.)

Here is another important approximation. Define the functions

$$\Omega^0(z) = \frac{1}{2}\left[\frac{1 - z}{(1 + z^2)^{1/2}}\right]$$

$$\Omega^1(z) = \frac{1}{2}[(1 + z^2)^{1/2} - z]$$

It so happens (but it is not really important) that Ω^0 is the ccdf of $Z = T/\sqrt{2}$, where T has Student's t distribution with 2 degrees of freedom. Ω^1 is the corresponding loss function, i.e., $\Omega^1(z) = \int_z^\infty \Omega^0(t)\,dt$. Suppose we approximate D by $\nu + \sigma Z$. (Unlike the normal approximation, this construction does not match the moments of D. In fact, while Z has zero mean, its variance is infinite.) The approximate performance measures are similar in form to the normal approximation's:

$$\bar{A} = \Omega^0(z)$$

$$\bar{B} = \Omega^1(z)\sigma \qquad \bar{I} = \Omega^1(-z)\sigma$$

where $z = (s - \nu)/\sigma$ is again the standardized value of s.

We call this the *maximal approximation.* It turns out that, for any D with $E[D] = \nu$ and $V[D] = \sigma^2$, this estimate of $\bar{B}$ is always *more* than the true average backorders. Likewise, $\bar{I}$ above is an upper bound on the true inventory. (See Problem 6.10.) Thus, given only ν and σ^2, this approach provides conservative estimates of performance.

Just as in the normal approximation, for fixed z, $\bar{B}$ and $\bar{I}$ are both proportional to σ. Thus, σ is again the primary determinant of performance, as measured by these worst-case estimates.

6.4.3 General (r, q) Policies

For an (r, q) policy, we also replace the actual distribution of IP by the *continuous* uniform distribution on the real numbers in the interval $[r, r + q]$. (Actually, it is more accurate to use the interval $[r + \frac{1}{2}, r + q + \frac{1}{2}]$. We use $[r, r + q]$ here to simplify the notation. For the more accurate method, just replace r by $r + \frac{1}{2}$ in all the formulas below.)

Suppose we use the normal approximation of D. The standardized analogue of G^2 is the function

$$\Phi^2(z) = \int_z^\infty (x - z)\Phi^0(x)\,dx$$

One can show that

$$\Phi^2(z) = \int_z^\infty \Phi^1(x)\,dx = \tfrac{1}{2}[(z^2 + 1)\Phi^0(z) - z\phi(z)] \tag{6.4.8}$$

Now set

$$z_r = \frac{r - \nu}{\sigma} \qquad z_{r+q} = \frac{r + q - \nu}{\sigma}$$

To derive the performance measures, there are two alternative approaches, which lead to the same results: Follow the analysis leading to the exact formulas (6.2.11) to (6.2.13), using the continuous approximations in place of the actual IP and D. Or, average the quantities in (6.4.4) to (6.4.6), letting s range over the interval $[r, r+q]$. (This second approach is easier.) Either method yields

$$\overline{A} = \left(\frac{\sigma}{q}\right)[\Phi^1(z_r) - \Phi^1(z_{r+q})] \qquad (6.4.9)$$

$$\overline{B} = \left(\frac{\sigma^2}{q}\right)[\Phi^2(z_r) - \Phi^2(z_{r+q})] \qquad (6.4.10)$$

$$\overline{I} = \tfrac{1}{2}q + \sigma z_r + \overline{B} \qquad (6.4.11)$$

For these formulas to be reliably accurate, the approximations of *both* D and IP must themselves be accurate. We have already discussed when the normal approximation of D works well and when it does not. As for IP, clearly, the continuous uniform approximation is reasonably close to the actual distribution, when (but only when) q is large.

Well then, when will q be large? Or rather, when can we reasonably restrict attention to large values of q? We have yet to discuss policy optimization (that will come in Section 6.5). But, as you might guess, on the basis of prior chapters or just common sense, large q's arise when there are substantial scale economies in supply, e.g., large fixed order costs.

Again, the importance of this issue depends on what we use the model for. For rough-cut system-design studies the approximation is generally adequate, regardless of the scale of q. Otherwise, when precise policy evaluation is crucial, nothing less than the exact formulas will do.

The formulas analogous to (6.4.9) to (6.4.11) for a general continuous approximation are

$$\overline{A} = \left(\frac{1}{q}\right)[F^1(r) - F^1(r+q)]$$

$$\overline{B} = \left(\frac{1}{q}\right)[F^2(r) - F^2(r+q)]$$

$$\overline{I} = \tfrac{1}{2}q + r - \nu + \overline{B}$$

where

$$F^2(x) = \textstyle\int_x^\infty F^1(t)\,dt$$

For example, the exponential distribution has $F^2(x) = \nu^2 e^{-x/\nu}$. In general, clearly, $\overline{B}$ is decreasing in both r and q, as in the exact formulas. Problem 6.11 asks you to show that $\overline{B}$ and hence $\overline{I}$ are *jointly* convex in the variables (r, q). This property is very useful in policy optimization.

The maximal approximation results in formulas just like (6.4.9) to (6.4.11), with Φ^1 replaced by Ω^1 and Φ^2 by

$$\Omega^2(z) = -\tfrac{1}{4}\{z[(1+z^2)^{1/2} - z] + \ln[(1+z^2)^{1/2} + z]\}$$

6.4.4 Approximate Performance Measures

Next, we examine a different type of approximation. These formulas are commonly used in practice. They appear in many introductory textbooks; indeed, they are often presented as *the* performance measures, not approximations. They are popular because they are simpler than the exact formulas. However, as we shall see, they are not much simpler, and they are not reliably accurate. It is necessary to know about them, because they are so widely known and used, but I do not recommend them.

First, consider the following approximations of $\bar{A}$ and $\bar{B}$:

$$\bar{A}_{+1} = \left(\frac{1}{q}\right) G^1(r) \qquad \bar{B}_{+1} = \left(\frac{1}{q}\right) G^2(r)$$

Compare these formulas to (6.2.11) and (6.2.12). Clearly, $\bar{A}_{+1}$ is similar to $\bar{A}$ in (6.2.11), but it omits the term $-(1/q)G^1(r + q)$. Likewise, $\bar{B}_{+1}$ omits the second term of $\bar{B}$ in (6.2.12). Because the omitted terms are negative, $\bar{A}_{+1} \geq \bar{A}$ and $\bar{B}_{+1} \geq \bar{B}$. These approximations *overestimate* the exact quantities. The errors can be severe. For example, for the exponential approximation, it is easy to show that $\bar{A}_{+1}/\bar{A} = \bar{B}_{+1}/\bar{B} = 1/(1 - e^{-q/v})$. This can be quite large when q/v is small. That is, these approximations are unreliable, *unless* we can be certain that q/v is large.

Second, consider the following approximations:

$$\bar{A}_{+2} = G^0(r) \qquad \bar{B}_{+2} = G^1(r)$$

Recall, $\bar{A}$ is the average of the q numbers $G^0(s)$, $r \leq s < r + q$, and $\bar{A}_{+2}$ replaces the average by the first one. Since G^0 is nonincreasing, $\bar{A}_{+2} \geq \bar{A}$. Likewise, $\bar{B}_{+2} \geq \bar{B}$. So, like those above, these approximations overestimate the true quantities. Whereas $\bar{A}_{+1}$ and $\bar{B}_{+1}$ are most accurate when q is large, $\bar{A}_{+2}$ and $\bar{B}_{+2}$ work best for small q. These approximations too can give wildly inaccurate results. For the exponential approximation, $\bar{A}_{+2}/\bar{A} = \bar{B}_{+2}/\bar{B} = (q/v)/(1 - e^{-q/v})$, which can be enormous, *unless* we know in advance that q/v is small.

By the way, $\bar{A}_{+2}$ is sometimes proposed as an alternative measure of customer service. It is the probability of running out of stock *during an order leadtime.* But, this does not measure customer service in any meaningful way. Customers might well care about $\bar{A}$ and $\bar{B}$, but not what happens during one of our leadtimes.

So, neither of these approximations is particularly reliable. As for simplicity, well, to evaluate a policy, either approximation requires about half the computational effort of the exact formulas. This is not a compelling improvement.

The approximations do have a slight advantage when it comes to selecting a policy to meet a specified requirement: For example, suppose q is already determined somehow, so the remaining problem is to choose r, and there is a given target value $1 - \omega_-$ for $\bar{A}$. Suppose we use the normal approximation for D. Using the exact formula (6.4.9) for $\bar{A}$, we must solve $\bar{A} = 1 - \omega_-$ for r, a nonlinear equation in one unknown. Using approximation $\bar{A}_{+2}$, the equation becomes $\Phi^0(z_r) = 1 - \omega_-$.

Now, it is not terribly difficult to solve the exact equation by numerical methods with a computer. The approximate equation, however, can be solved manually: Just read $z_r = (\Phi^0)^{-1}(1 - \omega_-)$ from a table of the standard normal distribution, and set $r = v + z_r\sigma$. Likewise, the analogous equation based on $\bar{A}_{+1}$ requires a single table lookup (in this case a table of Φ^1).

Indeed, these approximations first became popular in the days before computers were widely available. Armed only with a handbook of statistical tables and a slide rule, an analyst could solve the approximate equation readily, whereas the exact equation required tedious iterations. Today, however, this is no longer a good reason to use the approximations.

Also, since $\overline{A}_{+1}$ and $\overline{A}_{+2}$ overestimate $\overline{A}$, the r obtained from either approximation is larger than the solution to the exact equation, sometimes much larger. Thus, the approximations lead to higher-than-necessary inventory. This is a good reason to avoid them.

EXAMPLE 6.4.A

Reconsider the record store of Example 6.2.A in Section 6.2. Under the (r, q) policy with $q = r = 2$, we found that $\overline{A} = 0.19$, just meeting the service requirement of 0.2. A direct calculation (with the Poisson distribution, not the normal approximation) shows that $\overline{A}_{+1} = 0.22$. So, using this approximation, the manager would conclude that $r = 2$ does *not* meet the requirement, even though it really does. The manager would choose $r = 3$ with $\overline{I} = 2.73$, more than before.

6.5 Optimization

6.5.1 Formulation

As we have seen, the formulas for performance measures have the same general form for both Poisson and world-driven demand. The demand process affects performance solely through the distribution of D, the leadtime demand. Also, a continuous approximation of D leads to performance measures of nearly the same form.

In this section we impose a cost structure on the problem and show how to compute an optimal policy. We also investigate qualitative characteristics of optimal policies and optimal system performance. These methods and results apply to *all* of the specific demand models above. (They apply also to many of the more complex supply models of Chapter 7.)

The cost factors are the same as in the deterministic model of Section 3.3 of Chapter 3:

k = fixed cost to place an order (moneys)
h = cost to hold one unit in inventory for one unit of time (moneys/[quantity-unit · time-unit])
b = penalty cost for one unit backordered for one unit of time (moneys/[quantity-unit · time-unit])

(Because the average variable cost is the constant $c\lambda$ in all cases, it plays no role in determining an optimal policy, so for now we ignore it, treating $c = 0$.) All these factors are positive, unless stated otherwise. The total average cost, then, is

$$C(r, q) = k\overline{OF}(r, q) + h\overline{I}(r, q) + b\overline{B}(r, q) \qquad (6.5.1)$$

The goal is to determine (integer) values of r and q that minimize this function.

Similarly, we can formulate the average cost by using a continuous approximation. We call this $C(r, q)$ also. Here, it makes sense to treat the policy variables too as continuous. As we shall see, this case is easier, both conceptually and computationally.

6.5.2 The Base-Stock Model

Assume that there are no scale economies in supply; that is, $k = 0$. As discussed in Section 6.2, this is the case where a base-stock policy makes sense. Again, $s = r + 1$ is the base-stock level. The average-cost function becomes

$$C(s) = h\bar{I}(s) + b\bar{B}(s) \tag{6.5.2}$$

Figure 6.5.1 illustrates this function. For small s, $\bar{I}(s)$ is negligible and $\bar{B}(s)$ is nearly linear with slope -1; thus, $C(s)$ is nearly linear with slope $-b$ in this range. For large s, $\bar{B}(s)$ goes to zero, while $\bar{I}(s)$ becomes linear with slope $+1$, so $C(s)$ becomes linear with slope h. Finally, as noted in Section 6.2.2, $\bar{I}(s)$ and $\bar{B}(s)$ are both convex functions, so $C(s)$ is too.

We can express $C(s)$ in another useful form: Define the function

$$\hat{C}(y) = h[y]^+ + b[y]^-$$

for all real y. This is a nonnegative, piecewise-linear, convex function. Then,

$$C(s) = E[\hat{C}(s - D)]$$

6.5.2.1 Continuous Approximation: General Case

Suppose we approximate D by a continuous random variable, as in Section 6.4.2, and use the corresponding formulas for $\bar{B}(s)$ and $\bar{I}(s)$ in the cost function (6.5.2), treating s

FIGURE 6.5.1

Average cost function.

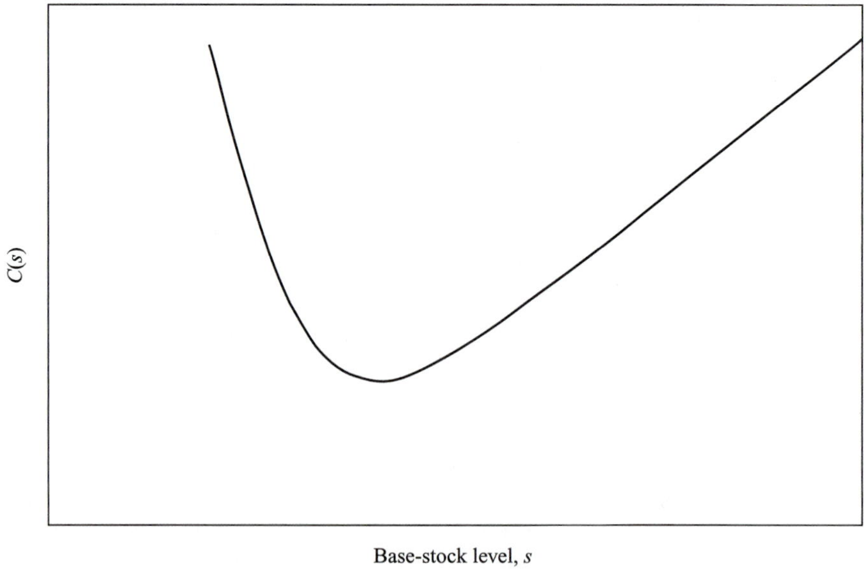

as a continuous variable. Now, the approximate ccdf F^0 is continuous and nonincreasing, so F^1 is continuously differentiable and convex, so $\bar{B}(s)$ and $\bar{I}(s)$ are too, hence so is $C(s)$. Thus, to minimize $C(s)$, we need only solve the equation $C'(s) = 0$.

Also, $dF^1(s)/ds = -F^0(s)$, so $\bar{B}'(s) = -F^0(s)$ and $\bar{I}'(s) = 1 - F^0(s)$. Thus, the optimality equation $C'(s) = 0$ reduces to

$$h[1 - F^0(s)] - bF^0(s) = 0$$

or

$$F^0(s) = \frac{h}{b + h} = 1 - \omega \tag{6.5.3}$$

where ω is the cost ratio $b/(b + h)$, as in Chapter 3. For simplicity, assume that D has a positive pdf $f(x)$, at least for $x \geq 0$. So, $F^0(x)$ is strictly decreasing, and (6.5.3) has a unique solution, say s^*. This is the optimal base-stock level. If the approximate D is positive ($F^0(x) = 1$ for $x \leq 0$), then s^* is positive.

To determine s^*, then, means to solve the single nonlinear equation (6.5.3), a numerical problem for which a variety of standard methods are available. In certain special cases, the solution can be computed in closed form, as shown below.

Recalling that $\bar{A}(s) = F^0(s)$, equation (6.5.3) prescribes the following simple rule for determining the optimal policy: *Set the base-stock level so that the stockout probability equals the critical ratio* $1 - \omega$. This is the same calculation required to meet a specified target level $1 - \omega_-$ for $\bar{A}$.

6.5.2.2 Normal Approximation

Specifically, consider the normal approximation of D. That is, use (6.4.5) and (6.4.6) for $\bar{I}(s)$ and $\bar{B}(s)$ in the cost function (6.5.2). In terms of $z = (s - \nu)/\sigma$ and the standard normal ccdf Φ^0, equation (6.5.3) now reads

$$\Phi^0(z) = 1 - \omega$$

That is, the optimal base-stock level can be written

$$s^* = \nu + z^*\sigma$$

where $z^* = (\Phi^0)^{-1}(1 - \omega)$. Computing the optimal policy, like meeting a specified target level, essentially reduces to a search through a standard-normal table or a computerized equivalent.

Thus, the *standardized* optimal base-stock level z^* depends only on the relative costs, not on ν and σ, hence not on the supply and demand processes. The leadtime-demand parameters tell us how to determine s^* from z^*, through the linear relationship above. Again, z^* is called the *safety factor*. It is positive and so $s^* > \nu$, when $\omega > ½$ or $b > h$. Generally, z^* is increasing in ω, becoming arbitrarily large as ω approaches 1. Indeed, as in Section 6.4.1, for $1 - \omega$ near 0, $z^* \approx [-2 \ln (1 - \omega)]^{1/2}$.

For the optimal $s = s^*$, the performance measures become

$$\bar{B}(s^*) = \Phi^1(z^*)\sigma \qquad \bar{I}(s^*) = \Phi^1(-z^*)\sigma$$

so the optimal cost is simply

$$C^* = h\Phi^1(-z^*)\sigma + b\Phi^1(z^*)\sigma = (b + h)[(1 - \omega)z^* + \Phi^1(z^*)]\sigma$$
$$= (b + h)\phi(z^*)\sigma$$
$$= b\Upsilon(z^*)\sigma$$

where $\Upsilon(z) = \phi(z)/\Phi(z)$. (The second equality uses the definitions of z^* and Φ^1, while the last uses the definition of ω.) Also, one can show that, for fixed h and $1 - \omega$ near 0, $C^* \approx h[-2 \ln (1 - \omega)]^{1/2}\sigma$.

Notice, C^* is the product of three terms: The first (b) is essentially a scale factor, measuring the overall magnitude of the cost coefficients. (If the monetary unit changed, say from £ to ¥, only this term would change.) The second term ($\Upsilon(z^*)$) depends on the relative costs of inventory and backorders through the ratio ω. These two terms summarize the *economics* of the problem. Only the last term (σ) depends on the *physical dynamics* of demand and supply. Thus, for fixed cost factors, *the performance measures and the optimal cost are all proportional to* σ.

This finding strengthens the earlier observation that σ is a primary determinant of performance. For example, σ is proportional to $\sqrt{L}$, so C^* is also. To the extent we improve the supply and demand processes so as to reduce σ, we can thereby reduce the overall cost of operating the system.

Indeed, suppose we somehow reduce σ to σ_-, while the cost factors remain unchanged. Then, the new optimal cost as a fraction of the old one is simply σ_-/σ. *The cost saving in percentage terms is entirely independent of the cost parameters.* Inventory and backorders both decrease by this same ratio.

6.5.2.3 Maximal Approximation

The maximal approximation yields similar results. Again, $s^* = \nu + z^*\sigma$, where z^* solves

$$\Omega^0(z) = \frac{1}{2}\left[\frac{1 - z}{(1 + z^2)^{1/2}}\right] = 1 - \omega$$

This equation can be solved explicitly:

$$z^* = \frac{\omega - 1/2}{[\omega(1 - \omega)]^{1/2}}$$

$$C^* = (b + h)[\omega(1 - \omega)]^{1/2}\sigma = (bh)^{1/2}\sigma$$

(Problem 6.15 asks you to verify these results.)

Because the maximal approximation provides an upper bound on $\overline{B}$ and $\overline{I}$, the corresponding value of $C(s)$ is an upper bound on the true cost for any s. Consequently, C^* here is an upper bound on the optimal cost. (Well, not quite: This allows fractional s^*. To get a true upper bound, restrict s^* to an integer; this yields a slightly higher value. For most practical purposes, however, we can treat C^* as an upper bound.)

So, the maximal optimal cost too is proportional to σ. This fact further emphasizes the centrality of σ.

6.5.2.4 Discrete Formulation

Return now to the exact, discrete formulation, using performance measures of form (6.2.5) and (6.2.6) within the cost function (6.5.2). Here, $C(s)$ is a function of the *integer* variable s.

Define s^* to be the *smallest* s that minimizes $C(s)$ over all integers s. Clearly, $0 \leq s^* < \infty$. Also, because C is convex, s^* is the unique value of s satisfying

$$\Delta C(s-1) < 0 \leq \Delta C(s)$$

Indeed, $\Delta C(s) < 0$ for all $s < s^*$, and $\Delta C(s) \geq 0$ for all $s \geq s^*$.

Now, using (6.2.5) and (6.2.6) and the definition of G^1, we have

$$\Delta C(s) = h\Delta \bar{I}(s) + b\Delta \bar{B}(s) = h[1 - G^0(s)] - bG^0(s)$$

So, s^* uniquely satisfies

$$G^0(s-1) > 1 - \omega \geq G^0(s) \tag{6.5.4}$$

Notice the similarity of this optimality condition to (6.5.3) above. Its interpretation is similar as well, recalling that $\bar{A}(s) = G^0(s-1)$: Choose s^* as small as possible, while keeping the probability of backorders $G^0(s)$ no greater than the critical ratio $1 - \omega$.

EXAMPLE 6.5.A, PART 1

Consider yet again the record store of Section 6.2. Suppose that the manager estimates $h = \$0.25$ and $b = \$1.75$ (both per CD-month). So, $\omega = 1.75/2.00 = 0.875$, $1 - \omega = 0.125$. The table in Example 6.2.A Part 1 in Section 6.2.2 indicates that $G^0(2) = 0.27$ and $G^0(3) = 0.11$, so $s^* = 3$. Also, $C^* = \$0.62$ (per month).

Solving (6.5.4) is essentially like solving a nonlinear equation, with minor adjustments to account for the integrality of s. It is straightforward to compute s^* through a standard bisection procedure, for example. (In special cases, G^0 can be inverted and s^* expressed in closed form. This is true, for instance, of a geometric distribution, which arises in the models of Section 7.3.)

6.5.3 The General (r, q) Model: Continuous Approximation

Turn now to the general case with $k > 0$. We wish to optimize the function $C(r, q)$ in (6.5.1). Suppose we approximate the actual distribution of D by a continuous one, and that of IP by a continuous uniform distribution. Now, both r and q are continuous variables.

In general, there are no explicit formulas for the optimal (r, q); to compute them requires numerical methods. But, as mentioned in Section 6.4, both $\bar{I}$ and $\bar{B}$ are convex functions of (r, q), and of course $\overline{OF}$ is, so C is also. Also, C is continuously differentiable. Therefore, *any nonlinear-optimization code can be used to minimize C.* (The Notes in Appendix A mention sources of such codes. It is possible to devise a specialized algorithm for this function C, but we shall not pursue this here.)

We can learn a good deal even without explicit formulas. The *model* combines the features of the EOQ model with planned backorders of Section 3.3 and the base-stock model with $k = 0$ of Section 6.5.2. The optimal *policy* and optimal *cost,* it turns out, are closely related to those of the two simpler models, and in remarkably simple ways.

Let r^* and q^* denote the optimal r and q, and $C^* = C(r^*, q^*)$ the optimal cost. Let q_k and C_k denote the optimal batch size and cost in the deterministic model; that is, $q_k = (2k\lambda/h\omega)^{1/2}$ and $C_k = h\omega q_k = (2k\lambda h\omega)^{1/2}$. For the base-stock model, let s^* denote the optimal base-stock level and $C_\sigma = C(s^*)$ the optimal cost. Also, $C_{\sigma+} = (bh)^{1/2}\sigma$ denotes the base-stock model's optimal cost under the maximal approximation. Finally, let $q_\sigma = C_\sigma/h\omega$ and $q_{\sigma+} = C_{\sigma+}/h\omega$.

THEOREM 6.5.1.

$$r^* \le s^* \le r^* + q^* \tag{6.5.5}$$

$$q_k \le q^* \le (q_k^2 + q_{\sigma+}^2)^{1/2} = \frac{(2k\lambda h\omega + bh\sigma^2)^{1/2}}{h\omega} \tag{6.5.6}$$

$$C_k \le C^* \le (C_k^2 + C_{\sigma+}^2)^{1/2} = (2k\lambda h\omega + bh\sigma^2)^{1/2} \tag{6.5.7}$$

$$q_k \le q^* \le q_\sigma + q_k \tag{6.5.8}$$

$$(C_k^2 + C_\sigma^2)^{1/2} \le C^* \le C_\sigma + C_k \tag{6.5.9}$$

Let us examine these results before proving them. (6.5.5) says that the interval $[r^*, r^* + q^*]$, i.e., the optimal range of IP, covers s^*. (6.5.6) and (6.5.7) are bounds on q^* and C^* that require knowledge of $\sigma^2 = V[D]$, but no more information about D. (6.5.8) and (6.5.9) provide refined bounds which do depend on D through C_σ.

The results indicate that the model inherits the sensitivity analyses of both the EOQ and the base-stock models, at least approximately. For example, q^* and C^* are bounded both above and below by functions proportional to $\sqrt{k}$. So, q^* and C^* are robust with respect to changes in k, just as in the EOQ model. Likewise, q^* and C^* are bounded by functions proportional to σ. So, σ degrades performance as before; lead-time-demand uncertainty can only increase cost, and only by a limited amount. In sum, *everything we have learned about the determinants of performance and the benefits of system improvements continues to apply here.* (See Problem 6.18 for more on sensitivity analysis.)

Also, the bounds on q^* suggest plausible heuristics for setting q; the simplest is q_k itself. We can use any such heuristic directly, or as the initial value in an optimization procedure. As for r, (6.5.5) indicates some value of the form $s^* - \beta q$, where $0 \le \beta \le 1$. (The proof below suggests setting β between $(1 - \omega)$ and ½.) Likewise, the bounds suggest reasonable approximations of C^* for rough-cut economic studies.

Here is a numerical example. Fix $\lambda = 10$ and $L = 1$, and use the normal approximation. The cost parameters are $k = 4$, $h = 1$, and $b = 24$. We examine several values of σ ranging from 0 to 8. (If demand were Poisson, $\sigma = \sqrt{\lambda L} \approx 3.16$, about the middle of this range.) Figure 6.5.2 shows the true optimal cost C^* (the heavy curve) and the bounds (6.5.9) (the lighter curves). Notice, C^* is increasing in σ, becoming nearly linear for large σ, as are both bounds. Figure 6.5.3 shows q^* along with the bounds (6.5.8). Evidently, q^* grows *very* slowly as σ increases, so q_k is a fairly close approximation. (The upper bound badly overestimates q^* for large σ. Its main value is in qualitative sensitivity analysis, as above.)

FIGURE 6.5.2

Optimal average cost (exact and bounds).

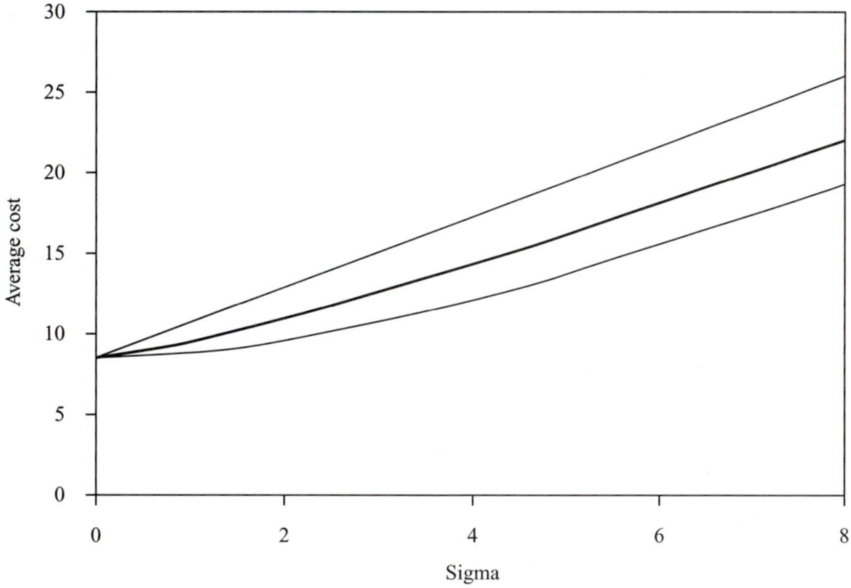

One additional property is worth mentioning: Define the function $C^*(q) = \min_r \{C(r, q)\}$, the optimal cost with q held fixed, and recall the EOQ error function $\epsilon(x) = \frac{1}{2}(x + 1/x)$, $x > 0$. Then,

$$\frac{C^*(q)}{C^*} \leq \epsilon\left(\frac{q}{q^*}\right) \tag{6.5.10}$$

(See Problem 6.19.) Chapter 3 presents a similar relation for the deterministic case, but with equality instead of inequality. Thus, the insensitivity property here is even stronger. If we choose some other q besides q^*, by error or by design, the cost penalty is modest, provided q is not too far away from q^*.

PROOF OF THEOREM 6.5.1. The proof is long, but it requires only basic calculus. Recall that $\overline{B}(r, q)$ and $\overline{I}(r, q)$ are simple averages of $\overline{B}(s)$ and $\overline{I}(s)$, respectively. Therefore, if $C(s)$ denotes the cost of a base-stock policy as in (6.5.2), the objective function can be written as

$$C(r, q) = \frac{k\lambda + \int_r^{r+q} C(s)\, ds}{q} \tag{6.5.11}$$

Let us first prove the bounds on C^*. Recall that $\hat{C}(y) = h[y]^+ + b[y]^-$, and define

$$C_-(s) = \hat{C}(s - E[D]) = \hat{C}(s - \nu)$$

$$C_+(s) = C_\sigma + \hat{C}(s - s^*)$$

FIGURE 6.5.3

Optimal batch size (exact and bounds).

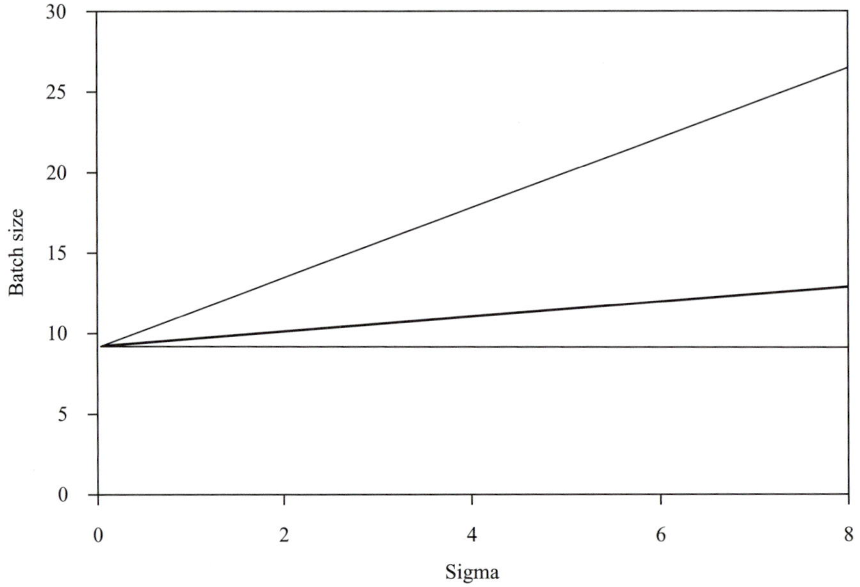

Thus, C_- and C_+ are translated versions of the convex, piecewise-linear function $\hat{C}$. See Figure 6.5.4. We claim that

$$C_-(s) \leq C(s) \leq C_+(s) \tag{6.5.12}$$

as in the figure. First, $C(s) = E[\hat{C}(s - D)]$, so Jensen's inequality (see Section C.2.2) yields the first inequality in (6.5.12). The second inequality is immediately apparent, since $C_+(s^*) = C_\sigma = C(s^*)$, and $C_+(s)$ is *steeper* than $C(s)$, both above and below s^*.

Now, replace $C(s)$ by $C_-(s)$ in the cost function (6.5.11), and call the result $C_-(r, q)$. It is easy to show (Problem 3.10) that this is precisely the cost function of the deterministic model, and (6.5.12) implies $C(r, q) \geq C_-(r, q)$ for all (r, q). Thus, $C^* \geq C_k$, which is the lower bound in (6.5.7).

The lower bound in (6.5.9) comes from applying a similar argument to the function $C_{-+}(s) = \max\{C_\sigma, C_-(s)\}$. (This is another piecewise-linear function, in this case with three pieces. It replaces the lowest parts of $C_-(s)$ with a horizontal segment at level C_σ.) Clearly, $C_{-+}(s) \leq C(s)$. So, substituting $C_{-+}(s)$ for $C(s)$ in (6.5.11) yields a lower bound on C^*, and direct calculation shows that this bound is $(C_k^2 + C_\sigma^2)^{1/2}$.

Likewise, replace $C(s)$ by $C_+(s)$ in (6.5.11), and call the result $C_+(r, q)$. Clearly, $C_+(r, q) = C_\sigma + C_-(r', q)$, where $r' = r - s^* + \nu$. Thus, the minimal value of $C_+(r, q)$ is $C_\sigma + C_k$. (The translation of r' leaves the minimum unchanged.) But (6.5.12) implies $C(r, q) \leq C_+(r, q)$ for all (r, q), so $C^* \leq C_\sigma + C_k$, which is the upper bound in (6.5.9).

For the upper bound in (6.5.7), fix D for the moment, and let $V = r - D$. Direct calculation yields

FIGURE 6.5.4

Piecewise linear approximations.

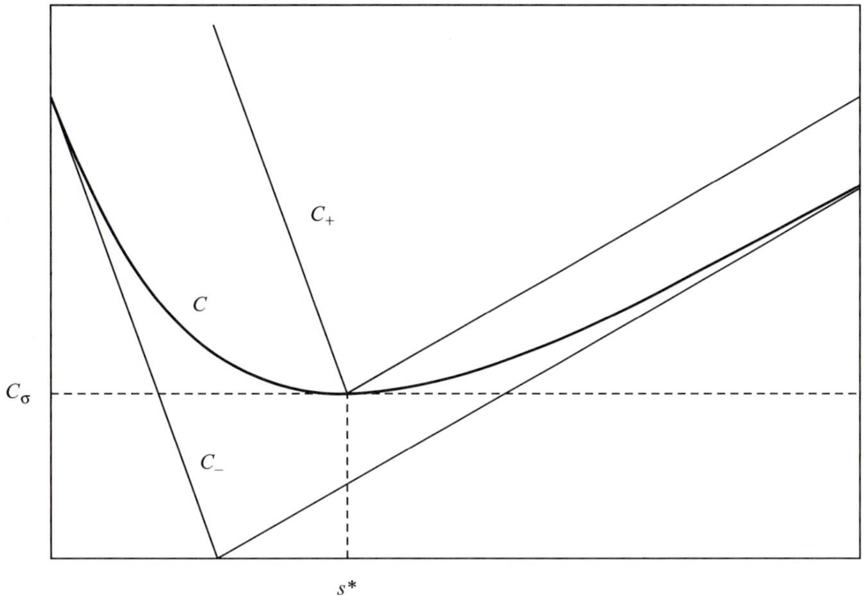

$$\int_r^{r+q} \hat{C}(s - D)\, ds = \int_V^{V+q} \hat{C}(y)\, dy$$
$$= \begin{cases} \tfrac{1}{2}b[V^2 - (q + V)^2] & V < -q \\ \tfrac{1}{2}[h(q + V)^2 + bV^2] & -q \le V \le 0 \\ \tfrac{1}{2}h[(q + V)^2 - V^2] & V \ge 0 \end{cases}$$

This quantity, clearly, is $\le \tfrac{1}{2}[h(q + V)^2 + bV^2]$ for all V. Therefore,

$$\int_r^{r+q} C(s)\, ds = \int_r^{r+q} E[\hat{C}(s - D)]\, ds = E[\int_r^{r+q} \hat{C}(s - D)\, ds]$$
$$\le \tfrac{1}{2}E[h(q + V)^2 + bV^2]$$
$$= \tfrac{1}{2}\{h(q + \bar{V})^2 + b\bar{V}^2 + (b + h)E[(V - \bar{V})^2]\}$$
$$= \tfrac{1}{2}\{h(q + \bar{V})^2 + b\bar{V}^2 + (b + h)\sigma^2\}$$

where $\bar{V} = E[V] = r - \nu$. Now, $C_-(r, q) = [k\lambda + \tfrac{1}{2}h(q + \bar{V})^2 + \tfrac{1}{2}b\bar{V}^2]/q$, so

$$C(r, q) \le C_-(r, q) + \frac{1}{2}\frac{(b + h)\sigma^2}{q}$$

The right-hand side has the same form as $C_-(r, q)$ itself with $k\lambda$ augmented by $\tfrac{1}{2}(b + h)\sigma^2$, so its minimal value is $\{2[k\lambda + \tfrac{1}{2}(b + h)\sigma^2]h\omega\}^{1/2} = (2k\lambda h\omega + bh\sigma^2)^{1/2}$. This, therefore, is an upper bound on C^*, as asserted.

FIGURE 6.5.5

Optimality condition.

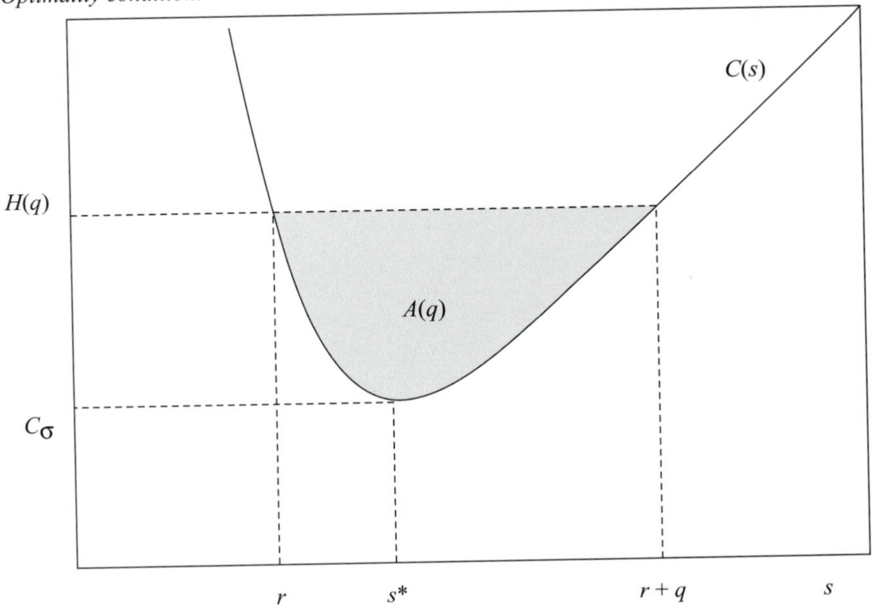

Now let us prove the bounds on q^*. The optimality conditions for minimizing $C(r, q)$ in (6.5.11) are $\partial C/\partial r = 0$ and $\partial C/\partial q = 0$. These equations reduce, respectively, to

$$C(r) \quad = C(r + q) \tag{6.5.13}$$

$$C(r, q) = C(r + q) \tag{6.5.14}$$

Figure 6.5.5 illustrates the idea: (6.5.13) says, for any fixed q, set r to equalize $C(r)$ and $C(r + q)$. So, on the graph of $C(s)$, these two points have equal heights and can be connected by a horizontal line. (By the convexity of $C(s)$, this implies $r \leq s^* \leq r + q$, which proves (6.5.5).) Let $H = H(q)$ denote this common *height*.

With r chosen to satisfy (6.5.13), the shaded *area* $A = A(q)$ is given by

$$\begin{aligned} A(q) &= qC(r + q) - \textstyle\int_r^{r+q} C(s)\, ds \\ &= qC(r + q) - [qC(r, q) - k\lambda] \end{aligned}$$

(This A is unrelated to the stockout probability $\bar{A}$.) The second optimality condition (6.5.14) is thus equivalent to

$$A(q) = k\lambda \tag{6.5.15}$$

Conceptually, we can determine q^* by manipulating the horizontal line defining H, adjusting it up or down, until the shaded area equals $k\lambda$.

Let $H_+(q)$ denote the analogue of $H(q)$ and $A_+(q)$ that of $A(q)$, using $C_+(s)$ instead of $C(s)$. Suppose we start with some q, and then increase it by the small amount dq. Then,

H increases by $dH = H'(q)\,dq$, and H_+ by $dH_+ = H'_+(q)\,dq$. Straightforward geometry reveals that $H'_+(q) = h\omega$. But, as mentioned above, $C_+(s)$ is steeper than $C(s)$, so $dH_+ \geq dH$; that is, $0 \leq H'(q) \leq h\omega$. (Problem 6.16 asks you for a more rigorous proof.) Thus,

$$H(q) = C_\sigma + \int_0^q H'_0(x)\,dx \leq C_\sigma + h\omega q = H_+(q)$$

The same increase dq changes A by $dA = A'(q)\,dq = (q)\,dH \leq (q)\,dH_+ = (h\omega q)\,dq = dA_+$. So,

$$A(q) = \int_0^q A'(x)\,dx \leq \int_0^q (h\omega x)\,dx$$
$$= \tfrac{1}{2}h\omega q^2 = A_+(q)$$

In particular, $A(q_k) \leq \tfrac{1}{2}h\omega q_k^2 = k\lambda = A(q^*)$, by (6.5.15). Since $A(q)$ is increasing, $q_k \leq q^*$, which is the lower bound in (6.5.6) and (6.5.8).

On the other hand, let $H_-(q)$ denote the analogue of $H(q)$, using $C_-(s)$ in place of $C(s)$. Since $C_-(s) \leq C(s)$, it is clear that $H(q) \geq H_-(q) = H_+(q) - C_\sigma = h\omega q$. In particular, using (6.5.14), $C^* = H(q^*) \geq h\omega q^*$, so $q^* \leq C^*/h\omega$. Consequently, (6.5.7) implies $q^* \leq (2k\lambda h\omega + bh\sigma^2)^{1/2}/h\omega$, which is the upper bound in (6.5.6). Similarly, (6.5.9) yields the upper bound in (6.5.8).

6.5.4 The General (r, q) Model: Discrete Formulation

6.5.4.1 Algorithm

Turn now to the exact formulation, where r and q are integer variables. There is no standard, tractable method to optimize a function of several integer variables. We now develop an algorithm specifically to optimize $C(r, q)$, as defined in (6.5.1). It is based on properties analogous to those of the continuous model in the proof of Theorem 6.5.1.

First, rewrite $C(r, q)$ in a form analogous to (6.5.11) above:

$$C(r, q) = \frac{k\lambda + \sum_{s=r+1}^{r+q} C(s)}{q} \tag{6.5.16}$$

where $C(s)$ is defined in (6.5.2). Think of $C(r, q)$ as the average of the costs of q base-stock policies, plus the fixed-cost term $k\lambda/q$.

Let C_1 denote the *smallest* value of $C(s)$ as s ranges over all the integers (of course, $C_1 = C(s^*)$), C_2 the *second smallest* value, C_3 the *third smallest,* and so on. That is, construct the sequence $\{C_1, C_2, \ldots\}$ by listing the values $C(s)$ in order, paying no attention to the order of the s's themselves. Because $C(s)$ is convex, the first q of these numbers correspond to *consecutive* values of s, for any q.

Fix the value of q for the moment, and let $r^*(q)$ denote the best value of r. By (6.5.16), for any r, $C(r, q)$ is the average of q consecutive values of $C(s)$, plus $k\lambda/q$. To determine $r^*(q)$, therefore, choose r such that $\{C(s) : r + 1 \leq s \leq r + q\}$ comprises the smallest q values of $C(s)$, that is, $C_1, \ldots, C_q$.

Furthermore, suppose we have determined $r^*(q)$ in this way. To find $r^*(q + 1)$, just find C_{q+1} and add it to the set $C_1, \ldots, C_q$. Moreover, by convexity, this C_{q+1} is $C(s)$ for some s just outside the interval $[r^*(q) + 1, r^*(q) + q]$. There are only two possibilities: Either $C_{q+1} = C(r^*(q))$, in which case $r^*(q + 1) = r^*(q) - 1$, or $C_{q+1} = C(r^*(q) + q$

$+ 1)$, so $r^*(q + 1) = r^*(q)$. Thus, $r^*(q)$ is nonincreasing in q, but it decreases no faster than q increases.

So, it is easy to optimize r for fixed q. We still need to optimize q. Let $C^*(q) = C[r^*(q), q]$ denote the optimal cost for fixed q, and

$$q^* = \min \{q > 0 : C_{q+1} \geq C^*(q)\}$$

It follows from (6.5.16) and the observations above that

$$\begin{aligned}(q + 1)C^*(q + 1) &= k\lambda + \Sigma_{j=1}^{q} C_j + C_{q+1}\\ &= qC^*(q) + C_{q+1}\\ &= (q + 1)C^*(q) - [C^*(q) - C_{q+1}]\end{aligned}$$

or

$$C^*(q + 1) = C^*(q) - \frac{C^*(q) - C_{q+1}}{q + 1}$$

Thus, $C^*(q + 1) < C^*(q)$ *if and only if* $C_{q+1} < C^*(q)$. Consequently, for $q < q^*$, $C^*(q) > C^*(q + 1)$, and so $C^*(q) > C^*(q^*)$. For $q \geq q^*$, one can show (by simple induction) that $C^*(q) \leq C^*(q + 1) \leq C_{q+1} \leq C_{q+2}$, and therefore $C^*(q) \geq C^*(q^*)$. Thus, q^* is optimal.

The following algorithm implements these ideas, and so determines an optimal policy:

Algorithm Optimize_rq

Step 0 (initialize):
  Determine s^* as above.
  Set $q \leftarrow 1, r \leftarrow s^* - 1, C^* \leftarrow k\lambda + C(s^*)$.
Step 1 (determine next smallest C(s)):
  Set $c_* \leftarrow \min \{C(r), C(r + q + 1)\}$.
Step 2 (test for termination):
  If $c_* \geq C^*$:
    Set $q^* \leftarrow q, r^* \leftarrow r$.
    STOP.
Step 3 (update):
  Set $q \leftarrow q + 1$.
  Set $C^* \leftarrow C^* - (C^* - c_*)/q$.
  If $C(r)$ was minimal in step 1:
    Set $r \leftarrow r - 1$.
  Go to step 1.

EXAMPLE 6.5.A, PART 2

Suppose that the CD's cost factors are again h = \$0.25 and b = \$1.75, but now k = \$0.15, so $k\lambda$ = \$0.54. Direct calculation yields the function $C(s)$:

s	$C(s)$
0	3.15
1	1.73
2	0.91
3	0.62
4	0.65
5	0.83
6	1.06

Step 0:
$s^* = 3, q = 1, r = 2.$
$C^* = 0.54 + 0.62 = 1.16.$

Step 1:
$c^* = \min\{0.91, 0.65\} = 0.65.$

Step 2:
$c_* = 0.65 < 1.16 = C^*$, so proceed to

Step 3:
$q = 1 + 1 = 2.$
$C^* = 1.16 - (1.16 - 0.62)/2 = 0.89.$
r remains 2.

Step 1:
$c_* = \min\{0.91, 0.83\} = 0.83.$

Step 2:
$c_* = 0.83 < 0.89 = C^*$, so proceed to

Step 3:
$q = 2 + 1 = 3.$
$C^* = 0.89 - (0.89 - 0.83)/3 = 0.87.$
r remains 2.

Step 1:
$c_* = \min\{0.91, 1.06\} = 0.91.$

Step 2:
$c_* = 0.91 > 0.87 = C^*$, so STOP with
$r^* = 2, q^* = 3, C^* = 0.87.$

Concerning the qualitative behavior of the optimal policy, it is generally true that $r^* < s^* \leq r^* + q^*$, analogous to (6.5.5) above. We suspect that analogues of the other parts of Theorem 6.5.1 also hold, although to our knowledge this has not been investigated.

6.5.4.2 Discussion

Evidently, Algorithm Optimize_rq starts with $q = 1$ and successively increments q until q^* is found. It is quite efficient when q^* happens to be relatively small, but when q^* is large, it may require a good deal of time. The algorithm can be extended, however, to start with any policy:

For instance, by analogy to the continuous model, a plausible initial value for q is q_k, rounded to an integer. A plausible r is an integer near $s^* - \beta q$, for some β between ½ and $1 - \omega$.

Given an initial policy, first find $r^*(q)$ for the initial q. This can be done with a simple search procedure based on the ideas above. Then, determine whether to increase or decrease q by comparing C_{q+1} to $C^*(q)$. If $C_{q+1} < C^*(q)$, then $q < q^*$, so proceed with Algorithm Optimize_rq, beginning with step 3. Otherwise, if $C_{q+1} \geq C^*(q)$, then $q \geq q^*$. It is not hard to modify the algorithm to decrease q until q^* is found. (Problem 6.21 asks you to work out the details.)

It is worth mentioning that the results above and Algorithm Optimize_rq do not really require $C(s)$ to be convex. The key property is that $-C(s)$ be unimodal (i.e., $C(s)$ is nonincreasing for $s < s^*$ and nondecreasing for $s \geq s^*$).

On the other hand, the algorithm is *not* guaranteed to work if there is a penalty cost on $\overline{A}$ instead of $\overline{B}$. (As discussed in Section 3.3.7, this is a peculiar objective, and it leads to peculiar results in the deterministic case.) In this case, the average cost can still be represented in the form (6.5.16), where $C(s)$ is redefined as

$$\begin{aligned} C(s) &= h\overline{I}(s) + b\overline{A}(s) \\ &= h[s - \nu + G^1(s)] + bG^0(s-1) \end{aligned}$$

Now, $-C(s)$ happens to be unimodal when D has a Poisson distribution, and in that case the algorithm works. In general, however, $-C(s)$ need not be unimodal. (One occasionally finds suggestions to the contrary in the literature; beware!) Without that property, it is much harder to find an optimal policy.

6.5.5 *A Service-Level Constraint*

Now, suppose there is an upper limit $1 - \omega_-$ on $\overline{A}$ instead of a backorder cost b. Also, $k > 0$, and both r and q are variables to be determined. The cost now includes only the first two terms of (6.5.1), $C(r, q) = k\overline{OF}(r, q) + h\overline{I}(r, q)$. The problem is to minimize this $C(r, q)$, subject to $\overline{A}(r, q) \leq 1 - \omega_-$.

In general, this is a hard problem. As mentioned in Section 6.2.3.3, for fixed q, it is easy to find the best r (namely, the smallest feasible value). Finding q^*, however, requires a full search.

Here is a heuristic: Set $b = h\omega_-/(1 - \omega_-)$, so that $\omega = b/(b + h) = \omega_-$, replace k by k/ω_-, and minimize the original $C(r, q)$ of (6.5.1) with no constraint, as above. This approach is relatively easy, and it works, in the sense that the resulting policy (r, q) has $\overline{A}$ near $1 - \omega_-$. (This is easiest to see for a continuous approximation, in which case $\overline{A} = 1 - \omega_-$ exactly. See Problem 6.17.)

On the other hand, there is no guarantee that this policy minimizes the true cost. Still, the policy is likely to perform fairly well. (For the deterministic case of Section 3.3.5, it recovers the optimal policy.) Moreover, as discussed in Section 3.3.7, $\bar{A}$ is usually an *ad hoc* proxy for more fundamental criteria. For these reasons, we believe the approach is a sound one.

6.6 Lumpy Demand

6.6.1 Discussion

Up to this point we have assumed that demands occur one unit at a time. Now, consider a system where demand **D** is a *compound-Poisson process:* Demand *epochs* form a Poisson process, denoted $\tilde{\mathbf{D}}$, but at each epoch the *amount* demanded is a random variable. This model describes demands that arrive in large, unpredictable lumps.

The amounts demanded at different epochs are identically distributed and independent of each other as well as of the timing of the epochs. For convenience, assume they are integer-valued. (Similar results hold for continuous quantities.) Let Y be the generic demand-quantity random variable. For technical reasons, assume $g_Y(1) > 0$ and $g_Y(0) = 0$. The demand-epoch rate is λ, so the overall demand rate is $\lambda E[Y]$.

Each demand increment can be filled separately. For example, if a demand of size $Y = 5$ occurs at a time t when $I(t^-) = 2$, the customer is willing to take the two units available, leaving a backlog of $B(t) = 3$. (This is not always true, of course; a customer may insist on all or nothing. This second scenario leads to a far more complex model, however, and only rarely to fundamentally different system behavior.) Moreover, the customer cares when each demand unit is filled; the time to fill the overall demand Y is unimportant. That is, the primary service measure remains $\bar{B}$, measured in units, *not* the number of waiting customers.

What policies make sense in this setting? The (r, q) policy works well for pure Poisson demand, so it is reasonable to adapt it to compound-Poisson demand. There are several different adaptations; we shall consider two. In both, a reorder point r triggers orders, as before, but the order quantities are determined differently.

First, there is the (r, s) policy. The second parameter s is called the *target stock level,* and $s \geq r + 1$. An order is placed whenever $IP(t^-)$ drops to r or less. The order size is $s - IP(t^-)$, which raises $IP(t)$ immediately to s. Thus, each order is for at least $s - r$ units, but some orders may be larger; the order size is random. (Such policies are frequently called (s, S) policies, with s in place of our r and S for s.)

The *second* type of policy is the (r, q) policy. Here, $q \geq 1$ is the *basic* batch size. Each order is a positive-integer multiple of q. When $IP(t^-) \leq r$, first order a batch of size q. If this is not enough to raise $IP(t)$ above r, add another batch of size q to the order. Keep adding batches in this way until $IP(t)$ is at least $r + 1$ (but no more than $r + q$). This kind of policy is useful when there is some "natural" order size, such as a truckload. (Sometimes this is called an (r, Nq) policy, where N indicates the random number of basic batches in an order.)

A bit of reflection should convince you that both types reduce to a standard (r, q) policy when the demand size is always one. Also, an (r, s) policy reduces to a base-stock policy when $s - r = 1$, and so does an (r, q) policy when $q = 1$.

As Chapter 9 shows, under standard cost assumptions, the best (r, s) policy is in fact optimal. This is not true of (r, q) policies. As noted above, there are special situations where an (r, q) policy is preferred, but otherwise, in general, an (r, s) policy performs better. However, the best (r, q) policy is often close to optimal.

The program here is the same as before: First, we evaluate the performance measures $\overline{A}$, $\overline{B}$, $\overline{I}$, and $\overline{OF}$. Then, we compute an optimal policy within each of the two policy classes. As we shall see, much of the earlier analysis for pure Poisson demand carries over to this model.

6.6.2 Policy Evaluation

To analyze performance, we follow the same four steps as in Section 6.2.3: Describe the distribution of *IP;* characterize the relationship between **IP** and **D;** determine the distribution of *IN;* finally, compute $\overline{A}$, $\overline{B}$, $\overline{I}$, and $\overline{OF}$ from *IN.*

There are two kinds of policies, and we perform the first step (describe *IP*) separately for each type. This is the *only* point where the two policy classes differ. The remaining steps cover both types at once.

Step 1: Begin with the second class, the (r, q) policies. The result is precisely the same as for the pure Poisson-demand case: The limiting inventory position *IP* has the uniform distribution on the integers in the interval $[r + 1, r + q]$.

The argument follows the proof of Lemma 6.2.1: Again, define $IP_c(t) = (r + q) - IP(t)$. Ignore transient states, i.e., assume $0 \leq IP_c(0) < q$. The process $\mathbf{IP}_c$ is a continuous-time Markov chain. It changes only at demand epochs, and if t is such a time, then

$$IP_c(t) = [IP_c(t^-) + Y] \bmod (q)$$

Now, it is not hard to show that $(1/q)\mathbf{e}'$, the uniform probability vector, is stationary for $\mathbf{IP}_c$. (This is basically the assertion of Problem 6.5, which is used in the proof of Theorem 6.3.2.) Also, the assumption that $g_Y(1) > 0$ ensures that $\mathbf{IP}_c$ is irreducible. Consequently, IP_c is uniformly distributed on the integers mod (q), and *IP* is uniform on the integers in the interval $[r + 1, r + q]$.

Now, consider an (r, s) policy. The distribution of *IP* is more complex here, but still fairly simple. Define the following sequence recursively:

$$m_0 = 0$$

$$m_j = 1 + \Sigma_{i=1}^{j} g_Y(i) m_{j-i} \qquad j \geq 1$$

(This is the discrete *renewal function* corresponding to g_Y.) *Define* $q = s - r$, and let $\boldsymbol{\iota}$ be the q-vector with components

$$\iota_i = \frac{(m_{i+1} - m_i)}{m_q} \qquad 0 \leq i < q$$

Then, $Pr\{IP = i\} = \iota_{s-i}$. (Here, *IP* does depend on g_Y.)

To see this, define $\mathbf{IP}_c$ as before, with $IP_c(t) = (r + q) - IP(t) = s - IP(t)$. At a demand epoch t

$$IP_c(t) = \begin{cases} IP_c(t^-) + Y & \text{if this quantity is} < q \\ 0 & \text{otherwise} \end{cases}$$

Again, the fact that $g_Y(1) > 0$ implies that $\mathbf{IP}_c$ is irreducible, and its stationary vector turns out to be precisely $\boldsymbol{\iota}$. (Problem 6.22 asks you to verify this fact.) The distribution of *IP* itself follows immediately.

Step 2: The demand process **D** again has independent increments. Therefore, for all *t,* the random variables $IP(t)$ and $D(t, t + L]$ are independent.

Step 3: For either policy, (6.2.7) remains valid:

$$IN(t + L) = IP(t) - D(t, t + L]$$

The limit argument in Section 6.2 also remains valid, so

$$IN = IP - D \tag{6.6.1}$$

where *IP* and *D* are independent. The leadtime demand *D* now has a compound-Poisson distribution (Section C.2.3.8). Also, *IN* describes the long-run frequency distribution of **IN,** by arguments parallel to those of Section 6.2.

Thus, the basic qualitative results for the pure Poisson-demand case continue to hold. While *IP* depends on the policy type, the identity (6.6.1) does not.

Step 4: First, consider an (r, q) policy. Because *IP* is uniform and (6.6.1) holds, the performance measures $\overline{A}$, $\overline{B}$, and $\overline{I}$ are precisely the same as in the Poisson-demand case, namely (6.2.11) to (6.2.13). The functions G^0, G^1, and G^2 now represent the actual compound-Poisson distribution of *D.* Also, in the formula for $\overline{I}$, $r - \lambda L$ now becomes $r - \lambda E[Y]L$. For a base-stock policy the simpler formulas of Section 6.2.2 apply.

As for $\overline{OF}$, actually an order can be defined in two ways: Each basic batch of size q can be viewed as a separate order. Under this interpretation, several orders are sometimes placed simultaneously. Alternatively, when several basic batches are ordered at once, they can be viewed as composing a single order. The correct interpretation depends on the economics of the situation. The first approach makes sense when each basic batch contributes to the workload, as when a separate vehicle must be used for each q, while the second applies when the workload is independent of the order size.

Under the first interpretation, where each basic batch is a separate order, the overall demand rate is $\lambda E[Y]$, so

$$\overline{OF} = \frac{\lambda E[Y]}{q}$$

which is analogous to the result for the pure Poisson-demand case. The second interpretation requires more care: At a typical demand epoch, an order occurs with probability

$$\Sigma_{i=r+1}^{r+q} Pr\{IP = i\} \cdot Pr\{Y \geq i - r\} = \Sigma_{j=0}^{q-1}\left(\frac{1}{q}\right)G_Y^0(j)$$

$$= \left(\frac{1}{q}\right)[E[Y] - G_Y^1(q)]$$

where, consistent with the earlier notation, $G_Y^1(d) = \Sigma_{j=d}^{\infty} G_Y^0(j)$. Since demand epochs occur at rate λ,

$$\overline{OF} = \left(\frac{\lambda}{q}\right)[E[Y] - G_Y^1(q)]$$

Here, $\overline{OF}$ is less than in the first interpretation.

Next, consider an (r, s) policy. Applying (6.6.1),

$$\begin{aligned}
\overline{A} &= Pr\{IN \leq 0\} \\
&= \Sigma_{d=r+1}^{s} Pr\{IP = d\} \cdot Pr\{D \geq d\} \\
&= \Sigma_{d=r+1}^{s} \iota_{s-d} G^0(d-1) \\
\overline{B} &= E[[IN]^-] \\
&= \Sigma_{d=r+1}^{s} \Pr\{IP = d\} \cdot E[[D-d]^+] \\
&= \Sigma_{d=r+1}^{s} \iota_{s-d} G^1(d) \\
\overline{I} &= E[IP] - E[D] + \overline{B} \\
&= \Sigma_{i=1}^{q} \frac{m_i}{m_q} + r - \lambda E[Y]E[L] + \overline{B}
\end{aligned}$$

Also, a demand epoch results in an order with probability $\Sigma_{i=1}^{q} \iota_{q-i} G_Y^1(i-1) = \iota_0 = 1/m_q$, so

$$\overline{OF} = \frac{\lambda}{m_q}$$

These formulas are not as simple as those for an (r, q) policy, but neither are they overly complex. Notice, $\overline{A}$ is a *weighted* average over q values of $G^0(d-1)$, where d ranges from $r+1$ to $r+q$, but the weights are no longer equal. Likewise, $\overline{B}$ is an unequally weighted average of q values of G^1.

Now, drop the assumption of Poisson $\tilde{\mathbf{D}}$, and suppose that $\tilde{\mathbf{D}}$ is a world-driven demand process. It turns out that *precisely* the same results hold. The only difference is in D. This has a compound distribution involving Y and the new $\tilde{D}$.

For an (r, q) policy, and in particular a base-stock policy, the normal and maximal approximations of Section 6.4 still apply. Using the general formulas for compound distributions of Section C.2.3.8, and letting $\tilde{\psi}^2$ denote the variance/mean ratio for $\tilde{\mathbf{D}}$,

$$\begin{aligned}
\nu &= E[D] \\
&= E[\tilde{D}]E[Y] \\
&= \lambda E[Y]L \\
\sigma^2 &= V[D] \\
&= E[\tilde{D}]V[Y] + V[\tilde{D}]E^2[Y] \\
&= \lambda(V[Y] + \tilde{\psi}^2 E^2[Y])L
\end{aligned}$$

The asymptotic variance-mean ratio for the overall demand process $\mathbf{D}$ is $\psi^2 = \sigma^2/\nu = (V[Y] + \tilde{\psi}^2 E^2[Y])/E[Y]$. This is larger than $\tilde{\psi}^2$, since $E[Y] > 1$. In the compound-Poisson case, with $\tilde{\psi}^2 = 1$, σ^2 reduces to $\lambda E[Y^2]L$, and $\psi^2 = E[Y^2]/E[Y] > 1$.

Thus, σ^2 reflects the uncertainties in both the timing of demands (through $\tilde{\psi}^2$) and the demand quantities (through $V[Y]$). As we have seen, the performance of the system depends largely on σ. Thus, the additional demand variation due to uncertain demand quantities does indeed degrade performance.

6.6.3 Optimization

Now, suppose we impose cost factors k, h, and p on the performance measures $\overline{OF}$, $\overline{I}$ and $\overline{B}$, respectively. Denote the total average cost by $C(r, q)$ or $C(r, s)$, depending on the policy class. We wish to minimize C *within* each class.

First, consider (r, q) policies. Here, $\overline{B}$ and $\overline{I}$ have the same form as in the Poisson-demand case. Also, assuming each basic batch counts as an order, $\overline{OF} = \lambda E[Y]/q$ too has the same form as before. Therefore, $C(r, q)$ is precisely the function in (6.5.1) (with $\lambda E[Y]$ replacing λ.) *All* the methods, formulas and bounds of Section 6.5 thus apply directly. (The second interpretation of an order, comprising all basic batches ordered together, requires more intricate methods; see Zheng and Chen [1992].)

Turning next to (r, s) policies, things are not quite so straightforward. It is possible to construct a continuous approximation of $C(r, s)$, but this does not help much. (The resulting cost function is typically *not* convex in the now continuous variables (r, s). Standard nonlinear optimization algorithms thus cannot guarantee a globally optimal solution.) As for the discrete formulation, there are indeed algorithms available to compute an optimal (r, s) policy. The best of these to date is that of Zheng and Federgruen [1991]. This procedure is similar to Algorithm Optimize_rq of Section 6.5 and not much harder to implement.

Some of the qualitative results of Section 6.5 can be extended directly to (r, s) policies: Since the best (r, s) policy costs no more than the best (r, q) policy, the upper bounds on C^* in Theorem 6.5.1 remain valid. Also, it is straightforward to prove the lower bound $C^* \geq C_\sigma$. We conclude, therefore, that *the impact of* σ *on overall performance is the same as before,* as described in Section 6.5, regardless of which type of policy is used.

Useful approximations have been developed; see Ass'ad and Beckmann [1988], for example. There are comparable results for the discrete-time context, discussed in Chapter 9. Also, there is a substantial body of empirical work exploring the behavior of optimal policies. See, for example, Archibald and Silver [1978], Naddor [1975], Wagner et al. [1965], and Zheng [1991].

6.7 Other Extensions

6.7.1 The Expected-Present-Value Criterion

Section 3.7 of Chapter 3 discusses the present-value criterion for deterministic models. We now explore an analogous criterion for stochastic models. We proceed quite briskly; our primary goal is to see what the results look like. This same approach, adapted to discrete time, underlies the models of Chapter 9, and we shall cover some of these concepts more carefully there.

The idea is conceptually straightforward: Take any of the models above, and select any specific control policy. Now, imagine *any one* particular scenario, a full realization (technically, a sample path) of the demand process over time. Given that scenario, and the rules embodied in the policy, certain cash flows will be incurred, and this cash-flow stream has a well-defined present value. Now, take the expectation of this present value over *all possible* scenarios, and call this the *expected present value* for the chosen policy. When the cash flows are expressed as costs, as they are here, call the result the *expected discounted cost.*

In the stochastic context this is not the only possible criterion. (See Singhal [1988], for instance.) It is the simplest one, however, and it is employed far more than any other.

We restrict attention to the model of Section 6.2.2: Demand is a Poisson process, and $k = 0$, so we follow a base-stock policy. As in Section 3.7, α denotes the interest rate. Also, for now, suppose the system starts at time $t = 0$ with no inventory and no orders outstanding.

We first evaluate the expected discounted order cost. With $k = 0$ there remains only the variable order cost, c. Interpret this as a purchase cost, and assume (reasonably) that we pay for goods when we receive them, after the leadtime, not when the order is placed. The policy orders s units at time $t = 0$, and we receive them at time $t = L$, so the discounted initial order cost is $e^{-\alpha L}cs$. From then on we order a unit each time a demand occurs. One can show that the expected discounted value of these continuing costs is $e^{-\alpha L}c(\lambda/\alpha)$.

Next, consider holding and backorder costs. (The cost factors h and b include only the real, physical costs $\underline{h}$ and $\underline{b}$, not financing costs, as discussed in Section 3.7.) There is nothing we can do to influence the initial costs during the time interval $[0, L]$, so ignore them. Second, assume the discounted expected costs of this type can be calculated as follows: For each time $t \geq L$, determine the expected *rate* at which cost is incurred; then, discount this quantity (multiply by $e^{-\alpha t}$) and integrate over t. (Technically, we are interchanging an expectation with an integral.) Now, following the derivations in Section 6.2 and Section 6.5, this expected cost rate is precisely $C(s)$ for $t > L$. The overall holding-backorder cost is thus $\int_L^\infty e^{-\alpha t}C(s)\,dt = (e^{-\alpha L}/\alpha)C(s)$.

We should also account for delays in receiving revenues due to backorders, as in Problem 3.27. But this involves complexities that we prefer to skip. (Section 9.4.7 works out the details for the discrete-time case.) So, assume that each customer pays us at his demand epoch, even if the demand is backlogged. (The cost $\underline{b}$ above can include a penalty that we pay continuously to each customer whose demand is backlogged.) Letting p denote the sales price, the total expected discounted revenue is $p\lambda/\alpha$, a constant which we omit.

Combining these results, the total expected discounted cost is

$$C_\alpha(s) = \left(\frac{e^{-\alpha L}}{\alpha}\right)[c\lambda + \alpha cs + C(s)]$$

This is no more complex than $C(s)$ itself. (All this presumes we start with $IP(0^-) = 0$. Otherwise, as long as $IP(0^-) \leq s$, the actual cost differs from the above by a constant. Indeed, as explained in Chapter 9, $C_\alpha(s)$ is the "right" objective in general.)

Now, let us optimize, as in Section 6.5. Suppose we use a continuous approximation. Differentiating $C_\alpha(s)$, we obtain the following equation for s^*:

$$F^0(s) = \frac{\underline{h} + \alpha c}{\underline{b} + \underline{h}}$$

This has precisely the same form as (6.5.3); only the cost ratio is different. For small α, indeed, this ratio approaches $1 - \omega$, the ratio in (6.5.3), so s^* has nearly the same value as in the average-cost model. Also, one can show that $\alpha C_\alpha(s^*)$ is approximately equal to the optimal average cost.

In sum, while the derivations involve different methods, the two criteria lead to closely related results. We observed the same close connections in Section 3.7.

This approach can be extended to more complex policies, demand processes, etc. See Problem 6.23, for instance.

6.7.2 Using Current Information about Demand

With world-driven demand, a base-stock or (r, q) policy is unlikely to be optimal if we actually see the world-system $\mathbf{W}$ as it evolves over time. Observing $W(t)$ provides information about future demands, which those policies ignore. We now suggest a new type of policy which does use such information. (Under standard economic assumptions, this form is optimal, as demonstrated in Section 9.7.) Exact calculations now become rather complex (Section 9.7 includes those too), so we develop a relatively simple approximation. This approach leads to an estimate of the value of observing $\mathbf{W}$.

Suppose there are no scale economies in supply, so a base-stock policy would be attractive *if* we were unable to observe the driving process. Assuming we do observe it, here is a plausible control rule: Reset the base-stock level s whenever $W(t)$ itself changes. That is, there is a *vector* $\mathbf{s} = (s_w)$ of fixed parameters, where w ranges over the state space of $\mathbf{W}$. At any time t where $W(t) = w$, follow a standard base-stock policy with base-stock level s_w. Call this a *state-dependent base-stock policy.*

This policy does what it can to keep $IP(t)$ as close as possible to $s_{W(t)}$. If $s_{W(t)}$ suddenly increases so that $s_{W(t)} > IP(t^-)$, the policy immediately orders, to bring $IP(t)$ up to $s_{W(t)}$. If $s_{W(t)}$ decreases and $s_{W(t)} < IP(t^-)$, it stops ordering until demand reduces $IP(t)$ to $s_{W(t)}$.

How might we evaluate such a policy? Note first, the familiar equation (6.2.7) still applies, i.e., $IN(t + L) = IP(t) - D(t, t + L]$. Here, $D(t, t + L]$ depends on $W(t)$. Specifically, let $(D|w)$ denote a generic random variable with the distribution of $D(t, t + L]$, conditional on $W(t) = w$; this is also the distribution of $D(L)$, conditional on $W(0) = w$. Then, $IN(t + L)$ has the same distribution as $IP(t) - (D|W(t))$. Thus, the *expected cost rate* at time $t + L$, viewed from time t, is given by $C_{W(t)}(IP(t))$, where

$$C_w(y) = E[\hat{C}(y - (D|w))]$$

and we again use the function $\hat{C}(y) = h[y]^+ + b[y]^-$ defined in Section 6.5.

Under a state-dependent base-stock policy, we never observe $IP(t) < s_{W(t)}$ (after ordering). Now let us approximate: Ignore the possibility that $IP(t) > s_{W(t)}$. That is, treat $IP(t) = s_{W(t)}$ for all t. The expected cost rate at time $t + L$ then becomes $C_{W(t)}(s_{W(t)})$.

Recall that $\boldsymbol{\xi}$ is the stationary vector of $\mathbf{W}$, so it specifies the fraction of time $\mathbf{W}$ spends in each of its states. In particular, ξ_w is the proportion of time during which we anticipate the (approximate) cost rate $C_w(s_w)$ a leadtime into the future. Thus, the average expected cost rate, denoted $C(\mathbf{s})$, is given by $C(\mathbf{s}) = E[C_W(s_W)] = \Sigma_w \xi_w C_w(s_w)$. This is in fact (by ergodic arguments like those of Section 6.2) the overall average cost, up to the approximation.

Now, suppose we aim to minimize $C(\mathbf{s})$ over $\mathbf{s}$. But $C(\mathbf{s})$ is separable in its variables. That is, to minimize it, we need only choose each s_w to optimize the corresponding

$C_w(s)$, independently of the others. Each of these one-dimensional problems can be solved using the methods of Section 6.5. Let $\mathbf{s}^+$ denote the resulting vector of base-stock levels. This is called the *myopic policy* for this model, because it optimizes the expected cost rate, looking ahead one leadtime into the future, ignoring all subsequent costs.

The myopic policy is a useful benchmark even when it is suboptimal. It tends to be close to optimal, when the conditional leadtime demand is fairly insensitive to the starting condition $W(0) = w$, so the s_w^+ are close together. Otherwise, it may perform poorly. Even then, it is related to the true optimal policy, which we denote $\mathbf{s}^*$. As we shall see in Section 9.7, it is always true that $\mathbf{s}^* \le \mathbf{s}^+$, and the shape of $\mathbf{s}^*$ (the way its components vary with w) is roughly parallel to that of $\mathbf{s}^+$.

The quantity $C(\mathbf{s}^+)$ provides a *lower bound* on the average cost of any policy, and hence on the actual optimal cost: This is the cost we would obtain, if at each time t we could reset $IP(t) = s_{W(t)}^+$, to achieve the best possible cost rate as measured by $C_{W(t)}$. Such actions may not be feasible, but certainly no policy could do better.

Of course, the cost of the best base-stock policy (using a constant base-stock level), which we still denote by C^*, is an *upper bound* on the true optimal cost. Thus, $C^* - C(\mathbf{s}^+)$ provides an estimate of the cost savings from using current information about **W**, or in other words, an estimate of the value of such information. This approximation is not always accurate (if anything, it overestimates the true savings or value), but it is vastly simpler than any more refined estimate.

Let us combine this approach with the normal approximation. Specifically, for each w, use a normal distribution with mean ν_w and variance σ_w^2 to approximate $(D|w)$. Also, let $\boldsymbol{\nu}$ be the column-vector $(\nu_w)_w$, and $\boldsymbol{\sigma} = (\sigma_w)_w$. From the results of Section 6.5.2, the myopic policy is determined by $s_w^+ = \nu_w + z^*\sigma_w$ for each w. (Recall, z^* is a function only of the cost parameters, and so is independent of w.) Also, $C_w(s_w^+) = \sigma_w(b + h)\phi(z^*)$. Thus, $C(\mathbf{s}^+) = (\boldsymbol{\xi}\boldsymbol{\sigma})(b + h)\phi(z^*)$, and

$$C^* - C(\mathbf{s}^+) = (\sigma - \boldsymbol{\xi}\boldsymbol{\sigma})(b + h)\phi(z^*)$$

This is a remarkably simple formula. Indeed, taking C^* as the base case, the (approximate) *relative* cost is $C(\mathbf{s}^+)/C^* = \boldsymbol{\xi}\boldsymbol{\sigma}/\sigma$, which is completely independent of the cost parameters.

Let us examine this ratio: Observe, σ_w^2 is the variance of the leadtime demand *assuming we know* **W** begins with $W(0) = w$. On the other hand, σ^2 is the leadtime-demand variance *presuming no knowledge* of the initial state (beyond $\boldsymbol{\xi}$ itself). Because σ^2 includes this additional source of uncertainty, we expect σ to be larger than the σ_w, at least on average. Indeed, decompose σ^2 using the conditional-variance formula:

$$\begin{aligned}
\sigma^2 &= V[D] \\
&= E_w V[D|w] + V_w E[D|w] \\
&= \Sigma_w\, \xi_w \sigma_w^2 + \Sigma_w\, \xi_w(\nu_w - \nu)^2 \\
&= (\boldsymbol{\xi}\boldsymbol{\sigma})^2 + [\Sigma\, \xi_w \sigma_w^2 - (\boldsymbol{\xi}\boldsymbol{\sigma})^2] + [\Sigma\, \xi_w \nu_w^2 - (\boldsymbol{\xi}\boldsymbol{\nu})^2]
\end{aligned}$$

The two expressions in brackets are variances, in this case the variances of the components of $\boldsymbol{\sigma}$ and $\boldsymbol{\nu}$, respectively. They are both nonnegative, so $\sigma^2 \ge (\boldsymbol{\xi}\boldsymbol{\sigma})^2$ and $\boldsymbol{\xi}\boldsymbol{\sigma}/\sigma \le 1$.

(This decomposition of σ^2 is entirely analogous to the analysis of variance in statistics. Here, the "dependent variable" is the leadtime demand, σ^2 is its total variance, and $(\boldsymbol{\xi\sigma})^2$ plays the role of the residual variance.)

Recall, similar ratios played a prominent role in Section 6.5. (We used the notation σ_{-}/σ). There, however, we were interested in improving the *physical systems* generating supplies and demands, whereas here we are using *information* more effectively. It makes intuitive sense that these two should be related, and indeed at this level of analysis we see no fundamental difference between them.

For example, reconsider the two-state MMP process of Section 6.3. Recall, $\lambda = 10$. Suppose $L = 0.1$. The (exact) overall leadtime-demand parameters are $\nu = 1, \sigma = 1.147$. The state-dependent parameters are $\boldsymbol{\nu} = (0.766, 1.234)'$, $\boldsymbol{\sigma} = (1.013, 1.222)'$. Since $\boldsymbol{\xi} = (0.5, 0.5)$, we obtain $\boldsymbol{\xi\sigma} = 1.118$. Thus, $\boldsymbol{\xi\sigma}/\sigma = 1.118/1.147 = 0.975$.

In this case the cost saving is (at most) about 2.5%. This is rather small, because **W** tends to change state quickly, so knowing the starting state provides only limited information about the leadtime demand. If L were smaller, the relative savings would be larger.

Recall, the results of Section 6.3 do not require that **D** be an MCDC process, and that is true here too: Again, think of $W(t)$ as summarizing our current information concerning future demand. This could be some continuous variable, for instance, instead of a discrete one. In that case we reinterpret all the vectors above as functions of the variable w. *In principle,* we need to describe all possible w's (the state space of **W**), together with their relative likelihoods over time ($\boldsymbol{\xi}$) and the corresponding leadtime-demand parameters ($\boldsymbol{\nu}$ and $\boldsymbol{\sigma}$). *In practice,* we can use the whole panoply of forecasting tools to estimate these quantities. In this spirit w might be some specific demand-related factor, and ν_w and σ_w simple functions of w, each with a few parameters to be estimated. With these data we can readily calculate σ, as well as the average standard deviation ($\boldsymbol{\xi\sigma}$), and then use them as above. Section 9.7 illustrates these ideas in the discrete-time context.

6.7.3 Periodic Review

Up to this point we have focused exclusively on continuous-review policies. Now, we briefly examine a periodic-review system, where orders can be placed only at designated times, separated by equal intervals (e.g., weekly). Chapter 9 takes up similar systems using a discrete-time formulation, but there the periods are fixed in advance. Here, we continue to model time as continuous.

Consider the basic system of Section 6.2.2, where demand is a Poisson process. Suppose we follow a (u, s) policy: The order interval u and the target stock level s are fixed policy variables. At each review point, we order enough to bring the inventory position up to s.

All else being equal, it is better to use an (r, q) policy, for that policy is more responsive to demand fluctuations than a (u, s) policy. However, all else may not be equal: An (r, q) policy requires information on the inventory position at all times, while a (u, s) policy requires such information only periodically, at each review point. Also, the supplier may prefer to ship orders, and/or we may prefer to receive them, at regular intervals, for reasons outside the model, e.g., to coordinate with other activities.

In this context, **IN** does not have a true limiting distribution, because of the cyclic behavior induced by the order policy. It does have a long-run frequency distribution, however, which we indicate by a random variable $\underline{\mathrm{IN}}$.

Suppose time 0 is a review point, and $IP(0^-) \leq s$, so $\mathrm{IP}(0) = s$. For each time t until the next review point ($0 \leq t < u$), equation (6.2.1) remains valid, i.e., $IN(t + L) = IP(t) - D(t, t + L]$, and $IP(t)$ and $D(t, t + L]$ are still independent. Moreover, $IP(t)$ is just $s - D(t)$, so $IN(t + L) = s - D(t + L)$. Clearly, subsequent cycles follow the same pattern. To get the distribution of $\underline{\mathrm{IN}}$, therefore, we need only average the distribution of $IN(t + L)$ over t. Let $\underline{D}$ denote the uniform mixture of $D(t + L)$ over t in the interval $[0, u)$. Then,

$$\underline{\mathrm{IN}} = s - \underline{D}$$

Notice, $\underline{IN}$ has the same form as IN in (6.2.3); only the leadtime-demand variable is different. The performance measures thus take the same form as in a base-stock policy.

Use $g(d|t)$, $G^0(d|t)$, etc. to describe the distribution of $D(t)$, i.e., the Poisson distribution with mean λt. Straightforward calculus leads to an expression for $g_{\underline{D}}$, the pmf of $\underline{D}$:

$$\begin{aligned} g_{\underline{D}}(d) &= \left(\frac{1}{u}\right)\int_0^u g(d|t + L)\, dt \\ &= \left(\frac{1}{\lambda u}\right)[G^0(d|L + u) - G^0(d|L)] \end{aligned}$$

Consequently,

$$G_{\underline{D}}{}^0(d) = \left(\frac{1}{\lambda u}\right)[G^1(d + 1|L + u) - G^1(d + 1|L)]$$

$$G_{\underline{D}}{}^1(d) = \left(\frac{1}{\lambda u}\right)[G^2(d|L + u) - G^2(d|L)]$$

Just as in (6.2.4) to (6.2.6),

$$\begin{aligned} \overline{A} &= G_{\underline{D}}{}^0(s - 1) \\ \overline{B} &= G_{\underline{D}}{}^1(s) \\ \overline{I} &= s - \lambda(L + \tfrac{1}{2}u) + \overline{B} \end{aligned}$$

since $E[\underline{D}] = \lambda(L + \frac{1}{2}u)$. And, of course, $\overline{OF} = 1/u$. These performance criteria, along with the cost factors, can be used to formulate an optimization model, along the lines of Section 6.5.

The following approximations are widely used:

$$\overline{A}_{+1} = \left(\frac{1}{\lambda u}\right)G^1(s|L + u)$$

$$\overline{B}_{+1} = \left(\frac{1}{\lambda u}\right)G^2(s|L + u)$$

Like those of Section 6.4.4, these approximations omit negative terms from the exact values. And, like those of Section 6.4.4, they are not reliable.

Suppose for the moment that u is fixed, and we set s optimally. As in the base-stock model, the optimal safety stock and cost are determined mainly by $\underline{\sigma}$, the standard deviation of $\underline{D}$. It is easy to show that

$$\underline{\sigma}^2 = V[\underline{D}] = \lambda L + \left(\frac{\lambda}{2}\right)u + \left(\frac{\lambda^2}{12}\right)u^2$$

This expression reveals the impact on performance of imposing a fixed review period. For small u, the last term is negligible, so the effect is similar to an increase in the leadtime from L to $L + \frac{1}{2}u$. For large u the effect is greater; $\underline{\sigma}^2$ becomes nearly quadratic in u, so $\underline{\sigma}$ becomes linear.

To apply the normal approximation (for any world-driven demand process), treat $D(t)$ as normal with mean $\nu_t = \lambda t$ and variance $\sigma_t^2 = \lambda\psi^2 t$. Setting $z_t = (s - \nu_t)/\sigma_t$ and $z_t^+ = (s + \nu_t)/\sigma_t$ gives

$$\begin{aligned}
\overline{A} &= \left(\frac{1}{u}\right)\int_L^{L+u} \Phi^0(z_t)\,dt \\
&= \left(\frac{1}{\lambda u}\right)[F^1(s|L+u) - F^1(s|L)] \\
\overline{B} &= \left(\frac{1}{u}\right)\int_L^{L+u} \sigma_t \Phi^1(z_t)\,dt \\
&= \left(\frac{1}{\lambda u}\right)[F^2(s|L+u) - F^2(s|L)] \\
\overline{I} &= s - \lambda(L + \tfrac{1}{2}u) + \overline{B}
\end{aligned}$$

where

$$F^1(s|t) = \sigma_t \Phi^1(z_t) - \tfrac{1}{2}\psi^2[\Phi^0(z_t) - e^{2s/\psi^2}\Phi^0(z_t^+)]$$

$$F^2(s|t) = \sigma_t^2 \Phi^2(z_t) - \tfrac{1}{2}\psi^2 F^1(s|t)$$

(It is not hard to verify these integrals.)

Notes

Section 6.2: Base-stock policies are discussed by Kimball in a memorandum written in the 1950s, published as Kimball [1988]. Whitin [1953] provides an early study of (r, q) policies. The basic results for the Poisson-demand model are set forth by Galliher et al.

[1959] and Hadley and Whitin [1963]. Concerning the PASTA property of Poisson processes, see Wolff [1982]. Theorem 6.2.4 appears in Svoronos and Zipkin [1991].

Section 6.3: The MCDC process of Section 6.3 is a special case of the point process introduced by Neuts [1979]. Song and Zipkin [1993a,1996c] discuss various applications. The main results (for various cases) are attributable to Sahin [1979,1983], Sivazlian [1974], Stidham [1974], Zipkin [1986a], and Browne and Zipkin [1991].

Section 6.4: The normal approximation has been in common use for decades; one early exposition is Whitin [1953]. The maximal approximation is attributable to Scarf [1958a]; see also Gallego and Moon [1993]. For more on the inaccuracies of standard performance approximations, see Herron [1978] and Zipkin [1986b].

Section 6.5: Most of the material on base-stock policies is adapted from well-known results on the mathematically equivalent news-vendor problem of Chapter 9. As for (r, q) policies, Zipkin [1986b] and Zhang [1998] demonstrate the convexity of $C(r, q)$. Theorem 6.5.1 and the other results of Section 6.5.3 are attributable to Zheng [1992] and Gallego [1998] (which also include more refined results). Algorithm Optimize_rq is attributable to Federgruen and Zheng [1992b]. (Some of the ideas were anticipated by Sahin [1982].) For the stockout-constraint model of Section 6.5.5, Platt et al. [1997] discuss an alternative heuristic.

Section 6.6: The results on (r, q) policies are primarily by Richards [1975] and Zheng and Chen [1992]. The approach here for (r, s) policies follows Iglehart [1963a] and Veinott and Wagner [1965].

Section 6.7: The notion of a myopic policy (Section 6.7.2) has uses in many areas. (It appears in Chapter 4 and again in Chapter 9 in the context of time-varying parameters.) Key references include Veinott [1965] and Heyman and Sobel [1984]. The use of it here to estimate the value of information appears to be new.

For the periodic-review model of Section 6.7.3, Rao [1994] shows that the average cost is convex in (u, s) and derives results similar to Theorem 6.5.1. Johnson et al. [1995] test a variety of approximations; they find that $\bar{A}_{+1}$ is unreliable.

Problems

6.1 Consider the model of Section 6.2.2: Demand is a Poisson process, and we follow a base-stock policy. Our customers, however, inform us in advance of their demands by the constant time L_D; in other words, customers *order* units from us for later delivery. (They will not accept early deliveries.) Thus, the customer orders themselves form a Poisson process, and the actual demands describe the same process shifted forward in time by L_D.

First, assume $L_D \geq L$. Argue that, in this case, we can operate a perfect flow system, meeting every demand as it occurs while carrying no inventory at all.

Now, assume $L_D < L$. Let us slightly alter the meaning of a base-stock policy: Supposing we start with $I(0) = s$, order a unit whenever a customer *order* occurs (not an actual demand). Let $S(t)$ denote the cumulative supply, the number of units received through time t. Clearly, $IN(t) = s + S(t) - D(t)$.

Consider a conventional system (i.e., with no L_D) with leadtime $L - L_D$, facing the same demand process as the original system, and using a base-stock policy with the same base-stock level s. Argue that $S(t)$ and hence $IN(t)$ is the same in the two systems for all t. (Conclude that the performance of the original system is identical to that of a standard system with the shorter leadtime $L - L_D$. The information our customers provide us here is thus valuable indeed.)

6.2 This problem explains the behavior observed in Figure 6.2.6. (Increasing q essentially increases backorders.) Suppose f is any convex function on the integers. Fix an integer s'. For each odd positive integer q let $F(q)$ denote the average of the quantities $f(s)$, taking s over q consecutive integers centered at s'. (For example, for $q = 3$, use $s = s' - 1, s'$, and $s' + 1$.) Show that $F(q)$ is increasing as a function of q.

6.3 Suppose demand forms a MMP process. The driving process $\mathbf{W}$ has three states, which we label *l*ow, *m*edium and *h*igh. The corresponding demand rates are $\lambda_l < \lambda_m < \lambda_h$. From states l and h transitions can occur only to state m; from m $\mathbf{W}$ changes to l with probability 1/3 and to h with probability 2/3. Each time $\mathbf{W}$ enters a state, it remains there for a random time; the mean times are 12 weeks for state l, 18 weeks for m, and 19 weeks for h.

Write down the matrices Q and Λ, and compute the stationary vector $\boldsymbol{\xi}$. Assuming the demand rates are $\lambda_l = 35$ units/week, $\lambda_m = 50$ units/week, and $\lambda_h = 75$ units/week, what is the overall mean demand rate λ?

6.4 Prove that the assumption of Section 6.3.3 is satisfied when $\mathbf{D}$ is a MMP process. (*Careful:* The demand rates λ_{ww} in some states may be 0. Some of them must be positive, however, because λ is.)

6.5 Verify directly the following assertion in the proof of Lemma 6.3.1: Suppose IP_c is a random variable distributed uniformly on the integers mod (q), and suppose D is an integer-valued random variable, independent of IP_c. Then, the random variable $[IP_c + D]$ mod (q) is also uniformly distributed on the integers mod (q).

6.6 Verify formulas (6.2.14) and (6.2.15) for the Poisson loss functions. (Prove them by induction.)

6.7 Consider the model of Section 6.2, but assume the leadtime $L = 0$. Assume we wish to preclude backorders entirely. What is the smallest value of r we can choose, and why? Assume we do choose r in this way. Argue that $\bar{I} = ½(q - 1)$. If we face an order cost k and a holding cost h, argue that the optimal q can be determined as in Problem 3.8. (In this case, then, the behavior of the system and the optimal policy depend on λ, but otherwise the specification of the demand process has no effect whatsoever.)

6.8 Verify equations (6.4.2) and (6.4.3) describing the standard normal loss function.

6.9 Verify equation (6.4.7) describing the sensitivities of the normal approximations of $\bar{I}$ and $\bar{B}$ to σ.

6.10 Assume that D has mean ν and variance σ^2, but otherwise we know nothing about its distribution. We can write

$$\bar{B} = E[[D - s]^+] = E[½\{|D - s| + (D - s)\}]$$

Use Jensen's inequality to argue that

$$E[|D - s|] \leq \{E[(D - s)^2]\}^{1/2}$$

Now, verify (with straightforward calculations) that

$$\bar{B} \leq ½[(1 + z^2)^{1/2} - z]\sigma = \Omega^1(z)\sigma$$

Show similarly that $\bar{I} \leq \Omega^1(-z)\sigma$.

6.11 Suppose we use continuous approximations for D and IP. Argue that

$$\overline{B}(r, q) = E[[D - (r + qU)]^+]$$

where U is a random variable uniform on [0, 1], independent of D. Then, show that $\overline{B}(r, q)$ is a convex function of the continuous variables (r, q). (Since $\overline{I}(r, q)$ is just $\overline{B}(r, q)$ plus a linear function of (r, q), it follows immediately that $\overline{I}$ too is convex.)

6.12 Verify that the average stocking time $\overline{IW}$ is given by $\overline{I}/\lambda$, following the argument in Section 6.2.4.

6.13 Use equation (6.2.16), relating the transforms of B and BW, to prove (6.2.17), relating their variances.

6.14 Verify the expression for $\frac{1}{2}E[B(B-1)]$ in equation (6.2.18).

6.15 Verify the formulas in Section 6.5.2.3 for z^* and C^* using the maximal approximation.

6.16 Within the proof of Theorem 6.5.1 there is a geometric argument that $0 \leq H'(q) \leq h\omega$. Here, we substantiate this result more rigorously.

Let $r(q)$ denote the optimal value of r for fixed q, that is, the r which satisfies (6.5.13). By the chain rule, $H'(q) = C'(r(q))r'(q)$. Now, differentiate (6.5.13) with respect to q, and use the implicit function theorem, to obtain an expression for $r'(q)$. Then, use the inequalities $-b \leq C'(r(q)) \leq 0$ and $0 \leq C'(r(q) + q) \leq h$ to argue that $0 \leq H'(q) \leq h\omega$.

6.17 For the continuous (r, q) model of Section 6.5.3, show that the optimality condition (6.5.13) is equivalent to $\overline{A}(r, q) = 1 - \omega$. Thus, as in the base-stock model, the optimal policy sets the stockout frequency to $1 - \omega$.

6.18 Consider the problem of finding an optimal (r, q) policy, using the normal approximation of D. We investigate what happens to (r^*, q^*) and C^* as the demand parameters change, keeping the cost factors fixed. Suppose that σ^2 depends linearly on λ, specifically, $\sigma^2 = \lambda/\lambda_1$ for some constant λ_1. Allow ν to change independently of λ and σ^2.

Let (r_1, q_1) denote the optimal policy and C_1 the optimal cost for $\lambda = \lambda_1$ (so $\sigma^2 = 1$) and $\nu = 0$. Show that, for all values of λ and ν,

$$r^* = \nu + r_1\sigma \qquad q^* = q_1\sigma \qquad C^* = C_1\sigma$$

Thus, r^* depends on ν and σ much as s^* does in the base-stock model. Also, both q^* and C^* are exactly proportional to σ.

6.19 This problem asks you to verify the inequality (6.5.10), showing that the optimal cost in the continuous (r, q) model is insensitive to suboptimal choices of q.

(*a*) Use the inequality $H(q) \geq h\omega q$ to show that, for any fixed q, $wH(q) - H(wq)$ is nondecreasing as a function of w, for $w > 0$.

(*b*) Use part (*a*) to show that, for any fixed q and $x > 0$, $\int_q^{xq} H(y)\,dy \leq \frac{1}{2}(x^2 - 1)qH(q)$. *Hint:* Change variables, setting $wq = y$.

(*c*) Use the definitions of $H(q)$ and $A(q)$ to show that

$$C^*(q) = \frac{k\lambda + \int_0^q H(y)\,dy}{q}$$

(*d*) Now use part (*b*) (with $x = q/q^*$) and part (*c*) to prove (6.5.10).

6.20 Consider the record store of Example 6.2.A. The problem now concerns Brahms' Fourth Symphony (played by Ormandy and the Philadelphia Orchestra). For this CD, demand is a Poisson process with rate 2.4 per month, and again $L = 0.5$. In this case $h = \$0.30$ and $b = \$2.70$.

(*a*) Assume that $k = 0$. Compute s^* and C^*.
(*b*) Now, assume $k = \$0.20$. Use Algorithm Optimize_rq to compute (r^*, q^*) and C^*.

6.21 Algorithm Optimize_rq in Section 6.5.4 starts with $q = 1$ and gradually increases q until it finds q^*. Suppose instead we start with a large q, and a test shows that $q > q^*$. Modify the algorithm to *decrease* q in increments of 1 until q^* is found.

6.22 Section 6.6.2 gives a formula for the limiting probability vector $\boldsymbol{\iota}$ of the process $\mathbf{IP_c}$ under an (r, s) policy. Verify this formula.

6.23 Consider the discounted-cost model of Section 6.7.1. This problem asks you to derive the corresponding cost function for an (r, q) policy with fixed order cost $k > 0$.

(*a*) Choose any $t \geq L$, and suppose $IP(t) = i$. Let T be the time until the next demand after t, and $C^T(i)$ the expected discounted holding and backorder cost in the time interval $[t + L, t + T + L)$, as viewed from time t. Argue that $C^T(i) = (1 - \gamma)(e^{-\alpha L}/\alpha)C(i)$, where $C(i)$ is the average cost of a base-stock policy, as before, and $\gamma = \lambda/(\lambda + \alpha)$.

(*b*) Now let $C^\infty(i)$ be the total discounted expected cost over all time, starting with $IP(0) = i$. Argue that these quantities satisfy the equations

$$C^\infty(i) = [k + e^{-\alpha L}c(r + q - i)] + C^\infty(r + q) \qquad i \leq r$$

$$C^\infty(i) = C^T(i) + \gamma C^\infty(i - 1) \qquad r < i \leq r + q$$

(*c*) Solve the equations for $r \leq i \leq r + q$ to obtain

$$C^\infty(r) = \frac{(k + e^{-\alpha L}cq) + \Sigma_{j=1}^{q}\gamma^{q-j}C^T(r + j)}{1 - \gamma^q}$$

$$C^\infty(0) = e^{-\alpha L}cr + C^\infty(r)$$

Compare this result with formula (6.5.16) for the average cost. Verify that this agrees with the cost of a base-stock policy derived in the text, assuming $k = 0$.

6.24 Suppose the demand process $\mathbf{D}$ is a Brownian motion with positive drift rate λ and variance rate $\psi^2\lambda$. (So $D(t)$ has a normal distribution with mean λt and variance $\psi^2\lambda t$.) Let $\nu = \lambda L$ and $\sigma^2 = \psi^2\lambda L$, as above. We follow an (r, q) policy.

Set $\beta = 2/\psi^2$, and for any fixed number a define the function $h(x|a) = 1 - e^{-\beta(x-a)}$, $x \geq a$. It can be shown that IP has the pdf

$$f(x) = \begin{cases} \left(\dfrac{1}{q}\right)[h(x|r) - h(x|r + q)] & x \geq r + q \\ \left(\dfrac{1}{q}\right)h(x|r) & r \leq x \leq r + q \end{cases}$$

($\mathbf{IP}$ *can* go above $r + q$, because $\mathbf{D}$ can have negative increments.) Define the functions

$$F^0(x) = \Phi^0\left(\frac{x - \nu}{\sigma}\right) - e^{\beta x}\Phi^0\left(\frac{x + \nu}{\sigma}\right)$$

$$F^1(x) = \textstyle\int_x^\infty F^0(t)\,dt$$

$$F^2(x) = \textstyle\int_x^\infty F^1(t)\,dt$$

(*a*) Show that F^0 has all the properties of a ccdf.

(*b*) Then, show that

$$\overline{A} = \left(\frac{1}{q}\right)[F^1(r) - F^1(r + q)]$$

$$\overline{B} = \left(\frac{1}{q}\right)[F^2(r) - F^2(r + q)]$$

$$\overline{I} = \beta + \tfrac{1}{2}q + r - \nu + \overline{B}$$

(Thus, the performance measures have the same form as before. So, the methods of Section 6.5 can be used to determine an optimal policy.)

(*c*) Express the functions F^1 and F^2 in terms of Φ^0, Φ^1, and Φ^2. What role does σ play in these formulas?

C H A P T E R

7 STOCHASTIC LEADTIMES: THE STRUCTURE OF THE SUPPLY SYSTEM

Outline

7.1 Introduction

7.1.1 Discussion

The previous chapter examined several stochastic demand processes, but only the simplest type of supply process, where every order leadtime is the constant L. In reality, leadtimes are rarely constant; unpredictable events in the supply system cause unpredictable delays.

The impact of leadtime uncertainty, it turns out, depends on the *structure* of the supply system and how it operates. In certain special cases, surprisingly, leadtime uncertainty has essentially no effect and can be ignored. Most often, however, leadtime fluctuations strongly degrade performance, just as demand uncertainty does. Furthermore, when the capacity of the supply system is limited, demand uncertainty induces longer and more variable leadtimes; in other words, limited capacity magnifies the impact of demand uncertainty.

Unpredictable events in the supply system can also generate quality defects. We learned in Chapter 3 that imperfect quality can hurt performance even in a completely deterministic system. Unpredictable quality has even more pronounced effects, especially in conjunction with stochastic demands and leadtimes. In limited-capacity systems, moreover, defects waste capacity, thus amplifying the effects of the other sources of uncertainty.

Even with these additional complicating features, the performance measures in many cases have the same form as in Chapter 6. Consequently, the optimization methods of Section 6.5 can be applied once again. Also, the impact of leadtime uncertainty and imperfect quality, as well as demand uncertainty, can be captured by the summary measure σ, suitably redefined.

7.1.2 Taxonomy

A supply system consists of production and transportation operations. We use the generic term *processors* to describe the individual operations. The system may be simple or complex; it may be part of our organization, or a different firm.

We focus on three distinct supply-system structures. These emphasize different characteristics of real systems. All are abstractions to some degree; real supply systems are often hybrids of these types, and include additional complicating features. To make sense of more complex systems, however, it is essential to understand these fundamental structures thoroughly.

Section 7.2 explores *parallel* processing systems: There is an infinite number of identical processors, which work independently. Each of our orders is handled by a different processor. The time a processor requires to process an order is, in general, stochastic. So, the order leadtimes are independent, identically distributed (i.i.d.) random variables. Clearly, such a system has no capacity limits. The constant-leadtime system of Chapter 6 is the special case with deterministic processing times.

It turns out that leadtime uncertainty has relatively little impact in a parallel supply system. For one special case (Poisson demand, a base-stock policy), indeed, performance is entirely insensitive to the leadtime distribution; the system is essentially equivalent to one with constant leadtimes. This is not so in general; for world-driven demand and/or an (r, q) policy, leadtime uncertainty does have an effect. Even so, this effect is not as strong as in other structures.

Section 7.3 treats *limited-capacity* supply systems. The simplest has a single processor, capable of working on one order at a time. More complex systems have several (but still finitely many) processors arranged in series, or in parallel, or in more intricate networks.

Limited capacity in conjunction with stochastic demand leads to congestion, and this in turn both increases order leadtimes and makes them less predictable. These congestion phenomena have dramatic effects on system behavior and performance, altogether missing in a pure parallel system. This impact is strongest and clearest in a *sequential* system, which preserves the sequence that orders arrive in. This category includes single-processor and series systems.

Section 7.4 introduces *exogenous, sequential* supply systems. Such a system is effectively uncapacitated, but for a different reason than a parallel system: Our orders constitute a negligible fraction of the system's total workload. Such systems share many of the characteristics of capacitated sequential systems; in particular, leadtime uncertainty plays a major role in performance. (A constant-leadtime system is also a special case of this structure.) Section 7.5 focuses on computing performance measures for certain important cases.

All these systems can be regarded as queueing systems. (We prefer the phrase *processing systems.* Processing is the function and purpose of these systems, while queues are unfortunate characteristics of them.) If you have studied the theory of queues, some will be familiar, others less so.

Processing systems by themselves are commonly used to represent the delivery of services. In the production-transportation context, a pure processing system models a service-like product. The outputs are typically customized; each unit has specific features ordered by the customer. In any case, all processing activities are triggered by customer demands, and each customer waits until his order is completed. This is called a *make-to-order* system.

Here, the processing system is part of a larger *make-to-stock* system, which can create goods and store them in anticipation of demand, in order to reduce customer waiting. Processing is triggered by orders, not demands. Clearly, this makes sense only if the goods are uniform, or nearly so. (A make-to-order system may have an inventory of units awaiting processing, but these are inputs, not outputs.)

7.1.3 Preview of the Analysis

For the moment, forget about the structure of the supply system; think of it as a black box. Each of our orders enters this black box; sometime later the order emerges, at which point we receive the goods ordered.

Consider a base-stock policy, and assume $IN(0) = I(0) = IP(0) = s \geq 0$. As in Section 6.2.2, the process describing our orders is identical to the demand process itself. Thus, equation (6.2.1) continues to apply:

$$IN(t) = s - IO(t)$$

Also, $IO(t)$ is precisely the number of orders in the supply system at time t, that is, its current *occupancy.* This is entirely independent of s; indeed, with $s = 0$, we have a pure (make-to-order) processing system.

Now, consider some particular supply system. The input to the system is a copy of the demand process. Suppose that the system with this input is sufficiently well behaved that it is ergodic, its equilibrium occupancy IO exists, and we can explicitly calculate the distribution of IO. Then, just as in (6.2.2),

$$IN = s - IO$$

From this we can calculate all the relevant performance measures, as in Section 6.2.2. Indeed, if g denotes the pmf of IO, G^0 its ccdf, and G^1 its loss function, the formulas for $\overline{A}$, $\overline{B}$, and $\overline{I}$ are virtually identical to (6.2.4) to (6.2.6):

$$\bar{A} = G^0(s - 1) \qquad \bar{B} = G^1(s)$$

$$\bar{I} = s - E[IO] + \bar{B}$$

And, of course, $\overline{OF} = \lambda$.

Consequently, many of the qualitative results of Chapter 6 remain valid. For instance, $\bar{B}$ is decreasing and convex in s, while $\bar{I}$ is increasing and convex. In a cost-minimization setting, therefore, the optimality condition (6.5.4) remains valid, and the optimal base-stock level essentially sets the backorder probability $G^0(s)$ to the critical ratio $1 - \omega$.

To understand the overall inventory system, therefore, we need to understand the supply system, no more and no less. For this purpose, we can and do apply the results of queueing theory. However, we need to understand the system quite thoroughly; the mean occupancy $E[IO]$ is not enough. As the results of Chapter 6 suggest, we need either the full distribution of IO, or perhaps an approximation based on $V[IO]$ as well as $E[IO]$.

Next, consider an (r, q) policy with $q > 1$. Conceptually at least, the same basic idea applies. However, the input to the supply system is no longer a copy of the demand process, but rather a filtered version of it. Consequently, the calculation of IO can be far more difficult. We shall see some cases where IO can be determined exactly and others where it can be approximated accurately.

This is the analytical approach used in most of the next two sections. Section 7.4, however, uses a different approach, more reminiscent of Section 6.2.3. There the focus shifts to the *time* an order spends in the supply system, instead of the occupancy.

7.2 Independent, Stochastic Leadtimes

This section explores supply systems with a parallel-processing structure. There is an infinite number of identical, independent processors. Each order is handled by a different processor. So, when two or more orders are in the system, they are processed simultaneously, without interacting in any way. The time required to process an order is, in general, stochastic. So, the order leadtimes are independent, identically distributed (i.i.d.) random variables. Let L denote a generic random variable with this common distribution; the mean leadtime is then $E[L]$.

In the standard code of queues, this is a $\cdot$/G/∞ system. The ∞ indicates an infinite number of parallel servers, the G stands for general independent service times, and the $\cdot$ means the input is yet to be specified. When we connect this system to the rest of the model, the input will be precisely the process describing orders, which depends on the demand process and the policy.

Of course, no real supply system has infinite processing capacity. The model is an approximation, a limiting case of systems with considerable, though finite, parallel structure, where the capacity limit is reached only rarely. The model gives a fairly accurate account, qualitatively and quantitatively, of the behavior of such systems.

7.2.1 Poisson Demand, Base-Stock Policy

Suppose that demand is a Poisson process. Consider a base-stock policy with base-stock level $s \geq 0$, and assume $IN(0) = I(0) = IP(0) = s$. So, the input (order) process is identical to the Poisson demand process. The code for the supply system is M/G/∞ (the M stands for Markovian, i.e., Poisson).

The central result for this model is Palm's Theorem: *The equilibrium occupancy IO has the Poisson distribution with mean* $\lambda E[L]$. So, *IO*, and hence the performance measures $\overline{A}$, $\overline{B}$, and $\overline{I}$ for any *s*, are precisely the same as in the constant-leadtime model of Section 6.2.2. They depend on the distribution of *L* only through its mean $E[L]$.

This is a powerful insensitivity result. The parallel-processing feature eliminates all effects of leadtime variability! To use the model, we need only estimate $E[L]$. The optimal base-stock level is identical to that of the constant-leadtime model. Also, we can use the normal approximation of Section 6.4, with $\nu = \sigma^2 = \lambda E[L]$. So, by the results of Section 6.5.2.2, the overall performance (e.g., optimal cost) of the system depends primarily on σ, and hence on the square root of $\lambda E[L]$.

The relationship $\overline{B} = \lambda \overline{BW}$ derived in Section 6.2.4 applies here as well, so the average customer waiting time $\overline{BW}$ also depends on *L* only through $E[L]$. On the other hand, Theorem 6.2.4 does *not* apply, except in the special case where *L* is constant. (That theorem requires, among other things, that the supply system be sequential, which is true only for constant *L*. In general, the distribution of customer waiting times, including its variance, does depend on the distribution of *L*.)

EXAMPLE 7.2.A

A personal-computer repair service provides "loaners" to its customers. That is, when a customer brings in a broken computer, the company lends the customer a replacement to use until the machine is fixed. The company provides excellent services, and its customers will go nowhere else, even when no loaner is available. Still, the company views the loaner program as an integral part of its overall service package, and so aims to keep enough loaners available that 95% of customers can get one.

The company employs a large number of technicians, each fully qualified to diagnose and repair virtually any computer problem. Each arriving job is assigned to one technician, who handles the entire job. Rarely does a job have to wait for an available technician. (When the workload gets unusually large, the company can expand its capacity by calling in regular technicians from days off or vacation, or occasionally part-time freelancers.)

Customer arrivals form a Poisson process. On average, 16 jobs arrive per day, and the average job requires 1.25 days to complete. There is a lot of variation among jobs. Many can be finished within hours, but a few require weeks. The company's owner wonders whether this variation should affect the number of loaners it maintains.

Since each job brings its own characteristic problems, it is reasonable to assume that the leadtimes (job-completion times) are i.i.d. Therefore, variation makes no difference. Given $\lambda = 16$ and $E[L] = 1.25$, *IO* has the Poisson distribution with mean $(16)(1.25) = 20$. The 95% availability target means $\overline{A} \leq 1 - \omega_{-} = 0.05$.

The performance of selected base-stock policies is as follows:

s	$\overline{A}$	$\overline{B}$	$\overline{I}$
21	0.44	1.34	2.34
22	0.36	0.98	2.98
23	0.28	0.70	3.70
24	0.21	0.49	4.49
25	0.16	0.33	5.33
26	0.11	0.22	6.22
27	0.08	0.14	7.14
28	0.05	0.09	8.09
29	0.03	0.05	9.05
30	0.02	0.03	10.03
31	0.01	0.02	11.02
32	0.01	0.01	12.01

So, to meet the performance target, the company should set $s = 28$. With this policy, the average inventory of loaners will be about 8. The normal approximation prescribes $s = 27.36$. Rounding this up to 28, the approximation predicts $\overline{A} = 0.037$ and $\overline{I} = 8.07$, quite close to the exact values.

By the way, while leadtime variation itself does not affect the result, the company can still gain by reducing the times of the longest jobs, for that will reduce $E[L]$.

The calculations above, and those of the other examples in this chapter, were performed in a simple spreadsheet, using the formulas in the text. You might want to set up your own spreadsheet to verify the results and explore the effects of parameter changes.

EXAMPLE 7.2.B, PART 1

Reconsider the classical record store of Example 6.2.A in Chapter 6. The leadtime there was the constant 0.5, but now suppose that it is really stochastic with $E[L] = 0.5$. Nevertheless, for a parallel supply system, the results are precisely the same as before.

7.2.2 World-Driven Demand

Next, consider a world-driven demand process, as in Section 6.3, still assuming a base-stock policy. It is difficult to obtain the exact distribution of *IO,* and even when it is possible, the calculations are rather complex.

Fortunately, the normal approximation of *IO* works well, provided $\lambda E[L]$ is fairly large. (Indeed, the approximation approaches the exact distribution in the limit, in a certain sense, as $\lambda E[L] \rightarrow \infty$. Such a result is called a *heavy-traffic approximation.*) The normal parameters are

$$\nu = \lambda E[L] \qquad \sigma^2 = \lambda E[L] + \lambda(\psi^2 - 1)E[L_{[2]}] \tag{7.2.1}$$

Here, ψ^2 is the asymptotic variance-to-mean ratio of the demand process, and $L_{[2]}$ indicates a random variable, the minimum of two independent copies of L. That is, $L_{[2]} = \min\{L^1, L^2\}$, where L^1 and L^2 are i.i.d. random variables, each with the same distribution as L. We shall say more about $L_{[2]}$ in a moment.

For a Poisson process, of course, $\psi^2 = 1$, so σ^2 reduces to the correct value, $\lambda E[L]$. For $\psi^2 \neq 1$, think of σ^2 the base value $\lambda E[L]$ plus a correction factor. The *sign* of this correction factor depends on $(\psi^2 - 1)$, which is a characteristic of the demand process; it does not depend on L. Thus, according to the approximation, IO is more variable than in the Poisson case $(\sigma^2 > \nu)$, precisely when demand is more variable than a Poisson process. The *magnitude* of the correction factor depends on the deviation of ψ^2 from 1, but also on $E[L_{[2]}]$, which reflects the distribution of L.

For constant L, $E[L_{[2]}] = E[L] = L$, so $\sigma^2 = \psi^2\lambda L$. The approximation is thus consistent with that of Section 6.4. In general, $0 < E[L_{[2]}] \leq E[L]$, and it is not hard to show that

$$E[L] - E[L_{[2]}] = \tfrac{1}{2}E[\,|L^1 - L^2|\,]$$

Thus, $E[L] - E[L_{[2]}]$ is a measure of the variation of L. If the distribution of L is spread out widely, this quantity is large. For example, if L has a uniform distribution on the interval $E[L] \pm u$, for some constant u with $0 < u \leq E[L]$, then $E[L] - E[L_{[2]}] = u/3$. (See Problem 7.1.)

The case $\psi^2 > 1$ leads to a seemingly paradoxical result: Greater variability in L actually reduces σ^2. In general, σ^2 always lies between $\lambda E[L]$ and $\psi^2\lambda E[L]$, as if the leadtime were fixed but the demand process were mixed with a Poisson process. This is the essential effect of stochastic, parallel processing.

The (approximate) optimal base-stock level s^* can again be determined as in Section 6.5.2.2. Also, the optimal cost is (approximately) proportional to σ and thus to the square root of λ.

Figure 7.2.1 illustrates the accuracy of the approximation. Demand is the two-state renewal process of Section 6.3.2, so $\lambda = 10$ and $\psi^2 = \tfrac{1}{2}$. The leadtimes have an exponential distribution, in which case $E[L_{[2]}] = \tfrac{1}{2}E[L]$. The figure shows two values of $E[L]$, ½ and 1. Evidently, the approximation works well in this case, even though $\lambda E[L]$ is rather small.

7.2.3 Lost Sales

For most of this chapter, as in Chapter 6, stockouts lead to backorders. Now, consider the lost-sales case: A demand that cannot be met immediately is lost forever (as in Section 3.3.8 and again in Section 7.3.4). Assume Poisson demand and a base-stock policy.

When $I(t) > 0$ so $IO(t) < s$, the system operates as before; each demand triggers an order. While $I(t) = 0$ and $IO(t) = s$, however, all demands are lost and no orders are placed. Consequently, $IO(t)$ never exceeds s. In effect, the supply system never uses more than s processors. We can assume there are only s of them.

Here is an equivalent control rule: *Every* demand generates an order, but the supply system ignores orders that arrive when all s processors are busy. This is another classic processing system called the *Erlang loss system.* Its code is M/G/s/s. (The first s indicates the number of processors, the second the maximum occupancy.)

FIGURE 7.2.1

Performance of Base-Stock Policies (Normal versus Exact).

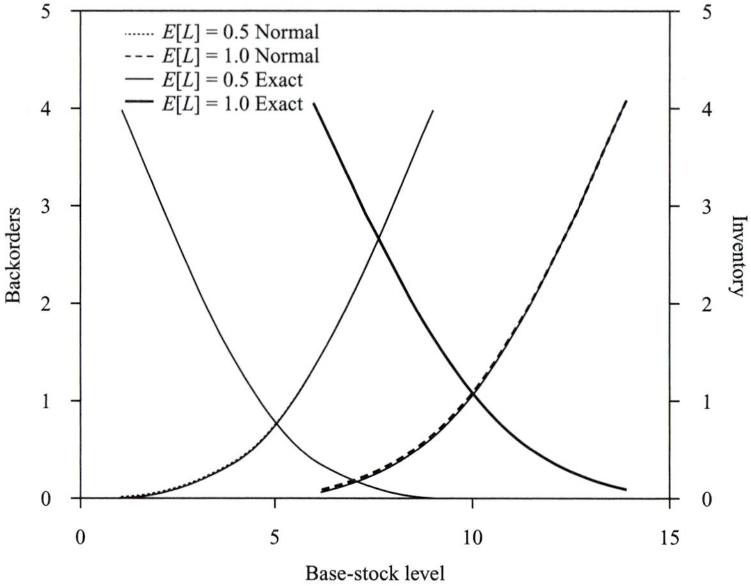

The equilibrium behavior of this system too is quite simple: Letting $\nu = \lambda E[L]$, the pmf of IO is given by

$$\begin{aligned} g_{IO}(d) &= \frac{(\nu^d/d!)}{\Sigma_{j=0}^{s}(\nu^j/j!)} \\ &= \frac{g(d)}{G(s)} \qquad d = 0, \ldots, s \end{aligned}$$

where g denotes the Poisson pmf with mean ν and G the corresponding cdf. So, g_{IO} is just a truncated version of g. Again, IO depends on the distribution of L only through its mean.

The stockout probability is $\overline{A} = g_{IO}(s)$, so the rate at which lost sales occur is $\lambda g_{IO}(s)$, and $\overline{OF} = \lambda(1 - \overline{A}) = \lambda[1 - g_{IO}(s)]$. The average inventory is

$$\overline{I} = \Sigma_{j=0}^{s} (s - j) g_{IO}(j) = s - \nu + \nu g_{IO}(s)$$

These criteria have fundamentally different forms than in the backorders model. Still, $\overline{A}$ is decreasing and convex in s, and $\overline{I}$ is increasing and convex. (See Problem 7.2.) So, given a service-level target or cost factors on $\overline{A}$ and $\overline{I}$, it is not hard to determine the optimal base-stock level.

EXAMPLE 7.2.B, PART 2

Suppose that next door to the classical record store is a popular CD outlet. One of its venerable Beatles albums is requested consistently at the rate of 3.6 per month (the same as Beethoven's Seventh!), according to a Poisson process. The mean leadtime is 2 weeks (also the same). The store aims to fill about 80% of demands directly from stock. Customers who cannot find the album in stock, however, walk out angrily and purchase it at a competing store across town.

Again, the average leadtime demand is $n = (3.6)(0.5) = 1.8$. Direct calculation yields the performance of alternative base-stock policies:

s	$\overline{A}$	$\overline{I}$
0	1.00	0.00
1	0.64	0.36
2	0.37	0.86
3	0.18	1.52
4	0.08	2.34
5	0.03	3.25
6	0.01	4.21

(Comparing this to the table in Example 6.2.A, Part 1, for each value of s, $\overline{A}$ is smaller and $\overline{I}$ larger than in the backlog case.) With a performance target of $\overline{A} \leq 1 - \omega_{-} = 0.2$, the store should set $s = 3$. (Recall, in the backlog case, the same performance target required $s = 4$.) This policy leads to an average inventory of 1.52.

By the way, you might question the 80% service target. A lost sale usually (very likely in this case) has a greater economic impact than a backorder. So, perhaps the popular store should aim higher, say at 95%.

These results apply in particular to the constant-leadtime system. We remarked in Section 6.2 that, for this system, assuming backorders, a base-stock policy is really optimal. This is not so in the lost-sales case. A base-stock policy is a useful heuristic, but no more than that. (Section 9.6.5 of Chapter 9 explains.)

7.2.4 Larger Batches

Return to the Poisson-demand, backlog model, but now consider an (r, q) policy with $q > 1$.

We need to specify precisely what happens to the individual units in a batch. Do they become separate entities in the supply system, or is the batch processed as a whole? In the first case, do we receive completed units immediately, or must we wait until the whole batch is finished? (We encountered this same issue in Section 3.4.) In the second case, does the batch size influence the leadtime, and if so how? (In any of these scenarios, the supply system becomes a *bulk queue,* where units arrive in groups, or are served in groups, or both; see Chaudhry and Tempelton [1983]. Such models tend to be difficult to analyze.)

Here, assume the simplest scenario, like that of Section 6.2: The supply system treats the batch as a whole, and the order leadtime is a random variable L, which does not depend on q. Even then, exact analysis is difficult. Here is an approximation, using the normal approximation of Section 7.2.2 within Section 6.4.3's evaluation scheme for (r, q) policies:

First, focus on the supply system: It treats each order as a distinct unit. Let $\widetilde{IO}(t) = IO(t)/q$ denote the supply system's occupancy in these units, i.e., the *number* of orders outstanding. An order is placed every q demands, so the input to the supply system is a renewal process, where each interdemand time has an Erlang-q distribution. This is an MCDC process; **IP** plays the role of **W.** Clearly, the input rate is $\tilde{\lambda} = \lambda/q$, and it is not hard to show that the variance-mean ratio is $\tilde{\psi}^2 = 1/q$. So, as in Section 7.2.2, for large λ, the limiting occupancy $\widetilde{IO}$ is approximately normal, with parameters

$$E[\widetilde{IO}] = \tilde{\lambda}E[L]$$

$$V[\widetilde{IO}] = \tilde{\lambda}E[L] + \tilde{\lambda}(\tilde{\psi}^2 - 1)E[L_{[2]}]$$

Consequently, $IO = q\widetilde{IO}$ too is approximately normal with parameters

$$\nu = qE[\widetilde{IO}] = \lambda E[L] \tag{7.2.2}$$

$$\sigma^2 = q^2 V[\widetilde{IO}] = \lambda E[L] + \lambda(q - 1)(E[L] - E[L_{[2]}])$$

Now, IP has the uniform distribution on the integers in $[r + 1, r + q]$, and we can approximate this by the continuous uniform distribution on $[r, r + q]$, as in Section 6.4.3. Also,

$$IN = IP - IO$$

However, IP and IO are *not* independent. As a further approximation, let us treat them as such. (More precisely, use σ^2 above to estimate $V[IN] - V[IP] = V[IO] - 2V[IP, IO]$, where $V[IP, IO]$ means the covariance of IP and IO. It turns out that the error thus introduced is negligible for large λ.) Given all these approximations, formulas (6.4.9) to (6.4.11) can be used directly to estimate performance. This approach works well when $\lambda E[L]$ is large.

The expression for ν is the same as in the constant-leadtime case, but σ^2 is quite different. Recall, $E[L] - E[L_{[2]}]$ measures leadtime variation. So, when $q > 1$, in sharp contrast to the case of $q = 1$, leadtime variation *does* affect σ^2 and hence system performance. The larger q is, the greater this impact is. Thus, the batch size and leadtime variation have a *joint effect* on performance.

Actually, (7.2.2) tends to overestimate $V[IN] - V[IP]$ for large q, and the following refinement works better:

$$\sigma^2 = \lambda E[L] + \min\{\lambda(q - 1)(E[L] - E[L_{[2]}]), \lambda^2 V[L]\} \tag{7.2.3}$$

(The second term in the minimum also appears in the analysis of sequential supply systems, as in Section 7.5.3. It arises here because, when q is large, there is rarely more than one order outstanding, so the supply system behaves almost sequentially.) This formula too expresses a joint effect of q and leadtime variation, but a limited one.

The optimization results of Section 6.5 do not apply straightforwardly here, because the performance formulas (6.4.9) to (6.4.11) depend on q directly, but also indirectly through σ. It remains true that, for fixed q, the formulas depend on r in the same way as before. For instance, $\overline{B}$ and $\overline{I}$ are convex in r, so it is easy to minimize the average cost over r for fixed q; moreover, the optimal cost includes a term that is roughly proportional to σ. But, for variable q as well as r, the optimality behavior of this system is uncharted territory.

The same ideas can be applied when demand itself is a world-driven process. Here, $\tilde{\psi}^2 = \psi^2/q$, where ψ^2 is the original variance-mean ratio of the demand process. A bit of algebra shows that (7.2.2) becomes

$$\sigma^2 = \lambda E[L] + \lambda(\psi^2 - 1)E[L_{[2]}] + \lambda(q - 1)(E[L] - E[L_{[2]}])$$

[It is not entirely clear what the analogue of the refined formula (7.2.3) should be.]

Incidentally, it is not hard to extend this approach to situations where the order size does influence the leadtime: Just specify L, and hence $E[L]$ and $E[L_{[2]}]$, as functions of q, and apply the results above.

7.2.5 Lumpy Demand

Now, suppose that demand is a compound-Poisson process. As in Section 6.6, let Y denote the generic batch-size random variable. Suppose we follow a base-stock policy. As in Section 7.2.4, each order comprises several units, and we must specify what happens to them in the supply system.

First, suppose that each order becomes a single, indivisible unit of work in the supply system, and its leadtime L is independent of Y. In this case, the number of orders outstanding $\widetilde{IO}$ has the same distribution as in the pure Poisson-demand model, the Poisson distribution with mean $\lambda E[L]$. Therefore, the total stock on order IO has a compound distribution, the distribution of $\widetilde{IO}$ compounded with g_Y. In sum, the results here are the same as in the constant-leadtime case. (It is possible to analyze an (r, q) policy also along these lines.)

Now, suppose that each unit goes to a different processor. The situation here is similar to that of Section 7.2.2; units arrive according to a complex demand process and are processed individually. The normal approximation of IO itself applies here too. The variation ratio is $\psi^2 = E[Y^2]/E[Y]$, and $\lambda E[Y]$ replaces λ in (7.2.1).

7.2.6 Imperfect Quality

Return once more to the case of Poisson demand and $q = 1$. Suppose that the supply system occasionally produces a defective unit. Each arriving unit has probability δ of being defective, independent of the others. A defective unit is entirely useless and must be discarded. Assume we discover defects immediately. This scenario is similar to that of Section 3.6 of Chapter 3. There, however, defects were predictable. Here, although δ is still the *long-run* fraction of defects, we do not know whether a unit is defective or not until it actually arrives; quality is uncertain as well as imperfect.

Consider what happens when a unit arrives and is found defective: The order for that unit has failed, in effect, so it makes sense to order another one immediately. When that second unit arrives, it too may turn out defective. If so, place yet another order. This sequence of events continues until we finally receive a nondefective unit. (This rule *is* a base-stock policy; it keeps $IP(t)$ constant. It is a reasonable heuristic, but even in the constant-leadtime case, it is not optimal overall. See Section 9.4.8 and Section 9.6.7 of Chapter 9.)

Call L the *nominal leadtime,* the time required for the supply system to deliver a unit, regardless of quality. Define L' to be the time needed to deliver a nondefective unit, the actual *effective leadtime.* The effective leadtimes for different orders are independent, so the system operates just like one with perfect quality, but with L' replacing L.

For simplicity, suppose also that the nominal leadtimes within an effective leadtime are independent. The random variable L' thus has a compound distribution, based on that of L. But, by the results of Section 7.2.1, only the mean counts, and this is given by

$$E[L'] = \frac{E[L]}{\xi}$$

where $\xi = 1 - \delta$. The effect of imperfect quality, then, is an inflation of the mean effective leadtime. Under the normal or maximal approximation, σ grows by a factor of $1/\sqrt{\xi}$, and performance deteriorates accordingly.

Imperfect quality also affects the cost parameters, depending on the payment arrangements. The required adjustments are the same as in Section 3.6. (It is possible, but much harder, to analyze the second inspection scheme of Section 3.6, where defects are discovered only when units are given to customers in response to their demands. Section 7.3.5.3 considers this scheme in the context of a different supply system.)

Finally, assume a constant leadtime L, and consider a general (r, q) policy. Here, an arriving batch may include both defective and nondefective units. Thus, the effects of poor quality cannot be captured exactly by an inflated leadtime, as above. That approach seems to work fairly well as an approximation, however (see Moinzadeh and Lee [1987]): That is, replace L by the constant $L' = L/\xi$, and then apply the calculations of Section 6.2.3.

7.2.7 Processing Networks

Suppose that the supply system consists of several stages or *nodes,* each a parallel-processing system like those above. The nodes are indexed $j = 1, \ldots, J$. Each order must pass through the nodes in this order, from 1 to J. Thus, the nodes are arranged in series, and we call the network a *series system.* (Unlike the series systems of Chapter 5, however, the supply system is a pure make-to-order system; there are no inventories of semi-finished goods at the nodes. Chapter 8 considers stochastic systems with internal inventories.) The processing time at node j is the random variable L_j. These times are independent of one another, both within each node and across nodes.

The total leadtime for each order is the random variable $L = \Sigma_j L_j$. Each order's leadtime, moreover, is independent of those of other orders. So, this system reduces to a single-node parallel supply system like those above.

It is worth mentioning one additional fact: Assume Poisson demand and a base-stock policy. Let IO_j denote the equilibrium occupancy of node j. Then, IO_j has the Poisson distribution with mean $\lambda E[L_j]$, and these random variables are independent. (This is consistent with what we already know, namely, that $IO = \Sigma_j IO_j$ has the Poisson distribution with mean $\lambda E[L]$.) Section 8.3.4.4 of Chapter 8 uses this fact.

These results extend to more complex network structures, where the processing sequence is not fixed: Suppose that each order starts at a randomly chosen node. Subsequently, on completing processing at node i, the order moves next to node j with some fixed probability, and exits the supply system (arrives in our inventory) with some other probability. So, any one order might encounter the same node several times, and other nodes not at all. Assume that every order does exit eventually. (In queueing-theory parlance, a network with this property is called *open.* There are other models called *closed* networks, which we do not consider here.)

Specifically, let r_{0j} be the probability that the initial node is j, r_{ij} the probability of moving from i to j, and r_{i0} the probability of exiting the system from i. These are called *routing probabilities.* The movements of orders in the network are independent of the processing times, and each such event is independent of the others.

These routing probabilities can be interpreted as quality defect rates. Suppose that the normal processing sequence, when all goes well, is nodes $1, 2, \ldots, J$, as in the series system above. That is, when processing is successful, an order moves from i to $i + 1$ for $i < J$, and from J it leaves the network. However, node i may induce a defect. In that case, the order may have to be reworked at node i (with probability r_{ii}), or worse, return to an earlier node (with probability r_{ij}, $j < i$). If the defect is serious enough, we may have to scrap the order and start a new one, which means returning to node 1. The imperfect-quality model of Section 7.2.6 is the special case with $J = 1$ and $\delta = r_{11}$. (In terms of network structure, this is called a *series system with feedback.*)

Again, assume Poisson demand and a base-stock policy. Beginning orders arrive at node j at rate λr_{0j}. Let $\boldsymbol{\lambda}_0$ denote the row-vector $(\lambda r_{0j})_j$. Let R denote the *routing matrix* $(r_{ij})_{i,j\neq 0}$. Also, let λ_j be the *total* arrival rate of orders to node j, and $\boldsymbol{\lambda}$ the row-vector $(\lambda_j)_j$. (We don't know these yet.) Thus, orders move from i to j at rate $\lambda_i r_{ij}$. For the λ_i to be defined consistently, then, requires $\lambda_j = \lambda r_{0j} + \Sigma_i \lambda_i r_{ij}$, or in matrix notation,

$$\boldsymbol{\lambda} = \boldsymbol{\lambda}_0 + \boldsymbol{\lambda} R$$

Now, *assume* that $I - R$ is a nonsingular matrix. This condition, in fact, ensures that each order leaves the network eventually. Then, the equations above have the unique solution

$$\boldsymbol{\lambda} = \boldsymbol{\lambda}_0 (I - R)^{-1} \tag{7.2.4}$$

(In the series system above, each $\lambda_j = \lambda$.) The λ_j are always nonnegative.

It turns out that each IO_j has the Poisson distribution with mean $\lambda_j E[L_j]$, just as if node j were an M/G/∞ system in isolation, and the IO_j are independent. Therefore, the total occupancy IO has the Poisson distribution with mean $\nu = \Sigma_j \lambda_j E[L_j]$. The performance of the system is thus identical to that of a constant-leadtime system with average leadtime demand ν. (In the one-node, imperfect-quality model, $I - R = (1 - \delta) = (\xi)$ and $r_{01} = 1$, so $\lambda_1 = \lambda/\xi$, and $\nu = \lambda E[L]/\xi$, consistent with the earlier result.)

Here is another way to express this result: Assume that each $\lambda_j \geq \lambda$ (as is always true for a series system with feedback), and let $\xi_j = \lambda/\lambda_j$. Define the mean effective leadtime $E[L_j'] = E[L_j]/\xi_j$, and set $E[L'] = \Sigma_j E[L_j']$. Then, $\nu = \lambda E[L']$. Thus, ν can be interpreted in terms of the total input rates λ_j, or equivalently the mean effective leadtimes $E[L_j']$.

The effects of quality on performance depend on the structure of R in an intricate way. Roughly, as the defect rates increase, the λ_j (or $E[L_j']$) become larger, hence performance deteriorates. Also, the impact of r_{ij} is greater for larger i and smaller j. A serious defect sends an order backward a long way, and that requires repeating the operations at all nodes in between. That is, r_{ij} affects *all* the λ_k, for $j \leq k \leq i$.

7.3 Limited-Capacity Supply Systems

7.3.1 Discussion

This section considers supply systems with *limited capacity* to process orders. The theory of queues covers a huge variety of such systems, almost any of which can serve as the supply system in a larger make-to-stock inventory system. Here, we discuss only a few important ones. Also, we omit the technicalities of the theory, concentrating on its main results.

The central insight of queueing theory is that *limited capacity and variation together cause congestion:* Consider a processing system that can process work at some finite rate. Suppose it receives an input stream that fluctuates over time. During a period when the input surges, the system experiences a short-term capacity shortage, and a backlog of work builds up. Even after the input subsides, it takes a while to work off the backlog. Greater and/or more frequent surges cause more such congestion. Variation in processing capacity, due to occasional breakdowns or other factors, increases congestion in the same way. All this is true even if the system's capacity is adequate to process its workload in the long run.

Let ρ represent the ratio of the long-run average workload-arrival rate to the average processing capacity. (These notions are a bit vague, but never mind; they will be quite precise later on.) So, "adequate capacity" certainly means $\rho \leq 1$. It turns out that system stability actually requires $\rho < 1$. This expresses another key insight: *In a system with input or processing variation, excess capacity is necessary for stability.* Moreover, the congestion in the system and its performance "explode" (become worse without limit) as ρ approaches 1. In fact, the total leadtime experienced by arriving units includes a term proportional to $\rho/(1 - \rho)$.

All this describes a stand-alone processing system, but the results are equally important for a make-to-stock system. The supply system must have excess capacity, and performance depends critically on ρ. The results below illustrate this clearly.

7.3.2 One Processor, Poisson Demand, Base-Stock Policy

Most of this section assumes Poisson demand and a base-stock policy. So, starting with $I(0) = IP(0) = s$, the input to the supply system is itself a Poisson process. Sections 7.3.8 and 7.3.9 consider other demand processes and policies.

This subsection, and several others below, treat the case of a single processor. The processor works on its inputs (orders) whenever there are inputs to work on, i.e., when $IO(t) > 0$, shutting off only when there are none. It processes orders sequentially, in their order of arrival. Systems with multiple processors are discussed later.

7.3.2.1 Markovian Processing

Suppose that, while the processor operates, it completes units according to a Poisson process with rate μ, the *processing rate*. This implies (Section C.5.6) that the unit processing times are independent and exponentially distributed with mean $1/\mu$. In this case, μ represents the capacity of the system, and $\rho = \lambda/\mu$. Assume $\rho < 1$, so the system is stable. The code for this processing system is M/M/1. (Both Ms stand for Markovian; the second one refers to the assumptions above about processing.)

Markovian processing means a great deal of variation. The exponential distribution puts substantial probability on very long times relative to its mean; its variance is $(1/\mu)^2$, the mean squared. It describes, for instance, the lengths of telephone calls, the run times of computer programs, and complex equipment repairs (as in Example 7.2.A). Most production processes are less variable. A processor that breaks down or produces defects frequently, however, may exhibit nearly Markovian behavior (see Section 7.3.5).

In this case (see Section C.5.4), the equilibrium occupancy IO has the *geometric distribution* with parameter ρ:

$$g(i) = (1 - \rho)\rho^i \qquad i \geq 0$$

Consequently, $E[IO] = \rho/(1 - \rho)$, and

$$\overline{A} = G^0(s - 1) = \rho^s \tag{7.3.1}$$

$$\overline{B} = G^1(s) = \left(\frac{\rho}{1 - \rho}\right)\rho^s$$

$$\overline{I} = s - E[IO] + -\overline{B} = s - \left(\frac{\rho}{1 - \rho}\right)(1 - \rho^s)$$

Notice, $\overline{A}$ and $\overline{B}$ are simple geometric functions of s.

Because $\rho = Pr\{IO > 0\}$, it is called the *utilization;* it gives the fraction of time the processor actually works. Evidently, the performance measures are strongly determined by ρ. When ρ is near 1, $E[IO] = G^1(0)$ becomes huge, and ρ^s decays slowly. Thus, s and hence $\overline{I}$ must be large to achieve adequate customer service, i.e., small $\overline{A}$ and/or $\overline{B}$.

Let us compare this system with a parallel-supply system, constructed so that both have the same $E[IO]$. (They do *not* have equal demand rates and processing times; in that case, $E[IO]$ would be larger for the sequential system.) Figure 7.3.1 displays $\overline{B}$ as a function of s for both systems, with $E[IO] = 10$ and 20. (The sequential system thus has $\rho = 10/11$ and 20/21, respectively.) The two systems perform similarly for small s, but as s increases, $\overline{B}$ decays much more slowly in the sequential model.

Figure 7.3.2 displays the stock-service tradeoff in the same format as Figure 6.2.4. (The horizontal and vertical scales are different in the new figure.) Comparing the two figures, we see that it is far more costly (in terms of $\overline{IW}$) to achieve adequate performance (as measured by $\overline{BW}$) when capacity is limited. Moreover, the shapes of the curves are different in the two figures: In Figure 6.2.4 the curves are slightly concave, whereas here they are convex. Thus, as we impose more stringent limits on $\overline{BW}$, the required $\overline{IW}$ increases faster in a limited-capacity system.

EXAMPLE 7.3.A, PART 1

Reconsider the computer-repair company of Example 7.2.A. Suppose the company has a single repair technician, who, however, works very fast. The repair times are exponential with mean just

FIGURE 7.3.1

Performance of base-stock policies (sequential versus parallel supply).

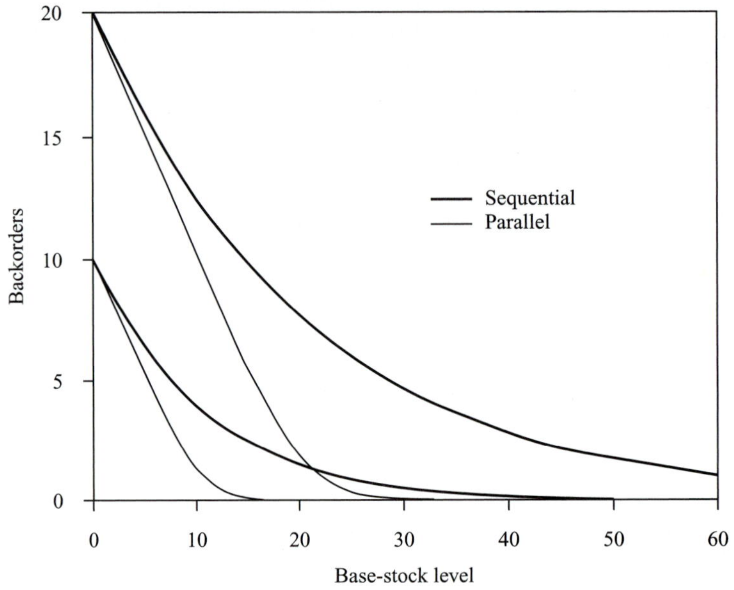

FIGURE 7.3.2

Stock-service tradeoff (M/M/1 system).

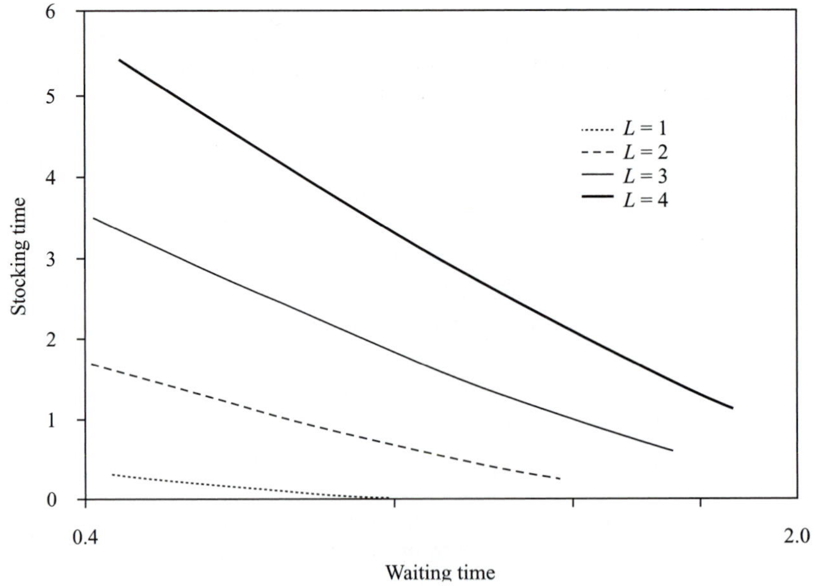

under 0.06 days, so that $E[IO] = 20$ as before. The performance of selected base-stock policies is as follows:

s	$\overline{A}$	$\overline{B}$	$\overline{I}$
58	0.059	1.18	39.18
59	0.056	1.12	40.12
60	0.054	1.07	41.07
61	0.051	1.02	42.02
62	0.049	0.97	42.97
63	0.046	0.92	43.92
64	0.044	0.88	44.88

To meet the requirement of $\overline{A} \le 0.05$, the company should set $s = 62$, far more than the 28 for the original parallel system. This policy has average inventory about 43, compared to 8 for the parallel system.

7.3.2.2 General Processing Times

Now, suppose the processing times are still i.i.d., but have an arbitrary distribution. The code for this processing system is M/G/1. Let S denote the generic processing-time random variable. Assume that $E[S]$, $E[S^2]$, and $E[S^3]$ are finite. Again, denote $\mu = 1/E[S]$ and $\rho = \lambda/\mu$, and assume $\rho < 1$.

There is no simple formula for g, the pmf of IO, but it can be computed by a recursive procedure: Let $g_{D(S)}$ denote the pmf of $D(S)$, the demand during a random time interval S, and $G^0_{D(S)}$ its ccdf. (Usually, $g_{D(S)}$ can be derived or computed easily.) Then,

$$g(0) = 1 - \rho$$

$$g(i + 1) = \frac{G^0_{D(S)}(i)g(0) + \sum_{j=1}^{i} G^0_{D(S)}(i + 1 - j)g(j)}{g_{D(S)}(0)} \qquad i \ge 0$$

From g, the ccdf G^0 and the loss function G^1 can be obtained directly. (In a moment we shall see an explicit formula for a special case.)

There are closed-form expressions for the mean and variance of the order waiting time, the time an order spends waiting for access to the processor before its own processing begins, denoted L_Q:

$$E[L_Q] = \frac{1}{2}(1 + \psi_S^2)\left(\frac{\rho}{1 - \rho}\right)\left(\frac{1}{\mu}\right) \tag{7.3.2}$$

$$V[L_Q] = E^2[L_Q] + \left(\frac{1}{3}\right)(\mu^3 E[S^3])\left(\frac{\rho}{1 - \rho}\right)\left(\frac{1}{\mu}\right)^2 \tag{7.3.3}$$

(ψ_S^2 is the square of the coefficient of variation of S; i.e., $V[S]/E^2[S] = \mu^2 V[S]$.) These are known as the Polleczek-Khintchine formulas. The total order leadtime L, then, has mean and variance

$$E[L] = E[L_Q] + E[S]$$

$$V[L] = V[L_Q] + V[S]$$

It turns out (see Section 7.3.8), moreover, that

$$E[IO] = \lambda E[L]$$

$$V[IO] = \lambda E[L] + \lambda^2 V[L]$$

These moments can be used to approximate the distribution of IO.

The formulas clearly reveal the impact of the system parameters on L_Q and hence on L and IO: In (7.3.2), the term $1/\mu = E[S]$ is a scale factor; the rest of the formula expresses $E[L_Q]$ as a multiple of $E[S]$. The utilization ρ again plays a dominant role through $\rho/(1-\rho)$; as ρ approaches 1, $E[L_Q]$ explodes. Processing variation has a linear impact via the term $\frac{1}{2}(1+\psi_S^2)$. These factors also affect $V[L_Q]$ in (7.3.3) through the $E^2[L_Q]$ term. The additional component of $V[L_Q]$ is similar in form, but it expresses processing variation by the third-moment factor $\frac{1}{3}\mu^3 E[S^3]$.

In the fortunate case of constant processing times, $\psi_S^2 = 0$ and $\mu^3 E[S^3] = 1$, and the formulas above reduce to

$$E[L_Q] = \frac{1}{2}\left(\frac{\rho}{1-\rho}\right)\left(\frac{1}{\mu}\right)$$

$$V[L_Q] = E^2[L_Q] + \frac{1}{3}\left(\frac{\rho}{1-\rho}\right)\left(\frac{1}{\mu}\right)^2$$

When S is exponential, $\psi_S^2 = 1$ and $\mu^3 E[S^3] = 6$, and we recover the results above for the M/M/1 system. Most production processes have values of ψ_S^2 between 0 and 1.

Now, suppose that S has a CPH distribution (Section C.5.5) with parameters $(\boldsymbol{\mu}, M)$, where $\boldsymbol{\mu}$ is a row-vector and M a square matrix. Assume $\boldsymbol{\mu}\mathbf{e} = 1$, so the unit processing time is positive with probability 1. Recall, $M^{-1} \geq 0$, and $E[S] = 1/\mu = \boldsymbol{\mu} M^{-1}\mathbf{e}$.

In this case, L too has a CPH distribution. Its parameters are $(\boldsymbol{\nu}, N)$, where

$$\boldsymbol{\nu} = \boldsymbol{\mu}[(1-\rho)\mathrm{I} + \lambda M^{-1}] \qquad N = M - \lambda \mathbf{e}\boldsymbol{\mu}$$

(Actually, N need not have all the required properties for a CPH distribution. Nevertheless, the distribution of L follows the CPH form.) Also, for $P = \lambda(\lambda I + N)^{-1}$ and $\boldsymbol{\pi} = \boldsymbol{\nu}P$, IO has a DPH distribution (Section C.4.4) with parameters $(\boldsymbol{\pi}, P)$. Therefore,

$$\bar{A} = G^0(s-1) = \boldsymbol{\nu}P^s\mathbf{e}$$

$$\bar{B} = G^1(s) = \boldsymbol{\nu}P(I-P)^{-1}P^s\mathbf{e} \qquad (7.3.4)$$

$$\bar{I} = s - \boldsymbol{\nu}P(I-P)^{-1}\mathbf{e} + \bar{B} \qquad s \geq 0$$

Notice the formal similarity between (7.3.4) and (7.3.1); the matrix P plays the same role here as the scalar ρ above. (Section C.4.4 discusses the implementation of calculations of this sort.)

7.3.3 Flexible Capacity

7.3.3.1 Load-Dependent Processing Rate

Next, consider a variant of the M/M/1 system, where the processing rate μ depends on the current occupancy of the system. Specifically, when $IO(t) = i$, the processing rate becomes μ_i. For example, the supply system may work faster when its workload grows large, in which case μ_i increases in i.

The process **IO** is a continuous-time Markov chain of a special kind, a *birth-death process* (see Section C.5.4). The distribution of IO can be computed readily: Define $\rho_0 = 1$, and

$$\rho_i = \frac{\lambda}{\mu_i} \qquad i > 0$$

$$R_i = \Pi_{j \le i} \rho_j \qquad i \ge 0$$

$$R = \Sigma_{i=0}^{\infty} R_i$$

The system is stable provided R is finite. (This is true, for instance, when ρ_i is bounded above by some constant < 1 for sufficiently large i.) In that case, the pmf of IO is given by

$$g(i) = \frac{R_i}{R} \qquad i \ge 0$$

From this, G^0 and G^1 can be computed directly. Problem 7.4 presents a special case.

7.3.3.2 Multiple Processors

Here is another special case: Reconsider the independent-leadtime model of Section 7.2.1, and assume L has the exponential distribution with mean $E[L] = 1/\mu$. Here, **IO** has precisely the form above with $\mu_i = i\mu$. In this case, IO has the Poisson distribution with mean $\lambda/\mu = \lambda E[L]$.

This agrees with the earlier result. What is interesting is the following alternative interpretation: Instead of infinitely many processors, each with a constant processing rate, there is a single processor, whose processing rate grows linearly with $IO(t)$. The process **IO** is precisely the same as before, so IO is also, even though the order leadtimes are certainly not independent. Thus, the result of Section 7.2.1 depends less on the independence assumption than on the expansion of processing capacity with the workload. (Under either interpretation the supply system has unlimited capacity.)

Next, suppose there is a finite number m of independent processors, each with constant processing rate μ. So, $\mu_i = \min\{i, m\}\mu$. The code for this system is M/M/m. Set $\nu = \lambda/\mu$ and $\rho = \nu/m = \lambda/m\mu$, and assume $\rho < 1$. Then,

$$g(i) = \begin{cases} \dfrac{\nu^i/i!}{R} & 0 \le i \le m \\[2ex] \dfrac{\nu^m/m!\rho^{i-m}}{R} & i > m \end{cases}$$

where

$$R = \Sigma_{i=0}^{m} \frac{\nu^i}{i!} + \left(\frac{\nu^m}{m!}\right)\left(\frac{\rho}{1 - \rho}\right)$$

So, $g(i)$ looks like a Poisson pmf for $i \leq m$, and a geometric pmf for $i > m$. The system combines features of the M/M/1 and M/M/∞ systems, and so does its solution.

EXAMPLE 7.3.A, PART 2

Suppose the computer-repair company has 15 technicians. The processing rate is now $\mu = 1.1731$, so that $\nu = 13.639$, $\rho = 0.9093$, and $E[IO]$ is about 20 as before. The performance of selected base-stock policies is as follows:

s	$\overline{A}$	$\overline{B}$	$\overline{I}$
39	0.065	1.30	20.30
40	0.059	1.18	21.18
41	0.054	1.07	22.07
42	0.049	0.97	22.97
43	0.044	0.89	23.89
44	0.040	0.81	24.81
45	0.037	0.73	25.73

To meet the requirement of $\overline{A} \leq 0.05$, the company should set $s = 42$, between the values (28 and 62) of the pure parallel and sequential systems. This policy has average inventory about 23, also between the values for those two systems.

7.3.3.3 Finite Sources of Demand

Now, return to the case of a constant processing rate. Suppose that there is a finite number of potential customers, say n, and when a customer's demand is backordered, that customer makes no further demands. Here is an example: The customers are pieces of equipment, say aircraft or machine tools, and a demand occurs when a critical part fails on one of them. The inventory is a stock of spare parts. The supply process is a repair system. When a demand is backordered, then the corresponding machine cannot operate, and hence cannot generate subsequent demands.

Again, **IO** is a birth-death process, but now the demand rate depends on the current state. Specifically, suppose each customer has demand rate λ/n, so the total demand rate when there are no backorders is just λ. In general, when $IO(t) = i$, the demand rate becomes

$$\lambda_i = \begin{cases} \lambda & i \leq s \\ \dfrac{\lambda(n + s - i)}{n} & s < i < n + s \\ 0 & i \geq n + s \end{cases}$$

We leave it as an exercise for you (Problem 7.10) to determine the distribution of *IO* and formulas for performance measures.

In modeling a spare-parts inventory, often the demand rate is treated as constant. This is an approximation of the model above. It is reasonable when (but only when) n is large.

7.3.4 Lost Sales

Consider a lost-sales system like that of Section 7.2.3, but with only one processor. The processing times are exponentially distributed with mean $1/\mu$, and set $\rho = \lambda/\mu$. (It is *not* necessary to assume $\rho < 1$; because of the lost-sales feature, this system is stable for any $\rho \geq 0$.)

Now, **IO** behaves like a single-processor system with a finite occupancy limit; $IO(t) = s$ precisely when $I(t) = 0$, in which case arrivals (demands) are lost. The code for this system is M/M/1/s. Its solution is simple. (You can verify it yourself: **IO** is a finite-state birth-death process, as discussed in Section C.5.4.)

$$g_{IO}(i) = \frac{\rho^i}{\sum_{j=0}^{s} \rho^j} \qquad i = 0, \ldots, s$$

In case $\rho = 1$ this is the uniform pmf. Otherwise,

$$g_{IO}(i) = \frac{(1 - \rho)\rho^i}{1 - \rho^{s+1}} \qquad i = 0, \ldots, s$$

For $\rho < 1$, $g_{IO}(i) = g(i)/G(s)$, where g and G are the pmf and cdf of the geometric distribution with parameter ρ. That is, g_{IO} truncates the solution of the corresponding backlog model, just as in Section 7.2.3.

Again, $\overline{A} = g_{IO}(s)$, so the lost sales rate is $\lambda g_{IO}(s)$, and $\overline{OF} = \lambda[1 - g_{IO}(s)]$. For $\rho = 1, \overline{I} = \frac{1}{2}s$, while for $\rho \neq 1$,

$$\overline{I} = s - \frac{\rho}{1 - \rho} + \frac{(s + 1)\rho^{s+1}}{1 - \rho^{s+1}}$$

Several related systems can be analyzed in the same way. For example, for a general processing-time distribution (Section 7.3.2.2) with $\rho < 1$, first calculate g for the backorders case, and then truncate it at s.

7.3.5 Imperfect Quality

7.3.5.1 Markovian Processing

Return to the M/M/1 system with backorders. Suppose now that each unit, on completing processing, turns out to be defective with probability δ. Aside from the different supply system, the scenario is the same as in Section 7.2.6. This model is a stochastic analogue of the finite-capacity deterministic model of Section 3.6.3 in Chapter 3. For now, assume we inspect each unit on receipt and discard the defectives. Again, $\xi = 1 - \delta$.

While the processor is working, the output of nondefective units is a thinned Poisson process, itself a Poisson process with rate $\xi\mu$ (Section C.5.6). Call this the effective processing rate. The system is thus identical to one with perfect quality but this slower processing rate. All the results of Section 7.3.2.1 apply, with $\rho = \lambda/(\xi\mu)$.

Just as in the deterministic model, defects waste production capacity. If the defect rate is too high, an otherwise stable system can be rendered unstable. Within the range of stability, however, the effects of poor quality are more significant than in the deterministic case. For example, the quantity $\rho/(1 - \rho)$ now becomes $\lambda/(\xi\mu - \lambda)$, which is very sensitive even to small δ if μ is near λ. The stochastic elements of the system, including quality itself, amplify the impact of bad quality. Also, the effects are stronger here than in the uncapacitated system of Section 7.2.6. Poor quality has the greatest impact in the presence of *both* uncertainty and limited capacity.

7.3.5.2 General Processing Times

These effects are even more pronounced in a supply system which, were it not for quality problems, would perform more reliably than the M/M/1 system. Consider an M/G/1 system with generic processing time S. Now, producing a defective unit has the same effect as requiring that unit to repeat the processing operation. Thus (using the same logic as in Section 7.2.6), the *effective* processing time is a new random variable S', where

$$E[S'] = \frac{E[S]}{\xi}$$

$$V[S'] = \frac{V[S]}{\xi} + \frac{E^2[S]\delta}{\xi^2}$$

$$\psi_{S'}^2 = \delta + (1 - \delta)\psi_S^2$$

Referring to (7.3.2), δ affects μ and ρ just as in the M/M/1 case, but there is an additional effect through $\psi_{S'}^2$: If the nominal processing time S is relatively predictable, with $\psi_S^2 < 1$, then $\psi_{S'}^2 > \psi_S^2$. In particular, if S is constant ($\psi_S^2 = 0$), then $\psi_{S'}^2 = \delta$. In sum, defects can induce variability in the processing times. This effect is absent in the M/M/1 model above, precisely because $\psi_S^2 = 1$ there. (Problem 7.11 obtains sharper results for the case where S has a CPH distribution.)

7.3.5.3 Delayed Inspection

Returning to the M/M/1 model, consider the postponed-inspection scenario of Section 3.6 (cases 3 and 4), where defects are discovered only when units are given to customers; units are inspected, in effect, by the customers themselves. When a demand occurs, withdraw a unit from inventory, and inspect it; if it is defective, discard it, and withdraw another unit, and so forth. It is possible that the entire inventory turns out defective, in which case the demand must be backlogged. When there are backorders outstanding and a unit arrives from the supply system, inspection occurs instantaneously, as before.

Compared to the immediate-inspection case, this one requires a more elaborate analysis (Problem 7.12). The results, however, are simple and intriguing: Setting $\rho_+ = 1 - (1 - \rho)\xi$,

$$\bar{B}(s) = \left(\frac{\rho}{1 - \rho}\right)\rho_+^s \qquad \bar{I}(s) = \left(\frac{\rho}{1 - \rho_+}\right)(1 - \rho_+^s)$$

Observe, $\overline{B}(s)$ has precisely the same geometric form as in the immediate-inspection scenario, and the constant $\rho/(1-\rho) = \overline{B}(0)$ is the same in both cases. Here, however, the geometric-decay rate ρ_+ is *larger* than ρ, so $\overline{B}(s)$ decreases more slowly as s increases. Intuitively, postponing inspection makes the system harder to manage, for it creates yet another source of uncertainty. When there is inventory on hand, some of it may be defective, and we do not know how much. So, we need more inventory to protect against backorders.

7.3.6 Processing Networks

7.3.6.1 Markovian Processing

Now, suppose the supply system is a network of J nodes. The initial node and movements between nodes are governed by routing probabilities r_{ij}, just as in Section 7.2.7. Again, the r_{ij} can be interpreted as defect rates. Here, however, each node consists of just a single processor that operates like the ·/M/1 system above. Let μ_j be the processing rate for node j. (The imperfect-quality system of Section 7.3.5.1 with immediate inspection is the special case with $J = 1$.) This model is called a *Jackson network,* after its inventor, Jackson [1957, 1963].

Assume that the matrix $I - R$ is nonsingular, so the network is open, and every order ultimately leaves it. Equation (7.2.4) then gives the total input rates λ_j. Set $\rho_j = \lambda_j/\mu_j$, and assume too that $\rho_j < 1$ for all j, so the capacity of each node is adequate to process its input.

As in Section 7.2.7, the equilibrium occupancies IO_j are independent. Here, however, each IO_j has the geometric distribution with parameter ρ_j, as if node j were an M/M/1 system operating in isolation. Now, IO is the sum of the IO_j, that is, the sum of independent, geometrically distributed random variables. Consequently, IO has a DPH distribution, and we can compute the performance measures using the matrix-algebraic formulas for G^0 and G^1, as in (7.3.4).

This distribution can be constructed directly, but there is a convenient alternative method: Let $L^= = \sum_{j=1}^J L_j$, where L_j is an exponentially distributed random variable with parameter $\nu_j = \mu_j - \lambda_j = \mu_j(1-\rho_j)$, and the L_j are independent. (Thus, L_j would be the leadtime at node j, if node j did operate in isolation.) So, $L^=$ has the CPH distribution with parameters $(\boldsymbol{\nu}, N)$, where $\boldsymbol{\nu}$ is the unit J-vector $\mathbf{e}_1'$, and N is the $J \times J$ matrix

$$N = \begin{pmatrix} \nu_1 & -\nu_1 & & & \\ & \nu_2 & -\nu_2 & & \\ & & \ddots & \ddots & \\ & & & \ddots & -\nu_{J-1} \\ & & & & \nu_J \end{pmatrix}$$

Then, $IO = D(L^=)$, which has the DPH distribution with parameters $P = \lambda(\lambda I + N)^{-1}$ and $\boldsymbol{\pi} = \boldsymbol{\nu} P$.

7.3.6.2 Constant Processing Times

Now, consider a series system where the processing time S_j at node j is the constant $1/\mu_j$. Let $S^* = \max\{S_j : 1 \leq j \leq J\}$, and consider an M/G/1 system with processing time S^* and input rate λ. It turns out that *the total order-waiting time L_Q is precisely the same in the series system and in this M/G/1 system.* So, L here is simply the sum of all the processing times $S = \Sigma_j S_j = \Sigma_j (1/\mu_j)$, plus L_Q in the M/G/1 system. Section 7.3.8 explains how to use this fact to compute the distribution of *IO.*

Let j^* indicate any node for which $S_{j^*} = S^*$. We call j^* a *bottleneck.* The bottlenecks determine L_Q. If we remove one of the other nodes, L is reduced by that node's processing time, but L_Q remains unaffected. Only if we remove all bottlenecks is L_Q itself reduced. Such behavior is quite different from the Markovian network above, where each node's contribution to L is independent of the others, and the removal of any node reduces waiting as well as processing time.

7.3.6.3 More Complex Networks

Certain more general networks also have simple solutions, for instance, when each node has several identical Markovian processors working in parallel, as in Section 7.3.3.2. Unfortunately, other important models do not. Even for a series system with nonexponential and nonconstant processing times, it is generally impossible to obtain the exact distribution of *IO.* (Approximations have been developed; see the Notes.)

Another important but problematic model is a *finite-buffer series system:* Imagine each node's queue occupying a physical storage area, or buffer, of limited capacity. When the buffer is full, the prior node is *blocked;* it is unable or forbidden to process any units, even if there are some available in its own queue. Even with exponential processing times, it is difficult to determine whether such a system is stable, let alone its performance characteristics. (Again, approximations are available; see the Notes.)

7.3.7 Multiple Input Sources

Consider any of the systems above. Suppose that, in addition to our orders, the supply system has to process other work. This forms another Poisson process with rate λ', independent of our orders. Assume that all units have the same processing-time distribution and otherwise are treated identically.

The overall input to the supply system is then a Poisson process with rate $\lambda_+ = \lambda + \lambda'$. Suppose we can compute the pmf $g_+(\cdot)$ of the total number of units in the system, IO_+. It turns out that each unit in the system has probability $\theta = \lambda/\lambda_+$ of being one of our orders, independently of the identities of the other units. Therefore, the *conditional* distribution of *IO,* given $IO_+ = n$, is binomial with parameters (n, θ). Deconditioning on *IO* yields

$$g(i) = \Sigma_{n=i}^{\infty} \binom{n}{1} \theta^i (1-\theta)^{n-i} g_+(n) \qquad i \geq 0$$

This technique is called *binomial disaggregation.*

For example, in the M/M/1 system with service rate μ, IO_+ has the geometric distribution with parameter $\rho_+ = \lambda_+/\mu$, as shown above. A simple calculation shows that *IO* is also geometric with parameter $\rho = \lambda/[\lambda + (\mu - \lambda_+)]$ and mean $\rho/(1-\rho) = \lambda/(\mu - \lambda_+)$.

More generally, suppose IO_+ has a DPH distribution with parameters $(\boldsymbol{\pi}_+, P_+)$, where $\boldsymbol{\pi}_+ = \boldsymbol{\nu}_+ P_+$ for some vector $\boldsymbol{\nu}_+$ with $\boldsymbol{\nu}_+\mathbf{e} = 1$. (Several models above have distributions of this form.) Then, IO also has a DPH distribution with parameters $(\boldsymbol{\pi}, P)$, where

$$P = \theta P_+[I - (1 - \theta)P_+]^{-1} \qquad \boldsymbol{\pi} = \boldsymbol{\nu}_+ P \tag{7.3.5}$$

(See Problem 7.5.) Formulas (7.3.4) then yield the performance measures.

7.3.8 Customer Waiting Time

Many of the supply systems above are *sequential;* they complete orders in the same sequence the orders are placed. The single-processor systems of Section 7.3.2 are sequential, as are the series networks of Section 7.3.6, but not a network with feedback. Suppose also that the total leadtime of an order is entirely unaffected by the arrivals and processing times of subsequent orders. This rules out the systems of Section 7.3.3 with load-dependent processing rates. Continue to assume Poisson demand, a base-stock policy, and backorders.

Under these conditions, Theorem 6.2.4 of Section 6.2.4 applies. (If you examine its proof carefully, you will find that it works.) That is, the backorders random variable B has the same distribution as $D(BW)$, the demand during a customer's waiting time. Setting $s = 0$ yields $IO = D(L)$ as a special case. These facts have several interesting and useful implications:

First, consider the Markovian processing network of Section 7.3.6.1. There, we constructed a random variable $L^{=}$ and found that $IO = D(L^{=})$. Therefore, for a series system (with no feedback), $L^{=}$ is identical to L, the actual leadtime experienced by units in the supply system. (With feedback, however, these two random variables have different distributions.)

Next, consider the series system with constant processing times of Section 7.3.6.2. Recall, S^* denotes the maximal processing time, and S the total processing time over the nodes. Here, IO is the sum of two independent random variables: The first is $D(S - S^*)$, which has a Poisson distribution with mean $\lambda(S - S^*)$. The second is the occupancy of the M/G/1 system with processing time S^*; we can compute or approximate its distribution as in Section 7.3.2.2. The full distribution of IO is the convolution of these two.

In general, the mean and variance of IO can be obtained easily from those of L:

$$E[IO] = \lambda E[L]$$

$$V[IO] = \lambda E[L] + \lambda^2 V[L]$$

Notice the crucial difference between a sequential system and the parallel-processing system of Section 7.2.2, both assuming Poisson demand: There, $V[IO] = E[IO] = \lambda E[L]$; the second term in $V[IO]$ above is absent. In a sequential system, however, the variance of the leadtime *does* play an important role. (Here, of course, L is not specified with the data of the model; it is determined by the interaction of the demand and supply processes.) In all the sequential systems above, moreover, $V[L]$ is positive, even in the M/G/1 model with constant processing times. And, given a sequential and a parallel model with equal values of $E[L]$, the sequential model will always produce larger values of $\bar{B}$, and hence $\bar{I}$, for all s. (See Problem 7.6. Figure 7.3.1 above illustrates this fact. Section 7.5 further explores the effects of $V[L]$ on performance.)

A similar relationship holds between the moments of B and BW:

$$E[B] = \lambda E[BW]$$

$$V[B] = \lambda E[BW] + \lambda^2 V[BW]$$

Section 7.5 explains how to compute the entire distribution of BW for certain important cases, including the M/G/1 system with CPH processing times and the series network with Markovian processing.

7.3.9 World-Driven Demand

When we relax the Poisson-demand assumption, there are basically four possibilities: First, for very special cases, there are simple, exact results. This is so, for instance, for GI/M/1 systems, where demand is a renewal process, and there is a single Markovian processor. Second, for a somewhat broader range of systems, it is possible to compute the distribution of IO numerically. There is an algorithm to solve the general MCDC/M/1 system, for example. Such specialized results and methods, while interesting and useful, are too special or too complex for us to cover here. Third, one can estimate performance via computer simulation.

Fourth, there are reasonably accurate approximations for a still broader class of systems. These are appropriate when we want to see the general pattern of system behavior, and so are willing to forego total precision. Consider a $\cdot$/G/1 supply system and a world-driven demand process, letting ψ_D^2 denote its variance/mean ratio. The following is a useful approximation for $E[L_Q]$:

$$E[L_Q] = \frac{1}{2}(\psi_D^2 + \psi_S^2)\left(\frac{\rho}{1-\rho}\right)\left(\frac{1}{\mu}\right) \qquad (7.3.6)$$

Notice, (7.3.2) is identical to (7.3.6) with $\psi_D^2 = 1$, so this approximation agrees with the exact result for the M/G/1 system. In general, the term $\frac{1}{2}(\psi_D^2 + \psi_S^2)$ represents an overall variation factor, combining the effects of demand and supply variability. The formula also works for lumpy demand, assuming each unit is processed individually, as in Section 7.2.5.

The approximation works especially well when ρ is large. In fact, this is a heavy-traffic approximation. The true value and (7.3.6) agree in the limit (in a certain sense) as $\rho \to 1$. Even for moderate ρ, the approximation often works well, though not always. (Researchers have developed a host of refinements to improve its accuracy; see Heyman and Sobel [1982], for example.)

Why do we use similar notation for ψ_D^2 and ψ_S^2? Let **S** indicate the *supply process,* that is, $S(t)$ is the cumulative output through time t, *assuming* the processor works continually, never stopping. Because the processing times S are i.i.d., **S** is a renewal process. It so happens that ψ_S^2 is precisely the long-run variance/mean ratio for this process. So,

ψ_D^2 and ψ_S^2 really do measure similar quantities. In fact, (7.3.6) applies more generally to a world-driven supply process **S**, i.e., one with the same properties as **D** discussed in Section 6.3. In that setting ψ_S^2 is *defined* as the variance/mean ratio.

The heavy-traffic theory also shows that, as ρ approaches 1, the distribution of L becomes exponential with $E[L]$ given by (7.3.6). (Of course, $E[L]$ includes $E[S]$ as well as $E[L_Q]$, but $E[L_Q]$ dominates for large ρ.) This suggests using the exponential distribution to approximate L.

How does this approximation work for the M/G/1 system? It is inexact, but close: The variance of an exponential variable is the square of its mean. For the M/G/1 system, the first term in $V[L_Q]$ is the square of the first term in $E[L_Q]$, and when ρ is near 1 these terms dominate the others.

As for IO, it remains true that $E[IO] = \lambda E[L]$, and (7.3.6) estimates $E[L]$. Actually, the following approximation works a bit better:

$$E[IO] = \frac{1}{2}(\psi_D^2 + \psi_S^2)\left(\frac{\rho}{1-\rho}\right) \tag{7.3.7}$$

(This agrees with the result for the M/M/1 system.) Moreover, by yet another result of heavy-traffic theory, the distribution of IO itself is approximately exponential. Section 7.3.11 explores this approximation further.

7.3.10 Larger Batches

7.3.10.1 Order-Driven Control

Things become considerably more difficult for an (r, q) policy with $q > 1$, even with Poisson demand. As mentioned in Section 7.2.4, the supply system then becomes a bulk queue, which is difficult to analyze.

The approximation scheme there is plausible here too: Approximate $\widetilde{IO}$ by an exponential distribution as in Section 7.3.9 above with $\psi_D^2 = 1/q$, and then use the result to approximate IO and IN as in Section 7.2.4. This approach should work well for a heavily loaded system (ρ near 1), but to our knowledge it has not been tested.

7.3.10.2 Direct Processor Control

In the models above, we control the supply system indirectly through the stream of orders we send it. The system works when it finds orders to work on, and it shuts off when the orders are exhausted. This is the scenario outlined in Section 7.1 and followed throughout most of the chapter.

Now, suppose we have a direct communication link to the supply system: Instead of placing orders, we can tell the system precisely what to do. For simplicity, suppose there is but a single processor with two possible states, on and off, so our instructions to it are signals to start or stop producing.

First, suppose we follow the analogue of a base-stock policy: When the net inventory falls below some fixed value s, start the processor, and stop it when the net inventory is s or more. A moment's thought should convince you that this system is identical to the order-driven one. Given the same demand sequence and unit processing times, the processor turns on and off at the same times, and **IN** is the same in the two cases. The order stream carries essentially the same information as the direct production signals.

Now, consider a more general policy: There are two policy variables, r and s, where $r < s$. Suppose the system starts at time 0 with $IN(0) = s$ and the processor off. Nothing happens until $IN(t)$ hits r. At that moment we turn the processor on. When $IN(t)$ hits s, we turn the processor off. Now the system is back at the starting point, and we continue in the same manner.

This policy makes sense when there is a setup cost to start (and/or a shutdown cost to stop) production, or simply a cost to send a signal of either kind. Increasing the range $s - r$ means that such costs are incurred less frequently. In this sense the policy is similar in spirit to an (r, q) policy; it exploits scale economies. (If $s = r + 1$, clearly, the policy reduces to a base-stock policy.) As we shall see, however, this direct-control system is considerably easier to analyze than a standard order-transfer system.

Call this an (r, s) policy. (The same notation is used for a related policy in Section 6.6.) The model is a stochastic version of the deterministic limited-capacity models of Chapter 3, Section 3.4.

As in Section 7.1, define $IO(t) = s - IN(t)$, and call **IO** the occupancy of the supply system. Again, **IO** does not depend on the particular values of r and s, but it does depend on the difference $s - r$, denoted by q. (Of course, q is not the batch size here. Indeed, q is the *minimal* number of units produced during a run; more units may be needed to compensate for demands occurring during the run.) Also, let **X** (capital χ) be the stochastic process indicating whether the processor is on or off; $\chi(t) = 1$ means on, while $\chi(t) = 0$ means off.

Now, assume that in all other ways the system functions just like the M/M/1 system above: Demand is Poisson, and the unit processing times are exponentially distributed. Problem 7.7 asks you to demonstrate that the joint process (**IO, X**) is a continuous-time Markov chain and to derive its stationary distribution. Specifically, letting $g(i, \chi) = \Pr\{IO=i, \mathbf{X}=\chi\}$, $\chi \in \{0, 1\}$, $i \geq 0$,

$$g(i, 0) = \frac{1 - \rho}{q} \qquad 0 \leq i < q$$

$$g(i, 1) = \frac{\rho(1 - \rho^i)}{q} \qquad 1 \leq i \leq q$$

$$g(i, 1) = \frac{\rho(1 - \rho^q)\rho^{i-q}}{q} \qquad i > q$$

Let us compute the performance measures: For simplicity, assume $r \geq 0$, so $s \geq q$. Then,

$$\bar{B} = E[[IO - s]^+] = \left(\frac{1}{q}\right)\left(\frac{\rho}{1 - \rho}\right)^2 (\rho^r - \rho^{r+q})$$

$$= \left(\frac{1}{q}\right)[G^2(r) - G^2(r + q)]$$

where G^2 is the second-order loss function for the geometric distribution. Likewise,

$$\begin{aligned}\bar{I} &= s - E[IO] + \bar{B} \\ &= \frac{1}{2}(q+1) + r - \left(\frac{\rho}{1-\rho}\right) + \bar{B}\end{aligned}$$

(Problem 7.7 also asks you to verify these expressions.) These formulas are precisely analogous to those for an (r, q) policy in Section 6.2.3, namely (6.2.12) to (6.2.13), but they use a geometric instead of a Poisson distribution. Finally, interpret $\overline{OF}$ as the frequency of production starts. Production commences at a transition from state $(q-1, 0)$ to $(q, 1)$, and this event occurs at rate

$$\overline{OF} = \lambda g(q-1, 0) = \frac{(1-\rho)\lambda}{q}$$

This measure too has the same form as before, except for the constant term $(1-\rho)$. (Indeed, the *average* run length is $q' = q/(1-\rho)$ units, and $\overline{OF} = \lambda/q'$.)

More generally, suppose the unit processing times have a CPH distribution, as in Section 7.3.2.2. The results have the same form as those above:

$$g(i, 0) = \frac{1-\rho}{q} \qquad 0 \le i < q$$

$$g(i, 1) = \frac{\boldsymbol{\nu} P(1 - P^i)\mathbf{e}}{q} \qquad 1 \le i \le q$$

$$g(i, 1) = \frac{\boldsymbol{\nu} P(1 - P^q)P^{i-q}\mathbf{e}}{q} \qquad i > q$$

$$\bar{B} = \left(\frac{1}{q}\right)[G^2(r) - G^2(r+q)]$$

$$\bar{I} = \tfrac{1}{2}(q+1) + r - \boldsymbol{\nu} P(I-P)^{-1}\mathbf{e} + \bar{B}$$

$$\overline{OF} = \frac{(1-\rho)\lambda}{q}$$

where G^2 is the second-order loss function of the DPH distribution with parameters $(\boldsymbol{\nu}, P)$. (An explicit formula for G^2 is given in Section 7.5 and Section C.4.4.)

Because the performance measures have the same form as in the constant-leadtime model, the qualitative results of Section 6.2.3 still apply; e.g., $\bar{B}$ is decreasing and convex in r. Also, the algorithm of Section 6.5.4 finds a cost-minimizing policy, and, up to a continuous approximation (see below), the bounds of Section 6.5.3 remain valid.

7.3.11 The Exponential Approximation

Recall, the normal approximation of IO works well for a constant-leadtime supply system, and more generally, for an independent-leadtime system. Perusing the results of this section, it is evident that the exponential distribution plays a similar role for limited-capacity systems:

For the world-driven-demand, single-processor system of Section 7.3.9, the distribution of *IO* is approximately exponential for large ρ. Geometric distributions appear in several places, and a geometric distribution has essentially the same shape as an exponential. In other places, *IO* has a DPH distribution, and the tail of a DPH distribution is approximately geometric, hence exponential. (For a Markovian network, in fact, $G^0(i) \approx \rho^{i+1}$ for large i, where $\rho = \max\{\rho_j\}$.) Finally, for the (r, s) policy of Section 7.3.10.2, the performance formulas look like those of Chapter 6 for an (r, q) policy, but using a geometric or DPH distribution, again essentially exponential in form.

Thus, the exponential distribution captures the basic, qualitative behavior of a limited-capacity system. That distribution has only one parameter, its mean $\nu = E[IO]$. To estimate it, we need *some* information about the supply and demand processes, but not all that much. For a single-processor system, for instance, we may use (7.3.7). In most cases, ν is nearly proportional to $1/(1-\rho)$. Also, the standard deviation is $\sigma = \nu$.

The performance measures for a base-stock policy are given in Section 6.4.2, but we repeat them here for convenience:

$$\overline{A}(s) = F^0(s) = e^{-s/\nu}$$

$$\overline{B}(s) = F^1(s) = \nu e^{-s/\nu}$$

$$\overline{I}(s) = s - \nu + \overline{B}(s) = \nu\left(\frac{s}{\nu} - 1 + e^{-s/\nu}\right)$$

So, to meet a target value $1 - \omega\_$ for $\overline{A}$, set $s = [-\ln(1-\omega\_)]\nu$. In that case, $\overline{I} = [-\ln(1-\omega\_) - \omega\_]\nu$. For average-cost minimization, following the approach of Section 6.5.2,

$$s^* = -\ln(1-\omega)\nu$$

$$C^* = hs^* = h[-\ln(1-\omega)]\nu$$

Let us examine the behavior of these formulas and compare them with those for the normal approximation. Since $\sigma = \nu$, it is clear that σ plays essentially the same role in both cases. It is a scale factor in the ratio s/σ, and it multiplies $\overline{B}$, $\overline{I}$, s^*, and C^*. So again, σ is a key determinant of system performance; the original system parameters (ρ, ψ_D^2, ψ_S^2, etc.) affect performance through σ.

However, σ reflects limited capacity, mainly through the explosive factor $1/(1-\rho)$, an effect absent in a parallel-processing system. Also, given two systems with Poisson demand and equal ν, one parallel and one sequential, σ is different in the two cases; $\sigma = \sqrt{\nu}$ for the parallel system, but $\sigma = \nu$ in the sequential case. In general, *the exponential approximation and the finite-capacity supply systems it describes do not exhibit statistical economies of scale.* For instance, if (7.3.7) is used, σ includes a term proportional to the demand-variance ratio ψ_D^2, not its square root. Likewise, σ grows at least as fast as λ, not $\sqrt{\lambda}$, even ignoring the factor $1/(1-\rho)$. That factor, of course, grows hyperbolically in λ, indicating strong *diseconomies* of scale.

In other words, while the benefits of system-improvement efforts can still be estimated through σ, those benefits are quite different here, and usually greater, than with a parallel system. In particular, one way to improve the system is to increase its capacity and thus lower ρ. Obviously, this has no meaning for an infinite-capacity system.

Furthermore, s and $\bar{I}$ are more sensitive to $\omega\_$ than their normal-approximation counterparts. In the normal case, s and $\bar{I}$ increase only as the square root of $-\ln(1 - \omega\_)$ as $\omega\_$ approaches 1, but here they are linear in this quantity. (s^* and C^* depend on ω in the same way.) This finding coincides with the discussion of Figure 7.3.2 in Section 7.3.2.1. A capacity limit implies that much more inventory is required to achieve good service.

Virtually every real supply system has elements of both models. No system truly has unlimited capacity, but capacity can often be adjusted in response to workload variations, at least to some extent. Given the choice, then, which is the "right" form, the normal or the exponential? There is no conclusive answer. If hard capacity limits are likely to be encountered frequently, then the exponential approximation is probably a better choice, but the normal is superior when capacity is relatively flexible.

There are more refined approximations, intermediate between these two. A gamma distribution, for instance, has two parameters, allowing (indeed requiring) a separate estimate of $V[IO]$ as well as $E[IO]$. It shares many of the qualitative characteristics of an exponential, but for large values of its shape parameter (n), it looks nearly normal. This approach is discussed further in Section 7.5 below. (Problem 7.4 explores a system where capacity is somewhat but not totally flexible. There, IO has a negative-binomial distribution, which can be fairly well approximated by a gamma.)

7.4 Exogenous, Sequential Supply Systems

7.4.1 Description

7.4.1.1 Examples and Summary

This section presents a different type of supply system. Here are some examples to motivate the idea:

Imagine that we operate a small retail store and order goods from a large manufacturer. Think of the supplier's production and transportation activities as a processing network. For simplicity, suppose this network is sequential; it delivers our orders in the same sequence as they are placed. Having read Section 7.3.6, we *could* create a network model of the kind discussed there to represent the supplier. The manufacturer doubtless has many other customers, so we would adjust the model accordingly, along the lines of Section 7.3.7.

Something seems out of balance: The great virtue of the models of Section 7.3 is that they capture the dynamic effects of orders on the supply system. Each order's leadtime depends on the congestion it finds in the supply system, which in turn depends on prior orders. The supply system is *endogenous* in this sense.

This is important in other contexts, but here such effects are negligible. While the supplier's overall workload, and hence the leadtimes we experience, may fluctuate over time, *our* demands and orders contribute little to these fluctuations. We can thus reasonably approximate the supplier's network as *exogenous,* ignoring the effect of our orders. As we shall see, this means we can do without much of the fine detail of a processing-network model.

Here is another example: Suppose leadtimes represent travel times. When we place an order, the corresponding goods are loaded onto a vehicle, say a truck, a train, or a ship. The vehicle then travels to us, over a highway, a track, or an ocean. The vehicles are identical for all orders, and they all follow the same route. The transit times can vary, however, because of local traffic conditions, switch failures, the weather, and so forth. Now, suppose that the traffic our vehicles add to the overall load on the transport system is negligible. Thus, we can again think of the supply system as exogenous. Also, suppose that none of our vehicles ever passes another, so the system is sequential.

These examples emphasize the two key properties of the systems considered here: The starting point is an exogenous supply system, whose evolution is independent of our demands and orders; the operation of this system determines our leadtimes. This system is sequential, so our orders do not cross in time. In practical terms, the difference between this scenario and the prior section's is one of *scale.* We are assuming, in effect, that the supply system is large relative to our operations. Of course, no real supply system is truly exogenous; like the parallel supply system of Section 7.2, this model is a limiting case, but a useful one.

EXAMPLE 7.4.A

A Japanese trading company purchases hardwoods from an international lumber company and distributes them to furniture makers throughout Japan. The supplier harvests logs in Southeast Asia, processes them into lumber, and ships them all over the world. For each of its major markets, including Japan, it fills orders in sequence. Although the trading company is large, it is only one among many customers of the lumber company. Thus, from the trading company's viewpoint, the supply system is essentially exogenous.

The advantage of this approach is that it allows us to apply essentially the same methodology used in Section 6.3 for the case of constant leadtimes. In particular, we can easily evaluate performance for *any* world-driven demand process using *any* (r, q) policy. This is in sharp contrast to the other stochastic-leadtime systems above, where non-Poisson demands or large batch sizes complicate matters significantly. Furthermore, the optimization methods and results of Section 6.5 all apply.

7.4.1.2 Formulation

We now describe the supply system in formal terms: The core of the model is a Markov process $\mathbf{Z} = \{Z(t) : t \geq 0\}$, which describes the state of the supply system. In addition, there is a stochastic process $\mathbf{L} = \{L(t) : t \geq 0\}$, which depends on $\mathbf{Z}$ in a quasi-Markov way: For each t, given $Z(t)$, the distribution of $L(t)$ depends on $Z(u)$ only for $u \geq t$, not $u < t$. That is, conditional on $Z(t)$, $L(t)$ is independent of the past of $\mathbf{Z}$, but certain common events may affect $L(t)$ and the future of $\mathbf{Z}$. Moreover, the joint process $(\mathbf{Z}, \mathbf{L})$ is well-behaved, in the sense of Section 6.2.1; it is ergodic and has a limiting distribution, represented by the random variable (Z, L).

For each t, $L(t)$ is a scalar with $0 \leq L(t) < \infty$. We call $L(t)$ the *virtual leadtime* at time t. If an order is placed at time t, its leadtime is $L(t)$; however, $L(t)$ is defined for all t.

Two additional assumptions are needed. First, (Z, L) is entirely independent of D; this is what exogenous means. Second, $t + L(t)$ is nondecreasing in t, which ensures that orders do not cross in time, i.e., the supply system is sequential.

FIGURE 7.4.1

Demands, orders, and receipts (stochastic leadtimes; exogenous, sequential supply).

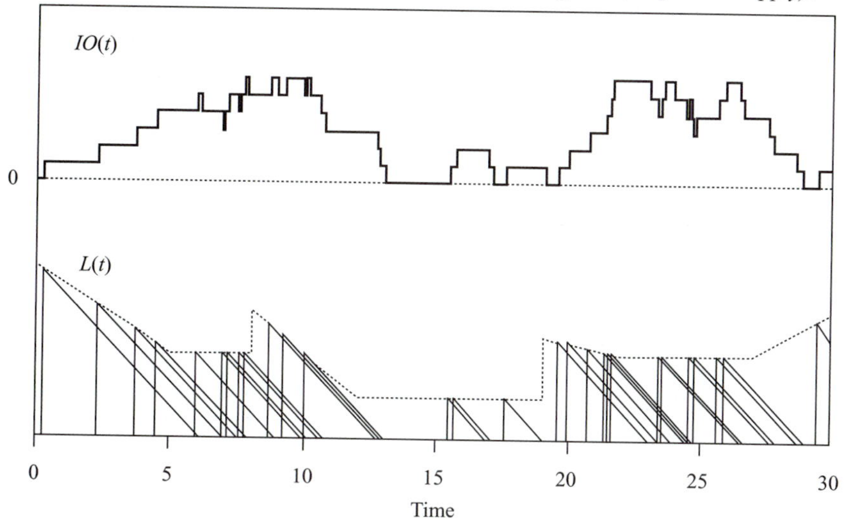

Figure 7.4.1 illustrates the interactions between demands, leadtimes, and orders, assuming a base-stock policy. The format is the same as Figure 6.2.1's. In the lower part of the figure, $L(t)$ is the dotted curve. Each demand is indicated by a vertical line of height $L(t)$, so the attached diagonal line meets the time axis at $t + L(t)$, when the corresponding order arrives. The upper part of the figure graphs $IO(t)$.

For example, consider a sequential processing network, like the manufacturer's system above, and assume its input is a Poisson process. (This is *not* **D;** remember, the supply system is exogenous.) Also, assume Markovian processing at each node. The state variable $Z(t)$ describes the current occupancy of each node (the exogenous analogue of the vector $[IO_j(t)]_j$ in Section 7.3.6). This **Z** is indeed a Markov process, specifically, a continuous-time Markov chain.

Let $L(t)$ be the time until all units now present depart the network; if the network is empty, $L(t) = 0$. Thus, each of our orders is a "virtual customer"; it rides along with one of the actual units, the one destined to leave the network last, adding nothing to that unit's processing times. Notice that **L** is dependent on **Z** in the manner above; $L(t)$ depends on $Z(t)$ and also the future processing times of units currently in the network, which also affect $Z(u)$, $u \geq t$. Under standard assumptions (e.g., stability), clearly, **(Z, L)** satisfies the conditions above.

Here is an alternative formulation of the same system: Imagine that, when a unit enters the network, it brings all the information needed to determine its processing times at the nodes. Now, $Z(t)$ includes, in addition to the occupancies, each unit's remaining processing times. This is sometimes called the "workload formulation." Given $Z(t)$, one can determine the entire future evolution of the network, insofar as it affects units already present at time t. Again, $L(t)$ is the time until all units now present depart. In this construction, $L(t)$ is a deterministic function of $Z(t)$.

These models may seem complex. Fortunately, we need them for conceptual purposes only. In the end, as we shall see, the performance of the system depends only on the distribution of L. For instance, although the original $(\mathbf{Z}, \mathbf{L})$ above and the workload formulation are different stochastic processes, they have the same equilibrium leadtime L, and that's what counts. (Incidentally, the workload formulation can be extended to a more general network, where the processing times have general distributions, and these times are independent over units.)

Here is a slight variation: Suppose $Z(t)$ includes, in addition to the information above, the processing times of the *next* unit to arrive. So, when a unit arrives, it inherits those processing times, and determines the following unit's times. Let $L(t)$ be the time until that next unit would depart, *if* it arrived at time t. (We may call this $L(t)$ the virtual sojourn time.) Here, provided the processing times are always positive, so are $L(t)$ and L. This is more realistic in most situations. Assuming markovian processing, in fact, L has the same distribution as $L^{=}$ in Section 7.3.6, i.e., a simple CPH distribution.

By the way, you might expect that observation of $Z(t)$ should affect our order decisions. Indeed it should. The story here is parallel to Section 6.3, where a world variable $W(t)$ drives demand: *Assume* that we do not have, or cannot use, current information about the supply system in the replenishment policy. When the supply system is some large network whose operations we cannot see, as in the examples above, this assumption makes perfect sense. So, it is reasonable to use a simple base-stock or (r, q) policy, depending on scale economies in supply, as before.

7.4.2 Analysis

First, we prove an analogue to Lemma 6.2.2:

LEMMA 7.4.1. For $t \geq 0$,

$$IN(t + L(t)) = IP(t) - D(t, t + L(t)] \tag{7.4.1}$$

PROOF. All and only those orders placed at time t or before arrive at or before time $t + L(t)$.

Now, consider a world-driven demand process satisfying the assumption of Section 6.3.3. Thus, Lemma 6.3.1 describes the limiting distribution of $(\mathbf{IP}, \mathbf{W})$, and for any *fixed* leadtime, Theorem 6.3.2 describes the limiting distribution of $\mathbf{IN}$ in terms of the leadtime demand.

For the actual stochastic-leadtime system, define the *leadtime demand* as the random variable $D = D(L)$. That is, start the processes $(\mathbf{W}, \mathbf{D})$ and $(\mathbf{Z}, \mathbf{L})$ in equilibrium at time 0, and observe the demand over the random time $L = L(0)$. Let $g(d|t)$ denote the pmf of $D(t)$, i.e., the leadtime demand for a constant leadtime t. Then, the pmf of D is

$$g(d) = E_L[\, g(d|L)\,] \qquad d \geq 0$$

That is, D is a mixture of the $D(t)$ over t, letting t be distributed as L.

We now show that the analogue of Theorem 6.3.2 describes $\mathbf{IN}$ in this case:

THEOREM 7.4.2. Under the assumptions above, the limiting distribution of the net inventory is described by the equation

$$IN = IP - D$$

where IP is uniformly distributed on the integers in the interval $[r + 1, r + q]$, D is the leadtime demand defined above, and IP and D are independent.

PROOF. We give an intuitive argument (which can easily be formalized): First, it is not hard to show that $IN(t + L(t))$ has the same limit as $IN(t)$ itself, namely IN. So consider the random variable $IP(t) - D(t, t + L(t)]$ in the right-hand side of (7.4.1). As $t \to \infty$, as in Lemma 6.3.1, $IP(t)$ goes to IP, a uniform random variable, independent of W. Also, since there is no interaction between the processes $(\mathbf{W}, \mathbf{D})$ and $(\mathbf{Z}, \mathbf{L})$, it is clear that $D(t, t + L(t)] \to D$. Combining these two limits yields the result.

This theorem is the exact analogue of the earlier results for constant leadtimes. It follows immediately that the performance criteria have exactly the same form. Let G^0 denote the ccdf of D, G^1 and G^2 its loss functions, and $\nu = E[D] = \lambda E[L]$.

COROLLARY 7.4.3.

$$\overline{A} = \left(\frac{1}{q}\right)[G^1(r) - G^1(r + q)] \tag{7.4.2}$$

$$\overline{B} = \left(\frac{1}{q}\right)[G^2(r) - G^2(r + q)] \tag{7.4.3}$$

$$\overline{I} = \frac{1}{2}(q + 1) + r - \nu + \overline{B} \tag{7.4.4}$$

Consequently, the average cost $C(r, q)$ has the same form as in Section 6.5, so the results there apply directly.

It is worth noting that, in the Poisson-demand, base-stock-policy case, the results coincide with those for an endogenous, limited-capacity system. The leadtime demand D here and IO there play the same role in performance, and $IO = D(L) = D$.

Here, of course, L is quite independent of the demand process, whereas there L is strongly affected by $\mathbf{D}$. Still, if the real supply system is not entirely exogenous, and we wish to study changes in λ, say, there is nothing to prevent us from specifying a different L for each λ to represent congestion, using what we know about endogenous systems. Strictly speaking, this is cheating, since the exogenous-supply model rules out such interactions. As an approximation, however, it is quite reasonable.

Many different processes $(\mathbf{Z}, \mathbf{L})$ can give rise to the same L. It is interesting and useful to see that *only* the distribution of L matters in the end, not finer details of the supply system. On the other hand, D reflects the *entire* distribution of L, not just its mean, unlike IO in the case of independent leadtimes. As Section 7.5.3 shows, this has major implications for the performance of the system.

The same approach works for lumpy demand, say a compound-Poisson process. The results are identical to those of Section 6.6, depending on the policy, with $D = D(L)$, as above.

7.4.3 (Approximate) Extensions

Although these results are more general than the two prior sections', the approach is somewhat inflexible. It cannot be extended easily to a lost-sales system, and imperfect quality also becomes problematic.

7.4.3.1 Lost Sales

Consider a lost-sales system. Reviewing the analysis above, troubles begin immediately: Lemma 7.4.1 no longer holds, because lost demands do not reduce the net inventory. The demand process effectively ceases to operate when $IN(t) = 0$. Since the rest of the analysis builds on the lemma, the entire approach breaks down. (The same is true of any system whose *effective* demand process, describing the demands actually filled, depends on the current value of $IN(t)$, including the finite-source demand model of Section 7.3.3.3.)

Here is an approximation, inspired by the results of the previous two sections: First, consider a base-stock policy. Let g and G indicate the distribution of D, as above, and estimate

$$\overline{A}(s) = \frac{g(s)}{G(s)}$$

$$\overline{OF}(s) = \lambda[1 - \overline{A}(s)]$$

$$\overline{I}(s) = \Sigma_{j=0}^{s} \frac{(s - j)g(j)}{G(s)}$$

These are precise analogues of the exact formulas of Section 7.2.3 and Section 7.3.4. For an (r, q) policy, simply average these quantities, again by analogy to prior results:

$$\overline{A}(r, q) = \left(\frac{1}{q}\right)\Sigma_{s=r+1}^{r+q} \overline{A}(s)$$

$$\overline{OF}(r, q) = \left(\frac{\lambda}{q}\right)[1 - \overline{A}(r, q)]$$

$$\overline{I}(r, q) = \left(\frac{1}{q}\right)\Sigma_{s=r+1}^{r+q} \overline{I}(s)$$

Here is an alternative approximation. These formulas *assume* that there is never more than one order outstanding. This assumption truly holds when $0 \leq r < q$, so in this case the formulas are exact.

$$\overline{A}(r, q) = \frac{G^1(r - 1)}{q + G^1(r)}$$

$$\overline{OF}(r, q) = \frac{\lambda}{q + G^1(r)}$$

$$\overline{I}(r, q) = \frac{[1/2(q + 1) + r - \nu + G^1(r - 1)]q}{q + G^1(r)}$$

(The derivation involves rather intricate methods and calculations, which we omit. See Hadley and Whitin [1963], pages 197–204.)

Which of these approximations works better? We know of no concrete evidence. We expect the first to be more accurate when q is small relative to r, and the second when q is relatively large.

Anyway, the (r, q) policy is a heuristic. See Section 9.6.5 of Chapter 9 for a more refined heuristic in the discrete-time setting.

7.4.3.2 Imperfect Quality

Return to the backorders case, but suppose the supply system sends us defective units, which we inspect and discover immediately. (If the supply system itself detects and corrects its own defects, simply include the resulting delays within L, based on the results of Section 7.3.5, and then use the no-defect model above. Here, in contrast, the supply system passes on some defective units to us.)

As in the lost-sales case, Lemma 7.4.1 breaks down, but for a different reason. The definition of $IP(t)$ becomes problematic: The inventory on hand consists of good-quality units, and backorders must be filled by such units. Some of the inventory on order, however, may ultimately turn out to be defective, and we do not know how much. Thus, the two components $IN(t)$ and $IO(t)$ of $IP(t)$ measure different things. We *cannot* simply add them to form $IP(t)$.

We do not yet know how to resolve this dilemma. For the constant-leadtime system, Section 7.2 provides exact (for $q = 1$) and approximate (for $q > 1$) methods. Chapter 9 presents a quite different approach. Perhaps these techniques can be adapted to cover the system here.

7.5 Leadtime-Demand Distributions

This section continues the study of exogenous, sequential supply systems, focusing on computational issues. Given **D** and L, what is the distribution of D? And, knowing D, can we efficiently compute its loss functions G^1 and G^2? We focus on a few specific cases.

Section 7.5.3 discusses certain approximations, and Section 7.5.4 treats the lumpy-demand case. All proofs are collected in Section 7.5.5.

7.5.1 Poisson Demand

First, assume that **D** is a Poisson process. Since $D = D(L)$, a formula like (6.2.16) describes the relation between the z-transform of D and the Laplace transform of L:

$$\tilde{g}_D(z) = \hat{f}_L[\lambda(1 - z)] \tag{7.5.1}$$

In addition, (6.2.16) itself characterizes the relation between B and BW.

We consider two particular leadtime distributions:

7.5.1.1 Gamma Leadtime

First, suppose that L has a gamma distribution (Section C.2.5.3). There are two parameters, μ and n, both positive numbers. $E[L] = n/\mu$ and $V[L] = n/\mu^2$. The Laplace transform is $\hat{f}_L(s) = [\mu/(\mu + s)]^n$. (A gamma distribution is often used in practice to approximate L. It requires estimates of $E[L]$ and $V[L]$ to fit μ and n, but no more information than that.)

Apply (7.5.1) to obtain

$$\tilde{g}(z) = \left(\frac{1 - p}{1 - pz}\right)^n$$

where $p = \lambda/(\lambda + \mu)$. Consulting Section C.2.3.6, we see that *the leadtime demand has the negative-binomial distribution* with parameters p and n. Section C.2.3.6 also shows how to compute the pmf and the loss functions.

EXAMPLE 7.5.A

The hardwood distributor of Example 7.4.A estimates the average leadtime for shipments of mahogany to be $E[L] = 1.5$ months, with a variance of $V[L] = 0.75$ months^2. Demand for mahogany is a Poisson process of rate $\lambda = 8$ (hundred board-meters/month). The supplier accepts orders only in units of 5 (hundred board-meters). The cost of holding inventory is $h = 1$ (thousand ¥/[(hundred board-meters)-month]), and the backorder penalty cost is $b = 9$ (in the same units). Since $q = 5$ is fixed, there is no need to include the order cost.

Use a gamma distribution to approximate L. Thus, $\mu = E[L]/V[L] = 1.5/0.75 = 2$ and $n = \mu E[L] = 2(1.5) = 3$. Thus, D has the negative-binomial distribution with parameters $n = 0.75$ and $p = 8/(8 + 2) = 0.8$. Using the negative-binomial formulas in Section C.1.3.6 within the performance measures of Section 7.4.2, we obtain the costs (in thousand ¥/month) of alternative (r, q) policies for $q = 5$:

r	$C(r, q)$
15	18.55
16	17.73
17	17.16
18	16.80
19	16.63
20	16.63
21	16.77
22	17.04
23	17.41
24	17.88
25	18.42

Evidently, $r = 19$ or 20 yields the lowest cost.

Let us explore the effects of leadtime variance on performance in this case. Figure 7.5.1 displays the results for $\lambda = 10$, $E[L] = 1$, and four values of $V[L]$. Evidently, performance deteriorates as the variance increases; in other words, there are real benefits to be gained by reducing leadtime variation.

For $n = 1$, the negative binomial reduces to a geometric distribution. This form appears too in the multiple-source system of Section 7.3.7, and it is worthwhile to compare the two cases. Here, p lies between 0 and 1 for *any* $\lambda > 0$, because $E[L] = 1/\mu$ is specified exogenously. There, the corresponding parameter is $\rho = \lambda/[\lambda + (\mu - \lambda_+)] = \lambda/(\mu - \lambda')$, where μ is the processing rate, λ' the arrival rate from other sources, and

FIGURE 7.5.1

Performance of base-stock policies (effect of leadtime variance).

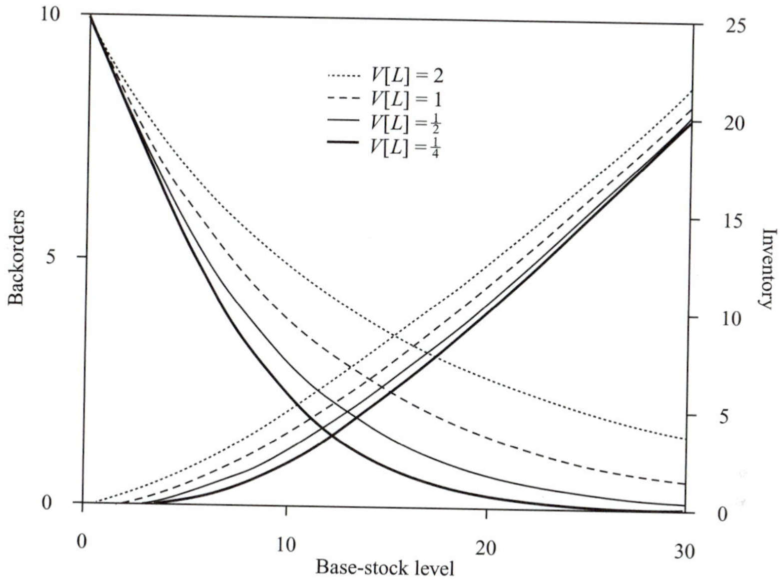

$\lambda_+ = \lambda + \lambda'$ the total arrival rate. So, ρ is more sensitive than p to λ. But, if μ and λ' are large relative to λ, this interaction effect is slight. The exogenous system is thus a limiting case of the multiple-source system, as the discussion of Section 7.4.1 suggests.

7.5.1.2 Phase-Type Leadtime

Next, suppose L has a (continuous) phase-type, or CPH, distribution. Such a distribution is specified by an m-vector $\boldsymbol{\mu}$ and an $m \times m$ matrix M. Assume $\boldsymbol{\mu}\mathbf{e} = 1$ for simplicity, so L has no mass at zero. (See Section C.5.5. As indicated there, some writers specify a CPH distribution using $-M$ in place of our M.) There is some overlap with the previous model: An Erlang distribution, and in particular an exponential, is a special case of both the gamma and the CPH distributions.

The advantages and disadvantages of the CPH distribution are quite different from those of the gamma. A gamma is ideally suited for fitting two moments, as noted above. A CPH distribution is rather awkward for direct estimation from data, because it has so many parameters. On the other hand, it offers another kind of flexibility: The distribution can model the physical supply system, using its state-transition diagram.

For example, suppose the supply system is a Markovian series network, as in Section 7.3.6.1. As explained in Section 7.3.8, the total leadtime is $L = L^{=}$, the sum of several independent exponential times, one for each node. So, $L^{=}$ has a CPH distribution, whose state-transition diagram looks just like the network itself; there is one state for each node, and the arcs link them in series.

THEOREM 7.5.1: If demand is a Poisson process, and L has a CPH distribution, then D has a discrete phase-type (DPH) distribution (Section C.4.4) with parameters $(\boldsymbol{\pi}, P)$, where

$$P = \lambda(\lambda I + M)^{-1} \qquad \boldsymbol{\pi} = \boldsymbol{\mu}P \tag{7.5.2}$$

(Problem 7.16 asks you to show that π and P have the required properties.)

The loss functions are given by

$$G^1(i) = \boldsymbol{\pi}(I - P)^{-1}P^i\mathbf{e} \tag{7.5.3}$$

$$G^2(i) = \boldsymbol{\pi}P(I - P)^{-2}P^i\mathbf{e} \qquad i \geq 0 \tag{7.5.4}$$

Therefore, for an (r, q) policy with $r \geq 0$,

$$\overline{A} = \left(\frac{1}{q}\right)\boldsymbol{\pi}(I - P)^{-1}(I - P^q)P^r\mathbf{e} \tag{7.5.5}$$

$$\overline{B} = \left(\frac{1}{q}\right)\boldsymbol{\pi}P(I - P)^{-2}(I - P^q)P^r\mathbf{e} \tag{7.5.6}$$

Section C.4.4 explains how to evaluate such quantities. For a base-stock policy with $q = 1$ and $s = r + 1$, these formulas reduce to

$$\overline{A} = \boldsymbol{\mu}P^s\mathbf{e}$$

$$\overline{B} = \boldsymbol{\pi}(I - P)^{-1}P^s\mathbf{e}$$

We encountered essentially the same formulas in (7.3.4).

Furthermore, using Theorem 6.2.4, we can fully describe the distribution of customer waiting times, BW: First, consider a base-stock policy with $s \geq 0$. Given the form of D, it follows immediately that $B = [D - s]^+$ has a DPH distribution with parameters $(\boldsymbol{\pi}P^s, P)$. Now, reverse the argument of Theorem 7.5.1, with B playing the role of D, to conclude that BW has a CPH distribution with parameters $(\boldsymbol{\mu}P^s, M)$. Thus, the *form* of BW is precisely the same as that of L, and they even share the same matrix parameter M; only their vector parameters differ.

For example, suppose L has an exponential distribution with parameter μ; here, $\boldsymbol{\mu} = (1)$ and $M = (\mu)$. Then, BW has a delayed exponential distribution, in particular, $F^0_{BW}(t) = p^s e^{-\mu t}$, $t > 0$, where $p = \lambda/(\lambda + \mu)$.

Similarly, for an (r, q) policy with $r \geq 0$, BW has a CPH distribution with matrix parameter M and initial vector $(1/q)\boldsymbol{\mu}P(I - P)^{-1}(I - P^q)P^r$.

7.5.2 World-Driven Demand

Next, suppose that demand is an MCDC process, as in Section 6.3. It is driven by a Markov chain $\mathbf{W}$ with generator $Q = Q^0 - \Lambda^D + \Lambda$, where the matrix Λ^D specifies the demand rates in all states. Again, $\boldsymbol{\xi}$ denotes the stationary vector of $\mathbf{W}$.

Recall, the distribution of D is difficult to compute when the leadtime L is constant. Now, suppose L has a CPH distribution with parameters $(\boldsymbol{\mu}, M)$, where $\boldsymbol{\mu}\mathbf{e} = 1$. With a *stochastic* leadtime of this form, D becomes relatively simple. Redefine

$$P = (\Lambda \oplus I + -Q \oplus M)^{-1}(\Lambda \otimes I) \qquad \boldsymbol{\pi} = (\boldsymbol{\xi} \otimes \boldsymbol{\mu})P$$

Here, $-Q \oplus M$ does *not* mean $-(Q \oplus M)$, but rather

$$-Q \oplus M = (-Q) \oplus \mathrm{M} = -Q \otimes I + I \otimes M$$

THEOREM 7.5.2. If demand is a MCDC process, and L has the CPH distribution above, then D has the DPH distribution with parameters ($\boldsymbol{\pi}$, P).

The expressions for P and $\boldsymbol{\pi}$ generalize (7.5.2) for the Poisson-demand case. (There, Q becomes the 1×1 matrix (0), $\boldsymbol{\xi} = (1)$, and $\Lambda = (\lambda)$.) Thus, formulas (7.5.5) to (7.5.6) for $\overline{A}$ and $\overline{B}$ apply immediately to this model. (Under a base-stock policy, BW again has a CPH distribution with matrix parameter M. The initial vector now involves powers of a larger matrix like P. See Song and Zipkin [1992].)

Evidently, the effort required to compute the performance measures depends on the complexity of the demand and supply models, through the sizes of the matrices Q and M. It is worth noting that, in the special case where demand is a renewal process, the calculations simplify somewhat: Assume that the interdemand times have a CPH distribution with parameters ($\boldsymbol{\kappa}$, K). So, $Q = -K(I - \mathbf{e}\boldsymbol{\kappa})$ and $\Lambda = K\mathbf{e}\boldsymbol{\kappa}$. Therefore, $\Lambda \otimes I = (K\mathbf{e} \otimes I)(\boldsymbol{\kappa} \otimes I)$, so

$$G^0(d) = \boldsymbol{\pi} P^d \mathbf{e} = \boldsymbol{\pi}_R P_R^d \mathbf{e} \qquad d \geq 0$$

where

$$P_R = (\boldsymbol{\kappa} \otimes I)(\Lambda \otimes I + -Q \oplus M)^{-1}(K\mathbf{e} \otimes I)$$

$$\boldsymbol{\pi}_R = \boldsymbol{\mu}[(\boldsymbol{\xi} \otimes I)(\Lambda \otimes I + -Q \oplus M)^{-1}(K\mathbf{e} \otimes I)]$$

Thus, D has the "reduced" parameters ($\boldsymbol{\pi}_R$, P_R). (One can show, with some effort, that the parameters ($\boldsymbol{\pi}_R$, P_R) have the required properties.) P_R has the same dimensions as M, and $\boldsymbol{\pi}_R$ is of the same size as $\boldsymbol{\mu}$, no matter how large Q is; the complexity of the end result depends on the complexity of the leadtime distribution only, not that of the demand process. For example, if the leadtime distribution is exponential, so M is a 1×1 matrix, then P_R is also a 1×1 matrix, and D has a (delayed) geometric distribution. True, we must invert a large matrix to compute P_R, but all subsequent calculations can be done on this smaller scale.

Here is a numerical example: Suppose L is the sum of two independent exponential variables with means ⅙ and ⅓ (e.g., the leadtime in a two-node series network). Thus, $\boldsymbol{\mu} = (1, 0)$, and

$$M = \begin{pmatrix} 6 & -6 \\ 0 & 3 \end{pmatrix}$$

Demand is the MMP process of Section 6.3.1 above. The matrices above are thus

$$\Lambda \otimes I = \begin{pmatrix} 0.5 & & & \\ & 0.5 & & \\ & & 19.5 & \\ & & & 19.5 \end{pmatrix}$$

$$-Q \otimes I = \begin{pmatrix} 20 & & -20 & \\ & 20 & & -20 \\ -20 & & 20 & \\ & -20 & & 20 \end{pmatrix}$$

$$I \otimes M = \begin{pmatrix} 6 & -6 & & \\ 0 & 3 & & \\ & & 6 & -6 \\ & & 0 & 3 \end{pmatrix}$$

Combine these as above to compute P. (The actual numbers in P are not especially illuminating.) Also, $\boldsymbol{\xi} \otimes \boldsymbol{\mu} = (\frac{1}{2}, 0, \frac{1}{2}, 0)$. Suppose we use a base-stock policy. Figure 7.5.2 compares the performance of this system to one with Poisson demand. Evidently, the more variable MMP process leads to higher backorders, but only slightly higher. (We explain why in a moment.)

7.5.3 Approximations

As indicated above, it is common practice to approximate the distribution of L using a convenient form, on the basis of estimates of its moments or a model of the supply system. An alternative method, also common practice, is to approximate D directly. Sup-

FIGURE 7.5.2

Performance of base-stock policies (effect of demand variation).

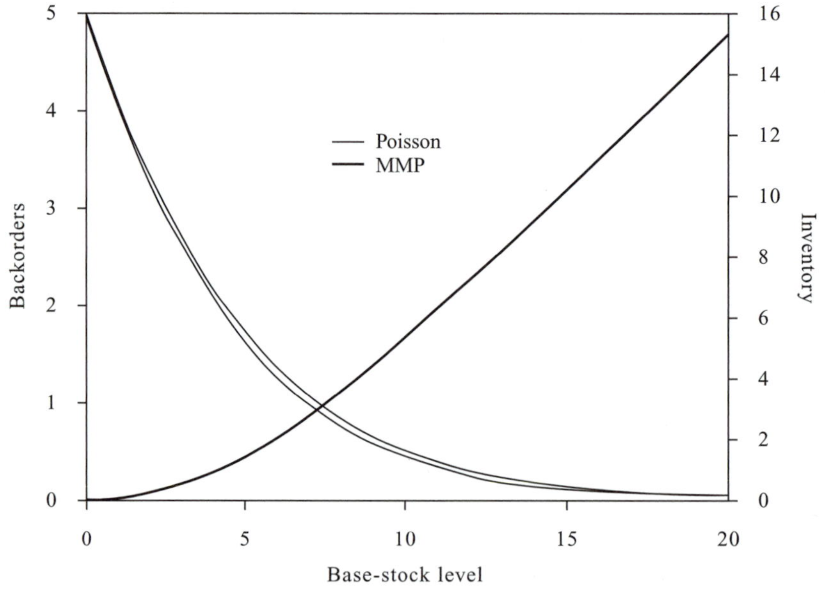

pose that we estimate λ, $\psi^2 = \psi_D^2$, $E[L]$ and $V[L]$. Then, the mean and (approximate) variance of D are

$$\nu = E[D] = \lambda E[L]$$
$$\sigma^2 = V[D] = \psi^2 \lambda E[L] + \lambda^2 V[L] \tag{7.5.7}$$

as in (6.3.1).

We can fit these estimates to several distributional forms. One is a negative-binomial distribution. (This requires $V[D] > E[D]$.) Another is a gamma distribution (for D itself, not L). This is another continuous approximation. It can be viewed as a refinement of the exponential approximation of Section 7.3.11. (It allows *any* positive $E[D]$ and $V[D]$.) The loss functions are given in Section C.2.5.3 and Problem 7.17. Also, for relatively small $V[L]$, we can even use the normal approximation. Finally, the maximal approximation provides a universal upper bound.

Once more, the optimal cost is nearly proportional to σ. So, $V[L]$ does affect system performance for a sequential system, unlike a parallel one. Also, σ is no longer proportional to the square root of λ; rather, for large λ, σ is roughly linear in λ. Thus, the system does *not* enjoy the statistical scale economies discussed in Section 6.4.1.

In the numerical example above, $E[L] = \frac{1}{2}$, $V[L] = (\frac{1}{6})^2 + (\frac{1}{3})^2 = 0.139$, $\lambda = 10$, and $\psi^2 = 1.45$. Thus, $\nu = 5$, $\sigma^2 = 21.1$, and $\sigma = 4.6$. For Poisson demand, again $\nu = 5$, but $\psi^2 = 1$, so $\sigma^2 = 18.9$ and $\sigma = 4.3$. Evidently, the values of σ in the two models are nearly the same; the second term in (7.5.7) dominates the first. This fact helps explain why the two curves in Figure 7.5.2 above are so similar.

7.5.4 Lumpy Demand

Section 6.6 gives performance formulas for the lumpy-demand case. The same formulas apply here, as indicated in Section 7.4.2, using the new leadtime demand D. In general, D has a compound distribution, built from those of $\tilde{D}$ and Y. Let us investigate the form of D for a few specific cases.

First, suppose $\tilde{D}$ has the Poisson distribution with mean ν (as in a constant-leadtime system), and Y the logarithmic distribution with parameter p (Section C.2.3.7). Then,

$$\begin{aligned}\tilde{g}_D(z) &= \exp\{-\nu[1 - \tilde{g}_Y(z)]\} \\ &= \exp\{-\nu[1 - \frac{\ln(1 - zp)}{\ln(1 - p)}]\} \\ &= \left(\frac{1 - p}{1 - zp}\right)^n\end{aligned}$$

where $n = \nu[-1/\ln(1 - p)]$. Thus, D has the negative-binomial distribution with parameters n and p. (We know of no compelling motivation for the logarithmic distribution, apart from this neat result. It is merely a coincidence that the negative-binomial distribution arises here and in the very different models of Section 7.5.1.1 and Problem 7.4.)

Next, suppose $\tilde{D}$ has the DPH distribution with parameters $(\tilde{\boldsymbol{\pi}}, \tilde{P})$, and Y itself has a DPH distribution with parameters $(\boldsymbol{\theta}, \Theta)$. (Since $g_Y(0) = 0$, $\boldsymbol{\theta}\mathbf{e} = 1$.) Then, D also has a DPH distribution with parameters $(\boldsymbol{\pi}, P)$, where

$$\boldsymbol{\pi} = \tilde{\boldsymbol{\pi}} \otimes \boldsymbol{\theta} \qquad P = I \otimes \Theta + \tilde{P} \otimes [(I - \Theta)\mathbf{e}\boldsymbol{\theta}]$$

(See Problem 7.20.) For example, suppose that Y has a geometric distribution, shifted up by 1 so that $g_Y(0) = 0$. So, $\boldsymbol{\theta}$ and Θ are both 1×1 arrays, $\boldsymbol{\theta} = (1)$, and $\Theta = (\theta)$ for some scalar θ with $0 < \theta < 1$. In this case,

$$\boldsymbol{\pi} = \tilde{\boldsymbol{\pi}} \qquad P = \theta I + (1 - \theta)\tilde{P}$$

The loss functions are given by (7.5.3) and (7.5.4). These can be used within the formulas of Section 6.6 for $\overline{A}$, $\overline{B}$, and $\overline{I}$, depending on the type of policy used. For an (r, q) policy, $\overline{A}$ and $\overline{B}$ are given by (7.5.5) and (7.5.6). (For an (r, s) policy, it is possible to compute $\boldsymbol{\iota}$ explicitly.)

In general, we can adapt the approximation of Section 7.5.3. Assuming compound-Poisson demand,

$$E[\tilde{D}] = \lambda E[L]$$
$$V[\tilde{D}] = \lambda E[L] + \lambda^2 V[L]$$

and the formulas for compound distributions of Section C.2.3.8 yield

$$E[D] = E[\tilde{D}]E[Y]$$
$$V[D] = E[\tilde{D}]V[Y] + V[\tilde{D}]E^2[Y]$$

Combining these two results gives

$$E[D] = \lambda E[Y]E[L]$$
$$V[D] = \lambda E[Y^2]E[L] + (\lambda E[Y])^2 V[L]$$

We can use these moments to fit a convenient distribution, such as a negative binomial, a gamma, or a normal.

This approach works approximately even when $\tilde{\mathbf{D}}$ is not a Poisson process. Starting with the approximation for $V[\tilde{D}]$ in (7.5.7), we obtain

$$E[D] = \lambda E[Y]E[L] \tag{7.5.8}$$
$$V[D] = \lambda(V[Y] + \tilde{\psi}^2 E^2[Y])E[L] + (\lambda E[Y])^2 V[L] \tag{7.5.9}$$

The term $\lambda(V[Y] + \tilde{\psi}^2 E^2[Y])$ in (7.5.9) represents the overall *demand variation*, as discussed in Section 6.6.2; this quantity is scaled by the average leadtime. The term $V[L]$ represents *supply variation*, which is scaled by the (squared) overall demand rate. The *total variation* in the system, $V[D]$, summarizes the contributions from all these sources.

7.5.5 Proofs

PROOF OF THEOREM 7.5.1. From (7.5.1) and the Laplace transform of L in Section C.5.5,

$$\tilde{g}(z) = \boldsymbol{\mu}[(1 - z)\lambda I + M]^{-1} M\mathbf{e} \tag{7.5.10}$$

Before proceeding further, let us derive (7.5.10) by another method. (We shall use this approach again later on.) Let **U** be the Markov chain whose time to absorption determines the distribution of L. So, the initial distribution of **U** is specified by the vector $\boldsymbol{\mu}$, and the transition rates of **U**, restricted to its transient (nonabsorbing) states, are given by $-M$. (Note, **U** is *not* the same as **Z** above, which describes the supply system.)

Consider the joint Markov chain (**D**, **U**). Define

$$g_{uu'}(d|t) = Pr\{D(t) = d,\ U(t) = u' \mid U(0) = u\}$$
$$G(d|t) = [g_{uu'}(d|t)]_{uu'}$$

(This includes only transient states u and u'.) By denoting $G' = \partial G/\partial t$, the dynamics of the joint process can be represented through the matrix differential equation

$$G(0|0) = I$$
$$G(d|0) = 0 \qquad d > 0$$

$$G'(0|t) = -G(0|t)(\lambda I + M)$$
$$G'(d|t) = -G(d|t)(\lambda I + M) + G(d-1|t)(\lambda I) \qquad d > 0$$

Now, consider the matrix z-transform

$$\tilde{G}(z|t) = \Sigma_{d=0}^{\infty} z^d G(d|t)$$

The dynamical equations above immediately yield the differential equation

$$\tilde{G}(z|0) = I$$
$$\tilde{G}'(z|t) = -\tilde{G}(z|t)[(1-z)\lambda I + M]$$

for each fixed z, whose solution is

$$\tilde{G}(z|t) = \exp\{-[(1-z)\lambda I + M]t\}$$

Now, the quantity $\boldsymbol{\mu} G(d|t)M\mathbf{e}$ describes *jointly* the probability that $D(t) = d$, and the absorption *rate* of **U** at time t. Thus,

$$g(d) = \int_0^\infty [\boldsymbol{\mu} G(d|t) M\mathbf{e}]\, dt$$
$$= \boldsymbol{\mu}\left[\int_0^\infty G(d|t)\, dt\right] M\mathbf{e}$$

Taking transforms of both sides,

$$\tilde{g}(z) = \boldsymbol{\mu}\left[\int_0^\infty \tilde{G}(z|t)\, dt\right] M\mathbf{e}$$
$$= \boldsymbol{\mu}\left[\int_0^\infty e^{-[(1-z)\lambda I + M]t}\, dt\right] M\mathbf{e}$$

which leads immediately to (7.5.10).

Now, the definition of P and some matrix manipulations yield the identity

$$\lambda M^{-1} = P(I - P)^{-1} \tag{7.5.11}$$

This fact and more matrix manipulations demonstrate that

$$[(1-z)\lambda I + M]^{-1} M = (I - P)(I - zP)^{-1} \tag{7.5.12}$$

Substituting this into (7.5.10) yields

$$\tilde{g}(z) = \boldsymbol{\mu}(I - P)(I - zP)^{-1}\mathbf{e}$$

This is the z-transform of a DPH distribution with parameters $(\boldsymbol{\pi}, P)$, where $\boldsymbol{\pi} = \boldsymbol{\mu}\mathrm{P}$, as claimed.

PROOF OF THEOREM 7.5.2. We use an argument parallel to the second demonstration of (7.5.10): Consider the joint process $(\mathbf{D}, \mathbf{W}, \mathbf{U})$. Define

$$g_{wu,w'u'}(d|t) = \Pr\{D(t) = d, W(\mathrm{t}) = w', U(t) = u'|W(0) = w, U(0) = u\}$$

$$G(d|t) = [g_{wu,w'u'}(d|t)]_{wu,w'u'}$$

(The matrix $G(d|t)$ has rows indexed by w and u, and columns indexed by w' and u'. Specifically, to index the rows, group together states with the same value of w, letting u vary over all the transient states of $\mathbf{U}$; the columns are indexed similarly, by grouping states with a common w'. As before, only transient states u and u' are included.)

Now, $\mathbf{W}$ and $\mathbf{U}$ are independent Markov chains, so the generator of $(\mathbf{W}, \mathbf{U})$, restricted to the transient states of $\mathbf{U}$, can be written in the form

$$Q \oplus (-M) = Q \otimes I + I \otimes (-M) = -(-Q \oplus M)$$

The dynamics of $G(d|t)$ can thus be represented as follows:

$$G(0|0) = I \otimes I$$

$$G(d|0) = 0 \otimes 0 \qquad d > 0$$

$$G'(0|t) = -G(0|t)(\,\Lambda \otimes I + -Q \oplus M\,)$$

$$G'(d|t) = -G(d|t)(\,\Lambda \otimes I + -Q \oplus M\,) + G(d-1|t)(\Lambda \otimes I) \qquad d > 0$$

Defining the matrix z-transform $(z|t)$ as above, we obtain

$$\tilde{G}(z|t) = \exp\{-[(1-z)(\Lambda \otimes I) + -Q \oplus M]t\}$$

Now in this case, the quantity $(\boldsymbol{\xi} \otimes \boldsymbol{\mu})G(d|t)(\mathbf{e} \otimes M\mathbf{e})$ describes jointly the probability that $D(t) = d$ and the absorption rate of $\mathbf{U}$. Thus,

$$\begin{aligned} g(d) &= \textstyle\int_0^\infty (\boldsymbol{\xi} \otimes \boldsymbol{\mu})G(d|t)(\mathbf{e} \otimes M\mathbf{e})\,dt \\ &= (\boldsymbol{\xi} \otimes \boldsymbol{\mu})[\textstyle\int_0^\infty G(d|t)\,dt](\mathbf{e} \otimes M\mathbf{e}) \\ &= (\boldsymbol{\xi} \otimes \boldsymbol{\mu})[\textstyle\int_0^\infty G(d|t)\,dt](-Q \oplus M)(\mathbf{e} \otimes \mathbf{e}) \end{aligned}$$

(The last equation uses the fact that $(-Q \oplus M)(\mathbf{e} \otimes \mathbf{e}) = -Q\mathbf{e} \otimes \mathbf{e} + \mathbf{e} \otimes M\mathbf{e} = \mathbf{e} \otimes M\mathbf{e}$.) Thus,

$$\begin{aligned} \tilde{g}(z) &= (\boldsymbol{\xi} \otimes \boldsymbol{\mu})[\textstyle\int_0^\infty \tilde{G}(z|t)\,dt](-Q \oplus M)(\mathbf{e} \otimes \mathbf{e}) \\ &= (\boldsymbol{\xi} \otimes \boldsymbol{\mu})\textstyle\int_0^\infty \exp\{-[(1-z)(\Lambda \otimes I) + -Q \oplus M]t\}\,dt\,(-Q \oplus M)(\mathbf{e} \otimes \mathbf{e}) \\ &= (\boldsymbol{\xi} \otimes \boldsymbol{\mu})[(1-z)(\Lambda \otimes I) + -Q \oplus M]^{-1}(-Q \oplus M)(\mathbf{e} \otimes \mathbf{e}) \end{aligned}$$

This expression is analogous to (7.5.10).

The analogues of (7.5.11) and (7.5.12) here are

$$(-Q \oplus M)^{-1}(\Lambda \otimes \mathrm{I}) = P(I - P)^{-1}$$

$$[(1 - z)(\Lambda \otimes I) + -Q \oplus M]^{-1}(-Q \oplus M) = (I - P)(I - zP)^{-1}$$

Hence,

$$\tilde{g}(z) = (\boldsymbol{\xi} \otimes \boldsymbol{\mu})(I - P)(I - zP)^{-1}(\mathbf{e} \otimes \mathbf{e})$$

This is the z-transform of the DPH distribution with parameters $(\boldsymbol{\pi}, P)$, where $\boldsymbol{\pi} = (\boldsymbol{\xi} \otimes \boldsymbol{\mu})P$, as claimed.

Notes

Section 7.1: The use of a queueing system as a part of a make-to-stock system seems to have been suggested first by Karush [1957], Morse [1958], and Scarf [1958b]. Recent books on the theory of queues include Gross and Harris [1985], Hall [1991], Heyman and Sobel [1982], and Walrand [1988].

Section 7.2: The same paper by Scarf [1958b] introduces the use of Palm's theorem in this context. Many extensions of this model are reviewed in Nahmias [1981]. The distribution of customer waiting times is discussed by Berg and Posner [1990], Higa et al. [1975], and Sherbrooke [1975].

Exact (but intricate) results for certain world-driven demand processes (Section 7.2.2) are provided by Ramaswami and Neuts [1980] and Scarf [1958b]. The normal approximation and the formula for σ are discussed by Whitt [1982,1992], Glynn and Whitt [1991], and the references therein. The paradoxical effects of leadtime variation in this context are discussed further by Wolff [1977].

The lost-sales model of Section 7.2.3 is by Karush [1957]. Smith [1977] presents an approximation technique. Johansen and Thorstenson [1993] show how to compute the optimal policy for the case of exponential leadtimes. For the (r, q) policies of Section 7.2.4, Galliher et al. [1959] and Sahin [1983] derive exact (but intricate) results. Song and Zipkin [1996a] evaluate the approximation (7.2.3). Yano and Lee [1995] review the literature on lot-sizing models with imperfect quality.

Section 7.3: Models with state-dependent processing rates (as in Section 7.3.3) can be found in Gross and Harris [1971]. See Whitt [1983] and Harrison and Nguyen [1990] as well as Walrand [1988] for approximations of processing networks. Baker [1992] and Dallery and Gershwin [1992] provide overviews of finite-buffer systems. The direct-processor-control system (Section 7.3.10.2) is studied in Baker [1973] and Sobel [1969]. Refinements of the exponential approximation can be found in Abate et al. [1995].

Section 7.4: The concept of an exogenous supply system and the results here come from Zipkin [1986a], drawing on earlier work by Ehrhardt [1984], Kaplan [1970], and Nahmias [1979]. Song and Zipkin [1996b] investigate policies that do use current information about the supply system.

Section 7.5: The derivations involving CPH distributions use ideas from Neuts [1981] and Zipkin [1988]. Explicit formulas have been derived for many other distributions; Bagchi, Hayya, and Ord [1984] and Bagchi [1987] provide reviews. See Bagchi et al. [1986] for further discussion of the effects of leadtime variation. Feeney and Sherbrooke [1966] study the system with independent leadtimes and compound-Poisson demand.

Problems

7.1 Consider the random variable $L_{[2]}$ introduced in Section 7.2, the minimum of two independent copies of L. Argue that its ccdf is given by the *square* of F_L^0, the ccdf of L itself. Use this fact to show that, if L has a uniform distribution on the interval $E[L] \pm \upsilon$, then $E[L_{[2]}] = E[L] - \upsilon/3$.

7.2 Consider the lost-sales model of Section 7.2.3, assuming Poisson demand and independent leadtimes. Show that $\bar{A}$ is decreasing and convex as a function of s for $s \geq 0$.

Hint: First, verify that $\bar{A}(s)$ satisfies the recursion

$$\bar{A}(s) = \frac{\bar{A}(s-1)}{\bar{A}(s-1) + s/\nu}$$

or

$$\bar{A}(s-1) = \bar{A}(s)[\bar{A}(s-1) + \frac{s}{\nu}] \qquad s > 0$$

Use this to demonstrate that

$$[\bar{A}(s) + \frac{s+1}{\nu}]\Delta\bar{A}(s) = [1 - \bar{A}(s)]\Delta\bar{A}(s-1) - \frac{\bar{A}(s)}{\nu}$$

Now, show directly that $\Delta\bar{A}(0) = -1/(1+\nu) < 0$, and then argue by induction that $\Delta\bar{A}(s) < 0$. Next, show that

$$[\bar{A}(s+1) + \frac{s+2}{\nu}]\Delta^2\bar{A}(s)$$

$$= [1 - \bar{A}(s)]\Delta^2\bar{A}(s-1) - 2\Delta\bar{A}(s)[\Delta\bar{A}(s) + \frac{1}{\nu}]$$

Use another induction to argue that $\Delta\bar{A}(s) > -1/\nu$ and $\Delta^2\bar{A}(s) > 0$.

7.3 Consider the M/G/1 system of Section 7.3.2.2. This problem concerns the modeling of the unit production time S, when the processor breaks down occasionally. Suppose the machine is always up whenever a unit begins production, and during production the machine completes units at the rate μ_0, as in the M/M/1 system. While the machine is producing, however, it tends to break down at the constant rate β_d. The repair time is exponentially distributed with mean $1/\beta_u$.

Model the distribution of S, including time waiting for repair, as a CPH distribution. Compute its mean and variance in terms of the parameters specified above. Also, describe the distribution of L, and compute its mean.

7.4 Consider the system with load-dependent processing rate of Section 7.3.3.1. Suppose that, for some constants $\mu > \lambda$ and $n \geq 1$, $\mu_i = \mu[i/(n - 1 + i)]$, $i \geq 1$. Thus, the processing rate starts small, with $\mu_1 = \mu/n$, but increases gradually, approaching the limit μ as i grows large. This is an intermediate case between the fixed-rate M/M/1 system and the proportional-rate M/M/∞ system.

Treating **IO** as a birth-death process, show that *IO* has the negative-binomial distribution with parameters n and $p = \lambda/\mu$.

7.5 Consider the system with multiple input sources of Section 7.3.7, and suppose IO_+ has a DPH distribution. Verify that *IO* has a distribution of the same form with parameters specified by equation (7.3.5). *Hint:* Work with z-transforms. Show that $\tilde{g}(z) = \tilde{g}_+[\theta z + (1 - \theta)]$.

7.6 As pointed out in Section 7.3.8, in a sequential supply system with Poisson demand, $IO = D(L)$. Use this fact along with Jensen's inequality to prove the following: Given a sequential system and a parallel system with equal values of $E[L]$, the sequential system always has larger $\overline{B}(s)$ for all s.

7.7 Consider the direct processor-control system of Section 7.3.10.2 operating under an (r, s) policy.
(a) Explain why the process (**IO**, **X**) is a continuous-time Markov chain, and draw its state-transition diagram. Verify that the pmf $g(i, \chi)$ given in the text satisfies the balance equations.
(b) Given this distribution of (**IO**, **X**), derive the formulas given in the text for $\overline{I}$ and $\overline{B}$.

7.8 Consider the simple lost-sales systems in Section 7.2.3 and Section 7.3.4, assuming a base-stock policy. For each of these two systems, verify the formula given for $\overline{I}$.

7.9 Consider the following variant of the M/M/1 system: Suppose that, when a demand occurs and finds no inventory available, the customer leaves (the demand becomes a lost sale) with probability $1 - \beta$ and waits (the demand is backlogged) with probability β. Which performance criteria are relevant here? Argue that **IO** is a birth-death process, and derive the distribution of *IO*. Use this result to obtain formulas for the performance criteria.

7.10 Consider the system of Section 7.3.3.3 with a finite number of customers. Determine the distribution of *IO*. Use this to derive formulas for $\overline{B}$ and $\overline{I}$.

7.11 Consider the M/G/1 system, where each unit is defective with probability δ, as in Section 7.3.5.2. Assume units are inspected when they are received and defects discarded. For the case where the original ("nominal") processing time S has a CPH distribution, show that the effective processing time S' also has a CPH distribution, and compute its parameters.

7.12 Consider the M/M/1 system with defect rate δ under the inspection scheme of Section 7.3.5.3, where units are inspected and defects discovered only at demand epochs. The process **IO** is a Markov chain. Its dynamics depend on s.
(*a*) For fixed s draw the state-transition diagram for **IO**. Argue that the transition rates q_{ij} have the following form:

$$
\begin{array}{ll}
\lambda(1 - \delta)\delta^{j-i-1} & i \leq s,\ i < j \leq s \\
\lambda\delta^{s-i} & i \leq s,\ j = s + 1 \\
\lambda & i > s,\ j = i + 1 \\
\mu & 0 < i \leq s,\ j = i - 1 \\
\mu(1 - \delta) & i > s,\ j = i - 1
\end{array}
$$

(*b*) Let $\rho = \lambda/(\xi\mu)$ and $\rho_+ = 1 - (1 - \rho)\xi$. Show that the following probabilities satisfy the balance equations, and so describe the distribution of *IO:*

$$\pi_0 = 1 - \rho$$

$$\pi_j = (1 - \rho_+)\rho\rho_+^{j-1} \qquad 1 \leq j \leq s$$

$$\pi_j = (1 - \rho)\rho_+^s\rho^{j-s} \qquad j > s$$

(*c*) Show that, as asserted in the text,

$$\bar{B}(s) = \left(\frac{\rho}{1 - \rho}\right)\rho_+^s$$

$$\bar{I}(s) = s - \left(\frac{\rho}{1 - \rho_+}\right)(1 - \rho_+^s)$$

7.13 Consider the M/M/1 system of Section 7.3.2.1, modified to describe a perishable product. Each unit of inventory may spoil at any time, according to a Poisson process of rate δ, where $\delta > 0$. (The unit spoils at the first event of this Poisson process, if that event occurs before the unit leaves the inventory to meet a demand.) These Poisson processes are independent of the demand and supply processes and of each other.

Explain that **IO** is a birth-death process, and determine its transition rates λ_i and μ_i. Express the ρ_i in terms of the ratios $\rho = \lambda/\mu$ and $\eta = \delta/\lambda$. Show that, for $i \geq s$, $R_i = \rho^i \Pi_{j=1}^s (1 + \eta j)$. Also, compute the R_i for $i < s$, and R itself.

7.14 Several situations are described below. The issue in each case is to decide which type of supply-system model to use: parallel, limited-capacity, or exogenous-sequential. Specify which kind you think is most appropriate, and explain why. (There need not be a single right answer. If you are unsure, describe what additional information you would seek to help decide the question.)

(*a*) You operate a small machine shop which makes spare parts used throughout a larger factory. One essential part is demanded frequently, and making it consumes a considerable fraction of your capacity.

(*b*) You order the raw materials used in a chemical process. One of the materials is supplied by many different chemical companies, and you routinely spread your orders among these companies. It is not uncommon for your orders to cross; that is, an order may be received from one company before another order placed later with a different company. There is no systematic, predictable difference between the companies' order-response times, however.

(*c*) You operate a small retail clothing store. You obtain one of your largest-selling lines from a single manufacturer. This supplier is large, with annual sales of several hundred million dollars. You are quite sure this company's president has never heard your name.

7.15 Suppose **D** is a Poisson process with $\lambda = 3$, and L has a gamma distribution with $E[L] = 2$, $V[L] = 2$. Determine the parameters of L and D. Suppose we wish to follow a base-stock policy with $\bar{A}(s) \leq 0.05$. What is the smallest value of s that achieves this performance requirement? (You can do the calculation by hand or by computer, using a spreadsheet program.)

7.16 Suppose M is the transition matrix of a CPH distribution. That is, M is a square, nonsingular matrix, whose off-diagonal entries are nonpositive, and $M\mathbf{e} \geq 0$. Show that $M^{-1} \geq 0$.

Define $P = \lambda(\lambda I + M)^{-1}$. Show that P is the transition matrix of a DPH distribution: $P \geq 0$, $(I - P)\mathbf{e} \geq \mathbf{0}$, and $(I - P)$ is nonsingular.

7.17 Suppose F^0 is the ccdf of a gamma distribution and f its pdf. Defining F^1 as in the text, use integration by parts to show that

$$F^1(x) = [\left(\frac{n}{\mu}\right) - x]F^0(x) + \left(\frac{x}{\mu}\right)f(x)$$

Use this to derive a formula for $F^2(x)$.

7.18 Suppose we obtain replenishments from one of the imperfect-quality supply systems of Section 7.2 and Section 7.3 with defect rate δ. We operate a base-stock policy. The average-cost model of Section 6.5 applies, and we compute an optimal policy using a continuous approximation, specifically, a normal or an exponential approximation. For each of these two cases explain the qualitative effects of changes in δ on the optimal cost. Use words and pictures artfully; keep the mathematics to a minimum.

7.19 Suppose that demand is a Poisson process with $\lambda = 5$, and the supply system is exogenous and sequential, where L has the exponential distribution with $E[L] = 0.2$. The cost factors are $h = 1$ and $b = 19$.

(*a*) What type of distribution does the leadtime demand D have? What are its parameters?
(*b*) Use an exponential approximation of D, and set $k = 0$ for now. Compute the optimal base-stock policy and the optimal cost.
(*c*) Using the exact discrete formulation, compute the optimal base-stock policy and the optimal cost. Compare the results to those of part (*b*).
(*d*) Now, set $k = 3$, and use Algorithm Optimize_rq of Section 6.5.4 to determine the optimal (r, q) policy and the optimal cost.

7.20 Consider a lumpy demand process as in Section 7.5.4, where $\tilde{D}$ has a DPH distribution with parameters $(\tilde{\boldsymbol{\pi}}, \tilde{P})$, and Y has a DPH distribution with parameters $(\boldsymbol{\theta}, \Theta)$ with $\boldsymbol{\theta}\mathbf{e} = 1$. Verify that D also has a DPH distribution with parameters $(\boldsymbol{\pi}, P)$, where

$$\boldsymbol{\pi} = \tilde{\boldsymbol{\pi}} \otimes \boldsymbol{\theta} \qquad P = I \otimes \Theta + \tilde{P} \otimes [(I - \Theta)\mathbf{e}\boldsymbol{\theta}]$$

7.21 Consider a service facility consisting of a single processor of limited capacity. As customers arrive, each brings a physical unit that requires processing. Every customer must wait with the unit to be serviced until the processor begins to process it. At that moment, the customer can leave. (This scenario describes, for instance, trucks carrying food or garbage to a processing plant.) Let $IO(t)$ describe the total occupancy of *units* in the system, including those waiting and the one being processed. Argue that the number of *customers* waiting is $B(t) = [IO(t) - 1]^+$, i.e., the backorders in an inventory system with base-stock level $s = 1$.

Now, suppose that the facility provides $s - 1$ storage bins, where $s > 1$. A customer can drop off his unit in a storage bin, when one becomes available, and then leave. Argue that $IO(t)$ is the same as before, but now $B(t) = [IO(t) - s]^+$, i.e., the backorders with base-stock level s. Thus, in this context, the storage bins play the same role as inventory, namely, to shield customers from congestion in the supply system.

C H A P T E R

8 Several Items with Stochastic Demands

Outline

8.1 Introduction

The last two chapters focus on a single product at a single location. Now we shift attention to structurally complex systems, as in Chapter 5, where several items (products and/or locations) are linked to form a network. In contrast to Chapter 5 (but as in Chapters 6 and 7) the demand process and the supply system may include random factors.

Such a network is sometimes called a *supply chain.* There has been a surge of interest recently in *supply-chain management,* as many companies have realized substantial benefits by restructuring their supply chains. To do this, one must understand how alternative control schemes and system designs work. This chapter summarizes the best analytical tools available to support supply-chain management at this conceptual level.

A supply chain is a type of *business process.* (This phrase also encompasses pure information-processing systems, where physical goods play a marginal role.) *Business-process reengineering* is a careful, systematic approach to network restructuring in order to enhance performance. Again, this chapter provides tools to support such endeavors.

We begin in Section 8.2 with a system composed of many independent items, each facing stochastic demand and supply conditions. The results generalize those of Section 5.2 of Chapter 5: We characterize overall system performance with the aid of a few simple aggregate statistics. These include the variety index J_* and a systemwide index of variation (the cost-weighted sum of the items' individual σ's). These results allow us to measure precisely and to understand intuitively the benefits of item consolidation.

The rest of the chapter treats systems whose items are linked, mainly through supply-demand relationships. We focus on a few special structures, namely, series, assembly, and distribution systems. Also, we discuss shared supply processes.

One key distinction among such systems concerns the flow of information and control. (We touched on this issue in Chapter 5, but here it becomes even more crucial.) When a structurally complex system is driven partly by random events, we need to understand clearly just who knows what and when, and how that information is used to control the various parts of the network.

The simplest case, conceptually, is a *centralized system.* Here, all relevant information in the network flows to a single point, where all decisions are made. These decisions are then transmitted throughout the network to be implemented. In a sense this situation is ideal; what could be better than a fully informed decision maker with full control over the system?

In practice, however (as mentioned in Section 5.8), centralization may be impractical or even dysfunctional: It requires a fast, reliable communication system, a powerful information-processing capability, and an organization willing and able to act in synchronized fashion. For a host of technical, economic, and cultural reasons, these elements are often lacking. To impose centralized control where it cannot be supported properly can have perverse effects.

For this reason we also consider relatively *decentralized systems,* where information and control are distributed throughout the network. We say "relatively" because, while the informational requirements of such systems are less formidable than those of a fully centralized system, they are fairly stiff all the same. There are many ways to decentralize, but not all of them work. For one thing, lacking a central authority, there must be some alternative mechanism to avoid chaos. All the control policies we consider are carefully sculpted to achieve reasonable degrees of coordination.

Sometimes, there is a clear reason to centralize information and control. Centralization allows us to *balance* the items' inventories in situations where otherwise, under purely local control, imbalances would arise. The exact meaning of balance depends on the context, but this general notion is broadly valid.

We begin with *series systems* in Section 8.3, focusing on those with no scale economies in supply. The root problem here, just as in a single-stage system, is the combination of demand uncertainty and supply leadtimes; again, this leads to a tradeoff between inventory and backorders. But now we have several possible stocking points, offering different degrees of stockout protection at different costs. We must decide not just how much inventory to keep, but also where to position it.

Interestingly, the distinction between centralized and decentralized systems disappears here. We start with a simple, plausible local control scheme, using a base-stock policy at each stage, and show that it is equivalent to a fully centralized system. Thus, centralized control can be implemented in a decentralized fashion.

We develop algorithms to evaluate any such policy and to select the best one. For the two-stage case we derive simple bounds on the optimal policy variables and the optimal cost. These results, along with some illustrative examples, help us understand intuitively the main drivers of effective control and system performance.

We obtain these results first for a basic model with Poisson demand and constant leadtimes. Later, we find that the same approach works, exactly or approximately, for compound-Poisson demand and *all* the supply systems of Chapter 7.

Then, we consider a system with fixed order costs. We start with a simple case, where *external* orders incur fixed costs, but *internal* shipments do not. Most of the earlier results extend directly to this system. Here, the first stage uses an (r, q) policy, while the others use base-stock policies. Again, centralized and decentralized control are equivalent. We then turn to the general case, where internal shipments too incur fixed costs. This system is more complex than the earlier ones. In particular, centralized and decentralized control are *not* the same. (Actually, centralized control is more general.) We develop a policy-evaluation method which covers both cases and a partial optimization algorithm, to compute the best reorder points given fixed order quantities.

Section 8.4 extends these ideas to *assembly systems.* Remarkably, an assembly system can be reduced to an equivalent series system. Thus, we can use the methods of Section 8.3 for policy evaluation and optimization. The policy we end up with, however, *cannot* be implemented with local information alone. We can *control* each item locally, but we require explicit *information* about others, in order to balance the items' inventories properly. Of course, it is possible to use a decentralized control scheme in this context, say a base-stock policy, though this approach is more costly. We show how to evaluate such a policy, again using series-systems techniques.

Next, we study a two-level *distribution system,* where one location (called the warehouse) receives goods from the outside source, and supplies in turn several others (the retailers). In structure this system is a hybrid of a two-stage series system and an independent-item (or parallel) system. This viewpoint is a fruitful one—we can interpret the operation and performance of the system in similar terms, as combining elements of series and parallel systems.

Here, even without fixed costs, the centralization-decentralization issue *does* matter. We treat local control in Section 8.5. Each location follows a base-stock policy, and the warehouse fills retailer orders on a first in, first out (FIFO) basis. We show how to evaluate such a policy and to determine the best one. This approach extends directly to arbitrary distribution networks and to systems with fixed external order costs.

The analysis reveals that warehouse inventory serves two distinct economic functions. It offers a low-cost form of stockout protection and a means of partially consolidating the retailers, i.e., of pooling their leadtime-demand uncertainties.

Section 8.6 discusses a distribution system operating under centralized control. We develop an approximation and a heuristic policy. One part of the policy is *myopic allocation,* a simple technique to divide outbound shipments from the warehouse among the retailers. The *balanced approximation* reduces the model to a two-stage series system, which we solve with the methods of Section 8.3. This yields both an estimate of the optimal cost and the remaining elements of the heuristic policy. The approximation and the policy work quite well, especially for systems with high demand volumes.

We find that, in general, a system with centralized control needs less warehouse inventory than a local-control system. The centralized system is able to substitute information for inventory to achieve some degree of retailer consolidation.

Section 8.7 discusses two kinds of shared supply processes. First, we solve a simple joint-replenishment problem. Then, we turn to systems with shared production capacity. These are similar, but not quite identical, to distribution systems. The section concludes with a general discussion of setup costs in systems with limited resources.

Finally, Section 8.8 explores variants of the base-stock policy for networks with limited-capacity processors. These policies are based on the celebrated *kanban system.* We find that, although these policies are more intricate than a base-stock policy, the simple models of Section 8.3 capture the fundamental economics of the system. Then, we discuss these ideas in the broader context of the just-in-time approach to operations.

8.2 Independent Items

Consider an inventory of several independent items, i.e., a parallel system, as in Section 5.2 of Chapter 5. Now, each item follows one of the scenarios of Chapters 6 and 7: Each faces a stochastic demand process and possibly also a stochastic supply system. The goal here, as in Section 5.2, is to understand aggregate-level system performance in terms of aggregate parameters. (You might want to review Section 5.2, which explains the uses of such aggregate-level analysis.)

Again denote

J = number of items
j = item index, $j = 1, \ldots, J$
λ_j = demand rate of item j
c_j = purchase cost of item j
p_j = sales price of item j

Use the total purchase-cost rate as an aggregate-demand statistic:

$$c\lambda = \Sigma_j\, c_j\lambda_j$$

8.2.1 Base-Stock Policies

Suppose there are no scale economies in ordering, and we use a base-stock policy for each item. There are two primary performance criteria for each item, average inventory and average backorders. Accordingly, define two aggregate performance measures:

$$cI = \text{average total investment in inventory} = \Sigma_j\, c_j\overline{I}_j$$

$$pB = \text{aggregate sales-value of backorders} = \Sigma_j\, p_j\overline{B}_j$$

where $\overline{I}_j$ and $\overline{B}_j$ denote average inventory and backorders of item j.

To study the relationship between cI and pB, we adapt the individual-item approach of Section 5.2.3. That is, specify two positive constants, η and β, and use these along with the coefficients in cI and pB to define each item's cost factors:

$$h_j = \eta c_j \qquad b_j = \beta p_j, j = 1, \ldots, J \tag{8.2.1}$$

Then, compute the optimal base-stock policy for each item separately. This determines the $\bar{I}_j$ and $\bar{B}_j$ and thus cI and pB. This pair (cI, pB) is efficient; that is, there is no smaller pB consistent with cI. Vary the ratio β/η and repeat this procedure to obtain other efficient pairs. The locus of such pairs describes an *aggregate inventory-backorders tradeoff curve*. This construct is very useful to managers, in the same ways as the tradeoff curve of Section 5.2.

This approach works, but it offers no broad insights into system behavior; in general, it cannot be reduced to an elegant formula like (5.2.4). For that, we must impose additional assumptions: First, suppose the markup ratio p_j/c_j is the same for all items. Then (as in Problem 5.4), we can use

$$\begin{aligned} cB &= \text{aggregate cost-value of backorders} \\ &= \Sigma_j\, c_j \bar{B}_j \end{aligned}$$

as the aggregate backorders measure, for it captures the same information as pB, and respecify the backorder costs as $b_j = \beta c_j$. (The meaning of β has changed now.) Also, suppose that each item's leadtime demand is normally distributed (approximately, as in Section 6.4).

Following the approach of Section 6.5.2.2 leads to

$$\omega_j = \frac{b_j}{b_j + h_j} = \frac{\beta c_j}{\beta c_j + \eta c_j} = \frac{\beta}{\beta + \eta} \equiv \omega$$

for all items. Consequently, all items share the optimal standardized base-stock level $z^* = (\Phi^0)^{-1}(1 - \omega)$. Thus, $\bar{I}_j = \sigma_j \Phi^1(-z^*)$, $\bar{B}_j = \sigma_j \Phi^1(z^*)$, and

$$cI = c\sigma\, \Phi^1(-z^*) \qquad cB = c\sigma\, \Phi^1(z^*) \tag{8.2.2}$$

where

$$c\sigma = \Sigma_j\, c_j \sigma_j$$

(The maximal approximation leads to similar results.)

To compute the tradeoff curve, then, we can bypass the specification of η and β; just let z^* range over all real values, and directly calculate (cI, cB) via (8.2.2). Notice, the relationship depends on the system data only through the aggregate parameter $c\sigma$, and the dependence is homogeneous; that is, $c\sigma$ acts as a scale factor for both cI and cB.

Figure 8.2.1 shows one such tradeoff curve, computed using the normal approximation. Here, $c\sigma$ is about 2.2. Figure 8.2.2 plots the same data, using a logarithmic scale for cB, to show more clearly the impact of reducing cB to a very small value. This approach is similar to the stock-service tradeoff figures of Chapter 6, but at an aggregate level.

FIGURE 8.2.1

Aggregate inventory-backorders tradeoff.

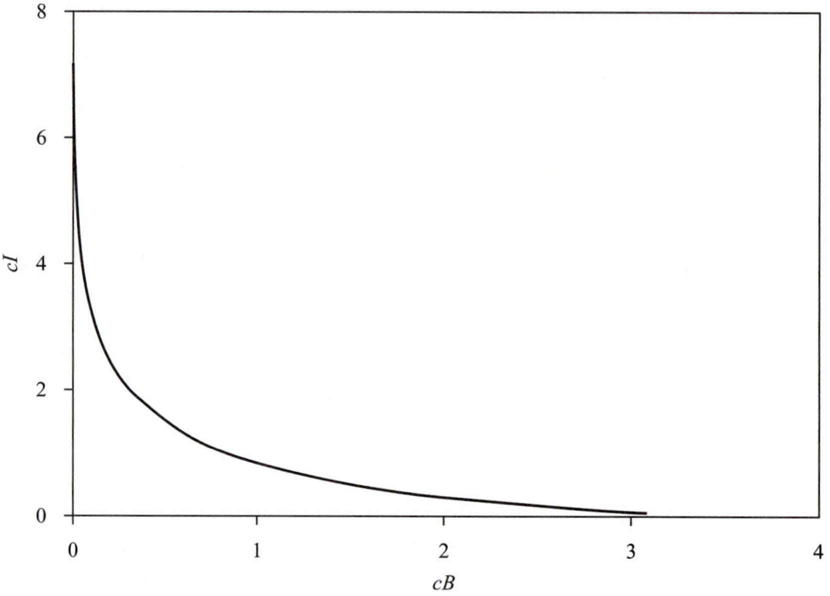

FIGURE 8.2.2

Aggregate inventory-backorders tradeoff (logarithmic scale).

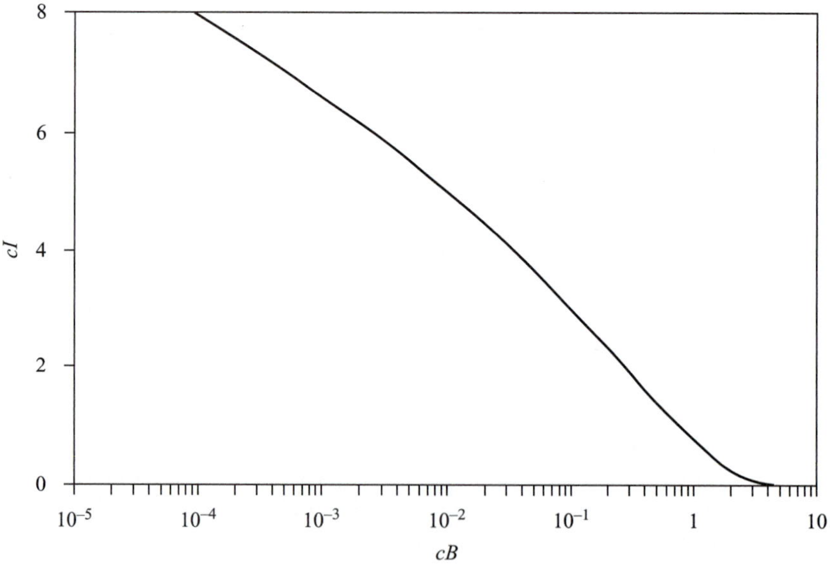

With given cost factors the optimal cost here becomes

$$C^* = c\lambda + (c\sigma)(\beta + \eta)\Phi(z^*) \tag{8.2.3}$$

Aside from the constant purchase cost $c\lambda$, the total cost also is proportional to $c\sigma$.

The aggregate parameter $c\sigma$, then, expresses the essential effect of multiple items, something like the variety index J_* of Section 5.2. Specifically, we cannot predict performance solely on the basis of an aggregate-demand statistic such as $c\lambda$. For example, if each item's demand process is Poisson, and all items share the common fixed leadtime L, then $\sigma_j = \sqrt{\lambda_j L}$, so $c\sigma = (\sqrt{L})\Sigma_j c_j \sqrt{\lambda_j}$. To estimate performance, then, requires information about the *distribution* of the λ_j over the items. Again, because of the concavity of the square-root function, we expect a system with few items having large λ_j to cost less than one with many low-demand items. (Remember, nevertheless, there may be solid marketing arguments for a differentiated product line.)

This point is clearest in the case of identical items. Suppose we keep the *total* demand rate λ constant, so $c\lambda$ is just the product of λ and the (common) cost rate c. Each $\lambda_j = \lambda/J$, so $\sigma_j = \sqrt{\lambda L/J}$ and $c\sigma = c\sqrt{J\lambda/L}$. Thus, apart from the constant term $c\lambda$, the total cost C^* is proportional to the square root of the number of items.

8.2.2 General (r, q) Policies

Now, suppose there are scale economies in supply, and we follow an (r, q) policy for each item. We need another aggregate performance measure (first introduced in Section 5.2):

$$\begin{aligned} wO &= \text{aggregate average workload} \\ &= \Sigma_j\, w_j \overline{OF}_j \end{aligned}$$

Let us extend the individual-item approach above: Specify κ, the unit cost of the resources measured in wO, and the cost factors

$$k_j = \kappa w_j \qquad j = 1, \ldots, J$$

in addition to η, β, and the h_j and b_j defined in (8.2.1). Then, find the optimal (r, q) policy for each item separately and combine the results to determine an efficient point (cI, pB, wO). By repeating this process for different values of κ/η and β/η, we can trace out an *aggregate tradeoff surface,* a two-dimensional surface in the three-space with coordinates (cI, pB, wO). This surface describes the best (smallest) possible value of any one of the measures, given the values of the other two.

Under the simplifying assumptions above, we obtain simpler results: Use the upper bound in (6.5.9) to approximate the optimal cost for each item. The (approximate) total cost becomes

$$C^* \approx \Sigma_j\, [c_j\lambda_j + C_{\sigma j} + C_{kj}]$$

where

$$\begin{aligned} C_{\sigma j} &= c_j\sigma_j(\beta + \eta)\Phi(z^*) \\ C_{kj} &= \sqrt{2(\kappa w_j)\lambda_j(\eta c_j)\omega} \end{aligned}$$

Summing these terms yields

$$C^* \approx c\lambda + c\sigma(\beta + \eta)\Phi(z^*) + \sqrt{2(\kappa\eta\omega)(wc\lambda)J_*} \tag{8.2.4}$$

where J_* is the variety index of Section 5.2.

Here we see, in one line, *all* the significant determinants of performance. The aggregate statistic $c\sigma$ has a scaling effect on one of the terms, just as in the base-stock model above, while the variety index plays the same role as in the deterministic model of Section 5.2. In the identical-item case, $J_* = J$, so again (apart from the constant $c\lambda$) C^* is proportional to $\sqrt{J}$.

8.3 Series Systems

8.3.1 Base-Stock Policy Evaluation: Poisson Demand, Constant Leadtimes

Consider a series system, like that of Section 5.3: There are J stages. The numbering of stages follows the flow of goods. Stage 1 receives supplies from an outside source. All other links are internal; each stage $j < J$ feeds its successor, stage $j + 1$. Each stage has its own associated supply system. When stage $j - 1$ sends a shipment toward stage j (or the source sends a shipment to stage $j = 1$), the shipment must pass through stage j's supply system before arriving at j. Every stage can hold inventory. Demand is stochastic; it occurs only at the last stage, J.

Until Section 8.3.4 we focus on the simplest case: Demand is a Poisson process with rate λ, and each stage j's supply system generates constant leadtimes, L'_j. There are no scale economies in supply and consequently no incentives to batch orders or shipments.

We shall consider natural extensions of the base-stock policy for a single stage. In a multistage system, there are two types of base-stock policy, local and echelon. As we shall see, although they seem quite different, they are equivalent in this context.

A *local base-stock policy* is a decentralized control scheme, where each stage monitors its own local inventory position, places orders with its predecessor, and responds to orders from its successor. Each stage j follows a standard, single-stage base-stock policy with parameter

$$s'_j = \text{local base-stock level for stage } j$$

a non-negative integer. The overall policy is described by the vector $\mathbf{s}' = (s'_j)_{j=1}$.

The policy works as follows: Stage J monitors its own inventory position. It experiences demands and places orders with stage $J - 1$ just like a single location operating alone, using a standard base-stock policy with base-stock level s'_J. Stage $J - 1$ treats these incoming orders as its own demands, filling them (releasing shipments, to arrive after time L'_J) when it has stock available and otherwise logging backorders to be filled later. It too follows a standard base-stock policy with parameter s'_{J-1} to determine the orders it places with stage $J - 2$. Stage $J - 2$ treats these orders as its demands, et cetera. Stage 1's orders go to the external source, which fills them immediately, so they arrive at stage 1 after time L'_1.

Suppose that each stage starts with inventory s'_j and an empty supply system. Then, each customer demand at stage J immediately triggers a demand at stage $J - 1$, which in turn generates a demand at stage $J - 2$, and so on. In this way demands propagate backward through the system, all the way to the external source. Thus, every stage experiences the original demand process.

Our goal is to evaluate such a policy. Define for $t \geq 0$

$$\begin{aligned}
I'_j(t) &= \text{local inventory at stage } j \\
B'_j(t) &= \text{local backorders at stage } j \\
IN'_j(t) &= \text{local net inventory at stage } j \\
&= I'_j(t) - B'_j(t) \\
IO_j(t) &= \text{inventory on order at stage } j \\
IOP'_j(t) &= \text{local inventory-order position at stage } j \\
&= IN'_j(t) + IO_j(t) \\
IT_j(t) &= \text{inventory in transit to stage } j \text{ (number of units in stage } j\text{'s supply system)} \\
ITP'_j(t) &= \text{local inventory-transit position at stage } j \\
&= IN'_j(t) + IT_j(t)
\end{aligned}$$

The "orders" in the definitions of $IO_j(t)$ and $IOP'_j(t)$ refer to those generated by the local base-stock policy. The other variables describe actual, physical quantities. Notice the difference between stock on order $IO_j(t)$ and stock in transit $IT_j(t)$: $IO_j(t)$ includes all outstanding stage-j orders, but $IT_j(t)$ includes only those that stage $j - 1$ has been able to fill already; i.e., those that have begun their passage through stage j's supply system. The difference is precisely the local backorders at $j - 1$. Of course, $IT_1(t) = IO_1(t)$, because the outside source responds immediately to orders from stage 1. Thus, setting $B'_0(t) \equiv 0$, for all j and t,

$$IO_j(t) - IT_j(t) = IOP'_j(t) - ITP'_j(t) = B'_{j-1}(t)$$

Each stage's inventory-order position remains constant at $IOP'_j(t) = s'_j$, but the inventory-transit position $ITP'_j(t)$ changes over time.

There are several possible approaches to performance evaluation. One, parallel to those of Sections 6.2.2, 7.2, and 7.3 in earlier chapters, focuses on the supply-system occupancies $IT_j(t)$. The definitions above imply

$$\begin{aligned}
B'_j(t) &= [-IN'_j(t)]^+ \\
&= [IO_j(t) - IOP'_j(t)]^+ \\
&= [B'_{j-1}(t) + IT_j(t) - s'_j]^+
\end{aligned}$$

So, *given* the $IT_j(t)$, the random variables $B'_j(t)$ satisfy the recursion

$$\begin{aligned}
B'_0(t) &= 0 \\
B'_j(t) &= [B'_{j-1}(t) + IT_j(t) - s'_j]^+
\end{aligned} \tag{8.3.1}$$

Now, it is difficult to characterize the $IT_j(t)$ directly. So, we shall utilize a different approach here. [There will be other uses for (8.3.1) later on.]

Consider the look-ahead approach of Section 6.2.3: A direct conservation-of-flow argument, like that underlying (6.2.7), indicates that

$$\begin{aligned} IN_j'(t + L_j') &= IN_j'(t) + IT_j(t) - D(t, t + L_j'] \\ &= ITP_j'(t) - D(t, t + L_j'] \\ &= s_j' - B_{j-1}'(t) - D(t, t + L_j'] \end{aligned} \tag{8.3.2}$$

Let $L_0 = 0$ and

$$L_j = \Sigma_{i \leq j} L_i'$$

This is the *backward echelon leadtime* for stage j (*not* the forward echelon leadtime used in Chapter 5). Rewrite (8.3.2) at shifted times:

$$IN_j'(t + L_j) = s_j' - B_{j-1}'(t + L_{j-1}) - D(t + L_{j-1}, t + L_j]$$

Using $B_j'(t + L_j) = [-IN_j'(t + L_j)]^+$, we obtain the recursion

$$\begin{aligned} B_0'(t) &= 0 \\ B_j'(t + L_j) &= [B_{j-1}'(t + L_{j-1}) + D(t + L_{j-1}, t + L_j] - s_j']^+ \end{aligned} \tag{8.3.3}$$

The interval $(t + L_{j-1}, t + L_j]$ has length L_j', and the intervals are disjoint. Therefore, $D(t + L_{j-1}, t + L_j]$ in (8.3.3) has the *Poisson distribution* with mean $\lambda L_j'$, and these random variables are *independent.* This distribution does not depend on t, so the $B_j'(t + L_j)$ are also stationary.

To describe the equilibrium behavior of the system, therefore, we can simply omit the time indicators in (8.3.3). Let

D_j = leadtime demand for stage j, a generic random variable having the Poisson distribution with mean $\lambda L_j'$; these D_j are independent

Then,

$$\begin{aligned} B_0' &= 0 \\ B_j' &= [B_{j-1}' + D_j - s_j']^+ \end{aligned} \tag{8.3.4}$$

Once we have the B_j', we can determine the I_j' through

$$\begin{aligned} I_j' &= \mathrm{IN}_j' + B_j' \\ &= s_j' - B_{j-1}' - D_j + B_j' \end{aligned}$$

We can now compute $E[B_j']$ and the $E[I_j']$, the performance measures of primary interest.

Note that the calculation is not that easy. We start with D_1, which has a Poisson distribution. To get the distribution of B_1', we shift and then truncate that of D_1. Next, we form the sum $B_1' + D_2$ by numerical convolution, then shift and truncate it to get B_2'. The subsequent steps are similar.

Here is a useful, relatively simple approximation: It requires only $E[D_j]$ and $V[D_j]$, and is called accordingly a *two-moment approximation.* Start by setting $E[B_0'] = V[B_0'] = 0$.

We know how to compute $E[B_1']$ and $V[B_1']$, since D_1 has a Poisson distribution. Suppose we have estimates of $E[B_{j-1}']$ and $V[B_{j-1}']$ for $j \geq 2$. Since B_{j-1}' is independent of D_j,

$$E[B_{j-1}' + D_j] = E[B_{j-1}'] + E[D_j]$$

$$V[B_{j-1}' + D_j] = V[B_{j-1}'] + V[D_j]$$

Using these quantities, approximate $B_{j-1}' + D_j$ with a negative-binomial distribution, and then compute $E[B_j']$ and $V[B_j']$ through (8.3.4) and the methods of Section 7.5.1.1. Continue in this manner to $j = J$. (We *can* use the negative-binomial distribution here, because every $V[B_j'] \geq E[B_j']$; see Problem 8.1.) This approximation, it turns out, is quite accurate.

We also need $E[IT_j]$. On average, we send λ units into stage j's supply system per unit time, and each unit stays there for time L_j', so $E[IT_j] = \lambda L_j'$. Notice, this is also $E[D_j]$.

To evaluate a policy in economic terms, we specify cost factors:

h_j' = inventory holding-cost rate at stage j
b = backorder cost rate at stage J

(There may also be a variable order cost c, but the average order cost is then just $c\lambda$, a constant, so we ignore it. Likewise, we ignore constants representing the variable costs of shipments between stages. On the other hand, we apply the holding cost h_j' not just to actual inventory at j but also to stock in transit to $j + 1$; on average this "pipeline holding cost" is just the constant $h_j'E[IT_{j+1}] = h_j'\lambda L_{j+1}'$.) The total average cost is thus

$$E\left[\Sigma_{j=1}^{J} h_j'(I_j' + IT_{j+1}) + bB_J'\right] \tag{8.3.5}$$

where $IT_{J+1} = 0$.

Let us review: The main result so far is (8.3.4). This recursion concisely expresses the linkages between stages. Each stage j operates much like an isolated single-stage system. The random variable $B_{j-1}' + D_j$ plays the role of the leadtime demand; the local base-stock level s_j' reduces stage-j backorders while increasing inventory in the usual way. What links the stage to its predecessors is the term B_{j-1}', which augments its "own" leadtime demand D_j.

Reflect for a moment on the managerial issues here: Customers see only the final-stage backorders B_J', and only those incur cost directly in (8.3.5). Only final-stage inventory provides *direct* protection against these backorders. The inventories at prior stages have *indirect* impacts; reducing B_j' reduces B_{j+1}', which reduces B_{j+2}', and so on through B_J'. (Problem 8.2 asks you to formalize this notion, specifically, to show that each $E[B_j']$ is nonincreasing and convex in all the s_i'.) Although direct stockout protection is more effective, it costs more; typically, the h_j' are increasing in j (as explained in Section 5.3.2).

To manage the system effectively, then, we must address some rather subtle tradeoffs. The overall issue remains the balance of inventory and backorders, but there are now alternative places to hold inventory with different costs and benefits. Clearly, we cannot choose the s_j' independently, for if we keep more stock at one stage, we need less at the others.

As we shall see now, there is another way to look at the system's dynamics and costs, which expresses these interactions in simpler terms. This approach sets the stage for the policy-optimization method developed later.

8.3.2 Echelon-Based Calculations

Define

$$
\begin{aligned}
B(t) &= \text{system backorders} \\
&= B'_J(t) \\
I_j(t) &= \text{echelon inventory at stage } j \\
&= I'_j(t) + \Sigma_{i>j}\,[IT_i(t) + I'_i(t)] \\
IN_j(t) &= \text{echelon net inventory at stage } j \\
&= I_j(t) - B(t) \\
IOP_j(t) &= \text{echelon inventory-order position at stage } j \\
&= IN_j(t) + IO_j(t) \\
ITP_j(t) &= \text{echelon inventory-transit position at stage } j \\
&= IN_j(t) + IT_j(t) \\
h_j &= \text{echelon inventory holding-cost rate at stage } j \\
&= h'_j - h'_{j-1}
\end{aligned}
$$

An *echelon base-stock policy* is a centralized control scheme. We monitor the echelon inventory-order positions $IOP_j(t)$. (These quantities, it turns out, summarize all the relevant information about the system.) We determine orders and interstage shipments so as to keep each $IOP_j(t)$ constant. In other words, each stage j applies a base-stock policy. The policy variables are

$$s_j = \text{echelon base-stock level for stage } j$$

Let $\mathbf{s} = (s_j)_{j=1}^J$.

We can reinterpret a local base-stock policy in echelon terms: Given $\mathbf{s}'$, set $s_j = \Sigma_{i\geq j}\, s'_i$. Now, the initial conditions $I'_j(0) = s'_j$ and $IT_j(0) = 0$ imply $IOP_j(0) = s_j$, so the echelon base-stock policy dictates that every stage order a unit precisely when a demand occurs. Thus, this policy is entirely equivalent to the original, local one.

Conversely, every echelon base-stock policy is equivalent to a local one. Given $\mathbf{s}$, if the s_j are nonincreasing, set $s'_j = s_j - s_{j+1}$ (where $s_{J+1} = 0$). In general, set $s_j^- = \min_{i\leq j}\{s_i\}$, and $s'_j = s_j^- - s_{j+1}^-$ (where $s_{J+1}^- = 0$). The policy $\mathbf{s}$, it turns out, is equivalent to $\mathbf{s}^- = \{s_j^-\}_{j=1}^J$, whose components are nonincreasing.

To see this, consider a two-stage system ($J = 2$), and assume $s_1 < s_2$. Suppose the system starts with no inventory at stage 1 and inventory s_1 at stage 2. Stage 2 immediately orders $s_2 - s_1$, but stage 1 has no inventory, so it backlogs those orders. In fact, stage 1's echelon inventory position is already at its base-stock level s_1, so it orders only in response to subsequent demands. Thus, the initial backlog at stage 1 stays there forever, that is, it remains at least $s_2 - s_1$. Stage 1 never holds inventory, and the inventory at stage 2 never exceeds s_1. In sum, the physical flow of units is precisely the same as in the policy $\mathbf{s}^-$, where $s_2^- = s_1^- = s_1$, and therefore as in the local policy with $s'_1 = 0$ and $s'_2 = s_1$.

This same logic extends to arbitrary J. In general, $s_{j+1} \geq s_j$ implies $s'_{j+1} = s_j^-$, so $s'_j = 0$. That is, whenever s_{j+1} exceeds s_j, stage j holds no inventory at all. By the way, $\mathbf{s}$ can even have some components $s_j = \infty$ for $j > 1$. Provided s_1 is finite, all of the s_j^- and s'_j are too. Of course, if $s_{j+1} = \infty$, then certainly $s_{j+1} \geq s_j$, so stage j never holds inventory.

In conclusion, *every* local base-stock policy is equivalent to some echelon base-stock policy, and *vice versa.* As we shall see in Chapter 9, the true *optimal* policy, based on fully centralized information, *is* an echelon base-stock policy. Thus, in this setting, there is no essential difference between centralized and local control; centralized control can be implemented locally.

To evaluate an echelon base-stock policy, we can convert it to the equivalent local one and apply the method above. Still, it is interesting and useful to develop a scheme that works directly at the echelon level: As in (8.3.2), conservation of flow implies that

$$\begin{aligned} IN_j(t + L_j') &= IN_j(t) + IT_j(t) - D(t, t + L_j'] \\ &= ITP_j(t) - D(t, t + L_j'] \end{aligned}$$

Also, the definitions of the state variables imply (Problem 8.3)

$$ITP_j(t) = \min\{s_j, IN_{j-1}(t)\} \tag{8.3.6}$$

Rewriting these identities at shifted times yields a recursion analogous to (8.3.3):

$$\begin{aligned} ITP_1(t) &= s_1 \\ IN_j(t + L_j) &= ITP_j(t + L_{j-1}) - D(t + L_{j-1}, t + L_j] \\ ITP_{j+1}(t + L_j) &= \min\{s_{j+1}, IN_j(t + L_j)\} \end{aligned}$$

In equilibrium this becomes

$$\begin{aligned} ITP_1 &= s_1 \\ IN_j &= ITP_j - D_j \\ ITP_{j+1} &= \min\{s_{j+1}, IN_j\} \end{aligned} \tag{8.3.7}$$

Also, the definitions of the state variables and straightforward algebra yield an alternative expression for the average cost (8.3.5):

$$C(\mathbf{s}) = E[\Sigma_{j=1}^{J} h_j IN_j + (b + h_J')B] \tag{8.3.8}$$

Here is an equivalent way to organize these calculations. (It is not really easier, but it connects (8.3.7) to the optimization algorithm below.) Define the functions

$$\begin{aligned} \hat{C}_j(x|\mathbf{s}) &= E[\Sigma_{i\geq j} h_i IN_i + (b + h_J')B | IN_j = x] \\ C_j(y|\mathbf{s}) &= E[\Sigma_{i\geq j} h_i IN_i + (b + h_J')B | ITP_j = y] \\ \underline{C}_j(x|\mathbf{s}) &= E[\Sigma_{i\geq j} h_i IN_i + (b + h_J')B | IN_{j-1} = x] \end{aligned}$$

The conditioning events refer to (8.3.7). For example, to compute $C_j(y|\mathbf{s})$, fix $ITP_j = y$, and continue the recursion from that point. The $\mathbf{s}$ here just serves as a reminder that the policy is fixed.

These functions can be determined recursively: First, $\underline{C}_{J+1}(x|\mathbf{s}) = (b + h_J')[x]^-$. For $j = J, J - 1, \ldots, 1$, given $\underline{C}_{j+1}$, compute

$$\begin{aligned} \hat{C}_j(x|\mathbf{s}) &= h_j s + \underline{C}_{j+1}(x|\mathbf{s}) \\ C_j(y|\mathbf{s}) &= E[\hat{C}_j(y - D_j|\mathbf{s})] \\ \underline{C}_j(x|\mathbf{s}) &= C_j(\min\{s_j, x\}|\mathbf{s}) \end{aligned}$$

By (8.3.7) this algorithm does compute the functions correctly. The average cost (8.3.8) is precisely $C(\mathbf{s}) = C_1(s_1|\mathbf{s})$.

8.3.3 Base-Stock Policy Optimization

A slight variant of the algorithm above determines the *best* echelon base-stock policy: Set $\underline{C}_{J+1}(x) = (b + h'_J)[x]^-$. For $j = J, J-1, \ldots, 1$, given $\underline{C}_{j+1}$, compute

$$\hat{C}_j(x) = h_j x + \underline{C}_{j+1}(x)$$
$$C_j(y) = E[\hat{C}_j(y - D_j)]$$
$$s_j^* = \text{argmin}\ \{C_j(y)\}$$
$$\underline{C}_j(x) = C_j(\min\ \{s_j^*, x\}) \qquad (8.3.9)$$

At termination, set $\mathbf{s}^* = (s_j^*)$ and $C^* = C_1(s_1^*)$. We prove below that these quantities describe the optimal policy and the optimal cost.

Evidently, this recursion is nearly identical to the policy-evaluation algorithm above, but there the s_j are predetermined constants, while here the s_j^* emerge within the calculation. (If the minimum over $C_j(y)$ is not unique, select the smallest minimizing value. Also, C_j may be a nonincreasing function; this happens when $h_j = 0$. If so, set $s_j^* = \infty$. As discussed above, an infinite s_j does have a sensible meaning. In that case $\underline{C}_j = C_j$.) The construction of $\underline{C}_j$ from C_j is illustrated in Figure 8.3.1.

In general, the optimal-policy vector $\mathbf{s}^*$ need not be nonincreasing. As in Section 8.3.2, however, it is equivalent to a nonincreasing vector $\mathbf{s}^{-*}$, where $s_j^{-*} = \min_{i \le j} \{s_i^*\}$. This policy, and hence the corresponding local policy $\mathbf{s}'^*$, can be determined only when the entire algorithm is completed. Only then can we see which stages hold stock and which do not.

Now, let us prove that the algorithm does find the best policy:

LEMMA 8.3.1. For all j, C_j and $\underline{C}_j$ are convex functions. Also, for any fixed echelon base-stock policy $\mathbf{s}$, $C_j(\cdot|\mathbf{s}) \ge C_j(\cdot)$ and $\underline{C}_j(\cdot|\mathbf{s}) \ge \underline{C}_j(\cdot)$.

PROOF. We argue by induction on j. Certainly, $\underline{C}_{J+1}$ is convex and $\underline{C}_{J+1}(\cdot|\mathbf{s}) = \underline{C}_{J+1}$. So, suppose that $\underline{C}_{j+1}$ is convex and $\underline{C}_{j+1}(\cdot|\mathbf{s}) \ge \underline{C}_{j+1}$ for any $j \ge 1$. First, $\hat{C}_j$ is clearly convex, and the expectation defining C_j preserves convexity, so C_j is convex. And since C_j is convex, so is $\underline{C}_j$. (This is clear from Figure 8.3.1: $\underline{C}_j(y)$ is decreasing and convex for $y < s_j^*$ and constant for $y \ge s_j^*$.) Also, from $\underline{C}_{j+1}(\cdot|\mathbf{s}) \ge \underline{C}_{j+1}(\cdot)$, it follows immediately that $C_j(\cdot|\mathbf{s}) \ge C_j(\cdot)$, and this implies

$$\underline{C}_j(y|\mathbf{s}) = C_j(\min\ \{s_j, y\}|\mathbf{s})$$
$$\ge C_j(\min\ \{s_j, y\})$$
$$\ge C_j(\min\ \{s_j^*, y\}) = \underline{C}_j(y)$$

(The last inequality is also evident from Figure 8.3.1: If we use some other value of s_j besides s_j^* to construct $\underline{C}_j$, we end up with a function that is greater than $\underline{C}_j$ itself.) This completes the induction.

FIGURE 8.3.1

Construction of revised cost function.

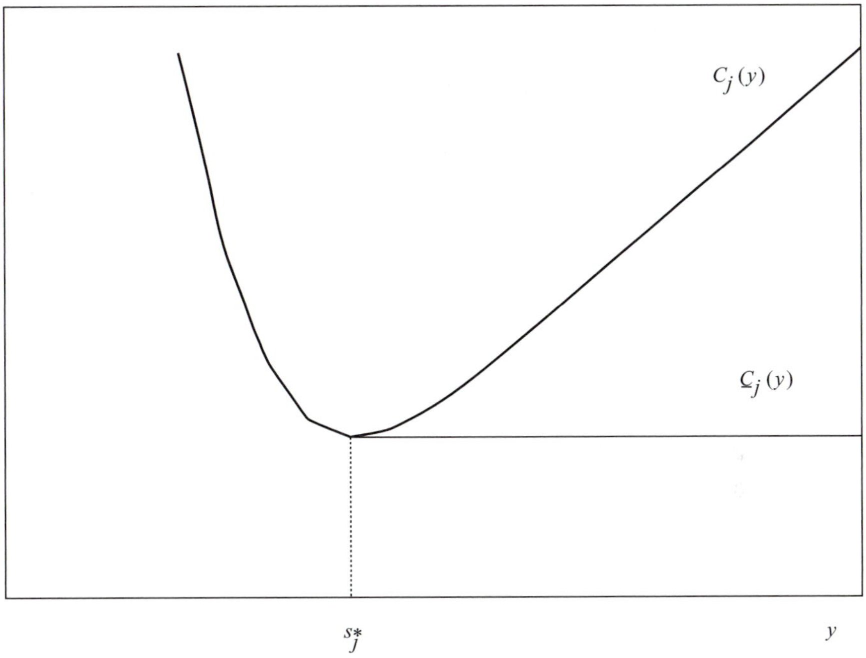

THEOREM 8.3.2. The policy determined by $\mathbf{s}^*$ is optimal among all base-stock policies.

PROOF. Comparing the algorithms in this and the previous subsections, it is apparent that $C_1(s_1^*)$ is in fact $C(\mathbf{s}^*)$, the average cost of the policy $\mathbf{s}^*$. And, the lemma tells us that no other policy has lower cost.

Recursion (8.3.9) deserves to be called *the fundamental equation of supply-chain theory.* It captures the basic dynamics and economics of serial systems.

It is remarkable that such a simple recursive scheme works at all: To determine s_j^*, we ignore nearly everything about upstream stages. We need to know the prior stage's holding cost h'_{j-1} to compute h_j, but that is all; s_j^* is completely unaffected by the D_i, $i < j$. (Still, we don't know what s_j^* means in local terms until we compute all the s_i^*.)

We can think of each C_j as the average-cost function of a single-stage system. This is literally true for $j = J$; the cost rates may seem odd (h_J plays the role of the holding cost and $b + h'_{j-1}$ the penalty cost), but the form is correct. For $j < J$ the term involving $\underline{C}_{j+1}$ replaces the usual penalty cost; $\underline{C}_{j+1}$ is sometimes called the *implicit penalty-cost function.*

How hard is it to implement the algorithm? It is helpful to know that every C_j is convex, so it is relatively easy to search for s_j^*. The evaluation of $C_j(y) = E[\hat{C}_j(y - D_j)]$ for $j < J$, however, is hard. It requires a direct numerical calculation.

8.3.4 Other Demand and Supply Processes

The same methods can be used to evaluate and optimize, exactly or approximately, under a variety of other model assumptions.

8.3.4.1 Compound-Poisson Demand

Suppose that demand is a compound-Poisson process. As in Section 6.6, each increment of demand can be filled separately. *All* the arguments and results above remain valid. Here, each D_j has a compound-Poisson distribution, but that is the only difference.

8.3.4.2 Exogenous, Sequential Supply Systems

Suppose that each stage has an exogenous, sequential supply system, as in Section 7.4. Let $L_j'(t)$ denote the virtual leadtime for stage j; a shipment to j begun at time t arrives at $t + L_j'(t)$. Assume these systems are independent of one another, as well as of the demand process, so the $L_j'(t)$ are independent over j. Let L_j' be the equilibrium leadtime (random variable) for stage j.

The analogue of (8.3.2) is now

$$IN_j'(t + L_j'(t)) = s_j' - B_{j-1}'(t) - D(t, t + L_j'(t)]$$

Set $L_0(t) = 0$, and, for $j > 0$, $L_j(t) = L_{j-1}(t) + L_j'(t + L_{j-1}(t))$. Thus, $L_j(t)$ is the total time required, starting at t, to pass through the first j supply systems. Rewrite the identity above at shifted times:

$$IN_j'(t + L_j(t)) = s_j' - B_{j-1}'(t + L_{j-1}(t)) - D(t + L_{j-1}(t), t + L_j(t)]$$

Thus, the backorders satisfy the following recursion, analogous to (8.3.3):

$$B_0'(t) = 0$$

$$B_j'(t + L_j(t)) = [B_{j-1}'(t + L_{j-1}(t)) + D(t + L_{j-1}(t), t + L_j(t)] - s_j']^+$$

The intervals $(t + L_{j-1}(t), t + L_j(t)]$ are disjoint, and their lengths $L_j'(t + L_{j-1}(t))$ are independent.

In equilibrium this recursion takes on precisely the same form as (8.3.4); that is,

$$B_0' = 0$$

$$B_j' = [B_{j-1}' + D_j - s_j']^+$$

The D_j have new meanings, however. Here, D_j has the distribution of $D(L_j')$, the demand over a random interval of time L_j', like D in Section 7.4. For Poisson demand,

$$E[D_j] = \lambda E[L_j'] \qquad V[D_j] = \lambda E[L_j'] + \lambda^2 V[L_j']$$

as in (7.5.7). Moreover, the D_j are independent. Similarly, (8.3.7) evaluates an echelon base-stock policy directly, and therefore algorithm (8.3.9) determines the best such policy. In sum, policy evaluation and optimization can be carried out just as in the fixed-leadtime case, using the new D_j in place of the old ones.

When each L_j' has a continuous phase-type (CPH) distribution, the recursion (8.3.4) can be performed exactly by using matrix-vector operations. See Problem 8.4.

8.3.4.3 Limited-Capacity Supply Systems

Return to the Poisson-demand case. Suppose each supply system consists of a single processor with exponential processing times and its queue, like the M/M/1 system of Section 7.3.2.1. Let μ_j be the processing rate for stage j's processor, and $\rho_j = \lambda/\mu_j$. The overall system now looks much like a processing network (Section 7.3.6.1), but now we can position inventory at each node, i.e., between pairs of successive processors, not just at stage J.

The derivation of (8.3.4) does not work here, so reconsider the alternative approach, starting with (8.3.1). The equilibrium version of that recursion is simply

$$B'_0 = 0$$
$$B'_j = [B'_{j-1} + IT_j - s'_j]^+ \tag{8.3.10}$$

Unfortunately, in general, it is hard to characterize the IT_j.

There is one case where it is easy, namely, when $\mathbf{s} = \mathbf{s}' = \mathbf{0}$. There, the system *is* a tandem network. (To see this, think about what happens when a demand occurs. The demand is passed back through stages $j < J$, creating a backorder at each one, all the way to the supplier, which releases a unit into stage 1's supply system. When the unit exits the stage-1 processor, stage 1 passes it along immediately to the stage-2 supply system, in order to fill the corresponding backorder. Likewise, each time a unit completes processing at stage $j < J$, it moves directly to the next supply system. Thus, the system works just like a standard tandem network.) Consequently, in this case, the occupancies IT_j are independent, and each IT_j has a geometric distribution with parameter ρ_j.

For general $\mathbf{s}' \geq \mathbf{0}$ we can use this same distribution to *approximate* the IT_j. That is, *assume* the IT_j are independent and geometrically distributed, and then apply (8.3.10). This approximation is quite accurate.

Notice the formal similarity of (8.3.10) and (8.3.4). Here, IT_j appears in place of D_j, but otherwise the recursions are the same. Similarly, one can derive an echelon-level recursion, analogous to (8.3.7):

$$ITP_1 = s_1$$
$$IN_j = ITP_j - IT_j$$
$$ITP_{j+1} = \min\{s_{j+1}, IN_j\}$$

Moreover, according to the approximation, the IT_j are independent, just like the D_j. So, using D_j to stand for the approximate IT_j, we can apply as is the methods of policy evaluation and optimization developed above. In particular, algorithm (8.3.9) finds the (approximately) best base-stock policy.

We remark that a base-stock policy need not be optimal here, in contrast to the constant-leadtime model. A base-stock policy often works well, but the true optimal policy is generally much more complex. We consider a more general (though still suboptimal) type of policy in Section 8.8.

8.3.4.4 Independent Leadtimes

The same approach works well when each supply system consists of multiple identical processors in parallel, so the leadtimes are independent, identically distributed random variables. The recursion (8.3.10) remains valid. As mentioned in Section 7.2.7, when $\mathbf{s} = \mathbf{s}' = \mathbf{0}$, the IT_j are independent, and IT_j has the Poisson distribution with mean $E[IT_j] = \lambda E[L'_j]$. We use this same distribution as an approximation in the general case.

According to this approximation, then, the performance of any policy is the same as in a constant-leadtime system; only the $E[L'_j]$ matter. As in Chapter 7, this is very different from the behavior of a sequential supply system, where the leadtime variances contribute significantly to performance.

8.3.4.5 Imperfect Quality

This approach can be used to analyze a system with imperfect quality: Stage i's supply system occasionally produces a defective unit, which is discovered immediately and must then return to the supply system of some earlier stage $j \leq i$. (Systems like this without internal inventories were discussed in Section 7.2.7 and Section 7.3.6.) Here, we must revise the base-stock policy slightly: A defect at stage i generates an implicit demand at all stages from j to $i - 1$, to account for the fact that a previously filled demand has now become, as it were, unfilled.

The approach, then, is to compute the IT_j as in an ordinary feedback network without internal inventories and to use the result as an approximation. In other words, compute the effective demand rates λ_j as in (7.2.4), and then proceed as above. This approximation seems to be reliably accurate.

The overall impact of poor quality is the same as in a network without internal inventories, depending on the nature of the supply systems: For uncapacitated parallel supply systems, poor quality increases the effective leadtimes. For limited-capacity sequential systems, defects reduce the effective processing rates.

8.3.5 Illustrations

This subsection presents some numerical examples, to provide insight into the behavior of the optimal policy.

8.3.5.1 Model Specification

We assume Poisson demand and constant leadtimes. Without loss of generality, we fix the time scale so that the total leadtime is $L = 1$, and the monetary unit so that the last stage's holding cost is $h'_J = 1$. The stages are spaced symmetrically, so each stage j's leadtime is $L'_j = 1/J$. We consider four numbers of stages, $J = 1, 4, 16, 64$; two demand rates, $\lambda = 16, 64$; and two penalty costs, $b = 9, 39$ (corresponding to fill rates of 90%, 97.5%).

We consider several forms of holding costs h'_j, depicted in Figure 8.3.2. The simplest form has *constant* holding costs, where all $h'_j = 1$. Here, there is no cost added from source to customer. This is a rather unrealistic scenario, but it is a useful starting point to help understand other forms. The *linear* holding-cost form has $h'_j = j/J$, or $h_j = 1/J$. Here, cost is incurred at a constant rate as the product moves from source to customer. This is quite realistic. *Affine* holding costs, where $h'_j = \alpha + (1 - \alpha)j/J$ for some $\alpha \in (0, 1)$, are even more realistic. Here, the material at the source has some positive cost, and the system then adds cost at a constant rate. This form is a combination of the constant and linear forms. Here, $\alpha = 0.75$.

FIGURE 8.3.2

Holding cost forms.

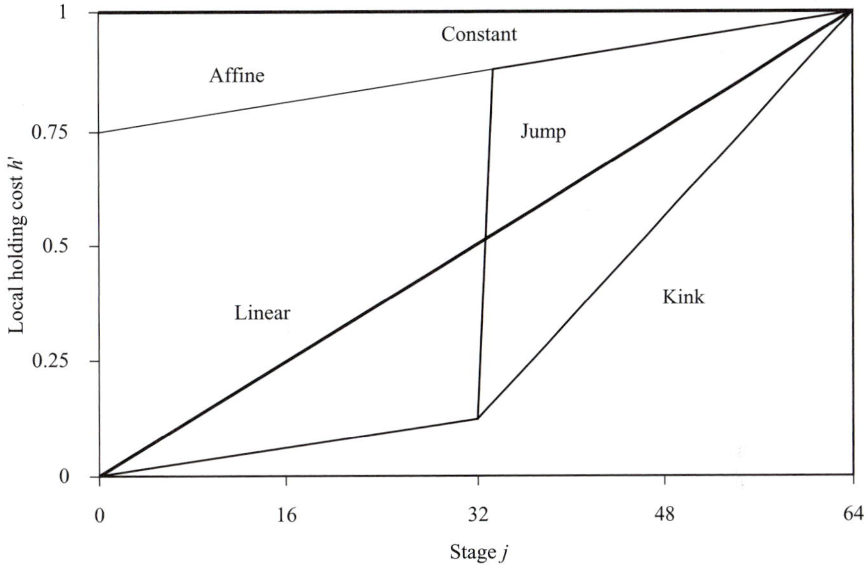

The last two forms represent deviations from linearity. The *kink* form is piecewise linear with two pieces. The system incurs cost at a constant rate for a while, but at some point shifts to a different rate, which remains constant from then on. Here, the kink occurs halfway through the process, at stage $J/2$. So, for some $\alpha \in (-1, 1)$, $h_j = (1 - \alpha)/J$, $j \leq J/2$, and $h_j = (1 + \alpha)/J$, $j > J/2$. Again, we set $\alpha = 0.75$. Finally, in the *jump* form, cost is incurred at a constant rate, except for one stage with a large cost. Here, the jump occurs just after stage $J/2$. So, $h_j = \alpha + (1 - \alpha)/J$, $j = J/2 + 1$, and $h_j = (1 - \alpha)/J$ otherwise, for some $\alpha \in (0, 1)$. We can view this as linear cost before $J/2$ and affine cost after. Here again, $\alpha = 0.75$.

8.3.5.2 Optimal Policy

For constant holding costs the optimal policy is simple: For $j < J$, $s_j'^* = 0$; only the last stage carries inventory. Stage J, in effect, becomes a single-stage system with leadtime L. The optimal policy is the same for all J. This is also the optimal policy for $J = 1$ under any other holding-cost form.

Figure 8.3.3*a* shows the optimal policy $\mathbf{s}^*$ for linear holding costs, $J = 64$, and two values each of λ and b. Several observations are worth noting: The curves are *smooth* and *nearly linear;* the optimal policy does *not* lump inventory in a few stages, but rather spreads it quite evenly. The departures from linearity are interesting too: The curves are *concave.* Thus, the policy focuses safety stock at stages nearest the customer.

Figure 8.3.3*b* shows the optimal policy for affine holding costs. For $j > 1$, the curves follow the same pattern as in the previous figure. (Indeed, the curves for $b = 9$ here are identical to those for linear costs and $b = 39$, because these two cases have identical

FIGURE 8.3.3

Optimal policy. (a) Linear holding costs; (b) affine holding costs; (c) kink holding costs; (d) jump holding costs.

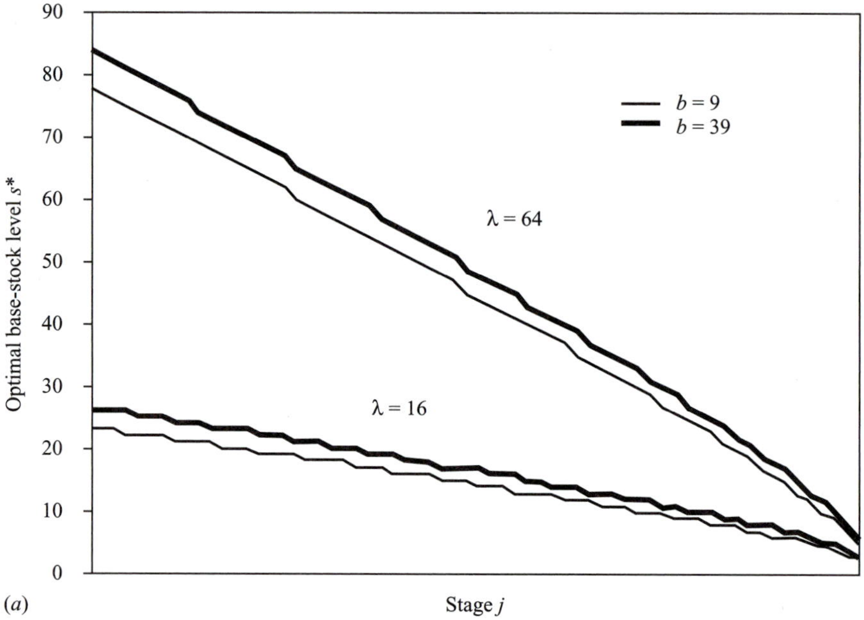

(*a*)

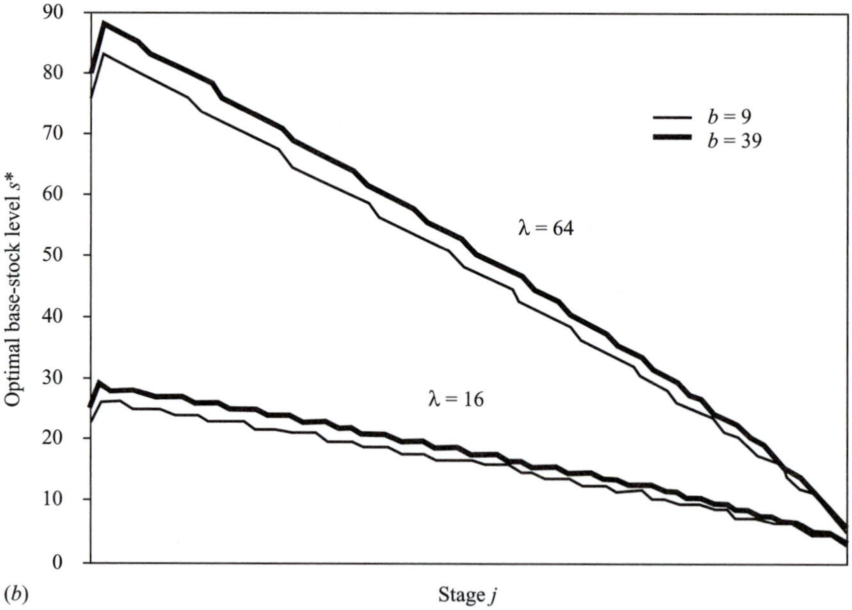

(*b*)

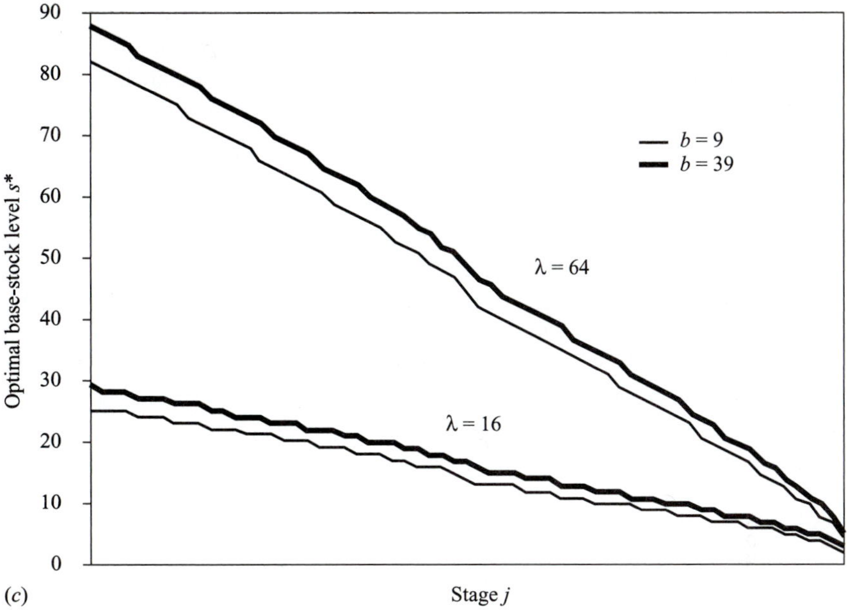
90
80
70
60
50
40
30
20
10
0
Optimal base-stock level s*
b = 9
b = 39
λ = 64
λ = 16
Stage j

(*c*)

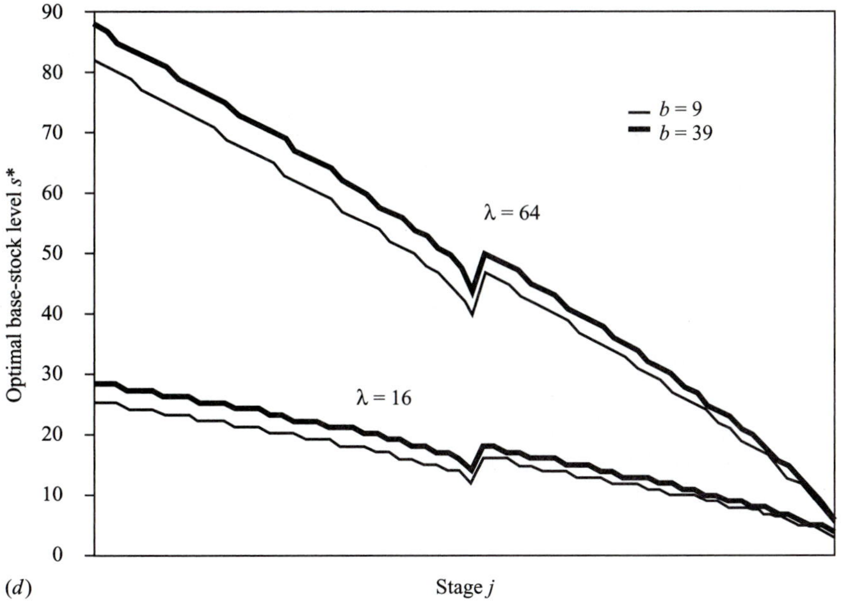
90
80
70
60
50
40
30
20
10
0
Optimal base-stock level s*
b = 9
b = 39
λ = 64
λ = 16
Stage j

(*d*)

ratios $h_j/(b + h'_J)$, $j > 1$.) However, the curves break down sharply at $j = 1$ (because h_1 is large). Therefore, the equivalent policy $\mathbf{s}^-$ is flat for small j, and so the policy holds *no* inventory at early stages. This solution is intermediate between those for constant and linear costs. As α increases and the costs move upward, stocks shift toward the customer. The total system stock decreases slightly. But, perhaps surprisingly, stocks near the customer actually increase.

Figure 8.3.3*c* displays $\mathbf{s}^*$ for kink holding costs. Downstream from the kink [before algorithm (8.3.9) encounters it], the curves exhibit the same pattern as in the linear case. Upstream from the kink, the policy again follows the linear pattern, almost as if the kink were the last stage. The net result is substantial stock at and just before the kink, where holding costs are low relative to later stages.

Finally, Figure 8.3.3*d* displays $\mathbf{s}^*$ for jump holding costs. From the jump on, the policy behaves much as in the affine case—smooth, concave decrease beyond the jump, but a sharp break downwards at the jump. Upstream from the jump, the policy again follows the pattern of the linear case. Thus, there is substantial stock just before the jump and none just after it.

8.3.5.3 Sensitivity Analysis

Figure 8.3.4 compares the $\mathbf{s}^*$ for different J's, each with linear holding costs, $\lambda = 64$, and $b = 39$. The curves follow the same patterns as before, as closely as the restricted numbers of stages allow. Indeed, the actual echelon stock at a stocking point is nearly identical to the $J = 64$ case. Closer inspection shows that the total system stock is slightly higher for larger J. Likewise, the optimal cost decreases in J, but quite slowly, as shown in Figure 8.3.5*a*.

Similar results hold for affine holding costs. Indeed, the optimal cost is even less sensitive to J. For kink holding costs (Figure 8.3.5*b*), the optimal cost is significantly lower at $J = 4$ than at $J = 1$, because of the availability of the low-cost stocking point at the kink. Larger J's yield relatively minor improvements. The jump form displays a similar pattern. Thus, for these two forms, it is important to position stock at the kink (or jump). Otherwise, the cost is quite insensitive to J.

These results suggest that *the system cost is relatively insensitive to stock positioning,* provided the overall stock level is about right, and obvious low-cost stocking points are exploited.

In Figure 8.3.5*a* and *b* the optimal cost for $\lambda = 64$ is about twice that for $\lambda = 16$ in every case. This is consistent with the notion that the optimal cost is nearly proportional to $\sqrt{\lambda}$, as in a single-stage system. We have also plotted, but omit here, the cumulative safety stocks $\Sigma_{i \le j} s'^*_j - \lambda j/J$. The curves for $\lambda = 64$ are about twice those for $\lambda = 16$. So, the safety stocks too are nearly proportional to $\sqrt{\lambda}$.

8.3.6 The Two-Stage System

Let us focus on a system with $J = 2$. For the last stage $j = 2$,

$$\hat{C}_2(x) = h_2 x + (b + h'_2)[x]^- = h_2[x]^+ + (b + h_1)[x]^-$$

$$C_2(y) = E[\hat{C}_2(y - D_2)]$$

FIGURE 8.3.4

Optimal policy: effects of J.

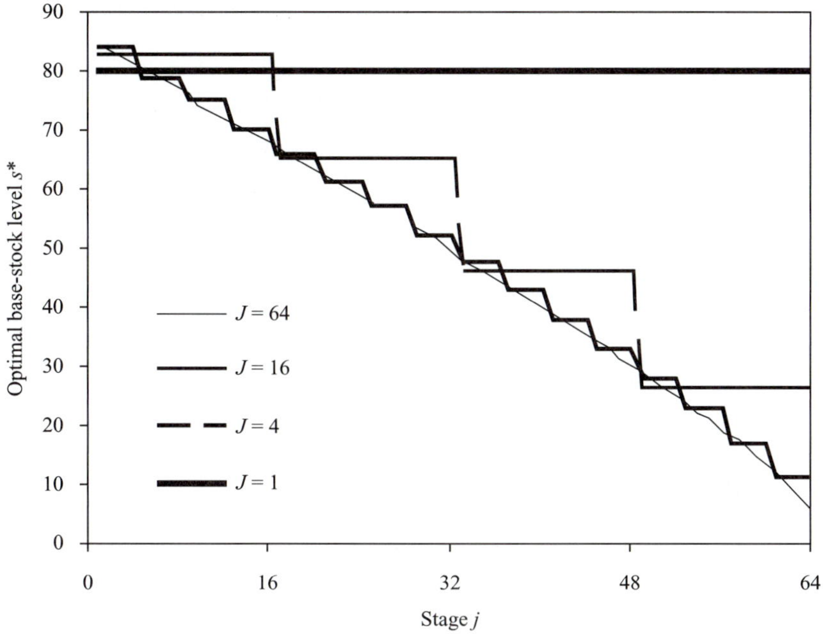

This is the cost function of a single-stage system, so it is easy to optimize. The stage-1 calculations are harder and less transparent. We shall derive simple bounds on $C_1(y)$, s_1^*, and the optimal cost C^*, and use them to gain additional insight into stock positioning.

Suppose we forbid stage 1 to hold inventory. That is, we restrict the feasible policies, fixing $s_1' = 0$. In echelon terms, we force $s_2 = \infty$, leaving s_1 free. Therefore, $\underline{C}_2(x)$ becomes $C_2(x)$ itself. Making this substitution in $\hat{C}_1$ and then C_1, we obtain the approximation

$$\begin{aligned} C_1^+(y) &= E[h_1(y - D_1) + C_2(y - D_1)] \\ &= h_1E[D_2] + h_2'(y - E[D]) + (b + h_2')E[[y - D]^-] \end{aligned}$$

where $D = D_1 + D_2$. This is the cost function of a single-stage system. Let s_1^+ denote the optimal value of y, and $C^{+*} = C_1^+(s_1^+)$.

Since we restricted the feasible policies, C^{+*} is an *upper bound* on C^*. Also, $\Delta C_2(y) \geq \Delta \underline{C}_2(y)$, so $\Delta C_1^+(y) \geq \Delta C_1(y)$ for all y. Consequently, s_1^+ provides a *lower bound* on s_1^*.

Now, assume that $h_2 > 0$, so s_2^* is finite. Observe, $C_1^+(y)$ coincides with $C_1(y)$ for $y \leq s_2^*$. So, suppose it turns out that $s_1^+ \leq s_2^*$. Then, $s_1^* = s_1^+ \leq s_2^*$. In this case, the corresponding local policy has $s_1'^* = 0$, i.e., stage 1 holds no stock. Otherwise, $s_2^* < s_1^+ \leq s_1^*$, so $s_1'^* > 0$, and stage 1 does hold stock.

Thus, *we can determine whether or not stage 1 should carry inventory by solving two single-stage systems,* one each for s_2^* and s_1^+. If not, we have actually solved the

Figure 8.3.5

Optimal cost. (a) Linear holding costs; (b) kink holding costs.

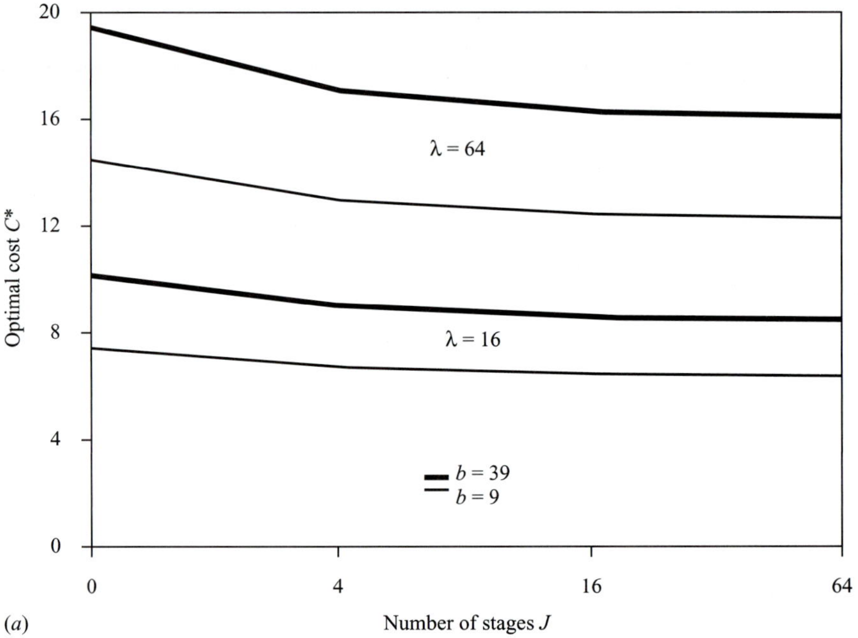

(*a*)

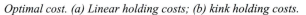

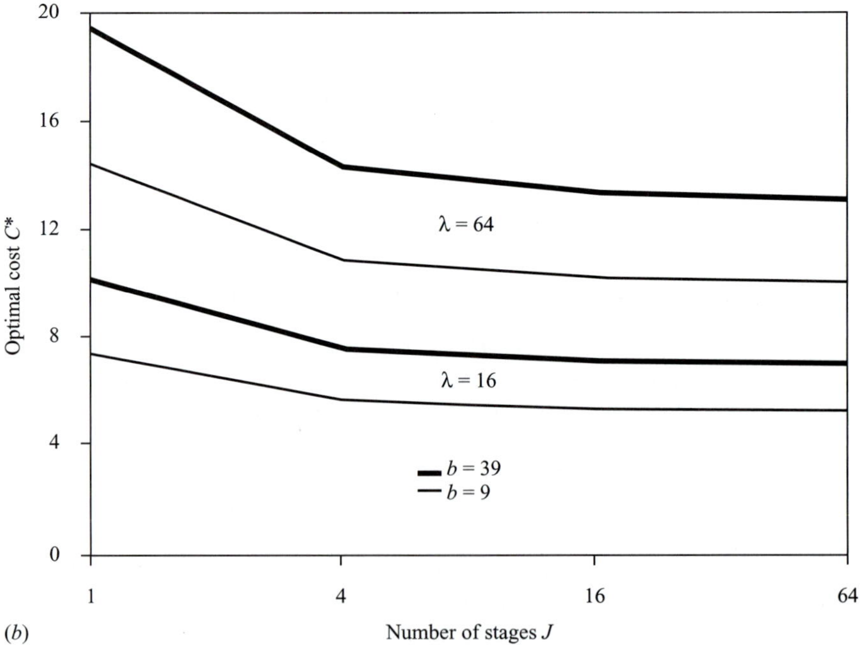

(*b*)

original model. If so, we have at least a lower bound on the amount of stock stage 1 should keep.

Some simple sensitivity analysis reveals how the distinction works: First, fix all parameters, including h'_2, but let h_1 vary between 0 and h'_2 (so $h_2 = h'_2 - h_1$). As h_1 changes, so does s_2^*, and in the same direction, but s_1^+ remains fixed. Indeed, as $h_1 \to h'_2$, $s_2^* \to \infty$, so $s_1^+ \le s_2^*$ for sufficiently large h_1. Conversely, as $h_1 \to 0$, $h_2 \to h'_2$, and since D is (stochastically) larger than D_2, $s_1^+ > s_2^*$ for sufficiently small h_1.

Thus, *stage 1 holds inventory when (but only when) it is* significantly *cheaper to hold it there than at stage 2.* The required difference, of course, depends on the other parameters.

Next, focus on the constant-leadtime case. Fix all parameters except L'_1. Only s_1^+ is affected by changes in L'_1, not s_2^*. When L'_1 is small, D is near D_2, so $s_1^+ \le s_2^*$. Conversely, for sufficiently large L'_1, $s_1^+ > s_2^*$. (This is true for *any* value of L'_2, but of course the distinction depends on L'_2. One can show that, as L_2 grows, the value of L'_1 required to make $s_1^+ \ge s_2^*$ grows also.)

That is, *stage 1 holds inventory when (but only when) its leadtime is substantial relative to stage 2's.* Otherwise, if its leadtime is negligible, inventory there serves no useful function. (A similar conclusion describes stochastic-leadtime models.)

Finally, applying the normal approximation to C_1^+, we see that the optimal cost is bounded above by a linear function of σ, where $\sigma^2 = V[D]$. Thus, the system parameters affect performance much as in a single-stage system.

8.3.7 *Economies of Scale*

Now, consider a system with scale economies in supply. There is a fixed cost k_j for shipments to stage j. We restrict attention to Poisson demand with constant or exogenous-sequential leadtimes.

8.3.7.1 Fixed Costs for External Supplies

First, suppose only $k_1 > 0$, but the other $k_j = 0$. That is, *internal* shipments generate no frictions, but *external* shipments from the outside supplier do. This special case is fairly simple:

An optimal policy has the form we might expect. Stages $j > 1$ follow a base-stock policy, as above, while stage 1 follows an (r, q) policy with parameters (r'_1, q_1), where $r'_1 + q_1 \ge 0$. Again, this is entirely equivalent to an echelon-based policy. That is, stages $j > 1$ follow an echelon base-stock policy; stage 1 monitors its echelon inventory-order position and applies an (r, q) policy to that quantity. (The echelon base-stock levels s_j are defined in terms of the s'_j as above for $j > 1$. Stage 1 uses the same q_1. Letting $s'_1 = r'_1 + q_1$ and $s_1 = s'_1 + s_2$, the echelon reorder point is $r_1 = s_1 - q_1$, so that $s_1 = r_1 + q_1$.)

To evaluate a policy of this type, we need only evaluate certain base-stock policies and then average the results, as in a single-stage system. These base-stock policies all have the same s_j, $j > 1$, but different s_1. Let $ITP_j(s)$ and $IN_j(s)$ denote the echelon-level random variables under a base-stock policy, as evaluated through (8.3.7), now viewed as functions of $s = s_1$. Also, abbreviate $(r_1, q_1) = (r, q)$.

Clearly, stage 1's (echelon) inventory-order position $\mathbf{IOP}_1$ behaves just like that of a single-stage system, so $ITP_1 = IOP_1$ is distributed uniformly over the integers $r + 1$ through $r + q$. Also, it is not hard to show that recursion (8.3.7) again describes the ITP_j and IN_j. From this it follows (Problem 8.8) that each ITP_j is a mixture of the $ITP_j(s)$, with $s = r + 1, \ldots, r + q$, using the equal mixing weights $1/q$, and IN_j is a similar mixture of the $IN_j(s)$. Consequently, $E[IN_j]$ is just the simple average of $E[IN_j(s)]$ over these s's, and $E[B]$ is the average of the $E[B(s)]$.

To compute the average cost of the policy, we can use these quantities directly. Alternatively, compute the functions $C_j(y|\mathbf{s})$ above. The actual average cost is then

$$C(r, q, \mathbf{s}) = \frac{k_1\lambda + \sum_{y=r+1}^{r+q} C_1(y|\mathbf{s})}{q} \tag{8.3.11}$$

These facts allow us to determine the best policy through a slight modification of algorithm (8.3.9). Compute the functions $C_j, j \geq 1$, and the $s_j^*, j > 1$. These s_j^* are in fact optimal. Moreover, the average cost of a policy using these base-stock levels and *any* (r, q) at stage 1 is just

$$C_1(r, q) = \frac{k_1\lambda + \sum_{y=r+1}^{r+q} C_1(y)}{q} \tag{8.3.12}$$

This looks just like (6.5.16), the cost of a single-stage model. Because C_1 is convex, Algorithm Optimize_rq of Section 6.5.4 minimizes $C_1(r, q)$ over (r, q). The minimal solution (r^*, q^*) and the s_j^* for $j > 1$ together constitute an optimal policy.

For a two-stage system we can obtain simple, intuitive characterizations of performance in the following way: Replace $C_1(y)$ in (8.3.12) by $C_1^+(y)$ from Section 8.3.6. Then apply Theorem 6.5.1, specifically, the bounds on the optimal single-stage cost (6.5.7) or (6.5.9). We then see, for instance, that σ drives performance as in the no-fixed-cost model; also, the optimal cost is bounded above by terms proportional to the square root of k_1. (Problem 8.10 asks you to work out the details.)

8.3.7.2 The General Case

Let us turn next to the general case, where all the k_j may be positive. Things now become more difficult. We do not even know what an optimal policy looks like. We describe a *plausible* type of policy. Here there *are* differences between local and centralized control. We outline first a local control scheme and then a centralized one. It turns out that the centralized policies include the local ones, but not *vice versa.* We present evaluation and (partial) optimization procedures for the more general centralized scheme.

Suppose each stage j uses a *local (r, q) policy* with parameters (r_j', q_j), where $r_j' + q_j \geq 0$. Each stage j monitors its own local inventory-order position, and orders batches of size q_j from its predecessor; these orders become the predecessor's demands. Assume that the policy is *nested,* meaning that, for $j < J$, r_j' and q_j are integer multiples of q_{j+1}. This is a reasonable restriction: Stage j experiences demands of size q_{j+1}, so it makes sense to order and to maintain stocks in similar units. Under this condition, if each $I_j'(0) = r_j' + q_j$ and $IT_j(0) = 0$, then $IN_j'(t)$ and $IOP_j'(t)$ remain integer multiples of q_{j+1} for all t. And, the policy *is* nested in the sense that, whenever stage j orders, so does $j + 1$.

Now, consider an *echelon (r, q) policy.* This works just like a local (*r, q*) policy, except that each stage monitors its *echelon* inventory-order position and bases its orders on that quantity. The policy variables are (r_j, q_j). Assume that the policy is *quasi-nested;* that is, q_j is an integer multiple of q_{j+1}. (This makes sense, for the reasons mentioned above. We can and do set each $I_j'(0)$ to an integer multiple of q_{j+1}, so $IN_j'(t)$ remains an integer multiple of q_{j+1} for all *t*.) As for the r_j, however, we require only that $r_j + q_j \geq 0$.

Given a local (*r, q*) policy, there is an equivalent echelon (*r, q*) policy: Use the same q_j, and set $s_j' = r_j' + q_j$, $s_j = \Sigma_{i \geq j} s_i'$, and $r_j = s_j - q_j$ (so that $s_j = r_j + q_j$). Clearly, the state variables have precisely the same values at all times under these two policies. Conversely, starting with an echelon-based policy, there is an equivalent nested local policy, *if* each $r_j - r_{j+1}$ is an integer multiple of q_{j+1}. (The argument parallels the earlier one for base-stock policies.) Otherwise, there is no equivalent local policy. Although it may not be obvious, the full freedom to choose the r_j in echelon (*r, q*) policies, beyond the restricted values of local policies, can indeed be valuable.

Intuitively, the relation between local and echelon policies can be seen by comparing the behavior of $\mathbf{IOP}_j'$ and $\mathbf{IOP}_j$. Both increase by q_j whenever stage *j* orders. But, $\mathbf{IOP}_j'$ decreases only when stage $j + 1$ orders, while $\mathbf{IOP}_j$ decreases with each actual customer demand. That is, under the echelon policy stage *j* learns about customer demands instantaneously, whereas under the local policy there is a delay in transmitting this information until enough demands accumulate to trigger an order by stage $j + 1$. If the echelon policy parameters satisfy the condition above, so that there is an equivalent local policy, then this delay is immaterial; the extra information is not used. Otherwise, there is a real difference. (We call the echelon policy "centralized," because it requires more information than stage-to-stage orders. Given that information, however, the control decisions are still taken locally.)

We now present a recursive method to evaluate an echelon (*r, q*) policy, analogous to (8.3.7). First, $ITP_1 = IOP_1$ is distributed uniformly over the integers $r_1 + 1$ through $r_1 + q_1$. Second, it remains true that

$$IN_j = ITP_j - D_j$$

Finally, recall that, for a base-stock policy, $ITP_{j+1} = \min\{s_{j+1}, IN_j\}$, which can be written as $s_{j+1} - ITP_{j+1} = [s_{j+1} - IN_j]^+$. The analogue here, it turns out, is

$$s_{j+1} - ITP_{j+1} = \pi(s_{j+1} - IN_j, q_{j+1}) \qquad (8.3.13)$$

where, for any positive integer *q*, the function $\pi(\cdot, q)$ is given by

$$\begin{aligned} \pi(x, q) &= \max\{x, (x) \bmod (q)\} \\ &= \begin{cases} x & x \geq 0 \\ (x) \bmod (q) & x < 0 \end{cases} \end{aligned}$$

This recursion is numerically intricate but conceptually straightforward.

To evaluate the shipment frequencies, we must determine just how shipment costs work. The policy may sometimes dictate shipping several batches of size q_j to stage *j* simultaneously. Does such a shipment incur only one fixed cost k_j or several, one for each batch? We encountered the same issue in Section 6.6, and again the correct answer depends on the actual situation. The analysis is much simpler, though the cost is greater, when each batch incurs its own cost, for then the average shipment cost to stage j is just $k_j\lambda/q_j$. The other case can be analyzed too, but only with more effort; we shall skip it.

This technique can evaluate any echelon (r, q) policy. What about optimization? Given *fixed* $\mathbf{q}$, we can find the optimal $\mathbf{r}$ (or equivalently $\mathbf{s} = \mathbf{r} + \mathbf{q}$) by an algorithm analogous to (8.3.9). Set $\underline{C}_{J+1}(x) = (b + h_J')[x]^-$. For $j = J, J-1, \ldots, 1$, given $\underline{C}_{j+1}$, compute

$$\hat{C}_j(x) = h_j x + \underline{C}_{j+1}(x)$$

$$C_j(y) = E[\hat{C}_j(y - D_j)]$$

$$\overline{C}_j(y) = \left(\frac{1}{q_j}\right) \Sigma_{z=0}^{q_j-1} C_j(y - z)$$

$$s_j^* = \text{argmin}\ \{\overline{C}_j(y)\}$$

$$\underline{C}_j(x) = C_j(s_j^* - \pi(s_j^* - x, q_j))$$

At termination, set $\mathbf{s}^* = (s_j^*)$ and $C^* = \overline{C}_1(s_1^*) + \Sigma_j k_j\lambda/q_j$.

To determine the best $\mathbf{q}$, a reasonable heuristic approach is to apply the methods of Chapter 5 to the corresponding deterministic system to obtain a good initial $\mathbf{q}$. Chen and Zheng [1994c] develop an alternative method, based on cost bounds (discussed below), which seems to work even better. Then, apply a local search, using the algorithm above at each step to optimize over $\mathbf{r}$.

There are ways to calculate a lower bound on the true optimal cost. (Problem 8.11 explores one idea.) By comparing this bound to the cost of a good (or the best) echelon (r, q) policy, we can estimate the policy's performance relative to *all* possible alternatives. In this way researchers have found that, for *some* systems, an echelon (r, q) policy performs quite well; the policy's cost exceeds the lower bound by only a few percent. We still lack strong results like those of Chapter 5, however. Specifically, we do not have a policy-construction heuristic that is *guaranteed* to perform well. This remains a pressing priority for research.

8.3.8 A Service-Level Constraint

Return to the case of no scale economies and Poisson demand. The models above measure customer service by outstanding backorders; to achieve adequate service, they penalize $E[B_J']$ by the cost b. Suppose instead there is a specified limit $1 - \omega_-$ on the fraction of demands backordered. We suggest the following simple approach, in the spirit of Section 6.5.5: Set b so that $b/(b + h_J') = \omega_-$, and proceed as above.

This approach works: Suppose we determine an optimal base-stock policy. Among other things, this policy chooses s_J' to minimize $h_J'E[I_J'] + bE[B_J']$, given the other s_j'. Consequently, as in Section 6.5.2, it sets the stockout probability $E[A_J']$ near $1 - \omega_-$. (Under a continuous approximation, $E[A_J'] = 1 - \omega_-$ exactly; the relation is approximate in a discrete model.) And $E[A_J']$ *is* the fraction of demands backordered.

Still, there is no guarantee that, among all feasible policies, this one minimizes the total average holding cost. But it is quite difficult to optimize in this sense, and the approach above is likely to perform well.

8.4 Assembly Systems

8.4.1 The Model

Recall, in the classification scheme of Chapter 5, an assembly system is a supply-demand network with a single end item J, such that every other item $j < J$ has just one successor. In contrast to a series system, however, an item j may have several predecessors, which compose the set $Pre\,(j)$. To make a unit of item j requires one unit each of *all* of its predecessors $i \in Pre\,(j)$.

Assume that customers demand only the end item, according to a Poisson or compound-Poisson process. There are no scale economies. Each item has its own constant leadtime, L'_j. (Recall, Chapter 5 allowed predecessor-specific leadtimes L'_{ij}. Here we assume that, for $i \in Pre\,(j)$, the L'_{ij} are equal to L'_j.) For instance, L'_j might represent a production activity that begins with an assembly operation, requiring all the components at the outset. So, it makes sense to take predecessor units from inventory and send them toward j only in complete kits, consisting of one unit each of *every* $i \in Pre\,(j)$, and we assume this from now on.

Figure 8.4.1 depicts such a system. The vertical lines show assembly operations, and the length of each arrow indicates the corresponding leadtime. Thus, the supply-system dynamics correspond to units moving at constant speed along the arrows. (We shall explain later the L''_j at the bottom.)

FIGURE 8.4.1

Assembly system.

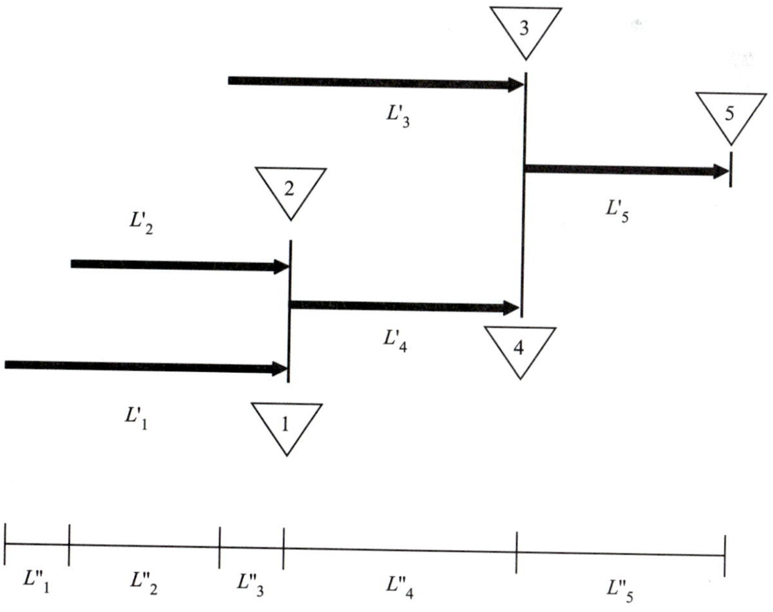

As in Section 5.4.2, we can interpret this picture as a project schedule, and this viewpoint provides some insight into the meaning of effective control. Suppose we operate the system entirely without inventories. When a demand occurs, we must order all the components and assemble them from scratch. Clearly, we want to schedule these events as indicated in the figure. This approach fills the demand as soon as possible, but given that requirement, it performs all activities as late as possible. Specifically, we order item 1 immediately, but wait a while before ordering item 2, so that the two units arrive together to be assembled into item 4. We order item 3 even later (but before the arrival of 1 and 2), so it arrives just when item 4 is ready.

Can a local control scheme realize this tight schedule? Consider what happens under a local base-stock policy with base-stock levels zero. A demand propagates backward through the network, so we order *all* raw materials (items 1, 2, and 3) immediately. Items 2 and 3 thus arrive too soon, before they can be used. Of course, we could modify this policy, either by delaying the demand signals or by instructing each item to wait before acting on its signals. But such modifications violate the spirit of pure local control.

The same issues arise when we do maintain inventories. Purely local information is inadequate to operate the system intelligently. (And the simple modifications above do *not* suffice in general.) We need global information.

Nevertheless, as we shall see, an assembly system can be reduced to an equivalent series system. Once we construct this equivalent system, we can use the methods of Section 8.3 for policy evaluation and optimization. The best policy, it turns out, is much like an echelon base-stock policy. To manage each item, however, it utilizes more than just locally available information.

As explained in Section 8.1, there are situations that *require* a local policy, where centralized control is expensive or impossible to implement. As shown in Section 8.4.5 below, series-system methods can also be used to evaluate a local base-stock policy.

(We do not yet know how to extend these results to stochastic supply systems. Nor do we know how to incorporate fixed costs, except in one very special case, discussed in Problem 8.13.)

8.4.2 Echelon Analysis and Inventory Balance

Define echelon-level state variables with the same meanings as in Section 5.4.3 and Section 8.3.2. Item *i*'s echelon inventory is the systemwide stock of *i*, including the local inventory of *i* itself, but also all downstream items along the path from *i* to *J*, as well as their supply systems. The net echelon inventories and the echelon inventory-transit positions can be defined recursively as

$$IN_J(t) = I_J(t) - B(t) = I_J'(t) - B_J'(t)$$

$$ITP_j(t) = IT_j(t) + IN_j(t)$$

$$IN_i(t) = I_i'(t) + ITP_j(t) \qquad i \in Pre\,(j)$$

(The stock in transit IT_j is measured in units of the destination item *j*. So, one unit of IT_j includes a unit each of the $i \in Pre\,(j)$.) Also,

$$h_j = h_j' - \Sigma_{i \in Pre(j)} h_i'$$

The total average cost can again be written as (8.3.8); i.e.,

$$E\left[\Sigma_{j=1}^{J} h_j IN_j + (b + h_J')B\right] \qquad (8.4.1)$$

Next, define

$\underline{L}_j$ = forward echelon leadtime for item j, *including* j's own leadtime

As in Section 5.3.2, this is the minimal time required to move a unit of item j to the customer, but here we start at the beginning of j's leadtime, not the end. Thus,

$$\underline{L}_J = L_J'$$
$$\underline{L}_i = L_i' + \underline{L}_j \qquad i \in Pre\,(j)$$

Renumber the items so that $\underline{L}_j$ is decreasing in j. (For now assume there are no ties, so $\underline{L}_j$ is *strictly* decreasing.) Also, set $\underline{L}_{J+1} = 0$, and define

$$L_j'' = \underline{L}_j - \underline{L}_{j+1}$$

$$L_j = \Sigma_{i \le j} L_i'' = \underline{L}_1 - \underline{L}_{j+1}$$

(L_j is the backward echelon leadtime. This definition is consistent with that of Section 8.3.) Observe that $L_j'' \le L_j'$ for all j. (Clearly, $L_J'' = L_J'$. For $i < J$, we have $i \in Pre\,(j)$ for some j, so $i + 1 \le j$, hence $L_i'' \le \underline{L}_i - \underline{L}_j = L_i'$.) Figure 8.4.1 illustrates this construction.

These concepts can help us delve deeper into the meaning of effective control. In Figure 8.4.1 the inventory of the end item 5 plays its usual role, to protect against demand surges and customer backorders. The inventories of its predecessors, items 3 and 4, provide indirect protection. But these internal inventories feed item 5 only in matched pairs. If there is more stock of item 4 than item 3 (or vice versa), the excess inventory is useless, at least in the near future. We would like to avoid such imbalances to the extent possible. Equivalently, we should aim to keep $IN_3(t)$ and $IN_4(t)$ roughly equal. For the same reason we should try to maintain equal (net echelon) inventories of items 1 and 2, the predecessors of item 4. In general, for each j, we should aim to equalize the $IN_i(t)$, $i \in Pre\,(j)$.

We cannot control these net inventories directly, however, so we must extend this notion of balance: What can we do now, at time t, to affect the net inventories of items 3 and 4? We can influence $IN_3(t + L_3')$ and $IN_4(t + L_4')$ by current shipments, so let us focus on the earliest of these times, $t + L_4'$. At that time we will have

$$IN_4(t + L_4') = ITP_4(t) - D(t, t + L_4']$$

What will item 3's net inventory be then? Well, *some* of $IT_3(t)$ will arrive by $t + L_4'$, but not all. Let $IT_3^-(t)$ denote that portion of $IT_3(t)$, namely, the units that entered item 3's supply system before time $(t + L_4') - L_3' = t - L_3''$. Letting

$$IN_3^+(t) = IT_3^-(t) + IN_3(t)$$

we have

$$IN_3(t + L_4') = IN_3^+(t) - D(t, t + L_4']$$

Thus, $IN_4(t + L_4') = IN_3(t + L_4')$ if and only if $ITP_4(t) = IN_3^+(t)$. Of these latter two quantities, we can control only $ITP_4(t)$ directly, and we can only increase it. So, if $ITP_4(t) > IN_3^+(t)$,

FIGURE 8.4.2

Equal forward echelon leadtimes.

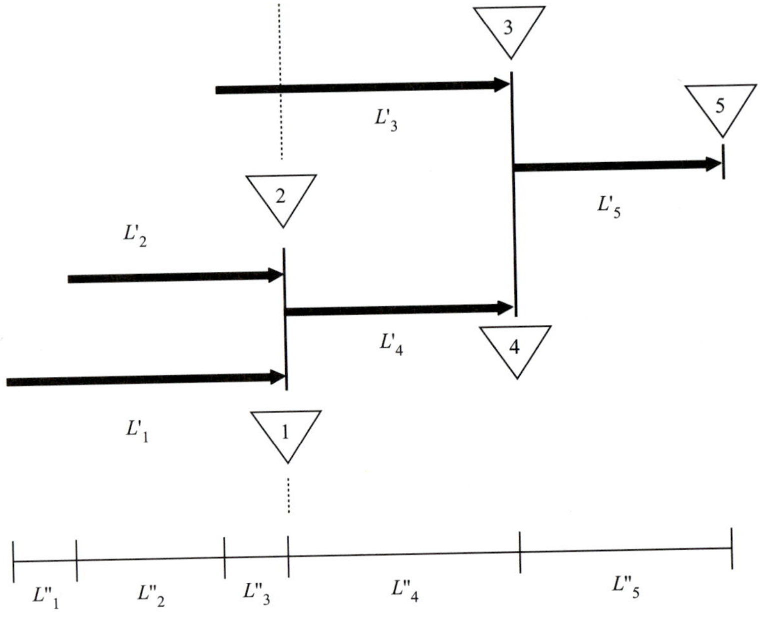

there is no reason to order more of item 4. Otherwise, if $ITP_4(t) < IN_3^+(t)$, we may wish to raise $ITP_4(t)$, but not beyond $IN_3^+(t)$.

We can visualize the idea here by drawing a vertical slice through the network, like the dashed line of Figure 8.4.2. To the right of the slice, downstream, is a subnetwork including all of item 4's supply system, but only part of item 3's. The points where the line crosses the leadtime arrows represent the same total leadtime to the end item. The echelon inventories downstream from these points are precisely $IN_3^+(t)$ and $ITP_4(t)$, and we want to equate these values as nearly as possible.

We can draw a slice *anywhere* in the network. Such a slice typically intersects several items' leadtimes. These intersection points are equidistant from the end item in terms of total leadtime. Now, consider the echelon inventory downstream from each intersection point, i.e., the total inventory along the path from the point to the end item. Ideally, we would like all these echelon inventories to be equal.

It is clear, then, that we cannot hope to operate the system intelligently using local information only. In the example above, the slice relates two items, 3 and 4, which happen to be close neighbors, but of course that need not be true in general. We may well wish to balance the inventories of items that are quite far apart in the network. In other words, we must coordinate actions explicitly across the entire system.

Fortunately, the requirements for effective coordination are less formidable than they seem at first glance. To see why, suppose some slice indicates balancing the inventories of seven different items. To achieve the necessary coordination, it makes sense to consider the items in pairs, that is, to balance the first with the second, the second with the third, and so on. This, it turns out, is sufficient; to control each item, we must pay attention to *one* other item. But which one? The new item-numbering scheme above provides the answer: For each item $j > 1$ we must take into account the status of item $j - 1$.

8.4.3 The Balanced Echelon Base-Stock Policy

We now define a class of plausible policies. The basic logic is the same as that of an echelon base-stock policy; there are policy variables s_j, which determine the overall inventory levels. We adjust that policy, however, to improve the balance among the inventories. We call the result a *balanced echelon base-stock policy.* The best policy of this type is truly optimal. (We shall not prove this fact.)

Recall, the original $IT_j(t)$ is the stock (in item j's units) shipped in the interval $[t - L'_j, t)$. Define

$$IT_j^-(t) = \text{portion of } IT_j(t) \text{ shipped in the interval } [t - L'_j, t - L''_j)$$
$$IN_j^+(t) = IT_j^-(t) + IN_j(t)$$

(Recall that $L''_j \le L'_j$. If the two are equal, then $IT_j^-(t) = 0$ and $IN_j^+(t) = IN_j(t)$.)

The policy works as follows: Item 1 uses an ordinary echelon base-stock policy with policy parameter s_1. For item $j > 1$ we adjust the base-stock policy using the variable $IN_{j-1}^+(t)$. Specifically, we decide the quantity to ship toward item j so as to bring $ITP_j(t)$ as close as possible to $\min\{s_j, IN_{j-1}^+(t)\}$. That is, if $ITP_j(t^-)$ is already more than this quantity before any shipments, we ship nothing. If $ITP_j(t^-)$ is less, we ship the difference, *provided* there is sufficient inventory of items $i \in Pre(j)$ to do so. And if one of those inventories is too small, we ship as much as possible, that is, we set $ITP_j(t) = \min_i \{IN_i(t){:}\ i \in Pre(j)\}$.

The rationale is similar to the one above for the example in Figure 8.4.2. If we slice the network at the beginning of item j's leadtime, the downstream net inventory of item j itself is $ITP_j(t)$, and that of item $j - 1$ is precisely $IN_{j-1}^+(t)$. There is no point in setting $ITP_j(t)$ any larger than $IN_{j-1}^+(t)$, for the excess inventory is useless.

Actually, we can simplify this rule somewhat. Initialize the system at time $t = 0$ as follows: First, given the vector of policy variables $\mathbf{s}$, compute the vector $\mathbf{s}^-$ as in Section 8.3.2, so that $\mathbf{s}^- \le \mathbf{s}$ and s_j^- is nonincreasing in j. (Again, the policy specified by $\mathbf{s}^-$ is equivalent to the original one, but we do not use this fact here.) Then, set

$$IN_J(0) = I'_J(0) = s_J$$

$$I'_i(0) = s_i^- - IN_j(0) \qquad i \in Pre(j)$$

so that

$$IN_i(0) = I'_i(0) + IN_j(0) = s_i^- \qquad i \in Pre(j)$$

For all $j > 1$,

$$ITP_j(0) = IN_j(0) = s_j^- \le s_{j-1}^- = IN_{j-1}(0) = IN_{j-1}^+(0)$$

In particular,

$$ITP_j(0) \le \min\{s_j, IN_{j-1}^+(0)\}$$

Thus, the policy ensures that, for all $t \geq 0$,

$$ITP_j(t) \leq \min\{s_j, IN^+_{j-1}(t)\} \tag{8.4.2}$$

(Only a demand can cause $IN^+_{j-1}(t)$ to fall, but this reduces $ITP_j(t)$ by the same amount.) For current purposes, the key part of (8.4.2) is

$$ITP_j(t) \leq IN^+_{j-1}(t) \qquad j > 1 \tag{8.4.3}$$

This condition is known as *long-run balance.*

THEOREM 8.4.1. Assume the long-run balance condition (8.4.3) holds for all t. Then, for all $j > 1$ and $i \in Pre(j)$, $IN_i(t) \geq IN^+_{j-1}(t)$.

(We postpone the proof until Section 8.4.6.) Thus, we never have to worry about the predecessor inventories; they are guaranteed to be sufficient. We need only compare $ITP_j(t)$ to $\min\{s_j, IN^+_{j-1}(t)\}$.

(Actually, from any initial conditions, if the system runs for a while, it will attain (8.4.2) at some finite time t. And, once the system enters this state, it will never leave. So, the theorem applies and the policy simplifies for sufficiently large t. To simplify the discussion, assume the special starting conditions above, so the theorem holds as stated.)

Consequently, (8.4.2) in fact holds as an equality:

$$ITP_j(t) = \min\{s_j, IN^+_{j-1}(t)\}$$

Notice the similarity to (8.3.6)! Also,

$$IN^+_j(t + L''_j) = ITP_j(t) - D(t, t + L''_j]$$

Following the approach of Section 8.3.2, rewrite these equations using a simple time shift:

$$ITP_1(t) = s_1$$
$$IN^+_j(t + L_j) = ITP_j(t + L_{j-1}) - D(t + L_{j-1}, t + L_j]$$
$$ITP_{j+1}(t + L_j) = \min\{s_{j+1}, IN^+_j(t + L_j)\}$$

In equilibrium this becomes

$$\begin{aligned} ITP_1 &= s_1 \\ IN^+_j &= ITP_j - D_j \\ ITP_{j+1} &= \min\{s_{j+1}, IN^+_j\} \end{aligned} \tag{8.4.4}$$

where D_j has the same distribution as $D(L''_j)$, and the D_j are independent. This has precisely the same form as (8.3.7)!

8.4.4 Policy Evaluation and Optimization

We are now ready to describe the *equivalent series system:* It has J stages, the same demand process and echelon cost rates h_j and b as the assembly system, but leadtimes L''_j. Thus, its leadtime demands D_j are precisely those above. By (8.4.4), therefore, its IN_j are precisely the IN^+_j of the original assembly system.

Suppose we apply the policy-evaluation algorithm of Section 8.3.2 to this series system, using the same policy parameters **s**. The average cost, in the assembly system's terms, is

$$E[\Sigma_{j=1}^{J} h_j IN_j^+ + (b + h_J')[IN_J^+]^-] \tag{8.4.5}$$

This is *not* the same as (8.4.1), the average cost of the assembly system. But $L_J'' = L_J'$, so $IN_J^+ = IN_J$ and $[IN_J^+]^- = B$. Also, by a simple conservation argument, $E[IT_j^-] = E[D(L_j' - L_j'')]$, so

$$E[IN_j^+] = E[IN_j] + E[IT_j^-] = E[IN_j] + E[D(L_j' - L_j'')]$$

Consequently, the computed cost (8.4.5) exceeds the true cost (8.4.1) by

$$\Sigma_{j=1}^{J} h_j E[D(L_j' - L_j'')] \tag{8.4.6}$$

This is a constant, independent of the policy. In sum, to evaluate a balanced base-stock policy in the assembly system, we need only compute the average cost (8.4.5) of the corresponding policy in the equivalent series system and then subtract the constant (8.4.6).

It follows immediately that, if we apply the optimization algorithm of Section 8.3.3 to the equivalent series system, the resulting policy vector **s*** is optimal also for the original assembly system. We're done!

Well, almost; there remains one loose end: What happens when two or more of the $\underline{L}_j$ are equal? We can resolve ties arbitrarily in renumbering the items. But then some of the L_j'' are 0, and the corresponding $D_j = 0$. What happens in the equivalent series system (or any series system) in this case? If $D_j = 0$, intuitively, inventories at stages $j - 1$ and j perform the same function, but stage j's is more expensive, so there is no reason to hold stock there. Indeed, $C_j(y) = h_j y + C_{j+1}(y)$, and so (since $h_j \geq 0$) $s_j^* \leq s_{j+1}^*$, which means stage j never holds inventory.

In the assembly system too, we choose $s_j^* \leq s_{j+1}^*$, but here this condition has a different meaning: *If* $j \in Pre\ (j + 1)$, we never hold inventory of item j, but otherwise we may. For instance, consider the system of Figure 8.4.1, but suppose items 1 and 2 have the same actual leadtime L_j', so $L_1'' = 0$. This implies $IN_1^+(t) = ITP_1(t)$. The policy thus dictates that $ITP_2(t) = \min\ \{s_2^*, ITP_1(t)\} = ITP_1(t) = s_1$. Consequently, we always maintain the *same* inventories of items 1 and 2. This is just what common sense suggests.

8.4.5 Local Base-Stock Policy Evaluation

Now suppose we are unable to implement the control scheme above, and instead use a local base-stock policy. To illustrate the idea, focus on a two-stage assembly system, where all items $j < J$ are raw materials, that is, direct predecessors of the end item J, with no predecessors of their own. Number the items as above, so among the materials, item 1 has the longest leadtime, and item $J - 1$ the shortest.

Again, we ship units to J only in kits. So, it is possible that some items have both (local) inventory and backorders simultaneously. Actually, the backorders of items $j < J$ are equal. If any (and hence all) of these items are backlogged, however, at least one has no inventory.

We can still define $IN_j'(t) = I_j'(t) - B_j'(t)$ and $IOP_j'(t) = IO_j(t) + IN_j'(t)$. Assuming $I_j'(0) = s_j'$, each customer demand generates a demand for each item, hence an order to the supplier for each raw material. Consequently, $IOP'_j(t) = s'_j$, and $IN'_j(t + L'_j) = s'_j - D(t, t + L'_j]$, $j < J$. It is clear, moreover, that

$$B'_j(t) = B'_{J-1}(t) = [\min_{i<J}\{IN'_i(t)\}]^- \qquad j < J$$

Define the L''_j and L_j as above. Let us evaluate the material backorders at time $t + L_{J-1}$. Notice, $(t + L_{J-1}) - L'_j = t + L_{j-1}$. Also, suppose the s'_j are nonincreasing for $j < J$ (which is reasonable), and set $s^{=}_{J-1} = s'_{J-1}$, and $s^{=}_j = s'_j - s'_{j+1}$, $1 \le j \le J - 2$. Then,

$$\begin{aligned} IN'_j(t + L_{J-1}) &= s'_j - D(t + L_{j-1}, t + L_{J-1}] \\ &= \Sigma_{j \le i < J}(s^{=}_i - D(t + L_{i-1}, t + L_i]) \end{aligned}$$

Consequently,

$$B'_{J-1}(t + L_{J-1}) = \max\{0, \Sigma_{j \le i < J}(D(t + L_{i-1}, t + L_i] - s^{=}_i) : j < J\}$$

In equilibrium this becomes

$$B'_{J-1} = \max\{0, \Sigma_{j \le i < J}(D_i - s^{=}_i) : j < J\}$$

This is precisely the form of the backorders in a $(J - 1)$-stage series system. (See Problem 8.2.) The $s^{=}_j$ play the roles of the local base-stock levels here, and the s'_j function as echelon base-stock levels. Then, as in (8.3.4), we have

$$B'_J = [B'_{J-1} + D_J - s'_J]^+$$

Thus, we can calculate $E[B'_J]$ and $E[I'_J]$ with the methods of Section 8.3. Also,

$$\begin{aligned} E[I'_j] &= E[IN'_j] + E[B'_j] \\ &= s'_j - E[D(L'_j)] + E[B'_{J-1}] \qquad j < J \end{aligned}$$

In sum, we can evaluate a local base-stock policy through an equivalent series system. (It is not clear how to find the best such policy, however, for $E[I'_j]$ is not related to $E[B'_j]$ as in the series system.) The same ideas extend directly to any assembly system. (See Problem 8.14 for another example.)

Evidently, it requires about the same effort to evaluate local and centralized policies, and we know how to optimize the latter. Remember too that, implementation issues aside, the best balanced echelon base-stock policy performs better than any local policy. Given a choice, therefore, a balanced policy is definitely better.

8.4.6 Proof of Theorem 8.4.1

(The argument involves state variables at times $t - L''_i$, which may be negative for small t. But the definitions can be extended to negative times: For $t < 0$ set $ITP_j(t) = IN_j(t) = IN_j(0)$ and $D(t) = 0$. The reasoning below is then valid for all t.)

For $i \le j$ define

$$\begin{aligned} IN_{ij}(t) &= ITP_i(t) - D(t, t + \underline{L}_i - \underline{L}_j] \\ &= ITP_i(t) - D(t, t + L_{j-1} - L_{i-1}] \end{aligned}$$

In the special case $i = j - 1$,

$$IN_{j-1,\,j}(t) = ITP_{j-1}(t) - D(t,\, t + L''_{j-1}] = IN^{+}_{j-1}(t + L''_{j-1})$$

Also, for $i \in Pre\,(j)$, $\underline{L}_i - \underline{L}_j = L'_i$, so

$$IN_{ij}(t) = ITP_i(t) - D(t,\, t + L'_i] = IN_i(t + L'_i)$$

Now, the long-term balance condition (8.4.3) implies

$$ITP_i(t) \le IN_{i-1,\,i}(t - L''_{i-1}) = ITP_{i-1}(t - L''_{i-1}) - D(t - L''_{i-1},\, t]$$

so (since $L''_{i-1} + \underline{L}_i = \underline{L}_{i-1}$)

$$\begin{aligned} IN_{ij}(t) &\le ITP_{i-1}(t - L''_{i-1}) - D(t - L''_{i-1},\, t + \underline{L}_i - \underline{L}_j] \\ &= IN_{i-1,\,j}(\mathrm{t} - L''_{i-1}). \end{aligned}$$

Apply this inequality repeatedly: For $i \in Pre\,(j)$,

$$\begin{aligned} IN_i(t) &= IN_{ij}(t - L'_i) \ge IN_{i+1,j}[(t - L'_i) + L''_i] \\ &\ge \cdots \ge IN_{j-1,j}[(t - L'_i) + (L''_i + \cdots + L''_{j-2})] \\ &= IN_{j-1,j}(t - L''_{j-1}) = IN^{+}_{j-1}(t) \end{aligned}$$

8.5 Distribution Systems: Local Control

8.5.1 The Basic Model

Consider a two-level distribution system. For the sake of concreteness, suppose there is a single product and several geographic locations. For convenience we modify the indexing scheme slightly: There are now $J + 1$ locations. All goods enter the network from an outside source and proceed first to location $j = 0$, called the *warehouse.* The warehouse in turn supplies J *retailers,* where customer demands occur, indexed $j = 1, \ldots, J$. All these locations may hold inventory. Each has its own supply system; for now the leadtimes are the constants L'_j. There are no scale economies (until Section 8.5.5).

Information flows in the opposite direction: As in a series system, each location follows its own local base-stock policy. Each retailer orders stock from the warehouse. *All* these orders together constitute the warehouse's demand process. The warehouse fills these demands (dispatches shipments to the retailers) sequentially, that is, on a first-come-first-served basis. The warehouse in turn places its own replenishment orders with the supplier.

Thus, information and control are decentralized or localized: Each retailer sees only its own demands, and the warehouse sees only the incoming order streams. Each location, including the warehouse, monitors only its own inventory-order position, and makes decisions on that basis. (The next section explores a centralized scheme.)

The demands at the retailers are independent Poisson processes $\mathbf{D}_j$, $j = 1, \ldots, J$. Assuming each location begins fully stocked (at its base-stock level), these demands propagate backward to the warehouse. The warehouse's demand process $\mathbf{D}_0$, therefore, is itself a Poisson process.

Denote

λ_j = demand rate for retailer j, $j = 1, \ldots, J$
λ_0 = demand rate for the warehouse $(j = 0) = \Sigma_{j=1}^{J} \lambda_j$
D_j = leadtime demand for location j, a random variable distributed as $D_j(L_j')$

The policy variables are the base-stock levels $s_j' \geq 0$.

This is a simplified version of a model-based planning system called METRIC, developed in the 1960s to help manage inventories of aircraft engines and other critical, expensive components for the United States Air Force. (There, a retailer represents an airbase, and the warehouse a central support facility.) Since then, METRIC has been refined and extended in several ways. It and its cousins have been adopted by other armed forces in the United States and other countries and also by several airlines. (In those applications a demand arises from the failure of an operating unit, and the supply systems represent repair activities as well as transportation. The real demand and supply processes are more complex than the model's; each airbase has a finite number of demand sources, the maximal number of operational units, as in Section 7.3.3.3, and each supply system has limited capacity. The model approximates reality, suppressing these complications.)

As explained in Chapter 5, the locations in the model can be relabeled as generic *items,* which can equally well represent different products or product-location pairs. In a multiproduct system the retailers correspond to distinct finished goods. The warehouse represents a uniform intermediate product, which can be transformed into any of the finished goods.

Real distribution systems typically move many products through a network of locations. The model here cannot represent that degree of complexity; our warehouse is limited to a single item. Sometimes, however, there are no strong links between the products like joint replenishment costs. Then, the products themselves are independent, and we can use a separate copy of the model for each one. METRIC-like models are frequently used in this way.

Incidentally, this approach works much better than a common alternative heuristic, which divides the world by location instead of by product. There, each location manages its inventories separately, ignoring the links to other locations. The heuristic tries to compensate for the missing links by imposing a service-level constraint on each location, usually based on an aggregate criterion like the average fill rate over all products. This sounds reasonable, but it is not enough; the aggregate constraints cannot adequately capture the location links.

8.5.2 Policy Evaluation

To evaluate a given policy, we follow a "top-down" approach, analogous to (8.3.2) to (8.3.4). We first analyze the warehouse and then the retailers.

The warehouse operates just like the first stage in a series system, so

$$B_0' = [D_0 - s_0']^+ \tag{8.5.1}$$

Next, consider retailer j. The logic of Section 8.3.1 leads to the following analogue of (8.3.4):

$$B'_j = [B'_{0j} + D_j - s'_j]^+ \tag{8.5.2}$$

where B_{0j} indicates the warehouse backorders generated by orders *from the individual retailer j*. Now, the warehouse is a system with multiple input sources, as in Section 7.3.7; the inputs are independent Poisson processes, and the warehouse fills demands in order. Consequently, the conditional random variable $(B'_{0j}|B'_0)$ has the binomial distribution with parameters B'_0 and $\theta_j = \lambda_j/\lambda_0$. From this and the distribution of B'_0 itself, directly calculate that of B'_{0j} by binomial disaggregation. Then, apply (8.5.2).

There is an equivalent way to express B'_{0j}: Let BW'_0 denote the time a warehouse demand waits on backorder, a random variable. As in Section 6.2.4, $D_0(BW'_0) = B'_0$. Also, because the warehouse treats all demands equally, BW'_0 is the waiting time for orders from *each* retailer, so $B'_{0j} = D_j(BW'_0)$. Thus, given the distribution of B'_0 from (8.5.1), we can extract that of BW'_0, and then compute that of B'_{0j}. (This idea is especially useful for some of the extensions discussed later.)

The two-moment approximation of Section 8.3.1 extends directly to the distribution system. The connection between levels is supplied by the identities

$$E[B'_{0j}] = \theta_j E[B'_0] \tag{8.5.3}$$

$$V[B'_{0j}] = \theta_j^2 V[B'_0] + \theta_j(1 - \theta_j)E[B'_0]$$

(The second equation uses the conditional-variance formula from Section C.2.2 in Appendix C.)

It is possible to define echelon inventories and related quantities. Indeed, one can show that local and echelon base-stock policies are equivalent. This approach offers no special advantages here, so we postpone it until the next section, where we make good use of it. (A base-stock policy, local or echelon, need *not* be optimal here. We know little about the true optimal policy.)

8.5.3 Optimization

Consider the problem of choosing a base-stock policy to minimize the long-run average cost. There is a holding-cost rate h'_j for each location; each retailer has its own backorder-cost rate b_j. (We use the notation C_j in a different way from Section 8.3.)

The total cost has several components: First, define

$$C_j(s'_0, s'_j) = h'_j E[I'_j] + b_j E[B'_j] \qquad j = 1, \ldots, J$$

This is the average cost at retailer j. It is a function of s'_0 as well as s'_j. Next, the average inventory in transit from the warehouse to retailer j is the constant $\lambda_j L'_j$; as above, we incur cost at rate h'_0 on this stock. As for the warehouse itself, the only relevant cost is the inventory holding cost. Sum these holding costs to obtain

$$C_0(s'_0) = h'_0(E[I'_0] + \Sigma_{j=1}^J \lambda_j L'_j)$$

Let **s**' denote the vector of retailer policy variables $(s_j')_{j=1}^J$. The total average cost is then

$$C(s_0', \mathbf{s}') = C_0(s_0') + \Sigma_{j=1}^J C_j(s_0', s_j')$$

Unfortunately, there is no simple, elegant procedure to optimize this function. (The recursive algorithm for series systems *cannot* be extended to distribution systems.) The most popular approach is a projection method: The main loop of the algorithm searches over possible values of s_0' to find the best. For each s_0', an inner loop determines the best values of the other s_j'.

The advantage of this approach is that, with s_0' temporarily fixed, the objective function $C(s_0', \mathbf{s}')$ separates by j, so the inner loop can optimize over each s_j' separately. Moreover, as a function of s_j' only, each of the $C_j(s_0', s_j')$ has the same form as the single-location cost function of Chapter 6 (in particular, it is convex), so it is easy to minimize. Furthermore, let $s_j'(s_0')$ denote the optimal value of s_j' for fixed s_0'. It is intuitively clear (and not hard to show) that each $s_j'(s_0')$ is nonincreasing in s_0'; as we add more stock at the warehouse, we need less at the retailers. So, if the search process increases s_0' sequentially, we need only consider ever smaller values of the s_j'.

We are still left with the problem of finding the optimal s_0', that is, of choosing s_0' to minimize $C(s_0', \mathbf{s}'(s_0'))$. Unfortunately, this is not a convex function of s_0'. Exhaustive search is the only sure method. (On the other hand, people who work with such models have found that a local search nearly always finds the global optimum.)

The normal approximation can be applied to this system. Let μ_j and σ_j^2 denote the mean and variance of D_j, $j \geq 0$. The normal approximation at the warehouse yields

$$E[B_0'] = \Phi^1(z_0)\sigma_0$$

$$E[B_0'(B_0' - 1)] = 2\Phi^2(z_0)\sigma_0^2$$

$$E[I_0'] = \Phi^1(-z_0)\sigma_0$$

where $z_0 = (s_0' - \mu_0)/\sigma_0$. Moreover,

$$E[B_{0j}'] = \theta_j E[B_0']$$

$$V[B_{0j}'] = \theta_j(1 - \theta_j)E[B_0'] + \theta_j^2 V[B_0'] \qquad j > 0$$

Now, approximate each $B_{0j}' + D_j$ by a normal distribution with the same mean and variance,

$$\underline{\mu}_j = E[B_{0j}'] + \mu_j$$

$$\underline{\sigma}_j^2 = V[B_{0j}'] + \sigma_j^2$$

The normal approximation for retailer j yields

$$E[B_j'] = \Phi^1(z_j)\underline{\sigma}_j$$

$$E[I_j'] = \Phi^1(-z_j)\underline{\sigma}_j$$

where $z_j = (s_j' - \underline{\mu}_j)/\underline{\sigma}_j$. We now have all the elements needed to evaluate the cost C of any policy.

Furthermore, if we set s_j' optimally, given s_0', then the cost for retailer j becomes

$$C_j^*(s_0') = (b_j + h_j)\Phi(z_j^*)\underline{\sigma}_j$$

where z_j^* solves $\Phi^0(z) = h_j/(b_j + h_j)$. (The function $C_j^*(s_0')$ depends on s_0' through $\underline{\sigma}_j$.) The total cost thus reduces to a function of one variable,

$$C(s_0') = h_0' E[I_0'] + \Sigma_{j>0} C_j^*(s_0')$$

It is straightforward to optimize this function numerically.

Gallego and Zipkin [1999b] report a numerical study of this approximation. They conclude that it is quite accurate.

To gain some insight into system performance, consider the case of identical retailers. Let L_r', h_r', and b denote the common values of the L_j', h_j', and b_j. Since $\theta_j = 1/J$,

$$V[B_{0j}'] = \frac{V[B_0'] + (J-1)E[B_0']}{J^2}$$

and

$$V[B_{0j}' + D_j] = \frac{V[B_0'] + (J-1)E[B_0'] + J\lambda_0 L_r'}{J^2}$$

Thus, if z^* represents the (common) optimal value of z for all retailers,

$$C_j(s_0', s_j'(s_0')) = \underline{\sigma}_j(b + h_r')\Phi(z^*) \tag{8.5.4}$$
$$C(s_0', \mathbf{s}'(s_0')) = h_0'(E[I_0'] + \lambda_0 L_r') + \underline{\sigma}_r(b + h_r')\Phi(z^*)$$

where $\underline{\sigma}_j$ is the standard deviation of $B_{0j}' + D_j$, and

$$\underline{\sigma}_r = \Sigma_j \underline{\sigma}_j = J\underline{\sigma}_j \tag{8.5.5}$$
$$= \{V[B_0'] + (J-1)E[B_0'] + J\lambda_0 L_r'\}^{1/2}$$

Let us examine the joint impact of s_0' and J on the total cost (8.5.4). First, fix $s_0' = 0$. In this case the retailers operate independently, as in the parallel system of Section 8.2, each with total effective leadtime $L_0' + L_r'$. Indeed, $V[B_0'] = E[B_0'] = \lambda_0 L_0'$, so $\underline{\sigma}_r = [J\lambda_0(L_0' + L_r')]^{1/2}$. Apart from the constant $h_0'\lambda_0 L_r'$, (8.5.4) reduces to the same form as (8.2.3); for fixed total demand λ_0, the total cost is proportional to $\sqrt{J}$. Now, raise s_0' to any positive value. This increases $E[I_0']$ and reduces $V[B_0']$, of course, but those effects are independent of J. Also, raising s_0' reduces one of the factors of J in $\underline{\sigma}_r$ ($E[B_0']$), leaving the other ($\lambda_0 L_r'$) constant. In sum, for any s_0', the overall cost (8.5.4) depends roughly on the square root of the number of retailers, but the strength of this dependence declines as s_0' increases.

Thus, warehouse stock performs two distinct functions: It may just be cheaper than retailer inventory, as in a series system. In addition, it serves to *pool some of the retailers' demand uncertainties;* it can be used to fill an order from *any* retailer, and this flexibility softens the impact of the warehouse's own leadtime, L_0'. Warehouse stock thus allows us to enjoy some of the advantages of consolidation, while still maintaining multiple retail locations.

EXAMPLE 8.5.A, PART 1

A Brazilian company makes *doce de leite* (literally, milk sweets, a wonderful concoction, something like caramel sauce only better) and ships it from its plant in the countryside to several locations in and around São Paulo. It is considering leasing a warehouse in the outskirts of the city and supplying its outlets from there.

There are $J = 16$ locations, all identical. Each faces Poisson demand at a rate of $\lambda = 0.625$ cases per day. The total leadtime to each location is $L = 4.4$ days. The cost rates are $b =$ R\$10 and $h =$ R\$0.62 per case-day. (The currency in Brazil is the *real,* abbreviated R\$.) There are no scale economies.

The current setup treats the locations as independent items (as in Section 8.2). The optimal base-stock level for each location is $s^* = 5$, with total cost over all locations (omitting the pipeline holding cost) of R\$38 per day.

If the company leases the warehouse, the leadtimes will be $L'_0 = 2.8$ and $L'_r = 1.6$. The back-order cost will remain $b = 10$, and the holding costs will be $h'_0 = h'_r = 0.62$. (Notice, the holding cost at the warehouse is the same as at the locations, and the total leadtime remains 4.4.) The best local base-stock policy is $s'_0 = 28$, and each $s'_j = 3$, with total cost $C =$ R\$26.4. Evidently, centralized inventory offers substantial savings in this case.

8.5.4 Extensions

Most of the extensions of the basic series-system model work here as well.

8.5.4.1 Compound-Poisson Demand

It is *not* a simple matter, however, to evaluate a distribution system with compound-Poisson demands. The warehouse itself is no problem: Suppose Y_j indicates the demand-size random variable for retailer j. The total demand at the warehouse, then, is also a compound-Poisson process; the demand-epoch rate is λ_0, and the demand size Y_0 is a mixture of the Y_j, using the mixing weights θ_j. Knowing this, we can determine the distribution of D_0, and then use (8.5.1) for B'_0.

The difficulty appears when we try to analyze the retailers. The binomial-disaggregation method breaks down, and the waiting time BW'_0 becomes quite complex. Exact analysis is therefore much harder here than in the pure Poisson-demand case.

We can extend the two-moment approximation, by invoking another rather crude approximation step: Suppose all retailers have the same demand-size distribution, so $Y_0 = Y_j = Y$. Now, *assume* that the backorders B'_0 always comprise an integral number of demand batches, say N'_0. (This is true for $s'_0 = 0$, but not otherwise.) Under this approximation, B'_0 has a compound distribution, built from those of N'_0 and Y. Given $E[B'_0]$ and $V[B'_0]$, $E[N'_0]$ and $V[N'_0]$ can be obtained from the identities

$$E[B'_0] = E[N'_0]E[Y]$$
$$V[B'_0] = E[N'_0]V[Y] + V[N'_0]E^2[Y]$$

Next, the number N'_{0j} of these batches originating at retailer j can be determined through binomial disaggregation, as in (8.5.3):

$$E[N'_{0j}] = \theta_j E[N'_0]$$
$$V[N'_{0j}] = \theta_j^2 V[N'_0] + \theta_j(1 - \theta_j)E[N'_0]$$

Finally, the moments of B'_{0j} can be derived from those of N'_{0j}:

$$E[B'_{0j}] = E[N'_{0j}]E[Y]$$
$$V[B'_{0j}] = E[N'_{0j}]V[Y] + V[N'_{0j}]E^2[Y]$$

Combining these three steps yields

$$E[B'_{0j}] = \theta_j E[B'_0] \tag{8.5.6}$$
$$V[B'_{0j}] = \theta_j^2 V[B'_0] + \theta_j(1 - \theta_j)E[B'_0]\,\frac{E[Y^2]}{E[Y]}$$

The factor $E[Y^2]/E[Y] > 1$ makes the variance here *larger* than in the Poisson-demand case.

Later, under the heading of independent leadtimes, we discuss a simpler and still cruder approximation. To avoid these difficulties, most of the discussion below assumes pure Poisson demands.

8.5.4.2 Exogenous, Sequential Supply Systems

Suppose each supply system is exogenous and sequential. The warehouse's system is independent of the retailers'. (The retailers' supply systems, however, need not be independent of one another. For instance, every retailer's supply system may include loading activities at the warehouse.)

Combining the ideas of Section 8.5.1 and Section 8.3.4.2 leads immediately to (8.5.1) and (8.5.2). D_j now means location j's demand over its (stochastic) limiting leadtime. Binomial disaggregation still works to derive B'_{0j} from B'_0.

8.5.4.3 Limited-Capacity Supply Systems

Next, suppose each supply system consists of a single processor, whose processing times are distributed exponentially. An approximation like the one in Section 8.3.4.3 works quite well: Treat the IT_j (for the warehouse as well as the retailers) as independent, geometrically distributed random variables with parameters $\rho_j = \lambda_j/\mu_j$, and then apply (8.5.1) and (8.5.2) (with IT_j playing the role of D_j). Equivalently, treat the supply systems as exogenous, with L'_j distributed exponentially with parameter $(1 - \rho_j)\mu_j$.

8.5.4.4 Independent Leadtimes

Suppose each supply system generates independent leadtimes. As in Section 8.3.4.4, approximate the IT_j as independent, Poisson-distributed random variables with $E[IT_j] = \lambda_j E[L'_j]$.

We can combine this approach with the two-moment approximation above. An even simpler approximation is sometimes used in this context: Compute $E[B'_{0j}]$ as in (8.5.3), but treat B'_{0j} as Poisson-distributed with this mean (and skip the calculation of its variance). Equivalently, replace BW'_0 by the constant $E[BW'_0]$. Or, again equivalently, treat the warehouse waiting times for successive demands as independent; thus, each retailer faces independent total order leadtimes. Under any of these three interpretations, $B'_{0j} + IT_j$ now has a Poisson distribution.

This simplified approach extends directly to compound-Poisson demand. That is, compute $E[B_0']$ in the usual way. Compute $E[BW_0'] = E[B_0']/(\lambda_0 E[Y_0])$, by the arguments of Section 6.2.4. Then, treating BW_0' as the constant $E[BW_0']$, determine the (compound-Poisson) distribution of each $B_{0j}' + IT_j$, and proceed to compute the $E[B_j']$.

This is sometimes called the METRIC approximation, for it was introduced in the original version of that model. It is fairly accurate, though less so than the two-moment approximation.

8.5.4.5 General Distribution Networks

These methods can be extended directly to *any* distribution system (a network of items indexed $j = 0, \ldots, J$, where each item $j > 0$ has a unique predecessor, and item 0 has none). Problem 8.16 asks you to work out the details.

Also, it is easy to incorporate exogenous demands for any or all items. In the two-level system, for instance, suppose demands occur at the warehouse as well as the retailers. Suppose these new demands form a Poisson process with rate λ_0', independent of the retailers' demands. Just add a dummy retailer to the network. Assign the warehouse's exogenous demands to the new retailer, and set the retailer's leadtime and base-stock level to zero. This augmented system, clearly, is equivalent to the original one.

8.5.5 Economies of Scale

Now, suppose every location has its own fixed cost k_j for shipments. As in Section 8.3.7, we begin with the special case where only *external* orders (here, from the warehouse) entail scale economies, so $k_0 > 0$ and the other $k_j = 0$. Accordingly, suppose the retailers all use base-stock policies, but the warehouse uses an (r, q) policy. (These are all local policies.)

This system is quite tractable: The warehouse operates like a single-location system with Poisson demand, so again IOP_0' is uniformly distributed. Furthermore, conditional on $IOP_0' = s_0' = s$, B_0' and the B_j' have the same distributions as under a pure base-stock policy with parameters $(s, \mathbf{s}')$. Consequently, the total cost can be written as a simple average, analogous to (8.3.11):

$$C(r, q, \mathbf{s}') = \frac{k_0\lambda_0 + \sum_{s=r+1}^{r+q} C(s, \mathbf{s}')}{q} \tag{8.5.7}$$

Again, to optimize this function, use a projection algorithm: For any fixed (r, q), compute the best s_j' separately for each j by minimizing a convex function. Using this technique as a subroutine, search for the optimal (r^*, q^*).

The general case, where there are also scale economies for *internal* shipments, so any of the k_j can be positive, is far more difficult. We briefly summarize the state of the art: As in Section 8.3.7.2, it is plausible to use a an (r, q) policy at each location. Such a policy may use either local or echelon information. (The difference appears only at the warehouse, of course.) It is no longer the case, however, that local (r, q) policies reduce to echelon (r, q) policies; these are two distinct policy classes. Neither one, moreover, always performs better than the other. There are methods to evaluate any such policy exactly. These techniques are intricate and computationally demanding, however, and become intractable for large J. There are also simpler approximations, which seem reasonably accurate. (Section 8.7.2.2 sketches one such approach.)

8.6 Distribution Systems: Central Control

The local base-stock policy of the last section is appealing in many ways. It seems reasonable, in particular, for the warehouse to fill demands sequentially. During periods when the warehouse has stock on hand, this just means filling demands as they occur. But consider what happens when the warehouse runs out of stock (a common event if it keeps little or no inventory): Suppose that, first, a single demand arrives from retailer 1. Retailer 2 generates the next 45 demands. At that point the warehouse receives a unit from its supply system. Where should it send this unit? Under the FIFO rule, the unit must go to retailer 1, because its demand occurred first, even though retailer 2 clearly needs it more.

The weakness of the local-control scheme, then, is that it relies on history rather than the current status of the system to make crucial decisions. This section describes an alternative approach, which requires and exploits fully centralized information. This approach seems to work well, especially for high-volume goods, specifically, when the total demand volume is large compared to the individual retailers' demand fluctuations. This is just the kind of situation where a capable information system can be justified economically. (For low-volume items the local-control mechanism suffices, because the retailers rarely compete for shipments, and major discrepancies like the example above are even rarer.)

For now assume the retailers have independent Poisson demands, and all leadtimes are constant. We point out later that these assumptions can be relaxed considerably.

8.6.1 Echelon Cost Accounting

This approach uses echelon-level information. Define

$$\begin{aligned} B_j(t) &= B_j'(t) \\ I_j(t) &= I_j'(t) \\ IN_j(t) &= I_j(t) - B_j(t) \\ ITP_j(t) &= IN_j(t) + IT_j(t) \\ h_j &= h_j' - h_0' \qquad j = 1, \ldots, J \\ ITP_r(t) &= \Sigma_{j=1}^J ITP_j(t) \\ IN_0(t) &= I_0'(t) + ITP_r(t) \\ ITP_0(t) &= IN_0(t) + IT_0(t) \\ h_0 &= h_0' \end{aligned}$$

Notice, $ITP_r(t)$ sums the net inventories at, and stocks in transit to, *all* the retailers; so $IN_0(t)$ includes all stock at, and downstream from, the warehouse.

The total cost rate at time t is given by

$$h_0'[I_0'(t) + \Sigma_{j=1}^J IT_j(t)] + \Sigma_{j=1}^J [h_j' I_j'(t) + b_j B_j'(t)]$$

In the spirit of (8.3.8) this can be rewritten as

$$h_0 IN_0(t) + \Sigma_{j=1}^{J} [h_j IN_j(t) + (b_j + h_j')B_j(t)]$$

Now, let us shift the way these costs are counted. Consider: There is nothing we can do at time t to affect retailer j before time $t + L_j'$. So, we lose nothing by shifting certain costs back in time, counting at time t the *expected* cost at retailer j at time $t + L_j'$. Thus, the total cost rate becomes

$$h_0 IN_0(t) + \Sigma_{j=1}^{J} E[h_j IN_j(t + L_j') + (b_j + h_j')B_j(t + L_j')] \tag{8.6.1}$$

(This type of transformation is widely used and widely useful. Section 9.6 justifies it in a simpler context, but it is valid here too.) Indeed, as in (8.3.2), we have

$$IN_j(t + L_j') = ITP_j(t) - D_j(t, t + L_j'] \tag{8.6.2}$$

Letting D_j denote retailer j's generic leadtime demand and

$$\hat{C}_j(x) = h_j x + (b_j + h_j')[x]^-$$

$$C_j(y) = E[h_j IN_j(t + L_j') + (b_j + h_j')B_j(t + L_j') \mid ITP_j(t) = y]$$

$$= E[\hat{C}_j(y - D_j)]$$

we can rewrite (8.6.1) in the compact form

$$h_0 IN_0(t) + \Sigma_{j=1}^{J} C_j(ITP_j(t)) \tag{8.6.3}$$

8.6.2 Myopic Allocation and the Balanced Approximation

Even with the reduction to (8.6.3), the true optimal policy is virtually impossible to compute and too complex to implement. We present a simple heuristic approach that seems to work well.

Consider a decision to ship stock from the warehouse to the retailers. It is helpful to separate the decision into two steps, *withdrawal* and *allocation.* First, we choose a quantity of stock to *withdraw* from the warehouse, the total amount to be shipped to all the retailers. Second, we decide how to *allocate* this amount among the retailers.

Let us focus further on the allocation step: Suppose we are at time t. There may be demands at t and/or an order arriving at the warehouse. Let IN_0^-, ITP_j^-, and ITP_r^- denote the values of the state variables after these events, but before any decisions. We then withdraw some specific amount. The effect is to raise $ITP_r(t)$ from ITP_r^- to a higher value, which we denote ITP_r. The problem, then, is to allocate ITP_r among the individual retailers' $ITP_j(t)$.

We propose the following heuristic allocation rule: Allocate so as to minimize the current total cost rate, as measured by (8.6.3). We call this rule *myopic allocation,* for it takes into account only current costs (or rather, the costs we count now), ignoring future developments.

Some additional notation will help express this method in clearer terms: Set $s_j^- = ITP_j^-$ and $s_r = ITP_r$. Also, let s_j denote the value of $ITP_j(t)$ after allocation. In these terms myopic allocation dictates solving the following optimization problem:

$$\begin{aligned} \text{Minimize} \quad & \Sigma_j C_j(s_j) \\ \text{subject to} \quad & \Sigma_j s_j = s_r \\ & s_j \geq s_j^- \qquad j = 1, \ldots, J \end{aligned} \tag{8.6.4}$$

Suppose we approximate the D_j by continuous random variables and treat the s_j as continuous variables. The model (8.6.4) then becomes a simple nonlinear program. The first-order optimality (or Karush-Kuhn-Tucker) conditions are as follows: Letting ζ be the dual variable corresponding to the equation, we require

$$C_j'(s_j) \geq \zeta \qquad j = 1, \ldots, J \tag{8.6.5}$$

Also, (8.6.5) is tight (holds as an equality) for all j with $s_j > s_j^-$.

Let us sketch what is involved in solving (8.6.4): Imagine that we start with each $s_j = s_j^-$ and then allocate in small increments, maintaining (8.6.5) throughout, until the equation in (8.6.4) is satisfied, i.e., until the entire quantity withdrawn has been allocated. First, identify the *smallest* of the $C_j'(s_j)$, and set ζ to that value. Slowly increase this s_j, thus increasing $C_j'(s_j)$ (by convexity), keeping $\zeta = C_j'(s_j)$, until ζ equals the *second smallest* of the $C_j'(s_j)$. Next, increase both of these s_j, keeping their $C_j'(s_j)$'s equal, and ζ equal to this common value, until ζ hits the *third smallest* $C_j'(s_j)$. Continue in this manner, stopping when the equation is satisfied exactly. The end result, clearly, is a feasible solution satisfying (8.6.5), hence an optimal solution.

[This is just the continuous analogue of an algorithm that solves the discrete version of (8.6.4), called *marginal allocation:* Starting with $s_j = s_j^-$, allocate one unit at a time, always choosing that j with the smallest current value of the first difference $\Delta C_j(s_j)$.]

There are more efficient ways to implement the procedure; the detailed mechanics need not concern us here. It is important to understand conceptually what solving (8.6.4) means: The optimal solution tries to *equalize the marginal costs* $C_j'(s_j)$ to the extent possible, subject to the limits imposed by the inequalities $s_j \geq s_j^-$. If s_r is sufficiently large (compared to $\Sigma_j s_j^-$), so we allocate something to every j, then all the marginal costs will be equal. Otherwise, some j's will receive no allocations, namely those with large initial inventory-transit positions s_j^-. In this sense myopic allocation tries to *balance* the retailer inventories. (This concept of balance is similar in spirit, though not in detail, to the notion of balance in assembly systems.)

In the case of identical retailers, the cost functions C_j are identical, so myopic allocation reduces to a simpler rule: Allocate stock to the retailers with the lowest inventory-transit positions. In other words, try to equalize the $ITP_j(t)$, specifically, make the smallest $ITP_j(t)$ as large as possible.

Let us now explore an approximation of the model as a whole: We continue to use (8.6.3) to measure the cost rate. Imagine that, at every point in time, we can costlessly and instantaneously redistribute inventory, backorders, and shipments in transit among the retailers. That is, we have a total value $ITP_r(t)$, which remains at its true value, but we can divide it among the individual $\text{ITP}_j(t)$ as we wish.

With these new rules in place, we know we can shift stock among the retailers at any time in the future, so we can and should focus solely on the current cost rate (8.6.3). That is, given this scenario, myopic allocation is truly optimal. In this setting, myopic allocation means solving a model like (8.6.4), but without the inequality constraints:

$$\text{Minimize} \quad \Sigma_j\, C_j(s_j) \tag{8.6.6}$$
$$\text{subject to} \quad \Sigma_j\, s_j = s_r \qquad j = 1, \ldots, J$$

Let $C_r^*(s_r)$ denote the optimal objective value as a function of s_r. The optimality conditions now become the simple equations

$$C_j'(s_j) = \zeta \qquad j = 1, \ldots, J$$

instead of (8.6.5). The solution to this model thus equates *all* the marginal costs $C_j'(s_j)$. The approximation thus assumes that the retailers' inventories are perfectly balanced at all points in time. For this reason we call it the *balanced approximation.*

Now, let us also apply the normal approximation: We have

$$C_j'(s_j) = h_j - (b_j + h_j')\Phi^0(z_j) = \zeta \tag{8.6.7}$$

or

$$\Phi^0(z_j) = \frac{h_j - \zeta}{b_j + h_j'}$$

where $z_j = (s_j - \nu_j)/\sigma_j$. The ratio involving ζ plays the same role here as $1 - \omega$ in a single-location model. The task, then, is to adjust ζ until the corresponding values of s_j satisfy $\Sigma_j\, s_j = s_r$.

Consider the *equal-cost case,* where all $h_j = h$, and all $b_j = b$. Here, (8.6.7) implies that all the z_j must be equal, say to z_r. Indeed,

$$s_r = \Sigma_j\, s_j = \Sigma_j\, (\nu_j + \sigma_j z_r)$$

so $z_r = (s_r - \nu_r)/\sigma_r$, where

$$\nu_r = \Sigma_j\, \nu_j \qquad \sigma_r = \Sigma_j\, \sigma_j$$

In short, we obtain the solution $s_j = \nu_j + \sigma_j z_r$ in closed form. (Notice, it is determined by s_r and the ν_j and σ_j, not the cost rates. If the retailers are fully identical, with the same ν_j and σ_j, the solution equates their inventory-transit positions s_j; in general, it equates the z_j, the standardized versions of the s_j. For that reason, it is sometimes called the *equal-fractile solution.*) Moreover, substituting this solution into the objective function yields

$$\begin{aligned} C_r^*(s_r) &= \Sigma_j\, C_j(s_j) = \Sigma_j\, \sigma_j[h\Phi^1(-z_r) + (b + h')\Phi^1(z_r)] \\ &= \sigma_r[h\Phi^1(-z_r) + (b + h')\Phi^1(z_r)] \\ &= C_r(s_r) \end{aligned}$$

where

$$C_r(s) = E[h(s - D_r) + (b + h')[D_r - s]^+]$$
$$h' = h_0 + h$$

and D_r represents a normally distributed random variable with mean ν_r and standard deviation σ_r. Thus, we can write the optimal cost of problem (8.6.6) in closed form; that form, moreover, is precisely the cost of a single-location model.

(The maximal approximation leads to similar results. The equal-fractile solution is again optimal. The random variable D_r now has the same form as the approximate D_j, i.e., $D_r = \nu_r + \sigma_r(T/\sqrt{2})$, where T has Student's t distribution with 2 degrees of freedom. Likewise, if we approximate the D_j by exponential random variables, D_r also has an exponential distribution with mean ν_r and standard deviation $\sigma_r = \nu_r$. More generally, we can use any family of distributions determined, like the normals, by a translation and a scale parameter, and obtain comparable results.)

With unequal costs, it turns out that a function of this same form approximates $C_r^*(s_r)$ with reasonable accuracy, at least when the cost rates are not too different. To do this, set h and b to the smallest retailer cost rates, i.e.,

$$h = \min_j \{h_j\} \qquad b = \min_j \{b_j\}$$

and $h' = h_0 + h$ in $C_r(s)$ above. (Clearly, the result is a lower bound on $C_r^*(s_r)$, but why should it be an accurate approximation? Intuitively, when s_r is large, so the system has ample inventory, we want to push most of that stock to the retailer with the lowest holding cost. Likewise, when s_r is small, we concentrate inventory in retailers with large penalty costs, leaving the retailers with small b_j to bear most of the burden of backorders. The approximation thus captures the system's actual behavior in extreme cases. Actually, we can construct a more accurate lower bound in a special case. Also, there is an alternative approach which sometimes works better. See Problem 8.17.)

Under the balanced approximation, then, the overall cost rate (8.6.3) now becomes

$$h_0 IN_0(t) + C_r(ITP_r(t))$$

This is just the cost rate of a two-stage series system. Thus, we can apply all the methods of Section 8.3 to this system. In particular, we can determine the optimal (echelon base-stock) policy. Shipments to the second stage (stage r) correspond to withdrawals in the original system; first-stage orders, of course, mean warehouse orders. (Recall, the balanced approximation is based on a relaxation of the original system, allowing us to redistribute stock in ways that are actually infeasible. So, the optimal cost of this series system is a lower bound on the true optimal cost—at least up to the normal approximation.)

We now propose a plausible heuristic policy for the original system: *Apply the balanced approximation, and solve the resulting series system. Use the optimal policy to determine both orders from the supplier and warehouse withdrawals, and use myopic allocation to divide the withdrawals among the retailers.* The average cost of this feasible policy, of course, is an upper bound on the optimal cost. Also, we propose to *use the optimal cost of the series system to estimate the performance of the original system.*

Intuitively, this approach should work well: Myopic allocation does all a policy can do to equalize the retailers' marginal costs. They will not be equal at all times, as the balanced approximation assumes, because demands decrement the $ITP_j(t)$ by random amounts, so the marginal costs may drift away from equality. One may hope, nevertheless, that the equalizing effects of allocation will compensate for such fluctuations, or nearly so. If so, the distortions induced by the balanced approximation will be minor. This is especially likely in high-volume systems, where there is ample stock flowing through the warehouse to correct imbalances in the retailer inventories, and relatively minor variation in the demands themselves.

There is strong empirical evidence that the approach does work well in such situations. Typically, the cost of the heuristic policy (estimated by computer simulation) and the balanced approximation's cost lie within a few percent of each other, and hence both are close to the true optimal cost.

8.6.3 Discussion

Let us reflect for a moment on the mechanics of the heuristic policy: It bases warehouse orders and withdrawals entirely on the aggregate state variables $ITP_0(t)$ and $ITP_r(t)$, ignoring the distribution of $ITP_r(t)$ among the retailers. The fact that the policy performs well implies that these quantities capture the most crucial system characteristics for decisions at that level. The individual $ITP_j(t)$ are important, of course, at the allocation level. It is only because myopic allocation manages them successfully that they can be ignored elsewhere.

Also, although the heuristic policy seems quite different from a local base-stock policy, the two operate similarly when the warehouse actually has inventory on hand. To see this, consider the identical-retailer case, assume that $s_0^* > s_r^* > 0$, and suppose we start at time 0 with inventory s_0^* at the warehouse and none at the retailers. We immediately withdraw s_r^* and allocate it myopically, so that each $ITP_j(0) = s_j^* = s_r^*/J$. Notice, the $C_j'(s_j^*)$ are equal. Now, suppose a demand occurs. According to the policy, we withdraw an equal amount of stock from the warehouse, if that much is available, or else all the remaining warehouse stock. We allocate that stock, clearly, to the retailer where the demand occurred, because its $C_j'(ITP_j(t))$ is now smaller than the others. The net result is precisely the same as under a base-stock policy. This pattern continues until the warehouse runs out of stock. Only in response to warehouse backorders do the two policies differ. The local policy allocates using the FIFO rule, while the centralized policy uses myopic allocation, which better reflects current conditions at the retailers.

Because the balanced approximation is accurate, the bounds of Section 8.3.6 and their interpretations all apply here. In particular, the performance of the system is strongly influenced by the parameters of D_0 and D_r, especially σ_0 and σ_r. Now, D_0 is the total system demand over the warehouse's leadtime, and σ_0^2 is its variance. It is tempting to interpret D_r too as measuring systemwide leadtime demand. But D_r is *not* $\Sigma_j D_j$. It has the same mean, ν_r, but σ_r^2 is *larger* than $V[\Sigma_j D_j]$. (They would be equal if, but only if, the D_j were perfectly correlated.) For instance, consider the identical-retailer case, where in particular the D_j have equal variances. Then, since the D_j are independent, we have $V[\Sigma_j D_j] = J\sigma_j^2$, but $\sigma_2^2 = J^2\sigma_j^2$.

This difference reflects the fact that, in the real system, retailer demands and inventories are *not* consolidated in a single location. (Even the balanced approximation does not actually pool the retailers. It aggregates the $ITP_j(t)$, not the $IN_j(t)$. In other words, it begins with the cost rate (8.6.3), which already reflects the separation of the retailers.) We enjoy *some* of the economies of scale that such consolidation would provide, as reflected in σ_0, but not all.

By the way, there is one sense in which the balanced approximation distorts the real system: In the identical-retailer case, suppose $h = 0$. The optimal policy for the two-stage series system, of course, tells us not to hold inventory at the warehouse. In other words, according to the balanced approximation, warehouse inventory has only one function, like internal inventory in a series system, to help save holding costs. We saw in Section 8.5 that, under local control, warehouse stock also helps to pool the retailers' demand uncertainties, but here that second function seems to disappear. This is not quite true. Simulation studies have shown that, even with $h = 0$, a small amount of warehouse stock can sometimes improve performance. The optimal warehouse stock is smaller than in a local-control system, though, and the performance improvement is slight. In sum, warehouse inventory still plays a risk-pooling role under centralized control, but the effect is weaker than in a local-control system.

EXAMPLE 8.5.A, PART 2

The Brazilian maker of *doce de leite,* having decided to lease the warehouse, is now considering a centralized control scheme, supported by a computer-based system.

The balanced approximation yields $s_0 = 0$, $s_r = 54$, with total cost $C = 20.8$. The best heuristic policy (found using simulation) has $s_0' = 6$, $s_r = 48$ (so each $s_j = 3$) with total cost $C =$ R\$21.6.

This policy uses much less warehouse inventory than the local-control scheme above ($s_0' = 6$ versus 28), and its cost is 20% less (R\$21.6 versus R\$26.4). The cost of this policy, moreover, is very close to the lower bound of R\$20.8, so the policy is nearly optimal.

8.6.4 Coupled Systems

Consider the special case where the warehouse cannot or does not hold stock. Under local control this means, in effect, that the retailers operate independently; each places its own orders with the supplier, and the effective leadtimes are the $L_j = L_0' + L_j'$. Section 8.2 shows how to evaluate such systems.

Here, however, the warehouse does play a key role, as a transshipment or break-bulk center. Orders are placed with the supplier from a central point. On receipt of an order at the warehouse, the order is immediately withdrawn and allocated among the retailers. The key advantage of centralized control is the ability to wait until that moment to allocate the order. The streamlined materials-handling techniques that make this possible are sometimes called *cross-docking,* because goods are transferred quickly from the inbound loading dock across the warehouse to outbound ones. This mode of operation is becoming increasingly popular. See Rosenfield and Pendrock [1980] for a general discussion of its managerial advantages. For instance, Wal-Mart runs its central ordering and distribution facilities in this manner, and this capability is a major element of its overall corporate strategy; see Stalk et al. [1992].

In other situations the warehouse need not be a physical location at all, but rather a control function. For instance, our arrangements with the supplier may allow us to order in bulk for all the retailers, but decide the disposition of the order only later, say after the supplier's production leadtime.

Consider the two-stage system we obtain through the balanced approximation. This system performs precisely as in the approximation of Section 8.3.6. Under the normal approximation, therefore, we can describe the best policy and its performance in closed form:

$$\nu = \nu_0 + \nu_r \qquad \sigma^2 = \sigma_0^2 + \sigma_r^2$$

$$\omega_0 = \frac{b}{b + h'}$$

$$\Phi(z_0^*) = \omega_0$$

$$s_0^* = \nu + \sigma z_0^*$$

$$C^* = h_0\nu_r + (b + h')\Phi(z_0^*)\sigma$$

Let us examine the key performance index σ in the identical-retailer case:

$$\begin{aligned} \sigma^2 &= \sigma_0^2 + \sigma_r^2 \\ &= \lambda_0 L_0' + J^2\left(\frac{\lambda_0}{J}\right)L_r' \\ &= \lambda_0(L_0' + JL_r') \end{aligned} \tag{8.6.8}$$

To understand this formula, consider two extreme cases: When $L_0' = 0$, the retailers operate independently, in effect, and each contributes its own cost to the total. In this case $\sigma = \sqrt{\lambda_0 JL_r'}$. Keeping the total demand rate λ_0 fixed, the overall cost is proportional to the square root of the number of retailers, as in the independent-item systems of Section 8.2. When $L_r' = 0$, on the other hand, we have $\sigma = \sqrt{\lambda_0 L_0'}$; the total cost is independent of the number of retailers, as if their demands were consolidated at one location.

The general case, where both L_0' and L_r' are positive, lies between these extremes. For a fixed total leadtime $L_0' + L_r'$, performance improves as L_0' grows (and L_r' shrinks). Let us compare (8.6.8) to (8.5.5), the formula for the local-control system under similar assumptions. The first term $V[B_0']$ there corresponds to $\lambda_0 L_0'$ here (since we carry no warehouse stock), and both expressions have the same last term, representing the retailers' leadtime-demand variances. The middle term $(J - 1)E[B_0']$ in (8.5.5), however, is entirely absent in (8.6.8). This term expresses retailer imbalances, which the balanced approximation approximates by zero. (As we have seen, this estimate is roughly correct, though it is a bit overoptimistic.) Thus, even a coupled system under centralized control achieves some, but not all, of the advantages of retailer consolidation. Centralized information (here) and warehouse stock (in a local-control system) have somewhat similar effects on performance. In other words, a capable information system serves as a partial substitute for inventory.

Lee et al. [1993] describe an interesting application of these ideas to product design. The model describes Hewlett-Packard's logistics network for distributing printers to markets in Europe. The printers are produced in the United States, shipped to a central point in Europe (corresponding to the warehouse), and then distributed to the several countries (retailers). The printers destined for different countries require slightly different features (e.g., power supplies), and initially these differences were built in during the production process. In effect, each retailer operated independently. Its leadtime L_j' was the production time plus the full shipment time from factory to market, and L'_0 was essentially zero.

Then, a new approach was suggested: Make a common printer for all countries, and insert the country-specific features only at the warehouse. This approach would allow HP to decide the destination of a particular printer only on its arrival in Europe, not at the American factory. Clearly, much of the original leadtime could be included in L'_0 and deducted from L'_j. An analysis along the lines above demonstrated substantial savings with the new approach, and partly for this reason the proposal was adopted.

This story illustrates a general design principle, sometimes called *delayed specialization:* Wait as long as possible before adding customer-specific features to products.

8.6.5 Extensions

The approach above extends immediately to the case of compound-Poisson demands. (Of course, the formulas for special cases must be adjusted appropriately. Recall, this case is problematic under local control, but under central control it is not.) However, the additional demand variation here may cause greater imbalance among the retailer inventories, so the balanced approximation may lose accuracy. The issue, again, is individual-retailer variation versus aggregate volume. Provided the systemwide demand volume is large compared to the retailers' demand fluctuations, the overall approach still works well.

Also, the approach does not actually require the demands to be independent across retailers; nothing changes if we have positively or negatively correlated demands. Of course, the distribution of D_0 must be adjusted appropriately; D_r remains the same. (This is another relative strength of this centralized approach; we have no idea how to analyze local-control policies without the independence assumption.) In the case of a coupled system, moreover, one can incorporate intertemporal correlation, as in the world-driven demand process of Section 6.3: The balanced approximation works as above, and the result is a model similar to that of Section 6.7.2.

The approach *should* perform well also for the other types of supply systems. (We are most comfortable making this assertion for exogenous-sequential supply systems, for the approach can be applied in that case with no additional approximations. We are less sure about the other types, because they do require approximation of the D_j. The empirical evidence to date is encouraging, but limited.) The crucial step in the analysis remains the same—add the *standard deviations* of the D_j to get σ_r.

Now, suppose there are economies of scale for external shipments, i.e., a fixed cost k_0 for warehouse orders. If we apply the balanced approximation as above, we end up with a two-stage series system like that of Section 8.3.6, and we know how to solve that model. The solution, it turns out, provides a good estimate of the optimal cost and a good policy for warehouse orders and withdrawals. To make the overall approach work, however, it is necessary to adjust the allocation policy.

To see why, consider a coupled system with Poisson demands and equal retailer costs. We use an (r, q) policy for warehouse orders here, so there may be a long interval between successive arriving orders. When an order arrives at the warehouse, it is withdrawn and allocated immediately. If we allocate myopically, we optimally balance the inventories *now,* but they may well slide out of balance in the future, long before the next order arrives.

Specifically, call the current time 0, and let us look ahead time $t \geq 0$. Denote $\nu_j(t) = \sigma_j^2(t) = E[D_j(L_j' + t)] = \lambda_j(L_j' + t)$. If we allocate s_j to retailer j, we would like the fractiles $z_j(t) = [s_j - \nu_j(t)]/\sigma_j(t)$ to be equal for *all t,* but that may not be possible. Myopic allocation tries to equalize the $z_j(0)$, but this may systematically induce unequal $z_j(t)$ for $t > 0$.

In the identical-retailer case, happily, there is no such difficulty. Equal $z_j(0)$ implies equal $z_j(t)$ for all t. (See Problem 8.18.) Myopic allocation continues to work well in this special case.

Otherwise, we must choose between balance now and balance later. For what time $t \geq 0$ would balanced inventories be most valuable? Consider the quantity $s_r - \nu - \lambda_0 t$. (In case the L_j' are equal (to L_r'), this is just the expected total retailer net inventory at time $L_r' + t$, assuming no further orders arrive in the interim. In general this is $E[\Sigma\ \{ITP_j(t) - D_j\}]$.) If this quantity is large, the system will have ample stock at time t, and it does not matter where the resulting holding costs are incurred. Likewise, if $s_r - \nu - \lambda_0 t$ is small, the system will be plagued with backorders at t, and it is of no consequence whether they are evenly or unevenly spread among the locations. Imbalance hurts the most at the moment the system runs out of stock, when this quantity hits zero, for then some retailers incur penalty costs at the same time that others pay holding costs. In short, we care most about imbalance for $t = (s_r - \nu)/\lambda_0$. (Actually, we need to revise this t slightly: If $s_r < \nu$, so t would otherwise be negative, reset $t = 0$. Also, there is no need to look beyond the next order arrival. So, if there is an outstanding order due to arrive before t, reset t to that arrival time; if not, compute the expected next arrival time, taking into account the number of demands needed to trigger the next order, and proceed accordingly.)

Then, use this t to redefine the myopic-allocation problem (8.6.4): Just replace D_j by $D_j(L_j' + t)$ in the cost functions C_j. It makes sense to call this *near-myopic allocation.* With this adjustment the overall approach performs well. (Different adjustments are needed for other cases, when the warehouse does hold stock or when the retailer costs are unequal, but the key idea remains the same: Balance the retailer inventories at some appropriate future time t.)

What about fixed costs for internal shipments? Alas, we know of no satisfactory approach to this problem.

8.7 Shared Supply Processes

This section discusses two types of shared supply processes. We cover the results briskly, only sketching certain fruitful directions of analysis.

8.7.1 The Joint-Replenishment Problem

Let us revisit the joint-replenishment problem of Section 5.5, where several items are linked through economies of scope, specifically, through shared fixed order costs. We focus on one special case: Each time we order, we pay the fixed cost k, regardless of the composition of the order. In the terminology of Section 5.5, there is a major setup cost, but no minor setup costs. The demands for the items are independent Poisson processes with rates λ_j. There is a constant leadtime L'_j for the units of item j within each order. (In many situations, all the items within an order are shipped and received together, in which case the L'_j are equal. Here, we allow for the possibility that certain items require special processing, and so have longer leadtimes.)

As in Section 5.5.2, construct an equivalent two-level distribution system: The items correspond to retailers. We add a fictitious item 0 representing the warehouse. The fixed cost $k_0 = k$ and leadtime 0 are assigned to item 0; the original items have no fixed costs and leadtimes L'_j. We never hold inventory of item 0.

Here is a plausible policy for this system, in the spirit of Section 8.5.5: Use a base-stock policy for the original items, and an (r, q) policy for item 0. Specify base-stock levels s'_j for the retailers (items), and start with $I'_j(0) = s'_j$. Also, fix $r = -q$, to ensure that the warehouse holds no stock, so $IOP'_0(0) = IN'_0(0) = I'_0(0) = r + q = 0$. Thus, there is only one policy parameter for item 0, namely q.

In terms of the original system, the policy works as follows: We place an order each time q demands accumulate over all the items. The composition of the order precisely reflects the demands since the last order.

This is just a special case of the system of Section 8.5.5, so the cost of any such policy can be expressed in the form (8.5.7). (Actually, it is simpler to evaluate a policy directly: Given q, $B'_0 = -IN'_0 = -IOP'_0$, so B'_0 is uniformly distributed on the integers 0 through $q - 1$. We can then proceed as in Section 8.5.2. Binomial disaggregation yields the distribution of the B'_{0j}, and we can apply (8.5.2) to obtain the B'_j.) Likewise, we can apply the straightforward policy-optimization approach outlined in Section 8.5.5.

Models of this basic flavor have been widely used for several decades by large oil companies, to supply filling stations with incidental products, such as motor oil and transmission fluid. These products are delivered by truck. Typically, a truck visits a single station, carrying all the products the station needs at the same time. The model represents that one station's problem. (In reality, of course, the trucks draw from centralized inventories, so the model includes only part of a larger distribution system.) The fixed cost k measures the cost of a delivery. Sometimes, the order size q is fixed to the capacity of a truck.

8.7.2 Shared Production Capacity

Next, consider a system with several items sharing a production facility of limited capacity. In a deterministic world this situation leads to the ELSP of Section 5.6.2. Here, the items' demands are independent Poisson processes, and we model the production facility by one of the limited-capacity supply systems of Section 7.3.

This is essentially a special kind of distribution system. The items play the roles of retailers, but with zero leadtimes (because goods leaving the production facility move immediately into inventory). The processing system, including its queue, corresponds to the warehouse's supply system. The warehouse itself, of course, cannot hold stock.

We say "essentially," because the analogy is not quite perfect: In a true distribution system the physical units in the warehouse's supply system are indistinguishable. Here, this is true only under two very special symmetry conditions, namely, (1) the items have the same processing requirements, i.e., the same unit processing times, and (2) a unit in process acquires its specific item identity only at the completion of processing. So, the results of Section 8.5 and Section 8.6 apply only under these conditions. Nevertheless, many of the basic ideas in those earlier sections can be fruitfully adapted here.

8.7.2.1 No Scale Economies

First, suppose there are no economies of scale in the system—no setup times or costs. Suppose we use the analogue of the local-control scheme of Section 8.5: Each item follows a base-stock policy and sends orders to the production facility. The facility responds to these orders using the first come, first served (FCFS) discipline.

For the moment, suppose the first symmetry condition above holds, so the items have identical processing requirements. (Because of the policy, the second condition is unnecessary.) The processing system itself has Poisson input, so it is relatively simple to analyze, as in Section 7.3. Then, binomially disaggregate its occupancy to obtain the outstanding orders for each item, as in Section 7.3.7. Finally, optimize each item's base-stock level separately. The identical-item case leads to a simple performance formula like (8.5.5); see Problem 8.19.

This same approach can be used even without the symmetry condition, at least in some cases. For instance, suppose there is a single processor. The processing times S_j for item j are i.i.d. random variables, but the S_j may differ over j. It turns out that the processing system behaves like the M/G/1 system of Section 7.3.2.2. Its overall processing time S is just the θ_j weighted mixture of the S_j. (In particular, $E[S]$, $E[S^2]$, and $E[S^3]$ are the corresponding weighted averages of the $E[S_j]$, $E[S_j^2]$, and $E[S_j^3]$, respectively.) So, suppose we compute or approximate its occupancy, IO. Dividing IO among the items requires a bit more care than before: Given $IO = n > 0$, each of the $n - 1$ units in the processor's queue has the same probability θ_j of being an order for item j, so binomially disaggregate these units as before. The unit in process, however, has probability ρ_j/ρ of belonging to item j, where $\rho_j = \lambda_j E[S_j]$ and $\rho = \Sigma_j \rho_j$. With this slight revision we can obtain the individual items' occupancies, and then proceed as above.

Instead of this local approach, we may prefer a centralized control scheme, along the lines of Section 8.6. Let us focus on the single-processor case. When both symmetry conditions above apply, we must allocate each unit of finished product as it emerges from the processor; otherwise, we allocate not stock but rather processor time. In both cases, analogues of myopic allocation seem to work well. With identical products, again, myopic allocation reduces to a simpler rule: When it comes time to allocate, whether stock or processing time, choose that product with the lowest net inventory. (In fact, this rule is truly optimal.)

There remains the decision when to operate the processor and when to shut it down, the analogue here of the warehouse's ordering decision. The following simple heuristic, essentially a base-stock policy, seems to work well: Monitor some aggregate measure of inventory, and turn the processor on when that measure falls below some fixed base-stock level; likewise, turn the processor off when the measure equals or exceeds the base-stock level. (In the identical-product case, the appropriate measure is total net inventory.) Also, one can determine a good value of the base-stock level and global performance measures, in the spirit of the balanced approximation.

8.7.2.2 Setup Costs and Times

Now, suppose there are economies of scale. Specifically, there is a cost and/or a time delay to switch production from one item to another. This system is very complex, and we can conceive of and analyze only rather crude heuristic policies.

We sketch one approach, which extends the local-control policy above: Each product uses an (r, q) policy to place orders, and the facility responds to those orders on a FCFS basis. (Many firms use control schemes of this general flavor, especially for batch-production processes, as found for instance in the chemical, petroleum, pharmaceutical, and food industries.)

For simplicity, suppose the products are identical, so each one has demand rate λ/J, and they all use the same policy variables (r, q). Also, there is a single processor, and the processing time for an order consists of two parts, a setup time τ and a processing time $1/\mu$ for each unit in the order, both constants. Thus, the total processing time takes the form $S = \tau + q/\mu$.

Now, the orders for each item form a renewal process; the times between orders have an Erlang distribution with parameters λ/J and q. Taking all the products' orders together, the overall input is a superposition of renewal processes. Approximate this by a Poisson process. (If J is large, this approximation is reasonably accurate, as mentioned in Section C.5.6.) The total order rate is $\underline{\lambda} = J(\lambda/J)/q = \lambda/q$. The processing system then becomes an M/G/1 system with constant processing time S and utilization $\underline{\rho} = \underline{\lambda}S = \lambda\tau/q + \rho$, where $\rho = \lambda/\mu$. The formulas of Section 7.3.2.2 then describe the order leadtime L.

Now, make another approximation: For each item, treat the processing system as exogenous. (Again, this is reasonable for large J.) Then, analyze each item by itself, as a single-item system with the stochastic leadtime L. For instance, use a two-moment approximation (normal, negative binomial, etc.), using $E[L]$ and $V[L]$ to compute the required parameters ν and σ^2.

The lot size q thus has two distinct effects here: Given L, q along with r determines the performance of each item in the usual way. However, q also affects $\underline{\lambda}$ and S, and these determine L itself. Indeed, for the overall system to be stable, we must have $\underline{\rho} < 1$, which is equivalent to $q > \lambda\tau(1 - \rho)$. And, when q just barely satisfies this lower bound, $\underline{\rho}$ is near 1, so $E[L]$ and $V[L]$ are large and overall performance suffers. Thus, even in the absence of a setup cost, there is a strong reason to avoid small values of q. (Consequently, there is a strong incentive to reduce the setup time τ.)

We see here in an explicit and extreme form the scenario outlined in Section 5.2 and Section 8.2, where each item's lot size determines the workload it imposes on some common resource. Here, the resource is the production facility, and its capacity is strictly finite. We cannot account for that limited resource, however, by a simple capacity constraint like (5.6.1). As the overall workload approaches the limit, the interaction of the system's uncertainties with its capacity causes congestion, and performance deteriorates rapidly.

This congestion effect is not just an artifact of this particular model, with all its simplifying assumptions and approximations. The effect is real. Indeed, it reflects the true impact of lot sizes in many situations better than simple fixed costs do.

Now, the explicit model above may be too hard to work with in practice. There may be no alternative to treating the items as independent, as in Section 8.2. (In those terms each item's w_j is τ, so $wO = \lambda\tau/q$.) Nevertheless, these observations should be kept in mind when selecting the aggregate resource cost κ. This parameter must reflect not just direct resource-usage costs, but also indirect congestion effects. There is no simple rule to accomplish this, to our knowledge, so it may be necessary to iterate. That is, if we choose a certain κ and the resulting workload is too large, we must adjust κ upward.

8.8 Kanban Systems

8.8.1 Definition

Kanban is a Japanese word meaning *card* or *ticket.* A *kanban system* is a production-control scheme that uses cards in a special way to regulate the flow of goods between stages. The idea was developed originally at Toyota Motors. The kanban system, along with other innovations in operations, has been one of the key factors underlying Toyota's remarkable growth over the last few decades. It is now widely used throughout industry in Japan and the rest of the world.

First we describe the mechanics of the kanban system. Then, we explore a more general control scheme. Finally, we discuss the kanban system in the broader context of the just-in-time approach to operations.

To illustrate the concept, consider a series system. Each stage's supply system consists of a single, finite-capacity processor and its queue. Demands occur one at a time, and there are no scale economies, so goods move through the system in individual units. (Actually, the scheme can work just as well in more complex system structures, and/or with larger batch sizes. As we shall see, however, the kanban system's main virtue is its effectiveness in dealing with capacity limits; it makes little sense in the context of an infinite-capacity supply system, like the exogenous and independent-leadtime models.)

Figure 8.8.1 depicts the subsystem associated with a single stage, including the *inventory* itself, the *processor,* and the processor's *queue.* There is also a *box* (sometimes called a post or a bulletin board), where cards are stored temporarily.

Each stage has a fixed, positive number of *cards,* which circulate around the subsystem. The key rule is this: At all times, every unit of stock in the subsystem *must* have one of these cards attached to it. Any additional cards are kept in the box.

Consider stage J. Suppose all of its cards are attached to units in inventory (so the processor, its queue, and the box must be empty). Now, suppose a demand occurs. We use one unit of inventory to fill the demand. As that unit departs, we detach its card and put it in the box. The card waits there, if stage $J-1$ has no inventory available. When stage $J-1$ does have inventory, we take one of those units, attach the card from the box, and place them together in stage J's queue. Since that queue is empty and the processor is idle, the unit moves immediately into the processor, which begins to work on it. (Had the processor been occupied, the unit would have waited its turn in the queue.) Once processing is complete, the finished unit, with its card still attached, moves into inventory. The cycle then begins anew.

The other stages work similarly: A card begins its cycle attached to a unit in inventory. When the unit is sent from inventory to the next stage, the card is detached and placed in the box. Only when there is a card available in the box can a unit be drawn from

FIGURE 8.8.1

One stage in a kanban system.

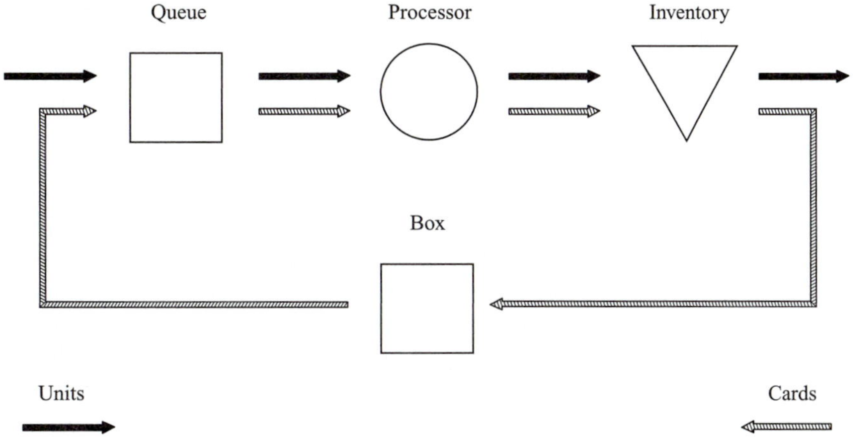

the previous stage. When that happens, the card is attached to the incoming unit. It remains attached during the entire time the unit remains in the stage, i.e., throughout the waiting time in the processor's queue, the actual processing time, and the time spent in inventory.

There is one difference: Units leave stage J to fill customer demands. At stage $j < J$, however, a demand occurs, in effect, only when one of stage $j + 1$'s cards enters its box. For instance, suppose there is no inventory at stage J, and all cards are attached to units in the processor and its queue. If a customer demand occurs, that demand is backlogged; no card moves into the box. In this situation, then, a customer demand does not trigger a demand at stage $J - 1$. Only later, when the processor completes a unit (which then immediately leaves to fill a backordered demand), does a card enter the box, thus generating a demand at stage $J - 1$.

The kanban system, then, is a particular type of policy, a rule specifying what to do under various circumstances. It is similar in many ways to a base-stock policy: Both are *pull systems:* Customer demands trigger all other events, directly or indirectly; demand information propagates backwards through the network, stage by stage, from the last to the first. In both cases there is one policy variable for each stage, the base-stock level or the number of cards, which determines that stage's maximal inventory.

The differences are noteworthy also: Under a base-stock policy a demand at one stage *always* triggers a demand at the prior stage. The kanban system, in contrast, generates a demand upstream when the stage *fills* one of its own demands. Thus, the demand-propagation mechanisms are the same when (but only when) the stage has inventory on hand; backlogged demands do not propagate upstream under the kanban system until later. Consequently, the number of cards has yet another role in the kanban system—it limits the occupancy of the stage's supply system. Under a base-stock policy, by contrast, the occupancy is unlimited.

This is the primary strength of the kanban policy. For instance, consider a two-stage system, where the first stage has a fast processor, but the second's processor is slower. Under a base-stock policy the queue at the second stage grows rapidly. No matter how large it gets, the policy instructs stage 1 to continue producing units and transmitting them to stage 2, as subsequent demands occur. The kanban policy, however, blocks the flow of units into stage 2 when it becomes too congested; equivalently, the policy blocks the transmission of demands to stage 1, and this ultimately stops stage 1's processor. In this way the kanban approach avoids excessive queues.

It should be clear that the basic logic here does not require the use of cards. We can use any other physical tokens instead. Some companies implement the policy with painted circles on the floor, marking the legal spaces in the queue; here, every unit in the queue *must* rest on one of these circles. Other firms embed the idea in a computer program; the logical equivalents of cards are sometimes called *electronic kanbans.*

(*Suggestion:* To make sure you understand the kanban mechanism, simulate manually the operation of a two- or three-stage system. Use pennies to represent physical units, and make cards out of paper, using a different color for each stage. You will also need markers, say dimes, to represent backlogged customer demands. Variation: Play this game with several friends. Choose one player to simulate customer demands; each of the others operates a single stage.)

8.8.2 The Generalized Kanban Policy

The kanban system is not perfect. Again consider a two-stage system, but now stage 1 has a slow processor, and stage 2's is relatively fast. We need little inventory at stage 2, so it makes sense to assign it only a few cards. But this also sharply limits the occupancy at stage 2. Consequently, stage 1's processor will frequently stop working, even when there are many customer backorders. And, since stage 1 responds slowly to its demands, stage 2's processor will often run out of work to do. To reduce such forced idleness, we can increase the number of cards at stage 2, but then stage 2's inventory may become too large. In contrast, base-stock policies allow us to regulate inventories precisely, while freely transmitting demand information to heavily loaded stages, where it is needed most.

Both the kanban and base-stock policies, then, have weaknesses as well as strengths. We now describe a more general class of policies, which includes the kanban and base-stock policies as special cases, and which captures the best features of both. Recall, in a kanban system, the number of cards in a stage affects its behavior in two ways, limiting both the inventory and the supply-system occupancy. The idea here is to separate these two roles, assigning them to different policy variables. We call this a *generalized kanban policy.*

Again use $s_j' \geq 0$ to denote the base-stock level, i.e., the maximum inventory, at stage j. Also, define

$$n_j = \text{supply-system occupancy limit for stage } j$$

This is a positive integer. These two policy variables can be set independently.

Initialize the system with $I_j'(0) = s_j'$ and $IT_j(0) = 0$. A generalized kanban policy is a pull system: Again, each stage generates demands at its predecessor; stage J responds to customer demands, while each of the other stages responds to the demands from its successor. The demand-transmission mechanism ensures that each supply system's occupancy remains within its limit, i.e., $IT_j(t) \leq n_j$. Otherwise, the policy operates just like a base-stock policy. That is, each stage fills its demands when it can and otherwise backorders them; also, each processor operates when it has work to do, i.e., when $IT_j(t) > 0$.

Specifically, a demand at stage j immediately triggers a demand at $j - 1$ unless it is blocked. Demands are blocked when

$$B'_{j-1}(t) + IT_j(t) = n_j \tag{8.8.1}$$

that is, when n_j earlier stage-($j - 1$) demands either remain unfilled or, though filled, have yet to pass through stage j's processor. Also, presuming we track these blocked demands, a process completion at stage j triggers a demand at $j - 1$ precisely when there are blocked demands waiting to be transmitted.

It turns out (Problem 8.21) that the following is an equivalent demand-blocking condition:

$$s'_j - IN'_j(t) \geq n_j \tag{8.8.2}$$

The number of blocked demands is just $[s'_j - IN'_j(t) - n_j]^+$. Thus, the one state variable $IN'_j(t)$ determines the demand-transmission mechanism at stage j. (This approach is easier to implement in some situations.)

The special case with each $s'_j = n_j$ is precisely a kanban policy; the number of cards is s'_j or n_j. [Condition (8.8.2) holds when there is no inventory, and blocked demands correspond to stage-j backorders.] Also, a base-stock policy is a limiting case with each $n_j = \infty$ (so demands are never blocked). Another special case, where all $s'_j = 0$, is a processing network with finite buffers (mentioned briefly in Section 7.3.6.3).

It is possible to implement a generalized kanban policy using physical tokens, analogous to kanbans. Figure 8.8.2 illustrates one such scheme: We now follow the flow of *demands,* or tokens representing them, in addition to units and cards. The cards play a somewhat different role here. Also, there are two boxes, a *delay box* and a *block box.* There are n_j cards, which circulate through the subsystem; at time $t = 0$ they all start in the block box.

When a demand arrives from the subsequent stage, it first goes to the block box. If it finds a card there, the two move together to the delay box, and the demand proceeds to the prior stage; otherwise, the demand is blocked, and it remains in the block box until a card arrives. The delay box works like a kanban system's box; a card there is a signal to move a unit from the prior stage's inventory into the queue. (So, $B'_{j-1}(t)$ is the number of cards in the delay box.) The card remains with the unit during its queueing time and processing time. After processing the card does *not* accompany the unit to inventory, but rather returns to the block box to await another demand.

The generalized kanban policy provides considerable freedom to modulate performance. Each s'_j has essentially the same impact as in a base-stock policy; as we increase it, we obtain better protection against backorders at the cost of larger inventories. Each n_j too affects inventory and backorders, but less directly. It mediates the backward transfer of demands. By increasing n_j, we reduce the chance of forced idleness at stage j, but increase its occupancy. (These properties should seem plausible intuitively; they can be proved rigorously, but we shall not do so.)

FIGURE 8.8.2

One stage under a generalized kanban policy.

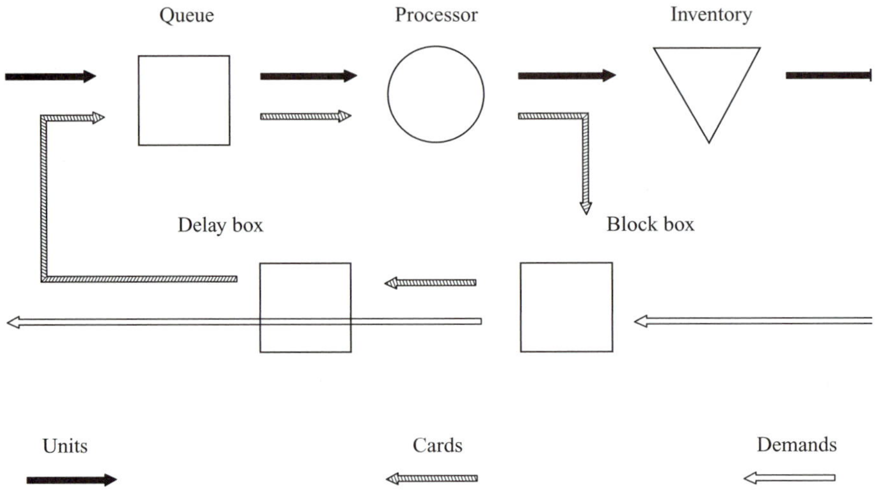

(A moment's thought should convince you that n_1 can be set arbitrarily. That is, provided $n_1 \geq 1$, the choice of n_1 has no effect on $IN_1'(t)$ or on events at downstream stages. This is because the external source always has stock available, so the stage-1 processor is never idle for lack of input. Thus, we can fix $n_1 = 1$; a larger n_1 does no harm, however, since $IT_1(t)$ incurs no holding cost.)

To illustrate, consider a two-stage system with Poisson demand and limited-capacity supply systems with exponential processing times, as in Section 8.3.4.3. Fix $\lambda = 1$ and $h_2' = 1$. Table 8.8.1 compares the best base-stock, kanban, and generalized kanban policies. The table has three parts, (*a*) to (*c*). The systems described in the three parts differ in their processing rates μ_j. Part (*a*) describes a base case with $\mu_j = 2$, so $\rho_j = ½$. Parts (*b*) and (*c*) explore the impacts of slower processing rates and thus larger ρ_j. Each part examines two values of h_1 and four values of *b*.

It is striking to observe that, in nearly all cases, the base-stock levels s_j' are identical across the three policy types; the occasional differences are slight. The overall costs too are quite close. [The greatest differences appear in part (*b*) of the table, describing a slow stage-2 processor. This is precisely where we expect an occupancy limit to help the most. Even then, the s_j' differ by at most 1, and the costs only by about 7%.]

Thus, the simple model of Section 8.3 seems to capture the fundamental economics of the system. The base-stock levels play the same roles in all three policies, with or without occupancy limits. This observation suggests using algorithm (8.3.9) as a heuristic method to determine the s_j' in a kanban or a generalized kanban policy.

Notice also that, in the generalized kanban policy, n_2 and s_2' are quite different in many cases; n_2 is much smaller in part (*b*), but larger in part (*c*). Moreover, they respond to parameter changes differently. For instance, s_2' is very sensitive to the backorder cost *b*, but n_2 is not; conversely, n_2 is much more sensitive than s_2' to μ_1.

TABLE 8.8.1

Base-Stock, Kanban, and Generalized Kanban Policies

		Base-Stock			Generalized Kanban				Kanban			
h_1	b	s'_2	s'_1	C^*	s'_2	n_2	s'_1	C^*	s'_2	n_2	s'_1	C^*
(*a*) Base Case: $\mu_j = 2$												
	10	5	0	5.35	5	8	0	5.35	5	5	0	5.38
0.8	20	6	0	6.44	6	10	0	6.44	6	6	0	6.46
	40	7	0	7.56	7	11	0	7.56	7	7	0	7.58
	80	8	0	8.70	8	13	0	8.70	8	8	0	8.71
	10	4	1	4.97	4	9	1	4.94	4	4	1	4.99
0.5	20	5	1	6.05	5	11	1	6.03	5	5	1	6.06
	40	6	2	7.16	6	9	2	7.12	6	6	2	7.13
	80	7	2	8.22	7	10	2	8.19	7	7	2	8.19
(*b*) Slow Stage 2: $\mu_2 = 1.2$												
	10	14	0	17.36	14	7	0	16.38	13	13	0	16.98
0.8	20	17	0	20.92	18	8	0	20.02	17	17	0	20.70
	40	21	0	24.57	21	8	0	23.74	21	21	0	24.46
	80	25	0	28.31	25	8	0	27.51	25	25	0	28.26
	10	14	0	15.86	14	8	0	15.33	14	14	0	15.62
0.5	20	17	0	19.42	18	8	0	18.94	17	17	0	19.28
	40	21	0	23.07	21	9	0	22.62	21	21	0	23.00
	80	25	0	26.81	25	9	0	26.38	25	25	0	26.78
(*c*) Slow Stage 1: $\mu_1 = 1.5$												
	10	5	2	7.24	5	19	2	7.21	5	5	2	7.26
0.8	20	6	3	8.80	6	20	3	8.77	6	6	3	8.79
	40	7	4	10.41	7	20	4	10.38	7	7	4	10.39
	80	8	4	12.01	8	19	4	11.98	8	8	4	11.99
	10	4	4	6.44	4	19	4	6.39	4	4	4	6.42
0.5	20	5	5	7.81	5	19	5	7.77	5	5	5	7.78
	40	6	6	9.20	6	19	6	9.18	6	6	6	9.18
	80	7	6	10.60	7	20	6	10.57	7	7	6	10.57

These patterns may be suggestive, but we cannot discern any clear guidelines for choosing n_2. On the other hand, it doesn't seem to matter much how we set n_2. The three policy types constrain n_2 in very different ways, yet their performance is nearly identical. In general, we must take care not to set n_2 too small, to avoid excessive forced idleness. (In these examples, all the policies easily satisfy this requirement, even the kanban policy, but that is because s'_2 is always comfortably large. If s'_2 were smaller, say because of a smaller b, we might well prefer a larger n_2.) If we err on the high side, the cost penalty is modest.

Caveat: This is a small test bed, and the conclusions should be regarded accordingly as tentative.

8.8.3 Analysis

There are a few tractable approximations for policy evaluation in the research literature. (See the Notes at the end of the chapter.) These are based on methods for finite-buffer processing networks.

8.8.4 The Larger Context: The Just-in-Time Approach

As we have seen, the kanban system is a *local* information and control system. All decisions are based on local information; the transmission of information, moreover, requires only short communication links (i.e., between successive stages). The mechanism is *simple.* The information itself and the rules that employ it are easy to describe and implement. Finally, the approach is *tangible.* At any moment, anyone—a worker or an observer—can see just what must be done.

We have seen other control schemes with these features. A base-stock policy is also local, simple, and tangible; so are a generalized kanban policy and a local (r, q) policy. It was only with the introduction of the kanban system, however, and the celebrated successes of Toyota and other companies using it, that we learned just how important these factors are. It was in contrast to the kanban system that the weaknesses of centralized control schemes like MRP, as discussed in Chapter 5, showed up clearly.

The kanban system is only one element of a broad approach to operations management called *just-in-time* (or JIT). Another key element is *kaizen,* a Japanese word that means *continuous improvement.* The idea here is to tinker with equipment and procedures so that they work better. Over time, many small reductions in setup times, processing times, and defects can add up to a much more capable process and vastly improved performance. Kaizen is everyone's responsibility. Even factory workers whose usual job is just to get work out the door should participate, for the people closest to the process can sometimes see problems and solutions that are invisible to others.

The kanban system addresses moment-to-moment control, while kaizen operates over a longer time scale. How are they connected? The main connection is psychological, or perhaps sociological: A local control system, precisely because it is transparent, supports the perception that the process belongs to everyone, and thus reinforces kaizen. This is no automatic mechanism, however; people don't work that way. A local control scheme cannot by itself engender kaizen; that requires training and incentives, not to mention patience. Conversely, an active kaizen program can survive some degree of centralized control.

In short, there is no need to apply the principle of local control dogmatically; indeed, it is foolish and dangerous to do so. *Some* longer communication links and more complex information are virtually always required.

Consider this scenario: There are 17 production stages. Stage 11 happens to be the bottleneck; it has the longest processing times. Now, the sales department learns of a demand surge upcoming in a month. Must we wait until then, relying on the kanban mechanism to transmit demands backward after they actually occur?

Of course not. In practice, typically, there is a higher-level planning-control function between the physical production activities and the market. The "demands" seen by the production process are not actual customer demands, but rather signals generated at this higher level. The planners do respond to real demands, but also to forecasts; also, they often try to damp demand fluctuations, in order to smooth the load on the production facility. Moreover, to anticipate longer-term changes in demand, they may increase or decrease the numbers of cards at some or all stages. In the scenario above, the planners may choose to generate demand signals before the demand surge occurs, or perhaps to increase the number of cards at the critical stage 11. This is one of the ways that MRP or MRP-like logic can be integrated with elements of JIT.

JIT also addresses the issue of managerial incentives: Many companies continue to judge managers along dimensions like throughput (total output per unit time) and utilization (fraction of time a facility is operating). If these are your objectives, it is clear what to do—keep all equipment working as hard as possible. It is equally clear that this rule leads to disaster: Inventory grows without limit. Sooner or later, something gives; either the plant breaks down by itself or somebody shuts it down. Under this *de facto* control policy, then, the system oscillates between massive overproduction and layoffs.

Now, *all* of the policies we have studied are smarter than this. Why not just impose one of them? Doesn't that settle the issue? *No:* When incentives systematically conflict with official policy, however refined, people often find ways to subvert the policy. The main message of JIT on this score is to look at existing incentives and to eliminate those that, however well intentioned, lead to perverse behavior. We should not have needed JIT to tell us this, of course, but we did. (This negative insight is crucial, but one would like more—a positive, constructive theory of incentives, a set of criteria designed to support intelligent operations. Academic research and business practice are just beginning to address this question.)

Notes

Section 8.1: Overviews of the subject are provided by Clark [1972] and the collections of Schwarz [1981], Axsäter et al. [1986], and Graves et al. [1993]. Davis [1993] elucidates the roles of uncertainties and inventories in complex networks from a managerial viewpoint. A good general discussion of centralized versus decentralized systems can be found in Rosenfield and Pendrock [1980]. Lee and Billington [1993] provide a cogent discussion of decentralized control in practice. Business process reengineering is described in Hammer [1990] and Davenport [1993].

Section 8.2: The notion of an aggregate tradeoff surface is discussed extensively in Gardner and Dannenbring [1979].

Section 8.3: The study of series systems with stochastic demand and constant leadtimes was initiated by Clark and Scarf [1960] and later refined by Federgruen and Zipkin [1984c], Rosling [1989], and Chen and Zheng [1994b]. The two-moment approximation is by Graves [1985].

The extension of the policy-evaluation scheme in Section 8.3.4 to exogenous, stochastic leadtimes is attributable to Svoronos and Zipkin [1991]. Buzacott et al. [1992], Lee and Zipkin [1992,1995] and Zipkin [1995] develop the approximation for limited-capacity supply systems; Graves [1985] and Sherbrooke [1986] develop the independent-leadtime approximation. Gallego and Zipkin [1999a] observe that the optimization algorithm can be used in these contexts. Song and Zipkin [1992] extend the policy-evaluation method to an MCDC demand process.

The numerical results of Section 8.3.5 are from Gallego and Zipkin [1999a]. The methods for (r, q) policies are attributable to Chen and Zheng [1994a] and Chen [1999].

Section 8.4: Rosling [1989] originated this approach to assembly systems, and Chen and Zheng [1994b] refined it.

Section 8.5: The original METRIC model was developed by Sherbrooke [1968]. Nahmias [1981] and Axsäter [1993a] review the literature. See Ahmed et al. [1992], Axsäter [1990], Schneeweiss and Schröder [1992], Sherbrooke [1992], and Tripp et al. [1991] for recent enhancements and applications. Muckstadt and Thomas [1980] demonstrate the inadequacy of the alternative heuristic discussed in Section 8.5.1. Recent results on exact and approximate methods for (r, q) policies can be found in Axsäter [1993b,1997] and Chen and Zheng [1998].

There is an interesting new stream of research, which unfortunately we have been unable to include because of space constraints, on systems under truly decentralized management. There, not only is the policy implemented locally, but also the policy variables are chosen by local managers, according to their own local incentives. See Cachon [1999] for a review.

Section 8.6: This approach to centralized control of distribution systems was initiated by Miller [1974] and Eppen and Schrage [1981], elaborated by Federgruen and Zipkin [1984a–c], Jackson [1988], and Erkip et al. [1990], and reviewed in Federgruen [1993].

Section 8.7: The joint-replenishment problem of Section 8.7.1 is attributable to Renberg and Planche [1967]. Centralized control schemes for the shared-production-capacity systems of Section 8.7.2.1 have inspired considerable research activity recently. See Zheng and Zipkin [1990], Menich and Serfozo [1991], Wein [1992], Zipkin [1995], Ha [1997], and Peña-Perez and Zipkin [1997]. The heuristic approach for the system with setups in Section 8.7.2.2 is explored by Williams [1984], Zipkin [1986c], and Karmarkar [1987b]; see Karmarkar [1993] for a review. Karmarkar and Rummel [1990] discuss in detail the role of congestion effects in fixed costs. There are other, more centralized approaches to this system, inspired by the ELSP; see Leachman and Gascon [1988], Gallego [1990], Katalan [1995], and Markowitz et al. [1995].

Section 8.8: For a general introduction to the kanban system and JIT see Schonberger [1982] or Shingo [1985,1989]. Zipkin [1991a] provides a critical guide to the popular literature. Berkley [1992] and Groenevelt [1993] review the research literature.

The generalized kanban policy of Section 8.8.2 is discussed by Buzacott [1989], Zipkin [1989], and Frein et al. [1995]. Even more general policies are analyzed by Buzacott and Shanthikumar [1992] and Cheng and Yao [1993]. Approximate policy-evaluation methods are developed by Buzacott and Shanthikumar [1992], Di Mascolo et al. [1996], and Mitra and Mitrani [1990,1991]. Even these generalized kanban policies need not be optimal. Veatch and Wein [1994] show that the true optimal policy can be quite complex, even in a two-stage system.

There is a considerable body of simulation-based research on more complex networks than those we treat in this chapter. For instance, Vargas and Dear [1990] study the effectiveness of alternative buffering methods in a setting much like MRP.

Problems

8.1 Justify the two-moment approximation of the series system in Section 8.3.1. Specifically, show that $V[B_j'] \geq E[B_j']$. (Use Theorem 6.2.4.)

8.2 Consider the series system of Section 8.3. Using (8.3.4), prove by induction that for all j

$$B_j' = \max\{0\,,D_j - s_j',\, (D_j - s_j') + (D_{j-1} - s_{j-1}'), \ldots, \Sigma_{i \leq j}(D_i - s_i')\}$$

From this fact argue that $E[B_j']$ is a nonincreasing, (jointly) convex function of all the s_i'. (Regard the s_i' as continuous variables.)

8.3 Consider the series system of Sections 8.3.1 and 8.3.2. Argue that

$$I_j'(t) = [IN_j(t) - IOP_{j+1}(t)]^+$$

Use this fact to verify (8.3.6); i.e., $ITP_{j+1}(t) = \min\{s_{j+1}, IN_j(t)\}$.

8.4 Consider a series system with exogenous, sequential leadtimes, as in Section 8.3.4.2. Assume that demand is Poisson, and L_j' has the CPH distribution with parameters $(\boldsymbol{\mu}_j', M_j')$. First, argue that D_j has a DPH distribution, and compute its parameters $(\boldsymbol{\pi}_j', P_j')$. (This is easy; the answers are in Section 7.5.) Now, define recursively the matrices and vectors $P_1 = P_1'$, $\boldsymbol{\pi}_1 = \boldsymbol{\pi}_1'$, and

$$\boldsymbol{\tau}_j = \boldsymbol{\pi}_j P_j^{s_j'} \qquad j \geq 1$$

$$\boldsymbol{\pi}_j = [\boldsymbol{\tau}_{j-1}, (1 - \boldsymbol{\tau}_{j-1}\mathbf{e})\boldsymbol{\pi}_j']$$

$$P_j = \begin{pmatrix} P_{j-1} & (I - P_{j-1})\mathbf{e}\boldsymbol{\pi}_j' \\ 0 & P_j' \end{pmatrix} \qquad j > 1$$

Prove by induction that B_j' has the DPH distribution with parameters $(\boldsymbol{\tau}_j, P_j)$. Then, write formulas for $E[B_j']$ and $E[I_j']$ in terms of these arrays.

8.5 Consider the same system as in the previous problem, and focus on the case $J = 2$. Show how to implement the optimization algorithm (8.3.9) using the arrays above: First, write down an explicit formula for $C_2(y)$ in terms of the data $(\boldsymbol{\pi}_2', P_2')$. Then, given s_2^* write down a formula for $C_1(y)$ in each of two cases, namely, $y = s_1 \leq s_2^*$ and $y = s_1 > s_2^*$. (Use the equivalence between local and echelon base-stock policies.)

8.6 For a two-stage series system, use the maximal approximation to obtain an explicit upper bound on C^*, using the results of Section 8.3.6. What does this tell us about the impact of σ on performance?

8.7 Show how to extend the bound of Section 8.3.6 to a three-stage system: Restrict the permissible policies to those with $s_2 = s_3 = \infty$. Argue that this leads to bounds on s_1^* and C^*. Express these bounds in closed form using the normal approximation.

8.8 Consider a series system with fixed costs, where all $k_j = 0$ except k_1. Suppose we follow a policy of the form proposed in the text, namely, an (r, q) policy at stage 1 and base-stock policies elsewhere. Show that the recursion (8.3.7) describes ITP_j and IN_j. Then, argue that each ITP_j is a mixture of the $ITP_j(s)$, with $s = r + 1, \ldots, r + q$, using the equal mixing weights $1/q$, and IN_j is a similar mixture of the $IN_j(s)$. Conclude that $E[IN_j]$ is just the simple average of $E[IN_j(s)]$ over these s's, and $E[B]$ is the average of the $E[B(s)]$.

8.9 For the model of Section 8.3.7.2, verify equation (8.3.13); i.e.,

$$s_{j+1} - ITP_{j+1} = \pi(s_{j+1} - IN_j, q_{j+1})$$

Hint: Recall that $IN_j = I_j' + ITP_{j+1}$. Consider the two cases $s_{j+1} - IN_j \geq 0$ and $s_{j+1} - IN_j < 0$ separately.

8.10 Consider a two-stage series system with a fixed cost k_1 at stage 1, but $k_2 = 0$. Replace $C_1(y)$ in (8.3.11) by $C_1^+(y)$ from Section 8.3.6. Then apply Theorem 6.5.1 in Chapter 6 to obtain a bound on the optimal cost. What does this result tell us about the determinants of performance? (Discuss *at least* the impacts of k_1 and λ.)

8.11 Consider a two-stage series system with fixed costs at both stages. This problem shows how to calculate a lower bound on the true optimal cost. Construct a pair of new systems as follows: System 1 also has two stages; system 2 has only one stage, which we call stage 2. We use superscripts to distinguish these systems' parameters:

$$\begin{array}{lll} k_1^1 = k_1 & k_2^1 = 0 & k_2^2 = k_2 \\ D_1^1 = D_1 & D_2^1 = D_2 & D_2^2 = D_2 \\ h_1^1 = h_1 & & \end{array}$$

For the stage-2 holding costs and backorder costs we select *any* h_2^1, h_2^2, b^1, and b^2, such that $h_2^1 + h_2^2 = h_2$ and $b^1 + b^2 = b$.

Now, consider *any* policy for the original system. Describe a policy for each of the new systems, such that, if all three systems face the same demands, the stages receive the same orders (in quantity and time) in all three systems. Argue that the sum of the costs in the two new systems equals the cost in the original system.

These policies are not necessarily optimal for the new systems, of course. Explain why it is relatively simple to optimize each of these systems separately. Then, argue that the sum of these optimal costs provides a *lower bound* on the true optimal cost of the original system. (To find the best such bound, we may search over possible values of h_2^1, h_2^2, b^1, and b^2, subject to $h_2^1 + h_2^2 = h_2$ and $b^1 + b^2 = b$. Let's not do that now.)

8.12 Consider the five-item assembly system shown in Figure 8.4.1. Suppose we follow a balanced echelon base-stock policy. For simplicity assume that the s_j are nonincreasing in j, so $\mathbf{s}'' = \mathbf{s}$, and we initialize the system at time $t = 0$ as explained in the text, so that $IN_j(0) = s_j$.

First set $\mathbf{s} = \mathbf{0}$. Suppose a single demand occurs at time t. Describe the response of the system according to the policy; that is, determine exactly when units of all items are shipped and received, and explain why (in terms of the policy's rules). Specifically, show that the policy realizes the ideal schedule mentioned in Section 8.4.1. That is, demand is filled at $t + L_J$, the earliest possible time, and given that as a requirement, the policy ships all units at the latest feasible times.

Now, suppose the s_j are strictly positive and strictly decreasing in j. Again, describe in detail the response of the system to a single demand at time t.

8.13 Consider an assembly system like that of Section 8.4, with Poisson demand at rate λ, but now there is a fixed cost k_1 for external orders of item 1. There are no economies of scale ($k_j = 0$) for the other items, even those obtained externally (i.e., those with no predecessors). Show how to analyze this system, combining the ideas of Sections 8.4 and 8.3.7.1. Specifically, suppose that item 1 follows an echelon (r, q) policy, and the others follow a balanced echelon base-stock policy. (This type of policy is indeed optimal.) Argue that the average cost of such a policy can be computed as in (8.3.11), that is, $k_1\lambda/q$ plus a simple average of the costs of certain (balanced) base-stock policies. Conclude that there is an equivalent series system with the same fixed cost k_1 for external supplies.

8.14 Show how to evaluate a local base-stock policy for the assembly system of Figure 8.4.1, using the techniques of Section 8.4.5. Specifically, explain that

$$B'_2(t + L_3) = \max\{0, (D_2 + D_3) - s'_2, (D_1 + D_2 + D_3) - s'_1\}$$

$$B'_4(t + L_4) = \max\{0, D_4 - s'_4, (D_3 + D_4) - s'_3, (D_2 + D_3 + D_4) - (s'_2 + s'_4), (D_1 + D_2 + D_3 + D_4) - (s'_1 + s'_4)\}$$

Then show how to compute B'_5 in terms of B'_4. Explain (in words) why it is intuitively reasonable to set $s'_4 \leq s'_3 \leq s'_2 + s'_4 \leq s'_1 + s'_4$. Finally, describe an equivalent series system, with which we can calculate $E[B'_5]$.

8.15 Consider a two-level distribution system with compound-Poisson demands, operating under a local base-stock policy. The text suggests an approach to two-moment approximation, leading to the equations (8.5.6). Verify these formulas.

8.16 Consider a general distribution system (a network of items indexed $j = 1, \ldots, J$, where each item $j > 1$ has a unique predecessor, and item 1 has none). Let $Suc\,(i)$ be the set of successors of item i. Demands occur only for end items (those with no successors), these are independent Poisson processes with rates λ_j, and the leadtimes are the constants L'_j. We follow a local base-stock policy with policy variables s'_j.

Our aim here is to extend the policy-evaluation techniques of Section 8.5.2 to this system, beginning with the exact approach. Suppose we know the distribution of B'_i for some item i. For $j \in Suc\,(i)$, let B'_{ij} denote that portion of B'_i due to demands for item j. Argue that we can obtain B'_{ij} through binomial disaggregation from B'_i. What are the appropriate weights θ_j? Then, show how to determine B'_j. We now have a recursive scheme to obtain the backorders for all items. Show how to apply the two-moment approximation here. (Clearly, these methods can be used also for the other supply processes of Section 8.5.4.)

8.17 To construct the balanced approximation in the unequal-cost case in Section 8.6.2, we used the smallest retailer cost rates for h and b in C_r. Call the resulting cost function C_r^- for now. Here, we explore alternative approximations of C_r^*, the optimal-cost function of problem (8.6.6). (We shall need to use the facts that C_r^* is strictly convex, and its derivative $C_r^{*'}(s)$ is precisely the dual variable ζ.)

(*a*) Suppose we use instead the σ_j-weighted averages of the original cost rates; i.e., $h = \Sigma_j\,(\sigma_j/\sigma_r)h_j$ and $b = \Sigma_j\,(\sigma_j/\sigma_r)b_j$. Call the resulting function C_r^+. Show that $C_r^+(s_r)$ measures the cost of the (feasible) equal-fractile solution to (8.6.6). Conclude that $C_r^+ \geq C_r^*$. (This approach sometimes works better.)

(*b*) Consider the special case where the retailers have proportional cost rates: There exist constants η, η', β, and c_j, such that $h_j = \eta c_j$ and $b_j + h_j' = (\beta + \eta')c_j$ for all j. (We have seen similar constructions in Chapter 5 and Section 8.2.) Letting $c^+ = \Sigma_j (\sigma_j/\sigma_r)c_j$, we have

$$C_r^+(s) = c^+ E[\eta(s - D_r) + (\beta + \eta')[D_r - s]^+]$$

Let s_r^0 be the value of s_r that minimizes C_r^* (so the corresponding $\zeta = 0$). Show that $C_r^+(s_r^0) = C_r^*(s_r^0)$. (So, this approximation agrees with the true value at least at one point. Notice, this same value must also minimize C_r^+.)

(*c*) Continuing with the proportional-cost case, let $c^- = \min\{c_j\}$. We have $C_r^-(s) = (c^-/c^+)C_r^+(s)$. Show that $C_r^*(s) \geq C_r^-(s) + [C_r^*(s_r^0) - C_r^-(s_r^0)] = C_r^-(s) + (c^+ - c^-)\sigma_r(\beta + \eta')\Phi(z_r^*)$, where z_r^* solves $\Phi(z) = \omega_r = (\beta + \eta_0)/(\beta + \eta')$ and $\eta_0 = \eta' - \eta$. (*Hint:* Let $\zeta^- = C_r^{-\prime}(s)$, and set s^- to solve $C_r^{*\prime}(s^-) = \zeta^-$. Thus, s^- is a function of s. Show that, if $s < s_r^0$, then $\zeta^- < 0$ and $s^- \geq s$, so $\zeta \leq \zeta^-$; while if $s > s_r^0$, then $\zeta^- > 0$ and $s^- \leq s$, so $\zeta \geq \zeta^-$.) Adding this constant to C_r^- thus provides a stronger lower bound on C_r^*, while retaining the same simple form.

8.18 Section 8.6.5 discusses a coupled system with identical retailer costs and a fixed cost for external orders. In this setting, the myopic allocation rule must be revised, in general. When the retailers are identical, however, no revision is necessary. Explain why. That is, argue first that, if the $z_j(0)$ are identical over j, so are the $z_j(t)$ for all t. Second, suppose we revise problem (8.6.4), replacing D_j by $D_j(L_j' + t)$ in the cost functions C_j. Show that the new problem is equivalent to the original.

Extend this idea to the case of compound-Poisson demands. Now, $\nu_j(t) = \lambda_j E[Y_j](L_j' + t)$ and $\sigma_j^2(t) = \lambda_j E[Y_j^2](L_j' + t)$. Show that the results above remain true for identical retailers, and more generally when the L_j' and the ratios $E[Y_j^2]/\lambda_j E^2[Y_j]$ are equal over j.

8.19 Consider the shared-production-capacity system of Section 8.7.2.1 with no economies of scale, local control, and identical products. Suppose we are able to determine the distribution of *IO*, the overall occupancy of the processor, and we then apply binomial disaggregation to obtain IO_j, the occupancy of item j's orders. Finally, approximate IO_j with a normal distribution. Show that the total optimal cost is proportional to $\underline{\sigma}$, where $\underline{\sigma}^2 = V[IO] + (J - 1)E[IO]$. Compare this formula with (8.5.5).

8.20 This problem extends the modeling approach of Section 8.7.2.2 to the case of nonidentical products and stochastic processing times: Item j has Poisson demand with rate λ_j and follows an (r, q) policy with variables (r_j, q_j). Its processing time S_j includes a random setup time T_j and a random unit processing time P_j; all these times are independent, even for the units within a batch. Approximate *each* item's orders by a Poisson process. Now, as explained in Section 8.7.2.1, the production facility becomes an M/G/1 system.

(*a*) Write down equations for $E[S_j]$ and $V[S_j]$ in terms of $E[T_j]$, $E[P_j]$, $V[T_j]$, $V[P_j]$, and q_j. Also, use these to compute $E[S_j^2]$.

(*b*) Let $\underline{\lambda}_j$ denote the order rate for item j, $\rho_j = \lambda_j E[P_j]$, $\underline{\rho}_j = \underline{\lambda}_j E[S_j]$, $\underline{\lambda} = \Sigma_j \underline{\lambda}_j$, $\rho = \Sigma_j \rho_j$, and $\underline{\rho} = \Sigma_j \underline{\rho}_j$. Write the simplest expression you can for $\underline{\rho}$ in terms of the data and the variables q_j. (Use the summary parameter ρ.)

(*c*) Let L_Q denote the time spent waiting in the queue itself (the total time L less the actual processing time). In our terms equation (7.3.2) can be written as $E[L_Q] = ½\underline{\lambda}E[S^2]/(1 - \underline{\rho})$. So, write the simplest expression you can for $\underline{\lambda}E[S^2]$, again using the data and the q_j. (It is possible to obtain a similar formula for $V[L_Q]$. Instead, approximate $V[L_Q]$ by $E^2[L_Q]$.)

(*d*) Finally, letting L_j be the total leadtime for item j, express $E[L_j]$ and $V[L_j]$ in terms of $E[L_Q]$ and the data.

8.21 Consider the generalized kanban policy of Section 8.8.2. Show that the following identity holds for all times t:

$$B'_{j-1}(t) + IT_j(t) = \min \{s'_j - IN'_j(t), n_j\}$$

(Argue that this is true for $t = 0$. Then, consider every possible event that changes one or more of the variables here. Show that each such event has the same effect on both sides.) Using this fact, argue that (8.8.1) and (8.8.2) are equivalent.

C H A P T E R

9 TIME-VARYING, STOCHASTIC DEMAND: POLICY OPTIMIZATION

Outline

9.1 Introduction

This chapter explores situations where demand is subject to both predictable and unpredictable variations. The scenario thus combines features that we studied separately in Chapters 4 and 6.

We begin in Section 9.2 with a heuristic analysis of a few extreme cases, in the same spirit as Section 4.2. Apart from that initial section, the primary goal in this chapter is to *prove* rigorously that the optimal policy takes on a certain form, depending on the details of the system. We have done nothing of the kind until now. In Chapter 6, for example, we argued that a base-stock policy is plausible under certain conditions, but here we show that, under similar conditions, it is truly the *best* among all possible policies.

To achieve this ambitious aim, along with the greater generality of time-dependent demand, we adopt a *discrete-time* formulation, as in Chapter 4, where all important events occur at prespecified time points. Also, we introduce the concept of *dynamic programming,* a powerful mode of formulation, analysis, and computation.

Here is the plan: Section 9.3 describes the basic setup. The costs in the model are just like those assumed previously—fixed and variable order costs, a holding cost for inventory, and a penalty cost for backorders. The demand at each time point is a random variable, whose distribution is a function of time. The demands at different points are independent (until Section 9.7).

Section 9.4 treats the special case without economies of scale, that is, with a *linear order cost.* The optimal policy is indeed a base-stock policy. It uses a distinct base-stock level for each time point. Otherwise, it works just like the base-stock policy of Chapter 6. It is not easy to calculate the optimal base-stock levels, so we explore a simple approximation, called the *myopic policy,* which often works well. This myopic approach is an important one, and we use it throughout the chapter. When the data are stationary, the optimal base-stock level too becomes stationary, as in Chapter 6.

The same policy structure remains optimal for certain variations of the basic model, namely, for lost sales instead of backorders, and for the broader objective of profit instead of cost. For imperfect supply quality, however, a base-stock policy is not optimal. We need to consider a larger class of rules called *inflated base-stock policies.*

In Section 9.5 the order cost includes a fixed component as well as a linear one. Here, an (r, s) policy is optimal. With time-varying data, both r and s change over time. In the infinite-horizon, stationary setting, a stationary (r, s) policy is optimal.

The models of Sections 9.3 to 9.5 have a minimal leadtime. Section 9.6 shows that the results remain valid for any constant leadtime, and also with sequential stochastic leadtimes. Here, finally, we have full analogues in discrete time of the continuous-time models of Chapters 6 and 7. We point out in Section 9.6.4 that simple structured policies are optimal in the continuous-time setting also. (These results do *not* extend to lost sales, however.)

The remainder of the chapter extends these results in various directions. Section 9.7 examines a system with world-driven demand, the discrete-time analogue of the complex demand process of Section 6.3, where the distribution of demand in each period depends on the current state of the world. The earlier results remain valid with minimal adjustments. With a linear order cost, for example, a base-stock policy is still optimal, but the optimal base-stock level reflects the current state of the world as well as time.

Section 9.8 treats a series system in discrete time. With linear shipment costs, an echelon-base-stock policy is optimal.

9.2 Extreme Cases

Suppose demand is a Poisson process, but its rate $\lambda = \lambda(t)$ is a known function of time. The cumulative demand $D(t)$, it turns out, has a Poisson distribution with mean $E[D(t)] = \int_0^t \lambda(v)\,dv$. Otherwise, the setup is like that of Chapter 6; the cost factors and the leadtime are constant. The goal is to analyze a few special cases, approximately and heuristically, as in Section 4.2.

9.2.1 Small or Fast Changes

When $\lambda(t)$ fluctuates slightly and/or quickly around an overall average λ, the changes have negligible effects on the demand process, as in the deterministic models of Section 4.2.1 and Section 4.2.2. So, it makes sense to ignore the current value of $\lambda(t)$ and treat the demand rate as the constant λ.

9.2.2 Slow Changes

Next, suppose $\lambda(t)$ changes slowly. Let $D(t|L) = D(t + L) - D(t)$ be the leadtime demand, a Poisson-distributed random variable with mean $E[D(t|L)] = \int_t^{t+L} \lambda(v)\,dv$. Defining $\underline{\lambda}(t) = (1/L)\int_t^{t+L} \lambda(v)\,dv$, we can write $E[D(t|L)] = \underline{\lambda}(t)L$. Since $\lambda(t)$ changes slowly, so does $\underline{\lambda}(t)$; indeed, $\underline{\lambda}(t)$ changes even more slowly.

For now, suppose there is no fixed order cost. It is plausible, then, to use a base-stock policy, with a base-stock level $s(t)$ that itself depends on time. Specifically, define the function

$$C(t, s) = E[\hat{C}(s - D(t|L))\,] \tag{9.2.1}$$

where $\hat{C}(y) = h[y]^+ + b[y]^-$ as before, and set $s(t) = s^+(t)$ to minimize $C(t, s)$ over s. That is, specify $s(t)$ as if $\underline{\lambda}(t)$ were really constant. This approach is parallel to that of Section 4.2.3. Because it looks ahead only a leadtime into the future and ignores subsequent costs, it is called the *myopic* approach. Also, estimate the optimal average cost by C^*, where

$$C^*(t) = c\lambda(t) + C[t, s^+(t)]$$

$$C^* = \lim_{T\to\infty}\left(\frac{1}{T}\right)\int_0^T C^*(t)\,dt$$

As demonstrated in Sections 9.4 and 9.6, when $\lambda(t)$ changes slowly, the myopic policy is close to optimal, and the estimate C^* is very accurate.

Under the normal approximation of $D(t|L)$, we obtain

$$s^+(t) = \nu(t) + \sigma(t)z^*$$

where

$$\nu(t) = \sigma^2(t) = \underline{\lambda}(t)L$$

and z^* solves the equation $\Phi^0(z) = 1 - \omega$ with $\omega = b/(b + h)$. Also,

$$C^*(t) = c\lambda(t) + (b + h)\phi(z^*)\sigma(t) \tag{9.2.2}$$

$$C^* = c\lambda + (b + h)\phi(z^*)\sigma_{-}$$

where λ is the average demand rate and σ_{-} the average of $\sigma(t)$ over t. The maximal approximation leads to similar results.

Here, as in Chapters 6 and 7, *system performance depends on the standard deviation of leadtime demand;* the mean $\nu(t)$ has no impact. Notice, σ_{-}^2 measures *residual,* unpredictable demand variation, *not* total variation. Raw observations of demand also include predictable variation, due to changes in $\nu(t)$, which does not belong in an estimate of σ_{-}^2.

An even cruder heuristic often works well: Notice, $\sigma(t)$ depends on the square root of $\underline{\lambda}(t)$, and so is robust with respect to demand changes; the mean $\nu(t)$ is linear in $\underline{\lambda}(t)$, so it is more sensitive. Consider some interval over which $\underline{\lambda}(t)$ changes only a modest amount, and let σ_{-} be the average of $\sigma(t)$ over that interval. Then, fix the safety stock to the constant $\sigma_{-}z^*$ and set $s(t) = \nu(t) + \sigma_{-}z^*$. Use (9.2.2) with this σ_{-} to estimate performance. Adjust σ_{-} only rarely, when $\underline{\lambda}(t)$ departs significantly from its original value.

Under this heuristic *the base-stock level moves in parallel with the mean leadtime demand.* This is the simplest way to account for demand changes, and it is used widely in practice. Moreover, apart from the order-cost term $c\lambda(t)$, the cost rate $C^*(t)$ remains constant.

Now, suppose there is a positive fixed cost $k > 0$. The analogue of the myopic approach above is this: Use an (r, q) policy with time-dependent policy variables $r(t)$ and $q(t)$. Choose these variables to minimize a cost function that combines (6.5.16) with (9.2.1):

$$C(t, r, q) = \left(\frac{1}{q}\right)[k\lambda(t) + \Sigma_{s=r+1}^{r+q} C(t, s)]$$

This method should work well provided the demand rate changes slowly, for the same reasons as in Section 4.2.3.

Or, set $r(t)$ and $q(t)$ using the simpler heuristics mentioned in Section 6.5.3. For instance, set $q(t) = [2k\lambda(t)/h\omega]^{1/2}$ by analogy to (4.2.1), and $r(t) = s^+(t) - \beta q(t)$ for some reasonable fraction β.

Or, even more crudely, fix $q(t)$ to some average value q, use some average σ_{-} of $\sigma(t)$, approximate $s(t) = \nu(t) + \sigma_{-}z^*$ as above, and set $r(t) = s(t) - \beta q(t) = \nu(t) + (\sigma_{-}z^* - \beta q)$. Adjust q and σ_{-} only in response to a substantial demand change. Here, *the reorder point moves in parallel with the mean leadtime demand.* This simple technique too is popular in practice.

Here is one way to estimate the average cost: Approximate $C^*(t) = C[t, r(t), q(t)]$ for each t separately, using the bounds of Theorem 6.5.1 together with the normal or maximal approximation. Then, average over time as in (9.2.2).

9.2.3 Other Supply Processes

The same ideas extend directly to systems with stochastic leadtimes, generated by either an independent-parallel or an exogenous-sequential supply process. Again, small and/or fast demand changes can be ignored, while slow changes can be handled by a myopic approach.

In the exogenous-sequential case, for instance, redefine $D(t|L)$ to be the leadtime demand starting at time t, i.e., the demand between t and $t + L$, where now L is the marginal leadtime, a random variable. In general, $D(t|L)$ is no longer Poisson, nor does it have any other any simple form, but we can approximate: Compute its mean and variance $\nu(t)$ and $\sigma^2(t)$ (Problem 9.1), and fit a standard distributional form, such as a normal or a gamma. Then, proceed with the methods above.

Recall, this supply system has unlimited capacity, and that makes it tractable. A finite-capacity supply process requires more care: Small and/or fast demand-rate changes can again be ignored. Slow changes too can be treated as above, but only when the changes are *very* slow, and the demand rate stays well below the system's capacity.

For instance, consider an M/M/1 system with processing rate μ. The direct analogue of the myopic approach sets $\rho(t) = \lambda(t)/\mu$, and replaces $D(t|L)$ in (9.2.1) by a geometric random variable with parameter $\rho(t)$. That is, pretend that the supply system reaches its equilibrium state at every point in time. (This is sometimes called the pointwise stationary approximation. For more on this and related techniques see Green and Kolesar [1991] and Whitt [1991].)

Clearly, this approach breaks down if $\lambda(t) > \mu$ for any t. Even when demand never exceeds capacity, the supply system itself responds slowly to changes in its input. For example, if $\lambda(t)$ is near μ for a while, the occupancy $IO(t)$ grows large, and this congestion will persist for some time even after $\lambda(t)$ falls lower. Thus, the equilibrium approximation is valid only when demand-rate shifts are slow enough for the supply system to recover quickly. This condition in turn depends on $\rho(t)$ itself; the supply system responds quicker when $\rho(t)$ remains well below 1.

These are stringent conditions. What if they do not apply, if $\lambda(t)$ sometimes exceeds capacity or changes faster than the supply system? First, *if* the base-stock level $s(t)$ is held constant, then the supply system behaves like a queue with nonstationary input. Methods to analyze such queues have been devised, e.g., by Rothkopf and Oren [1979]. However, it seems more sensible to build up inventory in advance of demand surges, as in Section 4.2.5, by increasing $s(t)$. But when and how much? We know no good, simple answers. The only way to get any answers, given the current state of the art, is by algorithmic methods (as outlined in Problem 9.4).

Sometimes it is possible to adjust the processing rate in response to the demand rate. Consider the following special case: We can and do set $\mu(t)$ proportional to $\lambda(t)$, so the ratio $\lambda(t)/\mu(t)$ is the constant $\rho < 1$. It turns out that this system is equivalent to one with stationary λ and μ, observed on a clock of variable speed. Thus, there is no reason to change the base-stock level. Assuming we do keep it constant, the analysis of Section 7.3.2.1 applies directly.

In sum, for a system with limited capacity and nonstationary demand, the current state of the art provides no single method to handle all cases. Some cases are easy, some are hard.

9.3 Discrete-Time Formulation

9.3.1 Dynamics

Now, and for most of the rest of the chapter, we envision a world of discrete time. The setup is much like that of Section 4.3.1: There is a sequence of *time points* $t = 0,1,\ldots,T$. The *horizon* T may be finite or infinite. *Time period* t is the interval from point t until just before point $t+1$.

Again denote

$z(t)$ = order size at time t
$d(t)$ = demand at time t, $t = 0,\ldots,T-1$

The demand $d(t)$ is now a nonnegative *random variable* with finite mean. Until further notice (in Section 9.7), the $d(t)$ are *independent* over t. For convenience, $d(t)$ is *continuous,* as is the control variable $z(t)$. (Apart from minor details, all the results remain valid in the discrete-quantity case.) Because demand is random, we must allow for backorders, so the state variable, as in Section 4.4.4, is

$x(t)$ = net inventory at time t, $t = 0, \ldots, T$

The initial net inventory is the constant x_0.

The sequence of events at each time $t < T$ is as follows:

1. We observe the net inventory $x(t)$.
2. We decide the order size $z(t)$.

Then, sometime during period t, the demand $d(t)$ occurs and the order $z(t)$ arrives. The system dynamics are described by equations identical in form to (4.3.2):

$$x(t+1) = x(t) + z(t) - d(t) \qquad t = 0, \ldots, T-1 \tag{9.3.1}$$

At the horizon T we observe $x(T)$, but that is all; there is no order $z(T)$ or demand $d(T)$.

This model is usually described in the literature as having a leadtime of zero. We haven't said exactly when orders arrive, and we don't really need to; (9.3.1) remains valid as long as each order arrives during its own period. If $z(t)$ arrives at the very end of period t, however, it makes sense to call the leadtime 1, not 0. This usage is consistent with Section 9.6, where we introduce an explicit leadtime. Whatever we call it, the leadtime is certainly short. Remember, a period can be *very* short, especially when the discrete-time model is constructed to approximate a continuous one. So, the model is quite special. Fortunately, virtually all the results carry over to more realistic models with longer leadtimes, as shown in Section 9.6.

The nature of the decision problem is quite different from that of Chapter 4. There, because the $d(t)$ were known in advance, we could determine the $z(t)$ all at once. Here, we choose each $z(t)$ at point t, based on what we know at step 2. At that moment, we know $x(t)$, which reflects all past demands, but not $d(t)$ or any later demands. It makes no sense to specify $z(t)$ any earlier, for that would ignore useful information.

What we want, then, is not a set of fixed decisions, but rather an order *policy,* a rule for making decisions based on current information. In contrast to Chapter 6, we place no advance restrictions on the form of the policy. One of our primary goals is *to determine which type of policy is best,* given the economics of the situation. Accordingly, we bypass the analysis of physical performance measures, such as average backorders. The costs associated with inventory, backorders, etc., enter the formulation from the beginning.

9.3.2 Costs

The cost parameters are

$k(t)$ = fixed order cost at time t
$c(t)$ = unit variable order cost at time t
$h(t)$ = inventory-holding cost rate at time t
$b(t)$ = backorder-penalty cost rate at time t
γ = discount factor, $0 < \gamma \leq 1$

Future costs are discounted at rate γ, as in Section 4.4.2. The cost factors indicate the original, undiscounted costs; unlike Section 4.4.2, we do *not* replace $k(t) \leftarrow \gamma^t k(t)$, etc.

Letting $\delta(z)$ denote the Heaviside function (1 when $z > 0$, 0 otherwise), the total order cost at time t is $k(t)\delta(z(t)) + c(t)z(t)$. The inventory-holding or backorder-penalty cost is assessed on $x(t)$ at step 1 of time t. This cost can be written compactly as $\hat{C}(t, x(t))$, where

$$\hat{C}(t, x) = h(t)[x]^+ + b(t)[x]^-$$

Actually, it is convenient to count this cost just *before* time t, at the *end* of period $t - 1$. The corresponding cost at the end of period t is $\hat{C}(t + 1, x(t + 1))$. This convention better reveals the links between causes and effects; the decision $z(t)$ affects $\hat{C}(t + 1, x(t + 1))$ but not $\hat{C}(t, x(t))$. In particular, ignore the constant $\hat{C}(0, x(0)) = \hat{C}(0, x_0)$.

Denote

$$y(t) = x(t) + z(t)$$

This is the inventory position just after ordering at step 2. Thus, (9.3.1) is equivalent to

$$x(t + 1) = y(t) - d(t) \qquad t = 0, \ldots, T - 1$$

Define the function

$$C(t, y) = E[\hat{C}(t + 1, y - d(t))]$$

Then, $C(t, y(t))$ measures the *expected* inventory-backorder cost, as viewed from step 2. We call $C(t, \cdot)$ the *one-period cost function.*

(This setup differs from the most common one in the literature, but the difference is purely cosmetic. There, $h(t)$ appears in place of our $h(t + 1)$, and $b(t)$ replaces our $b(t + 1)$.)

We have seen functions like $\hat{C}$ and C in earlier chapters. As before, for each t, $\hat{C}(t, y)$ and $C(t, y)$ are *convex* as functions of y. Such convexity properties were important in Chapters 6 to 8, and they are crucial here.

The strict discrete-time scenario can be relaxed somewhat, as in Section 4.4.3. Demands can occur and holding-backorder costs can accumulate throughout the period. The result is a slightly different one-period cost function $C(t, y)$. The new function, however, has the same form as the one above.

9.3.3 Salvage Value

Sometimes, when T is finite, it is convenient to include a special mechanism to "settle accounts" at the end. Specifically, when $x(T) < 0$, we *must* purchase stock to fill the remaining backorders $-x(T)$ at the unit purchase price $c(T)$. (Remember, the last real order is at time $T - 1$, so the meaning of $c(T)$ is unambiguous. There is no fixed cost for such purchases, i.e., $k(T) = 0$.) Also, if $x(T) > 0$, we can sell the leftover stock at the same price; thus, we receive total revenue $c(T)x(T)$, or equivalently, we pay a cost of $-c(T)x(T)$. In sum, regardless of the sign of $x(T)$, there is a terminal cost $-c(T)x(T)$.

The terminal-cost factor $c(T)$ is called the *salvage value.* Actually, we can do without it; we achieve the same effect by adding $c(T)$ to $b(T)$ and subtracting the same amount from $h(T)$. (Indeed, we can represent asymmetric terminal costs by adjusting $b(T)$ and $h(T)$ appropriately.) Nevertheless, the salvage-value construction is useful in certain situations. If there is no such mechanism, just set $c(T) = 0$.

9.4 Linear Order Costs

This section assumes that all $k(t) = 0$. Thus, the cost to order z at time t is the *linear* function $c(t)z$, $z \geq 0$.

We treat the problem in three parts, depending on the horizon T. First, we analyze a model with only two time points and one period, that is, with $T = 1$. Then, we extend the model to an arbitrary finite horizon. Finally, we consider an infinite horizon. In all these cases, it turns out, a base-stock policy is optimal.

Following that, we study three important extensions, namely, lost sales, profit maximization, and imperfect quality. The problems at the end of the chapter explore other extensions.

9.4.1 The Single-Period Problem

With $T = 1$ the problem is as follows: We must make a single order decision at time 0. During period 0 a random demand occurs and the order arrives. At time 1 the inventory-backorder cost $\hat{C}(1, x(1))$ is assessed and the terminal cost is realized. That's all. Because there is only one time period, we suppress the time index t. That is, we abbreviate $x_0 = x$, $d(0) = d$, $y(0) = y$, $c(0) = c$, $h(1) = h$, $b(1) = b$, $\hat{C}(1, x) = \hat{C}(x)$, and $C(0, y) = E[\hat{C}(y - d)] = C(y)$. We continue to use $c(1)$ for the salvage value, if any.

This may seem an artificially simple scenario, but it accurately portrays situations where the product has a short useful life. Examples include newspapers, magazines, and many foods and beverages. In fact, this is sometimes called the *newsboy* or *newsvendor problem.* In these applications the initial net inventory x $(= x_0)$ is most likely 0, but we allow x to have any value. (This generality will be helpful later.)

To choose the order quantity, we aim to balance the order cost, the inventory-backorder cost, and the terminal cost. Viewed from step 2 of time point 0, the discounted expected terminal cost at time 1 is

$$\gamma E[-c(1)x(1)] = -\gamma c(1)(y - E[d])$$

Thus, we face the following optimization problem in the single variable y:

$$\begin{aligned} &\text{Minimize} && c(y - x) + C(y) - \gamma c(1)(y - E[d]) \\ &\text{subject to} && y \geq x \end{aligned} \tag{9.4.1}$$

This is easy to solve for any given x. To determine an optimal policy, however, we must solve (9.4.1) for *every* value of x.

Define

$$\begin{aligned} H(y) &= cy + C(y) - \gamma c(1)(y - E[d]) \\ &= \gamma c(1)E[d] + c^{+}y + C(y) \end{aligned}$$

where $c^{+} = c - \gamma c(1)$. The objective of (9.4.1) is $H(y) - cx$, and the term cx is constant, so we can equivalently minimize $H(y)$. Recall, C is a convex function, and the other terms in H are linear, so H too is convex. Let s^* be the smallest y that minimizes $H(y)$ *globally,* ignoring the constraint $y \geq x$.

The optimal solution to (9.4.1) depends on the relation between x and s^*. If $x \leq s^*$, then $y = s^*$ is feasible and hence optimal. If $x > s^*$, then the optimal solution is $y = x$, because $H(y)$ is nondecreasing over the entire feasible range $y \geq x$. This is precisely a *base-stock policy* with base-stock level s^*. If the initial inventory is above s^*, don't order; if it is below s^*, order the difference, i.e., just enough to raise the inventory to s^*.

To compute s^*, we must solve $H'(y) = 0$. But $C(y)$ has the same form as the average-cost function of Section 6.5.2. Specifically, $C'(y) = [h - (b + h)F^0(y)]$, where F^0 is the ccdf of d $(= d(0))$. Consequently,

$$H'(y) = (c^+ + h) - (b + h)F^0(y)$$

and s^* solves

$$F^0(y) = \frac{c^+ + h}{b + h} \tag{9.4.2}$$

This is entirely analogous to equation (6.5.3). Only the cost ratio differs. The demand d plays the same role here as the leadtime demand in a continuous-time model. If we use a normal approximation for d with $\nu = E[d]$ and $\sigma^2 = V[d]$, and set z^* to solve $\Phi^0(z) = (c^+ + h)/(b + h)$, then $s^* = \nu + \sigma z^*$, and $H(s^*) = c\nu + \sigma(b + h)\phi(z^*)$.

Of course, (9.4.2) makes sense only when $c^+ < b$. If $c^+ \geq b$, i.e., $c \geq b + \gamma c(1)$, then $H(y)$ is nondecreasing, so set $s^* = -\infty$. The optimal policy tells us never to order, i.e., to get out of the business. It is cheaper to incur the penalty cost b plus the discounted terminal cost $\gamma c(1)$ than to purchase a unit at cost c. Likewise, assume $c^+ + h > 0$. Otherwise, $H(y)$ is nonincreasing; indeed, it is strictly decreasing (except in degenerate cases), and $s^* = +\infty$. Here, we can make unlimited profit by purchasing units at cost c and later selling them at price $c(1)$, even after deducting the holding cost h. Ruling out these bizarre cases, the fraction in (9.4.2) is strictly between 0 and 1.

Let $V(x)$ denote the optimal cost of problem (9.4.1), regarded as a function of x.

$$V(x) = -cx + V^+(x)$$

where

$$V^+(x) = H(\max\{s^*, x\})$$

The function $V^+(x)$ is depicted in Figure 9.4.1. (This is essentially a mirror image of Figure 8.3.1. Evidently, V^+ is constructed in much the same way as the function $\underline{C}_j$ in Section 8.3.3, only backwards.) It is clear (and easy to prove) that V^+ is a convex function, so V is too.

9.4.2 The Finite-Horizon Problem: Dynamic Programming

Now, suppose there are several periods, but still finitely many. The horizon T is a finite, positive integer, $T > 1$.

The problem here is more complex than in the single-period case. There are several interrelated decisions to make. In choosing $y(0)$ we need to consider the costs in future periods, not just the current one. Worse, when we reach point $t = 1$, we shall choose $y(1)$, which also affects future costs. But now, at $t = 0$, we haven't yet made that choice. So,

FIGURE 9.4.1

Optimal cost function (linear order cost).

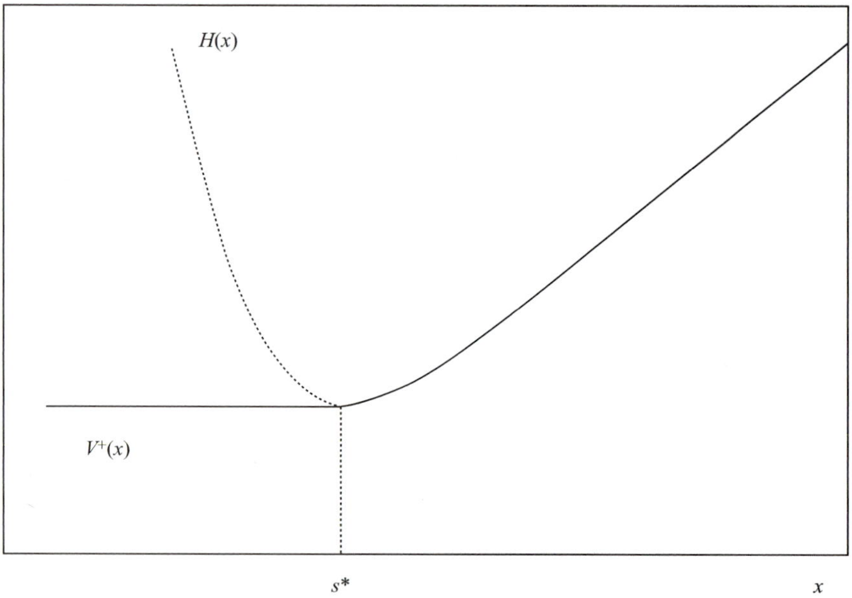

how can we intelligently select $y(0)$? And then there is $y(2)$, which should probably depend on $y(1)$ and $y(0)$, or maybe it's the other way around. . . . We seem to be trapped!

Fortunately, there *is* a way out. This is precisely the sort of dilemma addressed by *dynamic programming.* The key idea is to think *backward in time.*

Consider time point $T-1$. Once we arrive there, no matter what may have happened in the past, we shall face a single-period problem like the one above. We know how to solve that problem. The optimal base-stock policy tells us the best $y(T-1)$ for *any* $x(T-1)$.

Next, suppose we find ourselves at time $T-2$. We face a two-period problem. To account for the future, *assume* that we shall act optimally at $T-1$, according to the policy obtained already. With this information, as we shall see, we can determine the best $y(T-2)$ for all $x(T-2)$.

At time $T-3$, assume that we shall act optimally at *both* future points. Again, we can use this information to optimize $y(T-3)$. Continue working backward in this way, all the way to point $t=0$. At that point, we can determine the best $y(0)$ for the actual $x(0)=x_0$.

The fact that this approach works is sometimes called the *principal of optimality.* It should be intuitively clear, and it can be proven rigorously.

Here is a precise statement of the approach: Define the following functions for $t=0, \ldots, T$:

$V(t, x)$ = minimal expected discounted cost in periods $t, t+1, \ldots, T$, assuming period t begins with $x(t)=x$

We compute these functions recursively. In the process, we obtain the optimal policy. First (or rather, last),

$$V(T, x) = -c(T)x \tag{9.4.3}$$

Suppose we have determined $V(t + 1, x)$, along with the optimal policies for points $t + 1$ through $T - 1$. To address the problem at time t, given $x(t) = x$, define

$$H(t, y) = c(t)y + C(t, y) + \gamma E[V(t + 1, y - d(t))] \tag{9.4.4}$$

This quantity measures all the relevant costs if we choose $y(t) = y$. The first two terms (minus the constant $c(t)x$) represent the costs at time t itself. The last term is the expected value of all future costs, assuming we act optimally in the future, since $x(t + 1) = y - d(t)$. The problem at point t, then, is to choose y to minimize $H(t, y)$, subject to $y \geq x$. The solution to this problem for each x gives the optimal policy at time t. Then set

$$V(t, x) = -c(t)x + \min \{H(t, y) : y \geq x\} \tag{9.4.5}$$

Now, using $V(t, \cdot)$, we can proceed to compute $V(t - 1, \cdot)$ in the same way, then $V(t - 2, \cdot)$, and so on.

Equations (9.4.4) and (9.4.5), together with the boundary or terminal condition (9.4.3), describe a recursive scheme to compute the optimal-cost functions for all time points, as well as the optimal policy. They are *functional equations,* i.e., equations whose unknowns are the functions $V(t, \cdot)$ and $H(t, \cdot)$. This model is often called the *dynamic-programming formulation* of the problem. [Dynamic programming and *optimal control* are, essentially, alternative names for the same subject. We can just as well call (9.4.3) to (9.4.5) an optimal-control model.]

We're done, in principle. In practice, however, two difficulties arise:

First, x and y are continuous variables, and so, for each t, (9.4.4) prescribes an infinite number of expectations, and (9.4.5) an infinite number of optimizations. To solve functional equations of this kind typically requires numerical approximation techniques. One approach, the simplest conceptually, is to *discretize and truncate* the state space: Select a finite set of values for the $x(t)$, and similarly restrict the $d(t)$ and $y(t)$. This selection must be done carefully, of course, to obtain accurate results.

Second, the full optimal policy (the best y for every x and t, written out, say, in a large table) would be hard to understand and tedious to implement. Fortunately, it has a simple, appealing structure:

THEOREM 9.4.1. For all t:
(*a*) $H(t, y)$ is a convex function of y.
(*b*) A base-stock policy is optimal. The optimal base-stock level $s^*(t)$ is the smallest value of y minimizing $H(t, y)$.
(*c*) $V(t, x)$ is a convex function of x.

PROOF. By induction on t: We verified the result for $t = T - 1$ in Section 9.4.1. Suppose it is true for any $t + 1$. The first two terms of $H(t, y)$ are convex in y, as in the single-period problem. And, because $V(t + 1, x)$ is convex (by the induction hypothesis), so is the third term of $H(t, y)$. Thus, $H(t, y)$ is convex in y; we have established part (*a*). Parts (*b*) and (*c*) follow immediately, just as in the one-period model.

By the way, one can also show that $H(t, y)$ and $V(t, y)$ are continuously differentiable in y. So, $s^*(t)$ solves $H'(t, y) = 0$. (Here, H' is the derivative with respect to y.)

In sum, the optimal policy is characterized by a single parameter, the base-stock level $s^*(t)$, for each time point. In general, however, it is not easy to compute the $s^*(t)$. Even knowing the form of the optimal policy, we still must perform the recursive calculations indicated in (9.4.3) to (9.4.5) using numerical techniques.

9.4.3 The Myopic Policy

We can obtain useful and interesting information about the $s^*(t)$ by means of a slight transformation of the problem: Define

$$V^+(t, x) = c(t)x + V(t, x) \qquad t \le T$$

$$c^+(t) = c(t) - \gamma c(t+1)$$

$$C^+(t, y) = \gamma c(t+1)E[d(t)] + c^+(t)y + C(t, y) \qquad t < T$$

The following recursion is equivalent to (9.4.3) to (9.4.5):

$$V^+(T, x) = 0 \tag{9.4.6}$$

$$H(t, y) = C^+(t, y) + \gamma E[V^+(t+1, y - d(t))] \tag{9.4.7}$$

$$V^+(t, x) = \min\{H(t, y) : y \ge x\} \tag{9.4.8}$$

(Problem 9.2 asks you to verify the alternative expression for H in (9.4.7).) Evidently, $V^+(t, x)$ plays the same role here as $V^+(x)$ in the single-period problem. Indeed, we can write

$$V^+(t, x) = H(t, \max\{s^*(t), x\}) \tag{9.4.9}$$

Now, C^+ plays the role of the current period's cost in this transformed model. Let $s^+(t)$ be the smallest value of y that minimizes $C^+(t, y)$. The corresponding base-stock policy minimizes the current cost while ignoring the future, so we call it the *myopic policy*. Because $C^+(t, y)$ is just the actual one-period cost $C(t, y)$ plus a linear function of y and a constant, it is convex, and so easy to optimize. In particular, $s^+(t)$ solves an equation of the same form as (9.4.2):

$$F^0_{d(t)}(y) = \frac{c^+(t) + h(t+1)}{b(t+1) + h(t+1)} \tag{9.4.10}$$

This is essentially the same approach outlined in Section 9.2.2 in the continuous-time setting with a slow-changing demand rate. $s^+(t)$ reflects the data for period t in a simple manner, like s^* in a one-period model. For instance, suppose the cost factors are stationary, we approximate $d(t)$ using a normal distribution, denote $\nu(t) = E[d(t)]$ and $\sigma^2(t) = V[d(t)]$, and set z^* to solve $\Phi^0(z) = (c^+ + h)/(b + h)$. Then, $s^+(t) = \nu(t) + \sigma(t)z^*$, and $C^+(t, s^+(t)) = c\nu(t) + \sigma(t)(b + h)\phi(z^*)$.

The myopic and optimal policies are closely related:

THEOREM 9.4.2. For each t,

(a) $s^*(t) \le s^+(t)$; in particular, $s^*(T-1) = s^+(T-1)$.

(b) If $s^+(t) \le s^*(t+1)$, then $s^*(t) = s^+(t)$.

(c) If $s^+(t) \ge s^+(t+1)$, then $s^*(t) \ge s^*(t+1)$.

(d) If $s^+(t) \le s^+(t+1)$ and $s^*(t+1) \le s^*(t+2)$, then $s^*(t) \le s^*(t+1)$.

(e) $s^*(t) \ge \min_{u \ge t} \{s^+(u)\}$.

Theorem 9.4.2 part (a) tells us that the true optimal base-stock level always lies *at or below* the myopic level, never above; taking the future into account can only reduce the base-stock level. By part (b), the two levels coincide unless $s^+(t) > s^*(t+1)$. The only reason we might choose $s^*(t) < s^+(t)$ is to reduce the chance that $x(t+1) > s^*(t+1)$ in the next period, and that concern is relevant only when $s^*(t+1)$ is small. Indeed, by part (e), $s^*(t)$ is bounded below by the smallest subsequent myopic level. These results together imply that, if the $s^+(t)$ are nondecreasing in t, then $s^*(t) = s^+(t)$ for all t, i.e., the myopic policy is optimal. (See Problem 9.3.)

Parts (c) and (d) tell us that the general pattern of changes in the $s^*(t)$ follows closely that of the $s^+(t)$. When $s^+(t)$ goes down, so does $s^*(t)$. When $s^+(t)$ goes up, so does $s^*(t)$, unless we anticipate a decrease later on (i.e., unless $s^*(t+1) > s^*(t+2)$). Thus, since the $s^+(t)$ closely reflect changes in the data, so do the $s^*(t)$, but less directly; the $s^*(t)$ also anticipate future changes.

Also, when $s^*(t+1) < s^+(t)$, we are more likely to find $s^*(t) < s^+(t)$ when $V[d(t)]$ is large relative to $E[d(t)]$. The theorem doesn't directly support this statement, but the intuitive interpretation above does: If $E[d(t)]$ is large but $V[d(t)]$ is small, then there is little uncertainty in $x(t+1)$ given $y(t)$; even setting $y(t) = s^+(t)$, we can be fairly sure that $x(t+1) \le s^*(t+1)$. If $V[d(t)]$ is large, however, there is a greater chance that $d(t)$ will be small, hence $x(t+1) > s^*(t+1)$. To avoid that, the model pushes $s^*(t)$ down.

PROOF OF THEOREM 9.4.2.

(a) From (9.4.6) and (9.4.9) it is clear that $V^+(t+1, x)$ is nondecreasing in x, so $E[V^+(t+1, y-d(t))]$ is nondecreasing in y. So, $H'(t, y) \ge C^{+\prime}(t, y)$. In particular, $H'(t, s^+(t)) \ge 0$, so $s^*(t) \le s^+(t)$. For $t = T-1$ all these relations hold with equality.

(b) $V^+(t+1, x)$ is constant for $x \le s^*(t+1)$, so $E[V^+(t+1, y-d(t))]$ is constant and $H'(t, y) = C^{+\prime}(t, y)$ for $y \le s^*(t+1)$. In particular, $H'(t, s^+(t)) = 0$, so $s^*(t) = s^+(t)$.

(c) As in part (b), $H'(t, y) = C^{+\prime}(t, y)$ for $y \le s^*(t+1)$. If $s^+(t) \ge s^+(t+1) \ge s^*(t+1)$, then $H'(t, y) = C^{+\prime}(t, y) < 0$ for $y < s^*(t+1)$. This implies $s^*(t) \ge s^*(t+1)$.

(d) Again, $H'(t+1, y) = C^{+\prime}(t+1, y)$ for $y \le s^*(t+2)$. Since $s^*(t+1) \le s^*(t+2)$, it follows that $C^{+\prime}(t+1, s^*(t+2)) \ge 0$, so $s^*(t+2) \ge s^+(t+1)$. Applying part (b), $s^*(t+1) = s^+(t+1) \ge s^+(t) \ge s^*(t)$.

(e) The result is true for $t = T-1$. Suppose it is true for $t+1$. If $s^+(t) \le \min_{u \ge t+1} \{s^+(u)\} \le s^*(t+1)$, then by part ($b$) $s^*(t) = s^+(t) = \min_{u \ge t} \{s^+(u)\}$. If $s^+(t) > \min_{u \ge t+1} \{s^+(u)\}$, then in particular $s^+(t) > s^+(t+1)$, so by part (c) $s^*(t) \ge s^*(t+1) \ge \min_{u \ge t+1} \{s^+(u)\} = \min_{u \ge t} \{s^+(u)\}$.

Example 9.4.A illustrates these results.

EXAMPLE 9.4.A

We shall solve four models. In all cases, $T = 5$, $\gamma = 1$, and the holding and penalty costs are constant at $h(t) = 1$, $b(t) = 9$. The demands $d(t)$ have either Poisson or geometric distributions.

First, consider a pair of systems with constant $c(t)$, so every $c^+(t) = 0$. The mean demand $E[d(t)]$ stays constant at 40 until time 3, when it abruptly drops to 2, and remains constant thereafter. The systems differ only in their demand distributions, Poisson or geometric. Figure 9.4.2 displays the optimal and myopic policies.

In the Poisson-demand model, $s^*(t) = s^+(t)$ for all t; the myopic policy is optimal. In the geometric case, we see that $s^*(3) = s^+(3) = s^*(4) = s^+(4)$, as expected, but $s^*(2) < s^+(2)$ and even $s^*(1) < s^+(1)$, anticipating the drop in demand at time 3. It is remarkable, however, that the differences are so small. These anticipation effects die out at time 0, where again $s^*(0) = s^+(0)$.

Next, consider a pair of systems with constant mean demand $E[d(t)] = 30$. The order costs $c(t)$ change, however; they follow a general downward trend with fluctuations along the way. Figure 9.4.3 shows the results.

We see that $s^+(t)$ is large when we anticipate a higher cost in the next period, i.e., $c(t) < c(t + 1)$, so $c^+(t) < 0$, and small in the opposite case. The $s^*(t)$ follow the same pattern. Indeed, only for $t = 0$ and 2 do we observe $s^*(t) < s^+(t)$. Even then, the differences are slight, except in the geometric-demand case for $t = 0$.

In these four cases, the myopic policy is almost always nearly optimal. Such a close relation is typical. The myopic policy *can* be far from optimal, but only when the problem data change rapidly over time.

FIGURE 9.4.2

Optimal and myopic base-stock policies (stationary costs).

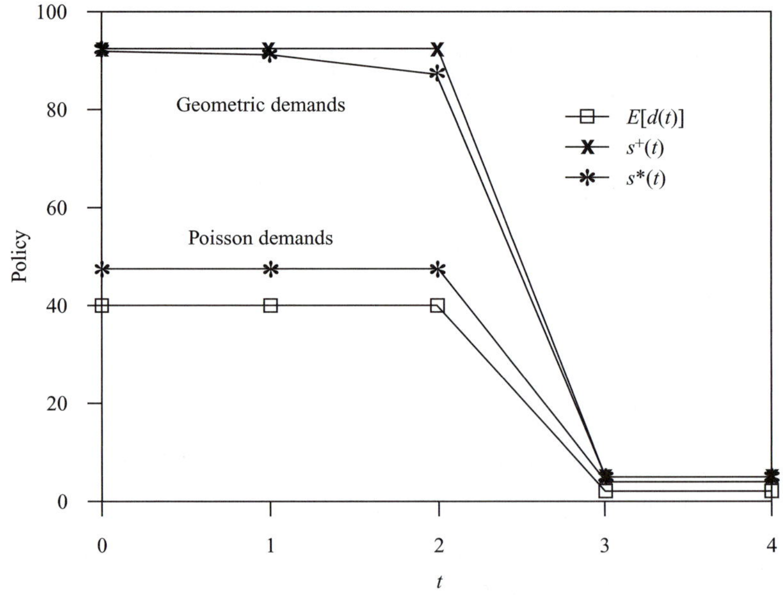

FIGURE 9.4.3

Optimal and myopic base-stock policies (stationary demands).

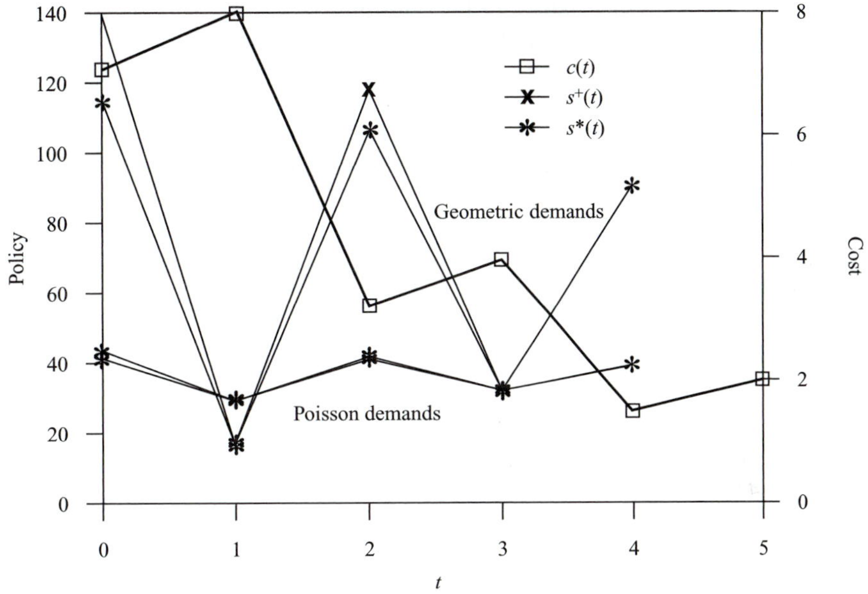

The myopic approach also provides a simple lower bound on the optimal cost: Let π denote *any* policy. The total expected cost starting with $x(0) = x$ using policy π can be written

$$V(0, x|\pi) = E[\Sigma_{t=0}^{T-1}\gamma^t\{c(t)(y(t) - x(t)) + C(t, y(t))\} - \gamma^T c(T)x(T)]$$

Each $y(t)$ here is determined by the policy and $x(t)$. The demands play an implicit role, through $x(t + 1) = y(t) - d(t)$. Using this identity to eliminate the $x(t)$ for $t > 0$, we get

$$V(0, x|\pi) = E[\ \Sigma_{t=0}^{T-1}\gamma^t C^+(t, y(t))\ ] - c(0)x$$

Equivalently, letting $V^+(0, x|\pi) = V(0, x|\pi) + c(0)x$

$$V^+(0, x|\pi) = E[\Sigma_{t=0}^{T-1}\gamma^t C^+(t, y(t))]$$

Now, $s^+(t)$ minimizes $C^+(t, y)$. Consequently, $V^+(0, x|\pi) \geq V_-(0)$ for all x, where

$$V_-(0) = \Sigma_{t=0}^{T-1}\gamma^t C^+(t, s^+(t))$$

This is true, in particular, for the optimal policy; i.e., $V^+(0, x) \geq V_-(0)$. With stationary cost parameters, under the normal approximation, the lower bound becomes

$$V_-(0) = c\Sigma_{t=0}^{T-1}\gamma^t\nu(t) + (b + h)\phi(z^*)\Sigma_{t=0}^{T-1}\gamma^t\sigma(t)$$

In fact, $V_-(0)$ provides a good approximation of $V^+(0, x)$, at least for not-too-large x, precisely when the myopic policy is close to the optimal one, i.e., usually. This is the discrete-time analogue of the cost approximation of Section 9.2.2.

9.4.4 The Infinite-Horizon Problem: Stationary Data

9.4.4.1 The Model and the Solution

Suppose the horizon T is infinite. Assume that the problem data (the costs and the demands) are stationary in time. So, $c(t) = c$, $C(t, y) = C(y)$, etc., and the $d(t)$ all have the same distribution. Let d denote a generic demand random variable. (These assumptions make sense only when the time periods are of equal length.)

Let us peer ahead to the solution. It turns out to be marvelously simple: Define

$$c^+ = (1 - \gamma)c$$

$$C^+(y) = \gamma c E[d] + c^+ y + C(y)$$

Let s^* be the smallest value of y minimizing $C^+(y)$, that is, s^* solves

$$F_d^0(y) = \frac{c^+ + h}{b + h} \qquad (9.4.11)$$

Assume that the cost ratio lies strictly between 0 and 1, so s^* is finite. Thus, s^* is the (stationary) myopic base-stock level.

THEOREM 9.4.3. The stationary base-stock policy with base-stock level s^* is optimal.

The myopic policy is optimal!

Because s^* remains constant over time, we can describe the policy as a *demand-replacement rule:* Assume that $x_0 \leq s^*$. The policy sets $y(0) = s^*$, so $x(1) \leq s^*$, so $y(1) = s^*$, and so on. Each $y(t) = s^*$, so $x(t + 1) = s^* - d(t)$, so $z(t + 1) = d(t)$. Thus, each order just replaces the prior period's demand. (If $x_0 > s^*$, wait until demand depletes the inventory so that $x(t) \leq s^*$; from then on the demand-replacement rule takes effect.) This is the way we interpreted a base-stock policy in earlier chapters. (When $s^*(t)$ changes over time, of course, this interpretation breaks down; a time-varying base-stock policy is *not* a demand-replacement rule.)

It is no harder to solve the infinite-horizon problem than the single-period problem; equation (9.4.11) is identical to (9.4.2). When $\gamma = 1$ (the average-cost case), the cost ratio in (9.4.11) becomes $h/(b + h) = 1 - \omega$, just as in (6.5.3). (As in the continuous-time model, the optimal policy does not reflect the order-cost rate c, because under any reasonable policy the average order cost is the constant $cE[d]$.)

The optimal cost is easy to compute also: The optimal average cost (for the case $\gamma = 1$) is given by

$$v^* = C^+(s^*) = cE[d] + C(s^*)$$

For the discounted-cost case ($\gamma < 1$), let $V^*(x)$ be the optimal discounted expected cost over the infinite horizon, and $V^{+*}(x) = V^*(x) + cx$. Then,

$$V^{+*}(x) = \frac{C^+(s^*)}{1 - \gamma} \qquad x \leq s^*$$

The remaining values take a bit more work. It is necessary to solve the functional equation

$$V^+(x) = C^+(x) + \gamma E[V^+(x - d)] \qquad x > s^*$$

This calculation requires numerical techniques. Under the normal approximation the basic quantity $C^+(s^*)$ becomes

$$C^+(s^*) = cv + \sigma(b + h)\phi(z^*)$$

9.4.4.2 Proof

Before justifying this result, we need to formulate the problem precisely. We distinguish between the two cases $\gamma < 1$ and $\gamma = 1$. When $\gamma < 1$ there is some hope that the total expected cost is finite over an infinite horizon, while if $\gamma = 1$ the total cost is certainly infinite under every policy, so we need a different criterion. (This is true, not just of inventory models, but of dynamic programs in general.)

In the *discounted-cost case* ($\gamma < 1$) suppose we choose a particular policy, say π, an ordering rule for each of an infinite number of periods. Let

$V(x|\pi)$ = total expected discounted cost using policy π, starting with $x_0 = x$

We can write

$$V(x|\pi) = E[\Sigma_{t=0}^{\infty} \gamma^t \{c(y(t) - x(t)) + C(y(t))\} \mid x(0) = x] \qquad (9.4.12)$$

The expectation is over all possible demand sequences. We want to choose a policy π^* that minimizes $V(x|\pi)$ for all x. Let $V^*(x)$ denote the optimal cost.

We have neglected some fine points in this formulation: Each sample path of the demand process contributes an infinite series to (9.4.12), and it is fair to ask whether such series converge finitely. One can show that, for any reasonable policy π, almost all the series do converge finitely (i.e., with probability 1). Moreover, the expectation is well defined and finite.

Turning to the *average-cost case* ($\gamma = 1$), we pose a different objective:

$$\begin{aligned} v(x|\pi) &= \text{expected long-run average cost using policy } \pi\text{, starting with } x_0 = x \\ &= E[\lim_{T\to\infty}\left(\frac{1}{T}\right)[\Sigma_{t=0}^{T-1}\{c(y(t) - x(t)) + C(y(t))\} - cx(T) \mid x(0) = x] \qquad (9.4.13) \end{aligned}$$

The goal is to find π^* minimizing $v(x|\pi)$ for all x.

Again, we have neglected certain technical issues. Everything works out satisfactorily for our problem. For other dynamic programs, however, these issues require more care. Indeed, the limit in (9.4.13) need not exist, and it is common to reformulate the criterion as

$$v(x|\pi) = \limsup_{T\to\infty}\left(\frac{1}{T}\right)E[\Sigma_{t=0}^{T-1}\{c(y(t) - x(t)) + C(y(t))\} - cx(T) \mid x(0) = x]$$

For our problem, this objective is equivalent to (9.4.13).

On the other hand, for reasonable problems (like ours) and reasonable policies, $v(x|\pi)$ is the same number for all x. In the long run, the effect of initial conditions disappears. So, we can denote the cost of policy π by $v(\pi)$ and the optimal cost by v^*.

Now that we have formulated the model, let us verify the solution outlined above.

PROOF OF THEOREM 9.4.3. We prove the result for $\gamma < 1$; the case $\gamma = 1$ is virtually identical. Substitute $x(t + 1) = y(t) - d(t)$ into (9.4.12) to obtain

$$V(x|\pi) = -cx + E[\,\Sigma_{t=0}^{\infty} \gamma^t C^+(y(t))]$$

Now, for every t and every possible $x(t)$, the base-stock policy with base-stock level s^* sets $y(t)$ to minimize $C^+(y(t))$, subject to $y(t) \geq x(t)$. (The argument is the same as in the single-period model.) Moreover, if $x(t) \leq s^*$ and we continue to apply this policy, we shall have $y(t+1) = s^*$, $y(t+2) = s^*$, etcetera. On the other hand, if $x(t) > s^*$, the policy sets $y(t)$ as small as possible, to $x(t)$. So, whatever value of $d(t)$ happens to occur, $x(t+1)$ will be as small as possible, and the feasible range for $y(t+1)$ as large as possible. The same is true for subsequent times. In sum, this policy minimizes $C^+(y(t))$ *for all t and for every demand sequence.* It certainly minimizes the expected discounted sum of these costs, and so is optimal.

This argument is quite easy and illuminating. It exploits certain special characteristics of the model. Other dynamic programs, unfortunately, cannot be analyzed in this way, including the fixed-cost model of the next section. We now *sketch* (omitting certain details) an alternative proof of Theorem 9.4.3, which illustrates the general approach required by more complex models. Again, we focus on the case $\gamma < 1$. (There is an argument along these lines for the average-cost case, but it is more intricate.)

This approach analyzes the *sequence* of finite-horizon models for increasing values of T. To identify a time point in this context, what matters is not its distance from time 0 but rather its distance from the horizon. Accordingly, we utilize a different indexing scheme for time. Specifically, set

$$n = T - t$$

So, n refers to that point in time when there are n periods *remaining* in the problem. Since the data are stationary, $V(n, \cdot) = V(T-t, \cdot)$, $s^*(n) = s^*(T-t)$, etc., have the same values for different T, provided that t is shifted accordingly to keep n constant. Equations (9.4.3) to (9.4.5) now become

$$V(0, x) = -cx \tag{9.4.14}$$

$$H(n, y) = cy + C(y) + \gamma E[V(n-1, y-d)] \tag{9.4.15}$$

$$V(n, x) = -cx + \min\{H(n, y) : y \geq x\} \tag{9.4.16}$$

There is another functional equation that plays a key role in the infinite-horizon dynamic program:

$$H(y) = cy + C(y) + \gamma E[V(y-d)] \tag{9.4.17}$$

$$V(x) = -cx + \min\{H(y) : y \geq x\} \tag{9.4.18}$$

The pair (9.4.17) and (9.4.18) is called the *optimality equation.* This is just (9.4.15) and (9.4.16) with the time index n removed. That difference is important, however, for the same functions H and V appear on both sides; these are unknowns to be solved for. Without further analysis, we do not know whether a solution exists, nor, if so, whether it is unique.

We plan to apply (but not prove) a general theorem about dynamic programs with stationary data. Stated in our terms, the result is this:

THEOREM 9.4.4. Assume

(i) The functions $V(n, \cdot)$ converge pointwise to a limit $V(\infty, \cdot)$; that is, for each x, $\lim_{n\to\infty} V(n, x) = V(\infty, x)$.
(ii) Substitute the limit function $V(\infty, \cdot)$ into (9.4.17), and call the result $H(\infty, \cdot)$; then, the pair $V(\infty, \cdot)$ and $H(\infty, \cdot)$ satisfies (9.4.18) and hence the entire optimality equation.

Let π^* be the policy indicating the optimal choice of y for each x in (9.4.18), using $H(\infty, \cdot)$ for $H(\cdot)$. Then,

(a) π^* is an optimal policy.
(b) The true optimal cost $V^*(\cdot)$ is given by $V(\infty, \cdot)$.

To verify assumptions (i) and (ii), several steps are required, which we state as a series of lemmas. After each one, instead of a formal proof, we merely indicate the main idea of the argument.

LEMMA 9.4.5. For $n \geq 1$.
(a) $H'(n, y) = C^{+\prime}(y) \qquad y \leq s^*$
(b) $s^*(n) = s^*$
(c) $V(n, x) \geq V(n-1, x) \qquad$ for all x
(d) $H(n, y) \geq H(n-1, y) \qquad$ for all y

The proof is a direct argument by induction.

LEMMA 9.4.6. $V(n, x) \leq V(x|\pi)$ for all n and any policy π

This result requires a simple, direct argument.

Thus, for each x, the sequence $\{V(n, x)\}$ is nondecreasing in n and bounded above, so it converges to a limit, $V(\infty, x)$. This establishes condition (i) of Theorem 9.4.4. Because $V(\infty, x)$ is the limit of convex functions, it too is convex.

LEMMA 9.4.7. The sequence $\{H(n, y)\}$ converges to $H(\infty, y)$. The functions $V(\infty, \cdot)$ and $H(\infty, \cdot)$ satisfy the optimality equation (9.4.17) and (9.4.18).

It is clear that $\{H(n, y)\}$ like $\{V(n, x)\}$ converges. But, it is hard to show that the limit is $H(\infty, y)$ and to verify (9.4.17) and (9.4.18). (The formal justification involves the Lebesgue dominated convergence theorem.) This result verifies condition (ii) of Theorem 9.4.4. Finally, it is easy to see that the policy π^* is precisely the base-stock policy with base-stock level s^*.

We have now completed the alternative approach to the proof of Theorem 9.4.3. It's hard work! The short cut in the original proof is certainly easier.

9.4.5 The Infinite-Horizon Problem: Nonstationary Data

The discussion above of the infinite-horizon model assumes that the data are stationary. What happens with nonstationary data? To say anything meaningful, the data must satisfy mild regularity conditions. (When $\gamma < 1$, for instance, it is sufficient that the cost factors be bounded in t, and the demands $d(t)$ be limited similarly.) Then, one can show that a base-stock policy is optimal, and Theorem 9.4.2 continues to relate the myopic and optimal policies.

In practice, it is useful to combine the finite- and infinite-horizon models, to avoid misleading horizon effects: It is often possible to specify the data with some confidence for a relatively short horizon T, but not for time points further into the future. However, the system is expected to continue operating well past T. Setting $V(T, x) = -c(T)x$ may thus distort the results.

Here is an alternative approach for the case $\gamma < 1$: Treat the data after T as stationary, estimate them as well as possible, and solve an infinite horizon model with the data; specifically, compute the optimal cost $V^*(x)$. Then, set $V(T, x) = V^*(x)$, and solve the finite-horizon model.

This same idea can be used with all the more elaborate models below.

9.4.6 Lost Sales

The models above assume that stockouts are backlogged. Now, consider the lost-sales case. The lost-sales assumption changes the formulation in only minor ways, and the key results remain valid. (These results do *not* extend to a longer order leadtime, however, as explained in Section 9.6.5.1 below.)

The net inventory $x(t)$ is now just the inventory, so $x(t) \geq 0$. The dynamics are

$$\begin{aligned} x(t+1) &= [x(t) + z(t) - d(t)\,]^+ \\ &= [\,y(t) - d(t)\,]^+ \qquad t = 0, \ldots, T-1 \end{aligned}$$

Imagine that, if $d(t) > y(t)$, the lost sales $d(t) - y(t)$ occur and $x(t+1)$ is set to 0 just at time $t + 1$. Reinterpret $b(t+1)$ as the unit cost of lost sales. So, the one-period cost function remains $C(t, y)$ as defined earlier. (Usually, $b(t+1)$ includes the unit sales price, so C includes revenue lost to shortages. This specification is consistent with the model of Section 9.4.5.2 below, which treats revenue explicitly.)

Also, *assume* that $b(t+1) + h(t+1) \geq \gamma c(t+1)$. This condition is nearly always true in practice; the sales price normally exceeds the unit cost. In theory, moreover, it *should* be true: Think of $b(t+1)$ as the unit cost charged by a special, emergency source, which delivers instantaneously at time $t+1$, in time to satisfy those prior-period demands $[y(t) - d(t)]^-$ that would be lost otherwise. Given that possibility, why not acquire extra emergency stock, hold it in inventory at cost $h(t+1)$, and use it at the end of period $t+1$? That transaction is equivalent to a regular order, and if it is cheaper, i.e., if $b(t+1) + h(t+1) < \gamma c(t+1)$, then we should always use it instead of the regular supply channel. In that case, we may as well replace $c(t+1)$ by $[b(t+1) + h(t+1)]/\gamma$.

The dynamic-programming formulation is almost identical to (9.4.3) to (9.4.5), but (9.4.4) now becomes

$$H(t, y) = c(t)y + C(t, y) + \gamma E[V\{t+1, [y - d(t)]^+\}]$$

It is convenient to work directly with the myopic formulation analogous to (9.4.6) to (9.4.8). Redefine

$$C^+(t, y) = c(t)y - \gamma c(t+1)E[[y - d(t)]^+] + C(t, y)$$

and replace (9.4.7) by

$$H(t, y) = C^+(t, y) + \gamma E[V^+\{t + 1, [y - d(t)]^+\}]$$

Using the definition of C, we can rewrite C^+ as

$$C^+(t, y) = b(t + 1)E[d(t)] + [c(t) - b(t + 1)]y$$
$$+ [b(t + 1) + h(t + 1) - \gamma c(t + 1)]E[[y - d(t)]^+]$$

Since $b(t + 1) + h(t + 1) \geq \gamma c(t + 1)$, this function is convex in y. Also, *extend* each function $V^+(t, x)$ to cover negative values of x, setting $V^+(t, x) = V^+(t, 0)$, $x < 0$. We can then rewrite $H(t, y)$ just as in (9.4.7):

$$H(t, y) = C^+(t, y) + \gamma E[V^+(t + 1, y - d(t))]$$

Let $s^*(t)$ minimize $H(t, y)$ over $y \geq 0$.

We claim that the base-stock policy with parameters $s^*(t)$ is optimal. To demonstrate this, we need to strengthen Theorem 9.4.1 slightly. Part (*c*) now says that the extended function $V^+(t, x)$ is convex *and nondecreasing* in x. Assume this for $t + 1$. Then, $H(t, y)$ is convex, and $V^+(t, x)$ is convex for $x \geq 0$, as before. Also, $V^+(t, x)$ is nondecreasing for $x \geq 0$, which implies that it is convex and nondecreasing for *all* x, completing the induction. (The nondecreasing property is essential; without it, the extended function would lose its convexity, and the proof would break down.)

Set the myopic base-stock level $s^+(t)$ to minimize $C^+(t, y)$. As before, this provides a simple upper bound on $s^*(t)$.

In the infinite-horizon model with stationary data the myopic policy is optimal. (The simple proof of Theorem 9.4.3, modified slightly, still works.) Here, $s^* = s^+$ minimizes

$$C^+(y) = bE[d] + (c - b)y + (b + h - \gamma c)E[[y - d]^+]$$

and so solves the equation

$$F_d^0(y) = \frac{c^+ + h}{b + h - \gamma c}$$

When this is compared to (9.4.11), it appears that the cost ratio is larger than in the backorders case, so s^* is smaller. But, the cost factor b has different meanings in the two models; it is likely to be bigger here, for a lost sale is worse than a delayed one. The larger b reduces the ratio and increases s^*.

9.4.7 Profit Maximization

The models above focus on operational costs; revenues are outside their scope. In many situations, however, the primary rationale for inventory is to support the exchange of goods for money. Fortunately, it is possible to extend the models to include revenues explicitly. The overall objective now broadens from cost to profit.

Suppose that demands are filled and revenues received just at the end of each period. Let

$p(t)$ = unit revenue (sales price) at the end of period $t - 1$

These are fixed, nonnegative constants.

Consider the lost-sales case first. The number of units sold at the end of period t is precisely

$$\min\{y(t), d(t)\} = d(t) - [d(t) - y(t)]^+$$

Viewed from step (2) of time t, the *expected* revenue is given by $R(t, y(t))$, where

$$R(t, y) = p(t+1)\{E[d(t)] - E[[d(t) - y]^+]\}$$

The relevant costs are the same as those in the earlier models. We can combine them with R to set up a model to maximize profit. Let us equivalently *minimize the negative of profit,* i.e., cost minus revenue. (This is a peculiar objective, but it is perfectly valid, and it will allow us to use the methods developed earlier.) Define the one-period profit function $P(t, y) = R(t, y) - C(t, y)$. To formulate the model, we need only replace C above by $-P = C - R$.

Observe that $R(t, y)$ is a *concave* function of y (i.e., $-R$ is convex). Therefore, $-P(t, y)$ is convex in y. (We actually need only $-P^+ = C^+ - R$ to be convex, and this is true under the reasonable condition $p(t) + b(t) + h(t) \geq \gamma c(t)$.) The analysis of the original (cost-minimization) model above thus remains valid; in particular, *a base-stock policy is optimal.*

Notice that subtracting R from C leaves the form of the function unchanged. There is a constant term $-p(t+1)E[d(t)]$, and the penalty-cost coefficient $b(t+1)$ is incremented by $p(t+1)$. This makes sense: When a sale is lost, we lose the corresponding revenue.

In the stationary infinite-horizon case, s^* satisfies

$$F_d^0(y) = \frac{(c^+ + h)}{(p + b + h - \gamma c)}$$

Now, suppose unfilled demands are backlogged. This case is harder, conceptually as well as technically. Suppose the price $p(t)$ changes over time. If a demand occurs in period $t - 2$, but can only be filled later, at the end of period $t - 1$, which price applies, $p(t-1)$ or $p(t)$? If $p(t) > p(t-1)$, it seems unfair to charge the higher price. Fair or not, if we do charge $p(t)$, why should customers be willing to wait?

Nevertheless, assume for simplicity that indeed $p(t)$ is the price for all demands and backorders *filled* at time t, even those due to earlier demands. To make this assumption more palatable, and to facilitate the analysis, we restrict the price parameters, requiring that

$$p(t) - \gamma p(t+1) + b(t) + h(t) \geq 0 \tag{9.4.19}$$

This condition holds when $p(t)$ is constant or decreasing. It allows price increases, but only modest ones.

If $x(t) \geq 0$, then $R(t, y)$ above still measures the expected revenue. If $x(t) < 0$, however, we can also collect revenue by filling outstanding backorders. Imagine that demand occurs before the order arrives. So, we could sell as many as $d(t) - x(t)$ units. Of these, we cannot fill more than $z(t) = y(t) - x(t)$. Thus, the number of units sold when $x(t) < 0$ is

$$\min\{y(t) - x(t), d(t) - x(t)\} = d(t) - [d(t) - y(t)]^+ - x(t)$$

In general, for any $x(t)$, the number of units sold is

$$d(t) - [d(t) - y(t)]^+ + [x(t)]^- = d(t) - [x(t+1)]^- + [x(t)]^-$$

and the total discounted revenue is

$$p(t+1)\{d(t) - [x(t+1)]^- + [x(t)]^-\}$$

Now, for time $t = 0$, the last term $p(1)[x(0)]^-$ is a constant, so we omit it. At time t we cannot influence $x(t)$, so we reassign the last term $p(t+1)[x(t)]^-$ to time $t-1$. (The same reasoning underlies the construction of $C(t, y)$.) The revenue at time t then becomes

$$\begin{aligned} p(t+1)\{d(t) - [x(t+1)]^-\} &+ \gamma p(t+2)[x(t+1)]^- \\ &= p(t+1)d(t) - p^+(t+1)[x(t+1)]^- \end{aligned}$$

where $p^+(t) = p(t) - \gamma p(t+1)$. Thus, the expected revenue as viewed from time t is $R(t, y(t))$, where we redefine

$$R(t, y) = p(t+1)E[d(t)] - p^+(t+1)E[[d(t) - y]^+]$$

Again let $P(t, y) = R(t, y) - C(t, y)$.

Let us formulate the dynamic program, analogous to (9.4.3) to (9.4.5). Here, $V(t, x)$ is minus the expected profit from time t onward.

$$\begin{aligned} V(T, x) &= -c(T)x \\ H(t, y) &= c(t)y - P(t, y) + \gamma E[V(t+1, y - d(t))] \\ V(t, x) &= -c(t)x + \min\{H(t, y) : y \geq x\} \qquad t < T \end{aligned}$$

It is convenient to work with the analogue of the myopic formulation (9.4.6) to (9.4.8). Defining $P^+(t, y) = R(t, y) - C^+(t, y)$, we have

$$\begin{aligned} V^+(T, x) &= 0 \\ H(t, y) &= -P^+(t, y) + \gamma E[V^+(t+1, y - d(t))] \\ V^+(t, x) &= \min\{H(t, y) : y \geq x\} \qquad t < T \end{aligned}$$

We can rewrite $-P^+$ as

$$\begin{aligned} -P^+(t, y) = \{c^+(t) + h(t+1)\}y &- \{h(t+1) - p(t+1)\}E[d(t)] \\ &+ \{p^+(t+1) + h(t+1) + b(t+1)\}E[[d(t) - y]^+] \end{aligned}$$

By (9.4.19) this is convex in y. Thus, we can invoke Theorem 9.4.1: Here too, *a base-stock policy is optimal.*

In the stationary infinite-horizon case, s^* satisfies

$$\begin{aligned} F_d^0(y) &= \frac{c^+ + h}{p^+ + b + h} \\ &= \frac{c^+ + h}{(p^+ - c^+ + b) + (c^+ + h)} \end{aligned}$$

For $\gamma = 1$ the cost ratio again reduces to $1 - \omega$. For $\gamma < 1$, the effect of including revenue in the model is to increment the backorder cost by p^+. Alternatively, since the factors h and b represent physical costs only, we can interpret c^+ as the financing cost for inventory and $p^+ - c^+$ as the corresponding financing cost for backorders.

This entire discussion presumes that the prices $p(t)$ are given constants. Problem 9.8 explores a scenario where they are decision variables. (The problem explores just that one scenario, however. The general case is difficult.)

9.4.8 Imperfect Quality

9.4.8.1 Discussion

Next, suppose that the supply system sometimes produces defective units. If we order $z(t) = z$ at time t, the amount of usable goods we actually receive is $\Xi(t, z)$, a random variable called the *yield*. Equivalently, $\Xi(t, z) = z - \Delta(t, z)$, where $\Delta(t, z)$ is the quantity of *defects*. We observe the yield when the order arrives. At that instant we pay for the nondefective goods, and only those (as in case 1 of Section 3.6.2), so the actual order cost is $c(t)\Xi(t, z)$. The yield in each period is independent of all other events, i.e., the demands and the other periods' yields. The yield distribution can depend on time, but for notational simplicity assume it does not; we write $\Xi = \Xi(z)$ and $\Delta = \Delta(z)$.

Before delving into details, let us try to see intuitively what is going on: The dynamics become

$$x(t + 1) = x(t) + \Xi(z(t)) - d(t) \tag{9.4.20}$$

There are *two* sources of uncertainty about $x(t + 1)$, the demand and the yield.

What happens if we follow a base-stock policy? Consider a stationary setting for simplicity, with base-stock level $s(t) = s$, starting with $x(0) \leq s$. We order $z(0) = s - x(0)$, so $x(1) = s - [\Delta(z(0)) + d(0)]$. The defects make $x(1)$ *less* than it would be otherwise. We do make up the difference at time 1, ordering $z(1) = s - x(1) = \Delta[z(0)] + d(0)$. But then $x(2) = s - [\Delta(z(1)) + d(1)]$, which is likely to be even smaller, because of the large $z(1)$. This pattern continues: At each time t, $z(t)$ replaces period $(t - 1)$'s defects as well as demand. Even so, period t's defects lead to a lower $x(t + 1)$ than we would otherwise expect. Knowing this, we most likely want to choose s *higher* than in the no-defect model.

How might we do better? Instead of ordering just to correct for past defects, we might aim to *anticipate* defects in the current period.

Consider the *deterministic-yield* case: There is a constant *yield rate* ξ, or a constant *defect rate* δ, as in Section 3.6. The actual yield $\Xi(z)$ is just the function ξz. The solution here is straightforward: Solve the no-defect model. A base-stock policy is optimal there; the optimal order size is $[s^* - x(t)]^+$. In the real system, *inflate* this quantity to anticipate defects; that is, set $z(t) = 0$ if $x(t) \geq s^*$ and $z(t) = [s^* - x(t)]/\xi$ otherwise, so that $x(t) + \Xi(z(t)) = \max\{s^*, x(t)\}$. The actual net inventories $x(t)$ and the costs are precisely the same as in the no-defect model. (This idea works even with nonstationary data.)

With random yields, of course, we can no longer anticipate perfectly. If we set $z(t) > 0$ so that $x(t) + z(t) > s^*$, and the yield turns out higher than expected, we may find $x(t + 1) > s^*$. This is an unwelcome outcome. It is not clear just how to anticipate properly.

Here is the plan: First, we consider a special case. A dynamic-programming analysis shows that, indeed, we should modify the base-stock rule to anticipate defects: We can decide *when* to order by comparing $x(t)$ to a certain base-stock level $s^*(t)$. When $x(t) < s^*(t)$, the actual *amount* to order is *more* than $s^*(t) - x(t)$. Unfortunately, the analysis cannot tell us just how much more; that requires a detailed calculation in each period.

Then, we explore a certain heuristic policy, called a linear inflation rule, inspired by the exact analysis but simpler to implement than the true optimal policy. We perform an approximate steady-state performance evaluation and, on the basis of that analysis, select the best such policy.

9.4.8.2 The Proportional-Yield Model—Exact Analysis

The collection $\{\Xi(z) : z \geq 0\}$ is a family of random variables, distinguished by the parameter z. How shall we model it? There are many possibilities. Let us focus on one simple case, that of *proportional yield:* The yield rate $\xi = \xi(t)$ in each period is a random variable between 0 and 1, *independent* of z, and $\Xi(z) = \xi z$. Given the yield rate, the yield is linear in the order size. (The yield rates in different periods are i.i.d.) Equivalently, there is a random defect rate $\delta = \delta(t)$, independent of $z(t)$.

This proportional-yield model is very special. Observe that $E[\Xi(z)] = E[\xi]z$ and $V[\Xi(z)] = V[\xi]z^2$; the mean is linear in the order quantity, but the variance is quadratic. This is a worst case. Imagine dividing the order into several equal portions. Then, each portion has the same yield; their yields are perfectly correlated. In effect, the order is thoroughly mixed, so that every portion is defective to the same degree. This says a great deal about the physical process generating the defects. Defects occur because of systematic causes only, which influence the entire order uniformly. Some physical processes do work this way, at least approximately, but others do not. There is no room here for independence, partial or total, among the portions. (If the portions were independent, $V[\Xi(z)]$ would be linear in z, like the mean.) Still, we focus on this model because of its simplicity.

The family of yields $\{\Xi(z) : z \geq 0\}$ has four appealing and important properties:

1. $\Xi(z)$ is *bounded,* specifically, $0 \leq \Xi(z) \leq z$. We never receive more than we ask for.
2. $\Xi(z)$ is *smooth.* That is, for any scalar function $f(\cdot)$, $E[f(\Xi(z))]$ preserves the smoothness properties of $f(\cdot)$. For instance, if $f(\cdot)$ is continuously differentiable, so is $E[f(\Xi(z))]$. This condition is natural in a world of continuous quantities.
3. $\Xi(z)$ is *stochastically increasing.* That is, if $f(\cdot)$ is nondecreasing, $E[f(\Xi(z))]$ is a nondecreasing function of z. Also, $z - \Xi(z) = \Delta(z)$ is stochastically increasing. If we order more, we are likely to receive more nondefective *and* defective goods.
4. $\Xi(z)$ is *stochastically convex.* That is, for any convex $f(\cdot)$, $E[f(\Xi(z))]$ is convex in z. Moreover, if $f(x, y)$ is jointly convex, then $E[f(x, \Xi(z))]$ is jointly convex in (x, z).

Now let us analyze the inventory system: Let $C(t, y)$ be the same function defined before, the one-period cost in the no-defect model, and $C^+(t, y)$ the myopic cost function. Define

$$\bar{C}(t, x, z) = E[C(t, x + \Xi(z))]$$
$$\bar{C}^+(t, x, z) = E[C^+(t, x + \Xi(z))]$$

By (9.4.20) the actual one-period cost is now $\bar{C}(t, x(t), z(t))$. The stochastic-convexity property ensures that $\bar{C}(t, x, z)$ and $\bar{C}^+(t, x, z)$ are jointly convex in (x, z) for each t.

Let us proceed directly to the myopic formulation of the dynamic program:

$$V^+(T, x) = 0$$

$$\bar{H}(t, x, z) = \bar{C}^+(t, x, z) + \gamma E[V^+(t+1, x + \Xi(z) - d(t))]$$

$$V^+(t, x) = \min\{\bar{H}(t, x, z) : z \geq 0\}$$

Notice that $\bar{H}$ can be written as $\bar{H}(t, x, z) = E[H(t, x + \Xi(z))]$, where

$$H(t, y) = C^+(t, y) + \gamma E[V^+(t+1, y - d(t))]$$

In the one-period model we can drop the time index. The problem is to choose $z \geq 0$ to minimize $\bar{H}(x, z) = \bar{C}^+(x, z)$, where $\bar{C}^+(x, z) = E[\, C^+(x + \Xi(z))\,]$. What does the optimal policy look like? Let s^* minimize $C^+(y)$, so s^* is the optimal base-stock level for the no-defects problem. Let $z^* = z^*(x)$ denote the true optimal order size, and $y^*(x) = x + z^*(x)$.

THEOREM 9.4.8. In the one-period problem

(a) $z^*(x) > 0$ if and only if $x < s^*$, and in general $y^*(x) \geq s^*$.
(b) For $x \leq s^*$, $y^*(x)$ is nonincreasing in x.
(c) The optimal cost $V^+(x)$ is convex in x.

Any rule with properties (a) and (b) we call an *inflated base-stock policy.* For x above s^*, order nothing. When x drops below s^*, order enough to bring $y = y^*(x)$ *above* s^*, to anticipate defects. Moreover, as x decreases further, $y^*(x)$ increases further above s^*.

PROOF.

(a) First, suppose $x \geq s^*$. Fix $z > 0$. For every realization of ξ, $\Xi(z) = \xi z \geq 0$, so $C^+(x + \Xi(z)) \geq C^+(x)$. Consequently, $\bar{C}^+(x, z) = E[C^+(x + \Xi(z))] \geq C^+(x) = \bar{C}^+(x, 0)$, so $z^*(x) = 0$. Conversely, suppose $x < s^*$. Fix $z < s^* - x$. Over the range $x \leq y \leq s^*$, $C^+(y)$ is nonincreasing, so for any realization of ξ, $C^+(x + \Xi(z)) = C^+(x + \xi z) \geq C^+(x + \xi(s^* - x))$. Therefore, $\bar{C}^+(x, z) = E[C^+(x + \Xi(z))] \geq E[C^+(x + \Xi(s^* - x))] = \bar{C}^+(x, s^* - x)$, so $z^*(x) \geq s^* - x$.
(b) Choose $x_1 < x_2 \leq s^*$, and let $z_1 = z^*(x_1)$ and $z_2 = z^*(x_2)$. Set $z' = x_2 - x_1 + z_2$, and consider z' as a potential value of z_1. We have

$$\frac{\partial \bar{C}^+(x, z)}{\partial z} = \left(\frac{d}{dz}\right) E[C^+(x + \Xi(z))]$$

$$= E[\left(\frac{d}{dz}\right) C^+(x + \Xi(z))]$$

$$= E[\xi C^{+\prime}(x + \xi z)]$$

Since $C^{+\prime}(\cdot)$ is nondecreasing, we have for every realization of ξ

$$\xi C^{+\prime}(x_1 + \xi z') = \xi C^{+\prime}(x_2 + \xi z_2 - \delta(z' - z_2))$$

$$\leq \xi C^{+\prime}(x_2 + \xi z_2)$$

where $\delta = 1 - \xi$. Therefore,

$$\begin{aligned}\frac{\partial \bar{C}^+(x_1, z')}{\partial z} &= E[\xi C^{+\prime}(x_1 + \xi z')] \\ &\le E[\xi C^{+\prime}(x_2 + \xi z_2)] \\ &= \frac{\partial \bar{C}^+(x_2, z_2)}{\partial z} = 0\end{aligned}$$

Thus, $z_1 \ge z'$, or $x_1 + z_1 \ge x_2 + z_2$.

(*c*) The function $\bar{H}(x, z)$ is jointly convex, and minimizing over z preserves convexity. (See Appendix A.)

Armed with these results for the one-period problem, we move on to the finite-horizon problem. A straightforward induction, as in Theorem 9.4.1, yields the following:

THEOREM 9.4.9. For all *t:*

(*a*) $H(t, y)$ is convex in y.

(*b*) The optimal policy for time t is an inflated base-stock policy; the optimal base-stock level $s^*(t)$ is the smallest value of y minimizing $H(t, y)$.

(*c*) $V^+(t, x)$ is convex in x.

In the infinite-horizon problem with stationary data, the optimal policy has this same form, and the optimal parameter s^* is stationary.

The myopic policy chooses $z \ge 0$ to minimize $\bar{C}^+(t, x, z)$. It is clear that this too is an inflated base-stock policy. The base-stock level here is $s^+(t)$, the value from the no-defect problem. We cannot conclude that $s^*(t) \le s^+(t)$, however, because $V^+(t, x)$ is *not* nondecreasing. It is nondecreasing for $x \ge s^*(t)$, but no longer constant for $x < s^*(t)$. For the same reason, in the infinite-horizon problem, the myopic policy is *not* generally optimal.

9.4.8.3 Linear-Inflation Heuristics

The theorems above tell us something about the optimal policy, but not everything. They leave open the precise value of the order quantity for $x < s^*(t)$. To compute $z^*(t)$ means to optimize $\bar{H}(t, x, z)$ numerically.

Consider the following heuristic: Fix some constant β with $0 < \beta \le 1$ and base-stock levels $s(t)$. In each period set

$$z(t) = \frac{[s(t) - x(t)]^+}{\beta}$$

We call this a *linear-inflation rule.* Evidently, it is one particular inflated base-stock policy. It embodies the main ideas of the theoretical analysis in a simple, unambiguous way. An ordinary base-stock policy is a linear-inflation rule with $\beta = 1$. The optimal policy for the deterministic-yield model is too; it uses $\beta = \xi$.

How should we pick β and the $s(t)$? Focus on the infinite-horizon model with stationary data and constant $s(t) = s$. Define

$$u(t) = s - x(t)$$

So, $z(t) = [u(t)/\beta]^+$, and the dynamics (9.4.20) can be expressed as

$$u(t+1) = u(t) - \Xi\left(\left[\frac{u(t)}{\beta}\right]^+\right) + d(t)$$

Our goal is to approximate the mean and variance of $u(t)$ in equilibrium. The steady-state random variable $u = s - x$ plays the same role as d in a no-defects model, and we shall approximate it with a normal distribution. Given these approximations, we can set s and β optimally.

We continue to assume proportional yield. (In fact, more general yield models can be analyzed similarly; see Problem 9.9.) For simplicity, set $\xi_1 = E[\xi]$ and $\xi_2 = V[\xi]$.

The key step in the approximation is to ignore the possibility of $u(t) < 0$, setting $z(t) = u(t)/\beta$. So, the dynamics become linear:

$$u(t+1) = u(t) - \frac{\xi(t)u(t)}{\beta} + d(t)$$

First, estimate $E[u]$: We have

$$E\left[\frac{\xi(t)u(t)}{\beta}\right] = \left(\frac{\xi_1}{\beta}\right)E[u(t)]$$

so

$$E[u(t+1)] = \left(\frac{1-\xi_1}{\beta}\right)E[u(t)] + E[d(t)]$$

In equilibrium

$$E[u] = \left(\frac{1-\xi_1}{\beta}\right)E[u] + E[d] = \left(\frac{\beta}{\xi_1}\right)E[d]$$

Now, turn to $V[u]$: Applying the conditional-variance formula, as in Section C.6.3,

$$V[u(t) - \frac{\xi(t)u(t)}{\beta}] = V\{E[(1 - \frac{\xi(t)}{\beta})u(t) \mid u(t)]\} + E\{V[(1 - \frac{\xi(t)}{\beta})u(t) \mid u(t)]\}$$

$$= V[(1 - \frac{\xi_1}{\beta})u(t)] + E[\xi_2\left(\frac{u(t)}{\beta}\right)^2]$$

$$= (1 - \frac{\xi_1}{\beta})^2 V[u(t)] + \left(\frac{\xi_2}{\beta^2}\right)E[u^2(t)]$$

$$= [(1 - \frac{\xi_1}{\beta})^2 + \left(\frac{\xi_2}{\beta^2}\right)]V[u(t)] + \left(\frac{\xi_2}{\beta^2}\right)E^2[u(t)]$$

We can use this to calculate

$$V[u(t+1)] = V[u(t) - \frac{\xi(t)u(t)}{\beta}] + V[d(t)]$$

but let us proceed directly to the equilibrium value:

$$V[u] = [(1 - \frac{\xi_1}{\beta})^2 + \left(\frac{\xi_2}{\beta^2}\right)]V[u] + \left(\frac{\xi_2}{\beta^2}\right)E^2[u] + V[d]$$

$$= [1 - (1 - \frac{\xi_1}{\beta})^2 - \left(\frac{\xi_2}{\beta^2}\right)]^{-1} \cdot \{\left(\frac{\xi_2}{\xi_1^2}\right)E^2[d] + V[d]\}$$

We plan to use these quantities within a normal approximation. Because $V[u]$ determines the ultimate performance of the system, we want to set β to make $V[u]$ small. Notice, $V[u]$ is the product of two terms, and the second one (in braces) is independent of β. The first term can be written as

$$\frac{\beta^2}{2\xi_1\beta - (\xi_1^2 + \xi_2)}$$

It is not hard to verify that the value of β that minimizes this function is

$$\beta^* = \frac{\xi_1^2 + \xi_2}{\xi_1} = \frac{E[\xi^2]}{E[\xi]}$$

Notice, $\beta^* < 1$, so the resulting policy *is* a linear-inflation rule. In the deterministic-yield case $\beta^* = \xi_1 = \xi$, the correct value. Otherwise, $\beta^* > \xi_1$. The best inflation factor is *larger* than in the deterministic case. We do anticipate defects, but only somewhat. Oddly, when the yield is highly variable, β^* is near 1, so the rule comes close to a base-stock policy.

Substituting β^* into $E[u]$ and $V[u]$, we get

$$E[u] = (1 + \frac{\xi_2}{\xi_1^2})E[d]$$

$$V[u] = (1 + \frac{\xi_2}{\xi_1^2})\{\left(\frac{\xi_2}{\xi_1^2}\right)E^2[d] + V[d]\}$$

Call these parameters ν and σ^2, and use them in the normal approximation: Set $s^* = \nu + \sigma z^*$ as usual. The optimal cost $C^+(s^*)$ is proportional to $\sigma = \sqrt{V[u]}$. When the yield is really random ($\xi_2 > 0$), σ is larger than the original $\sigma = \sqrt{V[d]}$. Yield uncertainty hurts performance. That uncertainty is expressed here by the ratio $\xi_2/\xi_1^2 = V[\xi]/E^2[\xi]$, the squared coefficient of variation of ξ.

As noted at the beginning, this is an approximate analysis. Still, the linear-inflation rule using β^* seems to work fairly well. The even simpler rule with $\beta = E[\xi]$ works well also.

9.5 Fixed-Plus-Linear Order Costs

This section allows positive fixed costs $k(t)$. Otherwise, the model is the same as before. It turns out that an (r, s) policy is optimal at each time point. (We saw this type of policy in Section 6.6.)

Again, we proceed in three major steps, depending on the horizon length, and then discuss extensions.

9.5.1 The Single-Period Problem

Again, suppress the time index t. So, the fixed cost becomes k. The formulation is parallel to that of Section 9.4.1. Defining the function H as before, we now need to solve

$$\begin{aligned} &\text{Minimize} \quad && k\delta(y - x) + H(y) \\ &\text{subject to} \quad && y \geq x \end{aligned} \tag{9.5.1}$$

Let s^* minimize H.

What is the optimal policy? Certainly, it is still best not to order when $x \geq s^*$. However, we may prefer not to order even when $x < s^*$, to avoid the fixed order cost. If we do not order, the cost above is just $H(x)$. If we do order, clearly, we want to set $y = s^*$, so the cost becomes $k + H(s^*)$. To decide between these two alternatives, then, we must compare the two numbers $H(x)$ and $k + H(s^*)$.

Recall that H is convex, so $H(x)$ is decreasing for $x < s^*$. Let r^* be that value of $x \leq s^*$ such that

$$H(x) = H(s^*) + k \tag{9.5.2}$$

Thus, $H(x) \geq H(s^*) + k$ for *all* $x \leq r^*$, so it is less costly to order. And, for $x > r^*$ (but $x \leq s^*$), $H(x) < H(s^*) + k$, so it is optimal not to order. To conclude, *the optimal policy is an (r, s) policy.* The optimal parameters are the reorder point r^* and the target stock level s^*.

Letting $V(x)$ denote the optimal cost, we have $V(x) = V^+(x) - cx$, where now

$$V^+(x) = \begin{cases} H(s^*) + k & x \leq r^* \\ H(x) & x > r^* \end{cases} \tag{9.5.3}$$

See Figures 9.5.1 and 9.5.2.

These functions are *not* convex. This does not affect the solution above, of course. Thinking ahead to the multiperiod problem, however, it is clear that we are going to have difficulties. In the linear-order-cost model the convexity of V was essential to the analysis. To prepare for later developments, then, we now reanalyze the single-period problem. As we shall see, the results above remain valid under a weaker condition on H than convexity. This property, called k-convexity, *is* preserved by V. It will play a central role in the subsequent analysis.

Let $f(x)$ be a function and m a nonnegative number. We say that f is *m-convex* if, for all x and all positive numbers ξ and υ,

$$f(x) + \frac{\xi[f(x) - f(x - \upsilon)]}{\upsilon} \leq f(x + \xi) + m \tag{9.5.4}$$

If f is differentiable, the following condition is equivalent: For all x and all positive ξ,

$$f(x) + \xi f'(x) \leq f(x + \xi) + m \tag{9.5.4'}$$

FIGURE 9.5.1

Cost function for one-period problem (fixed-plus-linear order cost).

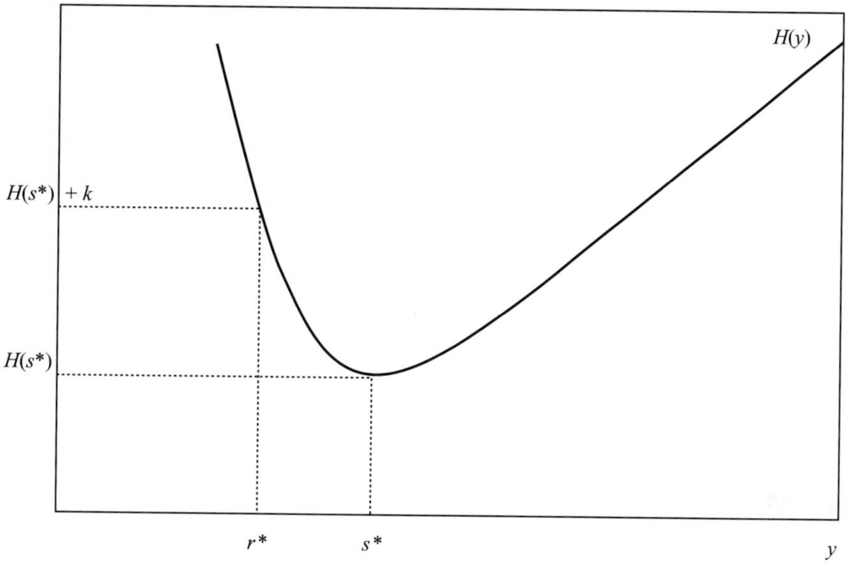

FIGURE 9.5.2

Optimal cost function (fixed-plus-linear order cost).

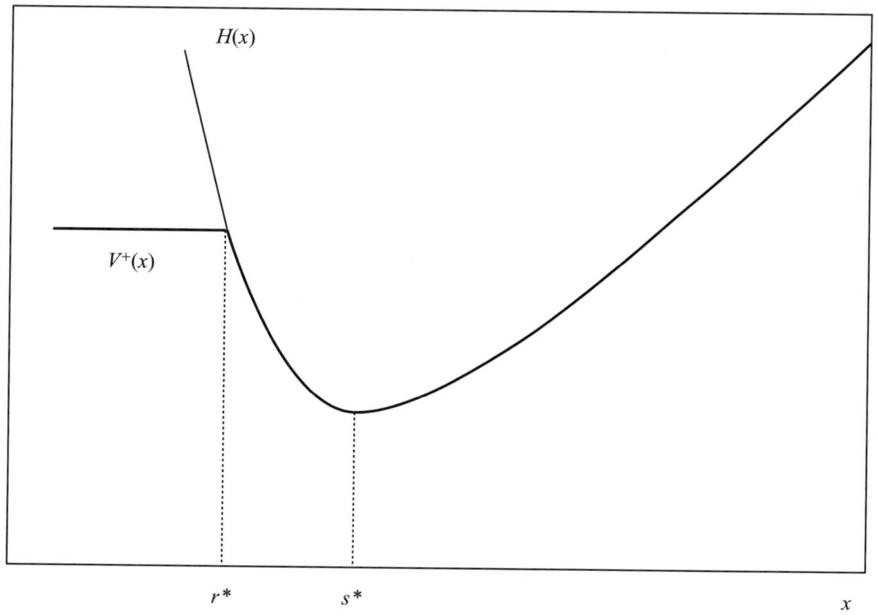

Let us try to understand this property intuitively: If f is actually convex, then (9.5.4) holds for $m = 0$; 0-convexity is equivalent to convexity itself. Also, the condition becomes weaker as m grows; that is, if f is m_1-convex and $m_2 > m_1$, then f is also m_2-convex. The expression on the left of (9.5.4) or (9.5.4′) can be viewed as a linear approximation of $f(x + \xi)$ for fixed x. When $m = 0$ and f is convex, we recover the familiar fact that the linear approximation *underestimates* the true value $f(x + \xi)$. When $m > 0$, the approximation may overestimate $f(x + \xi)$, but *the error is bounded* above by m. Figure 9.5.3 illustrates this property. The dotted line is the linear approximation.

We state some additional facts in the following lemma; the proof is left to Problem 9.11.

LEMMA 9.5.1.

(*a*) If $f(x)$ is m-convex, then so is the shifted function $f(x + \Psi)$, for any fixed Ψ (positive or negative).

(*b*) If f_1 is m_1-convex, f_2 is m_2-convex, and α_1 and α_2 are positive numbers, then the function $f = \alpha_1 f_1 + \alpha_2 f_2$ is m-convex, where $m = \alpha_1 m_1 + \alpha_2 m_2$.

(*c*) If $\tilde{f}$ is m-convex, and $f(x) = E[\tilde{f}(x - d)]$, then f is m-convex.

Now, let us return to our problem. Since H above is convex, it is certainly k-convex.

THEOREM 9.5.2. Let H be *any* continuous, k-convex function in problem (9.5.1). The optimal policy is an (r, s) policy with parameters (r^*, s^*), where s^* is the smallest y minimizing $H(y)$, and r^* is the largest $x \leq s^*$ satisfying (9.5.2).

FIGURE 9.5.3

An m-convex function.

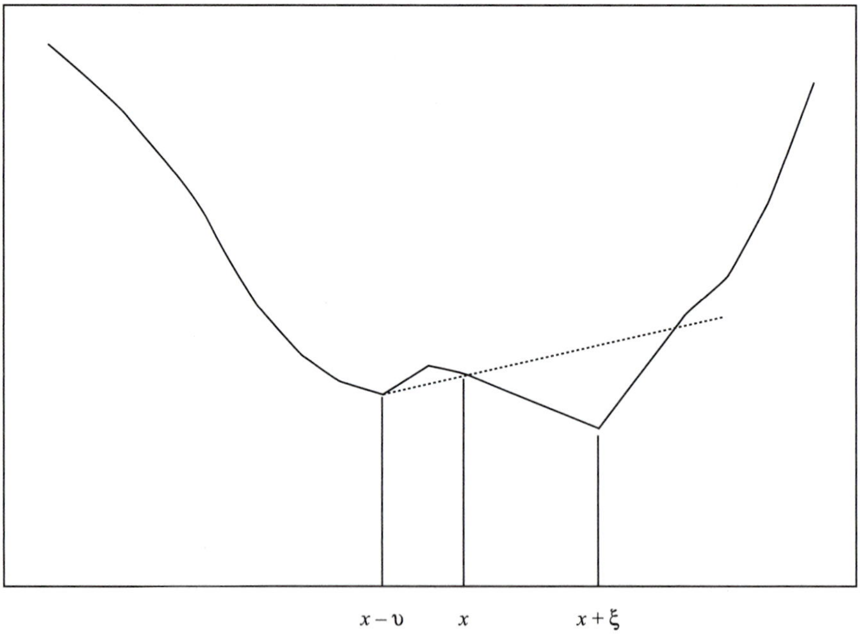

PROOF. Clearly, it is optimal not to order for $x \geq s^*$. Also, for $r^* < x < s^*$, we have $H(x) < H(s^*) + k$, by the definition of r^*, so again it is optimal not to order. So, we need only show that it is optimal to order up to s^*, i.e., $H(x) \geq H(s^*) + k$, for all $x \leq r^*$. But, suppose this inequality is violated at $x = r^* - \upsilon$ for some $\upsilon > 0$, and set $\xi = s^* - r^*$. Then, $H(r^*) > H(r^* - \upsilon)$, so

$$\frac{H(r^*) + \xi[H(r^*) - H(r^* - \upsilon)]}{\upsilon} > H(r^*) = H(r^* + \xi) + k$$

This violates the k-convexity of H at r^*.

Next, we show that k-convexity is preserved by $V^+(x)$.

THEOREM 9.5.3. Let H be any continuous, k-convex function, and define V^+ in terms of H, s^*, and r^*, according to (9.5.3). Then, V^+ is continuous and k-convex.

PROOF. Continuity is obvious. For k-convexity we need to consider three cases:

Case (i). $x + \xi \leq r^*$. Here, $V^+(w)$ is the constant $H(s^*) + k$ for all $w \leq x + \xi$, so the k-convexity condition (9.5.4) is immediate.

Case (ii). $x - \upsilon > r^*$. In this case $V^+(w) = H(w)$, $w \geq x - \upsilon$, and the result follows from the k-convexity of H.

Case (iii). $x - \upsilon \leq r^* < x + \xi$. We have $V^+(x - \upsilon) = k + H(s^*)$, and $V^+(x + \xi) = H(x + \xi) \geq H(s^*)$. As for x, there are two possibilities: If $V^+(x) \leq H(s^*) + k$, then

$$\frac{V^+(x) + \xi[V^+(x) - V^+(x - \upsilon)]}{\upsilon} \leq V^+(x) \leq H(s^*) + k \leq V^+(x + \xi) + k$$

If $V^+(x) > H(s^*) + k$, then $x > s^*$, and $V^+(x) = H(x)$. Also, setting $\upsilon' = x - s^*$, we have $\upsilon' < \upsilon$. Thus,

$$\frac{V^+(x) - V^+(x - \upsilon)}{\upsilon} = \frac{H(x) - H(s^*) - k}{\upsilon} < \frac{[H(x) - H(s^*)]}{\upsilon'}$$

Therefore, in view of the k-convexity of H,

$$V^+(x) + \frac{\xi[V^+(x) - V^+(x - \upsilon)]}{\upsilon}$$

$$< \frac{H(x) + \xi[H(x) - H(s^*)]}{\upsilon'}$$

$$\leq H(x + \xi) + k = V^+(x + \xi) + k$$

COROLLARY 9.5.4. Define V^+ as in the theorem, and set $V(x) = V^+(x) - cx$. Then, $V(x)$ is continuous and k-convex.

PROOF. Again, continuity is obvious. Also, V is the sum of a linear function and the k-convex function V^+, and so is k-convex by part (*b*) of Lemma 9.5.1.

9.5.2 The Finite-Horizon Problem

Next, consider a finite horizon T. There is now a fixed order cost in each period. We assume that this cost is constant over time, i.e., $k(t) = k > 0$. (See Problem 9.12 for the case of nonstationary $k(t)$.) The formulation of the dynamic program, analogous to (9.4.3) to (9.4.5) above, is the following:

$$V(T, x) = -c(T)x \tag{9.5.5}$$

$$H(t, y) = c(t)y + C(t, y) + \gamma E[V(t+1, y - d(t))] \tag{9.5.6}$$

$$V(t, x) = -c(t)x + \min\{k\delta(y - x) + H(t, y) : y \geq x\} \tag{9.5.7}$$

Again, these equations describe a recursive scheme to compute an optimal policy. The *form* of the optimal policy is characterized in part (*b*) of the following theorem, the direct analogue of Theorem 9.4.1:

THEOREM 9.5.5. For all t,

(*a*) $H(t, y)$ is a continuous, k-convex function of y.
(*b*) The optimal policy for point t is an (r, s) policy; the target stock level $s^*(t)$ is the smallest value of y minimizing $H(t, y)$, and the reorder point $r^*(t)$ is the largest value of $x \leq s^*(t)$ satisfying

$$H(t, x) = k + H(t, s^*(t))$$

(*c*) $V(t, x)$ is a continuous, k-convex function of x.

PROOF. The proof is parallel to that of Theorem 9.4.1: Use induction on t, starting with $t = T - 1$ and working backward. Assuming that $V(t+1, x)$ is k-convex, Lemma 9.5.1(*c*) implies that $EV[(t+1, y - d(t))]$ is too, hence so is $H(t, y)$. For parts (*b*) and (*c*), use the results for the one-period model.

Next, we derive relatively simple bounds on the optimal policy variables, analogous to the myopic policy of Section 9.4. We shall work with a transformed recursion, analogous to (9.4.6) to (9.4.8):

$$V^+(T, x) = 0 \tag{9.5.8}$$

$$H(t, y) = C^+(t, y) + \gamma E[V^+(t+1, y - d(t))] \tag{9.5.9}$$

$$V^+(t, x) = \min\{k\delta(y - x) + H(t, y) : y \geq x\} \tag{9.5.10}$$

Again, let $s^+(t)$ denote the myopic base-stock level, the smallest value of y that globally minimizes $C^+(t, y)$. Also, set $s^{++}(t)$ to the value of $y > s^+(t)$ that solves

$$C^+(t, y) = C^+(t, s^+(t)) + \gamma k$$

and $r^+(t)$ to the value of $y \leq s^+(t)$ that solves

$$C^+(t, y) = C^+(t, s^+(t)) + (1 - \gamma)k$$

These quantities directly reflect the data for period t. For example, if $d(t)$ shifts up or down by a simple translation, then $s^{+}(t)$, $s^{++}(t)$, and $r^{+}(t)$ all shift by the same amount. Also, as k grows, both $s^{++}(t)$ and $r^{+}(t)$ move further away from $s^{+}(t)$ and each other.

THEOREM 9.5.6. For each t, $s^*(t) \leq s^{++}(t)$ and $r^*(t) \leq r^{+}(t)$.

PROOF. The argument uses the following preliminary results: First, from the definition and k-convexity of V^{+}, one can show that, for all x and all $\xi > 0$,

$$V^{+}(t, x + \xi) - V^{+}(t, x) \geq -k$$

(This inequality generalizes the fact that, in the linear-cost case, $V^{+}(t, x)$ is nondecreasing in x.) From this it immediately follows that, for all y and all $\xi > 0$,

$$[H(t, y + \xi) - H(t, y)] - [C^{+}(t, y + \xi) - C^{+}(t, y)] \geq -\gamma k \tag{9.5.11}$$

Now, for $y > s^{++}(t)$, we have

$$\begin{aligned} H(t, y) - H(t, s^{+}(t)) &\geq C^{+}(t, y) - C^{+}(t, s^{+}(t)) - \gamma k \\ &> C^{+}(t, s^{++}(t)) - C^{+}(t, s^{+}(t)) - \gamma k = 0 \end{aligned}$$

Consequently, y cannot minimize H, and we conclude that $s^*(t) \leq s^{++}(t)$.

If $s^*(t) \leq r^{+}(t)$, then clearly $r^*(t) \leq r^{+}(t)$. So, suppose $s^*(t) > r^{+}(t)$. There are two cases to consider: First, assume $s^*(t) \leq s^{+}(t)$. For y with $r^{+}(t) < y \leq s^*(t)$

$$\begin{aligned} H(t, s^*(t)) - H(t, y) &\geq C^{+}(t, s^*(t)) - C^{+}(t, y) - \gamma k \\ &\geq C^{+}(t, s^{+}(t)) - C^{+}(t, y) - \gamma k \\ &> -(1 - \gamma)k - \gamma k = -k \end{aligned}$$

or $H(t, y) < H(t, s^*(t)) + k$. So, y cannot satisfy the equation for $r^*(t)$; thus, $r^*(t) \leq r^{+}(t)$. Second, assume $s^*(t) > s^{+}(t)$. For y with $s^{+}(t) < y \leq s^*(t)$

$$\begin{aligned} H(t, s^*(t)) - H(t, y) &\geq C^{+}(t, s^*(t)) - C^{+}(t, y) - \gamma k \\ &> 0 - k = -k \end{aligned}$$

while for y with $r^{+}(t) < y \leq s^{+}(t)$ we can use the same argument as in the first case above. In sum, $H(t, y) < H(t, s^*(t)) + k$ for all y with $r^{+}(t) < y \leq s^*(t)$, so again $r^*(t) \leq r^{+}(t)$.

Example 9.5.A illustrates the optimal (r, s) policy.

EXAMPLE 9.5.A

As in Example 9.4.A, we consider four systems with $\gamma = 1$, $h(t) = 1$, and $b(t) = 9$. The $d(t)$ have either Poisson or geometric distributions. In every case $k = 5$.

Figure 9.5.4 shows the optimal policy for a pair of models with stationary $c(t)$. The $E[d(t)]$ change, but not too much; they oscillate between 20 and 40. Observe, in both the Poisson- and geometric-demand models, the difference $q^*(t) = s^*(t) - r^*(t)$ remains nearly constant over t. In the Poisson-demand case, moreover, the changes in $r^*(t)$ are nearly parallel to the movements of $E[d(t)]$. This behavior is consistent with the heuristic proposed in Section 9.2. In the geometric-demand case too, $r^*(t)$ changes in the same direction as $E[d(t)]$, but the changes are more pronounced; indeed, $r^*(t)$ is nearly proportional to $E[d(t)]$. (Here, the standard deviation of $d(t)$ is no longer nearly constant; instead, it is close to $E[d(t)]$.

Next, we examine two systems with $E[d(t)]$ fixed at 30 but changing $c(t)$, as in Figure 9.4.3. The results are displayed in Figure 9.5.5. Both $r^*(t)$ and $s^*(t)$ anticipate changes in $c(t)$, much like the optimal base-stock level in the linear-cost case. But $r^*(t)$ changes somewhat less than $s^*(t)$, so the difference $q^*(t) = s^*(t) - r^*(t)$ grows and shrinks considerably as the data change, especially in the geometric-demand case. In contrast to demand changes, cost changes seem to have strong effects on all the policy variables.

Myopic-like heuristics for the stationary-cost, nonstationary-demand case have been developed by Askin [1981] and Bollapragada and Morton [1994a]. Numerical tests indicate that they perform well; their costs are only a few percent above optimal.

9.5.3 *The Infinite-Horizon Problem*

Now, suppose the horizon T is infinite and the data are stationary. The analogue of Theorem 9.4.3 turns out to be true: A stationary (r, s) policy is optimal, both for $\gamma < 1$ and $\gamma = 1$.

FIGURE 9.5.4

Optimal (r, s) policies (stationary costs).

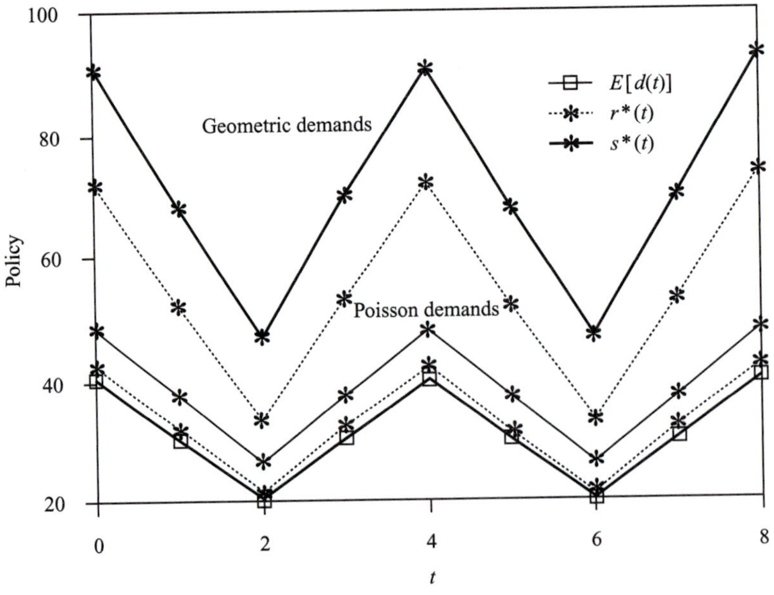

FIGURE 9.5.5

Optimal (r, s) policies (stationary demands).

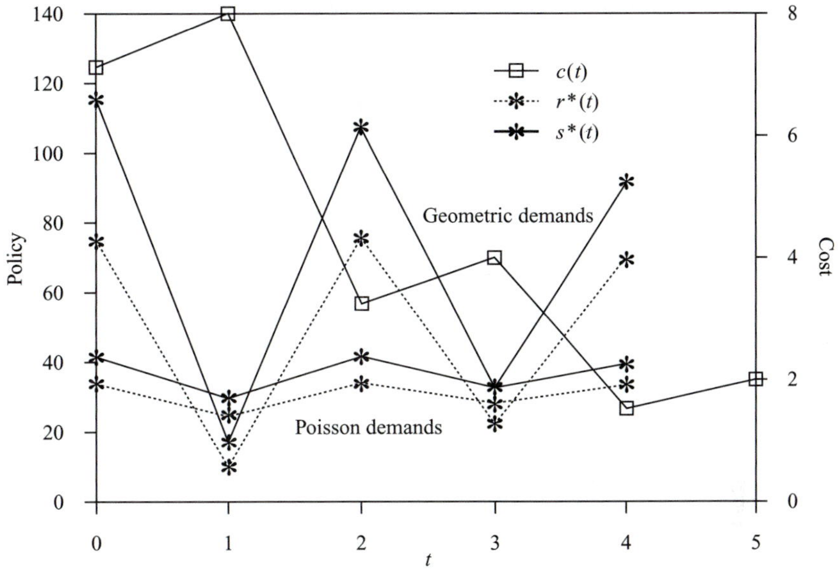

It is quite difficult to prove this fact, however. Nothing like the simple, direct proof of Theorem 9.4.3 works here.

The alternative approach, using Theorem 9.4.4, *can* be adapted to this model. The argument is essentially the same as that of Section 9.4.3. Certain details, however, are more problematic here. For instance, it is *not* generally true that the optimal policy variables $r^*(n)$ and $s^*(n)$ are constant, as in Lemma 9.4.5(*b*), nor even monotonic. However, they are bounded, so the sequence $\{[r^*(n), s^*(n)]\}$ has a limit point. This, it turns out, is enough. Any such limit point describes an optimal policy.

To compute an optimal (r^*, s^*), requires an algorithm. The situation is essentially the same as in the continuous-time setting: In the special case where the demand d is either 0 or 1, an (r, s) policy reduces to an (r, q) policy. To determine the best such policy, use Algorithm Optimize_rq of Section 6.5.4, with minor adjustments to account for discrete time. Otherwise, use the similar method mentioned in Section 6.6, similarly adjusted.

Alternatively, employ one of the algorithms for general dynamic programs. The simplest one, conceptually, is called *successive approximations:* Perform the finite-horizon recursion (9.4.14) to (9.4.16) (modified to include the fixed cost k, of course) for increasingly large n, until an appropriate termination condition is met. The terminal policy $[r^*(n), s^*(n)]$ estimates (r^*, s^*).

The upper bounds of Theorem 9.5.6 now become stationary; denote them by s^{++} and r^+. Thus, $s^*(n) \leq s^{++}$ and $r^*(n) \leq r^+$ for all n, and so $s^* \leq s^{++}$ and $r^* \leq r^+$. These bounds directly reflect the data of the problem, as discussed above.

Because it is hard to compute the optimal policy, researchers have investigated workable approximations. Here is a good one, called the *power approximation:* Assume $\gamma = 1$, and let $\nu = E[d]$ and $\sigma^2 = V[d]$. Set

$$q = 1.30\nu^{0.494}(k/h)^{0.506}[1+(\sigma/\nu)^2]^{0.116}$$

$$\theta = [(q/\sigma)(h/b)]^{1/2}$$

$$r = 0.973\nu + (0.183/\theta + 1.063 - 2.192\theta)\sigma$$

$$s = r + q$$

These formulas were obtained by solving a wide range of models, choosing a plausible functional form, and fitting the parameters with regression analysis. (The approximation works well provided q/ν is not too small, say above 1.5. Otherwise, use the following revision: Compute the optimal base-stock level, s^+. If $s^+ < s$, then replace s by s^+ and r by $s^+ - q$.)

Notice that the expression for q closely resembles the EOQ formula. The initial constant 1.30 is not far from $\sqrt{2}$, and the exponents of ν and k/h are close to ½. The last term is an inflation factor to account for demand variance. In broad terms, therefore, the formula is consistent with the bounds and numerical example of Section 6.5.3. This resemblance is remarkable, for the context there differs in several ways (e.g., continuous time). In the formula for r, the coefficient of ν is nearly 1; the reorder point moves in tandem with the mean demand.

9.5.4 Extensions

What happens if we extend the model as in Sections 9.4.6 to 9.4.8?

In the lost-sales case it is still true that an (r, s) policy is optimal. The $r^*(t)$ and $s^*(t)$ should be non-negative, of course, and we impose that as a constraint. In the one-period problem, for example, it is always true that $s^* \geq 0$, but if no $x \geq 0$ satisfies (9.5.2), set $r^* = 0$.

With the profit objective of Section 9.4.7, everything works fine, as above.

For the imperfect-quality model of Section 9.4.8 we do not know what the optimal policy looks like; as yet there are no results comparable to Theorem 9.4.8.

An analogue of the linear-inflation heuristic seems to work well for the stationary infinite-horizon model: Choose (r, s) and a constant β somehow. Then, if $x \leq r$, order $z = (s - x)/\beta$. We do not know how to extend the equilibrium analysis of Section 9.4.8.3 to help select the parameters. It seems quite effective, however, simply to treat the yield as deterministic. That is, choose the optimal (r^*, s^*) in the no-defects model, and $\beta = E[\xi]$.

9.6 Leadtimes

9.6.1 Constant Leadtime

Suppose there is a constant, positive-integer leadtime L. An order placed at t arrives by the end of period $t + L - 1$, in time to be counted in the net inventory at time $t + L$. As we shall see, this leadtime alters some of the data of the model, but not its overall form. *All* the qualitative results of the last two sections remain valid.

In these terms the original model has leadtime $L = 1$. As mentioned in Section 9.3.1, some writers define "leadtime" a bit differently, so that the original model's leadtime is 0, and the leadtime here is $L - 1$. This is a difference in labeling, not substance.

We slightly alter the timing conventions of Section 9.3: The cost $\hat{C}(t, \cdot)$ now occurs precisely *at* time t, not before. Also, assume that we pay the order cost, not when we *place* an order, but rather when we *receive* it, i.e., time L later. So, the effective order cost is $\gamma^L[k(t)\delta(z(t)) + c(t)z(t)]$. (These changes make the results come out a bit neater. They matter, of course, only when $\gamma < 1$. In the original model with $L = 1$ the only effect is to multiply every cost factor by γ, so the solution remains unchanged.) By the way, purchase costs commonly *are* paid on receipt of goods, not when the order is initiated. There are exceptions, e.g., some international transactions. It is easy to revise the results for those cases.

The leadtime imposes a lag between our actions and their effects. There is nothing we can do to influence the net inventory, and hence the holding-penalty costs, at times 0 through $L - 1$. So, it is reasonable to omit those costs from the problem. The cost at time L, moreover, can be affected *only* by the initial order $z(0)$; later orders, including $z(L)$ itself, take effect only after L. There is nothing lost, therefore, if we imagine that time L's inventory-backorder cost occurs *at* time 0.

In general, at time t, the current order $z(t)$ directly affects the net inventory at time $t + L$, and no later order does so. It makes sense, then, to *reassign* the corresponding inventory-backorder cost to point t. (This is an intuitive rationale; Section 9.6.2 presents a rigorous one.)

To implement this new accounting scheme, redefine the state and control variables:

$x(t)$ = inventory position at time t, before ordering
$y(t)$ = inventory position at time t, after ordering

With these definitions, the system dynamics remain as before, namely,

$$y(t) = x(t) + z(t)$$

$$x(t + 1) = y(t) - d(t)$$

Also, let us use a new symbol for the net inventory:

$\hat{x}(t)$ = net inventory at time t

The cost assigned to time t is now $\gamma^L\hat{C}(t + L, \hat{x}(t + L))$. (This assumes that the original cost factors $h(t + L)$ and $b(t + L)$ measure actual, undiscounted costs at time $t + L$. To count them correctly at time t, therefore, we discount by the factor γ^L.) We have

$$\hat{x}(t + L) = y(t) - D[t, t + L)$$

where $D[t, t + L)$ is the *leadtime demand* starting at t, specifically,

$$D[t, t + L) = \Sigma_{s=t}^{t+L-1} d(s)$$

Thus, the *expected* inventory-backorder cost at step (2) of time t is $C(t, y(t))$, where we redefine

$$C(t, y) = \gamma^L E[\hat{C}(t + L, y - D[t, t + L))]$$

For finite T this approach makes sense for $t \leq T - L$, but what about times near the horizon? For simplicity, imagine that the horizon extends to time $T + L - 1$; demands continue to occur and inventory-backorder costs continue to accrue until then. So, the same approach works for all $t < T$. Again, the last order is placed at time $T - 1$, and the inventory-backorder cost assigned to $T - 1$ is the actual cost at time $T + L - 1$. Also, for simplicity, assume there is no salvage value at time $T + L$.

Let us formulate the dynamic program as before: Now, $V(t, x)$ means the optimal cost under the revised accounting scheme, excluding the holding-penalty costs before time $t + L$, starting at time t with inventory position x. With the new definitions of V and C, the functional equations (9.4.3) to (9.4.5) or (9.5.5) to (9.5.7) remain valid as stated, except that all order-cost factors are multiplied by γ^L.

We now have a model of precisely the same form as the original. The symbols have new meanings, but that is the only difference. The new $C(t, y)$ is still convex in y. Thus, the main results of Section 9.4 and Section 9.5 still hold: *In the linear-order-cost case, a base-stock policy is optimal; with a fixed order cost, an (r, s) policy is optimal.* The myopic policy for the linear-cost model optimizes the function $C^+(t, y)$, constructed from C as before, and Theorem 9.4.2 remains valid.

Of course, the actual policies reflect the new data. The one-period cost $C(t, y)$ now involves an expectation over demand in L periods, not just one. For instance, in the linear-order-cost model, $s^+(t)$ solves an equation like (9.4.10), but the ccdf of the lead-time demand $D[t, t + L)$ plays the role of $F_D^0(y)$. Thus, the myopic policy is the discrete-time analogue of the heuristic approach of Section 9.2.2. For the reasons given there and in Section 9.4, the myopic policy is usually close to optimal.

In the infinite-horizon problem with stationary data and $k = 0$, the myopic policy *is* optimal, and s^* solves

$$F_D^0(y) = \frac{(c^+ + h)}{(b + h)}$$

as in (9.4.13), where $D = D[0, L)$. Interestingly, only the left-hand side depends on L, not the cost ratio. When $\gamma = 1$, the cost ratio again becomes $1 - \omega$. The solution here is essentially the same as that of equation (6.5.3).

The optimal cost retains the same form as before: For $\gamma = 1$,

$$v^* = C^+(s^*) = cE[d] + C(s^*)$$

For $\gamma < 1$, $V^*(x) = V^{+*}(x) - \gamma^L cx$, where

$$V^{+*}(x) = \begin{cases} \dfrac{C^+(s^*)}{1 - \gamma} & x \leq s^* \\ C^+(x) + \gamma E[V^{+*}(x - d)] & x > s^* \end{cases}$$

Under the normal approximation $C^+(s^*)$ again transparently reflects the system parameters: Letting $\nu = E[D]$ and $\sigma^2 = V[D]$,

$$C^+(s^*) = \gamma^L[\gamma c E[d] + c^+\nu + \sigma(b + h)\phi(z^*)]$$

(The first two terms reduce to $c\nu$ for $L = 1$, because $\nu = E[d]$, but not for $L > 1$.)

9.6.2 Constant Leadtime: Rigorous Argument

We now develop a rigorous justification for the cost-assignment scheme and the simple dynamic-programming formulation above.

Suppose we find ourselves at time t. What is the current state of the system? That is, what useful information about the past and the present is available? We need to track outstanding orders, in addition to the current net inventory. Specifically, for $L > 1$, let

$z_l(t)$ = order placed l periods ago, i.e., at time $t - l$, $l = 1, \ldots, L - 1$
$\mathbf{z}(t) = [z_l(t)]_{l=1}^{L-1}$.

The state is thus the pair $[\hat{x}(t), \mathbf{z}(t)]$. (The symbol $z(t)$ without a subscript continues to mean the order at time t. It is *not* part of the vector $\mathbf{z}(t)$. When $L = 1$, as in the original model, there are no outstanding orders, and $\mathbf{z}(t)$ is vacuous.) The dynamics are

$$\hat{x}(t + 1) = \hat{x}(t) + z_{L-1}(t) - d(t)$$

$$\mathbf{z}(t + 1) = [z(t), z_1(t), \ldots, z_{L-2}(t)]$$

In these terms the inventory position is $x(t) = \hat{x}(t) + \Sigma_{l>0} z_l(t)$. Also, define the functions

$$C^l(t, y) = \gamma^l E[C(t + l, y - D[t, t + l))]$$

Notice that $C^0(t, \hat{x}(t)) = \hat{C}(t, \hat{x}(t))$ is the actual (not reassigned) inventory-backorder cost at time t, and $C^L(t, y)$ is $C(t, y)$ defined above.

Define the functions

$\hat{V}(t, \hat{x}, \mathbf{z})$ = optimal cost from time t onward, starting in state $\hat{x}(t) = \hat{x}$ and $\mathbf{z}(t) = \mathbf{z}$
$\hat{C}(t, \hat{x}, \mathbf{z}) = C^0(t, \hat{x}) + C^1(t, \hat{x} + z_{L-1}) + C^2(t, \hat{x} + z_{L-1} + z_{L-2}) + \cdots + C^{L-1}(t, x)$

The latter represents all holding and penalty costs before time $t + L$. At time T, there are no further orders to place, but costs continue to accrue until time $T + L - 1$. These remaining costs are given by $\hat{C}(T, \hat{x}, \mathbf{z})$, and we set

$$\hat{V}(T, \hat{x}, \mathbf{z}) = \hat{C}(T, \hat{x}, \mathbf{z}) \qquad (9.6.1)$$

For $t < T$ the $\hat{V}(t, \cdot, \cdot)$ obey the functional equations

$$\hat{V}(t, \hat{x}, \mathbf{z}) = \min_{z \geq 0} \{\gamma^L k(t)\delta(z) + \gamma^L c(t) z + C^0(t, \hat{x}) \qquad (9.6.2)$$
$$+ \gamma E[\hat{V}(t + 1, \hat{x} + z_{L-1} - d(t), (z, z_1, \ldots, z_{L-2}))]\}$$

[Alternatively, we can set $\hat{V}(T + L - 1, \hat{x}, \mathbf{z}) = 0$ and apply (9.6.2) for all $t < T + L - 1$. For $t \geq T$, the optimal $z = 0$; an order placed so late costs money, since $c(t) \geq 0$, but never arrives. The recursion itself then implies (9.6.1).]

This dynamic program is *very* complex. We now show that it is equivalent to the simpler one above with the single state variable $x = \hat{x} + \Sigma_{l>0} z_l$ and optimal-cost function $V(t, x)$.

THEOREM 9.6.1.

$$\hat{V}(t, \hat{x}, \mathbf{z}) = \hat{C}(t, \hat{x}, \mathbf{z}) + V(t, x) \qquad 0 \leq t \leq T$$

Moreover, the optimal order quantity z in (9.6.2) is the same one that achieves the minimum in $V(t, x)$.

PROOF. We argue by induction on t: The result is true for $t = T$, by $V(T, x) = 0$ and (9.6.1). Suppose it is true for $t + 1$. Using this induction hypothesis, and the fact that

$$C^l(t, y) = \gamma E[C^{l-1}(t + 1, y - d(t))]$$

(9.6.2) becomes

$$\begin{aligned}\hat{V}(t, \hat{x}, \mathbf{z}) &= \min_{z \geq 0} \{\gamma^L k(t)\delta(z) + \gamma^L c(t)z + C^0(t, \hat{x}) + \gamma E[\hat{C}(t + 1, \hat{x} + z_{L-1} - d(t), \\ &\qquad (z, z_1, \ldots, z_{L-2})) + V(t + 1, x + z - d(t))]\} \\ &= \hat{C}(t, \hat{x}, \mathbf{z}) + \min_{z \geq 0} \{\gamma^L k(t)\delta(z) + \gamma^L c(t)z + C(t, x + z) + \gamma E[V(t + 1, x + z - d(t))]\} \\ &= \hat{C}(t, \hat{x}, \mathbf{z}) + V(t, x)\end{aligned}$$

9.6.3 Other Supply Systems

9.6.3.1 Exogenous, Sequential Systems

Now, suppose the leadtime is a random variable. That is, an order placed at time t will arrive at some future time $t + L(t)$, but $L(t)$ changes randomly over t. We allow $L(t) = 0$; in this case $z(t)$ arrives immediately, and is counted in time t's net inventory $\hat{x}(t)$. Assume that the $L(t)$ arise from a discrete-time version of the exogenous, sequential supply system of Section 7.4. That is, $t + L(t) \leq (t + 1) + L(t + 1)$, so orders never cross in time. Also, we can do nothing to influence the $L(t)$, and they are independent of the demands. Finally, the $L(t)$ are stationary; each has the same (marginal) distribution as a generic leadtime variable L.

Assume too that at each time t we have no information to help us predict $L(t)$. That is, even conditional on what we know at t, $L(t)$ has the same distribution as L. This can mean one of two things: Either $L(t)$ is independent of all past events, so there really is no such information; or, while such information *could* be extracted in principle, we cannot obtain or use it. (In case you are wondering, there *are* systems where $L(t)$ is independent of the past. Here is one: There is a sequence of i.i.d. non-negative-integer random variables $A(t)$. At each time t, all orders that have been outstanding for time $A(t)$ or more arrive immediately; that is, of the orders still outstanding, we receive those placed at $t - A(t)$ or earlier. Thus, $L(t) = \min\{u \geq t : A(u) \leq u - t\}$. The constant-leadtime model is the special case where all $A(t) = L$.)

Let us adapt the cost-accounting scheme above to this stochastic setting: *If* we knew that $L(t) = l$, it would make sense to assign to time t the holding-penalty cost at time $t + l$, by the argument for the constant-leadtime case. So, we assign a *fraction* of this cost to t, the fraction Pr $\{L = l\}$, and we do the same for every $l \geq 0$. (Again, the rationale here is intuitive. The idea can be supported rigorously, but we shall not do so.)

The actual cost at each fixed time u is distributed among earlier times $u - l$ with these same weights. Its cost is left unassigned with probability Pr $\{L > u\}$. This is exactly the probability that the order at time 0 arrives after u. Thus, this scheme, like the original one, omits those costs we cannot influence. As for terminal effects, assume that demands continue to occur and costs to accrue until the end of the last leadtime, i.e., until time $(T - 1) + L(T - 1)$. (This last assumption is not really necessary, but it simplifies the notation.)

We still pay for orders on receipt, so the effective order cost is $E[\gamma^L][k(t)\delta(z(t)) + c(t)z(t)]$. The expected inventory-backorder cost at time t now becomes $C(t, y(t))$, where

$$C(t, y) = E[\gamma^L \hat{C}(t + L, y - D[t, t + L))]$$

The expectation is over L as well as the demands. This function $C(t, y)$ is convex in y, for it is a positive-weighted average of convex functions. With this new C, the dynamic-programming formulation is precisely the same as before. So, again, all the previous results on optimal and myopic policies remain valid.

In the stationary, infinite-horizon case the cost function becomes

$$C(y) = E[\gamma^L \hat{C}(y - D))]$$

With $\gamma = 1$ this reduces to

$$C(y) = E[\hat{C}(y - D)]$$

and the optimal base-stock level s^* satisfies

$$F_D^0(y) = 1 - \omega$$

The random variable D is again $D[0, L)$, the demand over L periods, but now L is random. This is precisely analogous to the leadtime-demand random variable of Section 7.4. The optimal cost $cE[d] + C(s^*)$ now reflects the leadtime's variance as well as its mean, as in Chapter 7. (When $\gamma < 1$, s^* again solves a simple equation, but its form is a bit different from before, because of the random discount term γ^L. See Problem 9.13.)

9.6.3.2 Limited-Capacity Systems

Let us turn to a different model, a discrete-time analogue of the limited-capacity supply system of Section 7.3. There is now an upper limit $z_+(t)$ on the order quantity at time t. With a linear order cost, it turns out that a base-stock policy is still optimal. (See Problem 9.4.) Of course, $s^*(t)$ is different from, typically larger than, that of the original uncapacitated model.

This result remains valid for several extensions of the model: We can have limited capacity *and* a constant leadtime. Or, $z_+(t)$ can be random, realized at the same time as $d(t)$; here, if we order $z(t)$, we actually receive min $\{z(t), z_+(t)\}$. In the fixed-order-cost model, however, it is *not* always true that an (r, s) policy is optimal.

Also, a base-stock policy is optimal for the infinite-horizon model with stationary data. (Certain mild regularity conditions are needed; for instance, in the case $\gamma = 1$, we must assume that $E[d] < z_+$.) In general, exact policy evaluation and optimization are difficult.

There is a good approximation, however: Assume $\gamma = 1$. Let $u(t) = s - x(t)$, and let u be the corresponding steady-state random variable. This quantity plays the same role as D in the unlimited-capacity model, namely, $C(y) = E[\hat{C}(y - u)]$, and s^* solves $F_u^0(y) = 1 - \omega$. (In other words, $u(t)$ is the occupancy of a related discrete-time queue.) The *tail* of u, it turns out, is approximately exponential. That is, there are certain constants K and θ, such that $F_u^0(y) \approx Ke^{-y/\theta}$ for large y. (There are tractable numerical methods to estimate these constants; see Glasserman [1997].) Consequently,

$$s^* \approx \theta[ln\ (K) - ln\ (1 - \omega)]$$

$$C(s^*) \approx \theta h[(1 - \frac{E[u]}{\theta}) + ln\ (K) - ln\ (1 - \omega)]$$

This approximation is very accurate when ω is near 1. This is the discrete-time analogue of the exponential approximation of Section 7.3.11.

9.6.3.3 Independent Leadtimes

What about independent leadtimes, as in Section 7.2? There is no general optimality theory for such systems, to our knowledge. Such a theory would require a detailed scenario describing *when* we observe the leadtimes, or more generally how we obtain information about them. There are many alternatives. Each leadtime could be observed at the moment it begins, or ends. Or, partial information could be revealed during the leadtime. The optimal policy is probably different in each case, but complicated in every one.

Section 7.2 made no such assumptions, but that is because base-stock and (r, q) policies do not use leadtime information in any way. These are heuristic methods for what are, in fact, very complex problems.

For simplicity, let us return to the constant-leadtime case.

9.6.4 Relation to Continuous-Time Models

Suppose for the moment that time is continuous. The data are stationary, demand is a compound-Poisson process, there are no scale economies, and the leadtime is a positive constant. It turns out that a base-stock policy is indeed optimal, under either the discounted- or average-cost criterion. There are several ways to demonstrate this fact. We shall sketch three of them, omitting formal proofs:

First, the cost-reassignment scheme above is valid in continuous time. Thus, the function $C(y)$ above measures the inventory-backorder cost rate with $y(t) = IP(t) = y$. Then, the simple proof of Theorem 9.4.3 can be applied with only minor notational adjustments.

Second, we can discretize time. For any fixed period length we obtain a discrete-time model, and all the results above hold. (Of course, the discrete-time model's leadtime, one-period demand, and discount rate depend on the choice of period length.) Now, take a sequence of such models with successively shorter periods. The continuous-time model is the limit as the period length goes to zero. The optimality result, it turns out, is preserved in the limit.

Third, we can embed the process at demand epochs. This approach directly transforms the continuous-time problem into an equivalent discrete-time model. (The idea is essentially the same as constructing a discrete-time Markov chain to represent a continuous-time one, as discussed in Section C.5 of Appendix C. The continuous-time model is one instance of a general class called *semi-Markov decision processes* or *continuous-time dynamic programs.* The embedding technique is a standard one in that arena.) This discrete-time model has the same form as those above, so a base-stock policy is optimal.

The second and third approaches can be applied to other models above and below. (With rare exceptions, however, the first cannot.) With a fixed cost k, for instance, an (r, s) policy is optimal. In the Poisson-demand case, of course, this reduces to an (r, q) policy.

In sum, *the policies we chose to evaluate in Chapter 6 really are optimal,* at least for Poisson and compound-Poisson demand. Therefore, *the optimization methods of Section 6.5 find the best policy overall.*

Return to the discrete-time setting for the rest of the chapter.

9.6.5 Lost Sales and the Curse of Dimensionality

(No, this is not a new action movie, but the subject is just as exciting. Well, almost.) Suppose that unmet demands are lost instead of backlogged. Focus on the linear-order-cost case. Recall from Section 9.4.6 that, for the original scenario with $L = 1$, a base-stock policy is optimal. For $L > 1$, however, this is *not* so. The net-inventory dynamics now become (using the notation of Section 9.6.2)

$$\hat{x}(t + 1) = [\hat{x}(t) + z_{L-1}(t) - d(t)]^{+} \tag{9.6.3}$$

This relation is *nonlinear,* and that complicates things tremendously. It is still true that the current order $z(t)$ affects holding-penalty costs only at time $t + L$ and beyond, so we can ignore the earlier costs. However, because of the nonlinear dynamics, we can no longer express $\hat{x}(t + L)$ in terms of the inventory position $x(t)$ and $z(t)$. What matters is not just the *amount* of stock in the pipeline, but also *when* that stock is scheduled to arrive. (We encountered the same difficulty in Section 7.4.3.1.)

Consequently, the simple approach of Section 9.6.1 breaks down. Indeed, it is essentially impossible to solve the model exactly. We shall explain why and then explore heuristics.

Let us formulate the dynamic program. First, reassign time $(t + L)$'s holding-penalty cost to t: Given the current state $(\hat{x}, \mathbf{z})$ and the current order z, (9.6.3) can be rewritten as

$$\hat{x}(t + l + 1) = [\hat{x}(t + l) + z_{L-1-l} - d(t + l)]^{+} \qquad 0 \leq l < L \tag{9.6.4}$$

where $\hat{x}(t) = \hat{x}$ for $l = 0$ and $z_0 = z$ for $l = L - 1$. (9.6.4) recursively defines the random variables $\hat{x}(t + l)$. The expected cost at time $t + L$ as viewed from time t, then, is

$$C(t, \hat{x}, \mathbf{z}, z) = \gamma^{L} E[\hat{C}(t + L, \hat{x}(t + L - 1) + z - d(t + L - 1))]$$

The expectation is over all the $d(t + l)$, $0 \leq l < L$; here, $d(t + L - 1)$ appears explicitly, and the others are included implicitly through (9.6.4). Now, let $V(t, \hat{x}, \mathbf{z})$ be the minimal expected cost from t onward, omitting holding-penalty costs before time $t + L$. Then,

$$V(T, \hat{x}, \mathbf{z}) = 0$$

$$V(t, \hat{x}, \mathbf{z}) = \min_{z \geq 0} \{\gamma^{L} c(t) z + C(t, \hat{x}, \mathbf{z}, z) + \gamma E[V(t + 1, [\hat{x} + z_{L-1} - d(t)]^{+}, (z, z_1, \ldots, z_{L-2}))]\}$$

This recursion looks much like (9.6.2). Unfortunately, because the dynamics and hence the one-period cost C are so complex, we *cannot* reduce the state to the single variable x.

In principle, once again, the recursion prescribes a computational procedure to find the optimal policy. However, the state variable is now an L-vector. It is a sad fact that, in general, dynamic programs with high-dimensional states are *very* hard, indeed virtually impossible, to solve. (This point is vividly expressed by the phrase, *the curse of dimensionality.* If we discretize and truncate the state vector, using n values for each component, say, then the total number of states is n^L. The computational effort required is at least proportional to this number, which grows exponentially in L.)

Thus, *in practice,* there is no way to find the true optimal policy. Moreover, little is known about its structure; it is probably very complex and hard to implement. If we can't optimize, are there heuristic approaches that work well? Fortunately, the answer is yes. For simplicity, focus on the stationary, infinite-horizon model.

The key idea is to adapt the myopic approach to this system. Let $t = 0$ indicate the current time, so (9.6.4) becomes

$$\hat{x}(l+1) = [\hat{x}(l) + z_{L-1-l} - d(l)]^+ \qquad 0 \leq l < L \tag{9.6.5}$$

and the one-period cost becomes

$$C(\hat{x}, \mathbf{z}, z) = \gamma^L E[\hat{C}(\hat{x}(L-1) + z - d(L-1))]$$

Define the function

$$C^+(\hat{x}, \mathbf{z}, z) = \gamma^L c\{(\hat{x} + z) - \gamma E[\hat{x}(L)]\} + C(\hat{x}, \mathbf{z}, z)$$

The last term C is the (expected) holding-penalty cost. The first approximates the effect of z on current and future order costs. (The rationale for this approximation is subtle; we omit it.) So, C^+ includes all the short-term costs of the current order. The *myopic policy* selects z to minimize C^+. Numerical studies have found that this approach works quite well.

The myopic policy is *much* harder to implement here than in the backlog case. At each time point we must minimize C^+ anew. (In principle, we could determine the best z for every possible $(\hat{x}, \mathbf{z})$ in advance, but that would be tedious.) Just to evaluate C^+, we must use (9.6.5) recursively to compute the distributions of $\hat{x}(L-1)$ and then $\hat{x}(L)$. Still, this is much easier than computing the true optimal policy.

It is interesting and useful to explore the approach in detail: We can rewrite C^+ in the form

$$\begin{aligned} C^+(\hat{x}, \mathbf{z}, z) = \gamma^L\{&c(\hat{x} + z) + (h - \gamma c)E[\hat{x}(L-1) + z - d(L-1)] \\ &+ (b + h - \gamma c)\, E[[\hat{x}(L-1) + z - d(L-1)]^-]\} \end{aligned}$$

Assuming (as in Section 9.4.6) $b + h - \gamma c \geq 0$, this function is convex in z. So, once we have the distribution of $\hat{x}(L-1) - d(L-1)$, the minimization over z is fairly routine. The myopically optimal z satisfies $\partial C^+/\partial z \geq 0$, and $\partial C^+/\partial z = 0$ for $z > 0$. Equivalently, if

$$\Pr\{\hat{x}(L) = 0\}|_{z=0} \leq \frac{c^+ + h}{b + h - \gamma c}$$

set $z = 0$, and otherwise find $z > 0$ such that

$$\Pr\{\hat{x}(L) = 0\} = \frac{c^{+} + h}{b + h - \gamma c} \tag{9.6.6}$$

This relation generalizes the exact optimality condition for $L = 1$ in Section 9.4.6.

It turns out that the myopic policy leads the system to an "equilibrium" where (9.6.6) holds in every period. That is, perhaps after some initial periods with no orders, the system arrives at a state where (9.6.6) holds, and from then on (9.6.6) continues to hold. (See Problem 9.14.) Thus, the myopic policy aims to maintain a *constant stockout probability,* just as a base-stock policy does in a backlog system.

Let s_0^+ solve $F_D^0(y) = (c^+ + h)/(b + h - \gamma c)$. The myopic policy is related but not identical to the base-stock policy with base-stock level s_0^+. Letting x be the inventory position and $y = x + z$, it is clear from (9.6.5) that $\hat{x}(L) \geq y - D$, so

$$\Pr\{\hat{x}(L) = 0\} \leq \Pr\{y - D \leq 0\} = F_D^0(y)$$

Like the base-stock policy, the myopic policy orders nothing when $x \geq s_0^+$, and if $x < s_0^+$, the new y never exceeds s_0^+. However, y may be less than s_0^+. Thus, the myopic policy aims to keep the inventory position at *or below* s_0^+.

The two policies differ mainly in how they respond to unusually large or small demands. Recall, in a backlog system, a stationary base-stock policy can be viewed as a demand-replacement rule. The same is true in a lost-sales system, except that lost sales are not counted; the base-stock policy replaces filled demands. When the prior demand is large, the myopic policy typically orders *less* than the base-stock policy. That demand will likely lead to lost sales, now or in the near future, and once lost they are gone for good; a large order arriving at $t + L$ cannot help. Conversely, when the prior demand is very small, the base-stock policy orders that same small amount, but the myopic policy typically orders *more.* In sum, the sequence of orders generated by the myopic policy tends to be *smoother* than the filled demands themselves. (This property makes intuitive sense. It is probably true of the optimal policy too, but no one knows for sure.)

There are simpler heuristics than the myopic policy. The simplest is a base-stock policy. Unfortunately, except for special cases, we do not know how to evaluate such policies. (We have seen one case, the continuous-time model of Section 7.2.3, where base-stock policies *can* be evaluated and the best one selected readily.) Also, it is possible to approximate the myopic policy using simpler calculations. This approach is intermediate in complexity between a base-stock policy and the myopic policy. See Problem 9.15.

What about the overall performance of lost-sales systems? In the backorder case we understand the effects of the leadtime, the demand variance, and other basic parameters. Unfortunately, to our knowledge, there are no comparable results for the lost-sales case. It is a fair guess that these same parameters affect performance in similar ways, but this is just a guess.

This entire discussion presumes a constant leadtime. Certain limited-capacity supply systems are actually easier to comprehend. Consider the continuous-time model of Section 7.3.4 with Poisson demand, a single processor, no scale economies, and lost sales. Assume that we have direct control over the processor, as in Section 7.3.10.2, so we decide at each instant whether to turn it on or off. It turns out that a simple base-stock policy is optimal: For some s^* keep the processor on when inventory is less than s^* and off otherwise. The methods of Section 7.3.4 can thus be used to evaluate alternative policies and to find the best.

9.6.6 Profit Maximization

Even with $L > 1$, the profit-maximization model, like that of Section 9.4.7, is equivalent to the corresponding cost-minimization model.

In the lost-sales case, with $z(t) = z$, the number of units sold just before time $t + L$ is now

$$\begin{aligned} &\min \{\hat{x}(t + L - 1) + z, d(t + L - 1)\} \\ &= d(t + L - 1) - [d(t + L - 1) - \hat{x}(t + L - 1) - z]^+ \end{aligned}$$

so the expected discounted revenue is

$$R(t, \hat{x}, \mathbf{z}, z) = \gamma^L p(t + L)E[d(t + L - 1) - [d(t + L - 1) - \hat{x}(t + L - 1) - z]^+]$$

Subtract this from $C(t, \hat{x}, \mathbf{z}, z)$ to get $-P(t, \hat{x}, \mathbf{z}, z)$. This function has the same form as C. Thus, to account for revenue, just replace C by $-P$ in the model above.

In the backlog case, we cannot influence revenues at times $t < L$, so ignore them. The number of units sold at time $t + L$ is

$$\begin{aligned} &\min \{\hat{x}(t + L - 1) + z, d(t + L - 1)\} + [\hat{x}(t + L - 1)]^- \\ &= d(t + L - 1) - [\hat{x}(t + L)]^- + [\hat{x}(t + L - 1)]^- \end{aligned}$$

Ignore the last term for $t = 0$, and for $t > 0$ reassign it to $t + L - 1$. Next, reassign all of time $t + L$'s revenue to t. The expected revenue assigned to t, then, is $R(t, y(t))$, where now

$$R(t, y) = \gamma^L p(t + L)E[d(t + L - 1)] - \gamma^L p^+(t + L)E[[y - D[t, t + L)]^-]$$

From this point on, proceed as in Section 9.4.7. Provided the $p(t)$ satisfy (9.4.19), $-P^+(t, y)$ is again convex in y. So, the structure of the optimal policy remains the same as before, a base-stock or an (r, s) policy, depending on the order-cost function.

9.6.7 Imperfect Quality

What happens to the stochastic-yield model of Section 9.4.8 when $L > 1$? The state is now $[\hat{x}(t), \mathbf{z}(t)]$ and the dynamics (9.4.20) become

$$\hat{x}(t + 1) = \hat{x}(t) + \Xi[z_{L-1}(t)] - d(t)$$

As in the lost-sales model, the intricate dynamics make it impossible to reduce the state to a single variable. Thus, because of the curse of dimensionality, we cannot hope to solve the model exactly.

Let us try to adapt the linear-inflation heuristic: First, we would like to aggregate the state variables into one, analogous to the inventory position. But this is problematic, because the yields of outstanding orders are uncertain, as in Section 7.4.3.2. In the spirit of linearity, let us *deflate* the outstanding orders, i.e., multiply each one by a constant factor, and add the result to the net inventory. One reasonable deflation factor is $E[\xi]$ (the correct value for the deterministic-yield case). In sum, we redefine $x(t) = \hat{x}(t) + E[\xi]\ \Sigma_{l>0} z_l(t)$. This adjusted inventory position replaces the stock on order by its expected yield.

The overall heuristic uses this state variable to determine orders as before. In the stationary, linear-order-cost model, for example, fix s and β, and set $z(t) = [s - x(t)]^+/\beta$. It is possible, but messy, to extend the equilibrium analysis of Section 9.4.8.3 to $L > 1$. Or, we can treat *all* the yields as deterministic. That is, set s^* as in the no-defects model and $\beta = E[\xi]$. Perhaps surprisingly, this crude approach seems to work fairly well. In any event, it is the best alternative we know of to date.

9.7 World-Driven Demand

9.7.1 The Model

Until now we have assumed that the $d(t)$ are independent. Think about what this means: We know their distributions at the beginning. As time passes, demands are realized one by one. When we arrive at time t, the earlier realizations do *not* alter our initial beliefs about $d(t)$ or subsequent demands. This scenario is quite special.

Let us now explore a richer, more realistic demand model: Here, events occur as time passes, events which do affect future demands. Put another way, our information about the future evolves over time. Expressed yet another way, there is some system whose behavior drives demands.

To represent the significant events, or our information, or the system driving demands, we use a discrete-time Markov process $\mathbf{W} = \{W(t)\}$, called the *world.* The distribution of $d(t)$ now depends on the current value of $W(t) = w$. This means that the $d(t)$ are no longer independent; they are influenced by the $W(t)$, and the Markovian dependence among the $W(t)$ induces dependence in the $d(t)$. We even allow $d(t)$ and the next world state $W(t + 1)$ to be driven by common events, so $d(t)$ and $W(t + 1)$ may be dependent. We assume, however, that these are the *only* sources of dependence. That is, conditional on $W(t)$, the pair $[d(t), W(t + 1)]$ is independent of all past events. Equivalently, $(\mathbf{W}, \mathbf{D})$ is a Markov process (where $\mathbf{D}$ means cumulative demand, as usual).

This is the discrete-time analogue of the continuous-time world-driven process of Section 6.3. All the examples mentioned there (the weather, the economy, etc.) can be represented by using this construction. Indeed, the model here captures some of those situations better or more clearly:

For instance, $\mathbf{W}$ can represent competitive conditions for a new product or a mature one facing possible obsolescence. In those scenarios $\mathbf{W}$ includes short-term *transient* events. Once a product becomes obsolete, it usually stays so. Now, a continuous-time model can represent transient effects perfectly well, but the long-run average-cost objective, the focus of Chapter 6, is too crude to reflect them. Averaging suppresses everything that happens before obsolescence, during the most interesting part of the product's life cycle. The discounted-cost criterion does properly reflect the transient preobsolescence stage.

Likewise, Section 6.3 assumes that $\mathbf{W}$ is stationary. Here, that is not necessary (until we discuss the stationary, infinite-horizon model below). Thus, $\mathbf{W}$ can include demand-driving factors that change systematically over time, such as the weather over several seasons.

Also, many standard forecasting techniques embody a world-driven demand model, explicitly or implicitly. The most familiar techniques work in discrete time. For example, the popular exponential-smoothing method essentially views the world as scalar variable $W(t)$, representing the current demand forecast itself or some simple transformation of it, which evolves according to a Markov process. More elaborate techniques, designated by the acronym ARMA, model $W(t)$ as a vector. See Section C.6.4 of Appendix C.

Here is a related model: Demand has a stationary distribution of some particular, known form, but with an unknown parameter. For example, we may know that demand has a Poisson distribution, but not its actual mean. Here, $W(t)$ represents our current estimate of the parameter (more precisely, a sufficient statistic for it). The dynamics of $\mathbf{W}$ include some mechanism for updating the estimate (usually Bayes' rule) to incorporate each additional demand observation.

As we shall see, the qualitative results of earlier sections remain valid. For instance, in the linear-order-cost case, a base-stock policy is optimal. However, just as the optimal base-stock level depends on t in the original model, so here it reflects *all* relevant information about the future, namely, the current world state w as well as t.

9.7.2 Formulation and Analysis

Assume that the leadtime is the positive-integer constant L. Following Section 9.6, the one-period cost function is

$$C(t, w, y) = \gamma^L E[\hat{C}(t + L, y - D[t, t + L)) \mid W(t) = w]$$

Except in special cases, this function is hard to compute exactly. (The leadtime demand $D[t, t + L)$ is a complicated random variable, as in Section 6.3; it includes the effects of future values of $\mathbf{W}$, conditional on $W(t) = w$. Sometimes, depending on the form of $(\mathbf{W}, \mathbf{D})$, it is possible to estimate the moments of $D[t, t + L)$, and to use them to approximate C. Problem 9.16 computes the moments for the exponential-smoothing model, and Section 9.7.3 below illustrates their uses.) For now, however, we are concerned more with the *form* of the one-period cost, and that remains simple. The function $C(t, w, y)$ is *convex* in y for each (t, w).

Consider first the linear-order-cost case ($k = 0$) for a finite horizon T. Think through the dynamic-programming logic, applying the principle of optimality, to arrive at the following formulation:

$$V(T, w, x) = -\gamma^L c(T)x \tag{9.7.1}$$

$$H(t, w, y) = \gamma^L c(t)y + C(t, w, y) + \gamma E[V(t + 1, w', y - d(t)) \mid W(t) = w] \tag{9.7.2}$$

$$V(t, w, x) = -\gamma^L c(t)x + \min \{H(t, w, y) : y \geq x\} \tag{9.7.3}$$

The expectation in (9.7.2) is over the demand $d(t)$ *and* the next state $W(t + 1) = w'$, both conditional on $W(t) = w$. Again, $H(t, w, y)$ measures all the relevant costs, present and future, if we choose $y(t) = y$ at step (2) of time t. These equations describe a recursive scheme to compute an optimal policy.

Virtually the same argument as in Theorem 9.4.1 demonstrates that *a (state-dependent) base-stock policy is optimal:* In the induction, assume that $V(t + 1, w, x)$ is convex in x for each w. Write the expectation in (9.7.2) in two steps, as

$$E_{w'}\{E_{d(t)}[V(t + 1, w', y - d(t)) \mid W(t) = w, W(t + 1) = w']\}$$

The inner expectation is convex in y, as usual. The outer expectation is just a weighted average of convex functions, so it too is convex in y. Thus, the entire expectation preserves the convexity of $V(t + 1, w, x)$, and so $H(t, w, y)$ is convex in y. Consequently, a base-stock policy is optimal. The optimal base-stock level $s^*(t, w)$ is the smallest value of y that minimizes $H(t, w, y)$. Because H depends on w as well as t, so does s^*. Also, $V(t, w, x)$ is convex in x for all w, completing the induction.

Next, consider the infinite-horizon problem with stationary data. A base-stock policy is again optimal. The optimal base-stock level is $s^* = s^*(w)$, which depends on the current state w, but is stationary in time. (The proof is similar to the second argument for Theorem 9.4.3, the harder one involving Theorem 9.4.4.)

In the fixed-order-cost model ($k > 0$), an (r, s) policy is optimal. With finite horizon T the optimal policy variables are $r^*(t, w)$ and $s^*(t, w)$. Both depend on w as well as t. The proof follows closely that of Theorem 9.5.5. For infinite T and stationary data, $r^* = r^*(w)$ and $s^* = s^*(w)$.

By the way, all these results remain valid if we replace $c(t)$ by $c(t, w)$ in the formulation above. Here, the order cost depends on the current world state $W(t) = w$ as well as t. (We still pay for goods on receipt, but the cost is determined when the order is placed.) Likewise, the fixed cost can be $k = k(t, w)$ (subject to certain restrictions, along the lines of Problem 9.12.) Thus, we have a full theory of world-driven economics *and* demand.

Also, the results remain valid when the leadtime L is stochastic, as in Section 9.6.3.1. The calculation of $C(t, w, y)$ is different, and the γ^L factors above become $E[\gamma^L]$.

To summarize, the *form* of the optimal policy, whether a base-stock or an (r, s) policy, depends on the nature of the order cost, specifically on the presence or absence of a fixed cost. Regardless of the policy form, the optimal *values* of the policy variables reflect *information* about the present and future. That information includes the time index t, when, but only when, t is relevant. In an infinite-horizon setting with stationary data, t is irrelevant, for the time points all look alike, so the policy variables are stationary, independent of t. Otherwise, t is relevant; it provides information about time-varying data or horizon effects. Likewise, when there is other relevant information, expressed in the world state w, the policy variables depend on it. (Viewed in this way, the time index is one possibly relevant item of information, but there is nothing special about it.)

To *compute* the optimal policy is not easy, however. As mentioned above, it is hard to calculate $C(t, w, y)$. Even given the one-period cost, the state (w, x) now has at least one additional dimension besides x, so the recursion (9.7.1) to (9.7.3) requires more work than before for each t. The curse of dimensionality appears once again.

In modeling the world-demand system (**W, D**), then, we confront the classic tradeoff between accuracy and tractability. It is tempting to include everything we know about the drivers of demand in the world **W**. When we know a lot, however, the resulting model may be too complex to solve. We must use our best judgment and/or analytical skills to identify the really important factors and include only those.

Things do *not* become substantially simpler in the infinite-horizon model. The most direct approach is successive approximations. This method, mentioned earlier in Section 9.5.3, entails solving a sequence of finite-horizon models with increasingly long horizons.

9.7.3 The Myopic Policy and Cost Approximation

Reconsider the finite-horizon model with linear order costs. Define

$$C^+(t, w, y) = \gamma^{L+1}c(t+1)E[d(t)|W(t)=w] + \gamma^L c^+(t)y + C(t, w, y)$$

and set the myopic base-stock level $s^+(t, w)$ to minimize $C^+(t, w, y)$. One can show as in Theorem 9.4.2(*a*) that $s^+(t, w)$ is an upper bound on $s^*(t, w)$. Analogues of the other parts of Theorem 9.4.2 can also be derived. See Problem 9.17. (The same idea works with world-dependent order costs $c(t, w)$. The function C^+ involves a cost factor $c^+(t, w)$ which is a bit more intricate than before; see Problem 9.18.)

Moreover, the myopic approach yields a relatively simple lower bound on the optimal cost. Reasoning as in Section 9.4.3, $V^+(0, w, x) \geq V_-(0, w)$, where

$$V_-(0, w) = \Sigma_{t=0}^{T-1} \gamma^t E[C^+\{t, W(t), s^+(t, W(t))\} \mid W(0) = w]$$

The expectation in term t is over $[W(t) \mid W(0) = w]$. So, to compute this lower bound, we must know and use the dynamics of **W**.

Once again, $s^+(t, w)$ reflects the problem data in a simple way. Assume the cost factors are stationary. Estimate

$$\nu(t, w) = E[D[t, t+L) \mid W(t) = w]$$

$$\sigma^2(t, w) = V[D[t, t+L) \mid W(t) = w]$$

and approximate $D[t, t+L)$ using a normal distribution. Letting z^* solve $\Phi^0(z) = (c^+ + h)/(b+h)$, we obtain

$$s^+(t, w) = \nu(t, w) + \sigma(t, w)z^*$$

$$C^+(t, w, s^+(t, w)) = \gamma^L\{\gamma c E[d(t) \mid W(t) = w] + c^+\nu(t, w) + \sigma(t, w)(b+h)\phi(z^*)\}$$

$$V_-(0, w) = \gamma^L \Sigma_{t=0}^{T-1} \gamma^t E[\gamma c d(t) + c^+\nu(t, W(t)) + \sigma(t, W(t))(b+h)\phi(z^*) \mid W(0) = w]$$

In the exponential-smoothing model of Problem 9.16, the demand data are also stationary. We have $E[d(t) \mid W(t) = w] = aw + \underline{d}$ for positive constants a and $\underline{d}$, $\nu(t, w) = \nu(w)$ takes the form $\beta w + \underline{d}L$, a linear function of w, and $\sigma(t, w) = \sigma(w)$ is a constant σ_-, independent of w. So, the expressions above simplify to

$$s^+(w) = \beta w + (\underline{d}L + \sigma_- z^*)$$

$$C^+(w, s^+(w)) = \gamma^L\{\gamma c(aw + \underline{d}) + c^+(\beta w + \underline{d}L) + \sigma_-(b+h)\phi(z^*)\}$$

Here, the myopic base-stock level and cost estimate change linearly with the state variable w. Moreover, $E[W(t) \mid W(0) = w] = a^t w$, so (for $\gamma < 1$)

$$V_-(0, w) = \gamma^L \Sigma_{t=0}^{T-1} \gamma^t[(\gamma ca + c^+\beta)a^t w + (\gamma c + c^+L)\underline{d} + \sigma_-(b + h)\phi(z^*)]$$

$$= \gamma^L\left(\frac{1 - (\gamma a)^T}{1 - \gamma a}\right)(\gamma ca + c^+\beta)w + \gamma^L\left(\frac{1 - \gamma^T}{1 - \gamma}\right)[(\gamma c + c^+L)\underline{d} + \sigma_-(b + h)\phi(z^*)]$$

The lower bound too is a linear function of w.

In the infinite-horizon setting define $C^+(w, y)$ in the obvious way, and let $s^+(w)$ minimize this function over y. One can show that $s^*(w) \le s^+(w)$. The optimal and myopic policies are essentially the same ones discussed in Section 6.7.2.

The lower bound on the optimal cost for $\gamma < 1$ becomes

$$V_-(w) = \Sigma_{t=0}^{\infty} \gamma^t E[C^+\{W(t), s^+(W(t))\} \mid W(0) = w]$$

For the exponential-smoothing model under the normal approximation, this takes the form

$$V_-(0, w) = \gamma^L\left(\frac{\gamma ca + c^+\beta}{1 - \gamma a}\right)w + \frac{\gamma^L[(\gamma c + c^+L)\underline{d} + \sigma_-(b + h)\phi(z^*)]}{1 - \gamma}$$

We can simplify further: Suppose that $\mathbf{W}$ has a limiting, stationary distribution, represented by the random variable W, and at the beginning $W(0)$ has the same distribution. (Or, we don't know $W(0)$, and we are willing to assign it the stationary distribution.) Then, each $W(t)$ has this same distribution, so the lower bound becomes

$$V_- = \Sigma_{t=0}^{\infty} \gamma^t E[C^+\{W, s^+(W)\}]$$

$$= \frac{E[C^+\{W, s^+(W)\}]}{1 - \gamma}$$

For $\gamma = 1$, $W(t)$ goes to W regardless of initial conditions, so the optimal average cost is bounded by $v^* \ge v_-$, where

$$v_- = \lim_{T\to\infty}\left(\frac{1}{T}\right)\Sigma_{t=1}^{T-1} E[C^+\{W(t), s^+(W(t))\} \mid W(0) = w]$$

$$= E[C^+\{W, s^+(W)\}]$$

Under the normal approximation the lower bounds for $\gamma < 1$ and $\gamma = 1$, respectively, become

$$V_- = \frac{\gamma^L[(\gamma c + c^+L)E[d] + \sigma_-(b + h)\phi(z^*)]}{1 - \gamma}$$

$$v_- = E[c(d \mid W) + \sigma(W)(b + h)\phi(z^*)]$$

$$= cE[d] + \sigma_-(b + h)\phi(z^*)$$

where $E[d]$ is the overall mean demand and σ_- is the average of $\sigma(w)$.

These are discrete-time analogues of the cost approximation of Section 6.7.2. As emphasized there, the variation index σ_- represents the *residual variance* of leadtime demand, that is, the conditional variance given the information embodied in the current world-state w. This is typically less than the total leadtime-demand variance.

Specializing to the exponential-smoothing model, $\sigma(w)$ is just σ_- itself and $E[d] = \underline{d}$, so

$$V_- = \frac{\gamma^L[(\gamma c + c^+ L)\,\underline{d} + \sigma_-(b+h)\phi(z^*)]}{1-\gamma}$$

$$v_- = c\underline{d} + \sigma_-(b+h)\phi(z^*)$$

In sum, although exact optimization requires intricate calculations, we can obtain fairly simple, accurate estimates through approximation methods.

9.8 Series Systems

Consider a series system. We focus on a two-stage system ($J = 2$) for convenience, but the results extend to any J. Information and control are fully centralized.

Assume (until Section 9.8.4) that the costs to send goods from the source to stage 1 and from stage 1 to stage 2 are both linear. Shipments sent to stage j arrive after a leadtime of L_j. (In the terms of Chapter 8, we are abbreviating L_j' by L_j.)

As we shall see, an echelon base-stock policy is optimal. We saw this policy form in Section 8.3.

9.8.1 Formulation

The formulation extends that of Section 9.6.2. The following state variables describe the system:

$\hat{x}_j'(t)$ = (local) net inventory at stage j at time t
$z_{jl}(t)$ = shipment in transit to stage j sent l periods ago, i.e., at time $t - l$, $l = 1, \ldots, L_j - 1$
$\mathbf{z}_j(t) = (z_{jl}(t))_l$

(For $j = 1$, $\hat{x}_1'(t)$ is just the local inventory, so $\hat{x}_1'(t) \geq 0$.) The decision variables are

$z_j(t)$ = shipment sent to stage j at time t

We call $z_j(t)$ a shipment, not an order. The distinction is not important for stage 1, but it does matter for stage 2. Under centralized control there is no place for stage-2 orders that stage 1 cannot fill immediately. Only actual, feasible shipments count. Thus, we must constrain $z_2(t)$ to ensure that we ship from stage 1 no more than what is available there. Specifically, the constraints are

$$z_j(t) \geq 0 \qquad z_2(t) \leq \hat{x}_1'(t)$$

The dynamics are

$$\hat{x}_1'(t+1) = \hat{x}_1'(t) + z_{1,L_1-1}(t) - z_2(t) \tag{9.8.1}$$

$$\hat{x}_2'(t+1) = \hat{x}_2'(t) + z_{2,L_2-1}(t) - d(t)$$

$$\mathbf{z}_j(t+1) = [z_j(t), z_{j1}(t), \ldots, z_{j,L_j-2}(t)]$$

The shipment-cost rates are $c_j(t)$, the local holding-cost factors are $h'_j(t)$, and the backorder-cost rate is $b(t)$. The total shipment cost at time t is $c_1(t)z_1(t) + c_2(t)z_2(t)$. For simplicity, assume that this cost is paid at time t, not when the shipments arrive. (This departs from the convention of Section 9.6. If these costs actually occur later, replace $c_j(t)$ by the appropriately discounted value. If stage-1 shipments are outside purchases which we pay for upon arrival, for example, replace $c_1(t)$ by $\gamma^{L_1}c_1(t)$. But, stage-2 shipments are internal transfers, and those costs may occur at any time.) The total inventory-backorder cost is given by

$$h'_1(t)[\hat{x}'_1(t) + \Sigma_{l>0}z_{2l}(t)] + h'_2(t)[\hat{x}'_2(t)]^+ + b(t)[\hat{x}'_2(t)]^- \qquad (9.8.2)$$

This expression is analogous to (8.3.5). Here too, shipments in transit to stage 2 are charged at stage 1's holding-cost rate.

As in Chapter 8, it is convenient to work with echelon-level quantities. Define

$\hat{x}_j(t)$ = echelon net inventory at stage j at time t
$x_j(t)$ = echelon inventory transit-position at stage j at time t

Specifically,

$$\hat{x}_2(t) = \hat{x}'_2(t) \qquad x_2(t) = \hat{x}_2(t) + \Sigma_{l>0}\, z_{2l}(t)$$

$$\hat{x}_1(t) = \hat{x}'_1(t) + x_2(t) \qquad x_1(t) = \hat{x}_1(t) + \Sigma_{l>0}\, z_{1l}(t)$$

The condition $\hat{x}'_1(t) \geq 0$ now becomes $\hat{x}_1(t) \geq x_2(t)$, and the constraints can be written

$$z_j(t) \geq 0 \qquad x_2(t) + z_2(t) \leq \hat{x}_1(t)$$

From (9.8.1), the dynamics become

$$\hat{x}_j(t+1) = \hat{x}_j(t) + z_{j,L_j-1}(t) - d(t)$$

$$x_j(t+1) = x_j(t) + z_j(t) - d(t)$$

Also, let

$h_j(t)$ = echelon holding cost at stage j at time t

That is,

$$h_1(t) = h'_1(t) \qquad h_2(t) = h'_2(t) - h'_1(t)$$

Then, the inventory-backorder cost (9.8.2) becomes

$$h_1(t)\hat{x}_1(t) + h_2(t)\hat{x}_2(t) + [\mathrm{b}(t) + h_2(t)][\hat{x}_2(t)]^-$$

[This is analogous to (8.3.8).] Equivalently, the cost can be written as $h_1(t)\hat{x}_1(t) + \hat{C}_2(t, \hat{x}_2(t))$, where

$$\hat{C}_2(t, x) = h_2(t)x + [b(t) + h_2(t)][x]^-$$

The horizon extends to time $T + L_1 + L_2 - 1$; demands continue to occur and costs to accrue until then. For convenience, however, we assume that $h_1(t) = 0$, $t \geq T + L_1$. The last shipment to stage 2 is $z_2(T + L_1 - 1)$, and the last shipment to stage 1 is

$z_1(T-1)$; later shipments cannot arrive in time to meet demands. (These assumptions are not really necessary, but they make the formulation neater.)

We are now prepared to formulate the dynamic program: Let

$\tilde{V}(t, \hat{x}_1, \mathbf{z}_1, \hat{x}_2, \mathbf{z}_2) =$ optimal cost from time t onward, starting with $\hat{x}_j(t) = \hat{x}_j$ and $\mathbf{z}_j(t) = \mathbf{z}_j$

This is defined for states satisfying $\hat{x}_1 \geq x_2$, where the stage-2 inventory position x_2 is the sum over $(\hat{x}_2, \mathbf{z}_2)$, as above. We have

$$\tilde{V}(T + L_1 + L_2 - 1, \hat{x}_1, \mathbf{z}_1, \hat{x}_2, \mathbf{z}_2) = 0$$

and for $t < T + L_1 + L_2 - 1$, the $\tilde{V}$ satisfy the recursion

$$\begin{aligned}\tilde{V}(t, \hat{x}_1, \mathbf{z}_1, \hat{x}_2, \mathbf{z}_2) = \min \{&c_1(t)z_1 + c_2(t)z_2 + h_1(t)\hat{x}_1 + \hat{C}_2(t, \hat{x}_2) \\ &+ \gamma E[\tilde{V}(t+1, \hat{x}_1 + z_{1,L_l-1} - d(t), (z_1, z_{11}, \ldots, z_{1,L_1-2}), \\ &\hat{x}_2 + z_{2,L_2-1} - d(t), (z_2, z_{21}, \ldots, z_{2,L_2-2}))] \\ &: z_j \geq 0, x_2 + z_2 \leq \hat{x}_1\} \qquad (9.8.3)\end{aligned}$$

(We further constrain $z_2 = 0$ for $t \geq T + L_1$ and $z_1 = 0$ for $t \geq T$. Actually, provided the cost rates are all positive, these choices are optimal.)

Evidently, this is a very complex dynamic program with a large state space. Fortunately, it can be simplified radically. (The dreaded curse of dimensionality can be lifted sometimes!) We shall describe the solution and then prove that it really is optimal.

9.8.2 The Form and Calculation of the Optimal Policy

Define

$$C_2^l(t, y) = \gamma^l E[\hat{C}_2(t + l, y - D[t, t + l))]$$

and set $C_2(t, y)$ to $C_2^l(t, y)$ with $l = L_2$. Define the functions V_2 through the dynamic program

$$\begin{aligned}&V_2(T + L_1, x) = 0 \\ &H_2(t, y) = c_2(t)y + C_2(t, y) + \gamma E[V_2(t + 1, y - d(t))] \qquad (9.8.4) \\ &V_2(t, x) = -c_2(t)x + \min \{H_2(t, y) : y \geq x\}\end{aligned}$$

This recursion has exactly the same form as (9.4.3) to (9.4.5). In particular, $C_2(t, y)$ is convex in y, so a base-stock policy is optimal. Let $s_2^*(t)$ denote the optimal base-stock levels.

Also, let

$$\begin{aligned}\underline{H}_2(t, y) &= H_2(t, \min \{s_2^*(t), y\}) - H_2(t, s_2^*(t)) \\ \hat{C}_1(t, x) &= h_1(t)x + \underline{H}_2(t, x) \\ C_1^l(t, y) &= \gamma^l E[\hat{C}_1(t + l, y - D[t, t + l))]\end{aligned}$$

and set $C_1(t, y)$ to $C_1^l(t, y)$ with $l = L_1$. Define the functions V_1 through another dynamic program:

$$V_1(T, x) = 0$$
$$H_1(t, y) = c_1(t)y + C_1(t, y) + \gamma E[V_1(t+1, y - d(t))] \qquad (9.8.5)$$
$$V_1(t, x) = -c_1(t)x + \min\{H_1(t, y) : y \geq x\}$$

The function $\underline{H}_2$ is called the *implicit penalty cost,* like $\underline{C}_j$ in Section 8.3, and indeed it is constructed in the same way as $\underline{C}_j$. As in the proof of Lemma 8.3.1, since $s_2^*(t)$ minimizes $H_2(t, y)$ over y, $\underline{H}_2(t, y)$ is convex in y. (To form $\underline{H}_2$, unlike $\underline{C}_j$, we subtract a constant, the minimal value of H_2, but that does not affect convexity.) Consequently, $\hat{C}_1(t, y)$ and $\hat{C}_1^l(t, y)$ are convex in y, and a base-stock policy is optimal for (9.8.5) too. Let $s_1^*(t)$ denote the optimal base-stock levels.

As shown in Section 9.8.3, *the echelon base-stock policy with parameters $s_j^*(t)$ is optimal for the system as a whole.* In other words, to solve the complex dynamic program (9.8.3), we need only solve a pair of simpler ones, (9.8.4) and (9.8.5).

This policy describes actual shipments, not orders. For stage 2, we adjust the standard base-stock policy to respect feasibility. That is, we ship nothing if $x_2(t) \geq s_2^*(t)$, and otherwise we set $y_2(t) = x_2(t) + z_2(t)$ to $\min\{s_2^*(t), \hat{x}_1(t)\}$.

It is worthwhile to compare the calculations above with the algorithm of Section 8.3.3 for the continuous-time, stationary, average-cost model. There is an extra time dimension here, and in that respect the calculations are more complex, but the overall logic is the same: We start at the last stage and work backward to the first, solving a single-stage model at each one. Except for stage J, the data for each stage are constructed using the solution for the next stage.

Recall from Section 8.3 that, with stationary data, an echelon base-stock policy can be implemented by a local control scheme. That equivalence rests on the fact that a (local) base-stock policy replaces demands, so stage 2's orders provide stage 1 with complete demand information. With time-varying data, however, this is no longer true. To implement the policy, *each stage must have direct access to demand information.*

We can construct a myopic policy using simpler calculations: Define $c_j^+(t) = c_j(t) - \gamma c_j(t+1)$ and

$$C_2^+(t, y) = \gamma c_2(t+1)E[d(t)] + c_2^+(t)y + C_2(t, y)$$

and let $s_2^+(t)$ minimize $C_2^+(t, y)$ over y. Then, define the functions

$$\underline{C}_2^+(t, y) = C_2^+(t, \min\{s_2^+(t), y\}) - C_2^+(t, s_2^+(t))$$
$$\hat{C}_1^+(t, x) = h_1(t)x + \underline{C}_2^+(t, x)$$
$$C_1^{+l}(t, y) = \gamma^l E[\hat{C}_1^+(t + l, y - D[t, t + l))]$$
$$C_1^+(t, y) = \gamma c_1[t + 1)E[d(t)] + c_1^+(t)y + C_1^{+L_1}(t, y)$$

and let $s_1^+(t)$ minimize $C_1^+(t, y)$ over y. The myopic policy, then, is the echelon base-stock policy with base-stock levels $s_j^+(t)$. It turns out (see Problem 9.20) that $s_j^*(t) \leq s_j^+(t)$. The myopic policy works well, provided the data do not change too fast.

With an infinite horizon and stationary data, the myopic approach yields the optimal policy. (This can be proven by using Theorem 9.4.4.) Specifically, set $c_j^+ = (1 - \gamma)c_j$, $D_1 = D[0, L_1)$, and $D_2 = D[L_1, L_1 + L_2)$. Define

$$C_2(y) = \gamma_2^L E[\hat{C}_2(y - D_2)]$$

$$C_2^+(y) = \gamma c_2 E[d] + c_2^+ y + C_2(y)$$

and let s_2^* minimize $C_2^+(y)$ over y. Then, define

$$\underline{C}_2^+(y) = C_2^+(\min\{s_2^*, y\}) - C_2^+(s_2^*)$$

$$\hat{C}_1^+(x) = h_1 x + \underline{C}_2^+(x)$$

$$C_1(y) = \gamma^{L_1} E[\hat{C}_1^+(y - D_1)]$$

$$C_1^+(y) = \gamma c_1 E[d] + c_1^+ y + C_1(y)$$

and let s_1^* minimize $C_1^+(y)$ over y. Apart from a few details, this is precisely the algorithm of Section 8.3.3.

In the nonstationary model, the myopic policy in effect treats the current data as stationary over an infinite horizon, as in Section 9.4. Consequently, the bounds of Section 8.3.5, with minor adjustments to account for discrete time, can be used to describe the myopic policy.

9.8.3 *Proof*

We now argue rigorously that the policy determined by the recursions above is indeed optimal.

Let us obtain an explicit expression for $\hat{V}(T + L_1, \cdot, \cdot, \cdot, \cdot)$. Recall that, in (9.8.3), $z_2 = 0$ for $t \geq T + L_1$, and $z_1 = 0$ for $t \geq$ T. Also, $h_1(t) = 0$ for $t \geq T + L_1$. Therefore, the expected cost at time $t = T + L_1$ is

$$\hat{V}(T + L_1, \hat{x}_1, \mathbf{z}_1, \hat{x}_2, \mathbf{z}_2) = \hat{C}_2(T + L_1, \hat{x}_2, \mathbf{z}_2)$$

where

$$\hat{C}_2(t, \hat{x}_2, \mathbf{z}_2) = C_2^0(t, \hat{x}_2) + C_2^1(t, \hat{x}_2 + z_{2,L_2-1}) + \cdots + C_2^{L_2-1}(t, x_2)$$

We simplify (9.8.3) in three steps: (1) We apply the logic of Theorem 9.6.1 to reduce the vector $(\hat{x}_2, \mathbf{z}_2)$ to the scalar x_2. This step yields a dynamic program involving functions of the form $\check{V}(t, \hat{x}_1, \mathbf{z}_1, x_2)$. (2) We show that these functions are separable, specifically, that $\check{V}(t, \hat{x}_1, \mathbf{z}_1, x_2) = \hat{V}_1(t, \hat{x}_1, \mathbf{z}_1) + V_2(t, x_2)$ for some $\check{V}_1$. The function V_2 is the one defined above in (9.8.4). (3) We apply Theorem 9.6.1 once more to reduce $\check{V}_1(t, \hat{x}_1, \mathbf{z}_1)$ to $V_1(x_1)$, where V_1 is the function defined in (9.8.5).

Step 1. Observe that $z_2(t)$ affects the stage-2 costs measured by $\hat{C}_2(\cdot, \cdot)$ only at time $t + L_2$. So, we can reassign $\hat{C}_2(t + L_2, \cdot)$ to time t. More precisely, define $\check{V}(t, \hat{x}_1, \mathbf{z}_1, x_2)$ for $t \leq T + L_1$ by the recursion

$$\check{V}(T + L_1, \hat{x}_1, \mathbf{z}_1, x_2) = 0$$

$$\check{V}(t, \hat{x}_1, \mathbf{z}_1, x_2) = \min\{c_1(t)z_1 + c_2(t)(y_2 - x_2) + h_1(t)\hat{x}_1 + C_2(t, y_2)$$

$$+ \gamma E[\check{V}(t+1, \hat{x}_1 + z_{1,L_1-1} - d(t), (z_1, z_{11}, \ldots, z_{1,L_1-2}), y_2 - d(t))]$$
$$: z_1 \geq 0, x_2 \leq y_2 \leq \hat{x}_1\}$$

Then, by an inductive argument following that of Theorem 9.6.1, one can show that, for $t \leq T + L_1$,

$$\hat{V}(t, \hat{x}_1, \mathbf{z}_1, \hat{x}_2, \mathbf{z}_2) = \hat{C}_2(t, \hat{x}_2, \mathbf{z}_2) + \check{V}(t, \hat{x}_1, \mathbf{z}_1, x_2)$$

Moreover, the values of z_1 and y_2 that optimize $\check{V}$ are truly optimal.

Step 2. Now define the functions $\hat{V}_1(t, \hat{x}_1, \mathbf{z}_1)$ for $t \leq T + L_1$ by the recursion

$$\hat{V}_1(T + L_1, \hat{x}_1, \mathbf{z}_1) = 0$$
$$\hat{V}_1(t, \hat{x}_1, \mathbf{z}_1) = \min \{c_1(t)z_1 + \hat{C}_1(t, \hat{x}_1)$$
$$+ \gamma E[\hat{V}_1(t+1, \hat{x}_1 + z_{1,L_1-1} - d(t), (z_1, z_{11}, \ldots, z_{1,L_1-2}))]$$
$$: z_1 \geq 0\} \tag{9.8.6}$$

THEOREM 9.8.1. For all $t \leq T + L_1$

$$\check{V}(t, \hat{x}_1, \mathbf{z}_1, x_2) = \hat{V}_1(t, \hat{x}_1, \mathbf{z}_1) + V_2(t, x_2)$$

Moreover, the z_1 that solves (9.8.6) and the base-stock policy that solves (9.8.4), revised for feasibility as above, are truly optimal.

PROOF. By induction: The result is true by definition for $t = T + L_1$, so suppose it holds for any $t + 1$. Then,

$$\check{V}(t, \hat{x}_1, \mathbf{z}_1, x_2) = \min \{c_1(t)z_1 + h_1(t)\hat{x}_1 \tag{9.8.7}$$
$$+ \gamma E[\hat{V}_1(t+1, \hat{x}_1 + z_{1,L_1-1} - d(t), (z_1, z_{11}, \ldots, z_{1,L_1-2}))]$$
$$+ c_2(t)(y_2 - x_2) + C_2(t, y_2) + \gamma E[V_2(t+1, y_2 - d(t))]$$
$$: z_1 \geq 0, x_2 \leq y_2 \leq \hat{x}_1\}$$

We have two decision variables here, z_1 and y_2, linked only by the constraint $y_2 \leq \hat{x}_1$. Let us perform the optimization in two steps. First, fix z_1 and optimize over y_2. The problem we now face is to evaluate

$$-c_2(t)x_2 + \min \{H_2(t, y_2) : x_2 \leq y_2 \leq \hat{x}_1\} \tag{9.8.8}$$

[The function H_2 is defined in (9.8.4).] There are two cases to consider: If $\hat{x}_1 \geq s_2^*(t)$, then the base-stock policy with base-stock level $s_2^*(t)$ is feasible in (9.8.8), and so it is optimal. That is, we set $y_2 = \max \{s_2^*(t), x_2\}$. The value of (9.8.8) in this case is just $V_2(t, x_2)$. Otherwise, if $\hat{x}_1 < s_2^*(t)$, it is optimal to set $y_2 = \hat{x}_1$. (This solution is feasible, since $x_2 \leq \hat{x}_1$, and the convexity of H_2 implies that it is optimal.) Here, the value of (9.8.8) is

$$-c_2(t)x_2 + H_2(t, \hat{x}_1) = V_2(t, x_2) + [H_2(t, \hat{x}_1) - H_2(t, x_2)]$$
$$= V_2(t, x_2) + [H_2(t, \hat{x}_1) - H_2(t, s_2^*(t))]$$

Combining the two cases, we can write the value of (9.8.8) as

$$V_2(t, x_2) + [H_2(t, \min\{\hat{x}_1, s_2^*(t)\}) - H_2(t, s_2^*(t))] = V_2(t, x_2) + \underline{H}_2(t, \hat{x}_1).$$

Now, substitute this value into (9.8.7). Notice, the term $V_2(t, x_2)$ can be brought outside the minimization. Thus,

$$\begin{aligned}\check{V}(t, \hat{x}_1, \mathbf{z}_1, x_2) = V_2(t, x_2) + \min\{&c_1(t)z_1 + h_1(t)\hat{x}_1 + \underline{H}_2(t, \hat{x}_1) \\ &+ \gamma E[\hat{V}_1(t+1, \hat{x}_1 + z_{1,L_1-1} - d(t), (z_1, z_{11}, \ldots, z_{1,L_1-2}))] \\ &: z_1 \geq 0\}\end{aligned}$$

Recalling that $\hat{C}_1(t, \hat{x}_1) = h_1(t)\hat{x}_1 + \underline{H}_2(t, \hat{x}_1)$, we see that the minimum here is precisely $\hat{V}_1(t, \hat{x}_1, \mathbf{z}_1)$. The induction is complete.

Step 3. Examine the recursion (9.8.6) defining $\hat{V}_1$. This has *precisely* the form of the dynamic program (9.6.2) for a single-stage system, so we can apply Theorem 9.6.1 directly to simplify it. Specifically, defining

$$\hat{C}_1(t, \hat{x}_1, z_1) = C_1^0(t, \hat{x}_1) + C_1^1(t, \hat{x}_1 + z_{1,L_1-1}) + \cdots C_1^{L_1-1}(t, x_1)$$

and recalling the definition of V_1 in (9.8.5), we have

$$\hat{V}_1(t, \hat{x}_1, \mathbf{z}_1) = \hat{C}_1(t, \hat{x}_1, \mathbf{z}_1) + V_1(t, x_1) \qquad 0 \leq t \leq T$$

Moreover, the base-stock policy that solves (9.8.5) yields the optimal stage-1 shipments.

9.8.4 Extensions

It should be clear that the same logic applies to longer series systems ($J > 2$): Work backward from J to 1. For each stage, reduce the state vector (as in step 3 above), and then separate the optimal cost (as in step 2). In conclusion, an echelon base-stock policy is optimal.

Returning to the two-stage system, suppose there is an external fixed cost $k_1(t) = k_1 > 0$, but the internal fixed cost $k_2(t) = 0$. The entire argument above remains valid as stated. In the dynamic programs involving z_1 [(9.8.3), (9.8.5), and several others], the order cost includes a term $k_1\delta(z_1)$. So, the optimal policy is a base-stock policy for stage 2, computed using (9.8.4), and an echelon (r, s) policy for stage 1, obtained by solving (9.8.5).

A positive internal fixed cost $k_2(t)$, however, destroys the argument. (Step 2 breaks down.) We can say little about the optimal policy here. An echelon (r, s) policy (as described in Section 8.3) is certainly a plausible heuristic.

Now, consider an assembly system with linear shipment costs. In general, the optimal policy is quite complex. However, consider the infinite-horizon model with stationary data. *Provided* the initial state satisfies an analogue of the long-run balance condition (8.4.3), a balanced echelon base-stock policy is optimal. The best such policy, moreover, can be found by analyzing an equivalent series system.

What about other starting states? If we do use that policy, sooner or later the system will achieve the balance condition, and from then on, the policy is optimal. That suffices for the average-cost objective ($\gamma = 1$); the best balanced echelon base-stock policy is truly optimal. For the discounted-cost case ($\gamma < 1$), however, during that initial period the policy is suboptimal; the true optimal policy also reaches the balance condition, and it does so at lower cost. But, the optimal policy is very intricate; it is hard to calculate and hard to implement. It is reasonable, therefore, to use the balanced echelon base-stock policy as a heuristic for *all* starting states.

This seems to be as far as one can go in the direction of structural complexity, at least for now. For a distribution system, for example, it seems impossible to compute or even to describe the true optimal policy. (The curse of dimensionality once again asserts its power!) We must turn to approximations. The techniques of Section 8.6, for instance, can be adapted to the discrete-time system to yield a heuristic policy and a lower bound on the optimal cost.

Notes

Section 9.3: The discrete-time dynamic-programming formulations of this and the next two sections were introduced in the papers of Arrow et al. [1951] and Dvoretzky et al. [1952]. Since then, a massive literature has accumulated, extending the basic model in many directions. Porteus [1990] provides a thorough review.

Section 9.4: Karlin [1958] analyzes the linear-order-cost model. The myopic policy and its properties are attributable to Karlin [1960] and Veinott [1965]. See Morton and Pentico [1995] for empirical evidence on its performance and Lovejoy [1992] for an analytical performance bound. One source for Theorem 9.4.4 is Bertsekas and Shreve [1978].

The imperfect-quality model of Section 9.4.8 is by Henig and Gerchak [1990], and the linear-inflation rule is by Ehrhardt and Taube [1987] and Baker and Ehrhardt [1995]. The equilibrium approach of Section 9.4.8.3 borrows from Tang [1990] and Denardo and Tang [1992], who use similar ideas to analyze more complex systems. See Bollapragada and Morton [1994b] for a promising alternative approach. Yano and Lee [1995] review the related literature.

Section 9.5: Scarf [1960] introduced the notion of k-convexity to prove the optimality of an (r, s) policy. See Veinott [1966b] for an alternative approach; this paper also develops the bounds of Theorem 9.5.6. The infinite-horizon model was first tackled by Iglehart [1963a,b]. Zheng [1991] provides a relatively simple proof. The power approximation is attributable to Ehrhardt and Mosier [1984]; Ehrhardt [1984,1985] extends the idea.

Section 9.6: Karlin and Scarf [1958] showed how to extend the basic model to include a constant leadtime. As for stochastic leadtimes, Kaplan [1970], Nahmias [1979], Ehrhardt [1984], and Song and Zipkin [1996b] discuss exogenous supply systems, and Federgruen and Zipkin [1986] explore limited-capacity systems. The myopic approach to the lost-sales system of Section 9.6.5.1 is by Morton [1971] and Nahmias [1979]. See also Johansen and Thorstenson [1996].

Section 9.7: The world-driven demand model was introduced in Iglehart and Karlin [1962] and elaborated by Johnson and Thompson [1975], Lovejoy [1992], Song and

Zipkin [1993a,1996c], and Sethi and Cheng [1997]. See Azoury [1985] for the case of an unknown parameter with bayesian updating.

Section 9.8: The basic results for series systems are attributable to Clark and Scarf [1960] (as are many of the central concepts in the field, such as echelon inventory). Schmidt and Nahmias [1985] and Rosling [1989] extend the ideas to assembly systems. Chen and Zheng [1994b] provide elegant proofs for the infinite-horizon case. Iida [1998] shows that the myopic policy is effective when the data change slowly.

Eppen and Schrage [1981] and Federgruen and Zipkin [1984a,b,c] analyze distribution systems along similar lines. Bessler and Veinott [1966] and Karmarkar [1981,1987a] develop qualitative results for these and other structurally complex systems.

Problems

9.1 Consider the model of Section 9.2.3 with time-varying Poisson demand and an exogenous, sequential supply process. Using the conditional variance formula, verify the following expressions for the mean and variance of leadtime demand:

$$\nu(t) = E[\int_t^{t+L} \lambda(v)dv]$$

$$\sigma^2(t) = E[(\int_t^{t+L} \lambda(v)dv)^2] + \nu(t) - \nu^2(t)$$

9.2 Verify that expression (9.4.7) for the function H agrees with the original definition (9.4.4).

9.3 In the linear-order-cost model of Section 9.4, use parts (*a*) and (*e*) of Theorem 9.4.2 to argue that, if the $s^+(t)$ are nondecreasing in t, then $s^*(t) = s^+(t)$ for all t.

9.4 The linear-order-cost model of Section 9.4 is uncapacitated; there is no limit to the size of an order. Now, suppose there is an upper limit $z_+(t) > 0$. In this setting a base-stock policy works as follows: Do not order if $x(t) \geq s(t)$. Otherwise, order $z(t) = s(t) - x(t)$, unless this would violate the capacity constraint, in which case set $z(t) = z_+(t)$.

(*a*) For the one-period problem, show that a base-stock policy is optimal, and argue that $V(x)$ is convex.

(*b*) Show that a base-stock policy is optimal for the finite-horizon model, following the logic of Theorem 9.4.1.

9.5 Consider the linear-order-cost model of Section 9.4, but suppose that we can dispose of excess inventory at each time point. That is, if $x(t) > 0$, we can choose $z(t) < 0$, so $y(t) < x(t)$. The unit disposal cost is $-c_-(t)$, so the total disposal cost when $z(t) < 0$ is $c_-(t)z(t)$.

Normally, $c_-(t) \leq 0$, so $-c_-(t) \geq 0$. We do allow $c_-(t) > 0$. In that case the disposal "cost" $c_-(t)z(t)$ is negative; interpret disposal as sales, and $c_-(t)$ as the sales price. However, assume $c_-(t) \leq c(t)$, for otherwise we could earn unlimited profits by buying and immediately selling. Even with $c_-(t) > 0$, this scenario is different from the profit-maximization story of Section 9.4.7. Selling inventory is entirely separate from meeting demand.

Consider a policy of the following form: There are two parameters, $s(t)$ and $u(t)$, with $0 \leq s(t) \leq u(t)$. Set

$$y(t) = \begin{cases} s(t) & x(t) < s(t) \\ x(t) & s(t) \le x(t) \le u(t) \\ u(t) & x(t) > u(t) \end{cases}$$

The interval $[s(t), u(t)]$ is called a *control band,* and the policy a *control-band policy.* This rule tells us to act as necessary to restore $y(t)$ to the control band.

(*a*) Argue that a control-band policy with parameters s^* and u^* is optimal for the one-period problem. Show how to calculate s^* and u^*.

(*b*) Prove that a control-band policy is optimal for the finite-horizon model, and $s^*(t) \le s^+(t) \le u^*(t)$. (As you might expect, $s^*(t)$ is closer to $s^+(t)$ here than in the original model; the disposal option makes the myopic policy more attractive. It is also true that, for the infinite-horizon model with stationary data, a control-band policy with stationary parameters $[s^*, u^*]$ is optimal.)

9.6 In the formulation of Section 9.3, suppose $h(t)$ is the holding-cost rate on inventory $x(t)$ up to a given limit $x_+(t)$, but any inventory above that limit incurs the higher cost $h_+(t)$. (Problem 3.5 explores a similar scenario.) Show how to revise the function $\hat{C}(t, x)$ accordingly, and argue that this new function is convex in x.

From this point on the entire analysis of Sections 9.3 to 9.5 goes through, except for certain specific formulas like (9.4.2). For linear order costs, a base-stock policy is optimal; an (r, s) policy is optimal in the fixed-order-cost case. Evidently, these results remain valid for *any* convex cost function $\hat{C}(t, x)$ (assuming, of course, that $C(t, y)$ is finite).

9.7 Revise the proof of Theorem 9.4.3 to cover the average-cost case (with $\gamma = 1$).

9.8 In the profit-maximization model of Section 9.4.7 the prices $p(t)$ are given constants. Consider a situation where we control prices as well as order quantities. For simplicity, consider a one-period model, so there is but a single price p to select. Also, suppose the order cost is linear, and the initial inventory $x = 0$. The mean demand now depends on the price we set, according to the function $\nu(p)$. Assume that $\nu(p)$ is positive, decreasing, and convex for $p > 0$, and the mean revenue $p\nu(p)$ is concave. Also, assume that $\nu(p)$ has a multiplicative effect on demand, that is, $d = \nu(p)e$ for some random variable e with $E[e] = 1$.

Formulate a model to maximize the total expected profit. Fix p temporarily. Argue that a base-stock policy is optimal. Show that $\nu(p)$ has a multiplicative effect on the optimal base-stock level, that is, $s^* = s^*(\nu(p)) = \nu(p)s^*(1)$, and calculate the constant $s^*(1)$. Show too that the optimal cost $H(s^*)$ can be written as $\nu(p)[c + C^*(1)]$ for a positive constant $C^*(1)$.

Now, reduce the original model to one with the single variable p, and derive an equation whose solution yields the optimal price, p^*. Consider also a simpler model that ignores inventory-related costs, i.e., that maximizes $(p - c)\nu(p)$, and let $\underline{p}$ be its optimal price. Argue that $p^* > \underline{p}$. (Hence, $\nu(p^*) < \nu(\underline{p})$.)

9.9 As noted in Section 9.4.8.2, the proportional-yield model is quite special. This problem analyzes the linear-inflation rule of Section 9.4.8.3 for more general yields: Assume that there are nonnegative constants ξ_1, ξ_{21}, and ξ_{22} satisfying $0 < \xi_{22} + \xi_1^2 < \xi_1 < 1$, such that

$$E[\Xi(z)] = \xi_1 z \qquad V[\Xi(z)] = \xi_{21} z + \xi_{22} z^2$$

(In the proportional-yield model, $\xi_1 = E[\xi]$, $\xi_{21} = 0$, and $\xi_{22} = \xi_2 = V[\xi]$. A model with $\xi_{21} > 0$ and $\xi_{22} = 0$ approximates the case of independent unit defects.)

Adapt the analysis of Section 9.4.8.3 to cover this case. Show that, in equilibrium,

$$E[u] = \left(\frac{\beta}{\xi_1}\right)E[d]$$

$$V[u] = [1 - (1 - \frac{\xi_1}{\beta})^2 - (\frac{\xi_{22}}{\beta^2})]^{-1} \cdot \{(\frac{\xi_{21}}{\xi_1})E[d] + (\frac{\xi_{22}}{\xi_1^2})E^2[d] + V[d]\}$$

Argue that the optimal β^* is precisely the same as in the proportional-yield case. Give an expression for $V[u]$ using $\beta = \beta^*$. Specialize the results to $\xi_{22} = 0$.

9.10 Consider the imperfect-quality model of Section 9.4.8. Suppose that the order size z and the yield $\xi(z)$ are discrete. Specifically, $\{\Gamma_i\}$ is a sequence of 0-1 random variables, where $\Gamma_i = 1$ indicates that unit i is good (nondefective), and $\xi(z) = \Sigma_{i=1}^{z} \Gamma_i$. The Γ_i are symmetric (identically distributed, but not necessarily independent). Prove that $\xi(z)$ is stochastically convex. (*Hint:* Fix z, and condition on Γ_i, $i \leq z$. Pick any pair of 0-1 values γ_1 and γ_2, and condition further on the event $\{\{\Gamma_{z+1} = \gamma_1, \Gamma_{z+2} = \gamma_2\}$ *or* $\{\Gamma_{z+1} = \gamma_2, \Gamma_{z+2} = \gamma_1\}\}$. Argue that, conditional on all this, $\Delta^2 E[f(\xi(z))] \geq 0$. Then, decondition.)

9.11 Prove Lemma 9.5.1 (the basic properties of m-convex functions).

9.12 Consider the model of Section 9.5.2 with a finite horizon T. Suppose the fixed order costs $k(t)$ do depend on t. Suppose, however, that $k(t)$ is nonincreasing in t. Argue that an (r, s) policy is optimal. In the case where $\gamma < 1$ the result holds under an even weaker condition. What is it, and why is it sufficient?

9.13 Consider the stochastic-leadtime model of Section 9.6.3.1 with an infinite horizon, stationary data, a linear order cost, and $\gamma < 1$. Again, D is the leadtime demand. Define the function

$$F^0_{D\{\gamma\}}(y) = \frac{E[\gamma^L \mathbf{1}\{D > y\}]}{E[\gamma^L]}$$

$$= \Sigma_l \left(\Pr\{L = l\} \frac{\gamma^l}{E[\gamma^L]}\right) \Pr\{D > y \mid L = l\}$$

Argue that $F^0_{D\{\gamma\}}$ has the properties of a ccdf. Then, show that the optimal s^* satisfies the equation

$$F^0_{D\{\gamma\}}(y) = \frac{c^+ + h}{b + h}$$

9.14 Consider the lost-sales model of Section 9.6.5.1 with an infinite horizon, stationary data, a linear order cost, and $L > 1$. Define $Z[l, L)$ to be the total supply arriving from time l until just before L. That is, $Z[L - 1, L) = 0$, $Z[0, L) = x$, and

$$Z[l, L) = z_{L-1-l} + z_{L-2-l} + \cdots + z_1 \qquad 0 < l < L - 1$$

Letting $\hat{x}[l, L) = Z[l, L) + z - D[l, L)$, prove that

$$\hat{x}(L) = \max\{0, \hat{x}[l, L) : 0 \leq l < L\}$$

(*Hint:* State and verify by induction an expression for the conditional random variable $\{\hat{x}(L) \mid \hat{x}(m)\}$, $0 \leq m < L$. The logic here is the same as in Problem 8.2.)

Now, suppose the myopic policy chooses $z = z(0)$ at time 0 so that (9.6.6) holds exactly. Argue that, for any realization of $d(0)$,

$$\Pr\{\hat{x}(L+1) = 0 \mid d(0)\}|_{z(1)=0} \geq \frac{(c^+ + h)}{(b + h - \gamma c)}$$

so (9.6.6) will again hold at time $t = 1$. (Therefore, (9.6.6) will continue to hold for all $t > 0$.)

9.15 Consider again the lost-sales model of the previous problem. Using the representation above of $\hat{x}(L)$, argue that

$$\Pr\{\hat{x}(L) = 0\} \leq \min\{Pr\{\hat{x}[l, L) \leq 0\} : 0 \leq l < L\}$$

Let us use this to devise an approximation to the myopic policy: Let s_l^+ solve $F^0_{D[l,L)}(y) = (c^+ + h)/(b + h - \gamma c)$. (This is consistent with the definition of s_0^+ in the text.) Set $z_l^+ = [s_l^+ - Z[l, L)]^+$. (This is the order size for the base-stock policy, using base-stock level s_l^+ and treating $Z[l, L)$ as the inventory position.) Finally, set $z^+ = \min\{z_l^+ : 0 \leq l < L\}$. The new policy uses $z = z^+$ as the order size. Argue that, if $Z[l, L) \leq s_l^+$, then

$$\min\{Pr\{\hat{x}[l, L) \leq 0\} : 0 \leq l < L\} \geq \frac{c^+ + h}{b + h - \gamma c}$$

[From this we can't conclude anything about $Pr\{\hat{x}(L) = 0\}$ itself, but it probably comes close to solving (9.6.6).]

9.16 Consider the world-driven-demand model of Section 9.7. Suppose that **W** is a stable, first-order autoregressive process. That is, the dynamics of **W** are given by

$$W(t+1) = aW(t) + \tau e(t)$$

where a and τ are positive constants with $a < 1$, and $\{e(t)\}$ is a sequence of independent random variables, each with mean 0 and variance 1. Also, $d(t) = W(t+1) + \underline{d}$, for a positive constant $\underline{d}$. (This is the model underlying the exponential-smoothing technique of demand forecasting, as explained in Section C.6.4 of Appendix C.) Let $D = D[0, L)$. Express D as a linear combination of $W(0)$ and the $e(t)$. Then, demonstrate that

$$E[D \mid W(0) = w] = \beta w + \underline{d}L$$

$$V[D \mid W(0) = w] = \left(\frac{\tau^2}{(1-a)^2}\right)\{L - \left(\frac{\beta}{1+a}\right)[2 + (1-a)\beta]\}$$

where $\beta = a(1 - a^L)/(1 - a)$. Notice that the variance does not depend on w. It becomes nearly linear for large L, and we can approximate

$$V[D \mid W(0) = w] \approx \left(\frac{\tau^2}{(1-a)^2}\right)[L - \left(\frac{a}{1-a^2}\right)(2 + a)]$$

$$\approx \left(\frac{\tau^2}{(1-a)^2}\right)L$$

9.17 Consider the world-driven-demand model of Section 9.7 with linear order costs. Assume for convenience that **W** has a discrete state space. Argue that $s^*(t, w) \leq s^+(t, w)$, as in Theorem 9.4.2(a).

Also, prove the following analogue of Theorem 9.4.2(b): Suppose that $s^+(t, w) \le s^*(t+1, w')$ for all states w that are immediately reachable from w', i.e., such that $\Pr\{W(t+1) = w' \mid W(t) = w\} > 0$. Then, $s^*(t, w) = s^+(t, w)$.

9.18 Consider the world-driven-demand model of Section 9.7.2 with linear order costs $c(t, w)$ that depend on the current world state. Show how to compute $c^+(t, w)$ and $C^+(t, w, y)$. That is, set things up so that we can rewrite the dynamic program (9.7.1) to (9.7.3) in a form analogous to (9.4.6) to (9.4.8), i.e., in terms of functions $H(t, w, y)$, $C^+(t, w, y)$, and $V^+(t, w, x)$.

9.19 Consider the series system of Section 9.8. Justify the dynamics describing the echelon-inventory measures $\hat{x}_j(t)$ and $x_j(t)$ in Section 9.8.1. Also, demonstrate that the echelon-based inventory backorder cost $h_1(t)\hat{x}_1(t) + \hat{C}_2(t, \hat{x}_2(t))$ is equivalent to the original cost (9.8.2).

9.20 Consider the two-stage series system of Section 9.8, specifically, the myopic policy constructed in Section 9.8.2. Prove that $s_j^*(t) \le s_j^+(t)$. [This is easy for $j = 2$; just follow the proof of Theorem 9.4.2(a). Likewise, letting $s_j^{\#}(t)$ minimize

$$C_1^{\#}(t, y) = \gamma c_1(t+1)E[d(t)] + c_1^+(t)y + C_1(t, y)$$

argue that $s_1^*(t) \le s_1^{\#}(t)$. Then, show that $\underline{H}_2' \ge C_2^{+\prime}$, and use this to prove that $s_1^{\#}(t) \le s_1^+(t)$.]

APPENDIX A
OPTIMIZATION AND CONVEXITY

Outline

A.1 Introduction

This appendix provides a brief outline of selected concepts in the theory of mathematical optimization. These are essential tools in the analysis of inventory systems. The references cited in the Notes below provide more complete treatments of the subject.

A.2 Optimization

A.2.1 Definitions

Let X be a set, and $f = f(\mathbf{x})$ a real-valued function defined on X. We say that $\mathbf{x}^* \in X$ *minimizes* f on X, or is a *(global) minimizer* of f on X, if $f(\mathbf{x}^*) \leq f(\mathbf{x})$, $\mathbf{x} \in X$. The value $f(\mathbf{x}^*)$ is the *minimum* of f on X. We write $f(\mathbf{x}^*) = \min \{f(\mathbf{x}) : \mathbf{x} \in X\}$, and $\mathbf{x}^* = \operatorname{argmin} \{f(\mathbf{x}) : \mathbf{x} \in X\}$. Likewise, $\mathbf{x}^* \in X$ *maximizes* f on X and $f(\mathbf{x}^*)$ is the *maximum* of f on X, if $f(\mathbf{x}^*) \geq f(\mathbf{x})$, $\mathbf{x} \in X$. Clearly, $\mathbf{x}^*$ minimizes f, if and only if it maximizes $-f$.

Not every function has a minimizer and a minimum. (Consider $X = \Re$ (the real numbers), and $f(x) = e^x$.) Every function does, however, have an *infimum,* the greatest lower bound of the range $\{f(\mathbf{x}) : \mathbf{x} \in X\}$, written $\inf \{f(\mathbf{x}) : \mathbf{x} \in X\}$. Thus, $\inf \{e^x : x \in \Re\} = 0$, even though there is no x with $e^x = 0$. Also, $\inf \{x : x \in \Re\} = -\infty$. The corresponding concept for maximization is the *supremum,* written $\sup \{f(\mathbf{x}) : \mathbf{x} \in X\}$.

Suppose $X \subseteq \Re^n$. $\mathbf{x}^*$ is a *local minimizer* and $f(\mathbf{x}^*)$ a *local minimum* of f on X, if $f(\mathbf{x}^*) \leq f(\mathbf{x})$ for all $\mathbf{x} \in X$ in some *neighborhood* of $\mathbf{x}^*$.

Suppose $X \subseteq \Re^n$ is an open set and f a real-valued function defined on X. Assume that f is continuously differentiable. The *gradient* of f, denoted $\nabla f(\mathbf{x})$, is the n-vector of partial derivatives of f evaluated at $\mathbf{x}$; that is,

$$\nabla f(\mathbf{x}) = \left[\frac{\partial f(\mathbf{x})}{\partial x_j}\right]_{j=1}^{n}$$

Next, assume that f is twice continuously differentiable. The *Hessian* of f, denoted $\mathrm{H}f(\mathbf{x})$, is the $n \times n$ matrix of second partial derivatives of f evaluated at $\mathbf{x}$; that is,

$$\mathrm{H}f(\mathbf{x}) = \left[\frac{\partial^2 f(\mathbf{x})}{\partial x_i \partial x_j}\right]_{ij=1}^{n}$$

This matrix is symmetric.

In the one-dimensional case ($n = 1$) the gradient is just the derivative $f'(x)$, and the Hessian is the second derivative $f''(x)$. For any n suppose $f(\mathbf{x})$ is the *quadratic* function $\mathbf{c}'\mathbf{x} + \frac{1}{2}\mathbf{x}'Q\mathbf{x}$, where $\mathbf{c}$ is a constant n-vector and Q a constant, symmetric, $n \times n$ matrix. (The prime here denotes transpose.) Then, $\nabla f(\mathbf{x})$ is the linear function $\mathbf{c} + Q\mathbf{x}$, and $\mathrm{H}f(\mathbf{x})$ is the constant Q.

A.2.2 Optimality Conditions

In general it is hard to find a global minimizer, or even a local one. Optimality conditions help us to find them, or at least to recognize them. The following is the classic first-order necessary condition:

PROPOSITION A.2.1. Suppose f is continuously differentiable on the open set X. If $\mathbf{x}^*$ is a local minimizer, then

$$\nabla f(\mathbf{x}^*) = \mathbf{0} \tag{A.2.1}$$

This result suggests a method to find $\mathbf{x}^*$: Solve the system of n equations in n unknowns (A.2.1). There is no guarantee, however, that a solution, if one exists, really solves the problem. To resolve that issue, we need the concept of convexity, introduced in the next section.

Meanwhile, there are corresponding results for constrained optimization. We shall focus on the linear case: Suppose A is an $m \times n$ matrix with $m < n$ and $\mathbf{b}$ an m-vector. X_o is an open set in $\Re^n$, f is a real-valued, continuously differentiable function on X_o, and we want to minimize f over X_o, subject to the constraints

$$A\mathbf{x} = \mathbf{b} \tag{A.2.2}$$

(So, the actual set X is $X_o \cap \{\mathbf{x} : A\mathbf{x} = \mathbf{b}\}$.) Let A' denote the transpose of A.

PROPOSITION A.2.2. Under these assumptions, if $\mathbf{x}^*$ is a local minimizer of f over X, then there exists an m-vector $\boldsymbol{\zeta}^*$, such that

$$\nabla f(\mathbf{x}^*) + A'\boldsymbol{\zeta}^* = \mathbf{0} \tag{A.2.3}$$

If the rows of A (i.e., the columns of A') are linearly independent, moreover, $\boldsymbol{\zeta}^*$ is unique.

The components of $\boldsymbol{\zeta}^*$ are called *dual variables* or *Lagrange multipliers*. Here, (A.2.2) and (A.2.3) comprise $n + m$ equations in the $n + m$ unknowns $\mathbf{x}$ and $\boldsymbol{\zeta}$.

A.3 Convexity

A.3.1 Definitions and Properties

The *set* $X \subseteq \Re^n$ is *convex* if, for every pair of vectors $\mathbf{x}^1, \mathbf{x}^2 \in X$ and every scalar $\lambda \in [0, 1]$,

$$\mathbf{x} \equiv \lambda\,\mathbf{x}^1 + (1-\lambda)\mathbf{x}^2 \in X$$

Thus, X is convex if it contains the whole line segment connecting $\mathbf{x}^1$ and $\mathbf{x}^2$.

Examples. In $\Re^1$ an interval is convex; in $\Re^2$ a disk is convex; in $\Re^3$ a sphere is convex. In $\Re^n$ the set of solutions to a system of linear inequalities, i.e., $X = \{\mathbf{x} : A\mathbf{x} \le \mathbf{b}\}$, is convex. (Such a set is called a *convex polyhedron.*) Also, the intersection of two convex sets is itself convex. If X is convex and $\mathbf{y}$ is a constant vector, then the translated set $X + \mathbf{y} = \{\mathbf{x} + \mathbf{y} : \mathbf{x} \in X\}$ is convex.

Let f be a real-valued function defined on the convex set X. The *function* f is *convex* if, for every pair of vectors $\mathbf{x}^1, \mathbf{x}^2 \in X$ and every scalar $\lambda \in [0, 1]$, defining $\mathbf{x} \equiv \lambda\mathbf{x}^1 + (1-\lambda)\mathbf{x}^2$ as above,

$$f(\mathbf{x}) \le \lambda f(\mathbf{x}^1) + (1-\lambda) f(\mathbf{x}^2) \tag{A.3.1}$$

The expression on the right is an approximation of $f(\mathbf{x})$, obtained by linear interpolation between the values at $\mathbf{x}^1$ and $\mathbf{x}^2$. So, f is convex when the true value $f(\mathbf{x})$ always lies *at or below* this approximation. In other words, the graph of f lies below the line segment connecting $[\mathbf{x}^1, f(\mathbf{x}^1)]$ and $[\mathbf{x}^2, f(\mathbf{x}^2)]$ in $\Re^{n+1}$. For $X \subseteq \Re^1$ the graph of f in $\Re^2$ has a U-like shape; for $X \subseteq \Re^2$ the graph of f in $\Re^3$ is shaped like a bowl.

Here are some related definitions: f is *strictly convex* if the inequality (A.3.1) holds strictly (with $<$ replacing $\leq$) whenever $\mathbf{x}^1 \neq \mathbf{x}^2$ and $\lambda \in (0, 1)$. f is *concave* when $-f$ is convex, i.e., when (A.3.1) holds with the inequality reversed. Likewise, f is *strictly concave* when $-f$ is strictly convex.

Examples. A linear function is both convex and concave, but not strictly. For $X =$ the positive real numbers, and m a scalar constant with $m > 1$ or $m < 0$, the function x^m is strictly convex. If $0 < m < 1$, x^m is strictly concave, as is $\ln(x)$. For $X = \Re$, the functions $[x]^+ = \max\{0, x\}$ and $[x]^- = \max\{0, -x\}$ are both convex.

Convexity is preserved under certain transformations:

PROPOSITION A.3.1.

(*a*) If f is convex on X and $\mathbf{y}$ is a constant vector, then $f(\mathbf{x} + \mathbf{y})$ is convex on the translated set $X + \mathbf{y}$.
(*b*) If f and g are convex functions on X, then so are the functions $f(\mathbf{x}) + g(\mathbf{x})$ and $\max\{f(\mathbf{x}), g(\mathbf{x})\}$.
(*c*) If f is convex and μ is a scalar with $\mu \geq 0$, then $\mu f(\mathbf{x})$ is convex.
(*d*) If g is convex on X, and f is convex and nondecreasing on $\Re$, then $f[g(\mathbf{x})]$ is convex on X.
(*e*) If $\{f_m\}$ is a sequence of convex functions that converges pointwise to a function f (i.e., $f_m(\mathbf{x}) \to f(\mathbf{x})$ for each $\mathbf{x}$), then f is convex also.

From these basic laws, various other properties follow. Here is an important one, used extensively in Chapters 6 and 9:

COROLLARY A.3.2. Suppose $\hat{C}$ is a convex function on $X = \Re^n$, and $\mathbf{d}$ is a random variable taking values in $\Re^n$. Then, the function $f(\mathbf{x}) = E[\hat{C}(\mathbf{x} - \mathbf{d})]$ is convex.

PROOF: First, suppose that $\mathbf{d}$ has a finite range of values, say $\{\mathbf{d}_i\}$, with $\Pr\{\mathbf{d} = \mathbf{d}_i\} = p_i$. For each i, $\hat{C}(\mathbf{x} - \mathbf{d}_i)$ is convex in $\mathbf{x}$ [by part (*a*) of the Proposition], so $p_i\hat{C}(\mathbf{x} - \mathbf{d}_i)$ is too [by part (*c*)]. Consequently, $f(\mathbf{x}) = \Sigma_i p_i\hat{C}(\mathbf{x} - \mathbf{d}_i)$ is convex [by part (*b*)].

Next, consider the general case. The function f can be represented as the limit of a sequence $\{f_m\}$, where $f_m(\mathbf{x}) = E[\hat{C}(\mathbf{x} - \mathbf{d}^m)]$, and $\mathbf{d}^m$ is a random variable of finite range. (The expectation is an integral, and an integral *is* a limit of this sort.) Each f_m is convex (by the previous argument), so f is too [by part (*e*)].

There are equivalent characterizations of convexity when f is smooth to various degrees:

PROPOSITION A.3.3. Suppose X is open and convex, and the function $f: X \to \Re$ is continuously differentiable. Then, f is convex if and only if, for all $\mathbf{x}$ and $\mathbf{y}$ in X,

$$f(\mathbf{x}) \geq f(\mathbf{y}) + (\mathbf{x} - \mathbf{y})\,\nabla f(\mathbf{y}) \tag{A.3.2}$$

Also, f is strictly convex if and only if (A.3.2) holds strictly for $\mathbf{y} \neq \mathbf{x}$.

The right-hand-side of (A.3.2) is the first-order linear approximation of $f(\mathbf{x})$ centered at the point $\mathbf{y}$. So, f is convex when the true value $f(\mathbf{x})$ lies *at or above* the approximation. In the one-dimensional case, (A.3.2) becomes $f(x) \geq f(y) + (x - y)f'(y)$. An equivalent condition in this case is that $f'(x)$ be nondecreasing in x.

A square matrix Q is *nonnegative definite* if, for all $\mathbf{x}$, $\mathbf{x}'Q\mathbf{x} \geq 0$. Also, Q is *positive definite* when $\mathbf{x}'Q\mathbf{x} > 0$ for all $\mathbf{x} \neq \mathbf{0}$.

PROPOSITION A.3.4. Suppose f is twice continuously differentiable. Then, f is convex if and only if the Hessian $\mathrm{H}f(\mathbf{x})$ is nonnegative definite for all x. Also, if $\mathrm{H}f(\mathbf{x})$ is positive definite for all $\mathbf{x}$, then f is strictly convex.

In the one-dimensional case, the condition for convexity reduces to $f''(x) \geq 0$, while $f''(x) > 0$ implies strict convexity. In two dimensions, the convexity condition becomes $\partial^2 f(\mathbf{x})/\partial x_1^2 \geq 0$, $\partial^2 f(\mathbf{x})/\partial x_2^2 \geq 0$, *and* $|Hf(\mathbf{x})| \geq 0$; if all these inequalities are strict, then f is strictly convex.

One can similarly define convexity for a function f whose domain X is an interval of integers: f is convex if (A.3.1) holds whenever $\mathbf{x}$ itself is an integer. Equivalently, f is convex if the first difference $\Delta f(x) = f(x + 1) - f(x)$ is nondecreasing in x. Also, f is convex if the second difference $\Delta^2 f(x) = \Delta[\Delta f(x)] \geq 0$ for all x. f is strictly convex if these relations hold strictly. (This theory does *not* extend, however, to functions of several integer variables.)

A.3.2 Implications

Why do we care about convexity? The main reason is that it simplifies optimization. Assume that X is a convex set. The key results are the following:

PROPOSITION A.3.5. Suppose f is convex on X. If $\mathbf{x}^*$ is a *local* minimizer of f on X, then $\mathbf{x}^*$ is also a *global* minimizer.

PROPOSITION A.3.6. Suppose f is strictly convex on X. Then, f has at most one, *unique* local (and hence global) minimizer $\mathbf{x}^*$.

Thus, if we want to minimize f, and we know that f is convex, we need only search for a local minimum. And, if f is strictly convex, we know that the optimal point is unique, provided one exists.

Convexity also provides necessary and sufficient conditions for local optimality itself. First, some definitions: A function f is *locally convex* at $\mathbf{x}$ if it is convex on some neighborhood of $\mathbf{x}$.

PROPOSITION A.3.7. If $\mathbf{x}^*$ is a local minimizer of f, then f is locally convex at $\mathbf{x}^*$.

PROPOSITION A.3.8. Suppose f is continuously differentiable. If f is locally convex at $\mathbf{x}^*$ and $\nabla f(\mathbf{x}^*) = \mathbf{0}$, then $\mathbf{x}^*$ is a local minimizer of f.

In the last result, if f is in fact convex everywhere, then $\mathbf{x}^*$ is a true global minimizer, by Proposition A.3.5. The first-order *necessary* condition (A.2.1) thus becomes *sufficient* also. (We use this result in Chapter 3 and elsewhere.) There is a comparable result for linearly constrained optimization:

PROPOSITION A.3.9. Under the assumptions of Proposition A.2.2, if f is locally convex at $\mathbf{x}^*$, and $(\mathbf{x}^*, \zeta^*)$ satisfies (A.2.2) and (A.2.3), then $\mathbf{x}^*$ is a local minimizer of f on $\mathbf{X}$.

Again, if f is truly convex, then $\mathbf{x}^*$ is globally optimal.

Convexity is preserved by optimization, in the following sense:

PROPOSITION A.3.10. Suppose X and Y are convex sets, and $f = f(\mathbf{x}, \mathbf{y})$ is convex on $X \times Y$. Define $g(\mathbf{x})$ to be the minimal value of f for fixed $\mathbf{x}$, i.e., $g(\mathbf{x}) = \min \{f(\mathbf{x}, \mathbf{y}) : \mathbf{y} \in Y\}$. Then, g is convex on X.

This fundamental result is used throughout the book.

What if we aim to minimize a *concave* function? An element $\mathbf{x}$ of a convex set X is an *extreme point* if it is impossible to express $\mathbf{x} = \lambda\mathbf{x}^1 + (1 - \lambda)\mathbf{x}^2$ for $\mathbf{x}^1, \mathbf{x}^2 \in X$, where $\mathbf{x}^1 \neq \mathbf{x}$ and $\mathbf{x}^2 \neq \mathbf{x}$. For instance, if X is a closed interval, its extreme points are its end points; if X is a convex polyhedron, its extreme points are its vertices.

PROPOSITION A.3.11. If f is concave on X, and there exists a global minimizer, then some extreme point of X is a global minimizer.

Thus, to find the global minimum, we need only examine the extreme points. Even this is hard, in general, but it is easy in certain cases, depending on the structure of X. (This result is used in Chapter 4).

There are analogues of Propositions A.3.5 and A.3.6 for a function f defined on an interval of integers: A local minimizer here is a value x such that $f(x - 1) \geq f(x)$ and $f(x + 1) \geq f(x)$, or equivalently, $\Delta f(x - 1) \leq 0 \leq \Delta f(x)$. If f is convex, and x^* is a local minimizer, then x^* is also a global minimizer. If f is strictly convex, there is at most one unique local and global minimizer. (There are no such simple connections between local and global optimization, however, for functions of several integer variables.)

Notes

There are several accessible introductions to classical optimization, the main subject here, including Luenberger [1984] and Bazaraa and Shetty [1993]. For convex sets and functions the standard reference remains Rockafellar [1970].

We have entirely omitted the important topic of mathematical programming, including linear and integer programming. For good introductions see Chvátal [1983] and Nemhauser and Wolsey [1988]. The collection of survey articles compiled by Nemhauser et al. [1989] provides a useful overview.

To *solve* a real optimization model, there are several options: All the leading spreadsheet programs include optimization modules, which are quite adequate for small, routine models. For heavier-duty work (like the big models of Chapter 5), try one of the dedicated modeling languages with built-in links to powerful optimization codes, such as GAMS (Brooke et al. [1988]) and AMPL (Fourer et al. [1993]).

Appendix B
Dynamical Systems

Outline

B.1 Definitions and Examples

A *system* is a collection of related elements. A *dynamical system* is a system whose elements change over time. Here are some examples:

> *The solar system.* The sun and the planets, plus the moons, comets, asteroids, et cetera. These bodies are related mainly by gravity.
>
> *An electrical network.* Resistors, capacitors, transistors, and other such elements, connected by wires.
>
> *A production-distribution network.* The manufacturing and transportation facilities of a firm, and the inventories of physical items between them.

Here, of course, we are mainly interested in this third type of system, but the other two provide useful analogies.

These are *real* systems, but we are also interested in *models* of systems, primarily graphical and mathematical models. Both are called "systems" in common usage. This appendix explores *deterministic* systems exclusively; stochastic systems, whose behavior is affected by random events, are discussed in Appendix C.

No real system exists entirely alone (except the entire universe). So, to discuss a system entails a conceptual focus, implicit or explicit, on one part of the world, leaving out the rest. The *boundary* of a system distinguishes which elements are part of it and which are not. In most practical situations, it is obvious what the system is, that is, where its boundary belongs.

But not always. People can and do argue over the "right" scope of the system. Of course, this depends on the purpose of the discussion. For some purposes, the solar system can be regarded as gravitationally independent of the rest of the universe, but for others it can't. Likewise, sometimes it is useful to discuss a firm's own production-distribution network by itself, but sometimes it is essential to include customers and suppliers.

A *subsystem* is a system that is part of some larger system. The earth and its moon, for instance, compose a subsystem of the solar system. One particular item's inventory composes a subsystem of a logistics system. Typically, a subsystem operates somewhat independently of the rest of the system, so it is meaningful to focus attention on it.

B.1.1 Vocabulary

There is a general vocabulary for describing systems. We begin with four fundamental concepts, *input, output, state,* and *control.*

The *input* of a system is a stimulus or driving force, which enters the system from outside its boundary. The input may be the flow of a physical substance, or information from the environment.

For an electrical network, a battery might provide part of the input, in the form of a voltage source. If the circuit is designed to operate an electric motor, the input might also include signals indicating the desired speed of the motor. The inputs to a production system include the raw materials and information about customer demands for finished goods.

The *output* of a system measures the response or result of its operation. The definition of output depends on what aspects of the system's behavior interest us, or the purpose it is designed for. Also, the output must be something we can actually observe.

For the motor-driving circuit above, the output might be the actual speed of the motor. A production system's output may simply be its production rate. We may also wish to observe, say, the fill rate (the fraction of demands satisfied immediately).

The input and output, then, describe how a system interacts with its environment. The *state* of a system, in contrast, describes the internal workings of the system itself. The state is a complete description of the system's elements at a particular point in time. The key word here is *complete.* The state summarizes all available information about the system, past and present, that is useful in predicting its future evolution.

In a circuit, for example, the state describes the voltage at each node and the current on each arc of the network. The state of the solar system comprises the positions and velocities of the planets. In a production-distribution system the state includes, at least, the inventory level of each item at each location.

Sometimes, it is not obvious how to specify the state of a system; it may take some work to arrive at a satisfactory formulation. The "right" state description depends on the system's dynamics (discussed below). Astronomers care mainly about the positions of the planets, not their velocities. The velocities are necessary also, however, to predict future positions, because of the way gravity works.

Likewise, the appropriate state of a production-transportation system depends on how the system operates. If it is hard to change a production rate, then the state must include the current rate, in addition to the inventory levels. In a distribution network with delivery lags, the state must describe all shipments in transit, since those affect future inventory levels.

Finally, a *control* is some action taken in order to modify the behavior of the system. Sometimes, the control comes from outside the system, in which case it serves to modify the input. In other situations the control is intrinsic to the system itself, based on observing the actual output.

For example, the circuit above may include a device to compare the desired and actual speeds of the motor, and to adjust the input voltage accordingly. The control of a logistics system might order materials and adjust production rates, based on current inventory levels.

To complete the description of a system, we need some additional terminology, *initial conditions, dynamics, constraints,* and *objective.*

The *initial conditions* specify the starting state of the system.

The *dynamics* of a system describes how the state and the output evolve over time, in response to the input and the control. This is the fundamental core of a system.

The dynamics of the solar system embody Newton's (or Einstein's) laws of motion. Other physical laws (such as Ohm's and Kirchhoff's) govern the dynamics of an electric circuit. A logistics system's dynamics include stock-conservation laws: If we start this week with certain inventories (the current state), then decide specific amounts to order and produce (controls), and then demands occur (inputs), the dynamics specify the inventories that will be left next week.

Constraints place limits on the control actions or on the resulting values of the state. In most production systems a negative production quantity is meaningless, and positive values are limited by production capacity; constraints codify these facts. Also, while negative inventory does have a meaning (it can be interpreted as a backlog, as explained in Chapter 3), we may wish to forbid it nonetheless, and we can do this by imposing additional constraints.

Finally, the *objective* is a summary measure of the system's performance. In the case of a production-distribution system, for example, we may be interested in the total cost over a long time interval, or perhaps the average cost over time. The performance of the circuit might be measured as the average squared difference between the desired and actual motor speeds. The solar system has no objective (as far as we know).

B.1.2 Block Diagrams

To understand these four key components—input, output, state and control—and how they work together, it is helpful to introduce another type of vocabulary, the formalism of *block diagrams.* A block diagram is a picture of a system in the form of a network. Such diagrams can be drawn at different levels of detail or aggregation. These alternative pictures allow us to view a system from several different perspectives.

At the highest level of abstraction, we can view a system simply as a device for translating input into output. Figure B.1.1 expresses this view.

The system itself is the rectangle or *block* in the center of the diagram. The input and output are depicted by arrows. In a diagram like this we regard the system as a black box; we see nothing of its internal structure.

Figure B.1.2 provides a more detailed view of the system, including the state and the control as well as the input and output. All these components are now represented by arrows, and the blocks indicate transformations, through which each component affects the others.

The right-most block shows that the output is determined by a transformation of the state. The central block shows that the input and the control influence the state; also, the state affects itself.

FIGURE B.1.1

Block diagram: simplest.

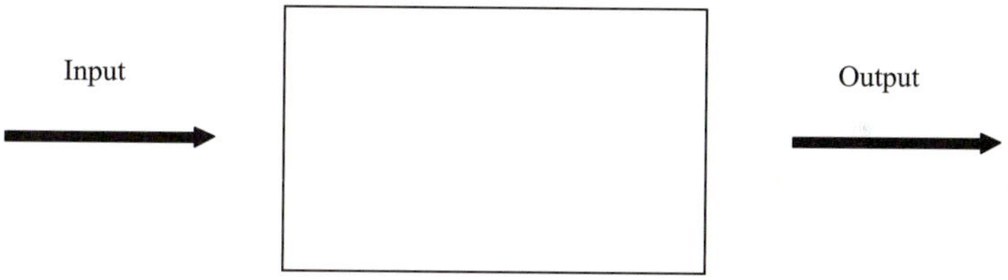

FIGURE B.1.2

Block diagram: more detail.

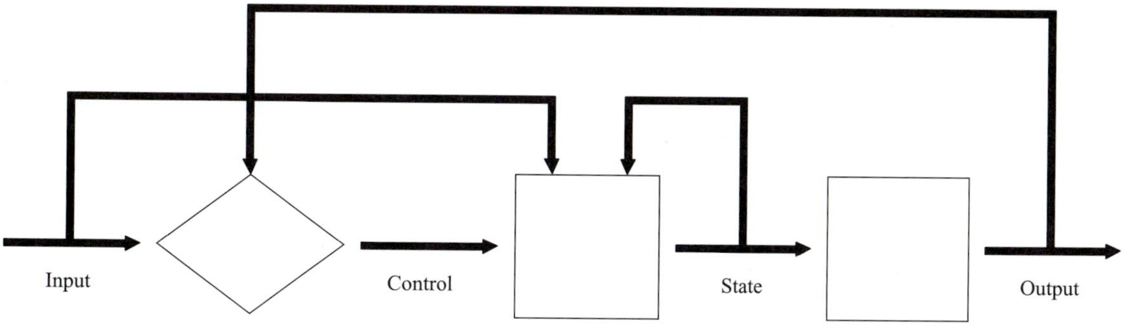

Finally, the left-most block tells us that the control depends on the input and also the output. Again, the diagram by itself does not tell us what happens inside the blocks, that is, the mechanisms of the corresponding transformations. (Some systems lack certain of the blocks and arrows shown in the figure. For example, as mentioned above, the solar system has no real input, output or control, only dynamics.)

There are yet more detailed diagrams, which show just how the blocks work. Alternatively, one can use a hierarchical diagram. This is actually a collection of diagrams, starting with figures like those above. It also includes additional diagrams, one for each of the blocks in Figure B.1.2, showing the details of the block's transformation. And, some blocks in these additional diagrams may be supplemented by yet more diagrams showing still greater detail.

B.2 Discrete-Time Systems

B.2.1 Formulation

Here is a fairly general mathematical model of a system. We model time as a sequence of discrete *time points.* (This notion is explained further in Chapter 4.) There is no explicit output, or rather, the state itself is the output.

T = time horizon
t = index for time points, $t = 0, \ldots, T$
$\mathbf{x}(t)$ = state
$\mathbf{z}(t)$ = control
$\mathbf{e}(t)$ = input

These last three are vectors. They need not have the same dimensions.

Initial conditions:

$$\mathbf{x}(0) = \mathbf{x}_0 \tag{B.2.1}$$

Dynamics:

$$\mathbf{x}(t+1) = \mathbf{g}[t, \mathbf{x}(t), \mathbf{z}(t), \mathbf{e}(t)] \qquad t = 0, \ldots, T-1 \tag{B.2.2}$$

Constraints:

$$\begin{aligned} \mathbf{x}(t) &\in X \qquad t = 0, \ldots, T \\ \mathbf{z}(t) &\in Z \qquad t = 0, \ldots, T-1 \end{aligned} \tag{B.2.3}$$

Objective:

$$\text{Minimize} \quad \Sigma_{t=0}^{T} f[t, \mathbf{x}(t), \mathbf{z}(t), \mathbf{e}(t)] \tag{B.2.4}$$

Here, $\mathbf{x}_0$ is a given vector, X and Z are subsets, $\mathbf{g}$ is a vector function of its arguments, and f is a scalar function of the same arguments. (For $t = T$, f is a function only of $\mathbf{x}(T)$.)

This formulation describes a *first-order* system, in that the next state $\mathbf{x}(t+1)$ depends only on the *current* state, control, and input, i.e., their values at time t, not at earlier times. Some systems, however, have higher-order dependence. Fortunately, it is possible to modify the formulation, to reduce a higher-order system to a first-order one. For example, suppose $\mathbf{x}(t+1)$ depends on $\mathbf{x}(t-1)$ as well $\mathbf{x}(t)$, $\mathbf{z}(t)$, and $\mathbf{e}(t)$. Redefine the state to be $\mathbf{y}(t) = [\mathbf{x}(t), \mathbf{x}(t-1)]$. Now, $\mathbf{y}(t+1)$ depends only on current values of the state, control, and input.

B.2.2 The Optimality Principle of Dynamic Programming

Here is a method to solve problem (B.2.1) to (B.2.4). The idea is to start at $t = T$ and then work backward in time.

Let $V(T, \mathbf{x}) = f(T, \mathbf{x})$, the cost of arriving at terminal state $\mathbf{x}(T) = \mathbf{x} \in X$. Now, define the functions

$$V(t, \mathbf{x}) = \text{minimal cost from time } t \text{ to time } T, \text{ starting at } \mathbf{x}(t) = \mathbf{x}$$
$$H(t, \mathbf{x}, \mathbf{z}) = f[t, \mathbf{x}, \mathbf{z}, \mathbf{e}(t)] + V\{t + 1, \mathbf{g}[t, \mathbf{x}, \mathbf{z}, \mathbf{e}(t)]\}$$

Given $V(t + 1, \cdot)$, and hence $H(t, \cdot, \cdot)$, compute $V(t, \cdot)$ by

$$V(t, \mathbf{x}) = \min_z\{H(t, \mathbf{x}, \mathbf{z}) : \mathbf{z} \in Z, \mathbf{g}[t, \mathbf{x}, \mathbf{z}, \mathbf{e}(t)] \in X\} \tag{B.2.5}$$

Continue all the way to $t = 0$. The optimal value of the objective is given by $V(0, \mathbf{x}_0)$. To construct the optimal solution, work forward in time. Set $\mathbf{z}(0)$ to the optimal $\mathbf{z}$ in (B.2.5) for $t = 0$ with $\mathbf{x} = \mathbf{x}_0$, and set $x(1)$ to the corresponding $\mathbf{g}[0, \mathbf{x}, \mathbf{z}, \mathbf{e}(0)]$. Set $\mathbf{z}(1)$ to the optimal $\mathbf{z}$ in (B.2.5) for $t = 1$ with $\mathbf{x} = \mathbf{x}(1)$, and set $\mathbf{x}(2)$ to the corresponding $\mathbf{g}[1, \mathbf{x}, \mathbf{z}, \mathbf{e}(1)]$. Continue in this manner all the way to $t = T$.

This method works, in principle. The fact that it does so is called *the optimality principle of dynamic programming.*

In practice, the exact recursive solution of (B.2.5) can be a *very* demanding computation. It is easy to make up problems which are essentially impossible to solve. Notice, (B.2.5) requires, for each t, solving a separate optimization problem for each $\mathbf{x}$. It is possible, however, to solve some important problems exactly, and various numerical approximation techniques can be applied to others.

Chapter 9 extends this idea to stochastic systems.

B.2.3 Linear-Quadratic Systems

Here is a special but important case. It has linear dynamics, quadratic objective, and no constraints.
Initial conditions:

$$\mathbf{x}(0) = \mathbf{x}_0$$

Dynamics:

$$\mathbf{x}(t + 1) = A\mathbf{x}(t) + B\mathbf{z}(t) + C\mathbf{e}(t) \qquad t = 0, \ldots, T - 1$$

Objective:

$$\text{Minimize } \Sigma_{t=0}^{T} ½[\mathbf{x}'(t)Q\mathbf{x}(t) + \mathbf{z}'(t)R\mathbf{z}(t)]$$

Here, A, B, C, Q, and R are matrices of appropriate dimensions. (It is also possible for them to depend on t, but we'll keep them stationary for simplicity.)

Let $\boldsymbol{\zeta}(t)$ be a vector of dual variables for the dynamic equations, and $\boldsymbol{\zeta}(T) = \mathbf{0}$. The optimality conditions are

$$Q\mathbf{x}(t + 1) = A'[\boldsymbol{\zeta}(t + 1) - \boldsymbol{\zeta}(t)]$$
$$R\mathbf{z}(t) = B'\boldsymbol{\zeta}(t)$$

along with the initial conditions and the dynamics. This constitutes a system of linear equations, which is not hard to solve. The optimal $\mathbf{z}(t)$, it turns out, can be expressed as a linear function of the initial vector $\mathbf{x}_0$ and the inputs $\mathbf{e}(\cdot)$.

This model is widely used to control physical systems, such as electric motors (one of the examples above) and the steering mechanisms of vehicles. There, both positive and negative values of the state variables and controls are meaningful (they just express opposite directions), and the goal of the system is to control deviations, which the quadratic objective captures.

Chapter 4 discusses the application of this approach to an inventory system.

B.3 Continuous-Time Systems

B.3.1 Formulation

It is also possible to express the problem of controlling a system in continuous time. This approach makes more sense in some situations. We shall just state the formulation:

Initial conditions:

$$\mathbf{x}(0) = \mathbf{x}_0$$

Dynamics:

$$\mathbf{x}'(t) = \mathbf{g}[t, \mathbf{x}(t), \mathbf{z}(t), \mathbf{e}(t)] \qquad t \in (0, T)$$

Constraints:

$$\mathbf{x}(t) \in X \qquad t \in [0, T]$$
$$\mathbf{z}(t) \in Z \qquad t \in [0, T]$$

Objective:

$$\text{Minimize } \int_0^T f[t, \mathbf{x}(t), \mathbf{z}(t), \mathbf{e}(t)]\, dt$$

The prime in the dynamics indicates the derivative with respect to t.

Notes

There are many books on systems. I have found especially useful Luenberger [1979] and Bertsekas [1995].

APPENDIX C
PROBABILITY AND STOCHASTIC PROCESSES

Outline

C.1 Introduction

This appendix is a review of probability and stochastic processes. It also introduces nomenclature, conventions, and notation used in the text. The material is mostly self-contained, but it is both selective and informal: Many important subjects are left untouched, and many definitions and arguments are intuitive rather than rigorous. The references in the Notes at the end provide fuller expositions.

The concept of probability is truly one of the great and beautiful ideas of science and human culture. It provides a clear, precise vocabulary for describing uncertainty and imprecision. Uncertainty and imprecision are central elements of inventory systems.

C.2 Probability and Random Variables

C.2.1 Discussion

Intuitively, a *random variable* is some quantity which, as of now, is not precisely known, but which will become known in the future. (There is a precise, technical definition, which we omit.) For example, in modeling inventory systems, we consider quantities like the following:

- The demand for a certain item over the next week
- The leadtime for a replenishment order placed now
- The demand for the item during the order leadtime
- Whether or not a particular unit of the item turns out defective

Typically, a random variable is indicated by a symbol, e.g., X.

The *range* of a random variable is the set of possible values the quantity can assume. For instance, for weekly demand, the range might be the integers between 0 and 200; the order leadtime's range might be all the non-negative real numbers; in the defective-unit example, the range might be $\{0, 1\}$, where 1 means defective and 0 means nondefective. An integer-valued random variable is called *discrete*, and a real-valued one is called *continuous*. The range too is indicated by a symbol, e.g., S_X or just S.

In addition to the range, the definition of a random variable includes the *probability* of each subset of possible values. For instance, the probability that the demand during the leadtime is exactly 93 might be 0.006, the probability that the leadtime exceeds 3.4 weeks might be 0.22, and the probability of a nondefective unit might be 0.95. The abbreviation Pr $\{\cdot\}$ means the probability of the event in brackets. If D denotes demand over the leadtime, for example, the first statement above becomes $\Pr\{D = 93\} = 0.006$.

The *realization* of a random variable is the value that actually occurs, when all uncertainties have been resolved. For instance, D above describes a demand quantity *before* the period in question. *After* that period, we might observe a demand of 103; this is the realization of D.

Sometimes we consider several related quantities, all uncertain. We can describe these as a collection of random variables or as a single, vector-valued random variable. (A *stochastic process*, defined later, is a special kind of collection of random variables.)

C.2.2 Discrete Random Variables: General Properties

Consider a discrete random variable X, whose range is S, a set of integers in some interval. The probabilities for X can be expressed by the *probability mass function* (abbreviated pmf). This is a function g_X defined on S, whose meaning is

$$g_X(x) = \Pr\{X = x\} \qquad x \in S$$

Thus, $g_X(x) \geq 0$, $x \in S$, and $\Sigma_{x \in S}\, g_X(x) = 1$. It is sometimes useful to extend the function g_X to all the integers, setting $g_X(x) = 0$ for $x \notin S$. When the symbol X is understood, we write g for g_X. (Some people refer to g_X as the probability density function; this phrase has a different but related meaning in the context of continuous random variables.)

A *mode* of g_X is a value x at which $g_X(x)$ is a local maximum. We say g_X is *unimodal* when it has only one mode (or more generally when all the modes are contiguous).

The *probability distribution* or *cumulative distribution function* (abbreviated cdf) of X is

$$G_X(x) = \Pr\{X \leq x\} = \Sigma_{y \leq x}\, g_X(y) \qquad x \in S$$

The *complementary cumulative distribution function* (or ccdf) is

$$G_X^0(x) = \Pr\{X > x\} = 1 - G_X(x) \qquad x \in S$$

Again, we write G and G^0 when X is understood.

The *mean* or *expectation* of X is

$$E[X] = \Sigma_{x \in S}\, x g(x)$$

(When S is infinite, the series need not converge, in which case $E[X]$ does not exist; even when $E[X]$ exists, it may be infinite. We nearly always assume that $E[X]$ exists and is finite. The same goes for similar series below.) More generally, if h is some function defined on S, the expectation of $h(X)$ is

$$E[h(X)] = \Sigma_{x \in S}\, h(x) g(x)$$

In particular, if n is a positive integer,

$$E[X^n] = \Sigma_{x \in S}\, x^n g(x)$$

is called the nth *moment* of X. $E[X]$ itself is the first moment. The *variance* of X is

$$V[X] = E[X^2] - (E[X])^2 = E[(X - E[X])^2]$$

A related quantity is the *second binomial moment* of X, $\frac{1}{2}E[X(X-1)]$. The *standard deviation* of X is the square root of its variance. For a random variable X with $E[X]$ positive, the *coefficient of variation* is the ratio of its standard deviation to its mean, i.e., $(V[X])^{1/2}/E[X]$.

The *z-transform* of X (also called the *probability generating function*, or pgf) is

$$\tilde{g}(z) = E[z^X]$$

(This function is defined for those z such that the expectation exists. Such z can be complex numbers as well as real ones.) This function has a number of important uses. For example, $E[X] =$

$(\partial\tilde{g}/\partial z)(1)$, and $\frac{1}{2}E[X(X-1)] = \frac{1}{2}(\partial^2\tilde{g}/\partial z^2)(1)$. Also, the z-transform completely characterizes a random variable's distribution (under mild technical conditions); that is, there is a one-to-one correspondence between pgf's and pmf's.

The *first-order loss function* (or *loss function*, for short) of X is

$$\begin{aligned} G^1(x) &= E[[X-x]^+] \\ &= \Sigma_{y\geq x}(y-x)g(y) \\ &= \Sigma_{y\geq x}G^0(y) \end{aligned}$$

(The last identity follows from summation by parts.) For a nonnegative X, $G^1(0) = E[X]$, so

$$G^1(x) = E[X] - \Sigma_{0\leq y<x}G^0(y) \qquad x \geq 0$$

(This form is convenient for computation.) The loss function is non-negative, nonincreasing, and convex in x. The *second-order loss function* is defined similarly:

$$\begin{aligned} G^2(x) &= \tfrac{1}{2}E[[X-x]^+[X-x-1]^+] \\ &= \tfrac{1}{2}\Sigma_{y\geq x}(y-x)(y-x-1)g(y) \\ &= \Sigma_{y\geq x}(y-x)G^0(y) \\ &= \Sigma_{y>x}G^1(y) \end{aligned}$$

For $X \geq 0$, $G^2(0) = \frac{1}{2}E[X(X-1)]$, so

$$G^2(x) = \tfrac{1}{2}E[X(X-1)] - \Sigma_{0<y\leq x}G^1(y) \qquad x \geq 0$$

Suppose h is a *convex* function, defined on an interval of real numbers including S. Then, for *any* random variable X with range S,

$$E[h(X)] \geq h(E[X])$$

This is *Jensen's inequality.*

Now, consider *two* related random variables X and Y with (two-dimensional) range S. The (joint) pmf of (X, Y) is the function

$$g_{X,Y}(x, y) = \Pr\{X = x, Y = y\} \qquad (x, y) \in S$$

The joint cdf is given by

$$G_{X,Y}(x, y) = \Pr\{X \leq x, Y \leq y\} \qquad (x, y) \in S$$

Similarly, one can define a joint pmf and cdf for three or more random variables.

The *conditional pmf* of x given $Y = y$ is a function of x, depending on a parameter y, defined for those y with $g_Y(y) > 0$:

$$g_{X|Y}(x \mid y) = \frac{g_{X,Y}(x, y)}{g_Y(y)}$$

The *conditional mean* of X given $Y = y$ is just the mean of X, computed using the conditional pmf $g_{X|Y}$ in place of g_X, and is denoted $E[X|Y = y]$, or $E[X|Y]$ for short. The *conditional variance* $V[X|Y]$ is computed similarly. The *conditional-variance formula* is often useful:

$$V[X] = E_Y\{V_X[X|Y]\} + V_Y\{E_X[X|Y]\} \qquad \text{(C.2.1)}$$

(The subscripts here indicate which variable the operator E or V applies to. For instance, in the first term, think of $V_X[X|Y]$ as a function of $Y = y$; the operator E_Y directs us to compute the mean of this function.)

The variables X and Y are *independent* when, for all x and y,

$$g_{X,Y}(x, y) = g_X(x)g_Y(y)$$

or equivalently

$$g_{X|Y}(x \mid y) = g_X(x)$$

The expectation of a function $h(x, y)$ is

$$E[h(X, Y)] = \Sigma_{(x,y)\in S}\, h(x, y)g(x, y)$$

An important example is the *covariance* of X and Y:

$$V[X,Y] = E[(X - E[X]) \cdot (Y - E[Y])] = E[XY] - E[X]E[Y]$$

When X and Y are independent, $V[X, Y] = 0$. (However, $V[X, Y]$ can be 0, even when X and Y are not independent. When $V[X, Y] = 0$, we say that X and Y are *uncorollated*.) For $Y = X$, $V[X, X] = V[X]$. It is always true that

$$E[X + Y] = E[X] + E[Y]$$

$$V[X + Y] = V[X] + 2V[X, Y] + V[Y]$$

Thus, when X and Y are independent, or more generally uncorollated,

$$V[X + Y] = V[X] + V[Y]$$

The *convolution* of two independent random variables X and Y is their sum $W = X + Y$. The convolution of the pmf's g_X and g_Y is the pmf of W, given by

$$g_W(w) = \Sigma_x g_X(x)g_Y(w - x)$$

In terms of z-transforms,

$$\tilde{g}_W(z) = \tilde{g}_X(z)\tilde{g}_Y(z)$$

Suppose X_i, $i = 1, 2, \ldots$ are independent random variables with the common pmf g_X. The *n-fold convolution* of g_X is the pmf of $W = \Sigma_{i=1}^{n} X_i$, and is written $g_W = g_X^{(n)}$.

C.2.3 Discrete Random Variables: Examples

Next, we review some important types of discrete probability distributions. (Section C.4.4 discusses another important family, the discrete phase-type distributions.)

C.2.3.1 Bernoulli Distribution

In this case $S = \{0, 1\}$. A random variable X of this kind represents a choice between yes and no, or on and off, or success and failure, etc. For instance, $X = 1$ might mean that a particular unit produced is defective, while $X = 0$ means the unit is good.

This distribution has a single parameter p, where $p = \Pr\{X = 1\}$. That is,

$$g(0) = 1 - p \qquad g(1) = p$$

Thus,

$$E[X] = p \qquad V[X] = p(1 - p) \qquad \tilde{g}(z) = (1 - p) + pz$$

C.2.3.2 Binomial Distribution

This type has two parameters, n and p, and $S = \{0,1, \ldots, n\}$. Here, X can be viewed as the sum of n independent random variables, each having a Bernoulli distribution with parameter p. For instance, X might indicate the number of defectives out of n total units produced.

Here,

$$g(x) = \binom{n}{x} p^x(1-p)^{n-x} \qquad x \in S$$

$$E[X] = np \qquad V[X] = np(1-\text{p}) \qquad \tilde{g}(z) = [(1-p) + pz]^n$$

Figure C.2.1 graphs three binomial pmf's, all with $n = 20$, but different values of p. In each case g is unimodal. Also, for $p = ½$, g is symmetric about the mean $½n$. In general, exchanging p and $1 - p$ results in a reflection of g about the vertical line at $x = ½n$. All binomial distributions have these properties.

C.2.3.3 Uniform Distribution

Here, there are two parameters a and b, both integers, with $a < b$. The range is $S = \{a+1, a+2, \ldots, b-1, b\}$. We say X has the uniform distribution on S, when X has equal probability of occurring at any of the integers in S. Thus,

$$g(x) = \frac{1}{b-a} \qquad x \in S$$

$$E[X] = ½(b + a + 1) \qquad V[X] = \frac{(b-a+1)(b-a-1)}{12}$$

(The inventory position in the model of Section 6.2.3 has this distribution, for example.)

FIGURE C.2.1

Probability mass functions (binomial: n = 20).

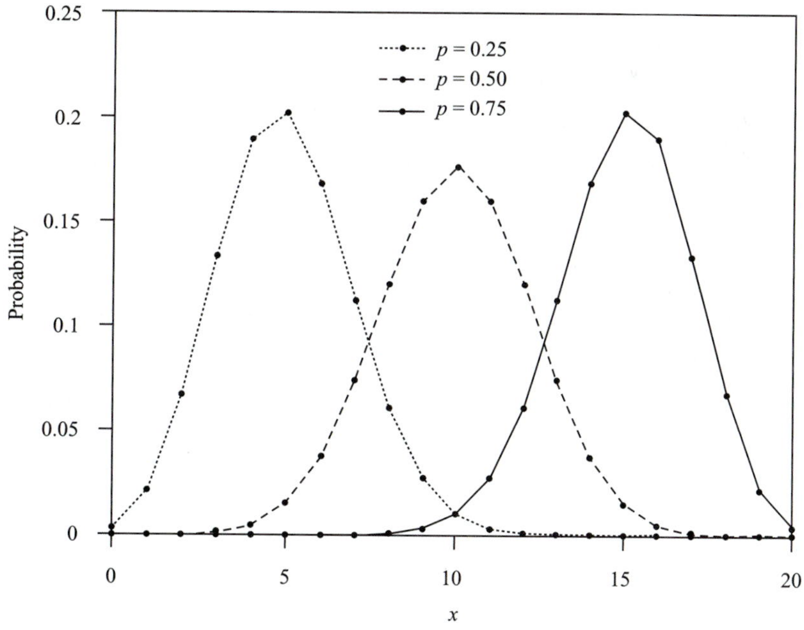

C.2.3.4 Poisson Distribution

A Poisson distribution has a single parameter $\lambda > 0$, and S is the non-negative integers. The pmf is

$$g(x) = \frac{\lambda^x e^{-\lambda}}{x!} \qquad x \geq 0$$

and

$$E[X] = V[X] = \lambda$$

Also,

$$\tilde{g}(z) = e^{-\lambda(1-z)}$$

The pmf is easy to compute by the recursion

$$g(0) = e^{-\lambda}$$

$$g(x) = \left(\frac{\lambda}{x}\right) g(x-1) \qquad x \geq 1$$

There is no closed form expression for G. The simplest way to compute it is to sum terms of g directly. (This approach is fast and accurate enough for most purposes, provided x is not too large. For large x, sophisticated numerical methods are required; see, e.g., Knüsel [1986] and Fox and Glynn [1988].) The loss functions can be written in terms of G^0 as

$$G^1(x) = -(x-\lambda)G^0(x) + \lambda g(x)$$

$$G^2(x) = \tfrac{1}{2}\{[(x-\lambda)^2 + x]G^0(x) - \lambda(x-\lambda)g(x)\}$$

[These identities are (6.2.14) to (6.2.15) in Chapter 6.]

Figure C.2.2 graphs the Poisson pmf for four different values of λ. Notice, g is unimodal in each case, and the mode occurs near the mean λ. (Specifically, when λ is a positive integer, both $\lambda - 1$ and λ are modes; otherwise, the single mode is the integer part of λ.) Several of the figures in Chapter 6 illustrate the loss function.

Consider a sequence of binomial distributions, with n increasing to ∞, but p adjusted to maintain a constant mean λ, i.e., $p = \lambda/n$. Then, the limit is a Poisson distribution with the same mean λ.

The Poisson distribution is used extensively to model the demand for an item over a fixed time interval, as discussed in Chapter 6.

C.2.3.5 Geometric Distribution

Here, S is the non-negative integers, and there is a single parameter p with $0 < p < 1$. Consider an infinite sequence of independent variables, each having the Bernoulli distribution with parameter p. (This is called a *Bernoulli sequence* or *Bernoulli process*.) Then, X is the number of 1's before the first 0 is observed.

The geometric distribution is commonly used to model the time until some event occurs, like the failure of a machine, where there is a constant probability of failure, regardless of the age of the machine. It arises also in Chapter 7, describing demand over a stochastic leadtime.

We have

$$g(x) = (1-p)p^x \qquad G^0(x) = p^{x+1} \qquad x \geq 0$$

$$E[X] = \frac{p}{1-p} \qquad V[X] = \frac{p}{(1-p)^2}$$

FIGURE C.2.2

Probability mass functions (poisson).

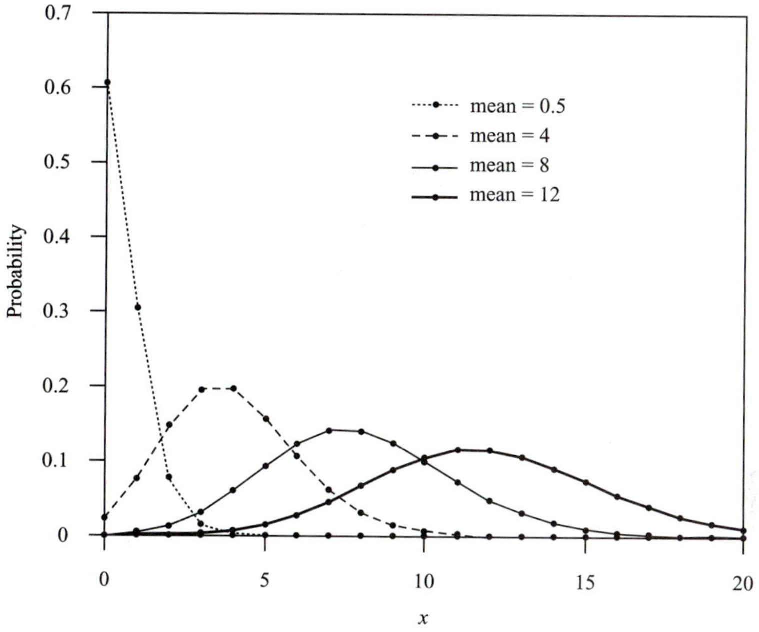

$$\tilde{g}(z) = \frac{1-p}{1-pz}$$

$$G^1(x) = \left(\frac{p}{1-p}\right)p^x \qquad G^2(x) = \left(\frac{p}{1-p}\right)^2 p^x \qquad x \geq 0$$

A slightly more general class of distributions arises in certain applications: Suppose the first Bernoulli random variable in the sequence has probability π of being 1, but all the rest have probability p. Then, X has a *delayed geometric distribution:*

$$g(0) = 1 - \pi \qquad g(x) = \pi(1-p)p^{x-1} \qquad x > 0$$

$$G^0(x) = \pi p^x \qquad x \geq 0$$

$$E[X] = \frac{\pi}{1-p} \qquad V[X] = \frac{\pi(1+p-\pi)}{(1-p)^2}$$

$$\tilde{g}(z) = (1-\pi) + \frac{z\pi(1-p)}{1-pz}$$

$$G^1(x) = \left(\frac{\pi}{1-p}\right)p^x \qquad G^2(x) = \left[\frac{\pi p}{(1-p)^2}\right]p^x \qquad x \geq 0$$

C.2.3.6 Negative-Binomial Distribution

Again, S is the non-negative integers. There are two parameters, n and p, with $0 < p < 1$ and $n > 0$.

Suppose n is a positive integer. We can think of X as the sum of n independent random variables, each having a geometric distribution. Equivalently, X is the number of 0's before n 1's occur in a Bernoulli sequence. Thus, X might represent the time until n identical machines fail. In this case,

$$g(x) = \binom{n-1+x}{x} p^x (1-p)^n \qquad x \in S$$

The same formula applies even when n is not an integer if the binomial coefficient is interpreted as

$$\binom{n-1+x}{x} = \frac{\Gamma(n+x)}{\Gamma(n)\Gamma(x+1)}$$

where Γ is the gamma function. The geometric distribution is the special case with $n = 1$.

We have

$$E[X] = \frac{np}{1-p} \qquad V[X] = \frac{np}{(1-p)^2}$$

$$\tilde{g}(z) = \left(\frac{1-p}{1-pz}\right)^n$$

Here is a useful recursion for the pmf:

$$g(0) = (1-p)^n$$

$$g(x) = \left(\frac{n-1+x}{x}\right) pg(x-1) \qquad x \geq 1$$

(Thus, even when n is not an integer, we never actually have to compute the function Γ.) There is no closed-form formula for G^0, G^1, or G^2. The loss functions can be expressed in terms of G^0 and g, however. Let $\beta = p/(1-p)$, so $E[X] = n\beta$.

$$G^1(x) = -(x - n\beta)G^0(x) + (x+n)\beta g(x)$$

$$G^2(x) = \tfrac{1}{2}\{[n(n+1)\beta^2 - 2n\beta x + x(x+1)]G^0(x) + [(n+1)\beta - x](x+n)\beta g(x)\}$$

Figure C.2.3 shows several negative-binomial pmf's, for $p = 0.75$ and four different values of n. (The case $n = 1$ is a geometric pmf.) Evidently, as n increases, the mean increases, and the distribution seems to become more spread out. Figure C.2.4 again examines four values of n, but now p is adjusted to keep the mean fixed at 9. Here, increasing n serves to concentrate the distribution; the variance decreases with n. In all cases, g is unimodal. Figure 7.5.1 illustrates the loss function.

The negative-binomial distribution is widely used to model demand over a (stochastic) leadtime, as in Chapter 7.

Consider a sequence of negative-binomial distributions with n increasing to ∞, but p adjusted to maintain a constant mean λ. This sequence converges to a Poisson distribution with the same mean. Thus, the Poisson distribution is a limiting case of the negative-binomial. (We mentioned a similar property above for the ordinary binomial distribution.)

FIGURE C.2.3

Probability mass functions (negative binomial: p = 0.75).

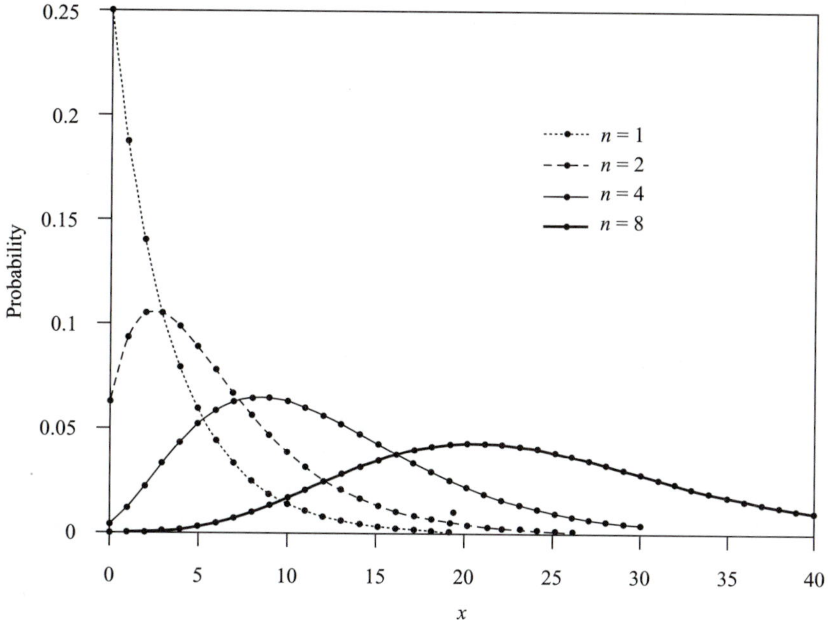

C.2.3.7 Logarithmic Distribution

Here, S is the positive integers. There is a single parameter p with $0 < p < 1$. Let $a = -1/\ln(1-p)$. The pmf is

$$g(x) = \frac{ap^x}{x} \qquad x \geq 1$$

One can show that

$$E[X] = \frac{ap}{(1-p)} \qquad V[X] = \frac{ap(1-ap)}{(1-p)^2}$$

$$\tilde{g}(z) = \frac{ln(1-zp)}{ln(1-p)}$$

While it is not obvious, $E[X]$ and $V[X]$ are both increasing in p; they increase to ∞ as $p \to 1$. As $p \to 0$, $E[X] \to 1$ and $V[X] \to 0$. Figure C.2.5 shows the pmf for four values of p. Evidently, g is monotone decreasing in all cases.

The logarithmic distribution is sometimes used to model the demand size, when an arriving customer may request more than one unit.

C.2.3.8 Compound Distributions

A compound distribution is built up from two other distributions. The following example illustrates the idea: During some time interval, several customers arrive, each demanding a certain amount of a product. The number of customers is a random variable N, and the amount demanded

FIGURE C.2.4

Probability mass functions (negative binomial: mean = 9).

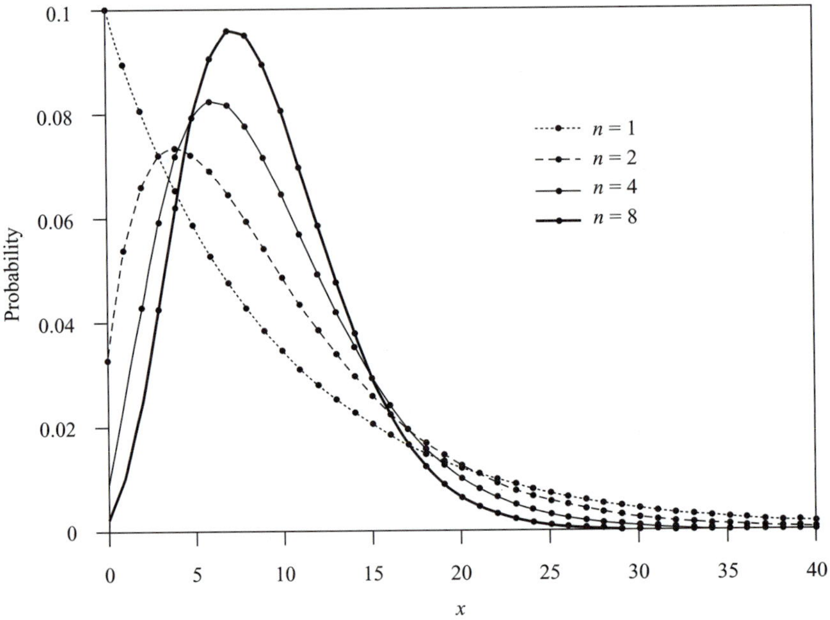

by customer n is another random variable Y_n. Each Y_n has the same distribution as a generic random variable Y, and the Y_n are independent of each other and of N. We are interested in the total demand, $X = \Sigma_{n=1}^{N} Y_n$.

The properties of X can be derived from those of N and Y:

$$g_{X|N}(x \mid n) = g_Y^{(n)}(x)$$

$$g_X(x) = \Sigma_{n=0}^{\infty} g_N(n) g_Y^{(n)}(x)$$

$$\tilde{g}_X(z) = \Sigma_{n=0}^{\infty} g_N(n)[\tilde{g}_Y(z)]^n = \tilde{g}_N[\tilde{g}_Y(z)]$$

$$E[X] = E[N]E[Y]$$

$$V[X] = E[N]V[Y] + V[N]E^2[Y]$$

[The second identity comes from the conditional-variance formula (C.2.1). Here, $E^2[Y]$ means $(E[Y])^2$.]

For example, suppose N has the Poisson distribution with mean $E[N] = \lambda$. We say X has a *compound-Poisson distribution.* In this case, the formulas above simplify to

$$\tilde{g}_X(z) = \exp\{-\lambda[1 - \tilde{g}_Y(z)]\}$$

$$V[X] = \lambda(V[Y] + E^2[Y]) = \lambda E[Y^2]$$

C.2.4 Continuous Random Variables: General Properties

The range S is now some interval of real numbers. Most of the basic properties of continuous random variables are similar to those in the discrete case, but there are some notable differences.

FIGURE C.2.5

Probability mass functions (logarithmic).

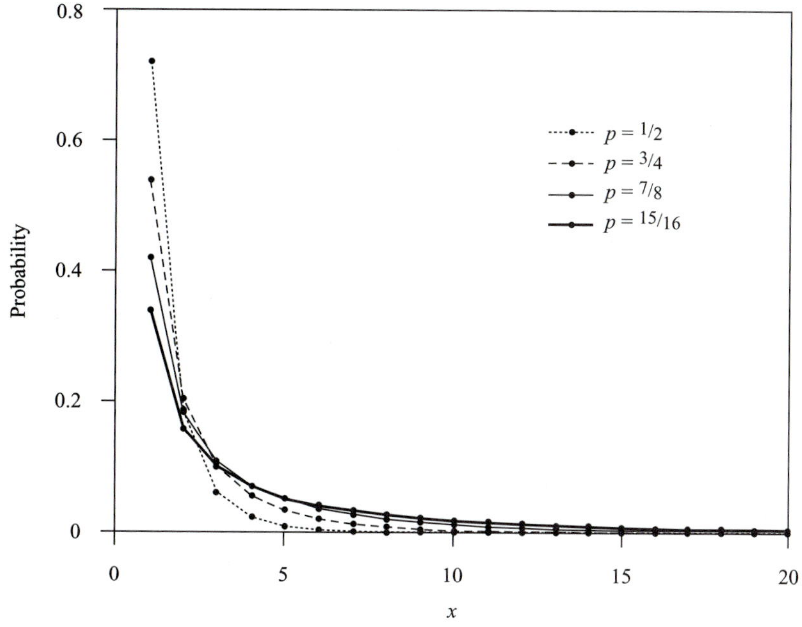

The probabilities can be described in terms of the *cumulative distribution function* (cdf), which has the same meaning as in the discrete case:

$$F_X(x) = \Pr\{X \le x\} \qquad x \in S$$

The *complementary cumulative distribution function* (ccdf) is again

$$F_X^0(x) = \Pr\{X > x\} = 1 - F_X(x) \qquad x \in S$$

The analogue of the probability mass function here is the *probability density function* (or pdf). This is a function f_X, such that

$$F_X(x) = \int_{-\infty}^{x} f_X(x)\,dx$$

The pdf exists only when F_X is smooth, which we assume. In particular, if F_X is differentiable, then $f_X(x) = F_X'(x)$.

When X is understood, we drop the subscript X, as in the discrete case.

Expectations involving continuous random variables are defined as in the discrete case, by using integrals in place of sums. Thus, the *mean* of X is

$$E[X] = \int_S x f(x)\,dx$$

and in general

$$E[h(X)] = \int_S h(x) f(x)\,dx$$

The *variance* of X is again $V[X] = E[X^2] - (E[X])^2$.

Now, assume S is the *non-negative* real numbers. The *Laplace transform* of X is

$$\tilde{f}(s) = E[e^{-sX}]$$

(Other transforms are used for random variables defined on the full real line.)

The *loss function* has the same meaning as before:

$$F^1(x) = E[[X - x]^+] = \int_x^\infty (y - x)f(y)\,dy = \int_x^\infty F^0(y)\,dy$$

The *second-order loss function* has a slightly different meaning:

$$F^2(x) = \tfrac{1}{2}E[([X - x]^+)^2] = \tfrac{1}{2}\int_x^\infty (y - x)^2 f(y)\,dy = \int_x^\infty F^1(y)\,dy$$

The joint cdf of two random variables X and Y is again given by

$$F_{X,Y}(x, y) = \Pr\{X \le x, Y \le y\}$$

The *joint pdf* is

$$f_{X,Y}(x, y) = \frac{\partial^2 F_{X,Y}(x, y)}{\partial y\, \partial x}$$

The conditional pdf, independence, and covariance are defined in terms of the joint pdf, exactly as in the discrete case, and their properties are the same also.

Let $\mathbf{X}$ denote a column vector $(X_i)_{i=1}^n$ of n random variables with joint pdf f. Some special notation and results can be used in this case: The *mean* of $\mathbf{X}$ is the column vector $E[\mathbf{X}] = (E[X_i])_{i=1}^n$. The *covariance matrix* of $\mathbf{X}$ is the $n \times n$ matrix $V[\mathbf{X}] = (V[X_i, X_j])_{i,j=1}^n$. This matrix is always symmetric and non-negative–definite.

Now, suppose m is any positive integer, and A is an $m \times n$ matrix. Define a new vector of random variables $\mathbf{Y}$ by the linear transformation

$$\mathbf{Y} = A\mathbf{X}$$

(That is, if we observe the realization of $\mathbf{X}$, say $\mathbf{X} = \mathbf{x}$, then the realization of $\mathbf{Y}$ is $\mathbf{y} = A\mathbf{x}$.) Then,

$$E[\mathbf{Y}] = AE[\mathbf{X}] \tag{C.2.2}$$

$$V[\mathbf{Y}] = AV[\mathbf{X}]A' \tag{C.2.3}$$

In particular, these formulas hold when $m = 1$, so A is a row-vector, and $\mathbf{Y}$ is a scalar. The formulas then give the mean and variance of a linear combination of several random variables.

C.2.5 Continuous Random Variables: Examples

Here are some important continuous distributions. Again, X denotes the random variable and S its range. (Continuous phase-type distributions are discussed in Section C.5.5.)

C.2.5.1 Uniform Distribution

This is the continuous analogue of the discrete uniform distribution above. The parameters are two real numbers a and b with $a < b$, and $S = [a, b]$. The pdf is

$$f(x) = \frac{1}{b - a} \qquad x \in S$$

Here, X is equally likely to be found anywhere in the interval $[a, b]$.

$$E[X] = \tfrac{1}{2}(b + a) \qquad V[X] = \frac{(b - a)^2}{12}$$

C.2.5.2 Exponential Distribution

Here, S is the non-negative real numbers. The exponential distribution is the continuous analogue of the geometric distribution. X represents the time until some event occurs, where, as long as it has not yet occurred, there is a constant "potential" of occurrence.

There is a single parameter $\mu > 0$, which measures that potential, and

$$f(x) = \mu e^{-\mu x} \qquad F^0(x) = e^{-\mu x} \qquad x \geq 0$$

$$E[X] = \frac{1}{\mu} \qquad V[X] = \frac{1}{\mu^2}$$

$$\tilde{f}(s) = \frac{\mu}{\mu + s}$$

$$F^1(x) = \frac{e^{-\mu x}}{\mu} \qquad F^2(x) = \frac{e^{-\mu x}}{\mu^2} \qquad x \geq 0$$

Analogous to a delayed geometric distribution, a *delayed exponential distribution* has $F^0(x) = \pi e^{-\mu x}$, $x > 0$, for some constant π, $0 \leq \pi \leq 1$.

C.2.5.3 Gamma Distribution

Again, S is the non-negative real numbers. There are two positive parameters, n and μ. Just as the negative-binomial distribution generalizes the geometric, so the gamma generalizes the exponential. In particular, a gamma distribution with $n = 1$ reduces to an exponential.

When n is a positive integer, X is the sum of n independent random variables, each having the exponential distribution with parameter μ. In this case, we say X has an *Erlang (or Erlang-n) distribution.*

For general $n > 0$,

$$f(x) = \frac{\mu(\mu x)^{n-1} e^{-\mu x}}{\Gamma(n)} \qquad x \geq 0$$

(Again, Γ is the gamma function.) Also,

$$E[X] = \frac{n}{\mu} \qquad V[X] = \frac{n}{\mu^2}$$

$$\tilde{f}(s) = \left(\frac{\mu}{\mu + s}\right)^n$$

There is no closed-form expression for the cdf F, in general, but it is available in many scientific and statistical software packages; also see Knüsel [1986]. In the Erlang case, where n is a positive integer,

$$F(x) = 1 - \Sigma_{i=0}^{n-1} \frac{(\mu x)^i e^{-\mu x}}{i!}$$

(This is also the Poisson ccdf with mean μx, evaluated at $n - 1$.) The loss functions can be expressed in terms of F^0 and f:

$$F^1(x) = \frac{(n - \mu x)F^0(x) + xf(x)}{\mu}$$

$$F^2(x) = \frac{\frac{1}{2}\{[(n - \mu x)^2 + n]F^0(x) + (n - \mu x + 1)xf(x)\}}{\mu^2}$$

A gamma distribution is often used to model the time until some event occurs. One can fit n and μ to *any* positive mean and variance.

Figure C.2.6 shows four gamma pdf's with a common mean of 1, but different values of n (so $\mu = n$). Evidently, the distribution becomes more concentrated near the mean for larger n.

C.2.5.4 Normal Distribution

Here, S is the entire real line. There are two parameters, ν and σ, with $\sigma > 0$.

$$E[X] = \nu \qquad V[X] = \sigma^2$$

The special case $\nu = 0$, $\sigma = 1$ is very important, and there is a special vocabulary and notation for it. The random variable is called Z instead of X. Z has the *standard normal distribution*. The pdf of Z is called the *standard normal pdf:*

$$\phi(z) = \left(\frac{1}{\sqrt{2\pi}}\right) \exp\left(-\frac{1}{2}z^2\right) \qquad z \in S$$

The corresponding cdf is the *standard normal cdf,* denoted $\Phi(z)$, and the ccdf is $\Phi^0(z)$. Thus,

$$\Phi^0(z) = \int_z^\infty \phi(x)\, dx$$

This integral cannot be evaluated in closed form, but it is available in many software packages; approximations can be found in Abramowitz and Stegun [1964], Chapter 26. The *standard normal loss functions* are

$$\Phi^1(z) = \int_z^\infty (x - z)\phi(x)\, dx = \int_z^\infty \Phi^0(x)\, dx$$

$$\Phi^2(z) = \int_z^\infty (x - z)\Phi^0(x)\, dx = \int_z^\infty \Phi^1(x)\, dx$$

FIGURE C.2.6

Probability density functions (gamma: mean = 1).

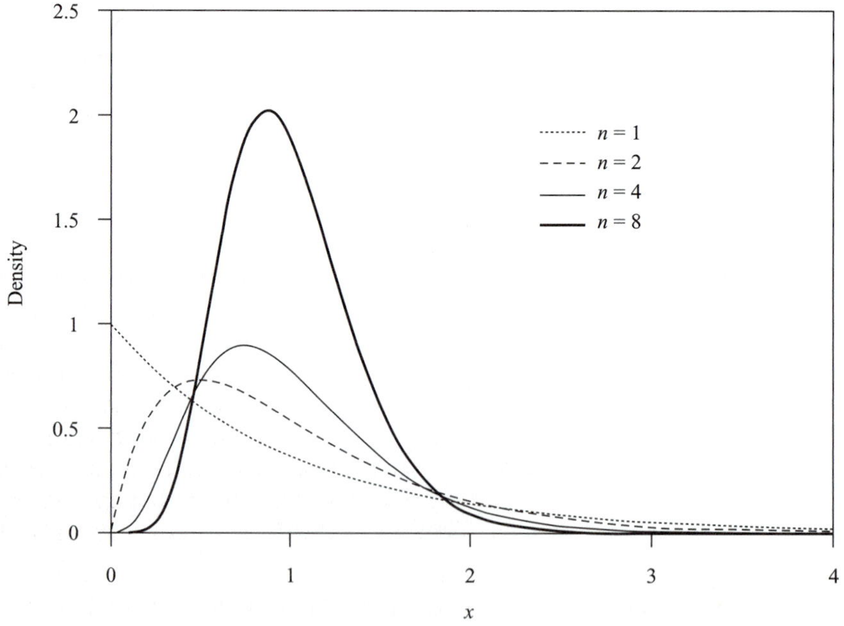

These functions have important symmetry properties:

$$\phi(-z) = \phi(z)$$

$$\Phi^0(-z) = 1 - \Phi^0(z) = \Phi(z) \tag{C.2.4}$$

$$\phi'(z) = -z\phi(z) \tag{C.2.5}$$

With these relations, the loss functions can be written in terms of ϕ and Φ^0 as

$$\Phi^1(z) = -z\Phi^0(z) + \phi(z)$$

$$\Phi^2(z) = \tfrac{1}{2}[(z^2 + 1)\Phi^0(z) - z\phi(z)]$$

Also, using (C.2.5), one can show that

$$\lim_{z\to\infty} \left\{\frac{z\Phi^0(z)}{\phi(z)}\right\} = 1$$

Thus, although there is no formula for $\Phi^0(z)$, for large z, $\Phi^0(z) \approx \phi(z)/z$, and so $\ln [\Phi^0(z)] \approx -\tfrac{1}{2}z^2$. By comparison, for an exponential distribution, $\ln [F^0(x)] = -\mu x$, and even for a gamma distribution one can show that $\ln [F^0(x)] \approx -\mu x$ for large x. Thus, the tail probability $\Phi^0(z)$ decays to 0 very fast as z gets large, faster than an exponential or a gamma tail. The loss functions $\Phi^1(z)$ and $\Phi^2(z)$ also decay to 0 relatively fast.

Now, for any ν and $\sigma > 0$, let $X = \nu + \sigma Z$. Then, X has the *normal distribution* with parameters ν and σ. Conversely, starting with X, $Z = (X - \nu)/\sigma$ has a standard normal distribution. Thus, if $z = (x - \nu)/\sigma$ is the *standardized value* or the *fractile* of x,

$$f_X(x) = \left(\frac{1}{\sigma}\right)\phi(z) \qquad F_X^0(x) = \Phi^0(z)$$

$$F_X^1(x) = \sigma\Phi^1(z) \qquad F_X^2(x) = \sigma^2\Phi^2(z)$$

The *central limit theorem* says roughly the following: Suppose X is the sum of many *independent* random variables. Then, the distribution of X is approximately normal. For example, suppose that demand for an item over some time period comes from many independent sources. Then, the total demand is approximately normal.

There is also the *multivariate normal distribution* for a *vector* of random variables. We begin with a special case: Let $\mathbf{Z} = (Z_i)_{i=1}^n$ be a column vector of independent random variables, each having the standard normal distribution above. Thus,

$$E[\mathbf{Z}] = \mathbf{0} \qquad V[\mathbf{Z}] = I$$

The joint pdf of $\mathbf{Z}$ is

$$\phi_n(\mathbf{z}) = (2\pi)^{-1/2n} \exp\left(-\tfrac{1}{2}\Sigma_{i=1}^n z_i^2\right) \qquad \mathbf{z} \in S$$

Now, let $\boldsymbol{\nu}$ denote an n-vector of constants and Σ a symmetric, nonsingular $n \times n$ matrix, and define the vector

$$\mathbf{X} = \boldsymbol{\nu} + \Sigma\mathbf{Z}$$

Then,

$$E[\mathbf{X}] = \boldsymbol{\nu} \qquad V[\mathbf{X}] = \Sigma^2$$

We say $\mathbf{X}$ has the (n-dimensional) multivariate normal distribution with parameters $\boldsymbol{\nu}$ and Σ. The pdf of $\mathbf{X}$ is given by

$$f(\mathbf{x}) = \left(\frac{1}{|\Sigma|}\right)\phi_n(\Sigma^{-1}(\mathbf{x} - \boldsymbol{\nu}))$$

where $|\Sigma|$ is the determinant of Σ.

Define $\mathbf{Y}$ by a further linear transformation

$$\mathbf{Y} = A\mathbf{X}$$

where A is an $m \times n$ matrix. For simplicity, suppose $m \leq n$ and A has full rank (its rows are linearly independent). Then, $\mathbf{Y}$ too has a multivariate normal distribution with parameters given by (C.2.2) and (C.2.3) above:

$$E[\mathbf{Y}] = AE[\mathbf{X}] = A\boldsymbol{\nu}$$

$$V[\mathbf{Y}] = AV[\mathbf{X}]A' = A\Sigma^2 A'$$

(When $m > n$, or more generally A is not of full rank, then $\mathbf{Y}$ has a *singular normal distribution*. It has a normal distribution on its range, the subspace generated by A.)

C.3 Stochastic Processes

C.3.1 Definition

A *stochastic process* is a model of a quantity that evolves over time, just like a dynamical system, but one influenced by random factors. In the study of inventory systems, stochastic processes are used to model demands and supplies that are affected by unpredictable events, as well as key variables such as net inventory.

Formally, a stochastic process is a collection of random variables $\mathbf{X} = \{X(t) : t \geq 0\}$, where $X(t)$ denotes the quantity of interest at time t. Time may be discrete, where t ranges over the nonnegative integers, or continuous. Each $X(t)$ itself may be discrete or continuous, or a vector of such variables. To define a stochastic process $\mathbf{X}$ means to specify, at least implicitly, the joint range and probability distributions of *all* these random variables. (Not every such collection meaningfully represents a quantity evolving over time. As time passes, the early $X(t)$ are realized, and we observe those realizations, at least partially, while later $X(t)$ remain uncertain. Thus, information is revealed gradually over time. There is a precise, technical way to express this notion, called a filtration. Suffice it to say that all the processes here work in this manner.)

A *sample path* of $\mathbf{X}$ describes a realization of all the random variables $X(t)$. Thus, a sample path is a definite function of time.

In principle, the ranges of the $X(t)$ may be different, but in most practical cases the $X(t)$ share a common range, denoted S, called the *state space* of $\mathbf{X}$. An element of S is a *state*. $X(t)$ itself is referred to as the *state variable*. (These usages are most appropriate for a Markov process, discussed below, but they are commonly applied to other processes too.)

There are many different kinds of stochastic processes. We now sketch some of the major distinctions.

C.3.2 Classification

C.3.2.1 Time

The time parameter t can be continuous (real) or discrete (integer). Depending on this choice, we say $\mathbf{X}$ is a *continuous-time process* or a *discrete-time process*.

The specification of time is a basic modeling choice, for a stochastic process just as for a deterministic system. In some cases there is a natural, predetermined time scale; observations and decisions may take place at regular (e.g., weekly), scheduled points in time, or they may occur continuously. Often, however, the choice is more one of convenience; one type may be easier to analyze than the other. Indeed, the differences between discrete- and continuous-time models are rarely fundamental. These modeling issues are discussed further in Chapters 4 and 9.

C.3.2.2 Space

Regardless of how we model time, the random variables $X(t)$ themselves may be discrete or continuous; in these cases, respectively, $\mathbf{X}$ is called a *discrete-state* or *continuous-state* process. With two ways each to model time and space, then, there are four possible combinations; all four are possible and useful.

A continuous-state process $\mathbf{X}$ can model the quantity (e.g., demand or inventory) of an infinitely divisible product, such as jet fuel. A discrete-state process, in contrast, models a discrete item, e.g., a jet. (These are not hard and fast rules, but rather modeling choices, just as with time, as discussed in Chapter 3.)

C.3.2.3 Continuity and Monotonicity

In the context of continuous time and space, a *continuous process* is one whose sample paths are all continuous functions. Examples include brownian motion and other diffusion processes. These are interesting and useful models, but they involve fairly sophisticated mathematics. We rarely use them here, beyond occasional passing references.

In continuous time (and either continuous or discrete space) a *jump process* is one whose sample paths are all step functions, i.e., constant except for certain distinct time points. Both the time points and the jump sizes may be random. Most of the continuous-time processes in the book are of this type. A jump process, then, has discontinuous sample paths. For technical reasons, we assume that such discontinuities are simple: All sample paths are right-continuous. That is, if there is a jump at time u, this jump *is* included in $X(u)$ but *not* in $X(t)$ for $t < u$. Also, each sample path has left limits, that is, the limit $\lim \{X(t): t \to u, t < u\}$ exists for all u. Denote this limit by $X(u^-)$.

A process with nondecreasing sample paths is called an *accumulation process*. We usually model demand as such a process, using the symbol $\mathbf{D} = \{D(t) : t \geq 0\}$ instead of $\mathbf{X}$. Here, $D(t)$ is the cumulative demand up to time t.

A jump-accumulation process with $X(0) = 0$, where every jump size is precisely 1, is a *counting process*. A counting process, then, is a continuous-time, discrete-state process; each sample path is a nondecreasing step function, starting at 0, with unit steps. A counting process models *events* occurring randomly over time; $X(t)$ counts the number of events during the time interval $(0, t]$. Many demand models are of this type. (Some writers call this a *point process*.)

C.3.2.4 Stationarity

An important distinction, both in continuous and in discrete time, is whether or not a process changes predictably over time. If so, the process is *nonstationary;* if not, it is *stationary.* More precisely, a process $\mathbf{X}$ is stationary if a shift in the time axis leaves its probability law unchanged. That is, first, the $X(t)$ all have the same (marginal) distribution, as viewed just before time 0. Second, for any fixed $u > 0$, the pair $[X(t), X(t + u)]$ has the same distribution for all t. Likewise, the distribution of any group of three or more variables remains constant over time. In particular, a stationary process has $E[X(t)] = E[X(0)]$, $t \geq 0$. (Of course, on any given sample path, the quantity $X(t)$ typically changes with t. Stationarity is a property of distributions, not sample paths.)

Here is a related definition: For any fixed $u > 0$, let $X_u(t) = X(t + u) - X(t)$, and $\mathbf{X}_u = \{X_u(t) : t \geq 0\}$. $X_u(t)$ is called the *increment* of $\mathbf{X}$ over the interval $(t, t + u]$. The process $\mathbf{X}$ has *stationary increments* if $\mathbf{X}_u$ is stationary for all $u > 0$. This is the natural concept of time-invariance for an accumulation process. It implies that $E[X(t)] = E[X(1)]t,\ t \geq 0$. For example, if the (cumulative) demand process has stationary increments, then demand during any week has the same distribution. (Sometimes, we loosely describe a process as "stationary" when we really mean stationary increments; the context usually makes the intended meaning clear.)

C.3.2.5 Ergodicity and Independence

Among stationary processes **X,** some have an important property, *ergodicity;* a process with this property is *ergodic.* The precise definition is rather technical, and we omit it, but its major consequence is worth mentioning: Consider any sample path, and calculate the long-run frequency distribution of $X(t)$ on that path. For example, if $X(t)$ is integer-valued, compute the long-run fraction of time $X(t)$ spends on each of the integers. If **X** is ergodic, then this frequency distribution is identical to the probability distribution of $X(0)$. (Actually, this identity holds for "almost all" sample paths, i.e., with probability 1.) In particular, the average of $X(t)$ over t is $E[X(0)]$.

Consider a stationary, discrete-time process **X,** and suppose that the $X(t)$ are mutually independent. Then, the property above holds; this is precisely the strong law of large numbers. An ergodic process, then, is one to which the strong law applies, whether or not the $X(t)$ are independent. (For example, let $Y(t) = X(t) + X(t + 1)$, where the $X(t)$ are independent. It is not hard to show that **Y** is ergodic, even though the $Y(t)$ are not independent.)

Ergodicity is a remarkable and useful property. The distribution of $X(0)$ embodies information on the likelihoods of *all* possible sample paths. The frequency distribution, in contrast, describes the behavior of **X** on *one* sample path. It is a striking fact that these two distributions are identical for certain (namely, ergodic) processes.

To appreciate this property, consider a stationary **X** that is *not* ergodic: Time is discrete, and the state space is $S = \{0, 1\}$. For $X(0)$, each value has probability ½. Then, for all $t > 0$, $X(t) = X(0)$. Thus, each sample path is either $\{0, 0, 0, \ldots\}$ or $\{1, 1, 1, \ldots\}$. So, the proportion of 0's is *never* ½, which is $Pr\{X(0) = 0\}$. (Here, of course, the $X(t)$ are not independent.) Such things are impossible for an ergodic process.

Turning now to a different property, a (discrete- or continuous-time) process **X** has *independent increments* if its increments over disjoint time intervals are independent. This implies that $X(t)$ and $X_u(t)$ are independent, for all t and u. That is, the current value provides no information about future increments. This property is especially relevant for an accumulation process, e.g., demand. In this case, the demands during different weeks are independent random variables.

C.3.2.6 Markov Processes

Appendix B explains the notion of the *state* of a system. The state constitutes a full description of the system at any point in time. In a deterministic system, the state summarizes all the available information relevant to predicting the future evolution of the system. There is a similar concept for stochastic systems. A stochastic process that has been formulated in terms of an appropriate state is called a *Markov process.*

Here is the basic idea: Suppose we find ourselves at time t. We observe the current value $X(t)$, and also we remember the realizations of past values, namely $X(s)$, $0 \leq s < t$. Suppose we are interested in some future value, say $X(t + u)$ for $u > 0$. Now, we cannot predict $X(t + u)$ perfectly, but the information we have may tell us something about $X(t + u)$. The question is, how much of that information is really salient? If **X** is a Markov process, then $X(t)$ itself embodies *all* the relevant information; the other $X(s)$ add no further information. In short, conditional on the present, the future is independent of the past. For this reason $X(t)$ is called the *state variable* or *state* of the process **X.** (An element of the state space S is also called a state; the context usually indicates which meaning applies.)

More formally, consider the two conditional random variables

$$[X(t+u) \mid \{X(s) : 0 \le s \le t\}]$$

$$[X(t+u) \mid X(t)]$$

The first one conditions on all the past realizations $X(s)$, while the second conditions only on the current state. For a Markov process **X,** these variables have the same distribution, for all t and u. (There are yet more formal definitions, but this will do.)

The dynamics of a Markov process can be expressed in relatively simple terms. For instance, in the discrete-time case, it suffices to specify the conditional distributions of $[X(t+1) \mid X(t)]$ for all t. The initial conditions give the distribution of $X(0)$.

Sometimes, starting with a non-Markov process **X,** there is a way to reformulate the model as a Markov process. This usually involves adding auxiliary variables. That is, we identify another process **Y,** such that the joint process **(X, Y)** *is* a Markov process. (This is entirely analogous to including velocities along with positions in a planetary system.) Such a reformulation is often critical in analysis.

A Markov process **X** is *time-homogeneous* if the conditional distribution of $[X(t+u) \mid X(t)]$ remains constant over t, for all fixed u. That is, the rules governing changes from present to future, i.e., the *dynamics* of the process, remain constant over time. Notice, **X** can be time-homogeneous without being stationary. (A stationary Markov process, however, is nearly always time-homogeneous.)

The simplest kinds of Markov processes are called *Markov chains.* These are the subjects of the next two sections.

C.4 Markov Chains: Discrete Time

C.4.1 Definition

A *Markov chain* is a discrete-time, discrete-state, time-homogeneous Markov process. Thus, the state space S is countable. Such models are simple but also flexible. A great variety of economic and physical phenomena can be represented in this framework.

The phrase *Markov chain* sometimes refers to other models. The state space S may be some more general set, such as the real numbers; we shall see examples in Section C.6. Or, the dynamics may be time-dependent. There is even a related continuous-time model, discussed in Section C.5. For now, Markov chain has the restricted meaning above.

As time passes, **X** jumps from state to state within S; such jumps are called *transitions.* The *transition probabilities* are the numbers,

$$p_{ij} = Pr\,\{X(t+1) = j \mid X(t) = i\} \qquad i, j \in S$$

Because **X** is time-homogeneous, these do not depend on t. By the Markov property, the p_{ij} fully specify the dynamics of **X.** By definition, the p_{ij} satisfy

$$p_{ij} \ge 0 \qquad i, j \in S$$

$$\Sigma_{j \in S}\, p_{ij} = 1 \qquad i \in S$$

Let us collect these probabilities in a matrix $P = (p_{ij})$. Each row i represents the current state, and the columns j correspond to the possible subsequent states. (If S is infinite, then P is an infinite matrix.) We call P the *transition probability matrix* of **X.** If **e** denotes a column vector of ones, the conditions above can be written

$$P \ge 0 \qquad P\mathbf{e} = \mathbf{e}$$

It is easy to see that, for any integer $u > 0$,

$$Pr\,\{X(t+u) = j \mid X(t) = i\} = (P^u)_{ij}$$

where the matrix P^u is the uth power of P. That matrix thus specifies the u-step transition probabilities.

To complete the specification of **X**, we need only initial conditions, i.e., the starting state $X(0)$, or more generally, the distribution of $X(0)$. Often, however, we are interested in the *family* of processes with a given S and P, covering all possible initial distributions; it is common to refer to the whole family as *a* Markov chain.

To aid modeling and intuition, it is useful to represent S and P by a directed graph called the *state-transition diagram:* There is a node for each state $i \in S$. There is an arc from node i to node j, when $p_{ij} > 0$. Thus, the arcs indicate which transitions can occur. (Sometimes the p_{ij} are attached to the arcs, but sometimes they are omitted to avoid clutter.)

For example, consider a three-state chain with $S = \{1, 2, 3\}$ and

$$P = \begin{pmatrix} \frac{1}{2} & 0 & \frac{1}{2} \\ \frac{1}{2} & 0 & \frac{1}{2} \\ \frac{1}{2} & \frac{1}{2} & 0 \end{pmatrix}$$

Figure C.4.1 shows the state-transition diagram. (There is an arc from node 1 to itself, because $p_{11} > 0$.)

When S is infinite, of course, we cannot draw the whole graph. Still, there may be a pattern or structure in P that can be indicated graphically. For example, suppose $S = \{0, 1, 2, \ldots\}$, and for all i

$$p_{i,i+1} = \tfrac{1}{4} \qquad p_{i+2,i} = \tfrac{3}{4}$$

$$p_{ij} = 0 \qquad \text{otherwise}$$

Figure C.4.2 shows the diagram. Fortunately, most Markov chains encountered in practice do have fairly simple structures, reflecting the dynamics of the systems they model. (This fact is important in analysis too, as explained later.)

C.4.2 The Dynamics of State Probabilities

For each $t \geq 0$, define the *row* vector $\boldsymbol{\pi}(t)$ whose components are

$$\pi_i(t) = \Pr\,\{X(t) = i\}$$

We call the $\boldsymbol{\pi}(t)$ *probability vectors.* Evidently, $\boldsymbol{\pi}(t)$ expresses the distribution of $X(t)$ in the form of a vector. The initial vector $\boldsymbol{\pi}(0)$ is part of the specification of **X.** For $t > 0$, $\boldsymbol{\pi}(t)$ describes $X(t)$ as viewed from just before time 0.

The definitions of the $\pi_i(t)$ and p_{ij} imply

$$\pi_i(t+1) = \Sigma_{j \in S}\, p_{ij}\pi_j(t) \qquad i \in S$$

In matrix-vector notation, this becomes

$$\boldsymbol{\pi}(t+1) = \boldsymbol{\pi}(t)P \tag{C.4.1}$$

or

$$\Delta\boldsymbol{\pi}(t) = \boldsymbol{\pi}(t)[-(I-P)] \qquad t \geq 0$$

FIGURE C.4.1

State-transition diagram (three states).

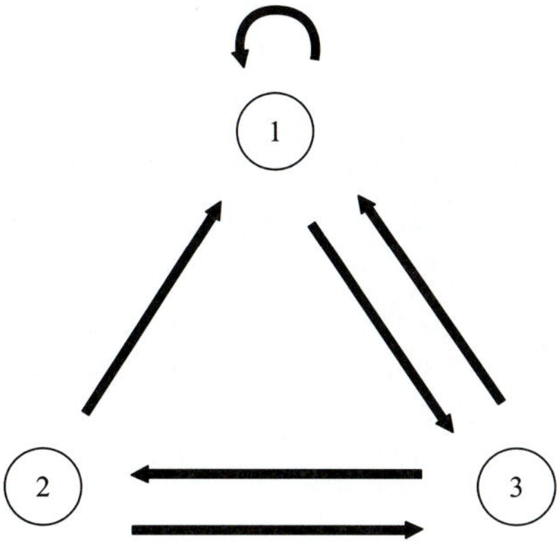

FIGURE C.4.2

State-transition diagram (infinite state space).

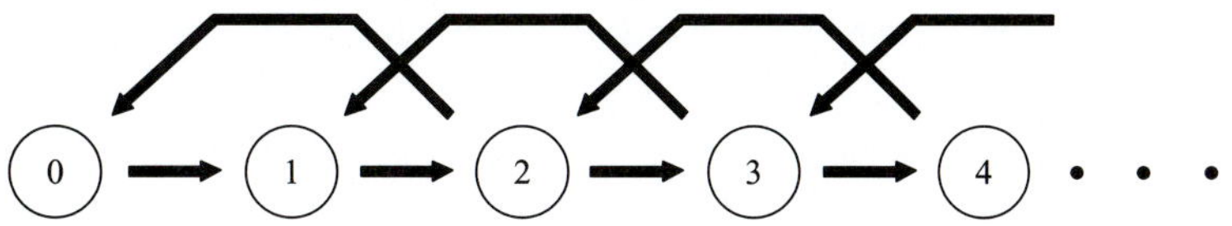

Here, I is the identity matrix. Thus, the $\pi(t)$ satisfy a discrete-time linear system. (It is the notational convention for Markov chains to use row vectors.) Thus, while $X(t)$ itself jumps unpredictably from state to state, the probabilities describing this behavior evolve in an orderly, predictable fashion.

Here are some key definitions:

DEFINITION. The probability vector π^{-} is *stationary* if it satisfies the system of linear equations

$$\pi = \pi P \tag{C.4.2}$$

If the process starts with $\pi(0) = \pi^{-}$, where π^{-} is stationary, then $\pi(t) = \pi^{-}$, $t \geq 0$. In this case, and only then, **X** is a stationary process. Equations (C.4.2) are called the *balance equations.*

DEFINITION. The probability vector π^{∞} is *limiting* if, for every initial vector $\pi(0)$,

$$\lim_{t\to\infty} \pi(t) = \pi^{\infty}$$

A limiting vector, if it exists, is clearly unique.

The analysis of Markov chains addresses the following fundamental questions: When does a stationary probability vector exist? If one exists, when is it unique, and how can we compute it? When does a limiting probability vector exist? Is it stationary? How do these vectors describe the sample-path behavior of the chain?

For certain chains, the answers are simple, but for others they are not.

C.4.3 Classification and Analysis

C.4.3.1 Finite State Space

First, assume S is *finite.* This case is relatively easy. For instance, the first question above has a straightforward answer:

PROPOSITION C.4.1. There exists at least one stationary vector.

To address the other questions, we need to consider carefully what types of transitions can occur.

DEFINITION. State j is *reachable* from state i if, in the state-transition diagram, there is a path from i to j. States i and j *communicate* if each is reachable from the other.

In terms of P, j is reachable from i if $(P^u)_{ij} > 0$ for some $u > 0$. Clearly, we can partition S into subsets S_k, such that all the states within each subset communicate, but states in different subsets do not.

In Figure C.4.1, all three states communicate, so there is only one subset, S itself. Figure C.4.3 shows a seven-state chain with three subsets; the subsets are indicated by rectangles and indexed by letters.

Also, we say that one subset is reachable from another, if *any* state in the second subset is reachable from *any* state in the first. (In this case, clearly, *every* state in the second is reachable from *every* state in the first.) However, two subsets cannot communicate, or else we would combine them into one. In Figure C.4.3, subsets S_B and S_C are reachable from S_A.

DEFINITION. A subset S_k is *transient* if some other subset is reachable from it. Otherwise, S_k is *recurrent.*

A transient subset is literally transient; if **X** starts in the subset, sooner or later **X** must leave it, never to return. Conversely, if **X** starts in a recurrent subset, it stays there forever. There is always *at least* one recurrent subset. In Figure C.4.3, S_B and S_C are recurrent, while S_A is transient. (The states in a transient subset are themselves called *transient;* likewise, there are *recurrent* states.)

DEFINITION. A Markov chain is *reducible* if there is more than one recurrent subset. Otherwise, it is *irreducible.*

The long-term behavior of a reducible chain thus depends crucially on its initial conditions; starting in one recurrent subset, **X** can never reach another one. The chain in Figure C.4.3 is reducible, while the one in Figure C.4.1 is irreducible.

PROPOSITION C.4.2. An irreducible chain has a unique stationary probability vector, $\boldsymbol{\pi}^-$.

Conversely, a reducible chain has several stationary vectors.

PROPOSITION C.4.3. In an irreducible chain, the stationary vector $\boldsymbol{\pi}^-$ describes the long-run frequency distribution of **X** for almost every sample path, regardless of $\boldsymbol{\pi}(0)$.

Next, consider the chains in Figure C.4.4. The first cycles indefinitely through three states. The second is less predictable, but still it alternates between the *groups* of states $\{1, 2\}$ and $\{3, 4\}$. (Both are irreducible.) Such chains are called *periodic.* We shall skip the formal definition; the intuitive idea should be clear. A chain without such systematic cycles is called *aperiodic.*

PROPOSITION C.4.4. An irreducible, aperiodic chain has a (unique) limiting probability vector, $\boldsymbol{\pi}^\infty$. Furthermore, $\boldsymbol{\pi}^\infty = \boldsymbol{\pi}^-$.

A chain with all these properties is called *ergodic.* Recall, Section C.3.2.5 discusses this term in the context of a general stochastic process. Here, the usage is a bit different. An irreducible chain with $\boldsymbol{\pi}(0) = \boldsymbol{\pi}^-$ has the key property of an ergodic process in the original sense, by Proposition

FIGURE C.4.3

A reducible chain.

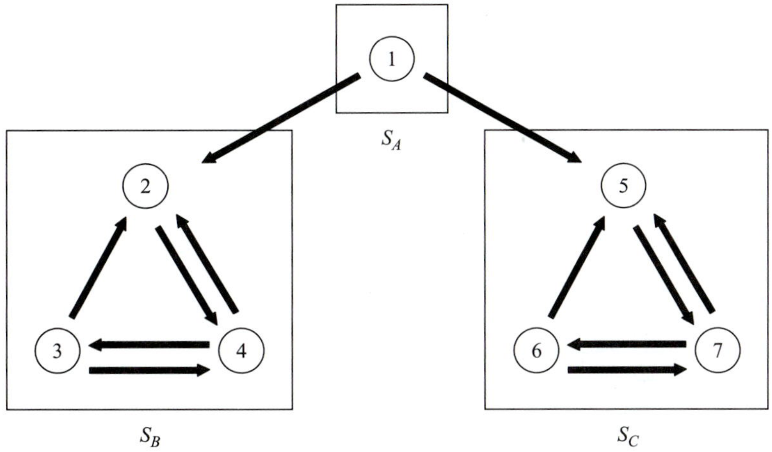

C.4.3. The new definition requires in addition that the chain be aperiodic. It describes the entire family of processes, allowing for different $\boldsymbol{\pi}(0)$.

When **X** is irreducible, so $\boldsymbol{\pi}^{-}$ exists uniquely, this vector is the unique solution to the balance equations (C.4.2) together with the *normalization equation*

$$\boldsymbol{\pi}\mathbf{e} = 1 \tag{C.4.3}$$

(You might worry that there are more equations than unknowns, but in fact there is a redundancy in the balance equations, which the normalization equation resolves.) So, we can compute $\boldsymbol{\pi}^{-}$ just by solving the linear system (C.4.2) and (C.4.3).

A transient state i always has $\pi_i^{-} = 0$. (Its long-run frequency must be 0.) Conversely, a recurrent state i has $\pi_i^{-} > 0$.

C.4.3.2 Countable State Space

Now we turn to the general case of *countable* $S = \{0, 1, 2, \ldots\}$. The definitions of reachability and communication among states remain the same as above. We need to refine the notions of transient and recurrent subsets, however.

Suppose $X(0) = i$. We say that state i is *transient* if there is a positive probability that **X** never returns to i in the future, i.e., for $t > 0$; otherwise, i is *recurrent.* It turns out that either all states in a subset are transient or all are recurrent, so we can again refer to subsets as transient or recurrent. (In the case of finite S this definition is consistent with the earlier one.)

It may be the case now that *all* subsets are transient. For example, consider Figure C.4.5. Here, each state has its own subset (no two states communicate), and each is transient. Also, reconsider Figure C.4.2, but change the probabilities to

$$p_{i,i+1} = 0.99 \qquad p_{i+2,i} = 0.01$$

$$p_{ij} = 0 \qquad \text{otherwise}$$

Here, all states communicate, so there is a single subset, but it is clearly transient; $X(t)$ almost always increases, and only rarely jumps down. In such cases we say that **X** itself is transient. Here, there is no stationary vector; Proposition C.4.1 fails.

FIGURE C.4.4

Periodic chains.

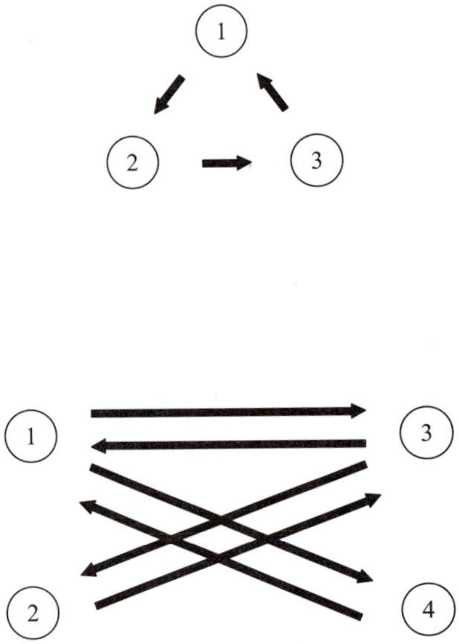

FIGURE C.4.5

Periodic chains.

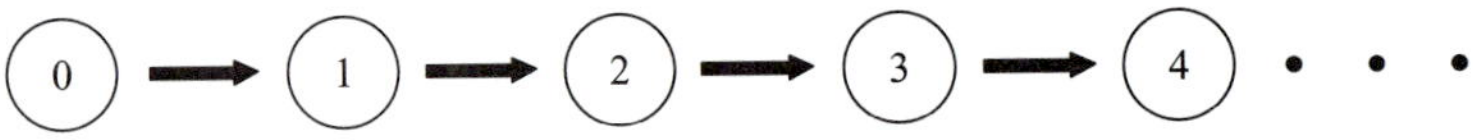

Given this new definition of recurrent subsets, the notions of reducible and irreducible chains remain the same as before; that is, a nontransient chain is irreducible if it has only one recurrent subset.

There are now two distinct kinds of recurrent subsets: Suppose $X(0) = i$, where i is recurrent. So, $\mathbf{X}$ will return to i in the future, with probability 1. Consider the *first-return time,* that is, the earliest time $t > 0$ with $X(t) = i$. If the *mean* of the first-return time is finite, i is *positive recurrent*; otherwise, if the mean is infinite, i is *null recurrent.* It turns out that either all states in a recurrent subset are positive recurrent or all are null recurrent, so these terms characterize subsets. (For finite S, *every* recurrent subset is positive recurrent.) Null-recurrent subsets appear only rarely; we shall see an example in the next section.

We now make an assumption:

ASSUMPTION. There is at least one positive-recurrent subset.

(Recall, this is always true when S is finite.) It turns out that, under this condition, the results above for the finite-state case remain valid: There *is* a stationary vector (as in Proposition C.4.1). If the chain is irreducible, the stationary vector is unique (Proposition C.4.2), and it characterizes the long-run frequency distribution of $\mathbf{X}$ (Proposition C.4.3). If the chain is also aperiodic, there is a limiting vector, which equals the stationary vector (Proposition C.4.4).

There is no direct general method to check positive recurrence. However, it turns out that the assumption above holds, *if and only if* a stationary vector exists. One (and usually the easiest) way to check the assumption, then, is to try to solve the balance and normalization equations (C.4.2) and (C.4.3); success means the assumption holds. Unfortunately, there is now an infinite number of equations in an infinite number of variables; there is no general procedure to solve such systems. Fortunately, many chains have special structure, and it is often possible to exploit that structure to solve the system.

C.4.3.3 Absorbing Chains

Let us now define an important class of Markov chains. The state space S can be finite or infinite.

An *absorbing state i* is one having $p_{ii} = 1$, so $p_{ij} = 0, j \neq i$. Thus, once $\mathbf{X}$ arrives in an absorbing state, it never leaves. Clearly, every absorbing state forms its own subset, and each is positive recurrent. An *absorbing Markov chain* is one where every state is either transient or absorbing; therefore, $\mathbf{X}$ will enter an absorbing state sooner or later, and then stay put.

An absorbing chain is irreducible, then, when it has precisely one absorbing state. In this case, the long-run behavior of the chain is obvious and uninteresting. (The absorbing state has $\bar{\pi}_i = 1$.) Its short-term ("transient") behavior, however, can be interesting indeed, as we see next.

C.4.4 Discrete Phase-Type Distribution

Next, we describe a type of probability distribution defined in terms of an absorbing chain. Consider a finite-state, absorbing, irreducible chain $\mathbf{X}$, i.e., with a single absorbing state. Renumber the states, if necessary, so that the absorbing state comes last.

We revise the notation slightly: Use P to denote, not the full transition matrix, but rather only the submatrix corresponding to transient states, leaving out the last row and column; let P_{all} denote the full matrix. So,

$$P_{all} = \begin{pmatrix} P & (I - P)\mathbf{e} \\ \mathbf{0} & 1 \end{pmatrix}$$

(Here, I and $\mathbf{e}$ have the dimensions of P, not P_{all}. The $\mathbf{0}$ is a row-vector of 0's.) The chain is absorbing, it turns out, if and only if $I - P$ is nonsingular.

Similarly, let $\boldsymbol{\pi}_{all}(t)$ denote the full probability vector, and $\boldsymbol{\pi}(t)$ the subvector corresponding to transient states. Abbreviating $\boldsymbol{\pi} = \boldsymbol{\pi}(0)$, we have $\boldsymbol{\pi}_{all}(0) = (\boldsymbol{\pi}, 1 - \boldsymbol{\pi}\mathbf{e})$. It is easy to check that

$$P^t_{all} = \begin{pmatrix} P^t & (I - P^t)\mathbf{e} \\ \mathbf{0} & 1 \end{pmatrix}$$

so

$$\boldsymbol{\pi}_{all}(t) = \boldsymbol{\pi}_{all}(0)P^t_{all} = (\boldsymbol{\pi}P^t, 1 - \boldsymbol{\pi}P^t\mathbf{e})$$

In particular, the $\boldsymbol{\pi}(t)$ satisfy a linear recursion of the same form as (C.4.1):

$$\boldsymbol{\pi}(t + 1) = \boldsymbol{\pi}(t)P$$

This system is stable (the eigenvalues of P all lie inside the unit disk), so $\lim_{t\to\infty}\boldsymbol{\pi}(t) = \mathbf{0}$.

Let T be the first time the chain enters the absorbing state, that is, the *time until absorption*. Observe, for each $t \geq 0$, the event $\{T > t\}$ is equivalent to $\{X(t)$ is in a transient state$\}$. Consequently,

$$G^0(t) = \boldsymbol{\pi}(t)\mathbf{e} = \boldsymbol{\pi}P^t\mathbf{e} \qquad \text{(C.4.4)}$$

The random variable T has a *discrete phase-type distribution* with parameters $(\boldsymbol{\pi}, P)$, or for short, $T \sim \text{DPH}(\boldsymbol{\pi}, P)$. Any finite row-vector $\boldsymbol{\pi}$ and matrix P of the same dimensions specify such a distribution, under the following conditions:

$$\boldsymbol{\pi} \geq \mathbf{0} \qquad \boldsymbol{\pi}\mathbf{e} \leq 1$$

$$P \geq 0 \qquad P\mathbf{e} \leq \mathbf{e} \qquad I - P \text{ is nonsingular}$$

By using (C.4.4), it is not hard to show that

$$g(0) = 1 - \boldsymbol{\pi}\mathbf{e} \qquad g(t) = \boldsymbol{\pi}(I - P)P^{t-1}\mathbf{e} \qquad t > 0$$

$$\tilde{g}(z) = (1 - \boldsymbol{\pi}\mathbf{e}) + z\boldsymbol{\pi}(I - P)(I - zP)^{-1}\mathbf{e}$$

$$E[T] = \boldsymbol{\pi}(I - P)^{-1}\mathbf{e} \qquad ½E[T(T-1)] = \boldsymbol{\pi}P(I - P)^{-2}\mathbf{e}$$

$$G^1(t) = \boldsymbol{\pi}(I - P)^{-1}P^t\mathbf{e} \qquad G^2(t) = \boldsymbol{\pi}P(I - P)^{-2}P^t\mathbf{e}$$

To evaluate these quantities requires no more, but no less, than standard numerical tactics for solving linear systems. To compute $G^0(t)$, for instance, start with the column-vector $\mathbf{e}$. Premultiply by P to obtain $P\mathbf{e}$; premultiply again to obtain $P^2\mathbf{e}$; continue in this manner to obtain $P^t\mathbf{e}$. Then, multiply by the row-vector $\boldsymbol{\pi}$ to yield $G^0(t)$. To compute $G^1(t)$, follow the same procedure, but at the last step use the row-vector $\boldsymbol{\pi}(I - P)^{-1}$ instead of $\boldsymbol{\pi}$.

This approach works well for small t. For large t, something else is required. Here are two approaches: First, compute the power-of-two powers of P (P, P^2, P^4, P^8, etc.) by direct multiplication. Then, following the binary representation of t, premultiply $\mathbf{e}$ by the appropriate subset of these matrices to obtain $P^t\mathbf{e}$, and proceed as above. (For example, $P^{18}\mathbf{e} = P^{16}P^2\mathbf{e}$.)

Alternatively, start by computing the spectral decomposition of P. That is, express P in the form $P = ADA^{-1}$, where D is a "simple" matrix. (Often, D is a diagonal matrix.) Then, $P^t = AD^tA^{-1}$. Because D is simple, it is easy to compute D^t directly for any t.

Some of the formulas become simpler in the special case where $\boldsymbol{\pi}$ can be written as $\boldsymbol{\pi} = \boldsymbol{\psi}P$ for some probability vector $\boldsymbol{\psi}$ with $\boldsymbol{\psi}\mathbf{e} = 1$. Then,

$$g(t) = \boldsymbol{\psi}(I - P)P^t\mathbf{e} \qquad t \geq 0$$

$$\tilde{g}(z) = \boldsymbol{\psi}(I - P)(I - zP)^{-1}\mathbf{e}$$

For example, a geometric distribution has precisely this form; there is only one transient state, $P = (p)$, and $\boldsymbol{\psi} = (1)$. Thus, this subclass of DPH distributions generalizes the geometric distributions; the matrix P plays the same role as the scalar p. Similarly, a general DPH distribution is the matrix analogue of a delayed geometric distribution (see Section C.2.3.5). Here, $\boldsymbol{\pi}$ is analogous to π, and P to p.

Phase-type distributions are quite flexible: Consider the sum, or a mixture, or the minimum, or the maximum, of several independent random variables, each with a DPH distribution. Each such combination also has a DPH distribution. Also, any distribution on the nonnegative integers can be approximated as closely as desired by a DPH distribution.

C.5 Markov Chains: Continuous Time

C.5.1 Definition and Dynamics

A *continuous-time Markov chain* $\mathbf{X}$ is a discrete-state, continuous-time, time-homogeneous Markov process. (This is identical to the earlier definition of a Markov chain, except for the continuous time parameter.)

Here is one way to specify such a process: Suppose we are given

- A discrete-time Markov chain $\mathbf{X}^E$ with state space S and transition matrix P, where each $p_{ii} = 0$
- A vector $\boldsymbol{\theta} = (\theta_i)_{i \in S}$, where each $\theta_i > 0$

Construct the process $\mathbf{X} = \{X(t) : t \geq 0\}$ as follows: The state space of $\mathbf{X}$ too is S. The *sequence* of values is precisely that of the discrete-time chain $\mathbf{X}^E$. The *time* $\mathbf{X}$ spends in state i on each visit there, however, is a random variable, distributed exponentially with parameter θ_i. These times are independent of $\mathbf{X}^E$ and of each other.

So, on entering state i, $\mathbf{X}$ stays there for an exponential amount of time with mean $1/\theta_i$. Then, a transition occurs to another state, according to the probabilities in the matrix P. The discrete-time chain $\mathbf{X}^E$ is said to be *embedded* in $\mathbf{X}$ (which explains the superscript E). This $\mathbf{X}$, then, is a continuous-time Markov chain.

Here is another, equivalent way to specify the data and to construct $\mathbf{X}$, without reference to $\mathbf{X}^E$: Define the matrix $Q = (q_{ij})$, where

$$q_{ij} = \begin{cases} \theta_i p_{ij} & j \neq i \\ -\theta_i & j = i \end{cases}$$

Notice that $P\mathbf{e} = \mathbf{e}$ implies $Q\mathbf{e} = \mathbf{0}$. Q is called the (infinitesimal) *generator* of $\mathbf{X}$. Then, $\mathbf{X}$ operates as follows: Suppose $\mathbf{X}$ is now in state i. Over a small increment of time Δt, the probability of jumping to $j \neq i$ is approximately $q_{ij}(\Delta t)$, and that of staying at i approximately $1 - \theta_i(\Delta t)$. Moreover, these probabilities are independent of how $\mathbf{X}$ arrived at i and how long it has been there.

Thus, as long as $\mathbf{X}$ remains in state i, q_{ij} measures the potential of a jump to j, $j \neq i$; it is called the *transition rate* from i to j.

The generator Q thus fully describes the behavior of $\mathbf{X}$. To formulate $\mathbf{X}$, we can specify Q directly, bypassing P and $\boldsymbol{\theta}$. (Indeed, starting with a square matrix Q, having negative diagonal and non-negative off-diagonal entries, such that $Q\mathbf{e} = \mathbf{0}$, we can easily recover P and $\boldsymbol{\theta}$.)

The state-transition diagram for a continuous-time chain has nodes and arcs defined as in the discrete-time case: There is a node for each state, and an arc from i to j when $q_{ij} > 0$, $j \neq i$. (There is never an arc from i to itself, since $p_{ii} = 0$.) The transition rates q_{ij} are used as labels on the arcs, not the p_{ij}.

For example, suppose $S = \{1, 2, 3\}$ and

$$Q = \begin{pmatrix} -1 & 0 & 1 \\ 2 & -6 & 4 \\ 8 & 4 & -12 \end{pmatrix}$$

Figure C.5.1 shows the state-transition diagram.

Just as in the discrete-time case, define $\pi_i(t) = \Pr\{X(t) = i\}$ and the row-vector $\boldsymbol{\pi}(t) = [\pi_i(t)]_i$, $t \geq 0$. Let $\boldsymbol{\pi}'(t)$ denote the row-vector $[d\pi_i(t)/dt]_i$, the (componentwise) derivative of $\boldsymbol{\pi}(t)$ with respect to t. One can show that $\boldsymbol{\pi}(t)$ satisfies the system of linear differential equations

$$\boldsymbol{\pi}'(t) = \boldsymbol{\pi}(t)Q \qquad t \geq 0 \tag{C.5.1}$$

This is analogous to the difference equation (C.4.1) for the discrete-time case.

C.5.2 Analysis

A *stationary vector* $\bar{\boldsymbol{\pi}}$ in this context is one satisfying the *balance equations*

$$\boldsymbol{\pi}Q = \mathbf{0}$$

FIGURE C.5.1

State-transition diagram (three states, continuous time).

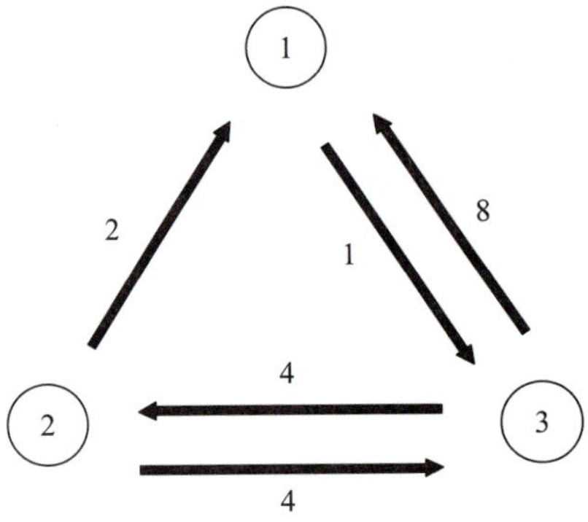

and the normalization equation

$$\boldsymbol{\pi}\mathbf{e} = 1$$

for then $\boldsymbol{\pi}(0) = \boldsymbol{\pi}^-$ implies $\boldsymbol{\pi}(t) = \boldsymbol{\pi}^-$, for all $t \geq 0$. A *limiting vector* $\boldsymbol{\pi}^\infty$ has the property that

$$\lim_{t\to\infty} \boldsymbol{\pi}(t) = \boldsymbol{\pi}^\infty$$

for all $\boldsymbol{\pi}(0)$.

Most of the key properties of $\mathbf{X}$ are inherited from the embedded discrete-time chain $\mathbf{X}^E$. $\mathbf{X}$ is irreducible or periodic, when $\mathbf{X}^E$ has the corresponding property. Furthermore, the definitions of recurrent, positive-recurrent, and null-recurrent subsets are the same as in the discrete-time case; and when S is finite, every recurrent subset is also positive-recurrent.

The only exception concerns positive-recurrence in the case of an infinite state space S. Now, we need *two* assumptions in place of the one in Section C.4.3:

ASSUMPTION 1. The embedded discrete-time chain $\mathbf{X}^E$ has at least one positive-recurrent subset.

This is the assumption of Section C.4.3 for the discrete-time case. Recall, this implies that $\mathbf{X}^E$ has a stationary vector, say $\boldsymbol{\pi}^{E-}$.

ASSUMPTION 2. The following quantity is finite:

$$\frac{1}{\theta} = \Sigma_{i\in S} \frac{\pi_i^{E-}}{\theta_i}$$

(Think of $1/\theta$ as the average time until $\mathbf{X}$ leaves its current state, with the current state chosen randomly according to $\boldsymbol{\pi}^{E-}$.) Clearly, both assumptions are satisfied automatically when S is finite.

Under these two assumptions, $\mathbf{X}$ has a stationary vector $\boldsymbol{\pi}^-$, given by

$$\pi_i^- = \frac{\pi_i^{E-}/\theta_i}{1/\theta}$$

or

$$\frac{\pi_i^-}{\theta} = \frac{\pi_i^{E-}}{\theta_i}$$

When additionally $\mathbf{X}^E$ (and hence $\mathbf{X}$) is irreducible, this is the unique stationary vector; in that case, $\boldsymbol{\pi}^-$ also describes the long-run frequency distribution. Under these conditions, furthermore, $\mathbf{X}$ has a limiting vector $\boldsymbol{\pi}^\infty = \boldsymbol{\pi}^-$.

(Interestingly, we do *not* need to assume $\mathbf{X}$ is aperiodic to obtain a limiting vector, in contrast to the discrete-time case. Even when the *sequence* of transitions is periodic, the random *times* between transitions dissipates the predictability of the process in the long run.)

C.5.3 Joint Independent Processes

Consider two independent continuous-time Markov chains $\mathbf{X}_1$ and $\mathbf{X}_2$, with finite but possibly different state spaces S_1 and S_2, and generators Q_1 and Q_2. Then, the joint process $\mathbf{X} = (\mathbf{X}_1, \mathbf{X}_2) = \{[X_1(t), X_2(t)] : t \geq 0\}$ is also a continuous-time Markov chain. But, what is its generator?

Here is some useful notation: Suppose $A = (a_{ij})_{ij}$ and B are finite, square matrices, where A is of dimensions $n \times n$ and B is $m \times m$. The *Kronecker product* of A and B is

$$A \otimes B = \begin{pmatrix} a_{11}B & \dots & a_{1n}B \\ \vdots & \vdots & \vdots \\ a_{n1}B & \dots & a_{nn}B \end{pmatrix}$$

The *Kronecker sum* of A and B

$$A \oplus B = A \otimes I + I \otimes B$$

The first I here has the dimensions of B, and the second the dimensions of A. Thus, $A \otimes B$ and $A \oplus B$ are both of dimensions $(mn) \times (mn)$.

It turns out that the generator of $\mathbf{X}$ is precisely $Q_1 \oplus Q_2$.

Let us sketch an explanation: Suppose $S_1 = \{1, \dots, n\}$ and $S_2 = \{1, \dots, m\}$. List the states of the joint process $\mathbf{X}$ in the order $(1, 1), (1, 2), \dots, (1, m); (2, 1), (2, 2), \dots, (2, m); \dots; (n, 1), (n, 2), \dots, (n, m)$. Now, at each transition of $\mathbf{X}$, only one of the component processes $\mathbf{X}_1$ and $\mathbf{X}_2$ changes; the other remains as it was. So, consider the transition rates for each type of change: If $\mathbf{X}_1$ were fixed, with Q_1 replaced by 0, the generator of $\mathbf{X}$ would be n copies of Q_2, arranged as blocks along the diagonal. This is precisely $I \otimes Q_2$. Likewise, if $\mathbf{X}_2$ were fixed, the generator of $\mathbf{X}$ would be $Q_1 \otimes I$. The actual generator is the sum of these two, namely $Q_1 \oplus Q_2$.

C.5.4 Birth-Death Processes

We now consider a simple but important type of continuous-time Markov chain, a *birth-death process*. Here, S is the non-negative integers. From each state, a transition can occur only to one of its nearest neighbors. Among discrete-state processes, a birth-death process is the closest analogue to a continuous process.

Such chains are used to model populations of people or animals. A transition upward represents a birth, and a transition downward a death (hence the name birth-death process). There are many other applications, e.g., to supply systems, as discussed below.

A birth-death process has an infinite S, but still is highly structured. Using this structure, we can determine whether the chain has a stationary vector and, if so, compute it:

Denote

$$\lambda_i = q_{i-1,i} \qquad \mu_i = q_{i,i-1} \qquad i > 0$$

For a birth-death process, all the other $q_{ij} = 0$, $i \neq j$. Assume all the μ_i are positive; this implies $\mathbf{X}$ is irreducible. For now, assume all the λ_i are positive also.

Define $\rho_0 = 1$, and

$$\rho_i = \frac{\lambda_i}{\mu_i} \qquad i > 0$$

$$R_i = \Pi_{j \le i}\, \rho_j \qquad i \ge 0$$

$$R = \Sigma_{i=0}^{\infty} R_i$$

The balance equations are equivalent to

$$\pi_i = R_i \pi_0 \qquad i \ge 0$$

The normalization equation then reduces to

$$1 = \Sigma_{i=0}^{\infty} \pi_i = R\pi_0$$

If R is finite, the equations have the unique solution

$$\pi_i = \bar{\pi}_i = \frac{R_i}{R} \qquad i \ge 0$$

and $\boldsymbol{\pi}^- = (\pi_i^-)_i$ is the unique stationary and limiting vector. Otherwise, if $R = \infty$, there is no solution, and the chain is either transient or null-recurrent.

For example, suppose all the $\lambda_i = \lambda$ and the $\mu_i = \mu$, where λ and μ are positive constants. (This case describes a simple queue, the M/M/1 system.) Then, $\rho_i = \rho = \lambda/\mu$, $i > 0$, so $R_i = \rho^i$, $i \ge 0$. Therefore, R is finite, if and only if $\rho < 1$, in which case $R = 1/(1 - \rho)$. Here, the stationary vector describes a geometric distribution with parameter ρ, that is, $\pi_i^- = (1 - \rho)\rho^i$, $i \ge 0$. If $\rho \ge 1$, there is no stationary vector. It turns out that $\mathbf{X}$ is transient when $\rho > 1$, and null-recurrent when $\rho = 1$.

Now, consider the case where some of the $\lambda_i = 0$. Let $s + 1$ be the smallest such i. Now, all states $i > s$ are transient. Ignoring these transient states, we can think of $\mathbf{X}$ as describing a *finite-state* chain on the state space $\{0, 1, \ldots, s\}$. This model is called a *finite birth-death process.* In this case, R is always finite (because $R_i = 0$, $i > s$), and the stationary vector is computed as above.

In the special case where $\lambda_i = \lambda$ and $\mu_i = \mu$, $i \le s$ (a finite M/M/1 queue), there is a stationary vector for *any* value of ρ. For $\rho \ne 1$, $R = (1 - \rho^{s+1})/(1 - \rho)$, so $\pi_i^- = (1 - \rho)\rho^i/(1 - \rho^{s+1})$, $i \le s$. For $\rho = 1$, $\boldsymbol{\pi}^-$ describes a uniform distribution: $\pi_i = 1/(s + 1)$, $i \le s$.

C.5.5 Continuous Phase-Type Distribution

Next, we introduce a *continuous* probability distribution, analogous to the *discrete* phase-type distribution of Section C.4.4. Just as the latter is defined in terms of a discrete-time Markov chain, this new distribution is constructed from a continuous-time chain.

Suppose $\mathbf{X}$ is a continuous-time Markov chain with generator Q_{all} and a specified initial vector $\boldsymbol{\mu}_{all}$. The last state is an absorbing state, and we partition the data as follows:

$$Q_{all} = \begin{pmatrix} -M & M\mathbf{e} \\ \mathbf{0} & 0 \end{pmatrix}$$

$$\boldsymbol{\mu}_{all} = (\boldsymbol{\mu}, 1 - \boldsymbol{\mu}\mathbf{e})$$

The vector $\boldsymbol{\mu}$ describes the initial probabilities of the transient states, so $\boldsymbol{\mu} \ge \mathbf{0}$, $\boldsymbol{\mu}\mathbf{e} \le 1$. As for M, its diagonal is positive, the off-diagonal entries are nonpositive, and $M\mathbf{e} \ge \mathbf{0}$; in addition, M is nonsingular. (The latter property ensures that $\mathbf{X}$ is an absorbing chain.)

Again, let T be the time until absorption. Arguing as in Section C.4.4, one can show that the ccdf of T is

$$F_T^0(t) = \boldsymbol{\mu} e^{-Mt}\mathbf{e}$$

That is, the subvector $\boldsymbol{\pi}(t)$ of $\boldsymbol{\pi}_{\text{all}}(t)$ solves the system of linear differential equations

$$\boldsymbol{\pi}'(t) = \boldsymbol{\pi}(t)(-M) \qquad t \geq 0 \tag{C.5.2}$$

with initial conditions $\boldsymbol{\pi}(0) = \boldsymbol{\mu}$, and $F_T^0(t) = \boldsymbol{\pi}(t)\mathbf{e}$. We say that T has a *continuous phase-type distribution* with parameters $(\boldsymbol{\mu}, M)$, or $T \sim \text{CPH}(\boldsymbol{\mu}, M)$.

If $\boldsymbol{\mu}\mathbf{e} < 1$, then $\Pr\{T = 0\} > 0$, so F_T is not purely continuous. Nevertheless, we include this case among the CPH distributions. Also, $-M$ is more commonly used as the matrix parameter than M itself; we find M more convenient.

One can show that $\Pr\{T = 0\} = 1 - \boldsymbol{\mu}\mathbf{e}$, and for $t > 0$, T has pdf

$$f(t) = \boldsymbol{\mu} M e^{-Mt}\mathbf{e} \qquad t > 0$$

Also,

$$\tilde{f}(s) = (1 - \boldsymbol{\mu}\mathbf{e}) + \boldsymbol{\mu} M(sI + M)^{-1}\mathbf{e}$$

$$E[T] = \boldsymbol{\mu} M^{-1}\mathbf{e} \qquad E[T^2] = \boldsymbol{\mu} M^{-2}\mathbf{e}$$

$$F_T^1(t) = \boldsymbol{\mu} M^{-1} e^{-Mt}\mathbf{e} \qquad F_T^2(t) = \boldsymbol{\mu} M^{-2} e^{-Mt}\mathbf{e}$$

The Laplace transform and the moments can thus be computed through matrix inversion. To calculate the ccdf F^0, we must solve the differential equations (C.5.2). While this is not a trivial task, there are standard numerical methods, which are widely available in scientific software packages.

Just as the DPH distribution generalizes the geometric, the CPH distribution can be viewed as the matrix analogue of the exponential distribution. Indeed, an exponential distribution with parameter μ *is* a CPH distribution; there is one transient state, $\boldsymbol{\mu} = (1)$, and $M = (\mu)$.

The CPH distributions are flexible in the same senses their discrete cousins are: They can model widely diverse phenomena, and they can approximate any distribution on the nonnegative reals.

C.5.6 Poisson Processes and Renewal Processes

A *Poisson process* is a counting process with stationary, independent increments. It has one parameter, $\lambda > 0$, called its *rate*. Let $\mathbf{D} = \{D(t) : t \geq 0\}$ denote the process. Then, $\lambda = E[D(1)]$, so $E[D(t)] = \lambda t$. This construct is widely used to model demands, among many other things; there, $D(t)$ is the cumulative demand through time t. The basic facts are set forth in Section 6.2.1 of Chapter 6. Here, we mention some additional properties.

A Poisson process is a special continuous-time Markov chain. The state-transition diagram is precisely Figure C.4.5; the only possible transitions are from i to $i + 1$, $i \geq 0$, and the transition rate on every such arc is λ. Thus, regardless of the current state i, the probability of a jump to state $i + 1$ (e.g., a demand occurring) during a short time Δt is about $\lambda(\Delta t)$. (This chain is transient.)

For each $t > 0$, the random variable $D(t)$ has the *Poisson distribution* with mean λt. Also, let T_1 denote the time of the first demand, and T_n the time between the $(n - 1)$st and nth demands, $n \geq 1$. Then, the T_n are independent random variables, each having the *exponential distribution* with mean $1/\lambda$.

These processes have some important conservation properties: Consider two independent Poisson processes $\mathbf{D}_1$ and $\mathbf{D}_2$ with rates λ_1 and λ_2, respectively. Then, the *superposition* $\mathbf{D}$, where $D(t) = D_1(t) + D_2(t)$, is also a Poisson process with rate $\lambda = \lambda_1 + \lambda_2$. Clearly, the superposition of more than two such processes is also Poisson.

Conversely, consider a Poisson process **D** with rate λ and a Bernoulli sequence $\{X_n: n \geq 1\}$ (Section C.2.3.5) with parameter p, independent of **D.** Now, construct a pair of processes $\mathbf{D}_1$ and $\mathbf{D}_2$ as follows: At the instant the nth point of **D** occurs, examine X_n. If $X_n = 1$, assign this point to $\mathbf{D}_1$, that is, increment $D_1(t)$ by one at the same instant; otherwise, if $X_n = 0$, assign the point to the other process $\mathbf{D}_2$. The pair $(\mathbf{D}_1, \mathbf{D}_2)$ is called a *splitting* of **D.** It turns out that both $\mathbf{D}_1$ and $\mathbf{D}_2$ are Poisson processes, with respective rates $\lambda_1 = p\lambda$ and $\lambda_2 = (1 - p)\lambda$, and they are independent.

Sometimes, we are interested only in $\mathbf{D}_1$; in effect, we "throw away" the points assigned to $\mathbf{D}_2$. The process $\mathbf{D}_1$ by itself is called a *thinning* of **D.** A thinning of a Poisson process, then, is itself a Poisson process.

Furthermore, consider a large number of independent, stationary counting processes, not necessarily Poisson processes, and consider the superposition of all of them. Provided certain regularity conditions are satisfied, this superposition behaves approximately like a Poisson process, at least over a relatively short time interval. (This fact is sometimes referred to as the central limit theorem for counting processes. It explains why so many actual, observed counting processes appear much like Poisson processes.)

A *renewal process* is a counting process whose interevent times T_n are independent, identically distributed random variables. The T_n can have any distribution. A Poisson process is the special case where the distribution of the T_n is exponential.

C.6 Stochastic Linear Systems in Discrete Time

C.6.1 Formulation

This section briefly discusses a discrete-time linear system whose input is stochastic. (In other ways the system is somewhat special; there is no control and no objective.)

Here is the basic notation:

t = index for time points, $t = 0, \ldots$
$\mathbf{x}(t)$ = state at time t, a real-valued n-vector
$\mathbf{e}(t)$ = input at time t, a real-valued m-vector

All vectors are column vectors. The $\mathbf{e}(t)$ represent pure noise. Specifically, the vectors $\mathbf{e}(t)$ are independent over t, and for all t,

$$E[\mathbf{e}(t)] = \mathbf{0} \qquad V[\mathbf{e}(t)] = I$$

Assume that each $\mathbf{e}(t)$ has a normal distribution. (This assumption is unnecessary for many of the results, but it helps to sharpen the discussion.) Thus, each $\mathbf{e}(t)$ is a vector of independent random variables, each with a standard normal distribution. The initial value $\mathbf{x}_0$ may be a fixed constant or more generally a random variable with a given normal distribution.

The system operates according to the following equations:

Initial conditions:

$$\mathbf{x}(0) = \mathbf{x}_0$$

Dynamics:

$$\mathbf{x}(t + 1) = A\mathbf{x}(t) + S\mathbf{e}(t) \qquad t = 0, \ldots$$

Here, A is a constant $n \times n$ matrix, while S is a constant $n \times m$ matrix. The collection $\mathbf{X} = \{\mathbf{x}(t) : t \geq 0\}$ describes a stochastic process. This is a Markov process, because the $\mathbf{e}(t)$ are independent over t. It is time-homogeneous, because A and S are constants.

Such models are used for many purposes. For instance, many standard demand-forecasting methods essentially fit a model of this form. We shall see some examples later on. Here, typically, demand in period t is one of the components of $\mathbf{x}(t)$ or some other simple function of $\mathbf{x}(t)$. There are powerful methods to estimate the required coefficients. These and related methods fall under the heading of *time-series analysis.*

C.6.2 Analysis

Because $\mathbf{x}_0$ and the $\mathbf{e}(t)$ are all normally distributed, so are the $\mathbf{x}(t)$. By (C.2.2) and (C.2.3), the mean and covariance matrix of the $\mathbf{x}(t)$ satisfy the following recursions:

$$E[\mathbf{x}(t+1)] = AE[\mathbf{x}(t)]$$

$$V[\mathbf{x}(t+1)] = AV[\mathbf{x}(t)]A' + SS' \qquad t = 0, \ldots$$

Consequently,

$$E[\mathbf{x}(t)] = A^t E[\mathbf{x}_0] \qquad t = 0, \ldots$$

It is not possible to write $V[\mathbf{x}(t)]$ in closed form, in general, but it can be computed easily using the recursion above.

What does system stability mean in this context? Here is a reasonable definition: The system is stable when $\mathbf{X}$ has a limiting distribution. A necessary and sufficient condition for stability, it turns out, is $A^t \to 0$. This is, of course, the same condition as in the deterministic case. Thus, all the eigenvalues of A lie inside the unit disk. In this case, letting $\mathbf{x}$ denote the limiting random variable, then $\mathbf{x}$ has a normal distribution, where

$$E[\mathbf{x}] = \mathbf{0}$$

and $V[\mathbf{x}]$ is the solution to the following matrix equation in the unknown V:

$$V = AVA' + SS'$$

(The equation does have a solution; there are numerical methods to compute it.) If $\mathbf{x}_0$ has this distribution, then $\mathbf{X}$ is stationary and ergodic.

The case where $\mathbf{x}(t)$ and $\mathbf{e}(t)$ are both scalars is instructive. Here, $\mathbf{X}$ is called a *first-order autoregressive process.* Write $\mathbf{x}(t) = x(t)$, $\mathbf{e}(t) = e(t)$, $A = (a)$ and $S = (s)$. So, the dynamics become

$$x(t+1) = ax(t) + se(t)$$

The stability condition in this case reduces to $|a| < 1$. Presuming stability, we have

$$E[x(t+1)] = aE[x(t)] = a^{t+1}E[x_0]$$

$$V[x(t+1)] = a^2 V[x(t)] + s^2$$

$$= a^{2(t+1)}V[x_0] + \left(\frac{1 - a^{2(t+1)}}{1 - a^2}\right) s^2$$

and, in the limit,

$$E[x] = 0$$

$$V[x] = \left(\frac{1}{1 - a^2}\right) s^2$$

C.6.3 Stochastic Coefficients

Continuing with the scalar model, suppose that the coefficient a is no longer a constant. In its place is a sequence $\{a(t)\}$ of i.i.d. random variables, independent of $\{e(t)\}$. The dynamics become

$$x(t + 1) = a(t)x(t) + se(t)$$

(However, s is still a constant.) Let a denote a generic random variable, distributed as the $a(t)$. Assume that $0 \leq a \leq 1$ and $E[a^2] < 1$.

Here, $x(t)$ is in general *not* normally distributed, but we can compute its moments: Since $a(t)$ is independent of $x(t)$,

$$E[x(t + 1)] = E[a(t)]E[x(t)] = E^{t+1}[a]E[x_0]$$

and by (C.2.1),

$$\begin{aligned} V[x(t + 1)] &= V[E[x(t + 1) \mid x(t)]] + E[V[x(t + 1) \mid x(t)]] \\ &= V[E[a(t)]x(t)] + E[V[a(t)]x^2(t) + s^2] \\ &= V[E[a]x(t)] + E[V[a]x^2(t) + s^2] \\ &= E^2[a]V[x(t)] + V[a]E[x^2(t)] + s^2 \\ &= E[a^2]V[x(t)] + V[a]E^2[x(t)] + s^2 \\ &= E[a^2]V[x(t)] + V[a]E^{2t}[a]E^2[x_0] + s^2 \end{aligned}$$

The variance can be simplified further, but let us proceed directly to the limiting values:

$$E[x] = 0$$

$$V[x] = \left\{\frac{1}{1 - E[a^2]}\right\} s^2$$

C.6.4 Applications to Demand Forecasting

The scalar model (with constant coefficients) is sometimes used for demand forecasting in a discrete-time setting. Here is one approach: At each time t, we forecast the demand during period t. Call the forecast $f(t)$. This is a point estimate. The actual demand $d(t)$ will typically deviate somewhat from the forecast. Call the deviation $\varepsilon(t) = d(t) - f(t)$. At time $t + 1$, having observed $d(t)$, compute the forecast for the next period (*update* the forecast) by

$$f(t + 1) = (1 - \alpha)f(t) + \alpha d(t) = f(t) + \alpha\varepsilon(t)$$

This approach is called *exponential smoothing*. The parameter α is called the *smoothing constant;* it is a positive number between 0 and 1. Thus, the updated forecast is a weighted average of the prior forecast and the actual, observed demand. If demand exceeds the forecast, so $\varepsilon(t) > 0$, revise the forecast upward by the fixed fraction α of the deviation; conversely, a negative deviation reduces the forecast. The initial forecast $f(0) = f_0$ is some given constant.

We can describe this procedure in terms of linear systems as follows: The state variable $x(t)$ is the forecast $f(t)$ itself. For now, think of the input as $e(t) = \varepsilon(t)$. So, the parameters are $a = 1$ and $s = \alpha$. The actual demand is $d(t) = f(t) + \varepsilon(t) = x(t) + (1/\alpha)e(t)$.

We haven't made any assumptions about the deviations $\varepsilon(t)$ which drive the demands. But, consider under what conditions this technique makes sense: A good forecast should be unbiased, which means $E[d(t)] = f(t)$, or $E[\varepsilon(t)] = 0$. Also, the forecast should take account fully of all current information, which means that $\varepsilon(t)$ is independent of $f(t)$, and therefore of all past deviations. Thus, the input sequence $\{e(t)\}$ has (or should have) two of the key properties assumed above, namely, $E[e(t)] = 0$ and independence. Now, *assume* that the deviations are stationary, so that $V[\varepsilon(t)]$ is a constant $V[\varepsilon]$, and redefine $s = \alpha(V[\varepsilon])^{1/2}$ and $e(t) = (\alpha/s)\varepsilon(t)$. Then, $V[e(t)] = 1$, and the system dynamics are $x(t + 1) = x(t) + se(t)$, as above.

Exponential smoothing is a popular technique in practice, perhaps too popular, in my opinion. It is certainly simple, and that is a virtue. And, it works well when the underlying model fits, i.e., when the real demand is generated by something like the model above. Otherwise, it may not. Unfortunately, it is sometimes presented as an all-purpose tool, appropriate for all occasions, free of model assumptions and restrictions. It is not. Also, numerous (and conflicting) rules of thumb are cheerfully proposed to select the smoothing constant. But rules of any kind are inappropriate here. The smoothing constant is a model parameter, and it should be estimated like any other. This does not mean that fancy methods are necessary; there is a role for simple heuristics in statistical estimation, provided they are understood as such.

Notice too that the system here is unstable, since $a = 1$. In particular,

$$\begin{aligned} d(t) &= \varepsilon(t) + f(t) = \epsilon(t) + [\alpha\varepsilon(t-1) + f(t-1)] \\ &= \varepsilon(t) + \alpha\varepsilon(t-1) + [\alpha\varepsilon(t-2) + f(t-2)] \\ &= \varepsilon(t) + \alpha[\varepsilon(t-1) + \cdots + \varepsilon(0)\,] + f(0) \end{aligned}$$

so $V[d(t)] = (1 + \alpha^2 t)V[\varepsilon]$. That is, the variance of future demand, as viewed from the present, is linearly increasing in t.

Another forecasting model is based on the first-order autoregressive process above. Suppose there is a constant base demand $\underline{d}$. Now, $x(t + 1)$ represents the deviation of actual demand $d(t)$ from $\underline{d}$; i.e., $x(t + 1) = d(t) - \underline{d}$, and $x(0) = x_0 = 0$. The dynamics of these deviations are given by

$$x(t+1) = ax(t) + se(t)$$

where $0 < a < 1$, so the system is stable. In these terms the forecast becomes $f(0) = \underline{d}$, and $f(t) = \underline{d} + E[x(t + 1) \mid x(t)] = \underline{d} + ax(t) = (1 - a)\underline{d} + ad(t - 1)$, $t > 0$. The two parameters $\underline{d}$ and a are estimated by statistical methods.

An *ARMA* process is a more general type of model, also used in forecasting. (ARMA stands for *autoregressive moving average.*) Again, there is a base demand $\underline{d}$, and we model the deviation $x(t + 1)$. Now, however, $x(t + 1)$ depends not just on $x(t)$, but also on the values at certain earlier times, say $x(t - 1)$ and $x(t - 2)$. Also, it depends on scalar noise factors over several time periods, say $e(t)$ and $e(t - 1)$. So, the stochastic process $\{x(t) : t \geq 0\}$ is certainly *not* a Markov process.

Such a process can be written as a linear system in the form above by formulating the state vector $\mathbf{x}(t)$ appropriately, treating past quantities as auxiliary variables. In the example above, set $\mathbf{x}(t) = [x(t), x(t-1), x(t-2), e(t-1)]'$, a vector with four components. Also, $\mathbf{e}(t) = e(t)$. Clearly, $\mathbf{x}(t + 1)$ depends only on $\mathbf{x}(t)$ and $\mathbf{e}(t)$, so $\mathbf{X}$ is indeed a Markov process.

Some of the dynamic equations are now definitional identities, for example, $x_2(t + 1) = x_3(t)$. So, some elements of A and S are fixed. Still, there are more parameters here than in the first-order autoregressive process. This is good, in that the model is more flexible, but bad, in that more data and effort are required to obtain good parameter estimates.

Most forecasting techniques are best viewed as statistical methods to fit dynamical systems of this kind. That is true even of more intricate techniques, which account for seasonal and trend factors.

Notes

Good introductory textbooks on probability and stochastic processes include Cox and Miller [1965], Heyman and Sobel [1982,1984], Karlin and Taylor [1975,1981], and Ross [1980]. The volumes by Feller [1957,1971] are classics in this area. For a collection of recent surveys of various topics see Heyman and Sobel [1990].

These books all discuss Markov chains, but Kemeny and Snell [1960] provide a focused treatment of the subject. On (both discrete and continuous) phase-type distributions, see Neuts [1981].

For introductions to time series analysis and forecasting, see Box and Jenkins [1976], Brown [1963], and Makridakis et al. [1983].

APPENDIX D
NOTATIONAL CONVENTIONS

Outline

D.1 Objectives and Conventions

The field of inventory theory is notorious for notational inconsistency. For example, a cursory scan of the literature reveals a wealth of symbols (*a, A, k, K, s, S,* and others), all used to indicate a fixed order cost. The symbols *R* and *s* are both widely used to denote a reorder point, albeit in slightly different contexts.

One does become accustomed to this notational promiscuity after a while, but for those approaching the material for the first time, it imposes a significant extra burden. Even for veterans it sometimes obscures ideas and the connections between them.

I have tried as best I can, therefore, to use consistent notational conventions throughout the book. Here are some examples:

> Lowercase letters are used throughout to indicate decision and policy variables. This is consistent with common usage in algebra, optimization, and mathematics generally. Thus, a lot size is denoted *q,* even though *Q* is seen more often in the literature. Cost coefficients and other constant parameters are also indicated by lower-case letters; *k,* not *K* or anything else, is the fixed order cost. Uppercase letters are reserved for important functions, random variables, and stochastic processes, as well as matrices.
>
> Boldface is used for **vectors** and **stochastic processes.**
>
> I have tried to impose some consistency between deterministic and stochastic models, even when this departs from common usage. Thus, λ denotes an average demand rate throughout, and μ an average production rate, not just where they *are* commonly used in this way (stochastic, continuous-time models), but also where they are *not* (like the EOQ model).
>
> Double letters indicate functions and processes associated with inventories (*IN* for net inventory, *IP* for inventory position, etcetera). This is the only solution I have found for a vexing problem: There are too many of these quantities, and they are all important. This usage of character strings borrows from computer languages; students seem to get used to the idea pretty quickly.

This approach has its drawbacks: Instructors will have to adapt their thinking and their notes; *after* the course, students will have to do some adapting to access the literature and to communicate with colleagues. (The latter problem is inevitable anyway, because of the field's general notational inconsistency.) For this I apologize. In my view, however, these are small prices to pay to avoid unnecessary obstacles to learning.

Consistency does have its limits, and I have run smack into one of them in selecting notation for the discrete-time control models of Chapters 4 and 9. There, inventory is essentially a decision variable, not a stochastic process. Should it be uppercase (as elsewhere in the book) or lowercase (consistent with the convention above, as well as the bulk of the literature)? I have chosen the second option. The result is *two* symbols for inventory, *I* and *x,* in different places. Alas!

There may remain other inconsistencies that my old, jaded eyes have missed. If so, I apologize again.

D.2 Symbols Used

Here is a list of the important symbols and their continuing usages. Occasional, transient usages are not included.

a_i	Unit resource requirement of item i (Section 5.7)
$a[t, u)$	Arc cost (Chapter 4)
A	Stockout indicator (equilibrium random variable); arcs in a network (Section 5.4)
$A(t)$	Stockout indicator (at time t) $= \mathbf{1}\{I(t) = 0\}$
$\overline{A}$	Stockout frequency
b	Backorder penalty-cost rate
B	Backorders (equilibrium random variable)
$\mathbf{B}$	Backorders (stochastic process)
$B(t)$	Backorders (at time t)
$\overline{B}$	Backorders (average)
BW	Customer waiting time (equilibrium random variable)
$\overline{BW}$	Customer waiting time (average)
c	Unit variable order cost
$\tilde{c}[t, u)$	Unit cost to order and hold (from time t until u, Chapter 4)
c^+	$(1 - \gamma)c$ (Chapter 9)
cB	Aggregate backorders value (Section 5.2, Section 8.2)
cI	Aggregate inventory value (Section 5.2, Section 8.2)
$C(\cdot)$	Total cost (e.g., average total cost, function of policy variables)
$\hat{C}(\cdot)$	Current holding-backorder-cost function; $\hat{C}(x) = h[x]^+ + b[x]^-$
$\underline{C}(\cdot)$	Truncated cost (Section 8.3.3)
$C^+(\cdot)$	Augmented cost for myopic formulation (Section 9.4)
$d(t)$	Demand (at time t, discrete time)
D	Leadtime demand
$\mathbf{D}$	Demand process
$D(t)$	Cumulative demand through time t
$D[t, u)$	Demand in the interval $[t, u)$
e	Base of natural logarithms
$\mathbf{e}$	Column-vector of ones
$E[\cdot]$	Expectation
f	Probability density function (pdf); arbitrary function
$\tilde{f}$	Laplace transform
F	Cumulative distribution function (or cdf, for continuous random variable)
F^0	Complementary cumulative distribution function (or ccdf, for continuous random variable)

F^1	Loss function (for continuous random variable)
F^2	Second-order loss function (for continuous random variable)
g	Probability mass function (pmf)
$\tilde{g}$	z-transform
G	Cumulative distribution function (or cdf, for discrete random variable)
G^0	Complementary cumulative distribution function (or ccdf, for discrete random variable)
G^1	Loss function (for discrete random variable)
G^2	Second-order loss function (for discrete random variable)
h	Inventory holding-cost rate
$\underline{h}$	Direct handling cost rate
$H(t, y)$	Total expected cost from t onward (Chapter 9)
i	Index for items, stages
I	Inventory (equilibrium random variable); identity matrix
$\mathbf{I}$	Inventory (stochastic process)
$I(t)$	Inventory (at time t)
$\overline{I}$	Inventory (average)
IN	Net inventory
IO	Inventory on order
IP	Inventory position
IP_c	$r + q - IP$
IT	Inventory in transit
ITP	Inventory-transit position
$\overline{IW}$	Average stocking time
j	Index for items, stages
J	Number of items, stages
J_*	Variety index (Section 5.2)
k	Fixed order cost
$k[t, u)$	Arc cost (Section 4.3)
L	Leadtime (constant or random variable)
$L(t)$	Virtual leadtime (at time t)
m	Number of processors (Section 7.3)
m_j	Renewal function (discrete) (Section 6.6)
M	Matrix parameter of CPH distribution
n	Shape parameter of gamma, negative-binomial distributions; customer index; reversed time index (Section 9.4)
N	Nodes in a network (Section 5.4)
$\overline{OF}$	Order frequency (average)
p	Unit sales price; probability (parameter of geometric distribution, etc.)
P	Transition probability matrix
$P(\cdot)$	Total profit

$\Pr\{\cdot\}$	Probability
$Pre\,(j)$	Predecessors (of item j, Section 5.4)
q	Order or batch size
Q	Generator matrix (of continuous-time Markov chain)
r	Reorder point
r_{ij}	Routing probability for network
R	Routing-probability matrix
$R(\cdot)$	Total revenue
s	Base-stock level; target stock level for (r, s) policy; time index
S	Processing time (random variable); arbitrary set
$Suc\,(j)$	Successors (of item j, Section 5.4)
t	Time variable
T	Time horizon
u	Time between orders, or cycle time; time index
$u(t)$	$s - x(t)$ (Section 9.4.8)
v	Safety stock
$v(t)$	Indicator variable for ordering (discrete time)
$V(t, x)$	Optimal expected cost from t onward (Chapter 9)
$V^{+}(t, x)$	$V(t, x) + c(t)x$ (Chapter 9)
$V[\cdot]$	Variance
$V[\cdot, \cdot]$	Covariance
w	State of the world (Section 6.3, Section 9.7); workload for an order (Section 5.2)
wO	Aggregate workload (Section 5.2)
W	World, a stochastic process driving demands (Section 6.3, Section 9.7)
$x(t)$	Inventory position (at time t, discrete time)
$\hat{x}(t)$	Net inventory (at time t, discrete time)
$y(t)$	Inventory position after ordering (at time t, discrete time)
Y	Demand size (random variable)
z	Standardized base-stock level; argument of z-transform
$z(t)$	Order quantity (at time t, discrete time)
$z_{+}(t)$	Capacity (at time t, discrete time)
α	Interest rate (continuous time)
β	Backorder-cost multiplier (Section 5.2 and Section 8.2); order-inflation factor (Section 9.4.8)
γ	Discount factor (discrete time)
Γ	Gamma function
δ	Defect rate; Heaviside function (Chapter 4)
Δ	Defects (Section 9.4.8); difference operator
$\epsilon(\cdot)$	EOQ error function, $\epsilon(x) = \frac{1}{2}(x + 1/x)$
ζ	Dual variable
η	Holding-cost multiplier (Section 5.2, Section 8.2)

θ	Demand ratio (Section 7.3.7, Section 8.5)
$\boldsymbol{\iota}$	Stationary vector of **IP** for (r, s) policy
κ	Fixed-cost multiplier (Section 5.2, Section 8.2)
λ	Demand rate
$\lambda(t)$	Demand rate (at time t)
Λ	Demand-rate matrix for MCDC process
μ	Production (service) rate; scale parameter of exponential or gamma distribution
$\boldsymbol{\mu}$	Vector parameter of CPH distribution
ν	Mean of leadtime demand
ξ	Yield rate (Section 9.4.8)
$\boldsymbol{\xi}$	Stationary vector of Markov chain
Ξ	Yield (Section 9.4.8)
π	Policy; pi, the number $3.14159 \cdots$
$\boldsymbol{\pi}$	Probability vector
ρ	Utilization ratio (of a limited-capacity system, e.g., a queue)
σ	Standard deviation of leadtime demand
τ	Setup time
Υ	Ratio ϕ/Φ
ϕ	Standard normal pdf
Φ	Standard normal cdf
Φ^0	Standard normal ccdf
Φ^1	Standard normal loss function
Φ^2	Standard normal second-order loss function
χ_0	Breakpoint (for quantity discounts)
$\mathbf{X}$	Stochastic process indicating whether processor is on or off (Section 7.3.10)
ψ^2	Variance-to-mean ratio of demand process
ω	Cost ratio $b/(b + h)$
ω_-	Lower limit on fill rate $1 - A$
Ω	Maximal approximation cdf (Chapter 6)
Ω^0	Maximal approximation ccdf
Ω^1	Maximal approximation loss function
Ω^2	Maximal approximation second-order loss function
$\mathbf{1}\{\cdot\}$	Indicator function
*	Optimal
′	Local (multiitem system); e.g., $I_j' =$ *local* inventory of item j $I_j =$ *echelon* inventory of item j
$\otimes$	Kronecker product
$\oplus$	Kronecker sum

Bibliography

Abate, J., G. Choudhury, and W. Whitt [1995]. Exponential approximations for tail probabilities in queues, I: Waiting times. *Operations Research* **43,** 885–901.

Abramowitz, M., and I. Stegun [1964]. *Handbook of Mathematical Functions,* National Bureau of Standards, Washington, DC.

Afentakis, P., B. Gavish, and U. Karmarkar [1984]. Computationally efficient optimal solutions to the lot-sizing problem in multistage assembly systems. *Management Science* **30,** 222–239.

Aggarwal, A., and J. Park [1993]. Improved algorithms for economic lot-size problems. *Operations Research* **41,** 549–571.

Aggarwal, S. [1974]. A review of current inventory theory and its applications. *International Journal of Production Research* **12,** 443–472.

_____ [1985]. MRP, JIT, OPT, FMS? *Harvard Business Review* **63** (September-October), 8–16.

Ahmed, M., D. Gross, and D. Miller [1992]. Control variate models for estimating transient performance measures in repairable item systems. *Management Science* **38,** 388–399.

Akella, R., S. Rajagopalan, and M. Singh [1992]. Part dispatch in random yield multistage flexible test systems for printed circuit boards. *Operations Research* **40,** 776–789.

Anily, S., and A. Federgruen [1990]. One warehouse multiple retailer systems with vehicle routing costs. *Management Science* **36,** 92–114.

APICS [1994]. MRP II software/vendor directory. *APICS—The Performance Advantage* **4,** 9 (September), 50–58.

Archibald, B., and E. Silver [1978]. (*s, S*) policies under continuous review and discrete compound Poisson demands. *Management Science* **24,** 899–908.

Arrow, K. [1958]. Historical background. Chapter 1 in Arrow et al. [1958].

Arrow, K., T. Harris, and J. Marschak [1951]. Optimal inventory policy. *Econometrica* **19,** 250–272.

Arrow, K., S. Karlin, and H. Scarf (eds.) [1958]. *Studies in the Mathematical Theory of Inventory and Production,* Stanford University, Stanford, CA.

_____ [1962]. *Studies in Applied Probability and Management Science,* Stanford University, Stanford, CA.

Arrow, K., S. Karlin, and P. Suppes (eds.) [1960]. *Mathematical Methods in the Social Sciences,* Stanford University, Stanford, CA.

Askin, R. [1981]. A procedure for production lot sizing with probabilistic dynamic demand. *AIIE Transactions* **13,** 132–137.

Ass'ad, M., and M. Beckmann [1988]. Approximate solution of inventory problems with Poisson demand, continuous review, and fixed delivery time. In Chikan, A., and M. Lovell (eds.) [1988]. *Economics of Inventory Management,* Elsevier, Amsterdam.

Åström, K. [1970]. *Introduction to Stochastic Control Theory,* Academic Press, New York, NY.

Atkins, D. [1990]. A survey of lower bounding methodologies for production/inventory models. *Annals of Operations Research* **26,** 9–28.

Atkins, D., and D. Sun [1995]. 98%-effective lot sizing for series inventory systems with backlogging. *Operations Research* **43,** 335–345.

Axsäter, S. [1982]. Worst case performance for lot sizing heuristics. *European Journal of Operations Research* **9,** 339–343.

_____ [1990]. Simple solution procedures for a class of two-echelon inventory problems. *Operations Research* **38,** 64–69.

_____ [1993a]. Continuous review policies for multi-level inventory systems with stochastic demand. Chapter 4 in Graves et al. [1993].

_____ [1993b]. Exact and approximate evaluation of batch-ordering policies for two-level inventory systems. *Operations Research* **41,** 777–785.

_____ [1997]. Simple evaluation of echelon stock (*r, q*) policies for two-level inventory systems. *IIE Transactions* **29,** 661–669.

Axsäter, S., and K. Rosling [1993]. Installation vs. echelon stock policies for multilevel inventory control. *Management Science* **39,** 1274–1280.

Axsäter, S., C. Schneeweiss, and E. Silver (eds.) [1986]. *Multi-Stage Production Planning and Inventory Control,* Springer-Verlag, Berlin.

Azoury, K. [1985]. Bayes solution to dynamic inventory models under unknown demand distribution. *Management Science* **31,** 1150–1160.

Bagchi, U. [1987]. Modeling lead time demand for lumpy demand and variable lead time. *Naval Research Logistics Quarterly* **34,** 687–704.

Bagchi, U., J. Hayya, and C. Chu [1986]. The effect of leadtime variability: The case of independent demand. *Journal of Operations Management* **6,** 159–177.

Bagchi, U., J. Hayya, and J. Ord [1984]. Modeling demand during lead time. *Decision Sciences* **15,** 157–176.

Baker, H., and R. Ehrhardt [1995]. A dynamic inventory model with random replenishment quantities. *Omega* **23,** 109–116.

Baker, K. [1973]. The inventory-queueing analogy and a Markovian production and inventory model. *Opsearch* **10,** 24–37.

_____ [1990]. Lot-sizing procedures and a standard data set: A reconciliation of the literature. Working Paper, The Amos Tuck School, Dartmouth College, Hanover, NH.

_____ [1992]. Tightly-coupled production systems—models, analysis, and insights. *Journal of Manufacturing Systems* **11,** 385–400.

_____ [1993]. Requirements planning. Chapter 12 in Graves et al. [1993].

Baker, K., P. Dixon, M. Magazine, and E. Silver [1978]. An algorithm for the dynamic lot size problem with time-varying production capacity constraints. *Management Science* **24,** 1710–1720.

Barbosa, L., and M. Friedman [1978]. Deterministic inventory lot size models—a general root law. *Management Science* **24,** 819–826.

Bazaraa, M., and C. Shetty [1993]. *Nonlinear Programming,* Wiley, New York.

Beckmann, M. [1961]. An inventory model for arbitrary interval and quantity distributions of demand. *Management Science* **8,** 35–57.

Berg, M., and M. Posner [1990]. Customer delay in M/G/∞ repair systems with spares. *Operations Research* **38,** 344–348.

Berkley, B. [1992]. A review of the kanban production control literature. *Production and Operations Management* **1,** 393–411.

Bertsekas, D. [1995]. *Dynamic Programming and Optimal Control,* Athena Scientific, Belmont, MA.

Bertsekas, D., and S. Shreve [1978]. *Stochastic Optimal Control: The Discrete Time Case,* Academic Press, New York.

Bessler, S., and A. Veinott [1966]. Optimal policy for a dynamic multi-echelon inventry model. *Naval Research Logistics Quarterly* **13,** 355–390.

Billington, P., J. McClain, and L. Thomas [1986]. Heuristics for multilevel lot-sizing with a bottleneck. *Management Science* **32,** 989–1006.

Bitran, G., T. Magnanti, and H. Yanasse [1984]. Approximation methods for the uncapacitated dynamic lot size problem. *Management Science* **30,** 1121–1140.

Bitran, G., and H. Yanasse [1982]. Computational complexity of the capacitated lot size problem. *Management Science* **28,** 1174–1186.

Blackburn, J. (ed.) [1991]. *Time Based Competition,* Irwin, Homewood, IL.

Blackburn, J., and R. Millen [1982]. Improved heuristics for multi-stage requirements planning. *Management Science* **28,** 44–56.

_____ [1985]. A methodology for predicting single-stage lot-sizing performance. *Journal of Operations Management* **5,** 433–438.

Blanchard, O. [1983]. The production and inventory behavior of the American automobile industry. *Journal of Political Economy* **91,** 365–400.

Blinder, A., and L. Maccini [1991]. Taking stock: A critical assessment of recent research on inventories. *Journal of Economic Perspectives* **5,** 73–96.

Bollapragada, S., and T. Morton [1994a]. A simple heuristic for computing non-stationary (*s, S*) policies. Working paper, Carnegie-Mellon University, Pittsburgh.

_____ [1994b]. Myopic heuristics for the random yield problem. Working paper, Carnegie-Mellon University, Pittsburgh.

Box, G., and G. Jenkins [1976]. *Time Series Analysis* (revised ed.), Holden-Day, San Francisco.

Bramel, J., and D. Simchi-Levi [1995]. A location-based heuristic for general routing problems. *Operations Research* **43,** 649–660.

Brooke, A., D. Kendrick, and A. Meeraus [1988]. *GAMS,* Scientific Press, Redwood City, CA.

Brown, R. [1963]. *Smoothing, Forecasting and Prediction of Discrete Time Series,* Prentice-Hall, Englewood Cliffs, NJ.

Browne, S., and P. Zipkin [1991]. Inventory models with continuous, stochastic demands. *Annals of Applied Probability* **1,** 419–435.

Burns, L., R. Hall, D. Blumenfeld, and C. Daganzo [1985]. Distribution strategies that minimize transportation and inventory costs. *Operations Research* **33,** 469–490.

Buzacott, J. [1989]. Queueing models of kanban and MRP controlled production systems. *Engineering Costs and Production Economics* **17,** 3–20.

Buzacott, J., S. Price, and J. Shanthikumar [1992]. Service level in multistage MRP and base stock controlled production systems. In G. Fandel, T. Gulledge, and A. Jones (eds.), *New Directions for Operations Research in Manufacturing,* Springer, Berlin.

Buzacott, J., and G. Shanthikumar [1992]. *Stochastic Models of Manufacturing Systems,* Prentice-Hall, Englewood Cliffs, NJ.

Cachon, G. [1999]. Competitive supply chain inventory management. In Tayur et al. [1999].

Chase, R., and N. Aquilano [1992]. *Production and Operations Management* (6th ed.), Irwin, Homewood, IL.

Chaudhry, M., and J. Templeton [1983]. *A First Course in Bulk Queues,* Wiley, New York.

Chan, L., A. Federgruen, and D. Simchi-Levi [1998]. Probabilistic analyses and practical algorithms for inventory-routing models. *Operations Research* **46,** 96–106.

Chen, F. [1999]. Optimal policies for multi-echelon inventory problems with batch ordering. *Operations Research* (in press).

Chen, F., and Y. Zheng [1994a]. Evaluating echelon stock (*r, nq*) policies in serial production/inventory systems with stochastic demand. *Management Science* **40,** 1262–1275.

_____ [1994b]. Lower bounds for multi-echelon stochastic inventory systems. *Management Science* **40,** 1426–1443.

_____ [1997]. One-warehouse, multi-retailer systems with centralized stock information. *Operations Research* **45,** 275–287.

_____ [1998]. Near-optimal echelon-stock (*r, nq*) policies in multi-stage serial systems. *Operations Research* **46,** 592–602.

Cheng, D., and D. Yao [1993]. Tandem queues with general blocking: A unified model and comparison results. *Discrete Event Dynamic Systems* **2,** 207–234.

Chikán, A. [1990]. *Bibliography of Inventory Literature,* International Society for Inventory Research, Budapest.

Chvátal, V. [1983]. *Linear Programming,* Freeman, New York.

Clark, A. [1972]. An informal survey of multi-echelon inventory theory. *Naval Research Logistics Quarterly* **19,** 621–650.

Clark, A., and H. Scarf [1960]. Optimal policies for a multi-echelon inventory problem. *Management Science* **6,** 475–490.

Cohen, M., and H. Lee [1988]. Strategic analysis of integrated production-distribution systems: Models and methods. *Operations Research* **36,** 216–228.

Cox, D., and H. Miller [1965]. *The Theory of Stochastic Processes,* Methuen, London.

Crowston, W., and M. Wagner [1973]. Dynamic lot size models for multistage assembly systems. *Management Science* **20,** 14–21.

Daganzo, C. [1991]. *Logistics Systems Analysis,* Springer-Verlag, Berlin.

Dallery, Y., and S. Gershwin [1992]. Manufacturing flow line systems: A review of models and analytical results. *Queueing Systems* **12,** 3–94.

Davenport, T. [1993]. *Process Innovation,* Harvard Business School Press, Boston, MA.

Davis, T. [1993]. Effective supply chain management. *Sloan Management Review* **34,** 4 (Summer), 35–46.

de Groote, X. [1994a]. Flexibility and marketing manufacturing coordination. *International Journal of Production Economics* **36,** 153–167.

_____ [1994b]. Flexibility and product variety in lot-sizing models. *European Journal of Operational Research* **75,** 264–274.

Denardo, E. [1982]. *Dynamic Programming,* Prentice-Hall, Englewood Cliffs, NJ.

Denardo, E., and C. Tang [1992]. Linear control of a Markov production system. *Operations Research* **40,** 259–278.

Diaby, M., H. Bahl, M. Karwan, and S. Zionts [1992]. A Lagrangian relaxation approach for very-large-scale capacitated lot-sizing. *Management Science* **38,** 1329–1340.

Di Mascolo, M., Y. Frein, B. Baynat, and Y. Dallery [1993]. Queueing network modeling and analysis of generalized kanban. Paper presented at the European Control Conference, Groningen, Netherlands.

Di Mascolo, M., Y. Frein, and Y. Dallery [1996]. An analytical method for performance evaluation of kanban controlled production systems. *Operations Research* **44,** 50–64.

Dobson, G. [1987]. The economic lot-scheduling problem: Achieving feasibility using time-varying lot sizes. *Operations Research* **35,** 764–771.

_____ [1992]. The cyclic lot scheduling problem with sequence-dependent setups. *Operations Research* **40,** 736–749.

Dobson, G., U. Karmarkar, and J. Rummel [1992]. A closed loop automatic scheduling system (CLASS). *Production Planning & Control* **3,** 130–140.

Dobson, G., and C. Yano [1994]. Cyclic scheduling to minimize inventory in a batch flow line. *European Journal of Operational Research* **75,** 441–461.

Dvoretzky, A., J. Kiefer, and J. Wolfowitz [1952]. The inventory problem. *Econometrica* **20,** 187–222.

Ehrhardt, R. [1984]. (*s, S*) policies for a dynamic inventory model with stochastic leadtimes. *Operations Research* **32,** 121–132.

_____ [1985]. Easily computed approximations for (*s, S*) inventory system operating characteristics. *Naval Research Logistics Quarterly* **32,** 347–359.

Ehrhardt, R., and C. Mosier [1984]. A revision of the power approximation for computing (*s, S*) policies. *Management Science* **30,** 618–622.

Ehrhardt, R., and L. Taube [1987]. An inventory model with random replenishment quantities. *International Journal of Production Research* **25,** 1795–1804.

Elmaghraby, S. [1978]. The economic lot scheduling problem (ELSP): Review and extensions. *Management Science* **24,** 578–598.

El-Najdawi, M. [1992]. A compact heuristic for common cycle lot-size scheduling in multi-stage, multi-product production processes. *International Journal of Production Economics* **27,** 29–42.

El-Najdawi, M., and P. Kleindorfer [1993]. Common cycle lot-size scheduling for multi-product, multi-stage production. *Management Science* **39,** 872–885.

Eppen, G. [1979]. Effects of centralization on expected costs in a multi-location newsboy problem. *Management Science* **25,** 498–501.

Eppen, G., F. Gould, and B. Pashigian [1969]. Extensions of the planning horizon theorem in the dynamic lot size model. *Management Science* **15,** 268–277.

Eppen, G., and R. Martin [1987]. Solving multi-item capacitated lot-sizing problems using variable redefinition. *Operations Research* **35,** 832–848.

Eppen, G., and L. Schrage [1981]. Centralized ordering policies in a multi-warehouse system with leadtimes and random demand. Chapter 3 in Schwarz [1981].

Erickson, R., C. Monma, and A. Veinott [1987]. Send-and-split method for minimum-concave-cost network flows. *Mathematics of Operations Research* **12,** 634–664.

Erkip, N., W. Hausman, and S. Nahmias [1990]. Optimal centralized ordering policies in multi-echelon inventory systems with correlated demands. *Management Science* **36,** 381–392.

Erlenkotter, D. [1989]. An early classic misplaced: Ford W. Harris' economic order quantity model of 1915. *Management Science* **35,** 898–900.

_____ [1990]. Ford Whitman Harris and the economic order quantity model. *Operations Research* **38,** 937–946.

Evans, J. [1985]. An efficient implementation of the Wagner-Whitin algorithm for dynamic lot-sizing. *Journal of Operations Management* **5,** 229–235.

Faaland, B., and T. Schmitt [1993]. Cost-based scheduling of workers and equipment in a fabrication and assembly shop. *Operations Research* **41,** 253–268.

Federgruen, A. [1993]. Centralized planning models for multi-echelon inventory systems under uncertainty. Chapter 3 in Graves et al. [1993].

Federgruen, A., M. Queyranne, and Y. Zheng [1992]. Simple power of two policies are close to optimal in a general class of production/distribution networks with general joint setup costs. *Mathematics of Operations Research* **17,** 951–963.

Federgruen, A., and M. Tzur [1991]. A simple forward algorithm to solve general dynamic lot sizing models with n periods in $O(n \log n)$ or $O(n)$ time. *Management Science* **37,** 909–925.

_____ [1993]. The dynamic lot sizing model with backlogging: A simple $O(n \log n)$ algorithm and minimal forecast horizon procedure. *Naval Research Logistics* **40,** 459–478.

_____ [1994]. Minimal forecast horizons and a new planning procedure for the general dynamic lot sizing model: Nervousness revisited. *Operations Research* **42,** 456–468.

Federgruen, A., and Y. Zheng [1992a]. The joint replenishment problem with general joint cost structures. *Operations Research* **40,** 384–403.

_____ [1992b]. An efficient algorithm for computing an optimal (*r, Q*) policy in continuous review stochastic inventory systems. *Operations Research* **40,** 808–813.

_____ [1995]. Efficient algorithms for finding optimal power-of-two policies for production/distribution systems with general joint setup costs. *Operations Research* **43,** 458–470.

Federgruen, A., and P. Zipkin [1984a]. Approximations of dynamic, multilocation production and inventory problems. *Management Science* **30,** 69–84.

_____ [1984b]. Allocation policies and cost approximations for multilocation inventory systems. *Naval Research Logistics Quarterly* **31,** 97–129.

_____ [1984c]. Computational issues in an infinite-horizon, multiechelon inventory model. *Operations Research* **32,** 818–836.

_____ [1986]. An inventory model with limited production capacity and uncertain demands. *Mathematics of Operations Research* **11,** 193–215.

Feeney, G., and C. Sherbrooke [1966]. The $(s - 1, s)$ inventory policy under compound Poisson demand. *Management Science* **12,** 391–411.

Feller, W. [1957]. *An Introduction to Probability Theory and its Applications,* Vol. 1, Wiley, New York.

_____ [1971]. *An Introduction to Probability Theory and its Applications,* Vol. 2 (2d ed.), Wiley, New York.

Fleischmann, B. [1990]. The discrete lot-sizing and scheduling problem. *European Journal of Operations Research* **44,** 337–348.

Florian, M., and M. Klein [1971]. Deterministic production planning with concave costs and capacity constraints. *Management Science* **18,** 12–20.

Florian, M., J. Lenstra, and A. Rinnooy Kan [1980]. Deterministic production planning: Algorithms and complexity. *Management Science* **26,** 669–679.

Fourer, R., D. Gay, and B. Kernighan [1993]. *AMPL,* Scientific Press, South San Francisco, CA.

Fox, B., and P. Glynn [1988]. Computing Poisson probabilities. *Communications of the ACM* **31,** 440–445.

Frein, Y., M. Di Mascolo, and Y. Dallery [1995]. On the design of generalized kanban control systems. *International Journal of Operations & Production Management* **15,** 158–185.

Gaalman, G. [1978]. Optimal aggregation of multi-item production smoothing models. *Management Science* **24,** 1733–1739.

Gallego, G. [1990]. Scheduling the production of several items with random demands in a single facility. *Management Science* **36,** 1579–1592.

_____ [1998]. New bounds and heuristics for (Q, r) policies. *Management Science* **44,** 219–233.

Gallego, G., and I. Moon [1993]. The distribution-free newsboy problem: Review and extensions. *Journal of the Operational Research Society* **44,** 825–834.

Gallego, G., and R. Roundy [1992]. The economic lot scheduling problem with finite backorder costs. *Naval Research Logistics* **39,** 729–739.

Gallego, G., and P. Zipkin [1999a]. Stock positioning and performance estimation in serial production-transportation systems. *Manufacturing & Service Operations Management* **1,** 77–88.

_____ [1999b]. Bounds, heuristics, and approximations for distribution systems. Working paper, Duke University, Durham, NC.

Galliher, H., P. Morse, and M. Simond [1959]. Dynamics of two classes of continuous review inventory systems. *Operations Research* **7,** 362–384.

Gallo, G., and S. Pallottino [1986]. Shortest path methods: A unifying approach. *Mathematical Programming Study* **26,** 38–64.

Gardner, E., and D. Dannenbring [1979]. Using optimal policy surfaces to analyze aggregate inventory tradeoffs. *Management Science* **25,** 709–720.

Gavish, B., and S. Graves [1977]. A one-product production/inventory problem under continuous review policy. *Operations Research* **28,** 1228–1236.

Glasserman, P. [1997]. Bounds and asymptotics for planning critical safety stocks. *Operations Research* **45,** 244–257.

Glynn, P., and W. Whitt [1991]. A new view of the heavy-traffic limit theorem for infinite-server queues. *Advances in Applied Probability* **23,** 188–209.

Graves, S. [1980]. The multi-product cycling problem. *AIIE Transactions* **12,** 233–240.

_____ [1981]. Multi-stage lot-sizing: An iterative procedure. Chapter 5 in Schwarz [1981].

_____ [1985]. A multi-echelon inventory model for a repairable item with one-for-one replenishment. *Management Science* **31,** 1247–1256.

_____ [1999]. A single-item inventory model for a nonstationary demand process. *Manufacturing & Service Operations Management* **1,** 50–61.

Graves, S., A. Rinnooy Kan, and P. Zipkin (eds.) [1993]. *Logistics of Production and Inventory,* Handbooks in Operations Research and Management Science, Vol. 4, Elsevier (North-Holland), Amsterdam.

Green, L., and P. Kolesar [1991]. The pointwise stationary approximation for queues with nonstationary arrivals. *Management Science* **37,** 84–97.

Groenevelt, H. [1993]. The just-in-time system. Chapter 13 in Graves et al. [1993].

Gross, D., and C. Harris [1971]. On one-for-one-ordering inventory policies with state-dependent leadtimes. *Operations Research* **19,** 735–760.

_____ [1985]. *Fundamentals of Queueing Theory* (2nd ed.), Wiley, New York.

Ha, A. [1997]. Optimal dynamic scheduling policy for a make-to-stock production system. *Operations Research* **45,** 42–53.

Hadley, G., and T. Whitin [1963]. *Analysis of Inventory Systems,* Prentice-Hall, Englewood Cliffs, NJ.

Hall, R. [1991]. *Queueing Methods for Services and Manufacturing,* Prentice-Hall, Englewood Cliffs, NJ.

Hammer, M. [1990]. Reengineering work. *Harvard Business Review* **68** (July-August), 104–112.

Hanssmann, F. [1962]. *Operations Research in Production and Inventory Control,* Wiley, New York.

Harris, F. [1913]. How many parts to make at once. *Factory, The Magazine of Management* **10,** 135–136, 152.

Harrison, J., and V. Nguyen [1990]. The QNET method for two-moment analysis of open queueing networks. *Queueing Systems* **6,** 1–32.

Hax, A., and D. Candea [1984]. *Production and Inventory Management,* Prentice-Hall, Englewood Cliffs, NJ.

Hayes, R., and D. Garvin [1982]. Managing as if tomorrow mattered. *Harvard Business Review* **60** (May-June), 70–79.

Heinrich, C., and C. Schneeweiss. [1986]. Multi-stage lot-sizing for general production systems. Chapter 9 in Axsäter et al. [1986].

Henig, M., and Y. Gerchak [1990]. The structure of periodic review policies in the presence of random yield. *Operations Research* **38,** 634–643.

Herer, Y., and R. Roundy [1997]. Heuristics for a one-warehouse multiretailer distribution problem with performance bounds. *Operations Research* **45,** 102–115.

Herron, D. [1978]. A comparison of techniques for multi-item inventory analysis. *Production and Inventory Management* (first quarter), 103–115.

Heyman, D., and M. Sobel [1982]. *Stochastic Models in Operations Research,* Vol. I, McGraw-Hill, New York.

_____ [1984]. *Stochastic Models in Operations Research,* Vol. II, McGraw-Hill, New York.

_____ (eds.) [1990]. *Stochastic Models,* Handbooks in Operations Research and Management Science, vol. 2, Elsevier (North-Holland), Amsterdam.

Higa, I., A. Gegerheim, and A. Machado [1975]. Waiting time in an $(S - 1, S)$ inventory system. *Operations Research* **23,** 674–680.

Holt, C., F. Modigliani, J. Muth, and H. Simon [1960]. *Planning Production, Inventories and Work Force,* Prentice-Hall, Englewood Cliffs, NJ.

Iglehart, D. [1963a]. Dynamic programming and stationary analysis in inventory problems. Chapter 1 in Scarf et al. [1963].

_____ [1963b]. Optimality of (s, S) policies in the infinite horizon dynamic inventory problem. *Management Science* **9,** 259–267.

Iglehart, D., and S. Karlin [1962]. Optimal policy for dynamic inventory process with nonstationary stochastic demands. Chapter 8 in Arrow et al. [1962].

Iida, T. [1998]. The infinite horizon non-stationary stochastic multi-echelon inventory problem and near myopic policies. Working paper, Tokyo Institute of Technology, Tokyo.

Jackson, J. [1957]. Networks of waiting lines. *Operations Research* **5,** 518–521.

_____ [1963]. Jobshop-like queueing systems. *Management Science* **10,** 131–142.

Jackson, P. [1988]. Stock allocation in a two-echelon distribution system, or "what to do until your ship comes in." *Management Science* **34,** 880–895.

Jackson, P., W. Maxwell, and J. Muckstadt [1985]. The joint replenishment problem with powers of two restrictions. *AIIE Transactions* **17,** 25–32.

_____ [1988]. Determining optimal reorder intervals in capacitated production-distribution systems. *Management Science* **34,** 938–958.

Jacobs, F. [1983]. The OPT scheduling system. *Production and Inventory Management* (3d quarter), 47–51.

Johansen, S., and A. Thorstenson [1993]. Optimal and approximate (Q, r) inventory policies with lost sales and gamma-distributed lead time. *International Journal of Production Economics* **30,** 179–194.

_____ [1996]. Optimal (r, Q) inventory policies with Poisson demands and lost sales: Discounted and undiscounted cases. *International Journal of Production Economics* **46,** 359–371.

Johnson, G., and H. Thompson [1975]. Optimality of myopic inventory policies for certain dependent demand processes. *Management Science* **21,** 1303–1307.

Johnson, M., H. Lee, T. Davis, and R. Hall [1995]. Expressions for item fill rates in periodic inventory systems. *Naval Research Logistics* **42,** 57–80.

Jones, P., and R. Inman [1989]. When is the economic lot scheduling problem easy? *IIE Transactions* **21,** 11–20.

Juran, J. [1988]. *The Quality Control Handbook* (4th edition), McGraw-Hill, New York.

Kaplan, R. [1970]. A dynamic inventory model with stochastic lead times. *Management Science* **16,** 491–507.

_____ [1986]. Must CIM be justified by faith alone? *Harvard Business Review* **64** (March-April), 87–97.

Karlin, S. [1958]. Optimal inventory policy for the Arrow-Harris-Marschak dynamic model. Chapter 9 in Arrow et al. [1958].

_____ [1960]. Dynamic inventory policy with varying stochastic demands. *Management Science* **6,** 231–258.

Karlin, S., and H. Scarf [1958]. Inventory models of the Arrow-Harris-Marschak type with time lag. Chapter 10 in Arrow et al. [1958].

Karlin, S., and H. Taylor [1975]. *A First Course in Stochastic Processes* (2nd ed.), Academic Press, New York.

_____ [1981]. *A Second Course in Stochastic Processes* (2nd ed.), Academic Press, New York.

Karmarkar, U. [1981]. Policy structure in multi-state production/inventory problems: An application of convex analysis. Chapter 16 in Schwarz [1981].

_____ [1987a]. The multilocation multiperiod inventory problem: Bounds and approximations. *Management Science* **33,** 86–94.

_____ [1987b]. Lot sizes, lead times and in-process inventories. *Management Science* **33,** 409–418.

_____ [1989]. Getting control of just-in-time. *Harvard Business Review* **67** (September-October), 122–131.

_____ [1993]. Manufacturing lead times, order release and capacity loading. Chapter 7 in Graves et al. [1993].

Karmarkar, U., and J. Rummel [1990]. The basis for costs in batching decisions. *Journal of Manufacturing and Operations Management* **3,** 153–176.

Karmarkar, U., S. Kekre, and S. Kekre [1987]. The dynamic lot-sizing problem with startup and reservation costs. *Operations Research* **35,** 389–398.

Karush, W. [1957]. A queueing model for an inventory problem. *Operations Research* **5,** 693–703.

Kashyap, A., and D. Wilcox [1993]. Production and inventory control at the General Motors Corporation during the 1920s and 1930s. *American Economic Review* **83,** 383–401.

Katalan, Z. [1995]. Production and service management under setup times and uncertainties. Ph.D. Dissertation, Columbia University, New York.

Kelly, F. [1979]. *Reversibility and Stochastic Networks,* Wiley, New York.

Kemeny, J., and J. Snell [1960]. *Finite Markov Chains,* Van Nostrand Reinhold, Princeton, NJ.

Kimball, G. [1988]. General principles of inventory control. *Journal of Manufacturing and Operations Management* **1,** 119–130.

Kling, R., and Iacono, S. [1984]. The control of information systems development after implementation. *Communications of the ACM* **27,** 1218–1226.

_____ [1989]. The institutional character of computerized information systems. *Office: Technology and People* **5,** 7–28.

Knüsel, L. [1986]. Computation of the chi-square and Poisson distribution. *SIAM Journal on Scientific and Statistical Computation* **7,** 1022–1036.

Krajewski, L., B. King, L. Ritzman, and D. Wong [1987]. Kanban, MRP, and shaping the manufacturing environment. *Management Science* **33,** 39–57.

Kropp, D., and R. Carlson [1984]. A lot-sizing algorithm for reducing nervousness in MRP systems. *Management Science* **30,** 240–244.

Lasdon, L., and R. Terjung [1971]. An efficient algorithm for multi-item scheduling. *Operations Research* **19,** 946–969.

Lawler, E., J. Lenstra, A. Rinnooy Kan, and D. Shmoys (eds.) [1985]. *The Traveling Salesman Problem: A Guided Tour of Combinatorial Optimization,* Wiley, New York.

Leachman, R., and A. Gascon [1988]. A heuristic scheduling policy for multi-item, single machine production systems with time-varying, stochastic demands. *Management Science* **34,** 377–390.

Lee, H., and C. Billington [1993]. Material management in decentralized supply chains. *Operations Research* **41,** 835–847.

Lee, H., C. Billington, and B. Carter [1993]. Hewlett-Packard gains control of inventory and service through design for localization. *Interfaces* **23,** 4 (July-August), 1–11.

Lee, H., and S. Nahmias [1993]. Single-product, single-location models. Chapter 1 in Graves et al. [1993].

Lee, H., and M. Rosenblatt [1987]. Simultaneous determination of production cycle and inspection schedules in a production system. *Management Science* **33,** 1125–1136.

Lee, Y., and P. Zipkin [1992]. Tandem queues with planned inventories. *Operations Research* **40,** 936–947.

_____ [1995]. Processing networks with planned inventories: Sequential refinement systems. *Operations Research* **43,** 1025–1036.

Lippman, S., and K. McCardle [1977]. The competitive newsboy. *Operations Research* **45,** 54–65.

Little, J. [1961]. A proof of the queueing formula $L = \lambda W$. *Operations Research* **9,** 383–387.

Love, S. [1972]. A facilities in series model with nested schedules. *Management Science* **18,** 327–338.

Lovejoy, W. [1992]. Stopped myopic policies in some inventory models with generalized demand processes. *Management Science* **38,** 688–707.

Luenberger, D. [1979]. *Introduction to Dynamic Systems: Theory, Models, and Applications,* Wiley, New York.

_____ [1984]. *Linear and Nonlinear Programming* (2nd ed.), Addison-Wesley, Reading, MA.

Lundin, R., and T. Morton [1975]. Planning horizons for the dynamic lot size model. *Operations Research* **23,** 711–734.

Maes, J., and L. Van Wassenhove [1988]. Multi-item single-level capacitated dynamic lot-sizing heuristics: A general review. *Journal of the Operational Research Society* **39,** 991–1004.

Mahajan, V., and Y. Wind [1986]. *Innovation Diffusion Models for New Product Acceptance,* Ballinger, Cambridge, MA.

Makridakis, S., S. Wheelwright, and V. McGhee [1983]. *Forecasting: Methods and Applications* (2nd ed.), Wiley, New York.

Markowitz, D., M. Reiman, and L. Wein [1995]. The stochastic economic lot scheduling problem: Heavy traffic analysis of dynamic cyclic policies. Working paper, MIT, Cambridge, MA.

Maxwell, W. [1964]. The scheduling of economic lot sizes. *Naval Research Logistics Quarterly* **11,** 89–124.

Maxwell, W., and J. Muckstadt [1985]. Establishing consistent and realistic reorder intervals in production-distribution systems. *Operations Research* **33,** 1316–1341.

Menich, R., and R. Serfozo [1991]. Optimality of routing and servicing in dependent parallel processing systems. *Queueing Systems* **9,** 403–418.

Miller, B. [1974]. Dispatching from depot repair in a recoverable item inventory system. *Management Science* **21,** 316–325.

Mitchell, J. [1987]. 98%-effective lot-sizing for one-warehouse, multi-retailer inventory systems with backlogging. *Operations Research* **35,** 399–404.

Mitra, D., and I. Mitrani [1990]. Analysis of a kanban discipline for cell coordination in production lines, I. *Management Science* **36,** 1548–1566.

_____ [1991]. Analysis of a kanban discipline for cell coordination in production lines, II: Stochastic demands. *Operations Research* **39,** 807–823.

Moinzadeh, K., and H. Lee [1987]. A continuous-review inventory model with constant resupply time and defective items. *Naval Research Logistics* **34,** 457–467.

Monahan, J. [1984]. A quantity discount pricing model to increase vendor profits. *Management Science* **30,** 720–726.

Montgomery, D., and L. Johnson [1976]. *Forecasting and Time Series Analysis,* McGraw-Hill, New York.

Morse, P. [1958]. *Queues, Inventories and Maintenance,* Wiley, New York.

Morton, T. [1971]. The near-myopic nature of the lagged-proportional-cost inventory problem with lost sales. *Operations Research* **19,** 1708–1716.

Morton, T., S. Lawrence, S. Rajagopolan, and S. Kekre [1988]. SCHED-STAR: A price-based shop scheduling module. *Journal of Manufacturing and Operations Management* **1,** 131–181.

Morton, T., and D. Pentico [1995]. The finite-horizon non-stationary stochastic inventory problem: Near-myopic bounds, heuristics, testing. *Management Science* **41,** 334–343.

Muckstadt, J., and R. Roundy [1993]. Analysis of multistage production systems. Chapter 3 in Graves et al. [1993].

Muckstadt, J., and L. Thomas [1980]. Are multi-echelon inventory methods worth implementing in systems with low-demand-rate items? *Management Science* **26,** 483–494.

Naddor, E. [1975]. Optimal and heuristic decisions in single and multi-item inventory systems. *Management Science* **21,** 1234–1249.

Nahmias, S. [1979]. Simple approximations for a variety of dynamic leadtime lost-sales inventory models. *Operations Research* **27,** 904–924.

_____ [1981]. Managing repairable item inventory systems: A review. Chapter 13 in Schwarz [1981].

_____ [1982]. Perishable inventory theory: A review. *Operations Research* **30,** 680–708.

_____ [1994]. Demand estimation in lost sales inventory systems. *Naval Research Logistics* **41,** 739–757.

Nemhauser, G., and L. Wolsey [1988]. *Integer and Combinatorial Optimization,* Wiley, New York.

Nemhauser, G., A. Rinnooy Kan, and M. Todd (eds.) [1989]. *Optimization,* Handbooks in Operations Research and Management Science, Vol. 1, Elsevier (North-Holland), Amsterdam.

Neuts, M. [1979]. A versatile Markovian point process. *Journal of Applied Probability* **16,** 764–779.

_____ [1981]. *Matrix-Geometric Solutions in Stochastic Models,* Johns Hopkins, Baltimore.

Orlicky, J. [1975]. *Material Requirements Planning,* McGraw-Hill, New York.

Peña-Perez, A., and P. Zipkin [1997]. Dynamic scheduling rules for a multiproduct make-to-stock queue. *Operations Research* **45,** 919–930.

Platt, D., L. Robinson, and R. Freund [1997]. Tractable (*Q, R*) heuristic models for constrained service levels. *Management Science* **43,** 951–965.

Porteus, E. [1985]. Investing in reduced setups in the EOQ model. *Management Science* **31,** 998–1010.

_____ [1986a]. Investing in new parameter values in the discounted EOQ model. *Naval Research Logistics Quarterly* **33,** 39–48.

_____ [1986b]. Optimal lot sizing, process quality improvement and setup cost reduction. *Operations Research* **34,** 137–144.

_____ [1990]. Stochastic inventory theory. Chapter 12 in Heyman and Sobel [1990].

Ramaswami, V., and M. Neuts [1980]. Some explicit formulas and computational methods for infinite-server queues with phase-type arrivals. *Journal of Applied Probability* **17,** 498–514.

Rao, A. [1989]. A survey of MRP II software suppliers' trends in support of JIT. *Production and Inventory Management* **30** (3d quarter), 14–17.

Rao, U. [1994]. Convexity and sensitivity properties of the (*R, T*) inventory control policy for stochastic demand models. Working paper, Cornell University, Ithaca, NY.

Raymond, R. [1931]. *Quantity and Economy in Manufacture,* McGraw-Hill, New York.

Renberg, B., and R. Planche [1967]. Un modèle pour la gestion simultanée des *n* articles d'un stock. *Revue d'Informatique et de Recherche Opérationelle* **1,** 6, 47–59.

Resh, M., M. Friedman, and L. Barbosa [1976]. On a general solution of the deterministic lot size problem with time-proportional demand. *Operations Research* **24,** 718–725.

Richards, F. [1975]. Comments on the distribution of inventory position in a continuous-review (*s, S*) inventory system. *Operations Research* **23,** 366–371.

Rockafellar, R. [1970]. *Convex Analysis,* Princeton University, Princeton, NJ.

Rosenblatt, M., and H. Lee [1986]. Economic production cycles with imperfect production processes. *IIE Transactions* **18,** 48–55.

Rosenfield, D., and M. Pendrock [1980]. The effects of warehouse configuration design on inventory levels and holding costs. *Sloan Management Review* **21,** 4, 21–33.

Rosling, K. [1986]. Optimal lot-sizing for dynamic assembly systems. Chapter 7 in Axsäter et al. [1986].

_____ [1989]. Optimal inventory policies for assembly systems under random demands. *Operations Research* **37,** 565–579.

_____ [1993]. 94%-effective lotsizing: User-oriented algorithms and proofs. Working paper, Linköping Institute of Technology, Linköping, Sweden.

Ross, S. [1980]. *Introduction to Probability Models* (2nd ed.), Academic Press, New York.

Rothkopf, M., and S. Oren [1979]. A closure approximation for the nonstationary M/M/*s* queue. *Management Science* **25,** 522–534.

Roundy, R. [1985]. 98% effective integer-ratio lot-sizing for one warehouse multi-retailer systems. *Management Science* **31,** 1416–1430.

_____ [1986]. A 98% effective lot-sizing rule for a multi-product, multi-stage production inventory system. *Mathematics of Operations Research* **11,** 699–727.

_____ [1989]. Rounding off to powers of two in continuous relaxations of capacitated lot sizing problems. *Management Science* **35,** 1433–1442.

_____ [1993]. Efficient, effective lot sizing for multistage production systems. *Operations Research* **41,** 371–385.

Sahin, I. [1979]. On the stationary analysis of continuous review (*s, S*) inventory systems with constant lead times. *Operations Research* **27,** 717–729.

_____ [1982]. On the objective function behavior in (*s, S*) inventory models. *Operations Research* **30,** 709–725.

_____ [1983]. On the continuous review (*s, S*) inventory model under compound renewal demand and random lead times. *Journal of Applied Probability* **20,** 213–219.

Salomon, M. [1990]. *Deterministic Lotsizing Models for Production Planning,* Ph.D. Dissertation, Erasmus University, Rotterdam.

Scarf, H. [1958a]. A min-max solution of an inventory problem. Chapter 12 in Arrow et al. [1958].

_____ [1958b]. Stationary operating characteristics of an inventory model with time lag. Chapter 16 in Arrow et al. [1958].

_____ [1960]. The optimality of (*s, S*) policies in the dynamic inventory problem. Chapter 13 in Arrow et al. [1960].

Scarf, H., D. Guilford, and M. Shelly (eds.) [1963]. *Multistage Inventory Models and Techniques,* Stanford University, Stanford, CA.

Schmidt, C., and S. Nahmias [1985]. Optimal policy for a two-stage assembly system under random demand. *Operations Research* **33,** 1130–1145.

Schneeweiss, C. [1974]. Optimal production smoothing and safety inventory. *Management Science* **20,** 1122–1130.

Schneeweiss, C., and H. Schröder [1992]. Planning and scheduling the repair shops of the Deutsche Lufthansa AG: A hierarchical approach. *Production and Operations Management* **1,** 22–33.

Schonberger, R. [1982]. *Japanese Manufacturing Techniques,* Free Press, New York.

Schwarz, L. [1973]. A simple continuous-review deterministic one-warehouse N-retailer inventory problem. *Management Science* **19,** 555–566.

_____ (ed.) [1981]. *Multi-Level Production/Inventory Control Systems: Theory and Practice,* North-Holland, Amsterdam.

Schwarz, L., and L. Schrage [1975]. Optimal and system-myopic policies for multi-echelon production/inventory assembly systems. *Management Science* **21,** 1285–1294.

Sethi, S., and F. Cheng [1997]. Optimality of (s, S) policies in inventory models with Markovian demand. *Operations Research* **45,** 931–939.

Sherbrooke, C. [1968]. METRIC: A multi-echelon technique for recoverable item control. *Operations Research* **16,** 122–141.

_____ [1975]. Waiting time in an $(S-1, S)$ inventory system—constant service time case. *Operations Research* **23,** 819–820.

_____ [1986]. VARI-METRIC: Improved approximations for multi-indenture, multi-echelon availability models. *Operations Research* **34,** 311–319.

_____ [1992]. *Optimal Inventory Modeling of Systems,* Wiley, New York.

Shingo, S. [1985]. *A Revolution in Manufacturing: The SMED System,* Productivity Press, Cambridge, MA.

_____ [1989]. *A Study of the Toyota Production System from an Industrial Engineering Viewpoint* (revised ed.), Productivity Press, Cambridge, MA.

Shulman, H., and D. Smith [1992]. Scheduling production to minimize holding costs. Working paper, AT&T Bell Laboratories, Holmdel, NJ.

Silver, E., and H. Meal [1973]. A heuristic for selecting lot size quantities for the case of a deterministic time-varying demand rate and discrete opportunities for replenishment. *Production and Inventory Management* (2nd quarter), 64–74.

Silver, E., and R. Peterson [1985]. *Decision Systems for Inventory Management and Production Planning* (2nd ed.), Wiley, New York, NY.

Simon, R. [1971]. Stationary properties of a two-echelon inventory model for low-demand items. *Operations Research* **19,** 761–773.

Singhal, V. [1988]. Inventories, risk and the value of the firm. *Journal of Manufacturing and Operations Management* **1,** 4–43.

Sivazlian, B. [1974]. A continuous-review (s, S) inventory system with arbitrary interarrival distribution between unit demand. *Operations Research* **22,** 65–71.

Smith, S. [1977]. Optimal inventories for an $(S-1, S)$ system with no backorders. *Management Science* **23,** 522–528.

Sobel, M. [1969]. Optimal average-cost policy for a queue with start-up and shut-down costs. *Operations Research* **17,** 145–162.

Sogomonian, A., and C. Tang [1993]. A modeling framework for coordinating promotion and production decisions within a firm. *Management Science* **39,** 191–203.

Song, J., and P. Zipkin [1992]. Evaluation of base-stock policies in multiechelon inventory systems with state-dependent demands. *Naval Research Logistics* **39,** 715–728.

_____ [1993a]. Inventory control in a fluctuating demand environment. *Operations Research* **41,** 351–370.

_____ [1996a]. The joint effect of leadtime variance and lot size in a parallel processing environment. *Management Science* **42,** 1352–1363.

_____ [1996b]. Inventory control with information about supply conditions. *Management Science* **42,** 1409–1419.

_____ [1996c]. Managing inventory with the prospect of obsolescence. *Operations Research* **44,** 215–222.

Stalk, G., and T. Hout [1990]. *Competing against Time,* Free Press, New York.
Stalk, G., P. Evans, and L. Shulman. [1992]. Competing on capabilities: The new rules of corporate strategy. *Harvard Business Review* **70** (March-April), 57–69.
Starr, M., and D. Miller [1962]. *Inventory Control: Theory and Practice,* Prentice-Hall, Englewood Cliffs, NJ.
Stidham, S. [1974]. Stochastic clearing systems. *Stochastic Processes and Their Applications* **2,** 85–113.
Svoronos, A., and P. Zipkin [1991]. Evaluation of one-for-one replenishment policies for multiechelon inventory systems. *Management Science* **37,** 68–83.
Swain, J. [1994]. Crunching numbers. *OR/MS Today* **21** (October), 48–61.
Tang, C. [1990]. The impact of uncertainty on a production line. *Management Science* **36,** 1518–1531.
Tayur, S., R. Ganeshan, and M. Magazine (eds.) [1999]. *Quantitative Models for Supply Chain Management,* Kluwer, Norwell, MA.
Tripp, R., et al. [1991]. A decision support system for assessing and controlling the effectiveness of multi-echelon logistics actions. *Interfaces* **21,** 4 (July-August), 11–25.
Vargas, G., and R. Dear [1990]. Buffering against multiple uncertainty sources in assembly manufacturing. *Journal of Manufacturing and Operations Management* **3,** 309–334.
Veatch, M., and L. Wein [1994]. Optimal control of a two-station tandem production/inventory system. *Operations Research* **42,** 337–350.
Veinott, A. [1965]. Optimal policy for a multi-product, dynamic, nonstationary inventory problem. *Management Science* **12,** 206–222.
_____ [1966a]. The status of mathematical inventory theory. *Management Science* **12,** 745–777.
_____ [1966b]. On the optimality of (s, S) inventory policies: New conditions and a new proof. *SIAM Journal on Applied Mathematics* **14,** 1067–1083.
_____ [1969]. Minimum concave cost solution of Leontief substitution models of multi-facility inventory systems. *Operations Research* **17,** 262–299.
Veinott, A., and H. Wagner [1965]. Computing optimal (s, S) inventory policies. *Management Science* **11,** 525–552.
Vollmann, T., W. Berry, and D. Whybark [1992]. *Manufacturing Planning and Control Systems* (3d ed.), Irwin, Homewood, IL.
Wagelmans, A., S. Van Hoesel, and A. Kolen [1992]. Economic lot sizing: An $O(n \log n)$ algorithm that runs in linear time in the Wagner-Whitin case. *Operations Research* **40,** S145–S156.
Wagner, H. [1993]. Plus ça change. . . . *Interfaces* **23,** 5 (September-October), 20–25.
Wagner, H., and T. Whitin [1958]. Dynamic version of the economic lot size model. *Management Science* **5,** 89–96.
Wagner, H., M. O'Hagan, and B. Lundh [1965]. An empirical study of exact and approximately optimal inventory policies. *Management Science* **11,** 690–723.
Walrand, J. [1988]. *An Introduction to Queueing Networks,* Prentice Hall, Englewood Cliffs, NJ.
Wein, L. [1992]. Dynamic scheduling of a multiclass make-to-stock queue. *Operations Research* **40,** 724–735.
Wemmerlov, U. [1982]. A comparison of discrete, single stage lot-sizing heuristics with special emphasis on rules based on the marginal cost principle. *Engineering Costs and Production Economics* **7,** 45–53.
Weng, Z. [1995]. Channel coordination and quantity discounts. *Management Science* **41,** 1509–1522.
Whitin, T. [1953]. *The Theory of Inventory Management,* Princeton University, Princeton, NJ.

Whitt, W. [1982]. On the heavy-traffic limit theorem for GI/G/∞ queues. *Advances in Applied Probability* **14,** 171–190.

_____ [1983]. The queueing network analyzer. *Bell System Technical Journal* **62,** 2779–2815.

_____ [1991]. The pointwise stationary approximation for $M_t/M_t/s$ queues is asymptotically correct as the rates increase. *Management Science* **37,** 307–314.

_____ [1992]. Understanding the efficiency of multi-server service systems. *Management Science* **38,** 708–723.

Williams, T. [1984]. Special products and uncertainty in production/inventory systems. *European Journal of Operations Research* **15,** 46–54.

Wolff, R. [1977]. The effect of service time regularity on system performanace. In K. Chandy and M. Reiser (eds.) *Computer Performance,* North-Holland, Amsterdam.

_____ [1982]. Poisson arrivals see time averages. *Operations Research* **30,** 223–231.

Yano, C., and H. Lee [1995]. Lot-sizing with random yields: A review. *Operations Research* **43,** 331–334.

Yurkiewicz, J. [1993]. Forecasting software survey. *OR/MS Today* **20** (February), 64–75.

Zangwill, W. [1966]. A deterministic multiproduct, multifacility production and inventory model. *Operations Research* **14,** 486–507.

_____ [1968]. Minimum concave cost flows in certain networks. *Management Science* **14,** 429–450.

_____ [1969]. A backlogging model and a multi-echelon model of a dynamic economic lot size production system. *Management Science* **15,** 506–527.

_____ [1987]. From EOQ towards ZI. *Management Science* **33,** 1209–1223.

Zhang, H. [1998]. A note on the convexity of service-level measures of the (r, q) system. *Management Science* **44,** 431–432.

Zheng, Y. [1991]. A simple proof for the optimality of (s, S) policies for infinite-horizon inventory problems. *Journal of Applied Probability* **28,** 802–810.

_____ [1992]. On properties of stochastic inventory systems. *Management Science* **38,** 87–103.

Zheng, Y., and F. Chen [1992]. Inventory policies with quantized ordering. *Naval Research Logistics* **39,** 285–305.

Zheng, Y., and A. Federgruen [1991]. Finding optimal (s, S) policies is about as simple as evaluating a single policy. *Operations Research* **39,** 654–665.

Zheng, Y., and P. Zipkin [1990]. A queueing model to analyze the value of centralized inventory information. *Operations Research* **38,** 296–307.

Zimmerman, J. [1997]. *Accounting for Decision Making and Control* (2d ed.), Irwin, Chicago, IL.

Zipkin, P. [1982]. Exact and approximate cost functions for product aggregates. *Management Science* **28,** 1002–1012.

_____ [1986a]. Stochastic leadtimes in continuous-time inventory models. *Naval Research Logistics Quarterly* **33,** 763–774.

_____ [1986b]. Inventory service-level measures: Convexity and approximation. *Management Science* **32,** 975–981.

_____ [1986c]. Models for design and control of stochastic, multi-item batch production systems. *Operations Research* **34,** 91–104.

_____ [1988]. The use of phase-type distributions in inventory-control models. *Naval Research Logistics Quarterly* **35,** 247–257.

_____ [1989]. A kanban-like production control system: Analysis of simple models. Working paper, Columbia University, New York.

_____ [1991a]. Does manufacturing need a JIT revolution? *Harvard Business Review* **69** (January- February), 40–50.

_____ [1991b]. Computing optimal lot sizes in the economic lot scheduling problem. *Operations Research* **39,** 56–63.
_____ [1995]. Processing networks with planned inventories: Tandem queues with feedback. *European Journal of Operations Research* **80,** 344–349.
_____ [1995]. Performance analysis of a multi-item production-inventory system under alternative policies. *Management Science* **41,** 690–703.

I N D E X